Race, Ethnicity, and Policing

Race, Ethnicity, and Policing

New and Essential Readings

EDITED BY

Stephen K. Rice and Michael D. White

INTRODUCTION BY

Robin S. Engel

New York University Press

NEW YORK AND LONDON

NEW YORK UNIVERSITY PRESS
New York and London
www.nyupress.org

Library of Congress Cataloging-in-Publication Data
Race, ethnicity, and policing : new and essential readings /
edited by Stephen K. Rice and Michael D. White.
p. cm.
Includes bibliographical references and index.
ISBN-13: 978-0-8147-7615-5 (cl : alk. paper)
ISBN-10: 0-8147-7615-9 (cl : alk. paper)
ISBN-13: 978-0-8147-7616-2 (pb : alk. paper)
ISBN-10: 0-8147-7616-7 (pb : alk. paper)
1. Racial profiling in law enforcement. 2. Police—Attitudes.
3. Crime and race. I. Rice, Stephen K. II. White, Michael D.
(Michael Douglas), 1951–
HV7936.R3R29 2010
363.2'3089—dc22   2009039286

New York University Press books are printed on acid-free paper,
and their binding materials are chosen for strength and durability.
We strive to use environmentally responsible suppliers and materials
to the greatest extent possible in publishing our books.

Manufactured in the United States of America

c   10 9 8 7 6 5 4 3 2 1
p   10 9 8 7 6 5 4 3 2 1

Contents

Introduction

Robin S. Engel

I was a brand-new assistant professor at the Pennsylvania State University (PSU) in the fall of 1998. Sometime during those first few months, a high-ranking official from the Pennsylvania State Police (PSP) whom I happened to meet casually asked me what I knew about racial profiling. My reply was honest: "Not much." It was through this chance encounter with a PSP official that my work in racial profiling research began. I suspect that many researchers around the country had similar "chance" meetings and conversations that shaped their research agendas for years to come. Being both curious and eager as I started my career, I began to research what was known about racial profiling. My search did not take very long. I learned that a handful of studies from the mid-1990s were conducted, but there were flaws in the methodology and conclusions generated. I realized that the study of traffic stops was in its infancy and there was still much to learn. I also realized rather quickly that the rich information we had learned from years of studying police behavior somehow was not included in the new discourse of "racial profiling." Even the use of the new term itself—racial profiling—implied that this was a *new* problem. Yet my years of study in graduate school of the body of research surrounding police behavior indicated otherwise.

I laid out a research plan for the PSP after receiving requests from police officials for information on racial profiling. After presenting this plan at a meeting with the PSP command staff, legal counsel, and political advisers, a PSP adviser took me aside and told me that if I could "figure this out," there would be requests from police agencies around the country. He described the political and legal complexities of the issues and the dire need for police agencies to better understand and incorporate racial profiling research into their agencies. It was at that meeting that I realized the true enormity of the issues that lie before the research community. I can think of few other topics in criminal justice where researchers have had such an immediate and dramatic impact on practitioners—and ultimately on the treatment of citizens. And so, my colleagues and I went to work. Within just a few short years, racial profiling research exploded in police agencies around the country; and so did the debate among academics, researchers, practitioners, politicians, and citizens. This discourse spanned academic disciplines—law professors, practicing attorneys, criminologists, sociologists, statisticians, and psychologists all entered the mix. As the field expanded, different methodologies, statistical techniques, and conclusions were generated. The research and conclusions produced were as diverse as the backgrounds of the investigators. All the while, the litigation and politicking surrounding racial profiling continued. Most important, the legitimacy of the police continued to be questioned as citizens demanded equitable treatment.

In 2002 I wrote an article with my colleagues Jennifer Calnon and Thomas Bernard that questioned the underlying context, methodologies, and conclusions of the early research available regarding racial/ethnic differences in police traffic stops. We argued that although issues surrounding racial/ethnic discrimination and bias have long been concerns in field, the collective knowledge we had accumulated in this was not used to frame the more current concerns regarding racial profiling. In contrast to the larger body of research on police decision making, "racial profiling" research was prompted by high-profile litigation, political pressure, widespread public disapproval of policing tactics, and recommendations from social scientists. I have argued that the result was a body of research that generally failed to ask the proper questions, was methodologically weak, and was inappropriately interpreted by social scientists, the media, politicians, and the courts.[1] Why was the study of "racial profiling" so different from the study of the police behavior more generally, which included estimating the impact of race on police decision making?

Part of the difference in the research methods and conclusions generated was due to differences in the perceived behavior itself. The practice of targeting racial minorities for routine traffic and pedestrian stops originated with the war on drugs, whose advocates promoted profiling as an effective policing tactic to detect drug offenders.[2] The concept of a "drug courier profile" that included race/ethnicity was traced by David Harris to a report produced by the Drug Enforcement Administration (DEA) that concluded that "large scale, interstate trafficking networks controlled by Jamaicans, Haitians, and Black street gangs dominate the manufacture and distribution of crack."[3] In 1986 the DEA established "Operation Pipeline," a highway drug interdiction program designed to train federal, state, and local law enforcement officials on the indicators of drug trafficking activities of motorists.[4] One of the alleged indicators of drug trafficking used in the training was the race/ethnicity of the driver.[5]

The perceived legitimacy of these law enforcement tactics, however, was short-lived. The combined effects of successful litigation, pressure from politicians and public interest groups, and widespread media attention surrounding the issue of racial profiling led to a crisis of legitimacy for police departments across the country. In an effort to prove or disprove the practice of racial profiling, the courts responded by requiring the collection of data in police departments facing litigation. The federal government and the social science community supported these data collection efforts.[6] Police departments responded—and the mass collection of traffic stop data began in earnest within police agencies across the country. But the questions quickly became: What should agencies do with these data? How should they be analyzed? What conclusions could be generated? Most important, citizens wanted to know how this research would lead to an elimination of racial/ethnic bias by police, and specifically the end of racial profiling practices. These were the questions left to the research community. Many of the proposed answers lie within the pages of this book.

Over fifteen years later, the social scientific research in this area has advanced significantly from the pioneer work that made "racial profiling" part of the American lexicon. Researchers responded by first broadening the inquiry to once again consider the examination of all racial/ethnic bias by the police. The scientific and practitioner communities now refer to "bias-based policing."[7] Inquiries span across all type of police-citizen encounters and examine different types of coercive outcomes. In *Race, Ethnicity, and Policing*, it is widely recognized that racial/ethnic bias by police may result in many different outcomes for citizens. Readers are first introduced to the delicate issues surrounding perceptions of race/ethnicity through a reprint from Jerome Skolnick's 1966 classic book *Justice Without Trial*. It is through his discussion of the symbolic assailant that readers are reminded that the issues surrounding race and policing are not simply the use of profiles to target drug traffickers on interstates. Rather, this field of study must grapple with the intricate nature of all social interactions and better understand how all in society—including police—respond to racial/ethnic groups. The reprint of Skolnick's work is a vivid reminder that officers' perceptions of race/ethnicity during their daily work often reflect our own biases. Further, it serves to encourage scholars to consider the issues surrounding "racial profiling" in a much broader context than simply debating a strategy of targeting minorities for purposes of drug interdiction. In addition, scholars have also come to understand that one of the most important considerations of police bias is the impact on citizens' perceptions of police legitimacy. As Tyler and Fagan remind readers, how citizens are treated during the course of police-citizen encounters is just as important as the outcomes they receive, and this treatment affects citizens' perceptions of fairness and legitimacy, and ultimately their compliance with the law.

Due to the landmark litigation against the state police in Maryland and New Jersey in the mid-1990s, this field of inquiry has been, for better or worse, inextricably linked to the political arena. In *Race, Ethnicity, and Policing*, the context of the field is provided through the selection and reprint of seminal works by John Lamberth and David Harris. In an original chapter, Delores Jones-Brown and Brian Maule further describe the legal and legislative literature that surrounds these issues.

Chapters also examine the role of race/ethnicity on multiple coercive outcomes, including police stops, searches, arrests, and use of force. While most scholarship examining "racial profiling" has focused exclusively on traffic stops and searches, *Race, Ethnicity, and Policing* expands the field of inquiry to the use of force literature. A classic in the field, James Fyfe's comparison of police use of deadly force in Memphis and New York had one of the most important and lasting effects in the field of criminal justice. Including this reprint reminds readers that racial/ethnic bias by the police can have deadly consequences. This point is further illustrated by an original contribution by Michael White and Jessica Saunders examining the impact of race/ethnicity on the use of less-lethal force, including electro-muscular disruption devices.

One of the greatest areas of growth and scholarship in bias policing research has been the enhancement of our methodology and statistical analyses. This field of study has evolved considerably over the last fifteen years. In this volume, Greg Ridgeway and John MacDonald meticulously document the journey of our field in search of an accurate comparison group (i.e., benchmark) to better understand levels of racial/ethnic disparities in police-citizen contacts across racial groups. They document the limitations of different approaches and caution researchers against making interpretations from statistical analyses that are often built on faulty assumptions. In another chapter, Meaghan Paulhamus and her coauthors reconsider some of these data collection and methodological issues. Both contributions remind scholars to be careful and deliberate in their interpretations of statistical analyses. The original research included in this collection does exactly that—for example, I, along with Charles Klahm and Rob Tillyer, remind scholars of the importance of considering previously unmeasured factors in traffic stop research (such as citizens' demeanor) that have been shown repeatedly to affect police behavior in other settings. The reprint of work produced by Patricia Warren and her colleagues further demonstrates the importance of using sophisticated statistical analyses balanced with careful consideration of the implication of those analyses. Using a different approach, Rod Brunson demonstrates the importance of incorporating qualitative methods into our investigations of bias policing. Compare this approach to the use of geographic information systems and spatial analyses demonstrated by Matt Nobles and it is obvious that the understanding of the impact of race/ethnicity on police behavior must take multiple forms and analytical methods.

Scholars are also turning their attention to ecological contexts in addition to their focus on individual police-citizen encounters. Ronald Weitzer convincingly describes the importance of the recent trend to consider neighborhood context. Likewise, Karen Parker and her colleagues describe how search rates differ across communities, while Fagan and his coauthors revisit pedestrian stops in New York City within a community context. It is obvious that the initial studies of racial profiling that examined a few miles of interstate patrolled by Maryland state troopers have evolved into a much larger focus on how and why place matters. The push to consider community context—particularly for pedestrian stops—has become a revitalized area of interest in this field.

Further, the importance of considering the impact that bias policing has on racial groups other than Blacks is noted. For example, in this collection Ramiro Martínez directs our attention to the understudied impact of police on Latinos and immigrants. Additional pieces by Brian Stults and his colleagues, along with Karen Parker and her colleagues, consider Hispanic disparities in coercive outcomes during police-citizen encounters. Likewise Stephen Rice and William Parkin describe potential issues that surround the policing of Muslim Americans.

Finally, a handful of scholars in the field have stepped back from this type of detailed research and asked the broader, important, and often neglected questions. For example, Michael White describes the issues that surround police accountability and the difficulty with changing racially biased behaviors. Matthew Hickman further challenges the hypocrisy of the notion of democratic policing in the United States, calling for a greater understanding of citizens' perceptions of fairness and legitimacy of police. Finally, *Race, Ethnicity, and Policing* concludes with a thought-provoking chapter in which Bernard Harcourt asks readers to consider whether the systematic targeting of particular offenders—regardless of their race/ethnicity—is an effective and legitimate policing technique. Harcourt essentially challenges the bases for the use of actuarial methods across the entire criminal justice system.

From the comprehensive detailing of specific methodologies and statistical approaches to the global assessments of what democratic policing "should be," the collection of work compiled in *Race, Ethnicity, and Policing* gives readers an overview of the myriad concerns generated in this field of study. I know of no other work that brings these pieces together more succinctly. The majority of the chapters represent original pieces from authors at the forefront of study in bias policing; these pieces are skillfully interwoven with reprints from seminal works. This book is unique in that all aspects of police bias are considered, and through its pages the history of the field of study unfolds. Readers will find the pioneer work, the search for the ever-elusive comparison "benchmark," and the latest statistical advances in the area.

Equitable treatment of citizens across racial/ethnic groups by police is one of the most critical components of a successful democracy. It is only when agents of the state are viewed as efficient, effective, *and legitimate* that citizens will comply with the laws that govern their society. Our communities have too often experienced the damage and utter destruction that has accompanied racial/ethnic bias (or perceived bias) by police. There are significant challenges facing law enforcement officials in their efforts to provide unbiased police services, and the research community has a central role to play in assisting police officials to overcome these challenges. The issues surrounding the study of racial/ethnic bias by the police are plentiful. In *Race, Ethnicity, and Policing*, readers are guided by the editors through the complexity of these issues, the ecological and political contexts that surround these issues, and the groundwork laid for future discussions.

Based on my review of the work included in this book, I have been given the opportunity to reflect back to my chance meeting with that PSP official, and his encouragement for me to "figure it out." While I can say that I know a lot more about race and policing than I did over a decade ago, I still have more questions than answers. The latest perplexing issue that I am examining is why Hispanic motorists across the country are more likely to be searched, but less likely to be found in possession of contraband compared to Whites. Some have indicated that the answer is obvious—police bias. I still search for the not-so-obvious answers. Is it possible that officers across the country, with different training, different policies, different supervisors, all have the same bias? Possibly. But are there other explanations that must be explored? Definitely. And so my quest to "figure it out" continues.

What I have learned from my peers working in this area is profound. Collectively, the field of study surrounding police bias has advanced considerably. An important sampling of that knowledge from multiple perspectives and academic disciplines is included in the pages before you. I have read these pages with interest and curiosity. It is only through a continual reflection of what we know that we can be led in new directions. The research and discussions within *Race, Ethnicity, and Policing* will provide researchers, students, and practitioners with that guidance. There is no other collection currently available that is as comprehensive and introspective. The body of work that lies before you in this book is quite impressive and very encouraging. Perhaps one day I will be able to say that our field has "figured it out" and that we can reliably measure, predict, and reduce racially biased policing practices. Without doubt, the work included in *Race, Ethnicity, and Policing* moves us closer to this goal.

NOTES

1. See Engel, Calnon & Bernard, 2002; Smith & Alpert, 2002; Tillyer, Engel & Wooldredge, 2008.
2. Harris, 2002; Tonry, 1995.
3. Harris, 1999.
4. GAO, 2000.
5. ACLU, 1999; Harris, 2002.
6. GAO, 2000; Ramirez, McDevitt & Farrell, 2000.
7. Fridell et al., 2001.

REFERENCES

American Civil Liberties Union (ACLU). (1999). *Arrest the racism: Racial profiling in America.* Retrieved March 14, 2005, from http://www.aclu.org/profiling/index.html.

Engel, R. S., Calnon, J. M., & Bernard, T. J. (2002). Theory and racial profiling: Shortcomings and future directions in research. *Justice Quarterly, 19,* 201–225.

Fridell, L., Lunney, R., Diamond, D., & Kubu, B. (2001). *Racially biased policing: A principled response.* Washington, DC: Police Executive Research Forum.

General Accounting Office. (2000). *U.S. customs service: Better targeting of airline passengers for personal searches could produce better results.* Washington, DC: GAO.

Harris, D. A. (1999). Driving while Black: Racial profiling on our nation's highways. Retrieved March 11, 2005, from http://www.aclu.org/profiling/report/index.html.

Harris, D. A. (2002). *Profiles in injustice: Why racial profiling cannot work.* New York: The New Press.

Smith, M. R., & Alpert. G. (2002). Searching for direction: Courts, social science, and the adjudication of racial profiling claims. *Justice Quarterly, 19,* 673–703.

Ramirez, D., McDevitt, J. & Farrell, A. (2000). *A resource guide on racial profiling data collection systems: Promising practices and lessons learned.* Washington, DC: U.S. Department of Justice.

Tonry, M. (1995). *Malign Neglect.* New York: Oxford University Press.

Tillyer, R., Engel, R. S., & Wooldredge, J. (2008). The intersection of racial profiling and the law. *Journal of Criminal Justice, 36,* 138–153.

Overview

Stephen K. Rice and Michael D. White

Information is readily available to us. Where shall wisdom be found?

Irrespective of limitations in the perspectives employed in extant scholarship (e.g., criminological, legalistic, economic), methodological shortcomings in assessing police profiling and bias (e.g., determining benchmarks, or "denominators"), or arguments regarding the appropriate framing of deeply felt cultural subtexts (e.g., Amadou Diallo, the Jena Six, Sean Bell, Abner Louima, Henry Louis Gates Jr., Genarlow Wilson, Jean Charles de Menezes, FBI interviews of Muslim Americans, the depiction of undocumented immigrants as criminal aliens), at day's end the study of race, ethnicity, and policing centers on whether police tend to respond to ascribed characteristics, to situations, or to a combination thereof as they do their jobs. This determination is critical to understanding the "social location" of police and the conditions under which the public choose to defer to, or to defy, authority.

Race, Ethnicity, and Policing: New and Essential Readings is structured to provide the reader with requisite knowledge in four areas that are critical to answering these questions. First, "The Context" provides an overview of key propositions from criminology, social psychology, sociology, and the law that are important in understanding possible typifications (categorizations) of "symbolic assailants" by police, how race and ethnicity are more nuanced than their treatment in most existing scholarship, how perceived procedural justice shapes public support for police and the effective rule of law, how early questions about "driving while black" and "driving while brown" entered the public lexicon, and how courts and legislatures have responded to claims of racial and ethnic bias in policing. Second, "The Methods" introduces the reader to the major techniques that have been utilized in the study of race/ethnicity, bias, and policing (i.e., quantitative, qualitative, visual) and provides an overview of current measurement and analysis controversies and recommendations for ways forward. Third, "The Research" immerses the reader in empirical scholarship spanning the methodological (e.g., the need for multiple data sources at multiple levels of analysis), the definitional (e.g., expanding conceptions of race/ethnicity beyond black and white toward intra-ethnic, intra-racial continua), and the behavioral (e.g., broadening the range of police activities that warrant examination). Finally, "The Future" outlines areas of inquiry that have remained largely untapped—topics such as the role of spatial dynamics and neighborhood characteristics on stop rates; calls for a greater focus on the experiences of Latinos, Muslim Americans, and other under-studied populations; the potential role for randomness (versus actuarialism) in police decision making; and the importance for police departments and researchers to better explicate accountability and the democratic ideal in policing.

In total, we are hopeful that *Race, Ethnicity, and Policing: New and Essential Readings* will afford a more holistic approach to the study of race, ethnicity, and policing —an approach that accounts for what we know about effective and ethical policing, is grounded in empiricism and forward-edge methodologies, and affords a humanist sensibility in understanding the contemplations of those who perceive injustice in their interactions with agents of social control.

NOTE

Epigraph: Harold Bloom, *How to read and why* (New York: Scribner, 2000).

The Context

Introduction to Part I

Stephen K. Rice

The following section is foundational: it provides the criminological, sociological, social-psychological, and legal lens through which to better understand the theoretical basis and empirical examination of race, ethnicity, and policing. The section also provides the reader with a conceptual road map to better "place" the methodological advancements and controversies outlined later in the volume, illustrates how scholarship tends to coalesce around different ecological contexts and units of analysis (e.g., the neighborhood versus the individual), and provides an appreciation of how varied orthodoxies influence the pictures that get drawn. The chapters by Tyler and Fagan, and Weitzer are tasked with providing these distinctions, while the chapter by Jones-Brown and Maule assesses police bias and profiling legislatively and jurisprudentially. The section also includes foundational work by Skolnick on "the symbolic assailant" and by Lamberth and Harris on early statistical assessments of minority motorists' experiences—assessments that have formed the basis for much of the public's interpretations of "driving while black/brown."

The first chapter in the section, Skolnick's seminal "A Sketch of the Policeman's Working Personality," advances a thesis that has informed decades of research on the social psychology of policing as an occupation: that through a confluence of pressures that include exposure to danger, problems of authority, police solidarity, and the need for efficiency, police officers develop distinct ways of perceiving the world around them. As a result, this "working personality" tends to facilitate a suspicious comportment on the part of officers—an orientation in which officers develop perceptual shorthands to classify certain individuals as potentially violent based on inputs such as language, dress, gesture, or not "belonging" within a street scene. Conditioned by an officer's inherent need for order (e.g., via regularity, predictability, and safety), these "symbolic assailants" come to be cast as differentially likely for police interrogation. In the years subsequent to Skolnick's publication, researchers have worked to assess the implications and by-products of this thesis, such as whether race and ethnicity are utilized by police in much the same way as language or gesture: as triggers for differential stop, search, and interrogation independent of observable behavior or situation. Either tacitly or explicitly, each of the contributions to *Race, Ethnicity, and Policing* focuses on this important question.

As with Skolnick's description of the "symbolic assailant," Lamberth's 1993 census of violators on the New Jersey Turnpike may too be considered seminal in light of its sizable impact on public perceptions of "driving while black/brown" and as one of the earliest efforts to apply research design and statistical analysis to claims of profiling by police (also see Paulhamus, Kane, and Piquero; and Ridgeway and MacDonald, this volume). To establish a benchmark, or "denominator" (i.e., the number of drivers of a particular race on the turnpike over a period of time), and to gauge driver behavior (i.e., violators vs. nonviolators, by race), Lamberth set up surveys that afforded both metrics: one a static assessment of drivers and race from predetermined observation points, the other being a novel "rolling survey" to assess speeding. Lamberth's findings indicated that African Americans represented fewer than 15% of the drivers on the turnpike, 15% of the speeders, but 35% of those who were stopped by police. As such, blacks were almost five times more likely to be stopped as were others, and by reviewing arrest data he determined that blacks were nearly seventeen times more likely to be arrested. Subsequent research in Maryland yielded similar results, including suggestions of racial bias in decisions to search. Largely through Lamberth's early efforts, swaths of roadway in New Jersey, Maryland, and other states have become central to national dialogues on race, ethnicity, fair procedures, and the effective rule of law.

Harris's chapter finds its footing in Lamberth's New Jersey and Maryland scholarship, incorporates additional empirical (albeit nonobservational) work by Harris and Lamberth on Ohio traffic stops (similarly indicating racial disproportionality in ticket issuance), and further contextualizes these findings by incorporating interviews with African Americans that are presented as illustrating the "frightening and embarrassing nature of the experiences, the emotional difficulties and devastation that often follow, and the ways that they cope, bring[ing] to life the statistics" (also see Brunson, this volume). The chapter moves on to place racial profiling in the broader context of race in the criminal justice system, provides an outline of legal principles that relate to allegations of profiling and the (sometimes-limited) recourse available to those who perceive unfair treatment, and ends with recommendations for ways forward. To this last point, Harris calls for additional local- and state-level enactment of measures similar to the Traffic Stops Statistics Act of 1997 so that complainants can more readily utilize the whole host of legal rights available to them (e.g., Equal Protection Clause, civil rights statutes, state law).

Tyler and Fagan provide a critical counter to long-standing sociological perspectives: that while such inputs are no doubt important to understanding relationships between minority groups and legal authorities, they are inadequate in capturing the street-level *mechanisms* by which individuals choose to comply with the law, cooperate with the police, and support the empowerment of police to use discretion. To this question, Tyler and Fagan point to the influence of perceived procedural justice in conditioning police legitimacy: "The procedural justice model of policing argues that the police can build general legitimacy among the public by treating people justly during personal encounters. This argument is based upon two empirical arguments. The first is that people evaluate personal experiences with the police by evaluating the fairness of police procedures. The second is that this means that by using fair procedures the police can increase their legitimacy, even if their policing activities involve restricting or sanctioning the people with whom they are dealing" (241). As such, the procedural justice model is contrasted with instrumental perspectives which assert that legitimacy is less a function of process than outcome: that the public is more attuned to credible sanctioning threats, the ebb and flow of crime control/ crime rates in a community, and the fair distribution of police services (or attunement to risk, performance, and distributive fairness, respectively). To test the relative influence of procedural versus instrumental judgments, Tyler and Fagan analyze responses to a panel study focusing on New York City residents that tap both the constructs and the characteristics of police legitimacy and cooperation. Consistent with the model, legitimacy is found to be linked to the justice of the procedures utilized by the police in exercising their authority, and legitimacy more relates to experiencing procedural justice than to the favorability of outcomes. Tyler and Fagan's findings inform related efforts that aim to place greater emphasis on measures of fairness in police-public interactions (e.g., Brunson; Rice and Parkin; and Hickman, this volume).

Reflective of individuals being couched within ecological contexts, Weitzer provides an important overview of major empirical findings about race, ethnicity, and policing at the level of the individual (e.g., age, gender, and social class predicting public attitudes and experiences) and in contexts to include neighborhoods, cities, and nations. Consistent with Martínez (this volume), Weitzer pays particular attention to imperfections and inaccuracies in the manner in which the "Latino" or "Hispanic" experience has been explored, in that it tends to mask differences such as national origin, immigrant versus native-born status, frames of reference regarding police conditioned by home country (e.g., benevolent or brutal), stratification, integration, and alienation. With regard to ecology, Weitzer provides a comprehensive review of evidence that suggests that place matters: that neighborhoods and cities (and perhaps nations) play at least as much of a role as individual-level characteristics in explaining public treatment by police. Weitzer also provides useful recommendations for the application of social disorganization theory, conflict theory, minority threat theory, and group position theory in the study of race, ethnicity, and policing. In total, the chapter illuminates voices that hope to better understand how the individual is embedded within space and place (e.g., Tyler and Fagan; Parker, Lane, and Alpert; and Stults, Parker, and Lane, this volume).

Harris's brief discussion of legal principles provides a segue to Jones-Brown and Maule's comprehensive overview of fundamental constitutional rights that inform the study of race, ethnicity, and policing (e.g., expectation of privacy, equal protection, freedom from unreasonable intrusion), the socio-legal background in which these rights are embedded, and the conditions under which judicial and legislative bodies have taken action to better protect these rights (e.g., *U.S. v. Brignoni-Ponce*, vis-à-vis the inadequacy of ethnicity alone in determining reasonable suspicion). The authors also contend that the U.S. Supreme Court has been ineffectual in establishing a similarly clear standard on the impermissible role of race as sole determinant of reasonable suspicion—a failure that, when coupled with decisions that have expanded the scope of police discretion, "make racially biased policing *legally invisible* in the absence of direct admissions or overt racial epithets by police during traffic or pedestrian stops" (emphasis added). Jones-Brown and Maule go on to outline cases that they characterize as having expanded police discretionary authority in ways that enhance the likelihood of racially biased policing. The chapter closes with a discussion of successful settlements of racial profiling lawsuits and with an accounting of national legislation that has facilitated data collection on the part of police departments or formally prohibited racial and ethnic profiling. In sum, the chapter provides a legal/legislative lens through which to better explore how and under what conditions citizens' demeanor affects the police-public dyad; whether nonnative, undocumented, or "special" populations experience unique vulnerabilities in their experiences with legal authorities; and how modifications to law and policy might better facilitate police accountability and a democratic ideal (e.g., Engel, Klahm, and Tillyer; Weitzer; Martínez; and White, this volume).

Chapter 1

A Sketch of the Policeman's Working Personality

Jerome H. Skolnick

A recurrent theme of the sociology of occupations is the effect of a man's work on his outlook on the world.[1] Doctors, janitors, lawyers, and industrial workers develop distinctive ways of perceiving and responding to their environment. Here we shall concentrate on analyzing certain outstanding elements in the police milieu, danger, authority, and efficiency, as they combine to generate distinctive cognitive and behavioral responses in police: a "working personality." Such an analysis does not suggest that all police are alike in "working personality," but that there are distinctive cognitive tendencies in police as an occupational grouping. Some of these may be found in other occupations sharing similar problems. So far as exposure to danger is concerned, the policeman may be likened to the soldier. His problems as an authority bear a certain similarity to those of the schoolteacher, and the pressures he feels to prove himself efficient are not unlike those felt by the industrial worker. The combination of these elements, however, is unique to the policeman. Thus, the police, as a result of combined features of their social situation, tend to develop ways of looking at the world distinctive to themselves, cognitive lenses through which to see situations and events. The strength of the lenses may be weaker or stronger depending on certain conditions, but they are ground on a similar axis.

Analysis of the policeman's cognitive propensities is necessary to understand the practical dilemma faced by police required to maintain order under a democratic rule of law. . . . A conception of order is essential to the resolution of this dilemma. We suggest that the paramilitary character of police organization naturally leads to a high evaluation of similarity, routine, and predictability. Our intention is to emphasize features of the policeman's environment interacting with the paramilitary police organization to generate a "working personality." Such an intervening concept should aid in explaining how the social environment of police affects their capacity to respond to the rule of law.

Emphasis will be placed on the division of labor in the police department . . . ; "operational law enforcement" cannot be understood outside these special work assignments. It is therefore important to explain how the hypothesis emphasizing the generalizability of the policeman's "working personality" is compatible with the idea

From *Justice Without Trial: Law Enforcement in a Democratic Society*, pp. 80–91, by Jerome H. Skolnick. ©1966 John Wiley and Sons. Reprinted with permission of John Wiley and Sons.

that police division of labor is an important analytic dimension for understanding "operational law enforcement." Compatibility is evident when one considers the different levels of analysis at which the hypotheses are being developed. Janowitz states, for example, that the military profession is more than an occupation; it is a "style of life" because the occupational claims over one's daily existence extend well beyond official duties. He is quick to point out that any profession performing a crucial "life and death" task, such as medicine, the ministry, or the police, develops such claims.[2] A conception like "working personality" of police should be understood to suggest an analytic breadth similar to that of "style of life." That is, just as the professional behavior of military officers with similar "styles of life" may differ drastically depending upon whether they command an infantry battalion or participate in the work of an intelligence unit, so too does the professional behavior of police officers with similar "working personalities" vary with their assignments.

The policeman's "working personality" is most highly developed in his constabulary role of the man on the beat. For analytical purposes that role is sometimes regarded as an enforcement specialty, but in this general discussion of policemen as they comport themselves while working, the uniformed "cop" is seen as the foundation for the policeman's "working personality." There is a sound organizational basis for making this assumption. The police, unlike the military, draw no caste distinction in socialization, even though their order of ranked titles approximates the military's. Thus, one cannot join a local police department as, for instance, a lieutenant, as a West Point graduate joins the army. Every officer of rank must serve an apprenticeship as a patrolman. This feature of police organization means that the constabulary role is the primary one for all police officers, and that whatever the special requirements of roles in enforcement specialties, they are carried out with a common background of constabulary experience.

The process by which this "personality" is developed may be summarized: the policeman's role contains two principal variables, danger and authority, which should be interpreted in the light of a "constant" pressure to appear efficient.[3] The element of danger seems to make the policeman especially attentive to signs indicating a potential for violence and lawbreaking. As a result, the policeman is generally a "suspicious" person. Furthermore, the character of the policeman's work makes him less desirable as a friend, since norms of friendship implicate others in his work. Accordingly, the element of danger isolates the policeman socially from that segment of the citizenry which he regards as symbolically dangerous and also from the conventional citizenry with whom he identifies.

The element of authority reinforces the element of danger in isolating the policeman. Typically, the policeman is required to enforce laws representing puritanical morality, such as those prohibiting drunkenness, and also laws regulating the flow of public activity, such as traffic laws. In these situations the policeman directs the citizenry, whose typical response denies recognition of his authority and stresses his obligation to respond to danger. The kind of man who responds well to danger, however, does not normally subscribe to codes of puritanical morality. As a result, the policeman is unusually liable to the charge of hypocrisy. That the whole civilian world is an audience for the policeman further promotes police isolation and, in consequence, solidarity. Finally, danger undermines the judicious use of authority. Where danger, as in Britain, is relatively less, the judicious application of authority is facilitated. Hence, British police may appear to be somewhat more attached to the rule of law, when, in fact, they may appear so because they face less danger, and they are as a rule better skilled than American police in creating the appearance of conformity to procedural regulations.

The Symbolic Assailant and Police Culture

In attempting to understand the policeman's view of the world, it is useful to raise a more general question: What are the conditions under which police, as authorities, may be threatened?[4] To answer this, we must look to the situation of the policeman in the community. One attribute of many characterizing the policeman's role stands out: the policeman is required to respond to assaults against persons and property. When a radio call reports an armed robbery and gives a description of the man involved, every policeman, regardless of assignment, is responsible for the criminal's apprehension. The raison d'être of the policeman and the criminal law, the underlying collectively held moral sentiments which justify penal sanctions, arises ultimately and most clearly from the threat of violence and the possibility of danger to the community. Police who "lobby" for severe narcotics laws, for instance, justify their position on grounds that the addict is a harbinger of danger since, it is maintained, he requires $100 a day to support his habit, and he must steal to get it. Even though the addict is not typically a violent criminal, criminal penalties for addiction are supported on grounds that he may become one.

The policeman, because his work requires him to be occupied continually with potential violence, develops a perceptual shorthand to identify certain kinds of people as symbolic assailants, that is, as persons who use gesture, language, and attire that the policeman has come to recognize as a prelude to violence. This does not mean that violence by the symbolic assailant is necessarily predictable. On the contrary, the policeman responds to the vague indication of danger suggested by appearance. Like the animals of the experimental psychologist, the policeman finds the threat of random damage more compelling than a predetermined and inevitable punishment.

Nor, to qualify for the status of symbolic assailant, need an individual ever have used violence. A man backing out of a jewelry store with a gun in one hand and jewelry in the other would qualify even if the gun were a toy and he had never in his life fired a real pistol. To the policeman in the situation, the man's personal history is momentarily immaterial. There is only one relevant sign: a gun signifying danger. Similarly, a young man may suggest the threat of violence to the policeman by his manner of walking or "strutting," the insolence in the demeanor being registered by the policeman as a possible preamble to later attack.[5] Signs vary from area to area, but a youth dressed in a black leather jacket and motorcycle boots is sure to draw at least a suspicious glance from a policeman.

Policeman themselves do not necessarily emphasize the peril associated with their work when questioned directly, and may even have well-developed strategies of denial. The element of danger is so integral to the policeman's work that explicit recognition might induce emotional barriers to work performance. Thus, one patrol officer observed that more police have been killed and injured in automobile accidents in the past ten years than from gunfire. Although his assertion is true, he neglected to mention that police are the only peacetime occupational group with a systematic record of death and injury from gunfire and other weaponry. Along these lines, it is interesting that of the 224 working Westville policemen (not including the sixteen juvenile policemen) responding to a question about which assignment they would like most to have in the police department,[6] 50 percent selected the job of detective, an assignment combining elements of apparent danger and initiative. The next category was adult street work, that is, patrol and traffic (37 percent). Eight percent selected the juvenile squad,[7] and only 4 percent selected administrative work. Not a single policeman chose the job of jail guard. Although these findings do not control for such factors as prestige, they suggest that confining and routine jobs are rated low on the hierarchy of police preferences, even though such jobs are least dangerous. Thus, the policeman may well, as a personality, enjoy the possibility of danger, especially its associated excitement, even though he may at the same time be fearful of it. Such "inconsistency" is easily understood. Freud has by now made it an axiom of personality theory that logical and emotional consistency are by no means the same phenomenon.

However complex the motives aroused by the element of danger, its consequences for sustaining police culture are unambiguous. This element requires him, like the combat soldier, the European Jew, the South African (white or black), to live in a world straining toward duality, and suggesting danger when "they" are perceived. Consequently, it is in the nature of the policeman's situation that his conception of order emphasizes regularity and predictability. It is, therefore, a conception shaped by persistent suspicion. The English "copper," often portrayed as a courteous, easygoing, rather jolly sort of chap, on the one hand, or as a devil-may-care adventurer, on the other, is differently described by Colin MacInnes:

> The true copper's dominant characteristic, if the truth be known, is neither those daring nor vicious qualities that are sometimes attributed to him by friend or enemy, but an ingrained conservatism, and almost desperate love of the conventional. It is untidiness, disorder, the unusual, that a copper disapproves of most of all: far more, even than of crime which is merely a professional matter. Hence his profound dislike of people loitering in streets, dressing extravagantly, speaking with exotic accents, being strange, weak, eccentric, or simply any rare minority—of their doing, in fact, anything that cannot be safely predicted.[8]

Policemen are indeed specifically trained to be suspicious, to perceive events or changes in the physical surroundings that indicate the occurrence or probability of disorder. A former student who worked as a patrolman in a suburban New York police department describes this aspect of the policeman's assessment of the unusual:

> The time spent cruising one's sector or walking one's beat is not wasted time, though it can become quite routine. During this time, the most important thing for the officer to

do is notice the normal. He must come to know the people in his area, their habits, their automobiles and their friends. He must learn what time the various shops close, how much money is kept on hand on different nights, what lights are usually left on, which houses are vacant . . . only then can he decide what persons or cars under what circumstances warrant the appellation "suspicious."[9]

The individual policeman's "suspiciousness" does not hang on whether he has personally undergone an experience that could objectively be described as hazardous. Personal experience of this sort is not the key to the psychological importance of exceptionality. Each, as he routinely carries out his work, will experience situations that threaten to become dangerous. Like the American Jew who contributes to the "defense" organizations such as the Anti-Defamation League in response to Nazi brutalities he has never experienced personally, the policeman identifies with his fellow cop who has been beaten, perhaps fatally, by a gang of young thugs.

Social Isolation

The patrolman in Westville, and probably in most communities, has come to identify the black man with danger. James Baldwin vividly expresses the isolation of the ghetto policeman:

> The only way to police a ghetto is to be oppressive. None of the police commissioner's men, even with the best will in the world, have any way of understanding the lives led by the people they swagger about in twos and threes controlling. Their very presence is an insult, and it would be, even if they spent their entire day feeding gumdrops to children. They represent the force of the white world, and that world's criminal profit and ease, to keep the black man corralled up here, in his place. The badge, the gun in the holster, and the swinging club make vivid what will happen should his rebellion become overt. . . .
>
> It is hard, on the other hand, to blame the policeman, blank, good-natured, thoughtless, and insuperably innocent, for being such a perfect representative of the people he serves. He, too, believes in good intentions and is astounded and offended when they are not taken for the deed. He has never, himself, done anything for which to be hated —which of us has?—and yet he is facing, daily and nightly, people who would gladly see him dead, and he knows it. There is no way for him not to know it; there are few things under heaven more unnerving than the silent, accumulating contempt and hatred of a people. He moves through Harlem, therefore, like an occupying soldier in a bitterly hostile country; which is precisely what, and where he is, and is the reason he walks in twos and threes.[10]

While Baldwin's observations on police-black relations cannot be disputed seriously, there is greater social distance between police and "civilians" in general regardless of their color than Baldwin considers. Thus, Colin MacInnes has his English hero, Mr. Justice, explaining:

The story is all coppers are just civilians like anyone else, living among them not in barracks like on the Continent, but you and I know that's just a legend for mugs. We are cut off: we're not like everyone else. Some civilians fear us and play up to us, some dislike us and keep out of our way but no one—well, very few indeed—accepts us as just ordinary like them. In one sense, dear, we're just like hostile troops occupying an enemy country. And say what you like, at times that makes us lonely.[11]

MacInnes' observation suggests that by not introducing a white control group, Baldwin has failed to see that the policeman may not get on well with anybody regardless (to use the hackneyed phrase) of race, creed, or national origin. Policemen whom one knows well often express their sense of isolation from the public as a whole, not just from those who fail to share their color. Westville police were asked, for example, to rank the most serious problems police have. The category most frequently selected was not racial problems, but some form of public relations: lack of respect for the police, lack of cooperation in enforcement of law, lack of understanding of the requirements of police work.[12] One respondent answered:

As a policeman my most serious problem is impressing on the general public just how difficult and necessary police service is to all. There seems to be an attitude of "law is important, but it applies to my neighbor—not to me."

Of the 282 Westville policemen who rated the prestige police work receives from others, 70 percent ranked it as only fair or poor, while less than 2 percent ranked it as "excellent" and another 29 percent as "good." Similarly, in Britain, two-thirds of a sample of policemen interviewed by a royal commission stated difficulties in making friends outside the force; of those interviewed 58 percent thought members of the public to be reserved, suspicious, and constrained in conversation; and 12 percent attributed such difficulties to the requirements that policemen be selective in associations and behave circumspectly.[13] A Westville policeman related the following incident:

Several months after I joined the force, my wife and I used to be socially active with a crowd of young people, mostly married, who gave a lot of parties where there was drinking and dancing, and we enjoyed it. I've never forgotten, though, an incident that happened on one Fourth of July party. Everybody had been drinking, there was a lot of talking, people were feeling boisterous, and some kid there—he must have been twenty or twenty-two—threw a firecracker that hit my wife in the leg and burned her. I didn't know exactly what to do—punch the guy in the nose, bawl him out, just forget it. Anyway, I couldn't let it pass, so I walked over to him and told him he ought to be careful. He began to rise up at me, and when he did, somebody yelled, "Better watch out, he's a cop." I saw everybody standing there, and I could feel they were all against me and for the kid, even though he had thrown the firecracker at my wife. I went over to the host and said it was probably better if my wife and I left because a fight would put a damper on the party. Actually, I'd hoped he would ask the kid to leave, since the kid had thrown the firecracker. But he didn't, so we left. After that incident, my wife and I stopped going around with that crowd, and decided that if we were going to parties where there was to be drinking and boisterousness, we weren't going to be the only police people there.

Another reported that he seeks to overcome his feelings of isolation by concealing his police identity:

> I try not to bring my work home with me, and that includes my social life. I like the men I work with, but I think it's better that my family doesn't become a police family. I try to put my police work into the background, and try not to let people know I'm a policeman. Once you do, you can't have normal relations with them.[14]

Although the policeman serves a people who are, as Baldwin says, the established society, the white society, these people do not make him feel accepted. As a result, he develops resources within his own world to combat social rejection.

Police Solidarity

All occupational groups share a measure of inclusiveness and identification. People are brought together simply by doing the same work and having similar career and salary problems. As several writers have noted, however, police show an unusually high degree of occupational solidarity.[15] It is true that the police have a common employer and wear a uniform at work, but so do doctors, milkmen, and bus drivers. Yet it is doubtful that these workers have so close knit an occupation or so similar an outlook on the world as do police. Set apart from the conventional world, the policeman experiences an exceptionally strong tendency to find his social identity within his occupational milieu.

Compare the police with another skilled craft. In a study of the International Typographical Union, the authors asked printers the first names and jobs of their three closest friends. Of the 1,236 friends named by the 412 men in their sample, 35 percent were printers.[16] Similarly, among the Westville police, of 700 friends listed by 250 respondents, 35 percent were policemen. The policemen, however, were far more active than printers in occupational social activities. Of the printers, more than half (54 percent) had never participated in any union clubs, benefit societies, teams, or organizations composed mostly of printers, or attended any printers' social affairs in the past five years. Of the Westville police, only 16 percent had failed to attend a single police banquet or dinner in the past year (as contrasted with the printers' five years); and of the 234 men answering this question, 54 percent had attended three or more such affairs during the past year.

These findings are striking in light of the interpretation made of the data on printers. Lipset, Trow, and Coleman do not, as a result of their findings, see printers as an unintegrated occupational group. On the contrary, they ascribe the democratic character of the union in good part to the active social and political participation of the membership. The point is not to question their interpretation, since it is doubtless correct when printers are held up against other manual workers. However, when seen in comparison to police, printers appear a minimally participating group; put positively, police emerge as an exceptionally socially active occupational group.

Police Solidarity and Danger

There is still a question, however, as to the process through which danger and authority influence police solidarity. The effect of danger on police solidarity is revealed when we examine a chief complaint of police: lack of public support and public apathy. The complaint may have several referents including police pay, police prestige, and support from the legislature. But the repeatedly voiced broader meaning of the complaint is resentment at being taken for granted. The policeman does not believe that his status as civil servant should relieve the public of responsibility for law enforcement. He feels, however, that payment out of public coffers somehow obscures his humanity and, therefore, his need for help.[17] As one police officer put it:

> Jerry, a cop, can get into a fight with three or four tough kids, and there will be citizens passing by, and maybe they'll look, but they'll never lend a hand. It's their country too, but you'd never know it the way some of them act. They forget that we're made of flesh and blood too. They don't care what happens to the cop so long as they don't get a little dirty.

Although the policeman sees himself as a specialist in dealing with violence, he does not want to fight alone. He does not believe that his specialization relieves the general public of citizenship duties. Indeed, if possible, he would prefer to be the foreman rather than the workingman in the battle against criminals.

The general public, of course, does withdraw from the workday world of the policeman. The policeman's responsibility for controlling dangerous and sometimes violent persons alienates the average citizen perhaps as much as does his authority over the average citizen. If the policeman's job is to ensure that public order is maintained, the citizen's inclination is to shrink from the dangers of maintaining it. The citizen prefers to see the policeman as an automaton, because once the policeman's humanity is recognized, the citizen necessarily becomes implicated in the policeman's work, which is, after all, sometimes dirty and dangerous. What the policeman typically fails to realize is the extent he becomes tainted by the character of the work he performs. The dangers of their work not only draw policemen together as a group but separate them from the rest of the population. Banton, for instance, comments:

> Patrolmen may support their fellows over what they regard as minor infractions in order to demonstrate to them that they will be loyal in situations that make the greatest demands upon their fidelity.
>
> In the American departments I visited it seemed as if the supervisors shared many of the patrolmen's sentiments about solidarity. They too wanted their colleagues to back them up in an emergency, and they shared similar frustrations with the public.[18]

Thus, the element of danger contains seeds of isolation which may grow in two directions. In one, a stereotyping perceptual shorthand is formed through which the police come to see certain signs as symbols of potential violence. The police probably differ in this respect from the general middle-class white population only in degree. This difference, however, may take on enormous significance in practice. Thus, the policeman works at identifying and possibly apprehending the symbolic assailant; the ordinary citizen does not. As a result, the ordinary citizen does not assume the responsibility to implicate himself in the policeman's required response to danger. The element of danger in the policeman's role alienates him not only from populations with a potential for crime but also from the conventionally respectable (white) citizenry, in short, from that segment of the population from which friends would ordinarily be drawn. As Janowitz has noted in a paragraph suggesting similarities between the police and the military, ". . . any profession which is continually preoccupied with the threat of danger requires a strong sense of solidarity if it is to operate effectively. Detailed regulation of the military style of life is expected to enhance group cohesion, professional loyalty, and maintain the martial spirit."[19]

Social Isolation and Authority

The element of authority also helps to account for the policeman's social isolation. Policemen themselves are aware of their isolation from the community, and are apt to weight authority heavily as a causal factor. When considering how authority influences rejection, the policeman typically singles out his responsibility for enforcement of traffic violations.[20] Resentment, even hostility, is generated in those receiving citations, in part because such contact is often the only one citizens have with police, and in part because municipal administrations and courts have been known to utilize police authority primarily to meet budgetary requirements, rather than those of public order. Thus, when a municipality engages in "speed trapping" by changing limits so quickly that drivers cannot realistically slow down to the prescribed speed or, while keeping the limits reasonable, charging high fines primarily to generate revenue, the policeman carries the brunt of public resentment.

That the policeman dislikes writing traffic tickets is suggested by the quota system police departments typically employ. In Westville, each traffic policeman has what is euphemistically described as a working "norm." A motorcyclist is supposed to write two tickets an hour for moving violations. It is doubtful that "norms" are needed because policemen are lazy. Rather, employment of quotas most likely springs from the reluctance of policemen to expose themselves to what they know to be public hostility. As a result, as one traffic policeman said:

> You learn to sniff out the places where you can catch violators when you're running behind. Of course, the department gets to know that you hang around one place, and they sometimes try to repair the situation there. But a lot of the time it would be too expensive to fix up the engineering fault, so we keep making our norm.

When meeting "production" pressures, the policeman inadvertently gives a false impression of patrolling ability to the average citizen. The traffic cyclist waits in hiding for moving violators near a tricky intersection, and is reasonably sure that such violations will occur with regularity. The violator believes he has observed a policeman displaying exceptional detection capacities and may have two thoughts, each apt to generate hostility toward the policeman: "I have been trapped," or "They can catch me; why can't they catch crooks as easily?" The answer, of course, lies in the different behavior patterns of motorists and "crooks." The latter do not act with either the frequency or predictability of motorists at poorly engineered intersections.

While traffic patrol plays a major role in separating the policeman from the respectable community, other of his tasks also have this consequence. Traffic patrol is only the most obvious illustration of the policeman's general responsibility for maintaining public order, which also includes keeping order at public accidents, sporting events, and political rallies. These activities share one feature: the policeman is called upon to direct ordinary citizens and therefore to restrain their freedom of action. Resenting the restraint, the average citizen in such a situation typically thinks something along the lines of "He is supposed to catch crooks; why is he bothering me?" Thus, the citizen stresses the "dangerous" portion of the policeman's role while belittling his authority.

Closely related to the policeman's authority-based problems as director of the citizenry are difficulties associated with his injunction to regulate public morality. For instance, the policeman is obliged to investigate "lovers' lanes" and to enforce laws pertaining to gambling, prostitution, and drunkenness. His responsibility in these matters allows him much administrative discretion since he may not actually enforce the law by making an arrest, but instead merely interfere with continuation of the objectionable activity.[21] Thus, he may put the drunk in a taxi, tell the lovers to remove themselves from the backseat, and advise a man soliciting a prostitute to leave the area.

Such admonitions are in the interest of maintaining the proprieties of public order. At the same time, the policeman invites the hostility of the citizen so directed in two respects: he is likely to encourage the sort of response mentioned earlier (that is, an antagonistic reformulation of the policeman's role) and the policeman is apt to cause resentment because of the suspicion that policemen do not themselves strictly conform to the moral norms they are enforcing. Thus, the policeman, faced with enforcing a law against fornication, drunkenness, or gambling, is easily liable to a charge of hypocrisy. Even when the policeman is called on to enforce the laws relating to overt homosexuality, a form of sexual activity for which police are not especially noted, he may encounter the charge of hypocrisy on grounds that he does not adhere strictly to prescribed heterosexual codes. The policeman's difficulty in this respect is shared by all authorities responsible for maintenance of disciplined activity, including industrial foremen, political leaders, elementary schoolteachers, and college professors. All are expected to conform rigidly to the entire range of norms they espouse.[22] The policeman, however, as a result of the unique combination of the elements of danger and authority, experiences a special predicament. It is difficult to develop qualities enabling him to stand up to danger and to conform to standards of puritanical morality.

The element of danger demands that the policeman be able to carry out efforts that are in their nature overtly masculine. Police work, like soldiering, requires an exceptional caliber of physical fitness, agility, toughness, and the like. The man who ranks high on these masculine characteristics is, again like the soldier, not usually disposed to be puritanical about sex, drinking, and gambling.

On the basis of observations, policemen do not subscribe to moralistic standards for conduct. For example, the morals squad of the police department, when questioned, was unanimously against the statutory rape age limit, on grounds that as late teenagers they themselves might not have refused an attractive offer from a seventeen-year-old girl.[23] Neither, from observations, are policemen by any means total abstainers from the use of alcoholic beverages. The policeman who is arresting a drunk has probably been drunk himself; he knows it and the drunk knows it.

More than that, a portion of the social isolation of the policeman can be attributed to the discrepancy between moral regulation and the norms and behavior of policemen in these areas. We have presented data indicating that police engage in a comparatively active occupational social life. One interpretation might attribute this attendance to a basic interest in such affairs; another might explain the policeman's occupational social activity as a measure of restraint in publicly violating norms he enforces. The interest in attending police affairs may grow as much out of security in "letting oneself go" in the presence of police, and a corresponding feeling of insecurity with civilians, as an authentic preference for police social affairs. Much alcohol is usually consumed at police banquets with all the melancholy and boisterousness accompanying such occasions. As Horace Clayton reports on his experience as a policeman:

> Deputy sheriffs and policemen don't know much about organized recreation: all they usually do when celebrating is get drunk and pound each other on the back, exchanging loud insults which under ordinary circumstances would result in a fight.[24]

To some degree the reason for the behavior exhibited on these occasions is the company, since the policeman would feel uncomfortable exhibiting insobriety before civilians. The policeman may be likened to other authorities who prefer to violate moralistic norms away from onlookers for whom they are routinely supposed to appear as normative models. College professors, for instance, also get drunk on occasion, but prefer to do so where students are not present. Unfortunately for the policeman, such settings are harder for him to come by than they are for the college professor. The whole civilian world watches the policeman. As a result, he tends to be limited to the company of other policemen for whom his police identity is not a stimulus to carping normative criticism.

Correlates of Social Isolation

The element of authority, like the element of danger, is thus seen to contribute to the solidarity of policemen. To the extent that policemen share the experience of receiving hostility from the public, they are also drawn together and become dependent upon one another. Trends in the degree to which police may exercise authority are also important considerations in understanding the dynamics of the relation between authority and solidarity. It is not simply a question of how much absolute authority police are given, but how much authority they have relative to what they had, or think they had, before. If, as Westley concludes, police violence is frequently a response to a challenge to the policeman's authority, so too may a perceived reduction in authority result in greater solidarity. Whitaker comments on the British police as follows:

> As they feel their authority decline, internal solidarity has become increasingly important to the police. Despite the individual responsibility of each police officer to pursue justice, there is sometimes a tendency to close ranks and to form a square when they themselves are concerned.[25]

These inclinations may have positive consequences for the effectiveness of police work, since notions of professional courtesy or colleagueship seem unusually high among police.[26] When the nature of the policing enterprise requires much joint activity, as in robbery and narcotics enforcement, the impression is received that cooperation is high and genuine. Policemen do not appear to cooperate with one another merely because such is the policy of the chief, but because they sincerely attach a high value to teamwork. For instance, there is a norm among detectives that two who work together will protect each other when a dangerous situation arises. During one investigation, a detective stepped out of a car to question a suspect who became belligerent. The second detective, who had remained overly long in the backseat of the police car, apologized indirectly to his partner by explaining how wrong it had been of him to permit his partner to encounter a suspect alone on the street. He later repeated this explanation privately, in genuine consternation at having committed the breach (and possibly at having been culpable in the presence of an observer). Strong feelings of empathy and cooperation, indeed almost of "clannishness," a term several policemen themselves used to describe the attitude of police toward one another, may be seen in the daily activities of police. Analytically, these feelings can be traced to the elements of danger and shared experiences of hostility in the policeman's role.

Finally, to round out the sketch, policemen are notably conservative, emotionally and politically. If the element of danger in the policeman's role tends to make the policeman suspicious, and therefore emotionally attached to the status quo, a similar consequence may be attributed to the element of authority. The fact that a man is engaged in enforcing a set of rules implies that he also becomes implicated in affirming them. Labor disputes provide the commonest example of conditions inclining the policeman to support the status quo. In these situations, the police are necessarily pushed on the side of the defense of property. Their responsibilities thus lead them to see the striking and sometimes angry workers as their enemy and, therefore, to be cool, if not antagonistic, toward the whole conception of labor militancy.[27] If a policeman did not believe in the system of laws he was responsible for enforcing, he would have to go on living in a state of conflicting cognitions, a condition which a number of social psychologists agree is painful.[28]

This hypothetical issue of not believing in the laws they are enforcing simply does not arise for most policemen. In the course of the research, however, there was one example. A Negro civil rights advocate became a policeman with the conviction that by so doing he would be aiding the cause of impartial administration of laws for Negroes. For him, however, this outside rationale was not enough to sustain him in administering a system of laws that depends for its impartiality upon a reasonable measure of social and economic equality among the citizenry. Because this recruit identified so much with the Negro community as to be unable to meet the enforcement requirements of the Westville Police Department, his efficiency was impaired, and he resigned in his rookie year.[29]

Police are understandably reluctant to appear to be anything but impartial politically. The police are forbidden from publicly campaigning for political candidates. The London police are similarly prohibited, and before 1887 were not allowed to vote in parliamentary elections or in local ones until 1893.[30] It was not surprising that the Westville chief of police forbade questions on the questionnaire that would have measured political attitudes.[31] One policeman, however, explained the chief's refusal on grounds that "A couple of jerks here would probably cut up, and come out looking like Commies."

During the course of administering the questionnaire over a three-day period, I talked with approximately fifteen officers and sergeants in the Westville department, discussing political attitudes of police. In addition, during the course of the research itself, approximately fifty were interviewed for varying periods of time. Of these, at least twenty were interviewed more than once, some over time periods of several weeks. Furthermore, twenty police were interviewed in Eastville, several for periods ranging from several hours to several days. Most of the time was not spent on investigating political attitudes, but I made a point of raising the question, if possible, making it part of a discussion centered around the contents of a right-wing newsletter to which one of the detectives subscribed. One discussion included a group of eight detectives. From these observations, interviews, and discussions, it was clear that a Goldwater type of conservatism was the dominant political and emotional persuasion of police. I encountered only three policemen who claimed to be politically "liberal," at the same time asserting that they were decidedly exceptional.

Whether or not the policeman is an "authoritarian personality" is a related issue, beyond the scope of this discussion partly because of the many questions raised about this concept. Thus, in the course of discussing the concept of "normality" in mental health, two psychologists make the point that many conventional people were high scorers on the California F scale and similar tests. The great mass of the people, according to these authors, is not much further along the scale of ego development than the typical adolescent who, as they describe him, is "rigid, prone to think in stereotypes, intolerant of deviations, punitive and anti-psychological—in short, what has been called an authoritarian personality."[32] Therefore it is preferable to call the policeman's a conventional personality.

Writing about the New York police force, Thomas R. Brooks suggests a similar interpretation. He writes:

> Cops are conventional people. . . . All a cop can swing in a milieu of marijuana smokers, interracial dates, and homosexuals is the night stick. A policeman who passed a Lower East Side art gallery filled with paintings of what appeared to be female genitalia could think of doing only one thing—step in and make an arrest.[33]

Despite his fundamental identification with conservative conventionality, however, the policeman may be familiar, unlike most conventional people, with the argot of the hipster and the underworld. (The policeman tends to resent the quietly respectable liberal who comes to the defense of such people on principle but who has rarely met them in practice.) Indeed, the policeman will use his knowledge of the argot to advantage in talking to a suspect. In this manner, the policeman puts on the suspect by pretending to share his moral conception of the world through the use of "hip" expressions. The suspect may put on a parallel show for the policeman by using only conventional language to indicate his respectability. (In my opinion, neither fools the other.)

NOTES

1. For previous contributions in this area, see the following: Chinoy, *Automobile Workers and the American Dream*; Walker and Guest, *The Man on the Assembly Line*; Hughes, *Men and Their Work*; Wilensky, *Intellectuals in Labor Unions*; Wilensky, "Varieties of Work Experience"; Kriesberg, "The Retail Furrier"; Burchard, "Role Conflicts in Military Chaplains"; Becker and Geer, "The Fate of Idealism in Medical School"; and Becker and Straus "Careers, Personality, and Adult Socialization."

2. Janowitz, *The Professional Soldier*.

3. By no means does such an analysis suggest that there are no individual or group differences among police. On the contrary, most of this study emphasizes differences, endeavoring to relate these to occupational specialties in police departments. This chapter, however, explores similarities rather than differences, attempting to account for the police officer's general disposition to perceive and to behave in certain ways.

4. William Westley was the first to raise such questions about the police, when he inquired into the conditions under which police are violent. Whatever merit this analysis has, it owes much to his prior insights, as all subsequent sociological studies of the police must. See Westley, "Violence and the Police"; also his unpublished dissertation, *The Police: A Sociological Study of Law, Custom, and Morality*.

5. See Piliavin and Briar, "Police Encounters with Juveniles."

6. A questionnaire was given to all police officers in operating divisions of the police force: patrol, traffic, vice control, and all detectives. The questionnaire was administered at police line-ups over a period of three days, mainly by the author but also by some of the police personnel themselves. Before the questionnaire was administered, it was circulated to and approved by the police officers' welfare association.

7. Indeed, the journalist Paul Jacobs, who has ridden with the Westville juvenile police as

part of his own work on poverty, observed in a personal communication that juvenile police appear curiously drawn to seek out dangerous situations, as if juvenile work without danger is degrading.

8. MacInnes, *Mr. Love and Justice*, p. 74.

9. Connell, *Handling of Complaints by Police*.

10. Baldwin, *Nobody Knows My Name*, pp. 65–67.

11. MacInnes, *Mr. Love and Justice*, p. 20.

12. Respondents were asked, "Anybody who knows anything about police work knows that police face a number of problems. Would you please state—in order—what you consider to be the two most serious problems police have?" On the basis of a number of answers, the writer and J. Richard Woodworth devised a set of categories. Then Woodworth classified each response into one of the categories. When a response did not seem clear, he consulted with the writers. No attempt was made to independently check Woodworth's classification because the results are used impressionistically and do not test a hypothesis. It may be, for instance, that "relations to the public" is sometimes used to indicate racial problems, and vice versa. "Racial problems" include only those answers having specific reference to race.

13. Banton, *The Police in the Community*.

14. Similarly, Banton found Scottish police officers attempting to conceal their occupation when on holiday. He quoted one saying: "If someone asks my wife, 'what does your husband do?' I've told her to say, 'He's a clerk,' and that's the way it went because she found that being a policeman's wife—well, it wasn't quite a stigma, she didn't feel cut off, but that a sort of invisible wall was up for conversation purposes when a policeman was there."

15. In addition to Banton, William Westley and James Q. Wilson noted this characteristic of police. See Westley, "Violence and the Police"; Wilson, "The Police and Their Problems: A Theory."

16. Lipset, Trow, and Coleman, *Union Democracy*.

17. On this issue there was no variation. The statement "the police officer feels" means that there was no instance of a negative opinion expressed by the police studied.

18. Banton, *The Police in the Community*, p. 114.

19. Janowitz, *The Professional Soldier*.

20. O. W. Wilson, for example, mentions this factor as a primary source of antagonism toward police. See his "Police Authority in a Free Society." In the current study, in addition to the police themselves, other people interviewed, such as attorneys in the system, also attribute the isolation of police to their authority.

21. See LaFave, "The Police and Nonenforcement of the Law."

22. For a theoretical discussion of the problems of leadership, see Homans, *The Human Group*, especially the chapter entitled, "The Job of the Leader," pp. 415–40.

23. The work of the Westville morals squad was analyzed in detail in an unpublished master's thesis by Woodworth, *The Administration of Statutory Rape Complaints: A Sociological Study*.

24. Clayton, *Long Old Road*, p. 154.

25. Whitaker, *The Police*, p. 137.

26. It would be difficult to compare this factor across occupations, because the indications could hardly be controlled. Nevertheless, I felt that the sense of responsibility to police officers in other departments was on the whole quite strong.

27. In light of this, the most carefully drawn lesson plan in the "professionalized" Westville police department, according to the officer in charge of training, is the one dealing with the police officer's demeanor in labor disputes. A comparable concern is now being evidenced in

teaching police the appropriate demeanor in civil rights demonstrations. See, e.g., Towler, *The Police Role in Racial Conflicts.*

28. Indeed, one school of social psychology asserts that there is a basic drive, a fundamental tendency of human nature, to reduce the degree of discrepancy between conflicting cognitions. For police officers, this tenet implies having to do something to reduce the discrepancy between their personal beliefs and behavior. The officers would have to modify their behavior and beliefs or introduce some outside factor to justify the discrepancy. If the officers modified behavior, so as not to enforce a law that is personally unacceptable, they would not hold their jobs for long. Practically, then, the officers may either introduce an outside factor or modify their beliefs. The outside factor would have to be compelling to reduce the pain resulting from the dissonance between the officers' cognitions. For example, the officer would have to convince themselves that the only way to make a living was by being a police officer or, instead, modify their beliefs. See Festinger, *A Theory of Cognitive Dissonance.* For a brief explanation of Festinger's theory, see Sampson, ed., *Approaches, Contexts, and Problems of Social Psychology,* pp. 9–15.

29. I thank Gwynne Pierson for pointing out the inaccuracy of the first edition's report of this incident.

30. Whitaker, *The Police.*

31. The questions submitted to the chief of police were directly analogous to those asked of printers in the study of the I.T.U. See Lipset et al., *Union Democracy,* pp. 493–503.

32. Loevinger and Ossorio, "Evaluation of Therapy by Self-Report: A Paradox," p. 392; see also Shils, "Authoritarianism: 'Right' and 'Left,'" in Christie and Jahoda (eds.), *Studies in Scope and Method of the Authoritarian Personality.*

33. Brooks, "New York's Finest," pp. 29–30.

REFERENCES

Baldwin, James. 1962. *Nobody knows my name.* New York: Dell.

Banton, Michael. 1964. *The police in the community.* London: Tavistock.

Becker, Howard S., and Blanche Geer. 1958. The fate of idealism in medical school. *American Sociological Review* 23: 50–56.

Becker, Howard S., and Anselm L. Straus. 1956. Careers, personality, and adult socialization. *American Journal of Sociology* 62: 253–363.

Brooks, Thomas R. 1965. New York's finest. *Commentary* 40: 29–30.

Burchard, Waldo. 1954. Role conflicts in military chaplains. *American Sociological Review* 23: 50–56.

Chinoy, Ely. 1955. *Automobile workers and the American dream.* Garden City: Doubleday.

Clayton, Horace R. 1965. *Long old road.* New York: Trident Press.

Connell, Peter J. 1961. *Handling of complaints by police.* Unpublished Manuscript.

Festinger, Leon. 1957. *A theory of cognitive dissonance.* Evanston, IL: Row-Peterson.

Homans, George. 1950. *The human group.* New York: Harcourt, Brace.

Hughes, Everett C. 1958. *Men and their work.* Glencoe, IL: The Free Press.

Janowitz, Morris. 1964. *The professional soldier: A social and political portrait.* New York: The Free Press.

Kriesberg, Louis. 1952. The retail furrier: Concepts of security and success. *American Journal of Sociology* 57: 478–485.

LaFave, Wayne R. 1962. The police and nonenforcement of the law. *Wisconsin Law Review*: 179–239.

Lipset, Seymour M., Martin H. Trow, and James S. Coleman. 1962. *Union democracy*. New York: Anchor Books.

Loevinger, Jane, and Abel Ossorio. 1959. Evaluation of therapy by self-report: A paradox. *Journal of Abnormal and Social Psychology* 58: 392.

MacInnes, Colin. 1962. *Mr. love and justice*. London: New English Library.

Piliavin, Irving, and Scott Briar. 1964. Police encounters with juveniles. *American Journal of Sociology* 70: 206–214.

Sampson, Edward S., ed. 1964. *Approaches, contexts, and problems of social psychology*. Englewood Cliffs, NJ: Prentice Hall.

Shils, Edward A. 1954. Authoritarianism: "Right" and "left." In *Studies in scope and method of the authoritarian personality*, eds. R. Christie and M. Jahoda, 24–49. Glencoe, IL: The Free Press.

Towler, Juby E. 1964. *The police role in racial conflicts*. Springfield: Charles C. Thomas.

Walker, Charles R., and Robert H. Guest. 1952. *The man on the assembly line*. Cambridge: Harvard University Press.

Westley, William. 1953. Violence and the police. *American Journal of Sociology* 59: 34–41.

Westley, William. 1951. *The police: A sociological study of law, custom, and morality*. University of Chicago, Department of Sociology.

Whitaker, Ben. 1964. *The police*. Middlesex: Penguin Books.

Wilensky, Harold L. 1956. *Intellectuals in labor unions: Organizational pressures on professional roles*. Glencoe, IL: The Free Press.

Wilensky, Harold L. 1964. Varieties of work experience. In *Man in a world at work*, ed. H. Borow, 125–154. Boston: Houghton Mifflin Company.

Wilson, James Q. 1963. The police and their problems: A theory. *Public Policy* 12: 189–216.

Wilson, Orlando W. 1964. Police authority in a free society. *Journal of Criminal Law, Criminology, and Police Science* 54: 175–177.

Woodworth, J. Richard. 1964. *The administration of statutory rape complaints: A sociological study*. University of California, Berkeley.

Chapter 2

Driving While Black

A Statistician Proves That Prejudice Still Rules the Road

John Lamberth

In 1993, I was contacted by attorneys whose clients had been arrested on the New Jersey Turnpike for possession of drugs. They told me they had come across 25 African American defendants over a three-year period all arrested on the same stretch of turnpike in Gloucester County, but not a single white defendant. I was asked whether, and how much, this pattern reflected unfair treatment of blacks.

They wanted to know what a professional statistician would make of these numbers. What were the probabilities that this pattern could occur naturally, that is, by chance? Since arrests for drug offenses occurred after traffic stops on the highway, was it possible that so many blacks were arrested because the police were disproportionately stopping them?

I decided to try to answer their questions and embarked on one of the most intriguing statistical studies of my career: a census of traffic and traffic violators by race on Interstate 95 in New Jersey. It would require a careful design, teams of researchers with binoculars and a rolling survey.

To relieve your suspense, the answer was that the rate at which blacks were stopped was greatly disproportionate to their numbers on the road and to their propensity to violate traffic laws. Those findings were central to a March 1996 ruling by Judge Robert E. Francis of the Superior Court of New Jersey that the state police were de facto targeting blacks, in violation of their rights under the U.S. and New Jersey constitutions. The judge suppressed the evidence gathered in the stops. New Jersey is now appealing the case.

The New Jersey litigation is part of a broad attack in a number of states, including Maryland, on what has been dubbed the offense of "DWB"—driving while black. While this problem has been familiar anecdotally to African Americans and civil rights advocates for years, there is now evidence that highway patrols are singling out blacks for stops on the illegal and incorrect theory that the practice, known as racial profiling, is the most likely to yield drug arrests. Statistical techniques are proving extremely helpful in proving targeting, just as they have been in proving systemic discrimination in employment.

From *Washington Post*, p. C01, August 16, 1998. © *Washington Post* 1998. Reprinted with permission of *Washington Post*.

This was not my first contact with the disparate treatment of blacks in the criminal justice system. My academic research over the past 25 years had led me from an interest in small-group decision making to jury selection, jury composition and the application of the death penalty. I became aware that blacks were disproportionately charged with crimes, particularly serious ones; that they were underrepresented on jury panels and thus on juries; and that they were sentenced to death at a much greater rate than their numbers could justify.

As I began the New Jersey study, I knew from experience that any research that questioned police procedures was sensitive. I knew that what I did must stand the test of a court hearing in which every move I made would be challenged by experts.

First, I had to decide what I needed to know. What was the black "population" of the road—that is, how many of the people traveling on the turnpike over a given period of time were African American? This task is a far cry from determining the population of a town, city or state. There are no Census Bureau figures. The population of a roadway changes all day, every day. By sampling the population of the roadway over a given period, I could make an accurate determination of the average number of blacks on the road.

I designed and implemented two surveys. We stationed observers by the side of the road, with the assignment of counting the number of cars and the race of the occupants in randomly selected three-hour blocks of time over a two-week period. The New Jersey Turnpike has four lanes at its southern end, two in each direction. By the side of the road, we placed an observer for each lane, equipped with binoculars to observe and note the number of cars and the race of occupants, along with a person to write down what the observers said. The team observed for an hour and a half, took a 30-minute break while moving to another observation point and repeated the process.

In total, we conducted more than 21 sessions between 8 a.m. and 8 p.m. from June 11 to June 24, 1993, at four sites between Exits 1 and 3 of the turnpike, among the busiest highway segments in the nation. We counted roughly 43,000 cars, of which 13.5 percent had one or more black occupants. This was consistent with the population figures for the 11 states from which most of the vehicles observed were registered.

For the rolling survey, Fred Last, a public defender, drove at a constant 60 mph (5 mph above the speed limit at the time). He counted all cars that passed him as violators and all cars he passed as nonviolators. Speaking into a tape recorder, he also noted the race of the driver of each car. At the end of each day, he collated his results and faxed them to me.

Last counted 2096 cars. More than 98 percent were speeding and thus subject to being stopped by police. African Americans made up about 15 percent of those drivers on the turnpike violating traffic laws.

Utilizing data from the New Jersey State Police, I determined that about 35 percent of those who were stopped on this part of the turnpike were African Americans.

To summarize: African Americans made up 13.5 percent of the turnpike's population and 15 percent of the speeders. But they represented 35 percent of those pulled over. In stark numbers, blacks were 4.85 times as likely to be stopped as were others.

We did not obtain data on the race of drivers and passengers searched after being stopped or on the rate at which vehicles were searched. But we know from police records that 73.2 percent of those arrested along the turnpike over a 3½-year period by troopers from the area's Moorestown barracks were black—making them 16.5 times more likely to be arrested than others.

Attorneys for the 25 African Americans who had been arrested on the turnpike and charged with possessing drug or guns filed motions to suppress evidence seized when they were stopped, arguing that police stopped them because of their race. Their motions were consolidated and heard by Judge Francis between November 1994 and May 1995.

My statistical study, bolstered by an analysis of its validity by Joseph B. Kadane, professor of statistics at Carnegie Mellon University, was the primary exhibit in support of the motions.

But Francis also heard testimony from two former New Jersey troopers who said they had been coached to make race-based "profile" stops to increase their criminal arrests. And the judge reviewed police in-service training aids such as videos that disproportionately portrayed minorities as perpetrators. The statistical disparities, Francis wrote, are "indeed stark. . . . Defendants have proven at least a de facto policy on the part of the State Police . . . of targeting blacks for investigation and arrest." The judge ordered that the state's evidence be suppressed.

My own work in this field continues. In 1992, Robert L. Wilkins was riding in a rented car with family members when Maryland State Police stopped them, ordered them out, and conducted a search for drugs, which were not found. Wilkins happened to be a Harvard Law School trained public defender in Washington. With the support of the Maryland ACLU, he sued the state police, who settled the case with, among other things, an agreement to provide highway-stop data to the organization.

I was asked by the ACLU to evaluate the Maryland data in 1996 and again in 1997. I conducted a rolling survey in Maryland similar to the one I had done before and found a similar result. While 17.5 percent of the traffic violators on I-95 north of Baltimore were African American, 28.8 percent of those stopped and 71.3 percent of those searched by the Maryland State Police were African American. U.S. District Judge Catherine Blake ultimately ruled in 1997 that the ACLU made a "reasonable showing" that Maryland troopers on I-95 were continuing to engage in a "pattern and practice" of racial discrimination.

Other legal actions have been filed in Pennsylvania, Florida, Indiana and North Carolina. Police officials everywhere deny racial profiling.

Why, then, are so many more African American motorists stopped than would be expected by their frequency on the road and their violation of the law? It seems clear to me that drugs are the issue.

The notion that African Americans and other minorities are more likely than whites to be carrying drugs—a notion that is perpetuated by some police training films—seems to be especially prevalent among the police. They believe that if they are to interdict drugs, then it makes sense to stop minorities, especially young men. State police are rewarded and promoted at least partially on the basis of their "criminal programs," which means the number of arrests they make. Testimony in the New Jersey case pointed out that troopers would be considered deficient if they did not make enough arrests. Since, as Judge Francis found, training points to minorities as likely drug dealers, it makes a certain sort of distorted sense to stop minorities more than whites.

But there is no untainted evidence that minorities are more likely to possess or sell drugs. There is evidence to the contrary. Indirect evidence in statistics from the National Institute of Drug Abuse indicates that 12 percent to 14 percent of those who abuse drugs are African American, a percentage that is proportionate to their numbers in the general population.

More telling are the numbers of those people who are stopped and searched by the Maryland State Police who have drugs. This data, which has been unobtainable from other states, indicates that of those drivers and passengers searched in Maryland, about 28 percent have contraband, whether they are black or white. The same percentage of contraband is found no matter the race.

The Maryland data may shed some light on the tendency of some troopers to believe that blacks are somehow more likely to possess contraband. This data shows that for every 1,000 searches by the Maryland State Police, 200 blacks and only 80 non-blacks are arrested. This could lead one to believe that more blacks are breaking the law—until you know that the sample is deeply skewed. Of those searched, 713 were black and only 287 were non-black.

We do not have comparable figures on contraband possession or arrests from New Jersey. But if the traffic along I-95 there is at all similar to I-95 in Maryland—and there is a strong numerical basis to believe it is—it is possible to speculate that black travelers in New Jersey also were no more likely than non-blacks to be carrying contraband.

The fact that a black was 16.5 times more likely than a non-black to be arrested on the New Jersey Turnpike now takes on added meaning. Making only the assumption that was shown accurate in Maryland, it is possible to say even more conclusively that racial profiling is prevalent there and that there is no benefit to police in singling out blacks.

|||||||||||||||||||||||||||||||||||||||||||||||||||||||||||||||||||||||||||||||||||

Chapter 3

The Stories, the Statistics, and the Law
Why "Driving While Black" Matters

David A. Harris

Each one of those stops, for me, had nothing to do with breaking the law. It had to do with who I was . . . It's almost like somebody pulls your pants down around your ankles. You're standing there nude, but you've got to act like there's nothing happening.[1]

It has happened to actors Wesley Snipes, Will Smith, Blair Underwood, and LeVar Burton. It has also happened to football player Marcus Allen, and Olympic athletes Al Joyner and Edwin Moses. African Americans call it "driving while black"—police officers stopping, questioning, and even searching black drivers who have committed no crime, based on the excuse of a traffic offense. And it has even happened to O. J. Simpson lawyer Johnnie Cochran.

In his pre-Simpson days, Cochran worked hand-in-hand with police officers as an Assistant District Attorney in Los Angeles, putting criminals behind bars. Cochran was driving down Sunset Boulevard one Saturday afternoon with his two youngest children in the back seat when a police car stopped him.[2] Looking in his rearview mirror, Cochran got a frightening shock: "the police were out of their car with their guns out." The officers said that they thought Cochran was driving a stolen car, and with no legal basis they began to search it. But instead of finding evidence, they found Cochran's official badge, identifying him as an Assistant District Attorney. "When they saw my badge, they ran for cover," Cochran said.[3]

The incident unnerved Cochran, but it terrified his young children. "[The officers] had their guns out and my kids were in that car crying. My daughter said, 'Daddy, I thought you were with the police.' I had to explain to her why this happened."[4]

Cochran's experience is a textbook example of what many African American drivers[5] say they go through every day: police using traffic offenses as an excuse to stop and conduct roadside investigations of black drivers and their cars, usually to look for drugs. Normally, if police want to conduct stops and searches for contraband they need probable cause or at least reasonable suspicion that the suspect is involved in an offense.[6] But with the Supreme Court's recent cases involving cars, drivers, and passengers, none of this is necessary. Traffic offenses open the door to stops, searches,

From *Minnesota Law Review* 84: 265–326. © *Minnesota Law Review* 1999. Reprinted with permission of *Minnesota Law Review*.

and questioning, based on mere hunches, or nothing at all.[7] And African Americans believe they are subjected to this treatment in numbers far out of proportion to their presence in the driving population.

But is this just a problem of perception, the product of years of mistrust between police and minorities? Is it a problem only in large urban centers? Are these claims supported by statistical evidence, or are they merely strong feelings born of anecdotes?

To answer these questions, a number of African Americans—all middle class, tax-paying citizens—described their experiences in interviews. The interviewees were drawn from Toledo, Ohio, an almost prototypical medium-sized Midwestern city.[8] Statistics from courts in Toledo and in three other Ohio cities—Dayton, Akron, and Columbus—were analyzed.[9] Research from other areas of the country was also reviewed.[10]

The interviews reveal that African Americans strongly believe that they are stopped and ticketed more often than whites, and the data from Ohio and elsewhere show that they are right. For example, the Toledo Police Department is at least twice as likely to issue tickets to blacks than to all other drivers.[11] The numbers in Akron, Columbus and Dayton are similar: blacks are about twice as likely to get tickets as those who are not black.[12] When adjusted to reflect the fact that 21% of all black households do not own vehicles, making blacks less likely to drive than others, these numbers increase to even higher levels. All of the assumptions built into this statistical analysis are conservative; they are structured to give the law enforcement agencies the benefit of the doubt. Statistics from cases in New Jersey and Maryland are similar. Sophisticated analyses of stops and driving populations in both states showed racial disparities in traffic stops that were "literally off the charts."[13]

Police departments engage in these practices for a simple reason: they help catch criminals. Since blacks represent a disproportionate share of those arrested for certain crimes,[14] police believe that it makes sense to stop a disproportionate share of blacks. Lt. Ernest Leatherbury, a spokesman for the Maryland State Police (a department that has been sued twice over race-based traffic stops), explained to the Washington Post that stopping an outsized number of blacks was not racism, but rather "an unfortunate byproduct of sound police policies."[15] Carl Williams, Superintendent of the New Jersey State Police, put the matter even more bluntly in an interview with the *Newark Star-Ledger*. With narcotics today, he said, "it's most likely a minority group that's involved with that."[16] In other words, officers may be targeting blacks and other minorities, but this is a rational thing to do.

This type of thinking means that anyone who is African American is automatically suspect during every drive to work, the store, or a friend's house. Suspicion is not focused on individuals who have committed crimes, but on a whole racial group. Skin color becomes evidence, and race becomes a proxy for general criminal propensity. Aside from the possibility of suing a police department for these practices—a mammoth undertaking, that should only be undertaken by plaintiffs with absolutely clean records and the thickest skin—there is no relief available.

Pretextual traffic stops aggravate years of accumulated feelings of injustice, resulting in deepening distrust and cynicism by African Americans about police and the entire criminal justice system. But the problem goes deeper. If upstanding citizens are treated like criminals by the police, they will not trust those same officers as investigators of crimes or as witnesses in court. Fewer people will trust the police enough to tell them what they know about criminals in their neighborhoods, and some may not vote to convict the guilty in court when they are jurors. Recent polling data show that not just blacks, but a majority of whites believe that blacks face racism at the hands of police.[17] "Driving while black" has begun to threaten the integrity of the entire process not only in the eyes of African Americans, but of everyone.

This chapter begins in part I by discussing the experiences of three of the African Americans who were interviewed for this chapter. Their stories, selected not because they are unusually harsh but because they are typical, speak for themselves. The frightening and embarrassing nature of the experiences, the emotional difficulties and devastation that often follow, and the ways that they cope, bring to life the statistics, which are discussed in part II. Part III then shows how the problem is connected to larger issues at the intersection of criminal justice and race. Part IV puts the problem of "driving while black" into its legal context and explains how the law not only allows but encourages these practices. Finally, part V concludes with a discussion of some approaches that might be taken to address the problem.

I. The Cost of Getting Stopped: Fear, Anger, and Humiliation

Talk to almost any black person any place in the country and you will hear accounts of pretextual traffic stops. Some say they have experienced it many times. All of those interviewed—not criminals trying to explain away wrongdoing, but people with good jobs and families[18]—described an experience common to blacks, but almost invisible to whites. The stories of several of these individuals illustrate what the experience is like and how it has impacted their lives.

Karen Brank, a licensed social worker in her early thirties with a young son, had never been in trouble with the police.[19] But one morning, on her way to work for a monthly staff meeting, all of that changed when Brank was pulled over for speeding. Brank recalls being one of several cars that were traveling down a main thoroughfare at about the same rate of speed.[20] The officer who stopped her told her she was going too fast. He then asked for her license and registration and took these items to the squad car. When he returned, the officer told Brank that there were outstanding warrants for her arrest for unpaid traffic tickets.[21] Brank remembered the tickets because she did not get many and told the officer that she had paid them weeks before.[22] But when she could not produce a receipt to prove payment (and who could have?), the officer said he would have to arrest her.[23]

Brank was stunned. Arrest me? she thought. What do you mean arrest me? I'm not a criminal—I'm on my way to work![24] This could not be happening—and yet it was. It turned out later that the warrants were incorrect. Brank had paid, but a clerical error had kept the tickets in the computer system.[25] Additional squad cars arrived, making the area around her car look like a crime scene. Mistake or not, minutes later Brank stood by the side of the road in handcuffs so tight that they left ugly red marks on her wrists for several days.[26] She was distraught, breaking down in tears standing next to a public street. She can still feel the sting of embarrassment.

> I was really upset. I was like, "Why are you guys handcuffing me about some tickets?" They had me standing outside with all these people passing by. It was so humiliating.[27]

Months afterward, the pain she experienced during these moments still becomes visible on her face as she recalls the incident. She was put into a squad car and sat there, afraid to say anything.

> I didn't say nothing, because I figured if I said anything, if I moved, that would just give them permission to beat me. And I did not want that to happen because I have a little boy.[28]

Brank watched as the police searched her car. She says that the other officers on the scene—perhaps four or five exchanged high fives with the arresting officer, accompanied by phrases like "good job" and "you got another one."[29] Eventually, she was taken downtown and released. Brank felt unable to go to work that day. In the days that followed, her co-workers could tell something was wrong, but for some reason she hesitated to tell them what had happened. "I didn't want anyone to know. I was so embarrassed."[30]

Brank is firmly convinced that she was singled out from the other cars around her, which she says were going the same speed, because she is black. She is sure that a white person would not have been handcuffed and humiliated the way she was. But the police officer who stopped her denies this. "The only reason I stopped her was because of a violation—speeding," he says, adding that he caught her on radar. "I don't care if you're black, blue, beige, brown, whatever—if you're violating the law, I'll stop you."[31] And he categorically denies that any high fives or congratulatory words were exchanged.[32]

James, a well-dressed, 28-year-old advertising account executive with a media company, also has been stopped for numerous traffic offenses. "I'm not one of those guys who says, 'Oh yeah, blacks, we've just got it bad,'" he says. But being stopped repeatedly by police is such an unchangeable part of life for him that "it's like the fact that I'm black."[33]

James described an incident that took place recently in an upscale neighborhood, where he had visited a friend.[34] After socializing for a while, James left the house and got in his car to leave. As soon as he pulled out of the driveway, James noticed that a police car was following him.[35] Although he drove with extra care, the officer pulled James over and questioned him, accused him of weaving, checked his license and registration, and threatened to give him a citation for not wearing a seat belt.[36] "I think he saw a black male in that neighborhood and he was suspicious," James says.[37] Months later, the anger James felt that night remains fresh.

> I feel like I'm a guy who's pretty much walked the straight line and that's respecting people and everything. But if cops will even bother me, that makes me think, well, it's

gotta be something . . . We just constantly get harassed. So we just feel like we can't go nowhere without being bothered . . . I'm not trying to bother nobody. But yet I got a cop pull me over says I'm weaving in the road. And I just came from a friend's house, no alcohol, no nothing. It just makes you wonder—was it just because I'm black?[38]

It would be a mistake to think that pretextual traffic stops are limited to younger blacks. Michael, 41, is tall, attractive, and well-spoken. He is the top executive in an important public institution and has been stopped by the police many times.[39] One afternoon, Michael was driving to a local high school to work out. As he approached the parking lot, he saw a parked police cruiser, so he drove with extra caution.[40] "As I pulled up and put it in park and turned the key off, this police car comes screeching up behind me—the lights flashing, the whole deal," Michael says.[41] The squad car blocked him in to the parking space, so he could not leave.[42] But when the officer walked up to the window, he immediately noticed Michael's official identification. Without offering any explanation for why he had treated Michael as if he were a dangerous criminal, the officer "just backed away and he was gone. Just disappeared."[43]

Michael was angry and frustrated at being treated this way, but it was not the first time it had happened. As he has done many times before, he distanced himself from the experience as a kind of emotional self-defense.

You've gotta learn to play through it. Even though you haven't done anything wrong, the worst thing you can do in a situation like that is to become emotionally engaged when they do that to you . . . Because if you do something, maybe they're going to do something else to you for no reason at all, because they have the power. They have the power and they can do whatever they want to do to you for that period of time . . . It doesn't make a difference who you are. You're never beyond this, because of the color of your skin.[44]

For many blacks, the emotional cost is profound. Karen Brank missed work and experienced depression. For some time afterwards, she felt a wave of fear wash over her every time she saw a police car in her rearview mirror.[45] In that one brief encounter, her entire sense of herself—her job, the fact that she is a mother and an educated, law-abiding person working on a master's degree—was stripped away. Kevin, an executive in his thirties with a large financial services corporation, a husband, and father with several young children, says his experiences have left him with very negative feelings about police.[46] "When I see cops today, I don't feel like I'm protected. I'm thinking, 'Oh shoot, are they gonna pull me over, are they gonna stop me?' That's my reaction. I do not feel safe around cops."[47]

To cope, African Americans often make adjustments in their daily activities. They avoid certain places where they think police will "look" for blacks.[48] Some drive bland cars.[49] "I drive a minivan because it doesn't grab attention," says Kevin. "If I was driving a BMW"—a car he could certainly afford—"different story."[50] Some change the way they dress.[51] Others who drive long distances even factor in extra time for the inevitable traffic stops they will face.[52]

But nowhere does the effect of racially biased traffic stops become more painful than when blacks instruct their children on how to behave when—not if—they are stopped by police. Michael remembers, "My dad would tell me, 'If you get pulled over, you just keep your mouth shut and do exactly what they tell you to do. Don't get into arguments, and don't be stupid. It doesn't make a difference [that you did nothing wrong]. Just do what they tell you to do.' "[53] Officer Ova Tate, a thirteen-year veteran police officer and an African American, told his teenage son not to expect special treatment because Tate is a police officer. "[If] you're black, you're out in the neighborhood, it's a fact of life you're going to be stopped. So how you deal with the police is how your life is going to be. They say you did something, say 'O.K.,' and let them get out of your life."[54] Karen Brank's son is young, but she says that when the time comes, she will know what to say to him. Perhaps thinking of her own experience, she acknowledges the emotional cost, but knows it cannot be avoided.

[The police] are supposed to be there to protect and to serve, but you being black and being male, you've got two strikes against you. Keep your hands on the steering wheel, and do not run, because they will shoot you in your back. Keep your hands on the steering wheel, let them do whatever they want to do. I know it's humiliating, but let them do whatever they want to do to make sure you get out of that situation alive. Deal with your emotions later. Your emotions are going to come second—or last.[55]

These instructions will undoubtedly give black children a devastatingly poor impression of the police, but African American parents say they have no choice. They know that traffic stops can lead to physical, even deadly, confrontations.[56] Christopher Darden, the African American prosecutor in the O. J. Simpson case, says that to survive traffic stops, he "learned the rules of the game years before . . . Don't move. Don't turn around. Don't give some rookie an excuse to shoot you."[57] This may seem like an overreaction, but given the facts of life on the street, it seems likely that most African American parents would agree.[58]

II. The Statistical Analysis

Talking with African Americans leaves little doubt that pretextual traffic stops have a profound impact on each individual stopped, and on all blacks collectively. There is also no doubt that blacks view this not as a series of isolated incidents and anecdotes, but as a long-standing pattern of law enforcement. For those subjected to these practices, pretextual stops are nothing less than blatant racial discrimination in the enforcement of the criminal law.

But is there proof that would substantiate those strongly held beliefs? What statistics exist that would allow one to conclude, to an acceptable degree of certainty, that "driving while black" is, indeed, more than just the sum of many individual stories?

Data on this problem are not easy to come by. This is, in part, because the problem has only recently been recognized beyond the black community. It may also be because records concerning police conduct are either irregular or nonexistent. But it may also be because there is active hostility in the law enforcement community to the idea of keeping comprehensive records of traffic stops. In 1997, Representative John Conyers of Michigan introduced H.R. 118, the Traffic Stops Statistics Act, which would require the Department of Justice to collect and analyze data on all traffic stops around the country—including the race of the driver, whether a search took place, and the legal justification for the search.[59] When the bill passed the House with unanimous, bipartisan support the National Association of Police Organizations (NAPO), an umbrella group representing more than 4,000 police interest groups across the country, announced its strong opposition to the bill.[60] Officers would "resent" having to collect the data, a spokesman for the group said. Moreover, there is "no pressing need or justification" for collecting the data.[61] In other words, there is no problem, so there is no need to collect data. NAPO's opposition was enough to kill the bill in the Senate in the 105th Congress. As a consequence, there is now no requirement at the federal level that law enforcement agencies collect data on traffic stops that include race. Thus, all of the data gathering so far has been the result of statistical inquiry in lawsuits or independent academic research.[62]

A. New Jersey

The most rigorous statistical analysis of the racial distribution of traffic stops was performed in New Jersey by Dr. John Lamberth of Temple University. In the late 1980s and early 1990s, African Americans often complained that police stopped them on the New Jersey Turnpike more frequently than their numbers on that road would have predicted. Similarly, public defenders in the area had observed that "a strikingly high proportion of cases arising from stops and searches on the New Jersey Turnpike involve black persons."[63] In 1994, the problem was brought to the state court's attention in State v. Pedro Soto,[64] in which the defendant alleged that he had been stopped because of his ethnicity.[65] The defendant sought to have the evidence gathered as a result of the stop suppressed as the fruit of an illegal seizure. Lamberth served as a defense expert in the case. His report is a virtual tutorial on how to apply statistical analysis to this type of problem.[66]

The goal of Lamberth's study was "to determine if the State Police stop, investigate, and arrest black travelers at rates significantly disproportionate to the percentage of blacks in the traveling population, so as to suggest the existence of an official or de facto policy of targeting blacks for investigation and arrest."[67] To do this, Lamberth designed a research methodology to determine two things: first, the rate at which blacks were being stopped, ticketed, and/or arrested on the relevant part of the highway, and second, the percentage of blacks among travelers on that same stretch of road.

To gather data concerning the rate at which blacks were stopped, ticketed and arrested, Lamberth reviewed and reconstructed three types of information received in discovery from the state: reports of all arrests that resulted from stops on the turnpike from April of 1988 through May of 1991, patrol activity logs from randomly selected days from 1988 through 1991, and police radio logs from randomly selected days from 1988 through 1991.[68] Many of these records identified the race of the driver or passenger.

Then Lamberth sought to measure the racial composition of the traveling public on the road. He did this through a turnpike population census—direct observation by teams of research assistants who counted the cars on the road and tabulated whether the driver or another occupant appeared black. During these observations, teams of observers sat at the side of the road for randomly selected periods of 75 minutes from 8:00 a.m. to 8:00 p.m.[69] To ensure further precision, Lamberth also designed another census procedure—a turnpike violation census. This was a rolling survey by teams of observers in cars moving in traffic on the highway, with the cruise control calibrated and set at five miles per hour above the speed limit. The teams observed each car that they passed or that passed them, noted the race of the driver, and also noted whether or not the driver was exceeding the speed limit.[70]

The teams recorded data on more than forty-two thousand cars.[71] With these observations, Lamberth was able to compare the percentages of African Americans drivers who are stopped, ticketed, and arrested, to their relative presence on the road. This data enabled him to carefully and rigorously test whether blacks were in fact being disproportionately targeted for stops.

By any standard, the results of Lamberth's analysis are startling. First, the turnpike violator census, in which observers in moving cars recorded the races and speeds of the cars around them, showed that blacks and whites violated the traffic laws at almost exactly the same rate; there was no statistically significant difference in the way they drove.[72] Thus, driving behavior alone could not explain differences in how police might treat black and white drivers.[73] With regard to arrests, 73.2% of those stopped and arrested were black, while only 13.5% of the cars on the road had a black driver or passenger.[74] Lambert notes that the disparity between these two numbers "is statistically vast."[75] The number of standard deviations[76] present—54.27—means that the probability that the racial disparity is a random result "is infinitesimally small."[77] Radio and patrol logs yielded similar results. Blacks are approximately 35% of those stopped,[78] though they are only 13.5% of those on the road—19.45 standard deviations.[79] Considering all stops in all three types of records surveyed, the chance that 34.9% of the cars combined would have black drivers or occupants "is substantially less than one in one billion."[80] This led Lamberth to the following conclusion:

Absent some other explanation for the dramatically disproportionate number of stops of blacks, it would appear that the race of the occupants and/or drivers of the cars is a decisive factor or a factor with great explanatory power. I can say to a reasonable degree of statistical probability that the disparity outlined here is strongly consistent with the existence of a discriminatory policy, official or de facto, of targeting blacks for stop and investigation. . . .

. . . Put bluntly, the statistics demonstrate that in a population of blacks and whites which is (legally) virtually universally subject to police stop for traffic law violation, (cf. the turnpike violator census), blacks in general are several times more likely to be stopped than non-blacks.[81]

B. Maryland

A short time after completing his analysis of the New Jersey data, Lamberth also conducted a study of traffic stops by the Maryland State Police on Interstate 95 between Baltimore and the Delaware border.[82] In 1993, an African American Harvard Law School graduate named Robert Wilkins filed a federal lawsuit against the Maryland State Police.[83] Wilkins alleged that the police stopped him as he was driving with his family, questioned them and searched the car with a drug-sniffing dog because of their race.[84] When a State Police memo surfaced during discovery instructing troopers to look for drug couriers who were described as "predominantly black males and black females,"[85] the State Police settled with Wilkins. As part of the settlement, the police agreed to give the court data on every stop followed by a search conducted with the driver's consent or with a dog for three years.[86] The data also were to include the race of the driver.

With this data, Lamberth used a rolling survey, similar to the one in New Jersey,[87] to determine the racial breakdown of the driving population. Lamberth's assistants observed almost 6,000 cars over approximately 42 randomly distributed hours. As he had in New Jersey, Lamberth concluded that blacks and whites drove no differently; the percentages of blacks and whites violating the traffic code were virtually indistinguishable.[88] More importantly, Lamberth's analysis found that although 17.5% of the population violating the traffic code on the road he studied was black, more than 72% of those stopped and searched were black. In more than 80% of the cases, the person stopped and searched was a member of some racial minority.[89] The disparity between 17.5% black and 72% stopped includes 34.6 standard deviations.[90] Such statistical significance, Lamberth said, "is literally off the charts."[91] Even while exhibiting appropriate caution, Lamberth came to a devastating conclusion.

> While no one can know the motivation of each individual trooper in conducting a traffic stop, the statistics presented herein, representing a broad and detailed sample of highly appropriate data, show without question a racially discriminatory impact on blacks . . . from state police behavior along I-95. The disparities are sufficiently great that taken as a whole, they are consistent and strongly support the assertion that the state police targeted the community of black motorists for stop, detention, and investigation within the Interstate 95 corridor.[92]

C. Ohio

In the Spring of 1998, several members of the Ohio General Assembly began to consider whether to propose legislation that would require police departments to collect data on traffic stops. But in order to sponsor such a bill, the legislators wanted some preliminary statistical evidence—a prima facie case, one could say—of the existence of the problem. This would help them persuade their colleagues to support the effort, they said. I was asked to gather this preliminary evidence. The methodology used here presents a case study in how to analyze this type of problem when the best type of data to do so is not available.

In the most fundamental ways, the task was the same as Lamberth's had been in both New Jersey and Maryland: use statistics to test whether blacks in Ohio were being stopped in numbers disproportionate to their presence in the driving population. Doing this would require data on stops broken down by race, and a comparison of those numbers to the percentage of black drivers on the roads. But if the goal was the same, two circumstances made the task considerably more difficult to accomplish in Ohio. First, Ohio does not collect statewide data on traffic stops that can be correlated with race. In fact, no police department of any sizeable city in the state keeps any data on all of its traffic stops that could be broken down by race.[93] Second, the state legislators wanted some preliminary statistics to demonstrate that "driving while black" was a problem in all of Ohio, or at least in some significant—and different—parts of the whole state. While Lamberth's stationary and rolling survey methods worked well to ascertain the driving populations of particular stretches of individual, limited access highways, those methods were obviously resource-and labor-intensive. Applying the same methods to an entire city—even a medium-sized one—would entail duplicating the Lamberth approach on many major roads to get a complete picture. It would be impractical, not to mention prohibitively expensive, to do this in communities across an entire state. Thus, different methods had to be found.

To determine the percentage of blacks stopped, data were obtained from municipal courts in four Ohio cities.[94] Municipal courts in Ohio handle all low-level criminal cases[95] and virtually all of the traffic citations issued in the state. Most of these courts also generate a computer file for each case, which includes the race of the defendant as part of a physical description. This data provided the basis for a breakdown of all tickets given by the race of the driver.

The downside of using the municipal court data is that it only includes stops in which citations were given. Stops resulting in no action or a warning are not included. In all likelihood, using tickets alone might underestimate any racial bias that is present because police might not ticket blacks stopped for nontraffic purposes. Since using tickets could underestimate any possible racial bias, any resulting calculations are conservative and tend to give law enforcement the benefit of the doubt. Similarly, the way the racial statistics are grouped in the analysis is also conservative because the numbers are limited to only two categories of drivers: black and nonblack. In other words, all minorities other than African Americans are lumped together with whites, even though some of these other minorities, notably Hispanics, have also complained about targeted stops directed at them. Using conservative assumptions means that if a bias does show up in the analysis, we can be relatively confident that it actually exists.[96]

The percentage of all tickets in 1996, 1997, and the first four months of 1998[97] that were issued to blacks by the Akron, Dayton, and Toledo Police Departments and all of the police departments in Franklin County[98] are set out in table 3.1.

With ticketing percentages used as a measure of stops, attention turns to the other number needed for the analysis: the presence of blacks in the driving population. Given the concerns about the use of Lamberth's method in a statewide, preliminary study, another approach—a less exact one than direct observation, to be sure, but one that would yield a reasonable estimate of the driving population—was devised.

TABLE 3.1
Ticketing of African Americans for 1996, 1997, and 1998*

City	Percentage of all tickets in city issued to African Americans
Akron	37.6%
Toledo	30.8%
Dayton	50.0%
Columbus/Franklin County**	25.2%

* Through April 30, 1998.
** Data for Franklin County include 1996 and 1997, but not 1998, and include tickets issued by all law enforcement units in the county, not just the city of Columbus.

Data from the U.S. Census breaks down the populations of states, counties, and individual cities by race and by age. This data is readily available and easy to use.[99] Using this data, a reasonable basis for comparing ticketing percentages can be constructed: blacks versus nonblacks in the driving age population. This was done by breaking down the general population by race and by age. By selecting a lower and upper age limit—fifteen and seventy-five, respectively[100]—for driving age, the data yield a reasonable reflection of what we would expect to find if we surveyed the roads themselves. The data on driving age population can also be sharpened by using information from the National Personal Transportation Survey,[101] a study done every five years by the Federal Highway Administration of the U.S. Department of Transportation. The 1990 survey indicates that 21% of black households do not own a vehicle.[102] If the driving age population figure is reduced by 21%, this gives us another baseline with which to make a comparison to the ticketing percentages. Both baselines—black driving age population, and black driving age population less 21%—for Akron, Dayton, Toledo, and Franklin County are set out in table 3.2.

The ticketing percentages in table 3.1 and the baselines in table 3.2 can then be compared by constructing a "likelihood ratio" that will show whether blacks are receiving tickets in numbers that are out of proportion to their presence in the driving age population and the driving age population less 21%.[103] The likelihood ratio will allow the following sentence to be completed: "If you're black, you're _____ times as likely to be ticketed by this police department than if you are not black." A likelihood ratio of approximately one means that blacks received tickets in roughly the proportion one would expect, given their presence in the driving age population. A likelihood ratio of much greater than one indicates that blacks received tickets at a rate higher than would be expected. Using both baselines—the black driving age population, and the black driving age population less 21%—the likelihood ratios for Akron, Dayton, Toledo,[104] and Franklin County[105] are presented in tables 3.3 and 3.4.

The method used here to attempt to discover whether "driving while black" is a problem in Ohio is less exact than the observation-based method used in New Jersey and Maryland. There are assumptions built into the analysis at several points in an attempt to arrive at reasonable substitutes for observation-based data. Since better data do not exist, all of the assumptions made in the analysis involve some speculation. But all of the assumptions are conservative, calculated to err on the side of caution. According to sociologist and criminologist Joseph E. Jacoby, the numbers used here probably are flawed because blacks are probably "at an even greater risk of being stopped" than these numbers show.[106] For example, blacks are likely to drive fewer miles than whites, which suggests that police have fewer opportunities to stop blacks for traffic violations.[107] In statistical terms, the biases in the assumptions are additive, not offsetting.[108]

What do these figures mean? Even when conservative assumptions are built in, likelihood ratios for Akron, Dayton, Toledo, and Franklin County, Ohio, all either

TABLE 3.2
Population Baselines

City	Black driving age population* (percentage of city total)	Black driving age population, less 21% of black households without vehicles**
Akron	22.7%	17.9%
Toledo	18.0%	14.2%
Dayton	38.0%	30.0%
Columbus/Franklin County***	16.0%	12.6%

* *Source*: U.S. Census Bureau.

** *Source*: Federal Highway Admin., U.S. Dep't of Transp., *1995 National Personal Transportation Survey,* (visited Sept. 27, 1999) http://www.bts.gov/ntda/npts; Letters from Eric Hill, Research Associate, Center for Urban Transportation, to David A. Harris (Sept. 28 & Oct. 9, 1998).

*** Data for all of Franklin County, not just the city of Columbus.

TABLE 3.3
Likelihood Ratio "If You're Black, You're ___ Times as Likely to Get a Ticket in This City Than If You Are Not Black"

City	Black driving age population*	Black driving age population, less 21% of black households without vehicles**
Akron P.D.	2.05	2.76
Toledo P.D.	2.04	2.67
Dayton P.D.	1.67	2.32
Columbus/Franklin County***	1.77	2.34

* *Source*: U.S. Census Bureau.

** *Source*: Federal Highway Administration, U.S. Department of Transportation, *1995 National Personal Transportation Survey* (visited September 27, 1999), http://www.bts.gov/ntda/npts; letters from Eric Hill, Research Associate, Center for Urban Transportation, to David A. Harris (September 28 and October 9, 1998).

*** Includes all police agencies in Franklin County, not just Columbus.

TABLE 3.4
Combined Population Baselines and Likelihood Ratios

City	Black driving age population*	Black driving age population, less 21% of black households without vehicles**
Akron	22.7%	17.9%
	2.05	2.76
Toledo	18.0%	14.2%
	2.04	2.67
Dayton	38.0%	30.0%
	1.67	2.32
Columbus/Franklin County***	16.0%	12.6%
	1.77	2.34

* *Source*: U.S. Census Bureau.

** *Source*: Federal Highway Administration, U.S. Department of Transportation, *1995 National Personal Transportation Survey* (visited September 27, 1999) http://www.bts.gov/ntda/npts; letters from Eric Hill, Research Associate, Center for Urban Transportation, to David A. Harris (September 28 and October 9, 1998).

*** Data for all of Franklin County, not just the city of Columbus.

approach or exceed 2.0. In other words, blacks are about twice as likely to be tick-eted as nonblacks. When the fact that 21% of black households do not own a vehicle is factored in, the ratios rise, with some approaching 3.0. Assuming that ticketing is a fair mirror of traffic stops in general, the data suggest that a "driving while black" problem does indeed exist in Ohio. There may be race-neutral explanations for the statistical pattern, but none seem obvious. At the very least, further study—some-thing as accurate and exacting as Lamberth's studies in New Jersey and Maryland—is needed.[109]

III. Why It Matters: The Connection of "Driving While Black" to Other Issues of Criminal Justice and Race

The interviews excerpted here show that racially biased pretextual traffic stops have a strong and immediate impact on the individual African American drivers involved. These stops are not the minor inconveniences they might seem to those who are not subjected to them. Rather, they are experiences that can wound the soul and cause psychological scar tissue to form. And the statistics show that these experiences are not simply disconnected anecdotes or exaggerated versions of personal experiences, but rather established and persistent patterns of law enforcement conduct. It may be that these stops do not spring from racism on the part of individual officers, or even from the official policies of the police departments for which they work. Neverthe-less, the statistics leave little doubt that, whatever the source of this conduct by po-lice, it has a disparate and degrading impact on blacks.

But racial profiling is important not only because of the damage it does, but also because of the connections between stops of minority drivers and other, larger is-sues of criminal justice and race. Put another way, "driving while black" reflects, il-lustrates, and aggravates some of the most important problems we face today when we debate issues involving race, the police, the courts, punishment, crime control, criminal justice, and constitutional law.

A. The Impact on the Innocent

The Fourth Amendment to the United States Constitution prohibits unreason-able searches and seizures, and specifies some of the requirements to be met in order to procure a warrant for a search.[110] Since 1961[111]—and earlier in the federal court system[112]—the Supreme Court has required the exclusion of any evidence obtained through an unconstitutional search or seizure. From its inception, the exclusionary rule has inspired spirited criticism. Cardozo himself said that "the criminal is to go free because the constable has blundered,"[113] capturing the idea that the bad guy, caught red handed, gets a tremendous windfall when he escapes punishment because of a mistake in the police officer's behavior. We need not even go all the way back to Cardozo to hear the argument that the exclusion of evidence protects—and rewards —only the guilty.[114]

The justification advanced for the exclusionary rule is that while the guilty may receive the most direct benefit when a court suppresses evidence because of a constitutional violation, the innocent—all the rest of us—are also better off. The right to be free from illegal searches and seizures belongs not just to the guilty, but to everyone. The guilty parties who bring motions to suppress are simply the most convenient vehicles for vindicating these rights, because they will have the incentive—escaping conviction—to litigate the issues. In so doing, the argument goes, the rights of all are vindicated, and police are deterred from violating constitutional rules on pain of failing to convict the guilty. One problem with this argument is that it takes imagination: the beneficiaries of suppressed evidence other than the guilty who escape punishment are ephemeral and amorphous. They are everybody—all of us. And if they are everybody, they quickly become nobody, because law-abiding, taxpaying citizens are unlikely to view ourselves as needing these constitutional protections. After all, we obey the law; we do not commit crimes. We can do without these protections—or so we think.

It is not my intention here to recapitulate every argument for and against the exclusionary rule. Rather, I wish to point out a major difference between the usual Fourth Amendment cases and the most common "driving while black" cases. While police catch some criminals through the use of pretext stops, far more innocent people are likely to be affected by these practices than criminals. Indeed, the black community as a whole undoubtedly needs the protection of the police more than other segments of society because African Americans are more likely than others to be victims of crime.[115] Ironically, it is members of that same community who are likely to feel the consequences of pretextual stops and be treated like criminals. It is the reverse of the usual Fourth Amendment case, in that there is nothing ghostlike or indefinite about those whose rights would be vindicated by addressing these police practices. On the contrary, the victims are easy to identify because they are the great majority of black people who are subjected to these humiliating and difficult experiences but who have done absolutely nothing to deserve this treatment—except to resemble, in a literally skin-deep way, a small group of criminals. While whites who have done nothing wrong generally have little need to fear constitutional violations by the police, this is decidedly untrue for blacks. Blacks attract undesirable police attention whether they do anything to bring it on themselves or not. This makes "driving while black" a most unusual issue of constitutional criminal procedure: a search and seizure question that directly affects a large, identifiable group of almost entirely innocent people.

B. The Criminalization of Blackness

The fact that the cost of "driving while black" is imposed almost exclusively on the innocent raises another point. Recall that by allowing the police to stop, question, and sometimes even search drivers without regard to the real motives for the search, the Supreme Court has, in effect, turned a blind eye to the use of pretextual stops on a racial basis. That is, as long as the officer or the police department does not come straight out and say that race was the reason for a stop, the stop can always be accomplished based on some other reason—a pretext. Police are therefore free to use blackness as a surrogate indicator or proxy for criminal propensity. While it seems unfair to view all members of one racial or ethnic group as criminal suspects just because some members of that group engage in criminal activity, this is what the law permits.

Stopping disproportionate numbers of black drivers because some small percentage[116] are criminals means that skin color is being used as evidence of wrongdoing. In effect, blackness itself has been criminalized.[117] And if "driving while black" is a powerful example, it is not the only one. For instance, in 1992, the city of Chicago enacted an ordinance that made it a criminal offense for gang members to stand on public streets or sidewalks after police ordered them to disperse.[118] The ordinance was used to make over forty-five thousand arrests of mostly African American and Latino youths[119] before Illinois courts found the ordinance unconstitutionally vague.[120] Supporters said that the law legitimately targeted gang members who made the streets of black and Latino neighborhoods unsafe for residents. Accordingly, the thousands of arrests that resulted were a net good, regardless of the enormous amount of police discretion that was exercised almost exclusively against African Americans and Hispanics.[121] Opponents, such as Professor David Cole, argued that the ordinance had, in effect, created a new crime: "standing while black."[122] In June of 1999, the U.S. Supreme Court declared the law unconstitutional, because it did not sufficiently limit the discretion of officers enforcing it.[123]

The arrests under the Chicago ordinance share something with "driving while black": in each instance, the salient quality that attracts police attention will often be the suspect's race or ethnicity. An officer cannot know simply by looking whether a driver has a valid license or carries insurance, as the law requires, and cannot see whether there is a warrant for the arrest of the driver or another occupant of the car. But the officer can see whether the person is black or white. And, as the statistics presented here show, police use blackness as a way to sort those they are interested in investigating from those that they are not. As a consequence, every member of the group becomes a potential criminal in the eyes of law enforcement.

C. Rational Discrimination

When one hears the most common justification offered for the disproportionate numbers of traffic stops of African Americans, it usually takes the form of rationality, not racism. Blacks commit a disproportionate share of certain crimes, the argument goes. Therefore, it only makes sense for police to focus their efforts on African Americans. To paraphrase the Maryland State Police officer quoted at the beginning of this chapter, this is not racism—it is good policing.[124] It only makes sense to focus law enforcement efforts and resources where they will make the most difference. In other words, targeting blacks is the rational, sound policy choice. It is the efficient approach, as well.

As appealing as this argument may sound, it is fraught with problems because its underlying premise is dubious at best. Government statistics on drug offenses, which are the basis for the great majority of pretext traffic stops, tell us virtually nothing about the racial breakdown of those involved in drug crime. Thinking for a moment about arrest data and victimization surveys makes the reasons for this clear. These statistics show that blacks are indeed overrepresented among those arrested for ho- micide, rape, robbery, aggravated assault, larceny/theft, and simple assault crimes.[125] Note that because they directly affect their victims, these crimes are at least some- what likely to be reported to the police[126] and to result in arrests. By contrast, drug offenses are much less likely to be reported, since possessors, buyers, and sellers of narcotics are all willing participants in these crimes. Therefore, arrest data for drug crimes is highly suspect. These data may measure the law enforcement activities and policy choices of the institutions and actors involved in the criminal justice system, but the number of drug arrests does not measure the extent of drug crimes them- selves.[127] Similarly, the racial composition of prisons and jail populations or the racial breakdown of sentences for these crimes only measures the actions of those institu- tions and individuals in charge; it tells us nothing about drug activity itself.

Other statistics on both drug use and drug crime show something surprising in light of the usual beliefs many hold: blacks may not, in fact, be more likely than whites to be involved with drugs. Lamberth's study in Maryland showed that among vehicles stopped and searched, the "hit rates"—the percentage of vehicles searched in which drugs were found—were statistically indistinguishable for blacks and whites.[128] In a related situation, the U.S. Customs Service, which is engaged in drug interdiction efforts at the nation's airports, has used various types of invasive searches from pat downs to body cavity searches against travelers suspected of drug use. The Custom Service's own nationwide figures show that while over forty-three percent of those subjected to these searches were either black or Hispanic, "hit rates" for these searches were actually lower for both blacks and Hispanics than for whites.[129] There is also a considerable amount of data on drug use that belies the standard beliefs.[130] The percentages of drug users who are black or white are roughly the same as the presence of those groups in the population as a whole. For example, blacks constitute approximately twelve percent of the country's population. In 1997, the most recent year for which statistics are available, thirteen percent of all drug users were black.[131] In fact, among black youths, a demographic group often portrayed as most likely to be involved with drugs, use of all illicit substances has actually been consistently lower than among white youths for twenty years running.[132]

Nevertheless, many believe that African Americans and members of other minor- ity groups are responsible for most drug use and drug trafficking. Carl Williams, the head of the New Jersey State Police dismissed by the Governor in March of 1999, stated that "mostly minorities" trafficked in marijuana and cocaine, and pointed out that when senior American officials went overseas to discuss the drug problem, they went to Mexico, not Ireland.[133] Even if he is wrong, if the many troopers who worked for Williams share his opinions, they will act accordingly. And they will do so by looking for drug criminals among black drivers. Blackness will become an indica- tor of suspicion of drug crime involvement. This, in turn, means that the belief that blacks are disproportionately involved in drug crimes will become a self-fulfilling prophecy. Because police will look for drug crime among black drivers, they will find it disproportionately among black drivers. More blacks will be arrested, prosecuted, convicted, and jailed, thereby reinforcing the idea that blacks constitute the majority of drug offenders. This will provide a continuing motive and justification for stopping more black drivers as a rational way of using resources to catch the most criminals. At the same time, because police will focus on black drivers, white drivers will receive less attention, and the drug dealers and possessors among them will be apprehended in proportionately smaller numbers than their presence in the population would predict.

The upshot of this thinking is visible in the stark and stunning numbers that show what our criminal justice system is doing when it uses law enforcement practices like racially biased traffic stops to enforce drug laws. African Americans are just 12% of the population and 13% of the drug users, but they are about 38% of all those arrested for drug offenses, 59% of all those convicted of drug offenses, and 63% of all those convicted for drug trafficking.[134] While only 33% of whites who are convicted are sent to prison, 50% of convicted blacks are jailed,[135] and blacks who are sent to prison receive higher sentences than whites for the same crimes. For state drug defendants, the average maximum sentence length is fifty-one months for whites and sixty months for blacks.[136]

D. The Distortion of the Legal System

Among the most serious effects of "driving while black" on the larger issues of criminal justice and race are those it has on the legal system itself. The use of pretextual traffic stops distorts the whole system, as well as our perceptions of it. This undermines the system's legitimacy, which effects not only African Americans but every citizen, since the health of our country depends on a set of legal institutions that have the public's respect.

1. DEEP CYNICISM

Racially targeted traffic stops cause deep cynicism among blacks about the fairness and legitimacy of law enforcement and courts. Many of those African Americans interviewed for this chapter said this, some in strong terms. Karen Brank said she thought that her law-abiding life, her responsible job, her education, and even her gender protected her from arbitrary treatment by the police. She thought that these stops happened only to young black men playing loud music in their cars. Now, she feels she was "naive," and has considerably less respect for police and all legal institutions.[137] For James, who looks at himself as someone who has toed the line and lived an upright life, constant stops are a reminder that whatever he does, no matter how well he conducts himself, he will still attract unwarranted police attention.[138] Michael describes constant police scrutiny as something blacks have to "play through," like athletes with injuries who must perform despite significant pain.[139]

Thus, it is no wonder that blacks view the criminal justice system in totally different terms than whites do. They have completely different experiences within the system than whites have, so they do not hold the same beliefs about it. Traffic stops of whites usually concern the actual traffic offense allegedly committed; traffic stops of blacks are often arbitrary, grounded not in any traffic offense but in who they are. Since traffic stops are among the most common encounters regular citizens have with police, it is hardly surprising that pretextual traffic stops might lead blacks to view the whole of the system differently. One need only think of the split-screen television images that followed the acquittal in the O. J. Simpson case—stunned, disbelieving whites, juxtaposed with jubilant blacks literally jumping for joy—to understand how deep these divisions are. Polling data have long shown that blacks believe that the justice system is biased against them. For example, in a Justice Department survey released in 1999, blacks were more than twice as likely as whites to say they are dissatisfied with the police.[140] But this cynicism is no longer limited to blacks; it is now beginning to creep into the general population's perception of the system. Recent data show that a majority of whites believe that police racism toward blacks is common.[141] The damage done to the legitimacy of the system has spread across racial groups, and is no longer confined to those who are most immediately affected.

Perhaps the most direct result of this cynicism is that there is considerably more skepticism about the testimony of police officers than there used to be. This is especially true in minority communities. Both the officer and the driver recognize that each pretextual traffic stop involves an untruth. When a black driver asks a police officer why he or she has been stopped, the officer will most likely explain that the driver committed a traffic violation. This may be literally true, since virtually no driver can avoid committing a traffic offense. But odds are that the violation is not the real reason that the officer stopped the driver. This becomes more than obvious when the officer asks the driver whether he or she is carrying drugs or guns, and for consent to search the car.[142] If the stop was really about enforcement of the traffic laws, there would be no need for any search. Thus, for an officer to tell a driver that he or she has been stopped for a traffic offense when the officer's real interest is drug interdiction is a lie—a legally sanctioned one, to be sure, but a lie nonetheless. It should surprise no one, then, that the same people who are subjected to this treatment regard the testimony and statements of police with suspicion, making it increasingly difficult for prosecutors to obtain convictions in any case that depends upon police testimony, as so many cases do. The result may be more cases that end in acquittals or hung juries, even factually and legally strong ones.[143]

2. THE EFFECT ON THE GUILTY

As discussed above, one of the most important reasons that the "driving while black" problem represents an important connection to many larger issues of criminal justice and race is that, unlike many other Fourth Amendment issues, the innocent pay a clear and direct price. Citizens who are not criminals are seen as only indirect beneficiaries of Fourth Amendment litigation in other contexts because the guilty party's vindication of his or her own rights serves to vindicate everyone's rights. Law-abiding blacks, however, have a direct and immediate stake in redressing the "driving while black" problem. While pretextual traffic stops do indeed net some number of law breakers, innocent blacks are imposed upon through frightening and even humiliating stops and searches far more often than the guilty. But the opposite argument is important, too: "driving while black" has a devastating impact upon the guilty. Those who are arrested, prosecuted, and often jailed because of these stops, are suffering great hardships as a result.

The response to this argument is usually that if these folks are indeed guilty, so what? In other words, it is a good thing that the guilty are caught, arrested, and prosecuted, no matter if they are black or white. This is especially true, the argument goes, in the black community, because African Americans are disproportionately the victims of crime.[144]

But this argument overlooks at least two powerful points. First, prosecution for crimes, especially drug crimes, has had an absolutely devastating impact on black communities nationwide. In 1995, about one in three black men between the ages of 20 and 29 were under the control of the criminal justice system—either in prison or jail, on probation, or on parole.[145] In Washington, D.C., the figure is 50% for all black men between the age of eighteen and thirty-five.[146] Even assuming that all of those caught, prosecuted, convicted and sentenced are guilty, it simply cannot be a good thing that such a large proportion of young men from one community are adjudicated criminals. They often lose their right to vote, sometimes permanently.[147] To say that they suffer difficulties in family life and in gaining employment merely restates the obvious. The effect of such a huge proportion of people living under these disabilities permanently changes the circumstances not just of those incarcerated, but of everyone around them.

This damage is no accident. It is the direct consequence of "rational law enforcement" policies that target blacks. Put simply, there is a connection between where police look for contraband and where they find it. If police policy, whether express or implied, dictates targeting supposedly "drug involved" groups like African Americans, and if officers follow through on this policy, they will find disproportionate numbers of African Americans carrying and selling drugs. By the same token, they will not find drugs with the appropriate frequency on whites, because the targeting policy steers police attention away from them. This policy not only discriminates by targeting large numbers of innocent, law abiding African Americans; it also discriminates between racial groups among the guilty, with blacks having to bear a far greater share of the burden of drug prohibition.

3. THE EXPANSION OF POLICE DISCRETION

As the discussion of the law involving traffic stops and the police actions that often follow showed, police have nearly complete discretion to decide who to stop. According to all of the evidence available, police frequently exercise this discretion in a racially biased way, stopping blacks in numbers far out of proportion to their presence on the highway. Law enforcement generally sees this as something positive because the more discretion officers have to fight crime, the better able they will be to do the job.

Police discretion cannot be eliminated; frankly, even if it could be, this would not necessarily be a desirable goal. Officers need discretion to meet individual situations with judgment and intelligence, and to choose their responses so that the ultimate result will make sense. Yet few would contend that police discretion should be limitless. But this is exactly what the pretextual stop doctrine allows. Since everyone violates the traffic code at some point, it is not a matter of whether police can stop a driver, but which driver they want to stop. Police are free to pick and choose the motorists they will pull over, so factors other than direct evidence of law breaking come into play. In the "driving while black" situation, of course, that factor is race. In other law enforcement areas in which the state has nearly limitless discretion to prosecute, the decision could be based on political affiliation, popularity, or any number of other things. What these arenas have in common is that enforcement depends upon external factors, instead of law breaking.

Arguments examining law enforcement discretion have great resonance in the wake of the impeachment of President Clinton. The President was pursued by Independent Counsel Kenneth Starr for four years. Starr had an almost limitless budget, an infinite investigative time frame, and an ever-expandable mandate to investigate a particular set of individuals for any possible criminal activity, rather than to investigate particular offenses. In other words, Starr had nearly complete discretion. This was foreseen in 1988 by Justice Scalia in his dissent in Morrison v. Olsen,[148] the case in which the Supreme Court held the independent counsel statute constitutional. In a long final section of his opinion, Scalia decried the Independent Counsel Act not only as unconstitutional but also as bad policy, precisely because it gave the prosecutor nearly unlimited discretion. Among the words Justice Scalia chose to express this idea were those of Justice Robert Jackson, who, as Attorney General, talked about prosecutorial discretion in a speech to the Second Annual Conference of United States Attorneys. Jackson could just as easily have been discussing police discretion to make traffic stops; in fact, he used that very activity as an illustration.

> Law enforcement is not automatic. It isn't blind. One of the greatest difficulties of the position of prosecutor is that he must pick his cases, because no prosecutor can even investigate all of the cases in which he receives complaints . . . We know that no local police force can strictly enforce the traffic laws, or it would arrest half the driving population on any given morning . . .
>
> If the prosecutor is obliged to choose his case, it follows that he can choose his defendants. Therein is the most dangerous power of the prosecutor: that he will pick people that he thinks he should get, rather than cases that need to be prosecuted. With the law books filled with a great assortment of crimes, a prosecutor stands a fair chance of finding at least a technical violation of some act on the part of almost anyone. In such a case, it is not a question of discovering the commission of a crime and then looking for the man who has committed it, it is a question of picking the man and then searching the law books, or putting investigators to work, to pin some offense on him . . . It is here that law enforcement becomes personal, and the real crime becomes that of being unpopular with the predominant or governing group, being attached to the wrong political views, or being personally obnoxious to or in the way of the prosecutor himself.[149]

By substituting "the police" for "the prosecutor" in this excerpt, one gets a strong sense of the unfairness of pretextual traffic stops. The person subjected to a pretextual stop is not targeted for his or her law breaking activity, but for other reasons—in this case, membership in a particular racial or ethnic group thought to be disproportionately involved in drug crimes. And the law leaves police absolutely free to do this.[150]

4. SENTENCING

"Driving while black" also distorts the sentences that African Americans receive for crimes. Research shows that blacks receive longer sentences than whites for the same crimes.[151] One might hope that, with the advent of guidelines systems designed to limit judicial discretion in sentencing through the use of strictly applied nonracial criteria, this discrepancy might begin to disappear, but it has not.[152]

A recent federal sentencing decision illustrates the point. In December of 1998, Judge Nancy Gertner of the Federal District Court for the District of Massachusetts sentenced a defendant named Alexander Leviner for the crime of being a felon in possession of a firearm.[153] Under the Federal Sentencing Guidelines, a major determinant of the sentence a defendant receives is his or her record of prior offenses. The worse the record, the greater the offender score; the greater the offender score, the longer the sentence.[154] Judge Gertner found that Leviner's record consisted "overwhelmingly" of "motor vehicle violations and minor drug possession offenses."[155] Since all of the available evidence indicated that African Americans experience a proportionally greater number of traffic stops than whites,[156] Judge Gertner reasoned that allowing Leviner's offender score to be inflated by these traffic stop-related offenses represented a continuation of the racial discrimination implicit in the prior offenses into the sentencing process.[157] The judge felt this was improper, and as a result accorded Leviner a "downward departure"—a cut in the usual sentence he could expect, given his criminal record.[158]

It is not clear whether Judge Gertner's decision will survive an appeal.[159] It may be true that police, in general, discriminate against black motorists in their use of traffic stops. But this does not mean that any of the particular stops Leviner experienced in the past were the result of bias. Thus, an appellate court may not find Leviner deserving of the downward departure. Nevertheless, Judge Gertner's opinion points out something important, and not just in Leviner's case. "Driving while black" can have grave consequences not just immediately, when drivers may be at best irritated and at worst arrested or abused, but in the long term, as a minor criminal record builds over time to the point that it comes back to haunt a defendant by enhancing considerably the sentence in some future proceeding. This is simply less likely to happen to whites.

E. Distortion of the Social World

"Driving while black" distorts not only the perception and reality of the criminal justice system, but also the social world. For example, many African Americans cope with the possibility of pretextual traffic stops by driving drab cars and dressing in ways that are not flamboyant so as not to attract attention.[160] More than that, "driving while black" serves as a spatial restriction on African Americans, circumscribing their movements. Put simply, blacks know that police and white residents feel that there are areas in which blacks "do not belong." Often, these are all-white suburban communities or upscale commercial areas. When blacks drive through these areas, they may be watched and stopped because they are "out of place." Consequently, blacks try to avoid these places if for no other reason than that they do not want the extra police scrutiny.[161] It is simply more trouble than it is worth to travel to or through these areas. While it is blacks themselves who avoid these communities, and not police officers or anyone else literally keeping them out, in practice it makes little difference. African Americans do not enter if they can avoid doing so, whether by dint of self-restriction or by government policy.

Another recent example shows even more clearly how "driving while black" can distort the social world. In 1998, the federal government launched "Buckle Up America" in an effort to increase seat belt use.[162] The goal of this national campaign was to make the failure to wear seat belts a primary offense in all fifty states.[163] In many states, seat belt laws are secondary offenses—infractions for which the police cannot stop a car, but for which they can issue a citation once the car is stopped for something else and the seat belt violation is discovered.[164] If seat belt laws are made primary instead of secondary laws, the reasoning is that this would increase seat belt use, which would save thousands of lives per year. Since studies have shown that young African Americans and Hispanics are more likely to die in automobile accidents than whites because of failure to wear seat belts,[165] any effort to increase seat belt use would likely benefit the black and Hispanic communities more than any other groups.

Given that less frequent use of seats belts has a high cost in the lives and suffering of people of color, one would think that any responsible black organization would do everything possible to support efforts like Buckle Up America. And that is what made the position taken by the National Urban League on the issue so puzzling, at least at first blush. The Urban League told the Secretary of Transportation that its "affiliates' willingness to fully embrace [the] campaign began to stall" because of concern that primary seat belt enforcement laws would simply give police another tool with which to harass black drivers.[166] The League said it could not sign on to the campaign without assurances "that the necessary protections will be put in to ensure that black people and other people of color specifically are not subject to arbitrary stops by police under the guise of enforcement of seat belt laws."[167]

This is a truly disturbing distortion of social reality. Faced with a request to join a campaign to save lives through encouraging the use of a known and proven safety device, the use of which might require some greater degree of traffic enforcement, the decision is not easy for African Americans. On the contrary, it presents an agonizing choice: encourage the seat belt campaign to save lives and hand the police another reason to make arbitrary stops, or oppose the campaign because of the danger of arbitrary police action, knowing that blacks will be injured and killed in disproportionate numbers because they use seat belts less frequently than others do. Stated simply, it is a choice whites do not have to make.

F. The Undermining of Community-Based Policing

Until recently, police departments concentrated on answering distress calls. The idea was to have police respond to reports of crime relayed to them from a central dispatcher. In essence, the practice was reactive; the idea was to receive reports of crimes committed and respond to them.[168]

But over the past few years, modern policing has moved away from the response model. It was thought to be too slow and too likely to isolate officers from the people and places in which they worked. The new model is often referred to as community policing. Though the term sometimes seems to have as many meanings as people who use it, community policing does have some identifiable characteristics. The idea is for the police to serve the community and become part of it, not to dominate it or occupy it. To accomplish this, police become known to and involved with residents, make efforts to understand their problems, and attack crime in ways that help address those difficulties. The reasoning is that if the police become part of the community, members of the public will feel comfortable enough to help officers identify troubled spots and trouble makers. This will make for better, more proactive policing aimed at problems residents really care about, and engender a greater degree of appreciation of police efforts by residents and more concern for neighborhood problems by the police.[169]

In many minority communities, the history of police/community relations has been characterized not by trust, but by mutual distrust. In Terry v. Ohio,[170] the fountainhead of modern street-level law enforcement, the Supreme Court candidly acknowledged that police had often used stop and frisk tactics to control and harass black communities.[171] As one veteran African American police officer put it, "Black people used to call the police 'the law.' They were the law . . . The Fourth Amendment didn't apply to black folks because it only applied to white folks."[172] For blacks, trusting the police is difficult; it goes against the grain of years of accumulated distrust and wariness, and countless experiences in which blacks have learned that police are not necessarily there to protect and serve them.

Yet, it is obvious that community policing—both its methods and its goals—depends on mutual trust.[173] As difficult as it will be to build, given the many years of disrespect blacks have suffered at the hands of the police, the community must feel that it can trust the police to treat them as law-abiding citizens if community policing is to succeed.[174] Using traffic stops in racially disproportionate numbers will directly and fundamentally undermine this effort. Why should law-abiding residents of these communities trust the police if, every time they go out for a drive, they are treated like criminals? If the "driving while black" problem is not addressed, community policing will be made much more difficult and may even fail. Thus, aside from the damage "driving while black" stops inflict on African Americans, there is another powerful reason to change this police behavior: it is in the interest of police departments themselves to correct it.

IV. The Legal Context: How the Law Allows and Encourages "Driving While Black" Stops

When they hear some of the personal stories concerning traffic stops, some lay people (almost always whites) are genuinely surprised. Aside from issues concerning the racial aspects of the problem, the same questions almost always come up: Can the police do this? Does the law allow police to stop any driver, any time they wish? Don't they have to have a reason, some rationale, to think the occupants of the car committed a crime? The answer usually surprises them. Yes, police need a reason to stop the car, but they virtually always have it, without seeing any criminal activity. And the law makes it very easy to proceed from the stop to questioning and searching, with no more evidence than a hunch.

For many years, the Supreme Court has allowed police to stop and search a vehicle without a warrant when they have probable cause to believe that it contains contraband or evidence of a crime.[175] The Court reasoned that since automobiles were inherently mobile, it made no sense to require officers to leave and obtain a warrant because the suspect would simply drive away. Over the years, the Court has broadened the rationale for the "automobile exception," saying that in addition to mobility, the fact that cars are heavily regulated and inherently less private means that warrants should not be required.[176]

But the automobile exception only represents the beginning of the Court's cases that allow police considerable discretion over cars, their drivers, and their passengers. In 1996, the Supreme Court addressed directly the constitutionality of pretextual traffic stops. The Court used Whren v. United States[177] to resolve a circuit split,[178] ruling that police can use traffic stops to investigate their suspicions, even if those suspicions have nothing to do with traffic enforcement and even if there is no evidence of criminal behavior by the driver upon which to base those suspicions. The officer's subjective intent makes no difference.[179] This is true, the Court said, even if a reasonable officer would not have stopped the car in question. As long as there was, in fact, a traffic offense, the officer had probable cause to stop the car.[180] The fact that traffic enforcement was only a pretext for the stop had no Fourth Amendment significance, and no evidence would be excluded as a result.[181] Since no one can drive for even a few blocks without committing a minor violation—speeding, failing to signal or make a complete stop, touching a lane or center line, or driving with a defective piece of vehicle equipment[182]—Whren means that police officers can stop any driver, any time they are willing to follow the car for a short distance.[183] In other words, police know that they can use the traffic code to their advantage, and they utilize it to stop vehicles for many nontraffic enforcement purposes.

But Whren does not stand alone. It represents the culmination of twenty years of cases in which the Court has steadily increased police power and discretion over vehicles and drivers. Once the police stop a car, utilizing Whren, the plain view exception may come into play.[184] During the traffic stop, officers have the opportunity to walk to the driver's side window and, while requesting license and registration, observe everything inside the car.[185] This includes not only the car and its contents, but the driver. If it is dark, the officers can enhance a plain view search by shining a flashlight into any area that would be visible if it were daylight.[186] If the officers observe an object in plain view and it is immediately apparent, without further searching, that it is contraband, they can make an arrest on the spot. During this initial encounter, they can also have both the driver[187] and the passenger[188] get out of the vehicle, without any reason to suspect them of any wrongdoing.

If there is an arrest, the police can go further. They can do a thorough search of the passenger compartment[189] and all closed containers inside.[190] They can also "frisk" the car if there is anything resembling a weapon in plain view.[191] Even if nothing is seen in plain view, police can question the driver and passengers without giving them Miranda warnings.[192] The officers are likely to keep the tone of the questioning amicable, but this is more than just carside chit-chat. It is a purposeful, directed effort to get the driver talking.[193] The answers may disclose something that seems suspicious.[194]

Police may continue questioning even after a driver answers every question satisfactorily and in a way that does not raise any suspicion of guilt. The real goal of the questioning is to gather information and impressions that will help the officers decide whether they want to search the car. In the event that they do, the officers will try to obtain the driver's consent.[195] A great number of vehicle searches begin with a request for consent. The initial friendly discussion helps put the driver in the frame of mind to respond to the troopers helpfully, making cooperation and consent more likely.[196] And this technique usually works. Whether out of a desire to help, fear, intimidation, or a belief that they cannot refuse, most people consent. The police need not tell the driver that she has a right to refuse consent,[197] or that she is free to go.[198] As one veteran state trooper told a reporter, in two years of stops, "I've never had anyone tell me I couldn't search."[199] And while a driver could surely limit consent —"You can look through my car, but not my luggage"—most of the searches are in fact quite thorough and include personal effects.[200]

But even if there is no contraband in plain view, and the driver refuses consent, the officers' quiver is still not empty: they may still use a dog trained to detect narcotics. Since the Supreme Court has declared that the use of these dogs does not constitute a search, police may use them without probable cause or reasonable suspicion of any kind.[201] This makes them ideal tools for the "no consent and no visible evidence" situation, because no consent or evidence—in fact, no justification at all—is necessary.[202] Any police department with the funds to pay for them has one or more "K-9 teams" available at all times.[203] The dogs can be called in to search when there is a refusal. Better yet, officers might short circuit the whole process by using the dog as soon as a car is stopped, without even seeking consent.[204] If the dog indicates the presence of narcotics by characteristic barking or scratching, that information itself constitutes probable cause for a full-scale search.

The upshot is that officers are free to exercise a vast amount of discretion when they decide who to stop. And as the statistics show, police stop African Americans more often than their presence in the driving population would predict, since blacks and whites violate the traffic laws at about the same rate.[205] There are two likely explanations for this. First, the decisions of the last twenty years surveyed here allowing police ever-greater power over vehicles, drivers and even passengers, come from the crime-control model of criminal procedure.[206] One can see this in numerous decisions, but especially in the consent search cases, Schneckloth v. Bustamonte[207] and Ohio v. Robinette.[208] In both, the Court used the rhetoric of balancing, but in reality gave short shrift to any interest other than law enforcement. It would be "thoroughly impractical" to tell citizens they have a right to refuse to consent to a search, the Court said in Schneckloth, because this might interfere with the ability of the police to utilize consent searches.[209] In other words, if people were told they did not have to consent, some might actually exercise this right and refuse. Because of law enforcement's interest in performing consent searches, it is preferable to enable the police to take advantage of citizens' ignorance of their rights. Robinette, decided more than twenty years later, sounded the same note. It would be "unrealistic" to tell citizens whom the police have no reason to detain that they are free to go before the police ask for consent to search.[210] This statement is unaccompanied by even the barest explanation or analysis, save reference to Schneckloth.[211] Years of cases like these make it obvious that the Court has control of crime at the top of its criminal law agenda, and it has decided cases in ways designed to enable the police to do whatever is necessary to "win."

Second, by making the power of the police to control crime its top priority in criminal law, the Court—whether intentionally or not—has freed law enforcement from traditional constraints to such a degree that police can use blackness as a proxy for criminal propensity.[212] In other words, officers are free, for all practical purposes, to act on the assumption that being black increases the probability that an individual is a criminal. The statistics presented here suggest that is exactly what the police are doing. But this means that all African Americans get treated as criminal suspects, not just those who have committed crimes. And there are virtually no data that tell us just how many innocent people police officers stop for each criminal they catch.

V. Ways to Address the Problem

With the Supreme Court abdicating any role for the judiciary in regulating these police practices under the Fourth Amendment, leadership must come from other directions and other institutions. What other approaches might be fruitful sources of change?

A. The Traffic Stops Statistics Act

At the beginning of the 105th Congress, Representative John Conyers of Michigan introduced House Bill 118, the Traffic Stops Statistics Act of 1997.[213] This bill would provide for the collection of several categories of data on each traffic stop, including the race of the driver and whether and why a search was performed.[214] The Attorney General would then summarize the data[215] in the first nationwide, statistically rigorous study of these practices. The idea behind the bill was that if the study confirmed what people of color have experienced for years, it would put to rest once and for all the idea that African Americans who have been stopped for "driving while black" are exaggerating isolated anecdotes into a social problem. Congress and other bodies might then begin to take concrete steps to channel police discretion more appropriately. The Act passed the House of Representatives in March of 1998 with bipartisan support, and then was referred to the Senate Judiciary Committee. When police op-position arose,[216] the Senate took no action and the bill died at the end of the session. Congressman Conyers reintroduced the measure in April of 1999.[217]

The Traffic Stops Statistics Act is a very modest bill, a first step toward address-ing a difficult problem. It mandated no concrete action on the problem; it did not regulate traffic stops, set standards for them, or require implementation of particular policies. It was merely an attempt to gather solid, comprehensive information, so that discussion of the problem could move ahead beyond the debate of whether or not the problem existed. Still, the bill attracted enough law enforcement opposition to kill it.[218] But even if the Act did not pass the last Congress and subsequent bills also fail, it seems to have had at least one interesting effect: it has inspired action at the state and local level.

B. State Legislation

As important as national legislation on this issue would be, congressional action is no longer the only game in town. In fact, efforts are underway in a number of states to address the problem. For example, last year in California, Assembly Bill (A.B.) 1264, a bill patterned on Representative Conyers' federal effort, passed both houses of the state assembly. Weakening amendments were attached during the leg-islative process, but A.B. 1264 nevertheless represented the first state-level legislative victory on this issue. Unfortunately, then-Governor Pete Wilson vetoed the bill. A new bill was introduced in the California State Assembly in 1999.[219] The bill passed both houses of the state legislature by large bipartisan margins, but it was vetoed by Governor Gray Davis, who then urged all California police departments to collect this data voluntarily.[220]

This is not the only effort underway. By mid-1999, two state bills had become law: one in North Carolina[221] and one in Connecticut.[222] Bills have also been introduced in Arkansas,[223] Rhode Island,[224] Pennsylvania,[225] Illinois,[226] Virginia,[227] Massachu-setts,[228] Ohio,[229] New Jersey,[230] Maryland,[231] South Carolina,[232] Oklahoma,[233] and Florida.[234] While all of these measures differ in their particulars, they are all varia-tions on Representative Conyers' bill—they mandate the collection of data and analy-ses of these data. But it is important to remember that legislative efforts can take other approaches. There is no reason not to consider other options, such as the use of funding as either carrot or stick or both, to require the enactment of state law that mandates implementation of specific law enforcement policies, or the like.

C. Local Action

Of course, legislative action is not required for a police department to collect data and to take other steps to address the "driving while black" problem. When a de-partment realizes that it is in its own interest to take action, it can go ahead without being ordered to do so. This is precisely what happened in San Diego, California. In February 1999, Jerome Sanders, the city's Chief of Police, announced that the de-partment would begin to collect data on traffic stops, without any federal or state requirement.[235] The Chief's statement showed a desire to find out whether in fact the officers in his department were engaged in enforcing traffic laws on a racially uneven basis. If so, the problem could then be addressed. If the numbers did not show this, the statistics might help to dispel perceptions to the contrary.[236]

Thus far, San Diego, San Jose, Oakland, and Houston are the largest urban jurisdictions to do this, but they are not alone.[237] Police in over thirty other cities in California, as well as departments in Michigan, Florida, Washington and Rhode Island are also collecting data.[238] Police departments, not courts, are in the best possible position to take action—by collecting data, by re-training officers, and by putting in place and enforcing policies against the racially disproportionate use of traffic stops. Taking the initiative in this fashion allows a police department to control the process to a much greater extent than it might if it is mandated from the outside. And developing regulations from inside the organization usually will result in greater compliance by those who have to follow these rules—police officers themselves.[239] This represents a promising new approach to the problem. The police must first, of course, realize that there is a problem, and that doing something about it is in their interest.

D. Litigation

Another way to address racial profiling is to bring lawsuits under the Equal Protection Clause and federal civil rights statutes. In Whren, the U.S. Supreme Court said that under the Fourth Amendment of the U.S. Constitution courts can no longer suppress evidence in pretextual stop cases. But the Court did leave open the possibility of attacking racially biased law enforcement activity under the Equal Protection Clause with civil suits. There are a number of such suits around the country that are either pending or recently concluded, including cases in Maryland,[240] Florida,[241] Indiana,[242] and Illinois.[243]

It is important not to underestimate the difficulty of filing a lawsuit against a police department alleging racial bias. These cases require an "attractive" plaintiff who will not make a bad impression due to prior criminal record, current criminal involvement, or the like. They also require a significant amount of resources. For this reason, organizations interested in this issue, particularly the American Civil Liberties Union, have taken the lead in bringing these cases.[244] Last but not least, it takes a plaintiff with guts to stand up and publicly sue a police department in a racially charged case. Most people would probably rather walk away from these experiences, no matter how difficult and humiliating, than get into a legal battle with law enforcement.

E. Search and Seizure Challenges under State Constitutional Provisions, Case Law, and Statutes

Another possibility is the use of state constitutional provisions, cases and statutes to challenge these stops. For example, in the New Jersey case for which Lamberth conducted his study, the defendant brought his motion to dismiss under state case law that is different from Whren.[245] New Jersey law affords more protection to its citizens than the federal Constitution does.[246] Under New Jersey case law, a judge can grant a motion to suppress when there is evidence of racial bias,[247] but the Fourth Amendment, as interpreted by the Supreme Court in Whren, would not allow this. A second example comes from New York. In People v. Dickson, a New York state judge recently reaffirmed that New York's state constitution prohibits the use of pretextual stops, in direct contradiction to Whren.[248] And in Whitehead v. State, the Maryland Court of Special Appeals ruled that even if the pretextual stop of the defendant met Whren's constitutional standard, the detention that followed the stop was too long, resulting in the suppression of evidence.[249] All of these cases represent promising approaches spurred by state court hostility to pretextual traffic stops, which made these courts willing to consider creative state law-based legal theories.

VI. Conclusion

Everyone wants criminals caught. Few feel this with more urgency than African Americans, who are so often the victims of crime. But we must choose our methods carefully. As a country, we must strive to avoid police practices that impose high costs on law abiding citizens, and that skew those costs heavily on the basis of race.

African Americans clearly feel aggrieved by pretextual traffic stops. It is virtually impossible to find black people who do not feel that they have experienced racial profiling. The statistics presented here show that this is more than just the retelling of stories based on isolated instances of police behavior. Rather, the patterns in the data are strong, even when the data are not ideal. These experiences have a deep psychological and emotional impact on the individuals involved, and they also have a significant connection to many of the most basic problems in criminal justice and race.

Surely a solution will not be easy to achieve. There are, after all, many among the law enforcement community and its supporters who disfavor even the most basic first steps toward an understanding of the problem through the collection of comprehensive, accurate data. Yet it is with these same people that the best hope for any solution rests. Changes in law enforcement policies, training, and supervision, and a determination from the top to end race-based policing are where the effort to come to grips with this problem will ultimately succeed or fail. And lest we lose hope, the first effort to legislate the collection of data—Rep. Conyers' H.R. 118—has spawned a dozen imitators on the state level.

The bottom line is that we—every citizen and every police officer—must realize that "driving while black" is a problem not just for African Americans, but for every American who believes in basic fairness. When blacks feel like criminals whenever they do something as common as driving a car, and when they feel so distrustful of the police that they will not believe officers testifying in court, things have come to a dangerous point. "Driving while black" destroys the ideal that holds us together as a nation: equal justice under law. And when that goes, we are all in trouble.

NOTES

1. Interview with Michael, in Toledo, Ohio (Oct. 1, 1998). Michael, 41, is an African American male who has been subjected to pretextual traffic stops. As with some of the other individuals quoted here, Michael asked that his last name not be used.

2. See Cochran & Grace: Johnnie Cochran—Driving While Black (Court TV television broadcast, Mar. 23, 1997) (transcript on file with author).

3. Id.

4. Id.

5. I have referred specifically throughout this chapter to African American drivers, but it is also common for Hispanic drivers to face pretextual traffic stops. In fact, some legal actions against discriminatory traffic stop practices have been brought exclusively on behalf of Hispanics. See, e.g., Chavez v. Illinois State Police, 94 C-5307, 1999 WL 592187, at *1 (N.D. Ill. Aug. 2, 1999) (ruling on a civil rights action alleging that Illinois state police stop disproportionate numbers of Hispanic drivers).

6. See infra notes 175–76 and accompanying text.

7. See infra notes 177–204 and accompanying text.

8. According to the 1990 census, Toledo has a population of about 333,000; it is 77% white and 19.7% African American, with a mixture of other ethnic groups rounding out the total. See U.S. Census (visited Oct. 13, 1999) <http://www.census.gov/population/censusdata>. While there have been occasional discussions on race-related issues and even (more rarely) flare-ups of racial tension, see for example, Toledo Is Sued Over Random Stopping of Blacks, N.Y. Times, Aug. 14, 1988, at A31 (describing federal civil rights suit over random stops of black youths in racially mixed neighborhoods), the racial climate has been relatively calm in Toledo for the last ten years. Some of the interviewees asked that their last names not be used because they wanted to avoid repercussions at their jobs.

9. See infra notes 94–108 and accompanying text.

10. See infra notes 63–92 and accompanying text.

11. See infra table 3.3.

12. See infra table 3.3.

13. Report of Dr. John Lamberth, Plaintiff's Expert at 9, Wilkins v. Maryland State Police (No. MJG-93–468) (D. Md. 1996) (on file with author).

14. According to some national crime statistics, this is a correct assumption. See Bureau of Justice Statistics, Sourcebook of Criminal Justice Statistics 408 tbl.4.10 (1995) (showing that blacks, who make up 12% of the population, are 31.3% of all those arrested). Blacks, on average, also serve longer prison terms. See id. at 474 tbl.5.25 (stating that average federal sentence in 1992 is 84.1 months for blacks, but 56.8 months for whites); David Cole, No Equal Justice: Race and Class in the American Criminal Justice System 4–5 (1999) (stating that statistics on crime and the criminal justice system show blacks are disproportionately convicted and incarcerated); Randall Kennedy, Race, Crime, and the Law 145 (1997) (arguing that "blacks, particularly young black men, commit a percentage of the nation's street crime that is strikingly disproportionate to their percentage in the nation's population."). But as I will show, this represents an overly simplistic view that does little to illuminate the actual picture of relevant criminal behavior. See infra notes 127–36 and accompanying text.

15. Michael Fletcher, Driven to Extremes: Black Men Take Steps to Avoid Police Stops, Wash. Post, Mar. 29, 1996, at A22.

16. Joe Donahue, Boss Warns Troopers: Don't Target Minorities, Newark Star-Ledger, Feb. 28, 1999, at 1. Williams was later fired by Governor Christie Whitman for those and other remarks in that interview. See Kathy Barrett Carter & Ron Marsico, Whitman Fires Chief of

State Police, Newark Star-ledger, Mar. 1, 1999, at 1; Robert D. McFadden, Whitman Fires Police Chief over Comments on Race, N.Y. Times, Mar. 1, 1999, at A23.

17. See Dan Barry & Marjorie Connelly, Poll in New York Finds Many Think Police Are Biased, N.Y. Times, Mar. 16, 1999, at A1 (stating that less than 25 percent of New Yorkers surveyed believe that police treat blacks and whites equally); David W. Moore & Lydia Saad, No Immediate Sign That Simpson Trial Intensified Racial Animosity, Gallup Poll Monthly, Oct. 1995, at 5 (reporting that 68% of blacks and 52% of whites said they believe police racism against blacks is common); Julia Vitullo-Martin, Fairness, Justice Not Simply a Matter of Black and White, Chi. Trib., Nov. 13, 1997, at 31 (noting recent poll by Joint Center for Political and Economic Studies that indicated that more than 80% of blacks and Hispanics, and 56% of whites, agree that police are far more likely to harass and discriminate against blacks than whites); see also Michael A. Fletcher, Criminal Justice Panel Defines Racial Issues, Wash. Post, May 20, 1998, at A13 (noting that panelists appearing before President Clinton's Race Advisory Board argued, with little dissent, that the criminal justice system exhibits many biases toward blacks and other minorities).

18. I deliberately chose to interview middle-class people. By doing so, I do not wish to deny or exclude the experiences of others who may not fit within this group, and certainly would not argue that their experiences are any less important than those of the people on whom I have focused. But I made this choice in an attempt to show that "driving while black" is not only an experience of the young black male, or those blacks at the bottom of the socioeconomic ladder. All blacks confront the issue directly, regardless of age, dress, occupation, or social station.

19. Interview with Karen Brank, in Toledo, Ohio (Aug. 21, 1998).

20. See id.

21. See id.

22. See id.

23. See id.

24. See id.

25. See id.

26. See id.

27. Id.

28. Id.

29. Id.

30. Id.

31. Interview with Anthony Mack, Ottawa Hills, Ohio Police Officer, in Toledo, Ohio (Sept. 1996).

32. See id.

33. Interview with James, in Toledo, Ohio (Oct. 30, 1998). James asked that his last name not be used in any publication.

34. Since James's friend lived with his parents, his mother was with them that night. See id. When responding to the accusation of weaving, James recalled that there was no drinking of alcohol or use of any drugs that night. See id. He never uses either alcohol or drugs. See id.

35. See id.

36. See id.

37. Id.

38. Id.

39. See Interview with Michael, supra note 1.

40. See id.

41. Id.

42. See id.

43. Id.

44. Id.

45. See Interview with Karen Brank, supra note 19.

46. See Interview with Kevin, in Toledo, Ohio (Nov. 6, 1998). Kevin requested that his last name not be used.

47. Id.

48. See Fletcher, supra note 15, at A1 (describing how blacks avoid areas in which they know they will stand out and attract police attention); Interview with Karen Brank, supra note 19 (describing how after her arrest following a traffic stop revealed warrants [which turned out to be mistaken] she has changed her driving itinerary to avoid the all-white suburb in which this happened); Interview with James, supra note 33 (stating that he consciously avoids white suburban communities in which police frequently stop blacks).

49. See Fletcher, supra note 15, at A1 (describing a well-known civil rights lawyer who rents bland cars for trips from Washington, D.C. to Richmond to avoid attracting police attention, even though he is older and graying).

50. Interview with Kevin, supra note 46

51. See Fletcher, supra note 15, at A1 (describing a journalist who wears a distinctive beret and removes it when driving to avoid police stops).

52. See id. (stating that one man who drives across southern Illinois always allows extra travel time because he is stopped so frequently).

53. Interview with Michael, supra note 1.

54. Interview with Ova Tate, Police Officer, in Toledo, Ohio (Aug. 28, 1998).

55. Interview with Karen Brank, supra note 19.

56. See, e.g., Doron P. Levin, 4 Detroit Officers Charged in Death, N.Y. Times, Nov. 17, 1992, at A1 (reporting that four officers were charged in connection with the beating death of Malice Green after a traffic stop); Kenneth B. Noble, The Endless Rodney King Case, N.Y. Times, Feb. 4, 1996, 4, at 5 (detailing the many trials and other proceedings in the case against the officers accused of beating Rodney King); No Federal Charges in Motorist's Death, N.Y. Times, Feb. 21, 1999, 1, at 26 (reporting that the U.S. Department of Justice decided not to file federal criminal charges in the death of Jonny Gammage, who was killed in a struggle with police outside Pittsburgh after a 1995 traffic stop).

57. Christopher A. Darden, In Contempt 110 (1996).

58. If anyone has a well-informed view of this problem, it would be Officer Ova Tate. Tate's dual perspective—as an African American and as a member of what he calls "the blue race" of the police department—gives him a unique vantage point. Interview with Ova Tate, supra note 54. Not so long ago, Tate says, whatever the Constitution said about equal rights for all, it applied only to whites, not blacks, and wholesale racial harassment by the police was common. See id. As a result, he says, "African Americans do not trust police officers, and they feel that they are starting off on the wrong foot in any dealings with them." Id. Tate explains by describing a stop by an imaginary intimidating police officer. The officer asks prying questions, orders the driver out of the car, and then asks if the driver is carrying drugs, all of which are perfectly legal actions. See id. A white person would simply wonder why the officer seems hostile. "But if you're black, it's another thing you file away about how police deal with blacks," he says. Id. Whites put such an experience "in general terms," because they have no history with the police. "If you're black, it's 'the police are no good, this is how the police deal with blacks.'" Id.

59. See Traffic Stops Statistics Act of 1997, H.R. 118, 105th Cong. (1997). The bill was re-introduced in 1999 as the Traffic Stops Statistics Study Act, H.R. 1443, 106th Cong. (1999). The new bill limits data collection to a national sample of police departments.

60. See Robert L. Jackson, Push Against Bias in Traffic Stops Arrested, L.A. Times, June 1, 1998, at A5.

61. See id.

62. As of this writing, North Carolina and Connecticut have passed bills requiring data collection, and a number of local police forces are preparing to do the same. Collection of data may begin late in 1999. See infra notes 221–22 and accompanying text.

63. Report of Dr. John Lamberth, Plaintiff's Expert, Revised Statistical Analysis of the Incidence of Police Stops and Arrests of Black Drivers/Travelers on the New Jersey Turnpike Between Exits or Interchanges 1 and 3 from the Years 1988 Through 1991, at 2, State v. Pedro Soto, 734 A.2d 350 (N.J. Super. Ct. Law. Div. 1996) (on file with author).

64. 734 A.2d 350.

65. Soto was a criminal case; the defendant and the others joining his motion had been stopped and contraband seized from them, resulting in their arrests. See id. at 352. There is no doubt that now this claim would not succeed if based on the Fourth Amendment to the Federal Constitution. Under Whren v. U.S., the Fourth Amendment would play no part in the decision because the motivation of the officer is immaterial, as long as a traffic offense was, in fact, committed. 517 U.S. 806, 813 (1996). As the case was eventually decided, the trial court granted the motion to suppress based on New Jersey's own law and constitution. See Soto, 734 A.2d at 352.

66. See Lamberth, supra note 63.

67. Id. at 2.

68. See id. at 3–6.

69. See id. at 6–7. The hours of observation—essentially daylight only—were selected because there would be enough light to make a racial identification, and because most of the stops in the cases at issue in Soto occurred during those hours. See Soto, 734 A.2d at 352.

70. See Lamberth, supra note 63, at 14.

71. See id. at 9.

72. See id. at 26.

73. Lamberth's finding was supported by the testimony of several state police supervisors and officers. All said that blacks and whites drive indistinguishably. See Soto, 734 A.2d at 354.

74. See id. at 352.

75. Lamberth, supra note 63, at 20.

76. The accepted convention for statisticians to conclude that a difference is real and not chance is the finding that if the same study was done many times, the present results would occur only five times out of a hundred. This .05 level is determined by computing the number of standard deviations that the observed result differs from the expected. The .05 level of statistical significance is reached at about two standard deviations. The probability drops to one in 100 when 2.58 standard deviations is reached. Lamberth, supra note 13, at 5.

77. Lamberth, supra note 63, at 21.

78. This does not count those who are stopped and arrested.

79. See Lamberth, supra note 63, at 24.

80. Id. at 25.

81. Id. at 25–26, 28.

82. Lamberth, supra note 13.

83. See Plaintiff's Complaint at 1, Wilkins v. Maryland State Police (No. MJG-93-468) (D. Md. Feb. 12, 1993) (on file with author).

84. For a more complete description of Wilkins v. Maryland State Police, see David A. Harris, "Driving While Black" and All Other Traffic Offenses: The Supreme Court and Pretextual Traffic Stops, 87 J. Crim. L. & Criminology 554, 563–566 (1997).

85. Criminal Intelligence Report from Allegany County Narcotic Task Force to Maryland State Police (Apr. 27, 1992) (on file with author).

86. See Settlement Agreement P 9, Wilkins v. Maryland State Police (No. MJG-93-468) (D. Md. Jan. 6, 1995) (on file with author).

87. In Maryland, Lamberth also attempted to use a stationary survey as he had in New Jersey, but the Maryland State Police refused to allow him to do so. See Lamberth, supra note 13, at 2 n.4.

88. See id. at 5.

89. See id. at 5 tbl.1.

90. See id. at 9. Statewide, State Police found drugs on virtually the same percentages of black and white drivers. See id. at 5. This means that even though blacks were much more likely to get stopped and searched than whites were, they were no more likely to have drugs, putting the supposed justification for these stops in grave doubt.

91. Id. at 9.

92. Id. at 9–10.

93. The one exception is the Ottawa Hills Police Department. Ottawa Hills is a small (approximately 4,000 residents and almost exclusively white) incorporated village in Lucas County, Ohio. Village policy requires that officers issue either a ticket or a written warning for each stop, and both warnings and tickets include a space to note the driver's race.

94. Data from Akron Municipal Court, Dayton Municipal Court, Toledo Municipal Court, and Franklin County Municipal Court, which includes Columbus, were used.

95. See Ohio Rev. Code Ann. 1901.20 (Anderson 1998) (detailing municipal court criminal and traffic jurisdiction). A small number of citations are handled by mayor's courts, which still exist in certain areas of the state. See id. 1905.01 (setting out jurisdiction of mayor's courts for ordinance and traffic violations).

96. For at least Toledo and Akron, these numbers represent the total number of traffic cases, not individual tickets; some cases include more than one ticket given to the driver on the same occasion. By sheer coincidence, the data for Toledo were produced twice—first, tabulating all tickets, and then all cases. The data tabulating cases came to me by accident. The data were different; in the data on tickets, blacks were 35% of those ticketed; in the data concerning cases, blacks were 31%. These data showed that blacks were more likely than nonblacks to receive more than one ticket in the same stop, an interesting fact in its own right. Because I am interested in measuring traffic stops and am using ticketing only as a way to estimate stops, I have used the data on cases; after all, even if more than one ticket is issued in any given encounter, the driver was only stopped once. It is of course possible that the fact that blacks receive more than one ticket per incident more often than whites is itself a reflection of race-based policing, but there may be other factors at work here as well, such as the fact that blacks tend to drive older cars than whites that may have more obvious safety violations, or the fact that blacks use seat belts less often than whites. Therefore, for purposes of this study, I have chosen to treat this difference as if it is not evidence of racial bias.

97. Data from Franklin County Municipal Court include only the years 1996 and 1997, but none from 1998.

98. Franklin County Municipal Court data include all communities in the county, not just Columbus, but were not listed in a way that allowed separate numbers to be broken out for individual police departments. See Memorandum from Michael A. Pirik, Deputy Chief Clerk, Franklin County Municipal Court, to David Harris (Aug. 28, 1998) (on file with author).

99. The data in this portion of the study were obtained from the Census Bureau's website. See U.S. Census (visited Oct. 13, 1999) <http://www.census.gov>.

100. Fifteen and seventy-five are arbitrary choices, but they are reasonable ones. Fifteen is generally the minimum age at which states allows juveniles to obtain a driving permit. While many people do drive above age seventy-five, it is also the age at which population in general begins to drop fairly dramatically. See U.S. Census (visited Oct. 13, 1999) <http://www.census. gov>. Also, the census data breaks people down by ages into five-year blocks, and both fifteen and seventy-five allow the analysis to use these existing break points.

101. See Federal Highway Admin., U.S. Dep't of Transp., 1995 Nationwide Personal Transportation Survey (visited Sept. 27, 1999) <http://www.bts.gov/ntda/npts>; see also Letter from Eric Hill, Research Associate, Center for Urban Transportation, to David A. Harris (Sept. 28, 1998) (on file with author). The NPTS contains other data that could also be used to sharpen the driving age population figures in the same way. For example, whites take an average of 4.4 private vehicle trips daily; blacks take an average of 3.9. This leads to the inference that, proportionately, there are likely to be fewer blacks in the driving population than whites at any given time. I have not used these figures in the analysis, but it would be reasonable to do so.

102. Letter from Eric Hill, Research Associate, Center for Urban Transportation Research, to David A. Harris (Oct. 9, 1998) (on file with author).

103. I credit John Lamberth with this idea, and for teaching me to work with this data. (He also performed some of the early analysis in the study and served as a constant check on my work. To say that I am thankful for his help does not fully express the depth of my gratitude. Of course, any errors made here should be attributed to me.) A likelihood ratio is arrived at by first calculating the ratio of blacks ticketed to blacks in the relevant population. Then the ratio of nonblacks ticketed to nonblacks in the same population is calculated. The first number is then divided by the second. For example, for ticketing by the Toledo Police compared to Toledo's black driving age population, blacks ticketed are 30.8%, and blacks in the driving age population are 17.9%; .308/.179 = 1.7206. Nonblacks are 69.2% of those ticketed, and 82.1% of the driving age population; .692/.821 = .8428. The likelihood ratio is 1.7206/.8428, or 2.04.

104. For a comparison of the Toledo Police Department with other local police departments in Lucas County, Ohio, see David A. Harris, "Driving While Black": Do We Have a Problem Here in Toledo?, Toledo City Paper, Apr. 1999, at 16.

105. With the exception of Franklin County, the data could be broken down separately for these city police departments, and data for suburban or special jurisdiction police departments could be eliminated from the analysis. For Franklin County Municipal Court, which covers Columbus, the data for all of the police departments in the county were aggregated and could not be separated by department.

106. E-mails from Joseph E. Jacoby, Bowling Green State University, to David A. Harris (Feb. 2 & 3, 1999) (on file with author).

107. See Federal Highway Admin., supra note 101 (reporting that whites average 4.4 vehicle trips daily and blacks average 3.9).

108. See E-mails from Joseph E. Jacoby to David A. Harris, supra note 106.

109. See Harris, supra note 84, at 580–82 (explaining that most police agencies do not keep track of any information that allows an estimate of how many innocent people are being stopped for every person apprehended through traffic stops).

110. U.S. Const. amend. IV.

111. See Mapp v. Ohio, 367 U.S. 643, 655 (1961).

112. See Weeks v. United States, 232 U.S. 383, 393 (1914), overruled by Mapp, 367 U.S. 643.

113. People v. Defore, 150 N.E. 585, 587 (N.Y. 1926).

114. See generally Akhil Reed Amar, Fourth Amendments First Principles, 107 Harv. L. Rev. 757, 793–800 (1994) (arguing that the exclusionary rule makes murderers better off at the expense of society); David Blumberg, The Case Against the Exclusionary Rule, 14 Hum. Rts. 41, 45 (1987) (finding that "the suppression of unconstitutionality seized evidence . . . makes it more likely that the outcome will be an incorrect one, that a guilty defendant will go free or receive an unduly lenient punishment"); Gary S. Goodpaster, An Essay on Ending the Exclusionary Rule, 33 Hastings L.J. 1065, 1068 (1982) (arguing that although the exclusionary rule generally does not free the guilty, it may help them receive reduced sentences); Dallin H. Oaks, Studying the Exclusionary Rule in Search and Seizure, 37 U. Chi. L. Rev. 665, 736–39 (1970) (noting that the exclusionary rule is subject to the criticism that it frees the guilty); Richard A. Posner, Rethinking the Fourth Amendment, 1981 Sup. Ct. Rev. 49, 53 (arguing that the exclusionary rule gives criminals "a right to conceal evidence of their crimes," a result not intended by the Fourth Amendment); James E. Spiotto, Search and Seizure: An Empirical Study of the Exclusionary Rule and Its Alternatives, 2 J. Legal Stud. 243, 276 (1973) (explaining that the exclusionary rule provides a remedy only for those arrested and charged with a crime).

115. See, e.g., Andrew Hacker, Two Nations: Black and White, Separate, Hostile, Unequal 183 (1992) (finding that blacks accounted for 50.8% of murder victims in 1990); U.S. Dep't of Justice, Criminal Victimization in the United States 1993, at 15 (1996) (showing by empirical study that the rate of victimization of blacks exceeds the rates for other racial groups).

116. See Developments in the Law—Race and the Criminal Process, 101 Harv. L. Rev. 1472, 1508 (1988) (reporting that in any particular year 97.9% of blacks and 99.5% of whites are not arrested).

117. See, e.g., Katherine K. Russell, The Color of Crime 122 (1998) (stating that the current use of racial labels for black crime implies that "there is something about Blackness that 'explains' criminality"); see also Samuel G. Freedman, Is the Drug War Racist?, Rolling Stone, May 14, 1998, at 35–36 (interviewing Glen Loury and Orlando Patterson, two African Americans described as "leading public intellectuals" in America, in which Loury declares that "we're criminalizing a whole class of young black men"). The following passage helps explain why treating people as criminal suspects on the basis of racial characteristics is morally repugnant, even if based on a statistical justification:

> In the United States at present, there are real and large differences among ethnic and racial groups in their average performance in school and in their rates of committing violent crimes. (The statistics, of course, say nothing about heredity or any other putative cause.) . . . A good statistical category-maker could develop racial stereotypes and use them to make actuarially sound but morally repugnant decisions about individual cases. This behavior is racist not because it is irrational (in the sense of statistically inaccurate) but because it flouts the moral principle that it is wrong to judge an individual using the statistics of a racial or ethnic group. The argument against bigotry, then, does not come from the design specs for a rational statistical categorizer. It comes from a rule system, in this case a rule of ethics, that tells us when to turn our statistical categorizers off. (Steven Pinker, How the Mind Works 313 [1997])

See also Phillip Martin, Officials Trying to Determine If Racial Profiling Tactics Are Being Employed by Federal Law Enforcement Officials; Arguments Exist That Both Support and Refute Crime Statistics (National Public Radio broadcast, June 10, 1999) (stating that while police justify profiling based on arrest statistics, these statistics actually measure police activity instead of offense rates and overlook the fact that 98% of all blacks are not arrested in any year) (transcript on file with author).

118. See Chicago Gang Congregation Ordinance, Chi. Mun. Code 8-4-015 (1992).

119. See Joan Biskupic, High Court to Review Law Aimed at Gangs, Wash. Post, Dec. 7, 1998, at A4 (reporting that while the law was enforced, 45,000 people, mostly African Americans and Hispanics, were arrested); David G. Savage, High Court May Move Back on "Move On" Laws, L.A. Times, Oct. 5, 1998, at A1 (noting that 45,000 arrests were made from the passage of the law until 1995); Lynn Sweet, Court to Sort Out Loitering Law, Chi. Sun-Times, Dec. 6, 1998, at 14 (stating that about 43,000 arrests were made of mostly blacks and Hispanics under the law).

120. For the full procedural history of the case before it reached the U.S. Supreme Court, see City of Chicago v. Morales, 687 N.E.2d 53, 57–59 (Ill. 1997), aff'd, 119 S. Ct. 1849 (1999).

121. See Tracey L. Meares & Dan M. Kahan, The Wages of Antiquated Procedural Thinking: A Critique of Chicago v. Morales, 1998 U. Chi. Legal F. 197, 212–13. The arrest of mostly minority group members under the ordinance will have many negative effects, including the "enervation" of the stigma that might otherwise attach to being arrested, the disproportionate involvement of blacks and other minorities in the criminal justice system, and reinforcement of white distrust and suspicion of all African American men, but the authors feel nonetheless that "the ordinance is an example of a policy tool that is a tolerably moderate way to steer children away from criminality." Id. at 213. Moreover, they assert that residents of crime-ridden minority neighborhoods understand these downsides and still agree. See id. In an earlier version of the argument, Kahan asserts that though the law may have a disproportionate impact on minorities, "giving up on the gang-loitering law will result in more, not less, racial disparity. When we deprive the police of effective law-enforcement tools, it is the members of these groups that suffer most." Dan M. Kahan, Defending the Gang-Loitering Law, Chi. Trib., Dec. 31, 1995, at 19.

122. David Cole, "Standing While Black," Nation, Jan. 4, 1999, at 24 ("Chicago calls the offense 'gang loitering,' but it might more candidly be termed "standing while black.'"). Professor Paul Butler recently wrote that police followed him in his own neighborhood up onto the front porch of his home in Washington, D.C. because the officers apparently had some doubts about whether a black man should be walking in the area; he called his own "offense" "walking while black." Paul Butler, Walking While Black: Encounters with the Police on My Street, Legal Times, Nov. 10, 1997, at 23. The police relented only when his neighbor came out and vouched for him. See id. at 24.

123. See City of Chicago v. Morales, 119 S. Ct. 1849, 1861 (1999) (holding that despite the ordinance's features that purported to limit police discretion, its broad sweep violated the requirement that a legislating body establish at least minimal guidance to govern enforcement of a criminal law under Kolender v. Lawson, 461 U.S. 352, 358 [1983]).

124. See supra note 15 and accompanying text; see also Fletcher, supra note 17, at A13 (noting that one panelist testifying before the President's race advisory board argued that police should use "'profiles' that include race because it is efficient to scrutinize groups who have higher crime rates").

125. See Bureau of Justice Statistics, U.S. Dep't of Justice, Source-book of Criminal Justice Statistics 1997, at 338 (1997).

126. Homicides are much more likely to be reported then rapes.

127. See Delbert S. Elliot, Lies, Damn Lies, and Arrest Statistics, 2–8, Sutherland Award Presentation, American Society of Criminology (Center for the Study of Prevention of Violence, Institute of Behavioral Science, University of Colorado at Boulder 1995) (on file with author) (criticizing the use of arrest statistics to understand criminal behavior); John Kitsuse & Aaron Cicourel, A Note on the Use of Official Statistics, 11 Soc. Probs. 131, 136–37 (1963) (noting that statistics on arrest, disposition, and incarceration may measure the behavior of criminal justice agencies within the system, but not the behavior of criminals themselves).

128. Lamberth, supra note 13, at 7–8. In a very helpful and insightful comment, Professor Richard Friedman pointed out to me that perhaps this lack of statistical difference between black and white hit rates, even though many more blacks were being searched, may mean that in fact police are doing exactly what they should be: responding to very subtle cues and simply finding more blacks carrying contraband because they are engaged in this activity. I disagree; there is simply no evidence that this is so. But even if it were true, the fact that many more blacks who are completely innocent of any wrongdoing must be stopped and searched in order to expose officers to these cues would make this method of operating an unacceptable policy choice.

129. See U.S. Customs Service, Personal Searches of Air Passengers Results: Positive and Negative, Fiscal Year 1998, at 1 (1998) (finding that 6.7% of whites, 6.3% of blacks, and 2.8% of Hispanics had contraband); see also David Stout, Customs Service Will Review Drug-Search Process for Bias, N.Y. Times, Apr. 9, 1999, at A18 (explaining that the Customs Service faces numerous lawsuits alleging discrimination on the basis of race and gender in the use of intrusive searches at airports).

130. Statistics on drug use are interesting for our purposes not just as a more accurate measure than arrest statistics on who may be drug involved, but as a reasonably good measure of the crime of drug possession, since users must at some point be in possession of drugs.

131. See Substance Abuse and Mental Health Servs. Nat'l Admin., U.S. Dep't. of Health and Human Servs., National Household Survey on Drug Abuse, Preliminary Results from 1997, at 13, 58 tbl.1A (finding that thirteen percent of all illicit drug users were black).

132. See National Inst. on Drug Abuse, Drug Use Among Racial/Ethnic Minorities, 64–66 figs.1–5 (1997) (showing past-year use of marijuana, inhalants, cocaine, and LSD by black twelfth graders lower than use by whites in every year from 1977 to 1997, and tobacco use by blacks lower since 1982); see also Bureau of Justice Statistics, U.S. Dep't of Justice, Drugs, Crime, and the Justice System 28 (1992) (reporting similar findings). It is important to note that these statistics only count those still in school; those who have dropped out or who were not in school on the particular day the information was gathered were not included. Therefore, we do not know about the rates of drug use among all young people. There could be a greater degree of drug use among those who have left school than those who have not; of course, this is probably just as true for white dropouts as it is for black dropouts. See Substance Abuse and Mental Health Servs. Admin., U.S. Dep't of Health and Human Servs., National Household Survey on Drug Abuse, Preliminary Estimates from 1995, at 13 (1997) (stating that among white, black, and Hispanic youth, "the rates of use are about the same").

133. See Carter & Marsico, supra note 16, at 1.

134. See Bureau of Justice Statistics, supra note 125, at 338 tbl.4.10, 422 tbl.5.46.

135. See id. at 426 tbl.5.51 (citing figures for 1994).

136. See id. at 428 tbl.5.55 (citing figures for 1994).

137. Interview with Karen Brank, supra note 19.

138. See Interview with James, supra note 33.

139. Interview with Michael, supra note 1.

140. See Neil MacFarquar, Police Get Good Ratings From Most, but Not All, New Yorkers, N.Y. Times, June 5, 1999, at B3 (reporting that a national survey conducted by the Bureau of Justice Statistics and the Office of Community Oriented Police Services of the U.S. Department of Justice indicated that almost two and one-half times as many blacks as whites say they are dissatisfied with their police).

141. See supra note 17 and accompanying text.

142. See Gary Webb, DWB, Esquire, Apr. 1999, at 118, 125.

143. See Jeffrey Rosen, One Angry Woman, New Yorker, Feb. 24 & Mar. 3, 1997, at 54, 64

(arguing that rising percentage of mistrials may be because, as one senior Justice Department official says, "'[Blacks] see black defendants and white prosecutors. They get stopped for no reason. Those are the things that stick out in your mind.'"; see also Roger Parloff, Race and Juries: If It Ain't Broke . . . , Am. Law., June 1997, at 5. Although Parloff argues persuasively that there does not seem to be any impending crisis caused by a dramatic increase in hung juries or acquittals, he reveals considerable factual support for the proposition that minority communities do exhibit more skepticism toward police that whites do. See id. Professor Paul Butler has made a related argument: black jurors ought to use the power of nullification, and refuse to convict obviously guilty black men in certain cases, because of the unjust way in which the system treats blacks. See Paul Butler, Racially Based Jury Nullification: Black Power in the Criminal Justice System, 105 Yale L.J. 677, 679 (1995).

144. See Randall Kennedy, The State, Criminal Law, and Racial Discrimination: A Comment, 107 Harv. L. Rev. 1255, 1260 n.20 (1994) (arguing for a "politics of distinction," in which law enforcement efforts, even if excessive, against law-breaking blacks are seen not as racial discrimination but as a net benefit to law-abiding blacks, because so much crime is intraracial); see also Regina Austin, The Black Community, Its Lawbreakers, and a Politics of Identification, 65 S. Cal. L. Rev. 1769, 1772 (1992) (explaining this idea as "the difference that exists between the 'better' elements of 'the [black] community' and the stereotypical 'lowlifes' who richly merit the bad reputations the dominant society accords them"). But see David Cole, The Paradox of Race and Crime: A Comment on Randall Kennedy's "Politics of Distinction," 83 Ga. L. Rev. 2547 (1995) (arguing that while Kennedy astutely recognizes the paradox posed by the fact that blacks, who are disproportionately victims of crime by other blacks suffer from both over-and under-enforcement of the criminal law, he is wrong to try to make the false choice of benefiting "good" over "bad" blacks).

145. Marc Mauer & Tracy Huling, Young Black Americans and the Criminal Justice System: Five Years Later 4 tbl.2 (1995) (on file with author).

146. Eric Lotke, National Ctr. for Insts. and Alternatives, Hobbling a Generation (1997) (on file with author).

147. See The Sentencing Project, Losing the Vote: The Impact of Felony Disenfranchisement Laws in the United States 2, 8–10 tbl.3 (1998) (on file with author) (arguing that 1.4 million black men are disenfranchised, representing 13% of the adult male black population, and 36% of all those disenfranchised; in seven states, one in four black males is permanently disenfranchised).

148. 487 U.S. 654 (1988).

149. Id. at 727–28 (Scalia, J., dissenting) (quoting Robert Jackson, The Federal Prosecutor, Address at the Second Annual Conference of United States Attorneys [Apr. 1, 1940]) (emphasis added).

150. See infra notes 177–83 and accompanying text. Ironically, the Court's opinion in Whren, the case that completely freed the police from any Fourth Amendment–based restriction on their discretion to make traffic stops, was written by Justice Scalia. See Whren v. United States, 517 U.S. 806 (1996).

151. Blacks receive longer sentences than whites in federal courts and are more likely to be incarcerated. See Bureau of Justice Statistics, supra note 125, at 395 tbl.5.19 & 396 tbl.5.20. Even controlling for offense level and criminal history, blacks received longer sentences than whites under the Federal Sentencing Guidelines. See David B. Mustard, Racial Ethnic and Gender Disparities in Sentencing: Evidence From the U.S. Federal Courts (available at http://www.terry.uga.edu/~mustard/sentencing.pdf).

152. See Mustard, supra note 151.

153. See United States v. Leviner, 31 F. Supp. 2d 23, 26 (D. Mass. 1998).

154. See A.L.I.-A.B.A., Federal Sentencing Guidelines 1 (1988) ("Factors in determining the appropriate sentence range . . . include . . . the defendant's criminal history.").

155. Leviner, 31 F. Supp. 2d at 24.

156. See id. at 33 & n.26.

157. See id. at 33.

158. See id. at 31, 34.

159. The United States has filed an appeal in the case. See Petition for Appeal, United States v. Leviner, No. 99–1172 (1st Cir. Mar. 17, 1999) (on file with author).

160. See Fletcher, supra note 15, at A1 (describing ways that blacks attempt to avoid police attention by staying out of black areas); Interview with Kevin, supra note 46 (stating that he drives a minivan specifically to avoid police scrutiny).

161. See Interview with Karen Brank, supra note 19 (stating that she avoids the white suburban community where she was stopped before); Interview with James, supra note 33 (stating that he avoids a white suburban area because of its reputation for stopping and harassing black motorists).

162. See Warren Brown, Urban League Quits Seat Belt Drive; Group Cites Fear of Increased Police Harassment of Minorities, Wash. Post, Dec. 11, 1998, at A14.

163. See id.

164. See, e.g., 625 Ill. Comp. Stat. Ann. 5/12–603.1(e) (West Supp. 1999) (stating that police cannot stop a vehicle "solely on the basis of a violation or suspected violation of this Section"); Mich. Comp. Laws Ann. 257.710(e)(5) (West Supp. 1999) (stating that enforcement of seat belt requirement may be done only as a "secondary action"); Ohio Rev. Code Ann. 4513.263(D) (Anderson Supp. 1998) (stating that the police may not stop a motorist solely for a seat belt violation).

165. See Susan P. Baker et al., Motor Vehicle Occupant Deaths Among Hispanic and Black Children and Teenagers, 152 Archives of Pediatrics & Adolescent Med. 1209, 1210–11 (1998) (noting that higher rates of death in motor vehicle accidents among young blacks and Hispanics than among whites, which could be attributable to "racial/ethnic and sex differences in the use of safety belts and child restraints"); see also Center for Disease Control and Prevention, U.S. Dep't of Health and Human Servs., Vital and Health Statistics: Health of Our Nation's Children, Series 10: Data from the National Health Interview Survey, No. 191, at 45 tbl.14 (1994) (reporting low rates of seat belt and restraint use for black children); Steve J. Niemcryk et al., Motor Vehicle Crashes, Restraint Use, and Severity of Injury in Children in Nevada, 13 Am. J. Preventative Med. 109, 111 tbl.2 (1997) (same).

166. Brown, supra note 162, at A14.

167. Id.

168. See, e.g., William J. Bratton, New Strategies for Combating Crime in New York City, 23 Fordham Urb. L.J. 781, 782 (1996) (describing the dominant mode of policing in the 1970s and 1980s as "largely reactive" or "rapid response" oriented, in which officers were "reacting to 911 calls, random patrol, riding around waiting for something to happen . . . and the reactive investigation," leaving police "ill-prepared" to face greater rates of crime and violence that came with the crack cocaine trade); Bureau of Justice Assistance, U.S. Dep't of Justice, Understanding Community Policing, A Framework for Action, Monograph, Aug. 1994, at 6 (explaining how rapid response policing "became an end in itself" and cut officers off from the community); Veronica Jennings, Community Policing Is on the Way, Wash. Post, July 2, 1992, at M1 (noting that community policing "puts the emphasis on preventing crime rather than on responding to radio dispatched calls").

169. See, e.g., Cole, supra note 14, at 192–93 (defining community policing as an effort to "make the police an integral part of the neighborhoods they serve"); Community Relations Serv., U.S. Dep't of Justice, Principles of Good Policing: Avoiding Violence Between Police and Citizens 5 (1993) ("Community policing is a philosophy in which the police engage the community to solve problems . . . based on a collaboration between police and citizens in nonthreatening and supportive interactions. These interactions include efforts by police to listen to citizens, take seriously the citizens' definitions of problems, and solve the problems that have been identified."); Bratton, supra note 168, at 784–85 (stating that community policing emphasizes "the three P's": partnership with the community, problem solving, and prevention of crime).

170. 392 U.S. 1 (1968).

171. See id. at 14–15 & n.11.

172. Interview with Ova Tate, supra note 54.

173. See Cole, supra note 14, at 192–93 ("Where such programs develop effective channels for communication between the police and the community about their respective needs, the programs can play an important role in restoring community trust and overcoming the adversarial relationship too many police departments have with disadvantaged communities.").

174. Unfortunately, strong negative feelings about police among members of minority groups, especially African Americans, is not a thing of the past. See Barry & Connelly, supra note 17, at A1 (citing a 1999 survey indicating that "fewer than a quarter of all New Yorkers believe police treat blacks and whites evenly").

175. See Carroll v. United States, 267 U.S. 132, 153, 156, 161–62 (1925) (holding that when law enforcement agents have probable cause, a warrantless search of the vehicle is justified "where it is not practicable to secure a warrant because the vehicle can be quickly moved out of the . . . jurisdiction").

176. See, e.g., California v. Carney, 471 U.S. 386, 390, 393 (1985) (creating an exception to the warrant requirement justified by a motor home's mobility and the fact that it has "a reduced expectation of privacy stemming from its use as a licensed motor vehicle subject to a range of police regulations inapplicable to a fixed dwelling").

177. 517 U.S. 806 (1996).

178. The federal circuits had divided, with some ruling that any time an officer could have made a traffic stop, based on a traffic infraction, it was legitimate. See Whren v. United States, 53 F.3d 371, 374–75 (D.C. Cir. 1995) aff'd, 517 U.S. 806 (1996); United States v. Botero-Ospina, 71 F.3d 783, 787 (10th Cir. 1995) (en banc); United States v. Johnson, 63 F.3d 242, 247 (3d Cir. 1995); United States v. Scopo, 19 F.3d 777, 782–84 (2d Cir. 1994); United States v. Ferguson, 8 F.3d 385, 389–91 (6th Cir. 1993) (en banc); United States v. Hassan El, 5 F.3d 726, 729–30 (4th Cir. 1993); United States v. Cummins, 920 F.3d 498, 500–01 (8th Cir. 1990); United States v. Trigg, 878 F.2d 1037, 1039 (7th Cir. 1989); United States v. Causey, 834 F.3d 1179, 1184 (5th Cir. 1987) (en banc). Two other circuits ruled that a traffic stop was sufficient to constitute probable cause only when a reasonable officer would have made the stop. See United States v. Cannon, 29 F.3d 472, 475–76 (9th Cir. 1994); United States v. Smith, 799 F.2d 704, 709 (11th Cir. 1986).

179. Whren, 517 U.S. at 813 (holding that "subjective intentions play no role in ordinary, probable cause Fourth Amendment analysis").

180. See id. at 812–19.

181. See id. at 818–19. The Court did say that while pretextual stops would no longer be the basis for the suppression of evidence, a pattern of pretextual stops showing racial bias could give rise to a civil suit for violation of the Equal Protection Clause and associated federal laws. See id.

182. To the same effect, see David A. Harris, Car Wars: The Fourth Amendment's Death on the Highway, 66 Geo. Wash. L. Rev. 556, 559–60 (1998) (arguing that vehicle codes "contain an almost mind-numbing amount of detailed regulation" of driving and vehicle equipment, and listing numerous offenses for which one could be stopped beyond the usual moving violations).

183. Police officers have known this for a long time. For example, one study from as far back as the 1960s quoted several officers on this line of thought. "You can always get a guy legitimately on a traffic violation if you tail him for a while, and then a search can be made." Lawrence P. Tiffany et al., Detection of Crime 131 (1967). "In the event that we see a suspicious automobile or occupant and wish to search the person or the car, or both, we will usually follow the vehicle until the driver makes a technical violation of a traffic law. Then we have a means of making a legitimate search." Id. at 133. While these statements were not legally correct even when they were made—not every traffic violation, alone, would create legal justification for a search—the thrust of the comments is correct: if a traffic violation is probable cause to stop, they can stop any driver, almost at will, because no one drives perfectly.

184. The plain view exception is so widely used that it sometimes goes unmentioned and is often misunderstood. Briefly stated, an officer can seize an item in "plain view" without a warrant, when the officer sees the object from a lawful vantage point, the officer has a right of physical access to it, and the item's contraband nature is immediately apparent, without any further searching. See generally Horton v. California, 496 U.S. 128, 136–37 (1990) (reviewing the "plain view" doctrine); Arizona v. Hicks, 480 U.S. 321, 326–27 (1987) (explaining the "immediately apparent" requirement); Coolidge v. New Hampshire, 403 U.S. 443, 464–67 (1971) (same). If all three of these things are true, there is probable cause for an immediate seizure.

185. Thus the officer can look into the car from a lawful vantage point, fulfilling the first criterion for the exception. This means more than simply being in a place from which the officer can see the evidence; in the words of Justice Stewart, "in the vast majority of cases, any evidence seized by the police will be in plain view, at least at the moment of seizure." Coolidge, 403 U.S. at 465. Rather, the officer must not have violated the Fourth Amendment in coming to the spot from which the evidence is seen. See id. at 465–66.

186. See United States v. Lee, 274 U.S. 559, 563 (1927) (determining that using artificial illumination to see what would be visible in daylight is not a search for Fourth Amendment purposes).

187. See Pennsylvania v. Mimms, 434 U.S. 106, 111 (1977).

188. See Maryland v. Wilson, 519 U.S. 408, 415 (1997).

189. The usual rule is that the stop of a vehicle for a traffic infraction, alone, will not justify a search of the vehicle. There must be something more if police wish to go further than simply hand out a citation, ask a few questions, or give a warning: evidence establishing probable cause or reasonable suspicion that a crime has been committed, or voluntary consent to search. New York v. Belton, 453 U.S. 454 (1981), changes this in any case in which police arrest a person inside the car. In Belton, when an officer pulled over a car for a traffic offense, he noticed the smell of burnt marijuana and saw an envelope with "Supergold" on it, a word he associated with marijuana. See id. at 455–56. The officer ordered all four of the occupants out of the car, arrested them, and stood them in separate places along the highway so that they could not touch each other. See id. at 456. The officer discovered marijuana when he opened the envelope and then searched the rest of the inside of the car, including the zipped pocket of a jacket which contained cocaine. See id. The Supreme Court used Belton to announce a bright-line rule: an officer may conduct a warrantless search of the passenger compartment of a vehicle, including any closed containers found inside, contemporaneous with a lawful arrest of any of the vehicle's occupants. See id. at 460–61. Note that the Court did not limit the

Belton rule to cases involving arrests of drivers. Rather, it used the words "occupant of an automobile," id. at 460, so arrests of passengers would seem to trigger the rule. This rule applies in every case, not just when there appears to be a danger either to the officer or to the integrity of the evidence; if the defendant is taken from a car and arrested, the officer may search the car, even though it is physically impossible for the defendant to get to the car to reach a weapon, destroy evidence, or escape.

190. See California v. Acevedo, 500 U.S. 565 (1991). Prior to 1991, the law's treatment of closed containers found during searches of vehicles depended upon the facts of each case. If police happened to find a closed container in a vehicle when they had probable cause to search the entire vehicle, they did not need a warrant to open and search the container. See U.S. v. Ross, 456 U.S. 798, 821–22 (1982) (holding that when police have probable cause to search an entire vehicle, a warrantless search of the vehicle and any containers that may contain the contraband sought is reasonable). If, on the other hand, they had probable cause to search a particular container and happened to find it in a vehicle, they did need a warrant. See United States v. Chadwick, 433 U.S. 1, 11–13 (1977) (holding that search of locked footlocker placed in automobile and later seized by police required a warrant); Arkansas v. Sanders, 442 U.S. 753, 761–66 (1979) (find that the "automobile exception" does not allow warrantless search of luggage just because it is located in a lawfully stopped vehicle). The Court clarified this situation in Acevedo, in which the police had probable cause to believe that contraband would be found in a particular kind of bag which happened to be deposited in a car trunk. See Acevedo, 500 U.S. at 579. The Court wiped away the dual set of rules which had governed; instead, one rule would determine the outcome in both types of situations. Speaking for the Court, Justice Blackmun said that "the protections of the Fourth Amendment must not turn on . . . coincidences." Id. at 580. Instead, the Court said, "police may search without a warrant if their search is supported by probable cause." Id. at 579. Even though police in Acevedo had probable cause to search the bag, it is important to note that they had the right to search the trunk into which they had seen the bag put only to the extent necessary to find the bag. Nevertheless, Acevedo allows a search of any areas of an automobile and the opening and search of any closed containers found there, as long as police have probable cause to believe the evidence, fruits or instrumentalities of crime will be found. See id.

191. Terry v. Ohio, 392 U.S. 1 (1968), and the cases that have followed it, for example, Minnesota v. Dickerson, 508 U.S. 336, 372–74 (1993) (reiterating Terry standard), Adams v. Williams, 407 U.S. 143, 145–46 (1972) (same), permit a brief detention when there is reason to believe that crime is afoot and that a particular person is involved. See Terry, 392 U.S. at 30. If outward appearances indicate that the suspect is armed and dangerous, or if the crime suspected is one that by its nature requires weapons, Terry allows a frisk—pat-down of the outer clothing of the suspect—for the purpose of finding weapons. See Dickerson, 508 U.S. at 373; Adams, 407 U.S. at 146; Terry, 392 U.S. at 24; see also Ybarra v. Illinois, 444 U.S. 85, 93–94 (1979) (reviewing the Terry standard). Michigan v. Long, 463 U.S. 1032 (1983), extended the idea of a frisk to automobiles. Police in Long stopped to investigate a car that had swerved into the ditch; the defendant, who appeared intoxicated, met them at the rear of his car. See id. at 1035. When the defendant moved toward his car at the request of the officers to get his registration, one of the officers observed a hunting knife on the floorboard near the driver's seat. See id. at 1036. The defendant was outside the car and could not reach the weapon, but the officer did a cursory search of the car's interior anyway—a "frisk" of the car—and found a pouch of marijuana. See id. Once the defendant had been arrested for the marijuana inside the car, a further search of the car's trunk revealed 75 pounds of marijuana. See id. According to the Supreme Court, this search comported with the Constitution. See id. Even though the weapon did not pose any current danger since the defendant was outside the vehicle, the

Court said it was reasonable to search areas in the car from which the defendant could get a weapon. See id. at 1049–50. If the police find contraband in the course of such a search, it need not be suppressed. See id. at 1050. The circumstances of the case, the Court said, justified a reasonable belief that the defendant posed a danger if he returned to his car. See id. It is difficult to understand the Court's conclusion. Among the "circumstances" on which the Court relies are the lateness of the hour, the rural location, and the defendant's careless driving and apparent intoxication. See id. The Court also felt that the restricted nature of the search also made it reasonable. See id. at 1051. But the fact remains that the defendant was outside his car and under the control of more than one police officer. He only moved toward the car in response to the officers' request for his license and registration. Thus, simply maintaining the status quo would have protected the officers fully and there was no need to search the car, and no need for a new rule of law.

192. To be sure, officers can do more than make a request to see one's license and registration. They may question the driver and attempt to get substantive answers. If this sounds like it might be custodial interrogation that would trigger the requirements of Miranda v. Arizona, 384 U.S. 436 (1966), think again. In Berkemer v. McCarty, 468 U.S. 420 (1984), the Supreme Court decided that the typical roadside encounter does not bring Miranda into play. According to the majority, the concerns that drive Miranda do not apply to the questioning of motorists by officers. See id. First, these encounters take place in public and usually involve only one or two officers. See id. at 438. Traffic stops do not include the secretive, police-controlled atmosphere of the station house and the driver is therefore unlikely to feel completely within the power of the police. See id. at 438–39. Indeed, he can even refuse to answer questions. See id. at 439. Second, these encounters are "presumptively temporary and brief" and would not create the same feeling of fear and loss of control that one might feel upon a full custodial arrest or a trip to police headquarters. Id. at 437–38. Miranda does not, of course, say that those in custody cannot be interrogated. Rather, it says only that if custodial interrogation takes place, the resulting statements can be used in the prosecution's case-in-chief only if they were preceded by the Miranda warnings or some equivalent. See Miranda, 384 U.S. at 478–79. Berkemer says this requirement does not apply to traffic stops. Officers may freely question motorists without giving them warnings, and any incriminating statements that result can come into evidence. In short, Miranda is just not a factor in traffic stops. Justice Marshall did, however, attempt to leave some room for future cases with more egregious facts, when he said for the majority in Berkemer that a traffic stop could under some circumstances become a custodial interrogation situation requiring warnings. See Berkemer, 468 U.S. at 440 ("If a motorist who has been detained pursuant to a traffic stop thereafter is subjected to treatment that renders him 'in custody' for practical purposes, he will be entitled to the full panoply of protections prescribed by Miranda.").

193. See Kate Shatzkin & Joe Hallinan, Highway Dragnets Seek Drug Couriers—Police Stop Many Cars for Searches, Seattle Times, Sept. 3, 1992, at B6; Webb, supra note 142, at 118, 125 (describing informal yet probing interrogation that is part of drug interdiction traffic stops).

194. See J. Andrew Curliss, A Nose for Dope: Trooper Has Knack for Drug Busts that Stand Up in Court, Dallas Morning News, July 18, 1996, at 1A (describing how an officer experienced at making highway drug arrests looks for suspicious answers to his questions); Joseph Neff & Pat Stith, Highway Drug Unit Focuses on Blacks, News & Observer (Raleigh), July 28, 1996, at A1 (noting how officers question those stopped, looking for suspicious answers).

195. Consent searches remain an important part of law enforcement's arsenal. In Schneckloth v. Bustamonte, the Supreme Court resolved the issue of whether a consent search required

only a voluntary giving of consent or whether the state would have to show "an intentional relinquishment or abandonment of a known right" because consent involved the waiver of a constitutional right. 412 U.S. 218, 235 (1973) (Brennan, J., & Marshall, J., dissenting) (citing Johnson v. Zerbst, 304 U.S. 458, 464 [1938]). In Schneckloth, police obtained consent and performed a search without giving either Fourth Amendment "warnings" or advice. Id. at 219–20. The Court resolved the issue by relying on the voluntariness standard traditionally used in the police interrogation area, noting that "two competing concerns must be accommodated . . . the legitimate need for such searches and . . . the requirement of assuring the absence of coercion." Id. at 227. Requiring the state to show that the defendant knew he had a right to refuse consent and nevertheless waived it, would "create serious doubt whether consent searches could continue to be conducted," because the prosecution would find it quite difficult to prove the defendant's awareness of his right to refuse. Id. at 229–30. The Court was unwilling to promulgate such a rule and was candid about its reasons: in many situations, where police have some evidence of illicit activity but not enough to constitute probable cause, "a search authorized by a valid consent may be the only means of obtaining important and reliable evidence." Id. at 227. Of course, another possibility is that in some cases, this "insufficient evidence" is not indicative of criminality at all. The Court rejected the obvious answer—having officers advise the defendant of his right to refuse before asking for consent—as impractical, because consent searches, as a "standard" part of law enforcement's investigatory arsenal, are typically used in a less "structured" atmosphere than a trial, or even the custodial interrogation situation of Miranda. Id. at 231–32. The Court assumed, rather than explain, why this makes the alternative of a warning impractical. The reason seems obvious: the Justices fear that citizens who would otherwise consent to a search might actually listen to a brief warning ("You don't have to let us, but we'd like to search your car.") and refuse, thus depriving the police of the use of this "standard investigatory technique" that allows searches in the absence of any other legal justification.

Ohio v. Robinette, the most recent case in this line, arose under different factual circumstances, but arrived at the same conclusion. 519 U.S. 33, 36 (1996). While the officer was engaged in ongoing questioning and investigation in Schneckloth, the officer in Robinette had actually completed any investigation and had resolved to let the defendant go with a verbal warning as shown by the officer's questioning of the defendant before the request for consent. See id. Nevertheless, the Supreme Court refused to see Robinette as any different than Schneckloth, and gave exactly the same kind of answer in almost the same words: Schneckloth's "it would be thoroughly impractical" to tell defendants of their right to refuse becomes "it [would] be unrealistic" in Robinette. Id. Both cases are almost nakedly result-oriented; Robinette is different only because it lacks even the small amount of analysis present in Schneckloth.

196. See Webb, supra note 142, at 125.

197. See Schneckloth, 412 U.S. at 227–28 (holding that lack of knowledge of the right to refuse a search does not necessarily negate the "voluntariness of the consent").

198. See Robinette, 519 U.S. at 34 (upholding the consent search even though the police failed to tell the defendant he was free to go).

199. Shatzkin & Hallinan, supra note 193, at B6.

200. See Webb, supra note 142, at 125 (explaining how officers who obtain consent literally "take your car apart with an air hammer" or an electric screwdriver); see also Curliss, supra note 194, at 1A (attesting to thoroughness of troopers' searches); Neff & Stith, supra note 194, at A1 (describing searches so thorough that cars are permanently damaged). See, e.g., Harris, supra note 84, at 566–68 (noting a pretextual stop by police resulted in an hour-long search of the car's interior, trunk, and engine compartment).

201. In United States v. Place, 462 U.S. 696 (1983), the Court assessed the constitutionality

of allowing a dog trained to find drugs to sniff the luggage of an airline passenger. Although a decision on the constitutional validity of dog sniffs was unnecessary to the resolution of the case, the Court found the detention of the defendant's luggage that preceded the sniff unreasonable. See id. at 705–06, 710. Accordingly the Court did not have to reach the issue of the constitutionality of the sniff. Even though the issue had neither been briefed nor argued the Court decided the issue anyway. See id. at 720–21 (Blackmun, J., concurring in the judgment). The Justices declared that having a trained dog sniff a defendant's luggage located in a public place (a significant limitation, making it not at all clear that Place should apply to dog sniffs of people, or to the public exteriors of homes) was not a search. See id. at 707. The Court offered two reasons. First, the dog was unintrusive. See id. Using the dog did not even entail the opening of the luggage and the exposure of personal effects to public view, as a search by hand at an airport security checkpoint does. See id. Second, the dog only gave the authorities limited information: whether drugs were, or were not, present. See id. The Court observed, "in these respects, the canine sniff is sui generis. We are aware of no other investigative procedure that is so limited both in the manner in which the information is obtained and in the content of the information revealed by the procedure." Id. Canine sniffs did not prove to be sui generis for very long. Just the next term, the Court put drug field testing kits in the same category. See U.S. v. Jacobsen, 466 U.S. 109, 142 (1984) (Brennan, J., dissenting).

202. Place is critically important to understanding how police conduct traffic stops and searches of cars. Since the Court has said that using a drug-sniffing dog is not a search for Fourth Amendment purposes, these dogs can be used without a warrant, without probable cause or reasonable suspicion—without any evidence at all to provide individualized suspicion. See Place, 462 U.S. at 707. This makes these dogs an indispensable part of the modern day police department's arsenal, because like consent searches they allow officers to search when the law would not otherwise allow it.

203. Police have a limited amount of time to bring drug dogs to the traffic stop. Drivers can only be detained for a reasonable amount of time in order to bring a dog to the scene. See Harris, supra note 84, at 575–76. In fact, the constitutional violation in Place occurred because the detention of the luggage was longer than reasonable to obtain the dog. See 462 U.S. at 707–10.

204. But see, e.g., Ohio v. Montoya, No. L-97-1226, 1998 Ohio App. Lexis 824, at *7 (Ohio Ct. App. Mar. 6, 1998) (suppressing evidence when an initial stop was justified by commission of traffic offense, but subsequent questioning "unlawfully expanded the scope" of the detention).

205. See supra notes 72, 88 and accompanying text.

206. See Herbert L. Packer, The Limits of the Criminal Sanction 149–246 (1968) (articulating the crime-control and due-process models in criminal procedure that "compete for priority in the operation of the criminal process"); see also Peter Arenella, Rethinking the Functions of Criminal Procedure: The Warren and Burger Courts' "Competing Ideologies," 72 Geo. L.J. 185, 202–03 (1983); John Griffiths, Ideology in Criminal Procedure or a Third "Model" of the Criminal Process, 79 Yale L.J. 359 (1970).

207. 412 U.S. 218 (1973).

208. 519 U.S. 33 (1996).

209. Schneckloth, 412 U.S. at 226–27, 230–32.

210. See Robinette, 519 U.S. at 39.

211. See id. (citing Schneckloth, 412 U.S. at 227).

212. See Harris, supra note 84, at 572 (stating that disproportionate use of traffic stops against African Americans indicates police "are using race as a proxy for the criminality or 'general criminal propensity' of an entire racial group"); Sherri Lynn Johnson, Race and the

Decision to Detain a Suspect, 93 Yale L.J. 214, 220, 236–239 (1983) (noting that police use minority race as a proxy for a greater possibility of criminal involvement, even though such use is problematic at best).

213. Traffic Stops Statistics Act of 1997, H.R. 118, 105th Cong. (1997).

214. See id. 2.

215. See id. 3.

216. See Jackson, supra notes 60, at A5.

217. Traffic Stops Statistics Study Act of 1999, H.R. 1443, 106th Cong. (1999). House Bill 1443 is different than its predecessor in a few ways, the most notable of which is that the study would cover a nationwide sample of jurisdictions. Compare H.R. 1443 2(a)(3) with H.R. 118 2.

218. See supra notes 60–61 and accompanying text.

219. See S.B. 78, Reg. Sess. (Cal. 1999) (requiring collection and analysis of data on routine traffic stops).

220. See Carl Ingram, Davis Vetoes Racial Data Legislation, L.A. Times, Sept. 29, 1999, at A3.

221. See An Act to Require the Division of Criminal Statistics to Collect and Maintain Statistics on Traffic Law Enforcement, N.C. Gen. Stat. 114–10 (Michie Supp. 1999).

222. See An Act Concerning Traffic Stops Statistics, 1999 Conn. Acts 99–198 (Reg. Sess.).

223. See H.R. 1261, 82d Gen. Assembly, Reg. Sess. (Ark. 1999) (requiring Arkansas State Police to compile and publish traffic stop data).

224. See H.B. 8430, Jan. Sess. (R.I. 1998) (requiring the superintendent of the state police to keep statistical data on traffic stops and publish it annually).

225. See H.R. 2617, 182d Gen. Assembly, Reg. Sess. (Pa. 1998) (requiring the attorney general to collect data on traffic stops).

226. See H.B. 1503, 91st Gen. Assembly, Reg. Sess. (Ill. 1999) (requiring all law enforcement agencies to compile data on traffic stops between July 1, 1999 and Dec. 31, 2000, which the Secretary of State shall study and report upon).

227. See H.R.J. Res. 687 & 736, 1999 Sess. (Va. 1999) (setting up a joint subcommittee of both houses of legislature to study pretextual traffic stops).

228. See S.B. 1180, 181st Leg., Reg. Sess. (Mass. 1999) (requiring the collection and study of information relating to routine traffic stops).

229. See H.B. 363, 123d Leg., Reg. Sess. (Ohio 1999) (requiring the statewide collection of statistics on all traffic stops).

230. See Con. Res. 102, 208th Leg., Reg. Sess. (N.J. 1998) (creating a task force to investigate use of racial profiling).

231. See S.B. 430, 1999 Reg. Sess. (Md. 1999) (establishing a task force to study stops for routine traffic violations).

232. See S.B 778, 113th Gen. Assembly, Reg. Sess. (S.C. 1999) (requiring the collection of traffic stop data by the Highway Patrol and the State Police).

233. See S.B. 590, 47th Leg., 1st Sess. (Okla. 1999) (requiring two-year study of traffic stops "to consider relationships of traffic stops to criminal offenses, races, ethnicity, gender, and age").

234. See H.R. 769, 1999 Reg. Sess. (Fla. 1999) (requiring the Florida Department of Law Enforcement to conduct a study of routine traffic stops identifying characteristics of individuals stopped).

235. See Michael Stetz & Kelly Thornton, Cops to Collect Traffic-Stop Racial Data, San Diego Union-Trib., Feb. 5, 1999, at A1.

236. See id.

237. I am currently consulting with a small jurisdiction in Northwest Ohio to help them set up a system for collecting comprehensive data on all stops, and to enable them to calculate the base rate by counting vehicles that pass through the municipality and the races of their drivers. This system should enable them to duplicate John Lamberth's work in New Jersey and Maryland.

238. See M. Charles Bakst, Little to Remember in 1999 General Assembly Session, Providence J.-Bull., June 20, 1999, at 1C (reporting that police are keeping data voluntarily on race of all drivers stopped); Margaret Downing, If You're Black or Brown, Driving a Nice Car Will Get You Noticed by Police in Houston, Houston Press, Sept. 2, 1999 (stating that the Houston Police Chief announced that officers must collect racial data on traffic stops); Angela Galloway, State Patrol to Note Race, Gender in Stops, Seattle Post-Intelligencer, Sept. 24, 1999 (noting the Washington State Patrol will record race and gender of every driver stopped); Patrick McGreevy, Council Asks Parks To Consider a Study on L.A.P.D. Racial Profiling, L.A. Times, Oct. 21, 1999, at B5 (reporting the Governor's letter urging the L.A.P.D. to join 34 other California cities in data collection); Pamela J. Podger, Cops Rap Veto of Traffic-Stop Tally, S.F. Chron., Sept. 30, 1999, at A23 (reporting that thirty-five California cities will collect data on traffic stops despite the governor's veto a bill making such collection mandatory); David Shepardson & Oralandar-Brand Williams, Cops Fight Race Targeting, Detroit News, July 12, 1999, at A1 (noting that Michigan State Police began recording the race of all motorists ticketed); Jill Taylor, Highway Patrol Plans To Collect Data To Debunk Profiling, Palm Beach Post, Oct. 3, 1999, at 14A (stating that the Florida Highway Patrol will collect data on race and ethnicity of all drivers stopped).

239. See Wayne R. LaFave, Controlling Discretion by Administrative Regulations: The Use, Misuse, and Nonuse of Police Rules and Policies in Fourth Amendment Adjudication, 89 Mich. L. Rev. 442, 451 (1990) (stating that police-made rules are most likely to be followed and enforced by police).

240. There are actually two Maryland cases—one in which attorney Robert Wilkins is the plaintiff and that led to the collection of the Maryland stop data, see Wilkins v. Maryland State Police, No. MJG-93–468 (D. Md. 1993), and a more recently filed class action.

241. Two civil actions brought in Florida failed. The judge in the combined cases denied class certification, meaning that the plaintiffs had to prove individual racial animus, a nearly impossible burden to carry. See Washington v. Vogel, 880 F. Supp. 1542, 1543–44 (M.D. Fla. 1995), aff'd, 106 F.3d 415 (11th Cir. 1997). When the plaintiffs could not make a prima facie showing, the court dismissed their cases. See id.

242. See Johnson v. City of Fort Wayne, 91 F.3d 922 (7th Cir. 1996).

243. See Chavez v. Illinois State Police, 27 F. Supp. 2d 1053, 1066–68 (N.D. Ill. 1998).

244. Both of the Maryland cases, Wilkins, No. MJG-93–468 (D. Md. 1993), and the Illinois case, Chavez, 27 F. Supp. 2d at 1066–68, were brought by the ACLU.

245. See State v. Pedro Soto, 734 A.2d 350 (N.J. Super. Ct. Law Div. 1996).

246. See Dixon v. Rutgers, 541 A.2d 1046, 1056 (N.J. 1988) ("The eradication of 'the cancer of discrimination' has long been one of our State's highest priorities."); State v. Kennedy, 588 A.2d 834, 840 (N.J. Super. Ct. App. Div. 1991) (holding that the suppression of evidence is the proper remedy when the police have targeted minorities for investigation and arrest); State v. Kuhn, 517 A.2d 162, 166 (N.J. Super. Ct. App. Div. 1986) (determining that police may not stop motorists based on race or any other invidious classifications).

247. See Kennedy, 588 A.2d at 840.

248. 690 N.Y.S.2d 390, 396 (App. Div. 1998).

249. 698 A.2d 1115, 1119 (Md. Ct. Spec. App. 1997).

Chapter 4

||||||||||||||||||||||||||||||||||||||||||||||||||||||||||||||||||||||||||||||||

Legitimacy and Cooperation
Why Do People Help the Police Fight Crime in Their Communities?

Tom R. Tyler and Jeffrey Fagan

1. Introduction

To be effective in lowering crime and creating secure communities, the police must be able to elicit cooperation from community residents. Security cannot be produced by either the police or community residents acting alone—it requires cooperation. Such cooperation potentially involves, on the part of the public, both obeying the law[1] and working with the police or others in the community to help combat crime in the community.[2]

How can cooperation be motivated, and, conversely, what factors defeat cooperation and for whom? To answer these questions, we contrast two models of cooperation. The first is a social control or instrumental model, which argues that people are motivated by self-interest.[3] The second is a legitimacy or social norms model, which hypothesizes that people's views about the institutional legitimacy of the police and the law also influence their cooperation.

The social control or instrumental perspective argues that people's actions are governed by their self-interest either in the form of sanctions or incentives.[4] Consistent with rational choice assumptions about human motivation, the police can encourage cooperative behavior by giving cooperation greater personal utility for community residents, for example by demonstrating that the police are effective in fighting crime[5] and/or that rule breakers are punished.[6] Shared beliefs among neighborhood residents that their community works collectively to address local problems have, for example, been shown to motivate community residents to work with each other to fight crime and disorder in their communities.[7] Prior studies of policing have used several approaches to assess instrumental aspects of policing, including estimates of the rate of crime, fear of crime and police effectiveness in sanctioning criminal behavior.[8]

Unfortunately, from the instrumental perspective, it is in some people's short-term self-interest to break, rather than to obey, the law.[9] Cooperation with law enforcement

From *Ohio State Journal of Criminal Law* 6: 231–275. © *Ohio State Journal of Criminal Law* 2008. Reprinted with permission of *Ohio State Journal of Criminal Law*.

agencies and other legal actors follows suit. That is, some people may see little immediate personal utility in supporting police efforts to control crime, reporting crimes and criminals, or helping in community efforts to fight crime. In addition, helping has short term costs. Those costs could potentially be minor inconveniences but could also involve serious danger of retaliation. Hence, strategies appealing to self-interest are often an inadequate basis for managing crime and security. Empirical research supports this argument by finding only weak correlations between risk and compliance,[10] as well as little connection between police performance and public cooperation with the police.[11]

How else, then, can the police obtain public cooperation? Past research suggests that most people also obey the law because they view it as legitimate.[12] That is, law expresses moral and social norms that are widely held by both dominant and subordinate social groups.[13] Accordingly, the legitimacy argument suggests that the police can gain leverage for the co-production of security by inculcating the popular perception that their actions and decisions are legitimate. This argument builds upon a long line of theory that argues for the centrality of legitimacy to the effectiveness of state actors.[14]

What is legitimacy? Legitimacy is a feeling of obligation to obey the law and to defer to the decisions made by legal authorities.[15] Legitimacy, therefore, reflects an important social value, distinct from self-interest, to which social authorities can appeal to gain public deference and cooperation.[16] In past research, legitimacy has been measured using items reflecting the perceived obligation to obey legal authorities, as well as trust and confidence in authorities.[17] Recent studies have also operationalized legitimacy via identification with the police.[18]

While past research supports the argument that legitimacy encourages deference, more recent research emphasizes the importance of the ability of the police to leverage and secure cooperation from the public. Cooperation takes several forms, from reporting crimes to the police to assisting the police in investigations. This study tests the potential value of legitimacy in motivating these forms of public cooperation with local legal authorities. We refer to this approach as "self-regulation" because it draws upon the norms, values and preferences of community residents. When people cooperate with the police and other legal actors because of norms or values they share with the law, their behavior may be linked more to intrinsic motivations and less to the influence of sanctions or incentives on behavior.[19] We hypothesize that legitimacy influences the willingness to cooperate with the police, independent of sanction risks or experiences with punishment.

Accordingly, this study assesses the contribution of legitimacy to cooperation with the police and other legal actors to fight crime and produce security. Specifically, we examine whether citizens' views about the legitimacy of the police shape two specific forms of cooperative behavior among community residents: cooperation with the police in their response to crime and working collaboratively and collectively with others in the neighborhood to maintain social order.

In exploring the influence of legitimacy, this study also distinguishes the influence of legitimacy from the influence of a second noninstrumental variable—identification with one's neighborhood. Research from social psychology demonstrates that one central reason that people cooperate generally is that they identify with their communities, linking their sense of self (identity) to the wellbeing of their group.[20] Following research in this tradition, we define identification with the community as "self-group merging."[21]

This study tests two hypotheses. The first is that perceived or attributed legitimacy influences citizen cooperation separately from the instrumental influences of public evaluations of police performance, such as perceptions of the ability of the police to detect wrongdoing and effectively fight crime.[22] Legitimacy is an important motivation for social control if it can contribute to our understanding of why people cooperate with the police beyond the influence of public assessments of police performance and the benefits that citizens enjoy from such performance. That is, we segregate the effects of police performance from the other components of police behavior and services. This hypothesis is tested separately for two aspects of cooperation: the willingness to help the police in their investigations of crime and the willingness of citizens to work with others in the community to collectively produce security.

Second, we examine whether the link between legitimacy and cooperation differs across ethnic groups. Researchers have identified racial differences in attitudes toward the police as a key characteristic of American communities, with minorities having lower levels of trust and confidence in the police.[23] We assess whether these differences influence the degree to which police legitimacy shapes cooperation within the majority and minority communities. Indeed, residents in poor neighborhoods with high concentrations of racial and ethnic minorities experience different forms and strategies of policing, differences that may produce different views of the police independent of the outcomes of police-citizen interactions.[24] We include these perceptions and experiences as explicit and separate components of a framework to explain differences by race in cooperation with the police and compliance with the law.

We argue, and show empirically in this chapter, that legitimacy develops from aspects of experience with policing that are distinct from instrumental judgments about police performance. We test the hypothesis that legitimacy is based upon public judgments about the policies and practices of the police. We test the notion that citizens' perceptions of the legitimacy of the police are, in reality, justice-based evaluations of the manner in which the police are thought to exercise their authority. A corollary question speaks to the policy implications of legitimacy-based cooperation. To motivate such cooperation it is important to identify the antecedents of legitimacy, i.e., the degree to which legitimacy rests on a normative base and is a reflection of judgments about the appropriateness of police behavior.

2. Background

A. Why Are the Police Legitimate?

Widespread suggestions that many among the American public lack high levels of "trust and confidence" in the legal system give special importance to legitimacy's role.[25] This lack of trust and confidence is found to be especially high in the case of the courts and the criminal justice system and less striking with the police.[26] However, all of these legal institutions show evidence of strong group differences—with minority group members expressing lower levels of trust and confidence.[27] Professors Lawrence Bobo and Devon Johnson show evidence from general population surveys that African Americans show the lowest levels of trust, and Whites the highest.[28] Hispanics occupy a middle range between these two groups. Discontent among minority populations is especially important since the need for both deference and cooperation is especially strong in these communities, where criminal activity is often found at its highest levels.[29] While always a concern, in recent years the need to maintain legitimacy has been especially important to the police, the courts, and the legal system in seeking to leverage citizen trust and cooperation into the co-production of security.

The argument that legitimacy is a normative judgment flows from the classic work of Weber.[30] He suggests that legitimacy develops from the manner in which authority is exercised. Weber argues that in modern society, authorities benefit when they are able to obtain cooperation from the people with whom they deal beyond the cooperation which they can obtain via their control of the power to shape behavior through the use of sanctions and incentives. It is desirable to also be able to secure cooperation through the manner in which they exercise their authority. In other words, they want to be able to call upon deference to authority that is "legitimized" in noninstrumental ways, such as via the procedures by which it is exercised. Similarly, Beetham regards legitimacy as the product of interactions between state and individual where both the subordinate and the empowered actor share social norms and the moral reasoning that informs them that the exercise of authority by the state is appropriate.[31]

These perspectives raise several challenges for empirical assessments of procedural justice by social scientists. Procedural justice reflects judgments about the manner in which authority is exercised. It includes judgments of the quality of decision-making, which includes neutrality: making decisions based upon facts and applying rules consistently. It also involves judgments about the quality of interpersonal treatment: respect, politeness, and consideration of one's views. Distributive justice also informs legitimacy; it involves the fairness and equity of the police delivery of services to persons across social and demographic groups. In this study, survey respondents were asked to indicate whether services were distributed fairly to people like the respondent. An unfair distribution could reflect either receiving too little or too much.

And, as with the general importance of legitimacy in shaping cooperation, it is again important to consider whether the role of procedural justice in shaping legitimacy differs between Whites and minorities. Based upon an analysis of people's personal experiences with the police, Tyler and Huo argue that both Whites and minorities evaluate their personal experiences similarly, by putting weight on procedural justice and trust,[32] while Tyler and Fagan argue that Whites and minorities rely upon generally similar procedural justice evaluations when making overall evaluations of the police and the law.[33] This study tests that argument using panel data from a general population.

B. The Influence of Personal Experience with the Police

Legitimate authority, when it exists, has a unique and important advantage when it motivates voluntary cooperation that is not dependent on instrumental criteria.[34] In other words it is not dependent upon people's judgments about the rewards or punishments that are likely to follow from engaging in cooperative behavior. To the degree that people are motivated by legitimacy, people cooperate because they feel it is the right thing to do, not because of material gains or loses.[35] This perspective has been echoed by later social theorists,[36] and is strongly supported by empirical evidence suggesting that legitimacy is based upon judgments about the procedural justice of the actions of authorities and institutions.[37]

The suggestion that the legitimacy of authorities is linked to evaluations of the procedures that they use to make decisions and to how they deliver services receives widespread support in studies of the psychology of legitimacy.[38] Those studies find that the key antecedents of assessments of the legitimacy of authorities are judgments about the fairness of the procedures those authorities use when making decisions. Studies further find that procedures are judged against ethical criterion of their appropriateness that are distinct from the favorability or fairness of the outcomes of such procedures.[39]

This literature suggests that evaluations of the procedural fairness and justice of the policies and practices of the police shape perceptions of their legitimacy.[40] Further, the same studies suggest that it is such evaluations of procedural justice, rather than evaluations of the distributive justice of the allocation of police services, that is the key ethical judgment underlying legitimacy.

The procedural justice model of policing argues that the police can build general legitimacy among the public by treating people justly during personal encounters. This argument is based upon two empirical arguments. The first is that people evaluate personal experiences with the police by evaluating the fairness of police procedures. The second is that this means that by using fair procedures the police can increase their legitimacy, even if their policing activities involve restricting or sanctioning the people with whom they are dealing.

Others reject the notion that interaction, irrespective of its quality, affects the appraisal of police legitimacy or performance. Professor Wesley Skogan has recently claimed that positive experiences from personal encounters do not improve public evaluations of the police.[41] Research in England by Professor Ben Bradford and colleagues tested Skogan's notion of asymmetry and produced the opposite result: the quality of interaction with police affects attributed legitimacy, and influences citizen engagement with police in the co-production of local security.[42]

The contrasting outcomes are a function of differences in their study designs and measurement strategies. Unlike most procedural justice research, Skogan does not distinguish between receiving a positive outcome and receiving positive treatment. Instead, Skogan conflates these factors, arguing that when people have a positive experience with the police, "including being treated fairly and politely, and receiving service that [is] prompt and helpful," there is no positive impact of that experience.[43] In contrast, he suggests that negative experiences lower trust and confidence in the police, although it is not clear from his research whether such lower evaluations either promote compliance with legal rules or cooperation with legal actors. Instead, Skogan suggests that these findings have pessimistic implications for policing, since they suggest no easy route to building public trust and confidence. As he says, "this is bad news indeed for police administrators intent on solidifying their support among, voters, taxpayers and the consumers of police services."[44]

Skogan's claim that positive experiences do not influence evaluations of the police contradicts the arguments of a recent National Research Council review of a rich body of empirical evidence on the determinants of effective policing.[45] This review went beyond the normative basis for valuing procedurally "fair policing" to cite evidence that policing that increased police legitimacy through procedural justice was both necessary and possible.[46]

Certainly, the implications of Skogan's argument are contrary to the argument based upon procedural justice research that the police ought to be trained to act in ways the public experiences as being just and encouraged to do so during personal encounters with members of the public. While much procedural justice research has not been longitudinal in nature, cross-cultural findings have been used to argue that treating people fairly builds their trust and confidence in the police.[47] And, some studies have been longitudinal in nature.[48]

In this study, we use panel data from interviews one year apart to test the two key empirical assumptions underlying procedural justice research. The first is that procedural justice is the central factor that shapes people's reactions to their experiences with the police. The second is that, if people experience positive procedural justice during a personal experience with the police, their trust and confidence in the police increases, independent of the valence of their personal outcomes.

While the Skogan study is based on a number of large datasets, all the studies he considers are cross-sectional. In other words all the judgments are measured at one point in time, after the experience. Skogan infers the impact of experience by comparing the mean trust and confidence of people varying in the nature of their recent personal experience with the police. Cross-sectional research frustrates statistical identification of the effects of procedural justice and outcomes on evaluations of police legitimacy by overlooking causal order.[49] Imagine, for example, that people's views about the legitimacy of the police shape their judgments about their experience, rather than that legitimacy judgments result from judgments about experience. Cross-sectional data cannot distinguish among these two arguments.

C. This Study

We test the impact of personal experience on evaluations of legitimacy and cooperation with the police using a longitudinal design in which people are interviewed both prior to and following their personal experiences with the police. Our hypothesis is that experiencing procedural justice will have positive consequences upon people's views about the police, irrespective of whether people received favorable or unfavorable outcomes.

The study has three goals. First, we extend prior arguments concerning the value of legitimacy in shaping compliance to include an examination of the influence of legitimacy on cooperative behavior. Tyler uses panel data and argues that legitimacy shapes general compliance.[50] Tyler and Fagan use cross-sectional data to extend this argument to cooperation, but do not distinguish cooperation with the police from cooperation with the community.[51] This study distinguishes among forms of cooperation and uses a panel design to test the influence of legitimacy on these different types of cooperation. That influence is compared to the influence of instrumental judgments about the police and identification with one's neighborhood.

Second, we explore the psychology of cooperation with the police. Several studies claim that ratings of procedural justice following experiences with police shape legitimacy; here, we test the extent to which this argument is true using panel data.[52] And while other studies use narrow or single indicia of procedural justice, we examine the role of two aspects of procedures that have received less empirical attention: the quality of police decision making and the quality of interpersonal treatment of citizens by police.[53]

Finally, we examine whether and how ratings of the fairness of procedures during personal experiences with the police enhance or attenuate perceived legitimacy. We consider the effects of police procedure on perceived legitimacy when either positive or negative outcomes are being delivered. Tyler and Huo argue, based upon cross-sectional surveys, that both prior legitimacy and procedural justice during personal experiences with the police impact subsequent legitimacy, a conclusion rejected by Skogan.[54] Here, we use longitudinal data to conduct a more efficient estimation and identification of these effects, and accordingly offer a more rigorous test of this argument that considers both direct and indirect influences of legitimacy.

Looking ahead, we show that the procedural justice-legitimacy connection provides a robust framework for understanding the basis of public cooperation with the police similar to the basis of compliance that has already been established. If so, then a general model of police behavior can be identified, a model which indicates how the police can conduct themselves so as to encourage public cooperation both via compliance with the law, and through active cooperation with the police. We assume this link is normative and widely shared, and accordingly will be evident among both White and minority respondents.

3. Research Design

A random sample of New York City residents were interviewed by telephone at two points in time.[55] The first wave of interviews occurred in 2002, the second in 2004. The Wave 1 sample of 1,653 respondents was drawn from a stratified random sample of residential telephone numbers in the City. Non-White residents were oversampled to produce a high proportion of Hispanic and African American respondents. Interviews were conducted in English or Spanish, based on the language preference of the respondent. The ethnicity of the respondent and the interviewer were not matched. When a home was reached, the adult in the household with the most recent birthday was interviewed. The response rate for the Wave 1 survey was 64% of eligible respondents.

Approximately one year following the first interview, attempts were made to re-contact and reinterview all of the respondents interviewed. Among those identified and recontacted, the response rate for the Wave 2 sample was 53% (n = 879). Although efforts were made to trace and re-interview those respondents who had moved, only those respondents still living within the same neighborhood were included in this analysis (n = 830). A comparison of the 830 re-interviewed to the original Wave 1 sample indicates no statistically significant differences in ethnicity, gender, age, income, or education.[56] Methodological details about the survey are provided in the appendix.

A. Measures

Respondents at each wave answered a series of questions presented over the telephone with fixed response alternatives. Questions examined a variety of issues, including police legitimacy; indices of police performance; the quality of the respondent's connection with their neighborhood; the distributive and procedural justice of the police; and cooperation with the police and with others in the neighborhood. The variables were assessed using identical questions at both waves.

In addition, respondents in Wave 2 were asked if they had had any personal contact with the police during the one-year period between interviews. Of the 830 Wave 2 respondents, 255 (30.7%) had had at least one personal experience. Those with personal experience were asked about the procedural justice of that experience, as well as the fairness of its outcome. The questions are presented in the appendix. Those respondents without experience were excluded from this analysis. As we discuss below, we estimate propensity scores to address non-randomness in the population of persons who did and did not have contact with the police at Wave 2. We developed separate propensity scores for police-initiated and citizen-initiated contacts. Citizen-initiated contacts included requests for information and attempts to file complaints with the police.

Dependent variables were a series of items asking about four types of cooperative behavior: willingness to help the police by reporting crime and criminals; willingness to help the police by working in community groups to fight crime; compliance with regulations (e.g., speeding); and compliance with laws (e.g., drug use).

The independent variables were organized in two domains: legal orientation and attitudes toward the police, and neighborhood crime problems and condition. The first domain included measures of judgments about the legitimacy of the police; judgments about police performance; and background information. The legitimacy of the police was assessed through scales indexing three dimensions: obligation to defer to police directives and to the law, trust and confidence in the police, and identification with the police.

Three aspects of police performance were measured: beliefs about the frequency with which the police caught those who broke rules/laws, judgments about how effective the police were in combating crime, and evaluations of neighborhood conditions. The second domain included questions about crime problems in the neighborhood, neighborhood ties, and the physical condition of the neighborhood. Respondents were also asked to indicate their age, education, income, and ethnicity. Gender was determined by the interviewer during the telephone interview.

The three indices of legitimacy—obligation, trust and confidence, and identification with the police—were found to be highly correlated (average $r = 0.50$, $p < .000$). Accordingly, a single overall indicator of legitimacy was formed. We also estimated three dimensions of crime and criminal justice conditions: fear of crime, neighborhood social and physical conditions, and sanction risk. Two dimensions—fear of crime and physical conditions—were correlated ($r = 0.44$, $p < .000$) and were collapsed into a single measure. These indicators were distinct from sanction risk ($r = .000$, $p = $ n.s.). As a result, we treated sanction risk as a distinct indictor.

B. Data Analysis

Data were analyzed using Ordinary Least Squares (OLS) to assess relationships across the two waves. In the first wave analysis, we estimated OLS regressions cross-sectionally to identify factors that shaped baseline measures of legitimacy, compliance and cooperation.

We next estimated OLS regressions to identify the effects of procedural justice and outcomes on Wave 2 legitimacy, cooperation, and compliance. Only 255 of the 830 respondents had police contact at Wave 2. Accordingly, we constructed propensity scores to account for the non-randomness of exposure to the police.[57] We estimated the probability of police contact using logistic regression with predictors including Wave 1 cooperation, legitimacy, the neighborhood crime and social conditions measures, and demographics.[58] We estimated separate propensity scores for police-initiated and citizen-initiated contacts, given obvious differences in the voluntariness of each type of contact. In estimating the effects of police contact on legitimacy and cooperation, we follow Bang and Robins[59] and Indurkhya et al.;[60] we use the *inverse* probability of treatment as the propensity score for the group with police contact, and the inverse of one minus the probability for the group without contact. This procedure allows us to adjust for collinearity between police contact and the factors that might predict each type of police contact.

4. Results

A. Is Cooperation Distinct from Compliance?

Two types of cooperation were examined: compliance with the law and cooperation with the police. Conceptually, there is some overlap in these constructs and items are likely to be internally correlated. Accordingly, we used principal components factor analyses with varimax rotation and maximum-likelihood estimation to identify a parsimonious set of non-redundant variables to better represent the underlying

TABLE 4.1
*Principal Components Factor Analysis on Cooperation and
Compliance Behaviors (Rotated Factor Scores)*[a]

Factor	1	2	3	4
If the situation arose, how likely would you be to . . .				
Call the police to report a crime that was occurring.			.82	
Help the police to find a criminal.			.72	
Report suspicious activity to the police.			.77	
Volunteer time to help the police.		.85		
Patrol the streets with others.		.83		
Attend community police meetings about crime.		.68		
How often do you follow rules concerning . . .				
Where you park your car.				.75
How you dispose of trash.				.74
Speeding or breaking traffic laws.				.61
Making too much noise at night.	.60			
Not buying stolen items on the street.	.81			
Not stealing from stores or restaurants.	.86			
Not using illegal drugs.	.85			
Explained Variance	25.08	18.28	9.94	9.88
Eigenvalue	3.26	2.38	1.29	1.28

[a] Wave 1 items only, N = 830. Pairwise deletion. Varimax rotation.

dimensions of the various items. This procedure yielded four non-overlapping dimensions. These analyses were done initially on the Wave 1 measures. Because we were interested in stability and change over time, the factor analyses included only the 830 respondents who completed both waves. However, an analysis of the larger group of Wave 1 only respondents produced a similar factor structure. The panel respondents are shown in table 4.1 (N = 830).

Four factors underlie the cooperation questions: helping to identify criminals; helping the community combat crime; complying with non-criminal regulations (parking laws, trash removal); and complying with more serious criminal laws (stealing; drug use). Compliance and cooperation appear to be largely distinct from one another, suggesting that the reasons why people obey the law may differ from why they may actively engage with police in the social regulation of crime. In fact, two factors within each of these domains were identified, suggesting further complexity and dimensionality in law-related behaviors. Accordingly, we extend prior analyses of law-related compliance to examine the social psychology of two dimensions of cooperation: helping the police and helping others in the neighborhood.

Based on the configuration of items in the factor analysis, we next constructed scales for each of the four factors. First, two helping subscales were created: helping to locate criminals and report crimes (three items, alpha = 0.69); and working with others in the community to fight crime (three items, alpha = 0.75). Two scales of compliance were created: following non-criminal regulations (three items; alpha = 0.55); and following criminal laws (four items—making excessive noise; buying stolen goods; taking items from stores; using drugs—alpha = 0.81). Table 4.2 shows that the four scales were generally moderately correlated at Wave 1: the average correlation was r = 0.09.

TABLE 4.2
Correlation Matrices for Cooperation and Compliance Scale
(Mean, Standard Deviation, R, two-tailed)[a]

	Mean (SD)	Correlations			
		1	2	3	4
Comply with minor laws	4.37 (0.78)	—			
Comply with major laws	4.59 (0.82)	0.39***	—		
Help the police fight crime	3.57 (0.60)	0.12***	0.16***	—	
Help neighbors	2.79 (0.85)	0.06	0.02	0.33***	—

Significance: * p < .05; ** p < .01; *** p < .001.
[a] Analysis only for Wave 1 data, N = 830.

Since the intensity and tactics of policing in New York City tended to vary by neighborhood social and demographic factors,[61] we also examined the properties of and correlations among these scales separately for minority and White samples. Results indicate that the scale properties and correlations are similar for White and non-White respondents.

B. Why Do People Cooperate with the Police and with Others in Their Communities?

Given the distinction between cooperation and compliance, we turn next to examining the social psychology of cooperation. Regression analysis was used to explore the psychological antecedents of cooperation. The analysis took advantage of the panel aspects of the study by examining the influence of time two measures of legitimacy, crime conditions, risk, and identification with neighborhood upon measures of cooperation controlling upon time one measures of the same judgments. In addition, time one measures of the appropriate form of cooperation were included. Finally, an interaction term was included to examine ethnicity effects (i.e., whether legitimacy had a different influence within the different ethnic groups).

The results are shown in table 4.3. They indicate that legitimacy shaped willingness to help the police ($p < .001$) and willingness to work with the community ($p < .001$). In neither case was there a significant legitimacy-by-ethnicity interaction, suggesting that the influence of legitimacy was similar among both majority and minority respondents.

These findings supported the hypothesis that those members of the public who evaluated the police as being more legitimate were more cooperative with the police. They were cooperative first because they helped the police by reporting crime and criminals and second because they worked with others in their community to fight crime. The panel nature of the design allows us to demonstrate that legitimacy at time one shapes behavior at time two. Hence, attitudes are influencing later actions.

1. ANTECEDENTS OF LEGITIMACY

The findings outlined above suggest the importance of understanding the factors that shape public judgments about the legitimacy of the police and the law, since whether or not people viewed the police as legitimate shaped whether or not they cooperated with police in their neighborhood. As before the panel nature of the design allows us to show that time one identification shapes later actions (measured at time two). In this study two models of the antecedents of legitimacy were contrasted: an instrumental performance model and a non-instrumental procedural justice model.

One model was a performance model of legitimacy. This model hypothesized that legitimacy itself was linked to the quality of police performance. If so, then the findings would not point to new approaches to motivating cooperation, since instrumental issues would define legitimacy. A performance model of policing would link public views about cooperation to their judgments of the effectiveness of police performance in fighting crime and urban disorder. It would suggest that to be viewed as legitimate the police need to communicate to those in the community that they can credibly punish wrongdoers, as well as that they are effectively fighting crime. The broken windows model of policing, for example, would link public evaluations of the police to public judgments about whether crime and disorder was being effectively dealt with by the police.[62]

This analysis compared such a performance based model to a model of legitimacy suggesting that legitimacy was linked to evaluations of the normative quality of police policies and practices—to the justice of police actions. Drawing upon the psychological literature, the normative approach linked legitimacy to assessments of the manner in which the police exercised their authority—to judgments about procedural

TABLE 4.3
OLS Regression on the Antecedents of Helping the Police and
Helping the Community (b, SE)[a]

	Help the Police			Help the Community		
	b	*SE*	*p*	*b*	*SE*	*p*
Wave 2						
Legitimacy	.236	.058	***	.263	.088	**
Legitimacy* Ethnicity[b]	.050	.069		.121	.105	
Crime conditions	.024	.042		.230	.063	***
Risk	.016	.024		.136	.036	***
Identification-neighborhood	−.001	.035		.182	.053	***
Wave 1						
Cooperation	.390	.031	***	.537	.030	***
Legitimacy	.027	.047		−.226	.072	**
Crime Conditions	.004	.041		−.184	.063	**
Risk	.001	.018		.010	.028	
Identification-neighborhood	.078	.029	**	−.060	.051	
Demographics						
Gender	−.010	.032		−.024	.048	
Age	.004	.015		.055	.022	*
Education	−.008	.012		.034	.018	
Income	−.010	.009		−.002	.014	
Ethnicity	.123	.205		.290	.310	
Adjusted R-squared		34%			43%	

[a] * $p < .05$; ** $p < .01$; *** $p < .001$. All respondents (n = 830).
[b] Ethnicity is a binary variable for non-White versus White (White = 0).

justice. While both distributive and procedural justice were potential normative bases for evaluating legal authorities, prior research suggests that the public evaluates legal authorities primarily against criteria of procedural justice.[63]

Because they have been important in past discussions of policing,[64] judgments of the distributive fairness of police actions, i.e., the degree to which the police were viewed as allocating their services fairly, were also included to test for a possible role of the alternative normative model—that the public reacts to the distributive fairness of the allocation of police services. Within the social psychological literature distributive and procedural justice are viewed as the two types of justice that are potential antecedents of cooperation.[65]

Drawing on psychological models of procedural justice, two dimensions were distinguished: judgments about the justice of the decision making aspects of procedures and judgments about the justice of the interpersonal treatment that people receive from authorities.[66] Justice involving the decision making element in procedures links procedural justice to issues such as the degree of neutrality, even-handedness, consistency in the application of rules, and the absence of personal bias or prejudice. Justice in interpersonal treatment links procedural justice to respect for people's rights and dignity and consideration of their needs and concerns. Distributive justice refers to the fairness of the distribution of services. In this case, respondents were asked whether they received a fair level of services, or whether they received too little or too much.

The relationship between the procedural justice of police policies and practices and public evaluations of the legitimacy of the police was tested using regression analysis. The focus of this analysis is on time two evaluations of legitimacy. This analysis again takes advantage of the panel aspects of the study by examining the influence of time two evaluations of quality of decision making; quality of interpersonal treatment; crime concerns; sanctioning risk; and distributive justice to the respondent upon time two legitimacy, controlling on time one evaluations of these same qualities. And, also controlling upon time one measures of legitimacy. Demographic variables were also included in the analysis as controls. Finally, the analysis included interaction terms to test whether the influence of the indices of procedural justice had a differential influence among White and minority respondents.

The results of the analyses indicated that public evaluations of the justice of police decision making and the justice of the manner that the police treat members of the public both shaped police legitimacy (see table 4.4). Respondents viewed the police as more legitimate if they made decisions fairly ($p < .001$) and if they treated people justly ($p < .001$).

2. PERSONAL EXPERIENCE WITH THE POLICE

During the year between the two interviews, 255 of the 830 respondents (31%) had at least one personal experience with the police. When asked to discuss their most recent experience, 45% talked about a situation in which they contacted the police for help; 21% talked about a situation in which they were stopped by the police; and 35% talked about a situation in which they contacted the police to make a complaint about some problem or situation.

TABLE 4.4
OLS Regression on the Antecedents of Legitimacy (b, SE)[a]

	b	SE	p
T2			
Quality of decision making	.141	.033	***
Quality of interpersonal treatment	.158	.030	***
QDM* ethnicity	.078	.056	
QIT* ethnicity	−.024	.054	
Police performance	.034	.026	
Sanctioning risk	.033	.015	*
Distributive justice to groups	.056	.019	**
T1			
Legitimacy	.475	.029	***
Quality of decision making	−.038	.016	*
Quality of interpersonal treatment	−.015	.017	
Police performance	−.025	.025	
Sanctioning risk	−.005	.012	
Distributive justice to groups	−.019	.018	
Demographics			
Gender	.003	.020	
Age	.030	.009	***
Education	−.007	.008	
Income	.009	.006	
Ethnicity	.087	.066	
Adjusted R-squared		71%	

[a] * $p < .05$; ** $p < .01$; *** $p < .001$. All respondents (n = 830).

It was possible to further test the role of procedural justice in shaping legitimacy and cooperation using this subgroup of respondents. In this analysis those respondents who had no personal experience were excluded. Respondents were asked to make four judgments about their personal experience: whether decisions were made via just decision making procedures; whether they received just interpersonal treatment; whether the outcome of their experience was fair; and whether the outcome of their experience was favorable.

While the prior analysis in this paper focused upon general judgments about the outcomes produced by the police (i.e., lowering crime), this examination of personal experiences uses a more direct focus upon the favorability of police decisions when dealing personally with the respondent. The two indices—outcome fairness and outcome favorability—were assessed. They were found to be highly correlated ($r = 0.83$), so the analysis focused upon a single indicator that combined outcome favorability and outcome fairness.

Using a variable reflecting the two aspects of procedural justice—quality of decision making and quality of interpersonal treatment—the analysis first examined the influence of procedural justice on decision acceptance. The goal of this analysis is to replicate the widely found linkage between procedural justice and decision acceptance.

This analysis considered only judgments made during the second, post-experience, interview. This parallels most research on the influence of procedural justice, which only considers post-experience judgments.[67] Respondents were asked about: overall procedural justice (a combined index of quality of decision making and quality of treatment), outcome favorability, decision acceptance, and the intention to complain.

Using that data it was found that those who received favorable/fair outcomes were more likely to accept them (p < .001), as were those who experienced procedural justice (p < .001). Further, those who received favorable/fair outcomes were less likely to want to complain (p < .001), as were those who experienced fair procedures (p < .001). Overall, 82% of the variance in decision acceptance and 37% of the variance in complaining behavior was explained.

So, as in prior studies, procedural justice encouraged decision acceptance and led people to feel less motivated to complain.[68] And, it had an influence that was distinct from the favorability/fairness of the outcome. In addition, people were more willing to accept favorable outcomes.

Does prior legitimacy shape decision acceptance? A regression analysis including outcomes, procedural justice, and prior legitimacy indicates that prior legitimacy plays no direct role in shaping decision acceptance or the likelihood of complaining. However, prior legitimacy is directly related to later judgments that the outcome was more favorable (r = .37, p < .001) and that the procedures were fairer (r = .50, p < .001). In a causal analysis prior legitimacy shapes both of these experience based evaluations and, through that indirect influence, has an impact upon decision acceptance and interest in complaining. Of course, if experience based judgments were not included in the model, prior legitimacy was linked to decision acceptance (r = .40, p < .001) and interest in complaining (r = −.23, p < .001).

Because the encounters were not observed, it is not possible to distinguish between two reasons for the connection between prior legitimacy and evaluations of personal experience. One reason is that the encounters may have been different. Those who view the police as legitimate, for example, may approach them more positively, and create better interactions. Or, they may have the same type of interactions, but perceive them more favorably. Without direct evidence it is not possible to distinguish between these two possibilities.

C. Must Regulation Undermine Legitimacy?

One of the most promising arguments developing from the models outlined is that the police can deliver negative outcomes to the public in ways that will enhance legitimacy, if they exercise their authority via fair procedures. This argument, advanced by Huo and Tyler and others,[69] has not been disputed by Skogan to the extent that he agrees that negative experiences influence people.[70] Interestingly, Skogan is concerned not so much with negative outcomes, the traditional focus of concern, but with the limitations of favorable outcomes. In the case of positive outcomes, he argues that positive experiences have little influence upon views about the police, while negative experiences have a large influence. Based upon an analysis of cross-section data comparing people with no experience to those with positive experience Skogan argues that favorable experiences do not enhance trust and confidence in the police.

However, as noted, Skogan does not distinguish within experiences, separating the effects of just procedures from that of favorable or unfavorable outcomes.[71]

To address this issue we need to examine whether the procedural justice of experience matters among those receiving positive and negative outcomes. The panel design further allows the relationship between procedural justice and decision acceptance to be examined taking account of prior legitimacy. A regression analysis was used to explore the influence of time one legitimacy and the procedural justice of the experience (a summary of the two experience based indices—decision making and treatment) upon time two legitimacy. And, as noted, the analysis distinguished between those respondents who received either favorable or unfavorable outcomes. First we need to examine whether procedural justice influences legitimacy. The results are shown in table 4.5. They indicate that both procedural justice and prior legitimacy shape post experience legitimacy. As we might expect, outcome favorability has no influence.

Table 4.5 presents a combined analysis for overall procedural justice and separate analyses for quality of decision making and quality of interpersonal treatment. Irrespective of which analysis is considered, no effects for outcome valence/fairness are found. However, the analysis that includes decision making and interpersonal treatment as two factors suggests that it is interpersonal treatment that is the most important factor shaping reactions to experiences.

The best way to address the question whether experience changed views about the legitimacy of the police was to look at change in legitimacy among those whose experience has a favorable or an unfavorable outcome (see table 4.6). This analysis directly tests the suggestion that favorable experiences do not increase trust and confidence in the police. In addition, we can also examine the influence experience among those who initiated their contact with the police, in comparison to those for whom the contact was initiated by the police.

TABLE 4.5

OLS Regression of Personal Experience and T1 Legitimacy on T2 Legitimacy for Persons with Police Contact (b, SE)[a]

| | T2 Legitimacy | | | | | |
	b	SE	p	b	SE	p
Procedural justice[b]	.17	.05	***	—		—
Quality of decision making	—	—		.00	.05	
Quality of interpersonal treatment	—	—		.16	.05	***
Outcome valence/outcome fairness	.03	.04		.02	.04	
Gender	−.02	.04		−.02	.04	
Age	−.06	.02	***	−.06	.02	
Education	.02	.02		.02	.02	
Income	.00	.01		.00	.01	
Ethnicity	.01	.05		.00	.05	
T1 Legitimacy	.47	.05	***	.46	.05	***
Adjusted R.-sq.		58%			58%	

[a] * p < .05; ** p < .01; *** p < .001.
[b] The Procedural Justice scale is a combination of the Quality of Decision Making and Quality of Interpersonal Treatment.

There are two approaches that we might potentially use in the analysis. First, can ignore those without personal experience. Second, we can assume that those people would, if they had had a personal experience, have had an average experience.[72] Those two approaches are shown in table 4.6, with all respondents shown in column one, and only those with experience in column two. Both analyses reinforce our prior finding—procedural justice shapes post-experience legitimacy, controlling upon pre-experience legitimacy. One way to understand the Skogan argument is that it predicts an interaction in which procedural justice has a lower impact at high levels of outcome favorability.[73] None of the regression equations find a significant interaction. This suggests that the influence of procedural justice is constant across outcome favorability.[74]

The legitimacy scale used in the analyses shown in tables 4.5 and 4.6 contained a combination of three elements of legitimacy: obligation; trust and confidence; and identification with the police. An examination of each element indicates that those who experienced fair procedures increased their ratings of police legitimacy on each of the three aspects of legitimacy from pre-experience to post-experience. They felt greater obligation to obey ($t = 2.84$, $p < .01$); had more trust and confidence in the police ($t = 4.94$, $p < .001$); and identified more strongly with the police ($t = 4.90$, $p < .001$).

Although the pattern reported is consistent with the argument that people became more favorable in their views following a positive experience, it is also possible that those with more favorable attitudes in the first place were more likely to personally deal with the police. We can test this possibility by comparing those who would later have personal experiences to those who would not in terms of the views

TABLE 4.6

OLS Regression of Procedural Justice on T2 Legitimacy, for All Respondents and Those with Police Contact by Type of Contact (b, SE)[a]

	All respondents			Any contact			Citizen-initiated contact			Police-initiated contact		
	b	SE	p	b	SE	p	b	SE	p	b	SE	p
Quality of treatment	.23	.08	***	.23	.09	**	.28	.11	**	.17	.07	*
Outcome favorably	.08	.06		.09	.07		.12	.08		.11	.06	
Treatment * outcome	−.03	.03		−.03	.03		−.07	.04		.07	.05	
Who initiated contact[c]	.02	.03		−.03	.06		—	—				
Gender	.03	.03		.03	.06		.07	.06			[b]	
Age	−.04	.02		.00	.04		−.02	.04			[b]	
Education	.00	.02		.00	.04		.03	.05			[b]	
White	−.05	.04		−.01	.07		−.02	.08			[b]	
T1 Legitimacy	.51	.05	***	.49	.10	***	.53	.11	***	.36	.12	***
T1 Cooperation with police	.03	.03		.06	.06		.03	.07			[b]	
T1 Cooperation with community	.00	.02		−.02	.03		−.04	.03			[b]	
Probably of contact	.72	.56		1.04	1.12		.73	1.23		.64	.61	
Adjusted R-squared	54%			62%			65%			52%		
N	804			254			209			46		

[a] * $p < .05$; ** $p < .01$; *** $p < .001$.
[b] Predictors excluded from stepwise regression model.
[c] Coded as 0 = Citizen-Initiated Contact (voluntary); 1 = Police-Initiated Contact.

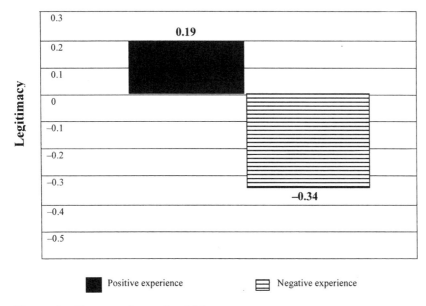

Fig. 4.1. Legitimacy and procedural fairness

they express at time one. A comparison of those who later had or did not have a personal experience in the year after the first interview indicates that the two groups did not differ in their ratings of police legitimacy at the time of the first interview (t = 1.86, n.s.).

Consistent with the argument that experience shaped attitudes at time two, those who had had a procedurally just encounter with the police made significantly higher ratings of police legitimacy than did those people who had no encounter during the year between the two interviews (t = 3.74, p < .001). And those who had had a procedurally unjust encounter with the police made significantly lower ratings of police legitimacy than did those people who had no encounter with the police (t = 7.61, p < .001). Figure 4.1 illustrates the separate and distinct influences of perceived fairness on attributed legitimacy. Using a simple binary metric, we classified respondents as having had positive or negative encounters with police. The legitimacy scores were adjusted for the T1 covariates, and centered at a mean of zero. Those with positive experiences attributed greater legitimacy to the police, while those with negative experiences attributed less legitimacy to the police. While we see some evidence of asymmetry, similar to Skogan, the importance of positive experiences on attributed legitimacy is apparent and distinct from the effects of negative encounters.

These findings suggest that, consistent with a procedure-based approach, legitimacy increases, even in the face of the delivery of negative outcomes. Those people who received a negative outcome via a just procedure increased their views about the legitimacy of the police and the law following a personal experience with a legal authority. They also suggest that differences in prior attitudes do not account for this effect. Conversely, legitimacy increased when the police delivered desirable outcomes, suggesting that the police can build support through fair treatment of the people with whom they deal.

5. Discussion

A. Why Do People Cooperate with the Police?

The first hypothesis is that legitimacy will influence people's willingness to cooperate with the police to fight crime in their communities. The results of the analysis suggest that legitimacy shapes willingness to cooperate with the police in fighting crime. The results for working with others in the community are more mixed. Among minorities legitimacy encourages working with others, but not among Whites. In both groups people who identify with their communities are more willing to cooperate with others in their community.

As noted in the introduction, recent discussions of crime and urban disorder suggest that the police have difficulty effectively managing crime without the support of the community.[75] This argument is consistent with the suggestion that the police have difficulty enforcing the law unless they can count on widespread cooperation from members of the public.[76] Both arguments emphasize the point that, while society creates legal authorities and institutions to manage problems of social order, the success of those authorities is ultimately linked to the attitudes and behaviors of people living within the communities involved. The work of the authorities is more difficult, and is sometimes impossible, without the active cooperation of the people in the community.

From the perspective of the people involved, the calculus behind decisions about whether and how much to cooperate with the police and the law mirrors the tradeoffs aptly described by the dilemmas widely studied within the social sciences. In particular, it reflects the issues involved in social dilemmas. It is often in people's self-interest to ignore or disobey laws and other social regulations, and to avoid helping the police by identifying criminals or engaging in community crime-prevention activities, since the latter behavior carries risks and has an uncertain positive payoff. On the other hand, if wrongdoing becomes widespread and the community generally fails to help the police to manage social order, everyone in the community suffers directly or indirectly. Hence, the mixed motive dynamics of the social dilemma—everyone would prefer not to help the community but have their neighbors do so—a view that, if widely acted on, leads to disorder and decline.

Typical approaches to resolving the social dilemma problem have been instrumental. They are based upon the belief that if the risks of rule breaking or the gains of cooperating with the police are increased people's self-interest calculus changes. And, as research makes clear, so does their behavior. We know that people are less likely to break the law if the risk of doing so is greater, just as they are more likely to act to help their community when the gains of cooperation are more certain.[77] The findings of this study confirm these instrumental influences by demonstrating that people are more cooperative with the police when they believe that police performance in fighting crime is more effective and that the police create a credible threat of punishment for wrongdoing.

While the potential value of instrumental approaches is clear, so are some of their limits. One limit is that, when they do influence behavior, the influence of instrumental calculations on behavior is, at best, small. Second, these strategies are most effective against instrumental crimes such as burglary and car theft, and in situations where surveillance is possible. Finally, even when they are effective, instrumental strategies are costly to implement, making them difficult to use during times of crisis, or in communities with limited resources.

Recognizing the limits of instrumental approaches, it has been argued that there are important advantages associated with self-regulatory models of order maintenance.[78] These models have the advantage of being based on people's own internal values, values that motivate behavior distinctly from the motivating influence of incentives and sanctions. To the degree that people are motivated by their values, they cooperate because they believe it is appropriate and proper, not because they believe it is in their immediate self-interest. One important value is legitimacy.

The value of a legitimacy based approach rests on the finding that appeals to legitimacy shape people's behavior. The findings outlined here show that they can. They demonstrate that people are more willing to cooperate with the police when they view the police as legitimate social authorities. If people view the police as more legitimate, they are more likely to report crimes in their neighborhood. In addition, minority group members are more likely to work with neighborhood groups.

B. How Is Legitimacy Created and Maintained? The Role of Procedural Justice

How can legitimacy be created and maintained? The second hypothesis is that procedural justice will be the central antecedent of legitimacy. The findings support this suggestion, and point to the justice of police policies and practices as key factors shaping police legitimacy. As is hypothesized based upon the psychological literature on procedural justice, people evaluate the legitimacy of the police largely in terms of their judgments about the fairness by which the police exercise their authority.[79] This does not mean that performance assessments are irrelevant—they are not. One factor shaping legitimacy is performance. However, once performance has been taken into account, legitimacy judgments are still shaped by procedural justice assessments.

In the past several decades those concerned with policing have focused on efforts to improve the objective quality of policing by developing better strategies for police efforts to fight crime, as well as improving the accountability of the police to the community for corruption, harassment, and abuse of authority. These efforts have lead to marked improvements in the objective quality of policing in the United States.[80] Despite these increases in the quality of policing, the police continue to have difficulty securing public cooperation, especially among minority group members, and in some cities police-community relations continue to be characterized by hostility and antagonism. These findings point to an alternative path to cooperation. This approach focuses on developing and maintaining the legitimacy of the police in the eyes of the public as another way that the police can be effective in fighting crime and urban disorder.

The findings of this study point directly to the value of process-based policing.[81] In a strategy of process-based policing the police strive to exercise their authority in ways that members of the public evaluate as fair. Such a strategy is not, of course, confined to policing. Similar arguments apply to the courts,[82] to government,[83] and to the management of for-profit organizations.[84] Research suggests that irrespective of context, legitimacy is strongly shaped by the procedural justice by which relevant authorities exercise their authority. These findings point to the value to the legal system of an empirically oriented analysis of the meaning of procedural justice. Knowing what is experienced by members of the public as fair or unfair is key to developing and maintaining public views that the legal system is legitimate.

While this study examines views about the police among the general public, it should be noted that the same findings about the importance of procedural justice emerge in studies in which the type of cooperation studied is deference to particular decisions during personal encounters with authorities.[85] These findings are confirmed among the subset of respondents in this study with their personal experience with the police. The findings of an analysis among that group indicate that legitimacy increases following personal experience with the police among both those with favorable and unfavorable outcomes, as long as those involved feel that the procedures used by the police were fair.

An example of the policy implications of these findings is found in recent research on racial profiling.[86] Thinking that one has been stopped by the police because of one's ethnicity reflects the belief that one has been profiled. This judgment has negative consequences during personal encounters with the police, because it encourages resistance and antagonism, as well as undermining the legitimacy of the police. On the community level, if members of the community believe that profiling is widespread, they are less supportive of the police.[87] These profiling effects emerge because people view profiling as an unfair policing procedure. Hence, procedural injustice leads to lowered legitimacy and diminished cooperation with the police. Conversely, if the police are procedurally fair when they deal with people, people are less likely to feel that they were profiled, and if people believe that the police are generally fair, they are less likely to think that profiling occurs. Hence, procedural justice provides a framework for understanding how people's views about police practices map onto police legitimacy and cooperation with the police.

C. Strengths and Weaknesses of This Study

The strength of the findings reported here flow from the fact that the data is panel data, which is a better type of correlational dataset for inferring causal relations than is cross-sectional data. In particular, a panel design allows for exogenous influences to be controlled. We have sharpened the distinction between fair treatment and fair outcome to assess their mutual influence that other studies blur or collapse. Additionally, our measures of legitimacy and cooperation are linked temporally to respondents' interactions with police, in effect allowing for the estimate of the effects of police contact as an intervention in citizens' everyday lives.

At the same time, our measures of public behavior rely on self-reports, whose vulnerability to bias and measurement error suggest caution. For example, we ask respondents to estimate how frequently they comply with the law and whether they cooperate with the police. There are obvious reasons that people might not accurately self-report their law related behavior. While there are reasons to believe that self-report data is reasonable in this context, it is important to acknowledge that its use is one weakness of this study.[88] Fortunately, more recent research using police records to index behavior supports the linkage of procedural justice to compliance through legitimacy.[89]

As in much survey research, our scenarios about cooperation are hypothetical. Because situations vary, respondents could not be asked if they had engaged in behavior. Instead, they were asked whether, if the situation arose, they would cooperate. For example, "If there were a criminal in your neighborhood, would you report them?" or "If the police held a community meeting, would you attend?" While made necessary by the situation, this hypothetical form is a weakness of the approach used in this situation. Nevertheless, research by social psychologists on behavioral intention or reasoned action suggests that predictions of future behaviors in survey research are sufficiently accurate to lend confidence to our conclusions.[90]

6. Conclusion

For the police to be successful in controlling crime and maintaining social order, they must have active public cooperation, not simply political support and approval. Cooperation increases not only when the public views the police as effective in controlling crime and maintaining social order, but also when citizens see the police as legitimate authorities who are entitled to be obeyed. Such legitimacy judgments, in turn, are shaped by public views about procedural justice—the fairness of the processes the police use when dealing with members of the public. These findings demonstrate the value to the police of having public legitimacy and indicate how such legitimacy can be sustained.

Appendix A

Method

The Wave 1 sample (n = 1,653) was racially and ethnically diverse: 34% White, 25% Hispanic; 28% African American; and 13% other Non-White. Data from the 2000 Census show that New York City's adult population at the time of the survey was 35% Non-Hispanic White, 27.0% Hispanic, 24.5% African American, and 13.5% Other Non-White and Non-Hispanic.[91] Accordingly, the Wave 1 sample closely approximated the racial and ethnic composition of the City. This diversity was maintained among those who were reinterviewed during the second time of the study (n = 879). In the time two sample 38% were White; 22% were Hispanic; 28% African American; and 11% other non-White. In addition, the Wave 1 and Wave 2 samples were closely matched on gender, age, education, and income. These demographics are outlined in the table below. Interviews were conducted by telephone, and lasted no more than 25–30 minutes. Respondents gave informed consent verbally prior to beginning the interview. Responses were recorded by interviewers directly into a database using preprogrammed response screens.

TABLE 4.A1
Sample Demographics

	T1	T2
Age		
18–24	14.0%	11.2%
25–34	26.4	22.3
35–54	38.2	38.9
55–64	9.9	12.7
65+	11.5	15.0
Education		
Less than HS	12.4%	11.8%
HS graduate	22.7	21.8
Some college	20.5	21.4
College graduate	31.4	31.6
Graduate work	13.0	13.4
Income		
Under $20,000	17.8%	17.7%
$20,000–$29,999	15.8	14.1
$30,000–$39,999	12.7	13.5
$40,000–$49,999	11.8	12.5
$50,000–$74,999	17.5	18.0
$75,000–$99,999	10.0	11.1
$100,000+	14.4	13.2
Race		
Hispanic	25.2%	22.2%
African American	28.0	28.2
White	33.8	38.2
Other Non-White	12.9	11.4
Gender		
Male	46.2%	44.2%

Items and Measures

COOPERATIVE BEHAVIOR

Two dimensions of cooperation were assessed: assisting the police in crime prevention and criminal investigations, and complying with the law. *Assistance* was assessed by asking respondents, if the situation arose, how likely they would be to: (a) call the police to report a crime; (b) help the police to find someone suspected of a crime; (c) report dangerous or suspicious activity; (d) volunteer time to help the police; (e) patrol the streets as part of an organized group; and (e) volunteer to attend community meetings to discuss crime. The response scale was: (4) very likely; somewhat likely; not too likely; and not likely at all (1).

For *compliance*, respondents were asked how frequently they followed rules concerning: (a) where they could legally park their car; (b) how to dispose of trash and litter; (c) making too much noise at night; (d) speeding or breaking other traffic laws; (e) buying possibly stolen items on the street; (f) not taking inexpensive items from stores; (g) using illegal drugs such as marijuana. The response scale was: (5) all of the time; almost all of the time; most of the time; some of the time; or none of the time (1).

Based upon the results of a principal components factor analysis with varimax rotation, four scales were created using the factor scores. Because of the small number of items within each of the four scales, Chronbachs alphas were only moderately high, within the 0.60–0.80 range, which is acceptable. The Wave 1 means and standard deviations for each scale are shown in table 4.A2.

ATTITUDES ABOUT THE POLICE

Legitimacy. The legitimacy of the police was assessed by asking about three issues: obligation; trust and confidence; and identification with the police. Obligation and trust and confidence measures were drawn from Tyler, while identification with the police was assessed following the approach of Tyler and Huo.[92]

Respondents were first asked whether or not they felt that they ought to obey the police in situations in which the police told them how to behave and/or when there were relevant laws. The scale included ten items, ranging from high (5) to low (1). The items were; "Overall, the NYPD is a legitimate authority and people should obey the decisions that NYPD police officers make"; "You should accept the decisions made by police, even if you think they are wrong?"; "You should do what the police tell you to do even when you don't understand the reasons for their decisions?"; "You should do what the police tell you to do even when you disagree with their decisions"; "You should do what the police tell you to do even when you don't like the way they treat you?"; "There are times it is ok for you to ignore what the police tell you to do (reverse scored)"; "Sometimes you have to bend the law for things to come out right (reverse scored)"; "The law represents the values of the people in power, rather than the values of people like you (reverse scored)"; "People in power use the law to try to control people like you (reverse scored)"; and "The law does not protect your interests (reverse scored)."

In addition, respondents were asked whether or not they had trust in the police as an institution. The scale used seven items, ranging from high (5) to low (1). The items were: "I have confidence that the NYPD can do its job well"; "I trust the leaders of the NYPD to make decisions that are good for everyone in the city"; "People's basic rights are well protected by the police"; "The police care about the well-being of everyone they deal with"; "The police are often dishonest (reverse scored)"; "Some of the things the police do embarrass our city (reverse scored)"; and "There are many things about the NYPD and its policies that need to be changed (reverse scored)."

Finally, they were asked whether they identified with police officers, i.e., generally sharing their values and respecting them as people. The scale included ten items, ranging from high (5) to low (1). The items were: "If you talked to most of the police officers who work in your neighborhood, you would find they have similar views to your own on many issues"; "Your background is similar to that of many of the police officers who work in your neighborhood"; "You can usually understand why the police who work in your neighborhood are acting as they are in a particular situation"; "You generally like the police officers who work in your neighborhood"; "If most of the police officers who work in your neighborhood knew you, they would respect your values"; "Most of the police officers who work in your neighborhood would value what you contribute to your neighborhood"; "Most of the police officers who work in your neighborhood would approve of how you live your life"; "I am proud of the work of the NYPD"; "I agree with many of the values that define what the NYPD stands for."

POLICE PERFORMANCE

Police performance was first measured via estimates of the likelihood that a rule breaker would be caught and punished for rule breaking; fear of crime; and judgments about neighborhood crime conditions.

Sanction risk. To determine the degree to which respondents felt that the police created an effective deterrent to rule breaking, they were asked how likely they thought it was that they would be caught and punished if they broke each of the seven laws used to determine cooperation. Seven items were used, ranging from (5) high to (1) low.

Crime concerns. Crime concerns were assessed in two ways: fear of crime and estimates of crime. To determine fear of crime respondents were asked a series of questions about how well the police managed crime in the respondent's neighborhood (three items, ranging from (4) high to (1) low). To evaluate neighborhood conditions respondents were asked about the existence of conditions such as "graffiti on neighborhood walls" and "empty beer bottles on the streets or sidewalks," as well as two questions about the rate of crime in the neighborhood (using eight items, ranging from (4) high to (1) low).

IDENTIFICATION WITH ONE'S NEIGHBORHOOD

In addition to measuring respondent judgments about the police, the degree to which respondents identified with their neighborhood was also assessed. Drawing upon the psychological literature on cooperation, which links cooperation to identification with a group,[93] identification with neighborhood was assessed using a seven item scale, ranging from (4) high to (1) low. The items were: "How important is the neighborhood in which you live to the way that you think of yourself as a person?";

"You are proud to live in your neighborhood"; "Things that people in your neighborhood stand for are important to you"; "When someone praises the achievements of others in your neighborhood, it feels like a personal compliment to you"; "Most of the people in your neighborhood respect your values"; "Most of the people in your neighborhood value what you contribute to the neighborhood"; and "Most of the people in your neighborhood approve of how you live your life."

EVALUATIONS OF POLICE ACTIONS

Based upon procedural justice theory, two distinct aspects of procedural justice were measured: the justice of decision making and the justice of interpersonal treatment. These assessments were asked for both global evaluations of police, and actions of police in the respondent's personal experience. This model reflects the findings of research in work settings.[94]

Justice of police decision making. The fairness of police decision making was assessed using five items, ranging from (5) agree strongly to (1) disagree strongly. The items were: "Usually accurately understand and apply the law"; "Make their decisions based on facts, not their personal biases and opinions"; "Try to get the facts in a situation before deciding how to act"; "Give honest explanations for their actions to the people they deal with"; "Apply the rules consistently to different people."

Justice of police interpersonal treatment. The justice of police treatment of residents of the community was assessed using four items, ranging from (5) agree strongly to (1) disagree strongly. The items were: "Treat people with dignity and respect"; "Respect people's rights"; "Consider the views of people involved"; and "Take account of the needs and concerns of the people they deal with."

Police distributive fairness to the respondent. Respondents were asked about the fairness of the delivery of police services to people like themselves. The scale ranges from (4) fair to (1) unfair.

JUDGMENTS ABOUT PERSONAL EXPERIENCE WITH THE POLICE

Next, those respondents who reported personal experience were asked a set of questions about that personal experience.

Justice of police decision making during personal experience. The justice of police decision making was assessed using six items, each with a four item response scale ranging from agree strongly (4) to disagree strongly (1). The items were: "Decisions about what to do were made fairly"; "I had the opportunity to describe my situation before decisions were made"; "I was treated the same way that others would be treated in a similar situation"; "The police made their decision based on facts"; "I received the same outcome that others would receive in the same situation"; and "My race/ethnicity did not influence how I was treated by the police."

Justice of police interpersonal treatment during personal experience. The justice of police interpersonal treatment was determined using six items, each with a four point response scale ranging from (4) agree strongly to (1) disagree strongly. The items were: "The police were honest in what they said to me"; "The police tried hard to do the right thing"; "The police tried to take my needs into account"; "The police cared about my concerns"; "The police treated me politely"; "The police respected my rights."

Fairness of the outcomes during personal experience. The fairness of the outcome during the personal experience was assessed using three items, each with a four point response scale ranging from (4) agree strongly to (1) disagree strongly (mean = 3.97; s.d. = 1.14; alpha = 0.94). The items were "I received a fair outcome"; "I received the outcome I deserved according to the law"; and "I received the outcome I feel I deserved."

Favorability of outcomes during personal experience. Three items were used, with a four point response scale ranging from (4) agree strongly to (1) disagree strongly. They were: "Overall, how satisfied were you with how the officer(s) handled your situation"; "How satisfied were you with the outcome of your experience"; and "From your perspective, was the outcome very good, somewhat good, somewhat bad, or very bad for you?"

The willingness to accept decisions following personal experience. A two item scale measured willingness to accept police decisions, with each item using a four point response scale ranging from (4) agree strongly to (1) disagree strongly. The items were: "I willingly accepted the decisions the police made"; and "In a similar situation in the future, I would like to see the situation handled in the same way."

Motivation to complain. Two items assessed motivation to question the decision, with each item using a four point response scale ranging from (4) agree strongly to (1) disagree strongly. "I considered going to others to complain about the actions of the police"; "I considered going to others to try to change the decisions the police made."

TABLE 4.A2
Scale Properties

	Mean	Standard Deviation	α
Compliance and Assistance			
Compliance with Minor Laws	3.40	0.73	
Compliance with Major Laws	3.63	0.88	
Helping the Police	2.57	0.60	
Helping Neighbors	1.78	0.85	
Legal Orientation[a]			
Legitimacy	3.62	0.58	0.61
Trust in Police	3.56	0.62	0.82
Attitudes Toward Police	3.96	0.69	0.87
Sanction Risk	3.54	0.96	0.87
Perceptions of Neighborhood and Crime			
Crime Problems in Neighborhood	2.76	0.67	0.73
Physical Disorder	2.04	0.67	0.82
Neighborhood Identification	1.78	0.60	0.77
Procedural Justice—General			
Fair Decisions	3.67	1.07	0.85
Respectful Treatment	3.82	0.99	0.83
Outcome Favorability	2.16	1.46	
Procedure Justice—Personal Experience[b]			
Fair Decisions	3.27	0.76	0.76
Respectful Treatment	3.22	0.96	0.94
Outcome Favorability	2.97	1.05	0.90
Willingness to Accept Police Decision	3.07	1.08	0.79
Motivation to Complain	3.36	0.97	0.80

[a] All of the reliabilities reported for the Legal Orientation measures were computed on the T1 sample.
[b] All of the reliabilities reported for Personal Experience were computed on the T1 sample.

NOTES

1. *See generally* TOM R. TYLER, WHY PEOPLE OBEY THE LAW (2006) [hereinafter TYLER, WHY PEOPLE OBEY] (discussing instrumental and normative perspectives on why people follow the law).

2. *See, e.g.,* Robert J. Sampson, Stephen W. Raudenbush & Felton Earls, *Neighborhoods and Violent Crime: A Multilevel Study of Collective Efficacy,* 277 SCIENCE 918, 918, 923 (1997) (finding, in study of Chicago neighborhoods, that informal social control among neighbors is linked with lower rates of violence).

3. Although our conceptual framework is compatible with economics perspectives on citizen interactions with criminal legal institutions and on crime, we avoid an explicit model of reward and sanction resulting from contacts with legal actors. We do claim that the costs of adverse interactions with police and poor outcomes are reduced incentives to cooperate with police and to comply with legal norms. *See* A. Mitchell Polinsky & Steven Shavell, *The Theory of Public Enforcement of Law, in* 1 HANDBOOK OF LAW AND ECONOMICS (2007); *see also* Oren Bar-Gill & Alon Harel, *Crime Rates and Expected Sanctions: The Economics of Deterrence Revisited,* 30 J. LEGAL STUD. 485 (2001).

4. *See* Daniel S. Nagin, *Criminal Deterrence Research at the Outset of the Twenty-First Century,* 23 CRIME & JUST. 1, 7 (1998) (discussing research that "points overwhelmingly to the conclusion that behavior is influenced by sanction risk perceptions—those who perceive that sanctions are more certain or severe are less likely to commit crime").

5. GEORGE L. KELLING & CATHERINE M. COLES, FIXING BROKEN WINDOWS 102–07 (1996) (advocating shift from "reactive, 911 policing and return to a model of policing" that emphasizes crime prevention and order maintenance).

6. *See, e.g.,* Nagin, *supra* note 4, at 34–35 (arguing that credibility of sanction policies depends in part on police and prosecutor resources and on sentencing and release decisions of judges and parole boards); *see also* DAVID H. BAYLEY & HAROLD MENDELSOHN, MINORITIES AND THE POLICE 58–86 (1968) (discussing Denver study indicating that racial minorities may be less willing to contact police for assistance because of perceptions of police attitude toward them).

7. Sampson et al., *supra* note 2, at 919 ("[S]ocially cohesive neighborhoods will prove the most fertile contexts for the realization of informal social control. . . . [T]he collective efficacy of residents is a critical means by which urban neighborhoods inhibit the occurrence of personal violence. . . ."). Conversely, weak social ties among neighborhood residents contribute to a rejection of legal norms and their underlying moral dimensions. *See* Robert J. Sampson & Dawn Jeglum Bartusch, *Legal Cynicism and (Subcultural?) Tolerance of Deviance: The Neighborhood Context of Racial Differences,* 32 LAW & SOC'Y REV. 777, 783, 800–01 (1998) (suggesting that perceived normlessness is greater in "inner-city contexts of racial segregation and concentrated disadvantage, where inability to influence the structures of power . . . breed[s] cynicism and perceptions of legal injustice"); David S. Kirk & Andrew V. Papachristos, Legal Cynicism and the Framing of Neighborhood Violence: Implications For "Neighborhood Effects" Research (Dec. 28, 2007) (unpublished manuscript), *available at* http://ssrn.com/abstract=1081894 (discussing link between "legal cynicism" and neighborhood rates of violence).

8. *See* NAT'L RES. COUNCIL, FAIRNESS AND EFFECTIVENESS IN POLICING 22–27 (Wesley Skogan & Kathleen Frydl eds., 2004) [hereinafter FAIRNESS AND EFFECTIVENESS IN POLICING].

9. TYLER, WHY PEOPLE OBEY, *supra* note 1, at 4, 20–21 (presenting instrumental perspective of compliance where individuals' compliance with law depends on likelihood of punishment).

10. *See* Robert J. MacCoun, *Drugs and the Law: A Psychological Analysis of Drug Prohibition*, 113 PSYCHOL. BULL. 497, 499–501 (1993) (discussing limited deterrence effect, in context of illicit drug use, stemming from limited public knowledge of criminal law system and weak correlation between perceived severity of sanction and criminal conduct).

11. *See* Jason Sunshine & Tom R. Tyler, *The Role of Procedural Justice and Legitimacy in Shaping Public Support for Policing*, 37 LAW & SOC'Y REV. 513, 519–21 (2003) (suggesting that police treatment of people in the community has a stronger effect on legitimacy than quality of police performance).

12. *See* TYLER, WHY PEOPLE OBEY, *supra* note 1, at 170–78 (suggesting psychology of legitimacy wherein people obey authorities and institutions that they trust).

13. *See generally* DAVID BEETHAM, THE LEGITIMATION OF POWER 15–17 (1991) (defining legitimacy along three dimensions, including rules that are "justified in terms of beliefs shared by both dominant and subordinate"); Tom R. Tyler, *Psychological Perspectives on Legitimacy and Legitimation*, 57 ANN. REV. PSYCHOL. 375 (2006) [hereinafter Tyler, *Psychological Perspectives*] (discussing ways in which legitimacy facilitates state exercise of power because individuals view authorities as morally or normatively appropriate).

14. BEETHAM, *supra* note 13, at 117–60, 118 (arguing that the "contemporary state . . . requires legitimation . . . to maintain its political system intact in the face of serious policy failure or challenge. . . ."). *See also* 1 MAX WEBER, ECONOMY AND SOCIETY 212–16 (Guenther Roth & Claus Wittich eds., Ephraim Fischoff et al. trans., 1968) (discussing legitimation of state power based on individuals' acceptance of and submission to that power and arguing for the value to the state of being viewed as legitimate among the populace).

15. BEETHAM, *supra* note 13, at 18 ("[L]egitimacy involves the demonstrable expression of consent on the part of the subordinate to the particular power relation in which they are involved, through actions which provide evidence of consent."); *see* TYLER, WHY PEOPLE OBEY, *supra* note 1, at 25 (stating that "legitimacy exists when the members of a society see adequate reason for feeling that they should voluntarily obey the commands of authorities"); Tyler, *Psychological Perspectives*, *supra* note 13, at 378 ("One aspect of values—obligation—is a key element in the concept of legitimacy. It leads to voluntary deference to the directives of legitimate authorities and rules."). *But see* 3 WEBER, *supra* note 14, at 941–54.

16. John R. P. French, Jr. & Bertram Raven, *The Bases of Social Power*, *in* STUDIES IN SOCIAL POWER 150, 158–62 (Dorwin Cartwright ed., 1959) (defining legitimacy as rooted in internalized values, such as expertise or social class, through which individuals feel obligated to accept the authority's power); HERBERT C. KELMAN & V. LEE HAMILTON, CRIMES OF OBEDIENCE: TOWARD A SOCIAL PSYCHOLOGY OF AUTHORITY AND RESPONSIBILTY 77–102 (1989) (discussing how obedience—where people follow orders out of a sense of duty—depends on legitimacy of authority); TOM R. TYLER & YUEN J. HUO, TRUST IN THE LAW: ENCOURAGING PUBLIC COOPERATION WITH THE POLICE AND COURTS 7–18 (2002) (advocating a "process-based model of regulation that encourages voluntary deference" to authorities based on fairness in exercise of authority); TYLER, WHY PEOPLE OBEY, *supra* note 1, at 23–30 (summarizing past studies suggesting that legitimacy exists when society internalizes normative reasons for voluntarily obeying the commands of authorities).

17. Tyler, *Psychological Perspectives*, *supra* note 13, at 379–80 (reviewing studies that indicate that authorities who exercise power fairly will be viewed as legitimate and have their decisions accepted).

18. TYLER & HUO, *supra* note 16, at 198–203 (advocating policing strategies that incorporate the process-based model, emphasizing fair and respectful treatment to encourage consent and cooperation).

19. Tom R. Tyler & John M. Darley, *Building a Law-Abiding Society: Taking Public Views About Morality and the Legitimacy of Legal Authorities into Account When Formulating Substantive Law*, 28 HOFSTRA L. REV. 707, 714–17 (2000) (discussing legitimacy as shaping "obe[dience of] laws because [people] regard deferring to social authorities as part of the obligations associated with citizenship").

20. TOM. R. TYLER & STEVEN L. BLADER, COOPERATION IN GROUPS 143–68 (2000) [hereinafter TYLER & BLADER, COOPERATION] (observing that procedural justice affirms the relationship between people and groups by "showing that the group to which they belong is . . . valuable . . . and that the group values them").

21. *See id.*

22. *Cf.* Wesley G. Skogan, *Asymmetry in the Impact of Encounters with Police*, 16 POLICING & SOC'Y 99, 118–19 (2006) (finding that citizen evaluations of police services are asymmetrically influenced by perceptions of negative treatment).

23. *See* BAYLEY & MENDELSOHN, *supra* note 6, at 109–42 (1969) (finding ethnicity, but not sex or social class, correlated with negative perception of police); RONALD WEITZER & STEVEN A. TUCH, RACE AND POLICING IN AMERICA 74–123 (2006) (examining views of racialized policing and perceptions of unequal justice); Steven A. Tuch & Ronald Weitzer, *The Polls—Trends: Racial Differences in Attitudes Toward the Police*, 61 PUB. OPINION Q. 642, 647–48 (1997) (discussing Los Angeles–area and national studies on Blacks' versus Whites' perceptions and experiences of police brutality).

24. *See* WEITZER & TUCH, *supra* note 23, at 119–23 (discussing roles of mass media and neighborhood crime concerns in shaping perceptions of racialized policing by Blacks and Hispanics); Faye Crosby, Stephanie Bromley & Leonard Saxe, *Recent Unobtrusive Studies of Black and White Discrimination and Prejudice: A Literature Review*, 87 PSYCHOL. BULL. 546 (1980) (reviewing studies on anti-Black prejudice); Jeffrey Fagan & Garth Davies, *Policing Guns: Order Maintenance and Crime Control in New York*, *in* GUNS, CRIME, AND PUNISHMENT IN AMERICA 21 (Bernard E. Harcourt ed., 2003); Jeffrey Fagan & Garth Davies, *Street Stops and Broken Windows: Terry, Race, and Disorder in New York City*, 28 FORDHAM URB. L.J. 457, 489–96 (2000) [hereinafter Fagan & Davies, *Street Stops*] (analyzing New York City study showing "greater intensity of enforcement and over-enforcement against minority citizens" and suggesting "conflation of race, poverty, and disorder in policing policy"); Leonard Saxe et al., *The Visibility of Illicit Drugs: Implications for Community-Based Drug Control Strategies*, 91 AM. J. PUB. HEALTH 1987, 1991–93 (2001) (discussing how differences in predictors for drug use versus visible drug sales affect policy).

25. TYLER & HUO, *supra* note 16, at 5 ("In recent years the perception has grown that the relationship between the public and legal authorities is becoming more negative."); GARY LAFREE, LOSING LEGITIMACY: STREET CRIME AND THE DECLINE OF SOCIAL INSTITUTIONS IN AMERICA (1998) (discussing postwar crime trends and impact on social and political institutions); Tom R. Tyler, *Public Mistrust of the Law: A Political Perspective*, 66 U. CIN. L. REV. 847, 848–53 (1998) [hereinafter Tyler, *Public Mistrust*] ("Recently, less than 10% of the American public expressed 'a great deal' of confidence in the American legal system.").

26. *See, e.g.*, Tyler, *Public Mistrust*, *supra* note 25, at 853 (discussing public opinion polls showing dissatisfaction with courts in general and local courts in particular).

27. JAMES GAROFALO, U.S. DEP'T OF JUSTICE, PUBLIC OPINION ABOUT CRIME: THE ATTITUDES OF VICTIMS AND NONVICTIMS IN SELECTED CITIES 28 (1977) (reporting, from National Crime Survey results, a "very large" gap between White and Black perceptions of police performance); HOWARD SCHUMAN ET AL., RACIAL ATTITUDES IN AMERICA 139–62 (1985) (discussing survey results on civil rights issues); Lawrence D. Bobo & Devon

Johnson, *A Taste for Punishment: Black and White Americans' Views on the Death Penalty and the War on Drugs*, 1 DU BOIS REV. 151, 156–57 (2004) (discussing "substantial differences between Blacks and Whites" on views of police behavior and prosecutor and court treatment); Michael J. Hindelang, *Public Opinion Regarding Crime, Criminal Justice, and Related Topics*, 11 J. RES. CRIME & DELINQ. 101 (1974); W. S. Wilson Huang & Michael S. Vaughn, *Support and Confidence: Public Attitudes Toward the Police*, *in* AMERICANS VIEW CRIME AND JUSTICE (Timothy J. Flanagan & Dennis R. Longmire eds., 1996).

28. *See* Bobo & Johnson, *supra* note 27, at 168–72.

29. Jeffrey Fagan, *Crime and Neighborhood Change*, *in* UNDERSTANDING CRIME TRENDS 81 (Arthur S. Goldberger & Richard Rosenfeld eds., 2008); Kenneth C. Land, Patricia L. McCall & Lawrence E. Cohen, *Structural Covariates of Homicide Rates: Are There Any Invariances Across Time and Social Space?*, 95 AM. J. OF SOC. 922, 954 (1990); Robert J. Sampson & Janet J. Lauritsen, *Violent Victimization and Offending: Individual-, Situational-, and Community-Level Risk Factors*, *in* 3 UNDERSTANDING AND PREVENTING VIOLENCE 1 (Albert J. Reiss, Jr. & Jeffrey A. Roth eds., 1994).

30. *See generally* WEBER, *supra* note 14.

31. *See* BEETHAM, *supra* note 13, at 15–16 ("Power can be said to be legitimate to the extent that . . . the rules can be justified by reference to beliefs shared by both dominant and subordinate. . . .").

32. TYLER & HUO, *supra* note 16, at 175–76 (arguing that "feelings of procedural justice and motive-based trust" enhance voluntary deference to authorities).

33. Sunshine & Tyler, *supra* note 11, at 531–33 ("[W]hite and African American assessments of legitimacy were influenced by distributive justice. . . .").

34. TOM R. TYLER, PSYCHOLOGY AND THE DESIGN OF LEGAL INSTITUTIONS 9–20 (2008) (explaining the deterrence model and noting its problems).

35. Tyler & Darley, *supra* note 19, at 708 (presenting "law-abiding society" as one in which people voluntarily defer to and cooperate with authority because of the belief that laws describe morally appropriate behavior).

36. *See* BEETHAM, *supra* note 13, at 26–29 (arguing that legitimate power provides moral and normative reasons for obedience, apart from incentives and sanctions); David Beetham & Christopher Lord, *Legitimacy and the European Union*, *in* POLITICAL THEORY AND THE EUROPEAN UNION (Albert Weale & Michael Nentwich eds., 1998).

37. TYLER, WHY PEOPLE OBEY, *supra* note 1, at 172 (concluding that "experiencing unfair procedures undermine[s] the role of legitimacy in maintaining compliance").

38. *See generally* E. ALLAN LIND & TOM R. TYLER, THE SOCIAL PSYCHOLOGY OF PROCEDURAL JUSTICE (1988) (discussing studies demonstrating that individuals' views of the system depend on justice of procedures as well as justice of outcome); TOM R. TYLER ET AL., SOCIAL JUSTICE IN A DIVERSE SOCIETY (1997) (discussing how fair procedures, and not just outcome fairness, is important to individual dignity and commitment to law); Tom R. Tyler & Heather J. Smith, *Social Justice and Social Movements*, *in* 2 THE HANDBOOK OF SOCIAL PSYCHOLOGY 595 (Daniel T. Gilbert et al. eds., 4th ed. 1998).

39. TYLER & HUO, *supra* note 16, at 57 (concluding from Chicago and California studies that "people are significantly more focused on the procedural justice of authorities' actions than [on] . . . the favorability or fairness of their own outcomes" during encounters with police or the court); Tom R. Tyler, *Procedural Justice, Legitimacy, and the Effective Rule of Law*, 30 CRIME & JUST. 283, 292 (2003) (observing that while fairness of outcome matters, procedural justice is "especially important in shaping people's willingness to defer to the decisions made by legal authorities"); Tom R. Tyler, *Social Justice: Outcome and Procedure*, 35 INT'L J. PSYCHOL. 117, 119–20 (2000) [hereinafter Tyler, *Social Justice*] (finding procedural justice factors

more important than outcomes of police interaction, such as arrest, for assessment of legitimacy); Tom R. Tyler, *What is Procedural Justice? Criteria Used by Citizens to Assess the Fairness of Legal Procedures*, 22 LAW & SOC'Y REV. 103, 117 (1988) [hereinafter Tyler, *What is Procedural Justice?*] (finding that individuals distinguish perceptions of fairness from favorability of outcome).

40. *See, e.g.*, TYLER & HUO, *supra* note 16, at 204–08 (emphasizing importance of fair procedures in increasing public acceptance of police authority); *cf.* WEITZER & TUCH, *supra* note 23, at 58–73 (discussing reasons behind perceptions of police misconduct).

41. Skogan, *supra* note 22, at 112 ("The impact of encounters is strongly asymmetrical. Having a positive experience helps little. . . . Having a bad experience hurts a great deal."). Skogan reaches these conclusions using cross-sectional survey data from a study of citizens in Chicago. *Id.* at 107–10. The absence of longitudinal or panel data suggests that citizen evaluations of policing could either precede or follow their encounter with police.

42. Ben Bradford, Jonathan Jackson & Elizabeth A. Stanko, *Contact and Confidence: Revisiting the Impact of Public Encounters with the Police*, 18 Policing and Society, 19: 20–46 (stating that "consistent with the procedural justice model[,] we also show that positively received contacts can improve perceptions of fairness and community engagement") (manuscript at 2, *available at* http://www.lse.ac.uk/collections/methodologyInstitute/pdf/JonJackson/policing _and_society_08.pdf).

43. Skogan, *supra* note 22, at 99.

44. *Id.*

45. FAIRNESS AND EFFECTIVENESS IN POLICING, *supra* note 8.

46. *Id.* at 109–54.

47. TYLER & HUO, *supra* note 16, at 198–208.

48. TYLER, WHY PEOPLE OBEY, *supra* note 1.

49. CHARLES F. MANSKI, IDENTIFICATION PROBLEMS IN THE SOCIAL SCIENCES (1995) (showing the importance of specification of causal order and the elimination of endogenous and simultaneous influences to establish causal ordering between behavioral factors); *see also* WILLIAM R. SHADISH, THOMAS D. COOK & DONALD T. CAMPBELL, EXPERIMENTAL AND QUASI-EXPERIMENTAL DESIGNS FOR GENERALIZED CAUSAL INFERENCE (2d ed. 2002).

50. TYLER, WHY PEOPLE OBEY, *supra* note 1, at 57–68.

51. Sunshine & Tyler, *supra* note 11, at 525–34.

52. *Id. See also* TYLER, WHY PEOPLE OBEY, *supra* note 1, at 94–112 (finding that personal experiences with police or court officials influences views about their legitimacy); TYLER & HUO, *supra* note 16, at 123–38 (suggesting that generalized legitimacy develops from experiences of fair and trustworthy conduct on the part of legal authorities); Sunshine & Tyler, *supra* note 11, at 534–36 (same).

53. In this study, we do not view these interactions as dynamic exchanges where both police and citizens respond to each others' behaviors. Such dyadic interactions are important and will bear on both how the police officer and the citizen react to each other, and also how each rates his or her behavior. However, the complications and challenges of a research protocol that would integrate such interactions in a study of citizens' reactions to police are daunting and should be obvious. Rather, we rely here on citizens' reports and evaluations of the quality of treatment they received from the police and set aside any effects of the citizens' behavior on the responses and reactions of the police officer in the situation or encounter.

54. TYLER & HUO, *supra* note 16, at 123–29 (reporting survey results suggesting that general favorable attitudes feed back into specific situations of interactions with legal authorities); Skogan, *supra* note 22, at 106.

55. The Random Digit Dialing method sampled only from eligible telephone numbers, and

did not include cell phones. If an answering machine was reached, respondents were recalled up to 20 times.

56. Data available from the authors.

57. *See* Richard Berk, Azusa Li & Laura J. Hickman, *Statistical Difficulties in Determining the Role of Race in Capital Cases: A Re-analysis of Data from the State of Maryland*, 21 J. QUAN-TITATIVE CRIMINOLOGY 365 (2005); Paul R. Rosenbaum & Donald B. Rubin, *The Central Role of the Propensity Score in Observational Studies for Causal Effects*, 70 BIOMETRIKA 41 (1983); *see also* RICHARD A. BERK, REGRESSION ANALYSIS: A CONSTRUCTIVE CRITIQUE (2004).

58. We used dummy variables for African American and Hispanic ethnicity to account for the disproportionate contact of non-White New Yorkers with the police during this period. *See* Fagan & Davies, *Street Stops*, *supra* note 24.

59. Heejung Bang & James M. Robins, *Doubly Robust Estimation in Missing Data and Causal Inference Models*, 61 BIOMETRICS 962, 965 (2005).

60. Alka Indurkhya, Nandita Mitra & Deborah Schrag, *Using Propensity Scores to Estimate the Cost-Effectiveness of Medical Therapies*, 25 STAT. MED. 1561 (2006).

61. Fagan & Davies, *Street Stops*, *supra* note 24.

62. KELLING & COLES, *supra* note 5.

63. Sunshine & Tyler, *supra* note 11; TYLER, WHY PEOPLE OBEY, *supra* note 1; Tom R. Tyler, *Public Trust and Confidence in Legal Authorities: What Do Majority and Minority Group Members Want from the Law and Legal Institutions?*, 19 BEHAV. SCI. & L. 215 (2001) [hereinafter Tyler, *Public Trust*].

64. Sunshine & Tyler, *supra* note 11.

65. Tyler, *Social Justice*, *supra* note 39.

66. Tyler, *Procedural Justice*, *supra* note 39.

67. TYLER & HUO, *supra* note 16; Skogan, *supra* note 22.

68. TYLER & HUO, *supra* note 16.

69. *See, e.g.*, TYLER & HUO, *supra* note 16.

70. Skogan, *supra* note 22, at 115, 119.

71. *Id.*

72. Using the time one measures we can predict 2% of the variance in the likelihood that a respondent will later have a police-initiated contact. Thus, contacts with the police at time two appear to be random. Time one values and cooperation have no influence upon the likelihood of later police-initiated contact, and the only significant demographic is gender, with men more likely to have police-initiated contact. With respondent-initiated contact we can also explain 2% of the variance. Again, time one values and cooperation have no influence upon the likelihood of a respondent later contacting the police. However, women, older respondents, and better-educated respondents are significantly more likely to initiate contact with the police.

73. *See* Skogan, *supra* note 22.

74. The analysis shown in table 4.6 also distinguishes between those who initiate contact and those who do not. The results are the same among both groups. Because the sample of police-initiated contacts was small (46 people) the equation testing that effect did not include background factors.

75. Sampson et al., *supra* note 2.

76. TYLER, WHY PEOPLE OBEY, *supra* note 1.

77. Nagin, *supra* note 4.

78. TYLER & HUO, *supra* note 16; Tom R. Tyler, *Promoting Employee Policy Adherence and Rule Following in Work Settings: The Value of Self-Regulatory Approaches*, 70 BROOK. L. REV.

1287 (2005); Tom R. Tyler & Steven L. Blader, *Can Businesses Effectively Regulate Employee Conduct? The Antecedents of Rule Following in Work Settings*, 48 ACAD. MGMT. J. 1143 (2005); Tyler & Darley, *supra* note 19.

79. TYLER, WHY PEOPLE OBEY, *supra* note 1; TYLER & HUO, *supra* note 16.

80. FAIRNESS AND EFFECTIVENESS IN POLICING, *supra* note 8.

81. *See* TYLER & HUO, *supra* note 16.

82. *Id. See also* Tyler, *Public Trust*, *supra* note 63.

83. Tom R. Tyler, *A Psychological Perspective on the Legitimacy of Institutions and Authorities, in* THE PSYCHOLOGY OF LEGITIMACY 416 (John T. Jost & Brenda Major eds., 2001).

84. Tyler, *Procedural Justice*, *supra* note 39.

85. *See* TYLER & HUO, *supra* note 16.

86. Tom R. Tyler & Cheryl J. Wakslak, *Profiling and Police Legitimacy: Procedural Justice, Attributions of Motive, and the Acceptance of Police Authority*, 42 CRIMINOLOGY 253 (2004).

87. *Id.* Tyler and Wakslak's study looks at the judgments of members of the community about the frequency of profiling. Their results indicate that when people think that profiling is more widespread in the community, they are less supportive of the police and less willing to cooperate with them in fighting crime.

88. The case of the reasonableness of self-report data about rule following is made in detail in TYLER, WHY PEOPLE OBEY, *supra* note 1, at 40–56. That discussion notes that research comparing the findings of self-report studies and studies that use actual criminal behavior as the dependent variable yield similar findings about the reasons for rule following.

89. Tom R. Tyler, Lawrence Sherman, Heather Strang, Geoffrey C. Barnes & Daniel Woods, *Reintegrative Shaming, Procedural Justice, and Recidivism: The Engagement of Offenders' Psychological Mechanisms in the Canberra RISE Drinking-and-Driving Experiment*, 41 L. & SOC'Y REV. 553 (2007).

90. Studies by social psychologists indicate that people's intentions to act in particular ways (e.g., "I will report criminals if I see them") are consistently found to be strong predictors of their actual behavior. *See* Icek Ajzen, *From Intentions To Actions: A Theory Of Planned Behavior, in* ACTION CONTROL: FROM COGNITION TO BEHAVIOR 11, 21 (Julius Kuhl & Jurgen Beckmann eds., 1985) (demonstrating that intention is the strongest predictor of human behavior, where intention is an immediate antecedent of behavior, activated by a cognitive representation of readiness to perform the behavior). *See also* ICEK AJZEN & MARTIN FISHBEIN, UNDERSTANDING ATTITUDES AND PREDICTING SOCIAL BEHAVIOR 54–60 (1980) (showing that a person's behavior is determined by his/her intention to perform the behavior and that this intention is, in turn, a function of his/her attitude toward the behavior and his/her subjective norm); Blair H. Sheppard, Jon Hartwick & Paul R. Warshaw, *The Theory of Reasoned Action: A Meta-Analysis of Past Research with Recommendations for Modifications and Future Research*, 15 J. CONSUMER RES. 325 (1988).

91. *See* POPULATION DIVISION, NEW YORK CITY DEP'T OF CITY PLANNING, DEMOGRAPHIC PROFILE 1990–2000, *available at* http://www.nyc.gov/html/dcp/html/census/demo _profile.shtml.

92. This study was based on survey responses from residents of Oakland and Los Angeles who were asked questions about recent personal experiences with the police and the courts. The questions used had fixed response alternatives. The particular items used are included in the appendix and were generally drawn from this prior research. For details, see TYLER AND HUO, *supra* note 16.

93. TYLER & BLADER, COOPERATION, *supra* note 20.

94. *Id.*

||||||||||||||||||||||||||||||||||||||||||||||||||||||||||||||||||||||||||||

Chapter 5

Race and Policing in Different Ecological Contexts

Ronald Weitzer

A recent trend in policing research is its focus on ecological context. Demographic factors continue to be studied, but the literature is no longer confined to assessing the influence of individual-level variables on either officer behavior or citizens' perceptions of the police. Scholars are increasingly realizing that place matters. This chapter examines current knowledge regarding the effects of three different contexts—neighborhoods, cities, and nations. But before proceeding to that discussion, I briefly summarize findings on selected individual-level predictors.

Demographic Factors

Race/ethnicity is one of the strongest predictors of citizen attitudes and experiences with the police. Blacks and Latinos are more likely than whites to believe that the police mistreat people, are racially biased, lack accountability, and need reform. At the same time, most studies document significant differences between Latinos and African Americans. Latinos tend to take an intermediate position between whites and blacks, more critical of the police than whites but less critical than blacks. This pattern has been described as a "racial hierarchy" in contrast to a more cohesive "minority-group orientation."[1] At the same time, although racial hierarchy is evident on many specific policing issues, there are some areas where the two minority groups are largely in agreement.[2]

One problem with the category "Latino" or "Hispanic" is that it masks internal differences between subgroups along the lines of ancestry and immigrant versus native-born status. One might expect immigrants to differ from native-born citizens in their frame of reference: that is, conceptions of police in immigrants' home countries (often corrupt and repressive) may be imported into the new country, in contrast to more indigenous influences among the native-born population. Yet the immigrant-native variable has almost never been examined.[3] Similarly neglected is the impact of national origin.[4] A couple of surveys reported that Puerto Ricans were more critical of the police than other Hispanic groups. Puerto Ricans were significantly more dissatisfied with the police working in their community[5] and more likely than other

Hispanic groups to believe that the police often abuse people verbally and physically, stop people without good reason, and engage in corruption.[6] Why? Puerto Ricans have lower incomes and higher poverty rates than other Hispanic groups (except Dominicans), and this level of deprivation likely contributes to their more critical views of the police. But these findings only scratch the surface: much more research is needed comparing Hispanic subgroups' orientations toward the police.

How can we explain differences between minority groups in their relations with the police? Surprisingly, this question has not been addressed by scholars, for the simple reason that so much of the literature has centered on black-white differences and neglected differences between minority groups. I argue that the *mode of incorporation* into a society affects how a particular group is treated by, and reacts to, the police.[7] Minorities differ considerably in the degree to which they are politically, culturally, and economically integrated in any given society and in their historical treatment by major institutions. The mode-of-incorporation perspective highlights key differences in the historical trajectory and contemporary stratification of different groups. As Lawrence Bobo writes: "Among racial minority groups, the level of alienation [from major social institutions] would vary based on differences in the persistence, pervasiveness across domains of life, and extremity of inequality of life chances. This argument implies that members of more recent and voluntarily incorporated minority groups will feel less alienation than members of long-term and involuntarily incorporated minority groups."[8] This proposition can be applied to criminal justice institutions: "Latinos occupy a disadvantaged middle ground where they are a less comprehensive and intensive focus of criminalization efforts than African Americans, but more at risk than whites."[9] Asian Americans' appear to have an even less contentious relationship with the police than the other minority groups, which is largely consistent with their mode of incorporation into American society. But this conclusion must be regarded as tentative since there are so few studies including Asians and, again, we must be careful to disaggregate the Asian population by national origin and nativity.

The mode-of-incorporation thesis is situated at the macro-structural and historical level of analysis and, as such, is not intended as a complete explanation of police-minority relations, but it offers considerable insight into group-level patterns and is a useful counterbalance to micro-level, individual, and situational explanations. It can also be used to help explain cross-national differences in police relations with ethnic minorities, an argument developed in the final section of the chapter.

Age is a consistent predictor of both experiences with and attitudes toward the police. Young people are more likely than older cohorts to have contact, and more adversarial contact, with police officers,[10] and to harbor critical opinions of the police.[11] While this age cleavage exists across racial and ethnic groups, minority youth are especially vulnerable to unwanted attention from the police. It is thus no surprise that they view the police more critically than white youth.[12]

Gender is typically not a predictor in its own right, but does play a role as it intersects with race and age. In the few studies that include race-age-gender interactions, young black males are significantly more likely to report bad experiences with officers and to hold negative opinions of the police than their counterparts—young black women, young white men, and older black men.[13] This *triple-jeopardy* pattern is also apparent among young Latino men.[14]

Social class is less consistent. Class position makes little difference among whites, whereas for African Americans the results are quite mixed. Some studies detect no significant class differences in blacks' attitudes toward the police; some find more favorable attitudes among middle-class blacks than among lower-class blacks; and others find that middle-class blacks are more critical than disadvantaged blacks. These mixed findings may be a function of the kinds of policing issues examined in various studies. It is possible that race trumps class on certain issues, while class significantly affects views on other issues. If so, it is not a question of race versus class in the abstract but is instead issue-specific.

The ecological frame of reference seems to play a role with regard to the relative impact of race and class. If the context is policing in one's neighborhood, the evidence indicates that residents of disadvantaged areas are more likely to negatively evaluate police services (e.g., response time, crime prevention, treatment of crime victims, police misconduct) than residents of middle-class communities.[15] But if the frame of reference is broader, say, citizens' views of general policing patterns throughout the nation, middle-class blacks tend to hold more critical views than their disadvantaged counterparts.[16] Why would middle-class African Americans hold more critical views on these issues? There are several possible explanations. First, better-educated persons have greater exposure to the media, including news coverage of instances of police misconduct. Greater media exposure appears to affect middle-class blacks' assessments of the scope of such problems to a much greater degree than their less-educated counterparts.[17] Second, middle-class discontent with the police may be related to their experiences *outside* their residential neighborhoods, where they may be viewed by officers as "out of place"[18] and treated more negatively than in their own residential neighborhoods.[19] This may be coupled with a sense of relative deprivation for those whose class status is invisible to police officers and who are treated on the basis of their race instead.[20] Policing is not unique: middle-class blacks perceive greater racial discrimination in employment and housing as well.[21]

Much more research is needed regarding the intersection of race and class in relation to citizen views and experiences of the police. At present, relatively little is known about the policing of middle-class African Americans and Latinos, as well as poor whites. But there is one domain in which social class has received increasing attention—namely, the class configuration of residential neighborhoods.

Neighborhood Context

Important recent studies indicate that the effects of demographic characteristics are reduced, but not necessarily eliminated, once neighborhood context is factored into the equation.[22] In other words, in terms of police treatment of citizens, where one lives matters as much or more than individual characteristics, and mobility outside one's neighborhood is also an important variable. Why is neighborhood an important unit of analysis?

Police practices vary, at least to some extent, from one locale to another.[23] Such variations are shaped, in part, by ecological conditions such as crime and socioeconomic status. Affluent neighborhoods tend to have low levels of crime and street disorder and the police tend to see such areas as hospitable, whereas inner-city neighborhoods are often the sites of multiple problems, including poverty, unemployment, dilapidation, street crime, one-parent families, and transience. The concentration of such conditions translates into severe community disorganization, marked by weak ties among neighbors and a low collective capacity to deal with local problems. This is social disorganization theory in a nutshell.

Social disorganization theory has been faulted for neglecting the possible impact of formal social control (e.g., police practices) and other external forces on intra-neighborhood arrangements.[24] A comprehensive social disorganization model would incorporate such external factors to more fully account for patterns of crime and disorder at the community level. At the same time, we can examine the effects of policing, in its own right, on the experiences and attitudes of community residents. A combination of *depolicing and harsh policing* is often characteristic of disorganized, poor neighborhoods. On the one hand, the police approach to these neighborhoods tends to be marked by unresponsiveness to calls from residents, poor service when they arrive at a call, or general underenforcement of the law.[25] On the other hand, residents of these communities are often the targets of overly aggressive police behavior. The National Research Council's comprehensive review concluded that "disadvantaged and higher crime neighborhoods are more likely to receive punitive or enforcement-oriented policing."[26] Such areas are marked by higher rates of police corruption, physical abuse of residents, and unjustified or questionable street stops.[27]

If police practices vary across different types of communities, it is reasonable to expect residents' views of the police to reflect this, and the evidence shows that this is indeed the case.[28] First, residents of high-crime areas may blame the police for crime and disorder,[29] and demand more vigorous policing. A large number of blacks and Hispanics, especially those living in disadvantaged neighborhoods, feel that their communities receive insufficient police protection.[30] Weitzer and Tuch's national survey found that 85 percent of Hispanics and 88 percent of African Americans favored more police surveillance of high-crime areas, and a New York City poll reported that 66 percent of Hispanics and 72 percent of blacks supported the planned installation of four hundred surveillance cameras throughout the city to enhance crime control.[31] Second, residents of such communities complain about harsh practices, including physical and verbal abuse and unwarranted stops of pedestrians and motorists.[32] There is evidence that police who patrol such communities often behave indiscriminately in their treatment of people: this is the dynamic of "ecological contamination" whereby mere residence in a particular community becomes a liability for all residents.[33] In sum, residents of these communities are doubly frustrated with the police, resulting in demands for both *more robust and more sensitive* policing.

Aggressive or insensitive policing in high-crime, minority neighborhoods is not inevitable. Some areas are characterized by a very different policing style: community policing. Community policing can take several forms, including foot patrols, school programs, and meetings where residents and officers work collaboratively to identify and devise solutions for local problems. Community policing may be considered an important part of neighborhood context, particularly in high-crime, disadvantaged areas, where it is more salient than in low-crime areas. If community policing lives up to its promise as trumpeted by advocates, we should expect it to have positive effects. Some studies show that sustained community policing and collaborative problem-solving mechanisms can enhance crime prevention and help build residents' confidence in the police.[34] It can backfire, however, if it is imposed in a way that residents find disingenuous, suspicious, or intrusive.[35]

In addition to the style of policing in a neighborhood, police practices may also vary according to the racial composition and class position of an area. Some studies find that neighborhood socioeconomic status is a strong predictor of both police behavior and residents' attitudes toward the police. In a Chicago study, after controlling for neighborhood racial composition and violent crime, residents of impoverished areas were significantly more likely than residents of other areas to report that officers performed poorly in preventing crime and maintaining order on the streets, responded poorly to crime victims, and were not responsive to local issues.[36] Dissatisfaction with the amount or quality of police services was also found to be highest, net of other factors, in disadvantaged neighborhoods in other cities.[37] Findings from these studies, which measured objective neighborhood conditions, are mirrored in studies based on residents' perceptions of neighborhood conditions. Residents who perceive their community as disorderly or crime-ridden hold more negative views of the police.[38]

Qualitative studies lend support to the quantitative findings describe above, confirming the impact of neighborhood context on police-community relations, but they also deepen our understanding by documenting the meanings residents attach to policing in their community, the reasoning people use in evaluating the police, and the kinds of changes they want to see in police practices. These studies highlight residents' lived experiences, illustrating what it feels like to be on the receiving end of verbal abuse, excessive force, and unwarranted or repeated stops.[39] Such research can also document neighborhood-level "multiplier effects" of instances of police actions that are conveyed within local social networks—that is, tapping into the neighborhood culture. It appears that residents of different kinds of neighborhoods operate with different universes of meaning regarding the police, at least on some issues—meanings born of personal and vicarious experiences and observations of police practices.

One illustration of clashing meanings is the following finding: When asked whether being African American "usually makes a difference" in how a person is treated by the police in Washington DC, large percentages of blacks and whites living in three neighborhoods agreed. Yet, when asked *why* race made a difference, black respondents tended to cite police racism whereas four-fifths of whites invoked blacks' involvement in crime, which they believed justified police bias—that is, "rational discrimination." Whites concede that differential treatment exists but place the onus on blacks, whereas African Americans blame the police. This important difference would have been masked had only the quantitative finding been presented, that 71 percent of white respondents believed police treat members of different races differently.[40]

Compared to residents of disadvantaged areas, minorities who reside in middle-class communities appear to have better relations with the police. Although the literature is scarce, it appears that blacks and Hispanics who live in predominantly white, middle-class neighborhoods, in cities as well as suburbs, report more favorable personal experiences with and attitudes toward the police than do their counterparts living in disadvantaged neighborhoods. A study comparing a Midwestern city with its surrounding suburbs documented this pattern: both whites and blacks living in the suburbs viewed the police more favorably than whites and blacks in the city, and suburban blacks had higher opinions of the police than urban whites. The researchers conclude that "it is residential location rather than racial attributes that can best explain satisfaction with [police] performance."[41] Recent research on other cities reaches similar conclusions: In El Paso, Texas, both Hispanics and whites residing in poor neighborhoods were more likely than people living in middle-class neighborhoods to report having observed a range of police abuses.[42] In Chicago, middle-class blacks and Hispanics who resided in disadvantaged neighborhoods held more negative views of the police than their middle-class counterparts in advantaged communities.[43] Holding individual race and class constant, neighborhood socioeconomic context was a predictor. And in Lexington and Louisville, Kentucky, whites and blacks living in disadvantaged neighborhoods expressed similar levels of dissatisfaction with the police, whereas in economically advantaged areas, blacks were less likely than whites to hold favorable attitudes toward the police.[44] In each of these studies, neighborhood-class position trumps individual-race or -class status for at least one of the racial or ethnic groups studied.

In my Washington DC study, police-community relations in a black middle-class neighborhood were at least as positive as they were for residents of a white middle-class neighborhood.[45] But when residents of the black middle-class community traveled outside their neighborhood, they received much more negative treatment from officers. For one thing, they were 3.4 times more likely to be stopped outside their neighborhood than inside, whereas the difference was much narrower for middle-class whites and for lower-class blacks in the study. And when they were stopped outside their community, their class status was relatively invisible to officers. As a twenty-three-year old woman from the middle-class neighborhood (Merrifield) compared her treatment inside the neighborhood and outside it while driving through a poor area:

> I've seen police on 14th Street [a poor area] with this attitude. They come out hard at you, but they really don't know what you're about. They stopped me on 14th Street and they were talking horrible. Once I started talking to them, they was like, "Oh, okay. It's not another person off the street." . . . I think they see [Merrifield] as a middle-class neighborhood . . . middle-class nuclear families, so they're more apt to be calmer. . . . If I lived on 14th Street they would deal with me harshly. . . . Not knowing me, just seeing me over there, I'd be treated differently until they got to [speak with] me.[46]

Similarly, Merrifield residents who had experienced or witnessed verbal or physical abuse by police officers reported that this largely occurred outside Merrifield in other parts of Washington DC.

These studies suggest that—in addition to crime rates and policing styles—a neighborhood's socioeconomic position may be a critical variable in terms of both police practices and police-community relations, perhaps trumping racial composition. Further research will help to clarify the role of neighborhood class versus racial configuration in relation to policing. What the existing literature does show is that neighborhood conditions are important predictors, over and above individual-level characteristics.

City Context

Do police-citizen relations also vary across cities? Surprisingly little comparative research has been done on policing at the city level. By this, I mean analysis of either variation *among cities* or variation on *city-level factors* that might affect policing. Most research is confined to a single-city or the nation as a whole. Yet there remain good reasons to expect cities to vary and to expect city-level variables to shape citizen assessments of the police. The question is twofold: Do city-level conditions affect (1) police practices and (2) residents' experiences and perceptions of the police—net of the effects of other variables? As it turns out, it is much easier to pose this question than to answer it, because of the tricky issue of identifying the proper variables to be measured. Below, I highlight some potentially important predictors.

Some classic studies by James Q. Wilson, Lawrence Sherman, and others demonstrate that policing policies, styles, and practices differ by city. Cities have distinctive historical legacies of policing, unique records of contentious events involving the police (e.g., riots, police killings, corruption scandals), and at least somewhat different police organization, policies, and leadership styles.[47] Such variables arguably affect differences in overall police-citizen relations from city to city. Yet surprisingly few comparative, multi-city studies examine these relations.[48]

There are additional city-level variables that may influence popular evaluations of the police. Conflict theory highlights certain macro-level conditions in shaping both social control practices and citizen evaluation of state institutions. In terms of social control, class-based conflict theory holds that "the more economically stratified a society becomes, the more it becomes necessary for dominant groups in society to enforce through coercion the norms of conduct which guarantee their supremacy."[49] The police are the premier institution in this coercive enterprise. At the city level, both absolute deprivation (poverty, unemployment, etc.) and relative deprivation (income inequality) may play a role in structuring residents' relations with the police. Economic distress may generate (1) an unstable situation conducive to intensified police control and (2) strains in police relations with disadvantaged residents. With regard to the first potential outcome, economic inequality in a city does appear to condition enhanced formal control, based on studies identifying inequality as a predictor of police force size[50] and killings of civilians.[51] Higher levels of inequality within a population are associated with a higher per capita number of police officers and a higher incidence of police killings.

Race-based conflict theory focuses on racial structures rather than aggregate economic patterns. A city's racial composition is one dimension of this structure. According to the "minority threat" thesis, the magnitude of formal control is related to the perceived threat that minority groups present to the dominant group in the city:[52] a large minority population elevates whites' fear of crime,[53] which generates more robust control over the minority. Although some studies report that black population size is not a predictor of formal control,[54] support for this thesis is found in several other studies. The larger the percentage of blacks in a city, the higher the per capita size of the police force,[55] expenditure on the police,[56] arrest rates,[57] and frequency of police killings of blacks.[58] These outcomes have been interpreted as indicators of heightened control over the black population.

A large or growing Hispanic population in a city might also be viewed as a threat by the dominant, white population, though the racial hierarchy thesis (described above) would predict that a sizeable Hispanic population would be perceived as less threatening than a large African American population. One study advanced this Hispanic-threat explanation for the association between police misconduct incidents and neighborhoods with large numbers of Hispanics, and this relationship can plausibly be extrapolated to the city level as well.[59] Another study, of 245 cities, reported an intriguing finding: An increase in the Hispanic population resulted in a decrease in the level of arrests of blacks, though the authors did not examine whether this was also associated with higher arrest rates for Hispanics.[60]

An assumption in the minority-threat literature is that demands for law and order emanate from the white majority population. An alternative and quite plausible explanation, not tested in these studies, is that the minority population itself may demand intensified social control. Data presented above show that a substantial majority of blacks and Hispanics desire robust law enforcement and crime control, so this interest is hardly unique to whites. At police-community meetings that I have attended in Washington DC, African Americans have been the most vocal in demanding more police patrols and proactive measures to fight crime, and this appears to be the case in other cities as well.[61] Especially in places where the minority population is sizeable, it may have significant political clout and capacity to pressure the authorities for changes, resulting in additional police resources or interventions in high-crime neighborhoods.[62] This minority-demand explanation stands in contrast to the minority-threat thesis, although the two are not mutually exclusive: the white majority may perceive a sizeable minority population as a threat, while both the majority and minority population call for intensified policing.

In cities with a large proportion of minority residents, this may also influence minority views of criminal justice institutions. A large minority population may increase members' exposure to others' (often critical) narratives about the police. A city where, say, two-thirds of the population is Hispanic (e.g., Miami, Florida) or African American (e.g., Albany, Georgia) might be expected to have a higher net level of ingroup dialogue regarding the police than a city with a small minority population and perhaps lacking a critical mass of residents who have had bad or cumulative experiences with local police officers. One study found that "an increase in the number of blacks in the neighborhood increases the opportunity for blacks to associate with others who have negative attitudes toward the police, and this results in an overall increase in their negative sentiment toward the police."[63] The study focused on neighborhood-level patterns, but the composition → association → discontent pattern may also operate, and even be magnified, at the city level.

To complicate matters, the effect of a city's racial composition may be affected by patterns of racial segregation. In other words, it may not be simply a matter of the size of the minority population but also its spatial proximity to or isolation from the white population that affects the amount of police control over the minority population. The segregation of minorities into urban ghettos may function as an informal mechanism of control, limiting their mobility and insulating whites from black crime.[64] Some studies report that residential segregation increased rates of intra-racial victimization but decreased inter-racial victimization.[65] Insulation from black crime may, in turn, reduce whites' demands for intensified formal control citywide. In cities with high racial segregation, "declines in white victimization [by blacks] should alleviate white pressure on political authorities to do something about crimes committed by blacks."[66] Relatively low racial segregation, by contrast, may increase whites' threat perception, thus generating more robust crime control. Support for this argument is reported in studies finding an association between higher levels of racial segregation and smaller police forces per capita[67] and lower arrest rates of blacks,[68] independent of crime rates.

Racial segregation may generate institutionalized police practices but may also indirectly influence residents' opinions of the police. If residential segregation decreases mobility and helps to contain crime in African American neighborhoods, and if police are evaluated in terms of their record in crime control, whites' approval of the police may be elevated in cities with high residential segregation. The effect of segregation on African Americans' opinions of the police may be more complex, however. If police under-enforce the law in residentially isolated black neighborhoods because crimes in such communities do not threaten those living elsewhere in the city (as suggested in the studies cited above), this may have *either* a positive or negative effect on the residents' attitudes toward the police: For those who want more intensive police patrolling and crime control, the depolicing associated with higher segregation would increase dissatisfaction with the city's police. For those who feel that officers frequently mistreat local residents or who have a generally unfavorable view of the police department, a diminished police presence in their neighborhood may be greeted with relief. The under-policing associated with segregation may not improve these residents' views of the police but it may temper their disapproval. The presence of *both* of these perspectives has been documented among residents of disadvantaged black neighborhoods.[69] In the context of these dual orientations, segregation (and its potential corollary, depolicing) may have a mixed effect on residents' opinions of the police. The dual orientations may cancel out and erase any discernable aggregate effect of high segregation on residents' attitudes toward the police. Researchers have yet to explore this question.

Another city-level variable that might be salient is the racial composition of a police department. Since the 1960s, a consensus has emerged among political leaders and police executives that racial diversification will lead to more impartial law enforcement and improved police relations with minority citizens, and a majority

TABLE 5.1
Percent African American, Selected Cities and Police Departments, 2000

	City	Police Department
Gary, IN	84%	59%
Detroit, MI	81	63
Birmingham, AL	73	55
Jackson, MS	70	70
Albany, GA	65	51
Atlanta, GA	61	57
Washington, DC	59	66

Percent Hispanic, Selected Cities and Police Departments, 2000

	City	Police Department
Laredo, TX	94%	98%
Brownsville, TX	91	82
El Paso, TX	77	72
Miami, FL	66	54

Sources: U.S. Census, 2000; Bureau of Justice Statistics, Law Enforcement Management, and Administrative Statistics, 2000.

of the American public agrees that diversification is a laudable goal.[70] Sherman hypothesized that "a department with more black officers behaves differently from a department with fewer black officers. As blacks comprise a larger portion of a police department, they may become less isolated and more influential in shaping the values and culture of the entire police department,"[71] potentially improving both police behavior and citizen perceptions of the police. If this hypothesis is true, we might expect majority-black, and majority-Hispanic, police departments to have a different orientation to the public than majority-white departments, all else being constant. Table 5.1 lists a number of cities where the majority of the population and police department is black or Hispanic. Police-citizen relations in these kinds of cities have only rarely been studied.[72]

Some older multicity studies explored the police composition question. Research on fourteen cities in 1968[73] and thirteen cities in 1975[74] found that cities with higher black representation on the police force were somewhat more likely to be associated with more positive views of the police among African Americans than in cities with lower black representation. However, the two studies were limited in several respects (1) all of the police departments were majority-white in composition, (2) the samples of cities were not designed to incorporate or control for other potentially important variables, and (3) the dependent variable was limited to a single item: police job performance or overall satisfaction with the police department. A recent multicity study found that police killings of civilians were not related to the ratio of Hispanic citizens to Hispanic officers or black citizens to black officers, but this study also neglected to include several potentially key city-level variables.[75] While the three studies are suggestive, more comparative research of this kind is needed to determine whether police diversification is a predictor.

Does the race of the mayor and police chief make a difference? It is possible that African American or Latino mayors and police chiefs have a positive symbolic effect on public opinion and/or constraining effect on police misconduct. Two multicity studies found that cities with black mayors featured greater institutional control over police officers[76] and lower rates of police killings of blacks[77] than cities with white mayors, and similar patterns may be associated with black police chiefs.

Highly publicized incidents of police misconduct that attract media coverage can dramatically shake citizens' confidence in a city's police department. This has been documented after controversial beatings and killings in New York City (involving Abner Louima, Amadou Diallo, and Patrick Dorismond) and in Los Angeles (after a 1979 killing of Eula Love and the 1991 Rodney King beating). Each incident was followed by a spike in unfavorable ratings of the police department.[78] After the Rodney King beating, for example, African American and Latino approval of the LAPD dropped a stunning fifty percentage points—from 64 to 14 percent among blacks, and from 80 to 31 percent among Latinos—and forty-three percentage points among white residents of Los Angeles.[79] Post-incident erosion of public confidence has been documented in other cities as well.[80] Following a videotaped and televised brutality incident in Cincinnati, the public was less likely to express favorable attitudes regarding both police use of force and other aspects of their job performance.[81]

In addition to specific incidents, public trust in the police may be affected by problems that receive protracted media coverage, such as an unfolding corruption scandal. This was evident during in the successive revelations of widespread corruption in the Rampart Division of the Los Angeles Police Department in 1999–2000. Officers were accused of stealing drugs from suspects, falsifying reports, framing people for crimes, perjury in court, and shooting unarmed suspects. Given that about seventy officers were implicated in these crimes, it is not surprising that fully 79 percent of blacks, 52 percent of Hispanics, and 42 percent of whites in Los Angeles thought that this wrongdoing was "symptomatic of a larger problem within the police department," while only a small minority of blacks and Hispanics believed that the offenses were "isolated incidents and not representative of the LAPD as a whole." The poll, taken at the height of the scandal, also reported that 90 percent of the city's residents thought that the scandal had "damaged the reputation" of the LAPD.[82] Overall approval of the LAPD fell dramatically between March 1999 (just prior to the story breaking) and April 2000—a full twenty-three percentage points for Latinos, and thirty points for African Americans.[83]

The effect of protracted media coverage was also examined in an Indianapolis study. Residents who reported high media consumption—during the course of a trial of officers accused of beating two citizens—were more likely to believe the officers were guilty, net of other factors.[84] A national survey tapped even longer-term exposure to media reporting on controversial policing events. Respondents were asked how often they "hear or read about (on the radio, television, or in the newspapers) incidents of police misconduct, such as police use of excessive force, verbal abuse, corruption, and so on." The greater the exposure to such reports, the lower the satisfaction with the police on a variety of issues (i.e., perceptions of four types of misconduct and four types of racially biased policing) and the greater the demand for a host of reforms in policing.[85] This finding suggests that public confidence in a police department is shaken not just by isolated incidents but also by long-term exposure to reports concerning misconduct.

It goes without saying that media coverage of events is not the sole predictor of post-incident changes in public opinion, yet the often-dramatic surge in unfavorable opinion in the wake of highly publicized events suggests that such incidents do indeed shake public confidence in the police. This factor should be included in city-level models. Research on the impact of urban contextual conditions would be limited if focused exclusively on socioeconomic and racial structures without also incorporating measures related to police practices that attract media coverage and are likely to independently affect popular confidence in the authorities.

National Context

There are very few systematic comparisons of police-minority relations in two or more nations.[86] Of course, comparing entire societies is fraught with problems, especially if there is significant internal variation within a society. But I would argue that it is nevertheless important to at least consider whether, and how, national context may impact the treatment of racial and ethnic minorities. Societies vary tremendously, and their police forces do as well. Examples of the kind of systematic, cross-national comparative analysis that I have in mind, though not centered on police-minority relations, would be David Bayley's study of Japan and America and Mercedes Hinton's study of Argentina and Brazil.[87]

Almost all of the literature is devoted to case studies of a single nation. What is clear from the case studies is that some types of societies are characterized by *extreme discord* between the police and ethnic minority groups. In some, the rift is so great that the police enjoy little or no legitimacy from the subordinate ethnic groups, who are estranged from all state institutions. These patterns are evident in "deeply divided societies" distinguished by a high degree of polarization along ethnic, racial, or religious lines, and a social control apparatus that is an instrument of the dominant ethnic group.[88] In divided societies, citizens' orientations toward the police are heavily shaped by their *loyalty to or estrangement from the state*. Examples include contemporary Iraq, the former Yugoslavia, British-ruled Northern Ireland, and white-ruled South Africa, Rhodesia, and Namibia.[89] Some of these cases featured armed conflict along ethnic lines, but others experienced long periods of relative stability —such as Rhodesia, Namibia, and South Africa prior to the outbreak of armed insurgency in the 1970s. Israel fits into the divided society model in some respects, but Israeli-Arab citizens are less alienated from the police than their counterparts in the societies mentioned above as well as in Gaza and the West Bank.[90]

In other words, what the police *represent politically* is important in shaping citizen orientations to the police. In divided societies, the symbolic status of the police, as a pillar of state domination over the subordinate ethnic group, is crucial. Insofar as the minority views the state and police as illegitimate and opposed to their interests, a substantial share of police resources will be devoted to preempting or repressing minority resistance. These cases demonstrate just how bad police-citizen relations can be, marked by a deep, unbridgeable gulf between state authorities and the subordinate ethnic population.[91]

The importance of the state is not confined to ethnically polarized societies. Citizens' orientations to the state are also crucial in nations where ethnic divisions are muted but where the entire population lacks confidence in the state. One study of nine nations in Latin America, for instance, found that citizens' trust in the political system (parliament, military, civil service, legal system, political parties) was the most robust predictor (among many other variables) of confidence in the police: the lower the level of trust in state institutions, the lower the confidence in the police.[92] The state may play the opposite role in more integrated, democratic societies, where it enjoys diffuse legitimacy and is not an object of fundamental contention.[93] Diffuse popular support for these political systems appears to have a positive spillover effect on citizens' support for the police.

Earlier in this chapter I argued that the mode of incorporation into a society influences how different minority groups are treated by, and react to, the police. A mode-of-incorporation framework can be usefully applied cross-nationally as well. Types of incorporation include assimilation, ethnic segmentation, multiculturalism, and vertical integration.[94] There is no need to describe these modes at length here, but it is important to identify the key ingredients shaping the different types. For an ethnic minority, the central variables include both historical and contemporary arrangements: (1) voluntariness of initial incorporation, (2) socioeconomic status, (3) ethnocultural orientation, (4) population size, and (5) political power—each in relation to that of the dominant ethnic group. In other words, it is the *group's* position vis-à-vis the dominant group, over and above individual or situational factors, that plays an important role in citizen orientations to the police at the macro level.

Weitzer and Tuch have applied the group-position thesis to the United States,[95] but it is equally germane to other multiethnic societies. For example, Muslims and Africans in some Western nations typically experience greater structural and cultural marginality and more tenuous relations with the police than either the dominant group or other minority ethnic groups in these societies (e.g., southern Europeans in the Netherlands or Belgium). These patterns have been documented in research on Moroccans, Turks, Algerians, Albanians, Pakistanis, and other immigrant groups in Belgium, France, Holland, and Germany, but these studies are just the tip of the iceberg, and they are typically confined to single-case studies rather than multi-nation comparisons.[96] One of the few comparative studies found that the Roma minority in Bulgaria, Hungary, and Spain experienced ethnic profiling—being stopped by the police more often than members of the dominant ethnic population and reporting more negative treatment during stops.[97] Much more research is needed comparing, for instance, Moroccans in Belgium and the Netherlands, Algerians in France, and Pakistanis in Britain in terms of their views of the police and their deeper orientation to the state.

Space limitations prevent a full elaboration of the ways in which nations might differ in the relationship of the police and ethnic and racial minorities, but I have sketched a framework for doing so. As indicated above, systematic, comparative analyses of two or more nations are few and far between in the policing literature, and much remains to be learned about the national-level causes and consequences of diverse patterns of police treatment of minority group members and the latter's perceptions of the police.

NOTES

1. Weitzer and Tuch, *Race and Policing in America.*
2. Weitzer and Tuch, *Race and Policing in America.*
3. An exception is Cheurprakobkit and Bartsch, "Police Work."
4. For a comparison of black Hispanics and white Hispanics, see Rice, Reitzel, and Piquero, "Shades of Brown."
5. Kaiser Foundation poll.
6. Weitzer and Tuch, *Race and Policing in America*, p. 52.
7. Alexander, "Theorizing the Modes of Incorporation."
8. Bobo, "Prejudice as Group Position," p. 461.
9. Hagan, Shedd, and Payne, "Race, Ethnicity, and Youth," p. 384.
10. Hurst, Frank, and Browning, "The Attitudes of Juveniles"; Leiber, Nalla, and Farnworth, "Explaining Juveniles' Attitudes."
11. Brown and Benedict, "Perceptions of the Police"; Brunson, "Police Don't Like Black People."
12. Taylor et al., "Coppin' an Attitude."
13. Skogan, "Asymmetry in the Impact"; Weitzer and Tuch, *Race and Policing in America.*
14. Weitzer and Tuch, *Race and Policing in America.*
15. Reisig and Parks, "Experience, Quality of Life"; Sampson and Bartusch, "Legal Cynicism"; Velez, "Role of Public Social Control"; Weitzer, "Citizens' Perceptions of Police Misconduct"; Weitzer, "Racialized Policing."
16. Weitzer and Tuch, "Race, Class, and Perceptions of Discrimination"; Weitzer and Tuch, "Perceptions of Racial Profiling"; Wortley, Hagan, and Macmillan, "Just Deserts?"
17. Wortley, Hagan, and Macmillan, "Just Deserts?"
18. Meehan and Ponder, "Race and Place"; Alpert, MacDonald, and Dunham, "Police Suspicion."
19. Weitzer, "Citizens' Perceptions of Police Misconduct."
20. Brooks and Jeon-Slaughter, "Race, Income, and Perceptions"; Weitzer and Tuch, "Perceptions of Racial Profiling."
21. Hochschild, *Facing Up to the American Dream*; Schuman et al., *Racial Attitudes in America.*
22. Reisig and Parks, "Experience, Quality of Life"; Sampson and Bartusch, "Legal Cynicism"; Schafer, Huebner, and Bynum, "Citizen Perceptions of Police Services"; MacDonald et al., "Race, Neighborhood Context, and Perceptions."
23. Klinger, "Negotiating Order in Police Work"; Smith, "Neighborhood Context of Police Behavior."
24. Kubrin and Weitzer, "New Directions in Social Disorganization Theory."
25. Klinger, "Negotiating Order in Police Work."
26. National Research Council, *Fairness and Effectiveness in Policing*, p. 189.
27. Alpert, MacDonald, and Dunham, "Police Suspicion"; Fagan and Davies, "Street Stops and Broken Windows"; Gelman, Fagan, and Kiss, "Analysis of the New York City"; Kane, "Social Ecology of Police Misconduct"; Mastrofski, Reisig, and McCluskey, "Police Disrespect Toward

the Public"; Mollen Commission, *Report of the Commission*; Smith, "Neighborhood Context of Police Behavior"; Terrill and Reisig, "Neighborhood Context and Police Use of Force."

28. RAND, *Police-Community Relations in Cincinnati*; Reisig and Parks, "Experience, Quality of Life"; Sampson and Bartusch, "Legal Cynicism"; Velez, "Role of Public Social Control."

29. Cao, Frank, and Cullen, "Race, Community Context, and Confidence," p. 13.

30. Velez, "Role of Public Social Control"; Weitzer and Tuch, *Race and Policing in America*.

31. Weitzer and Tuch, *Race and Policing in America*, p. 14; Quinnipiac, "New Yorkers Approve of NYPD."

32. Weitzer and Tuch, *Race and Policing in America*.

33. Smith, "Neighborhood Context of Police Behavior."

34. Reisig and Parks, "Experience, Quality of Life"; Skogan, *Police and Community in Chicago*; Terrill and Mastrofski, "Working the Street"; Weitzer and Tuch, *Race and Policing in America*.

35. Grinc, "Angels in Marble"; Williams, *Citizen Perspectives on Community Policing*; Weitzer, *Policing Under Fire*.

36. Sampson and Bartusch, "Legal Cynicism."

37. Reisig and Parks, "Experience, Quality of Life"; Schafer, Huebner, and Bynum, "Citizen Perceptions of Police Services"; Velez, "Role of Public Social Control."

38. Cao, Frank, and Cullen, "Race, Community Context, and Confidence"; Jesilow, Meyer, and Namazzi, "Public Attitudes Toward the Police"; MacDonald et al., "Race, Neighborhood Context, and Perceptions"; Skogan, "Asymmetry in the Impact"; Xu, Fiedler, and Flaming, "Discovering the Impact of Community Policing."

39. Brunson, "Police Don't Like Black People"; Weitzer and Brunson, "Strategic Responses to the Police"; Sharp and Atherton, "To Serve and Protect?"; Weitzer, *Policing Under Fire*; Weitzer, "Citizens' Perceptions of Police Misconduct"; Weitzer, "Racialized Policing"; Weitzer and Tuch, *Race and Policing in America*.

40. Weitzer, "Racialized Policing," pp. 135–137.

41. Kusow, Wilson, and Martin, "Determinants of Citizen Satisfaction," p. 663.

42. Holmes, "Perceptions of Abusive Police Practices."

43. Schuck, Rosenbaum, and Hawkins, "Influence of Race/Ethnicity, Social Class, and Neighborhood."

44. Wu, Sun, and Triplett, "Race, Class, or Neighborhood Context."

45. Weitzer, "Citizens' Perceptions of Police Misconduct"; Weitzer, "Racialized Policing."

46. Quoted in Weitzer, "Citizens' Perceptions of Police Misconduct," p. 842.

47. Wilson, *Varieties of Police Behavior*; Sherman, *Scandal and Reform*; Skolnick and Bayley, *New Blue Line*; see also Human Rights Watch, *Shielded from Justice*.

48. An exception is Skogan, "Asymmetry in the Impact."

49. Chambliss and Seidman, *Law, Order, and Power*, p. 33.

50. Jacobs, "Inequality and Police Strength."

51. Jacobs and Britt, "Inequality and Police Use of Deadly Force"; Jacobs and O'Brien, "Determinants of Deadly Force"; Sorenson, Marquart, and Brock, "Factors Related to Killings of Felons."

52. Blalock, *Theory of Minority-Group Relations*.

53. Jackson, *Minority Group Threat*; Chiricos, Hogan, and Gertz, "Racial Composition and Neighborhood Fear"; Liska, Lawrence, and Benson, "Perspectives on the Legal Order."

54. Parker, Stults, and Rice, "Racial Threat."

55. Liska, Lawrence, and Benson, "Perspectives on the Legal Order."

56. Jackson, *Minority Group Threat*.

57. Liska, Chamlin, and Reed, "Testing the Economic Production Model."

58. Jacobs and O'Brien, "The Determinants of Deadly Force"; Liska and Yu, "Specifying and Testing the Threat Hypothesis"; Smith, "Impact of Police Officer Diversity."

59. Kane, "Social Ecology of Police Misconduct."

60. Parker, Stults, and Rice, "Racial Threat."

61. For Chicago, see Skogan, *Police and Community in Chicago.*

62. Kane, "Social Control in the Metropolis."

63. Apple and O'Brien, "Neighborhood Racial Composition," p. 83.

64. Blalock, *Theory of Minority-Group Relations.* This effect is also evident in other highly segregated societies, such as Israel (Hasisi and Weitzer, "Police Relations with Arabs and Jews in Israel").

65. Messner and South, "Economic Deprivation, Opportunity Structure"; South and Felson, "Racial Patterning of Rape."

66. Kent and Jacobs, "Minority Threat and Police Strength," p. 736.

67. Liska, Lawrence, and Benson, "Perspectives on the Legal Order"; Kent and Jacobs, "Minority Threat and Police Strength." Some studies, however, report no segregation effect, such as Stults and Baumer, "Racial Context and Police Force Size."

68. Liska and Chamlin, "Social Structure and Crime Control"; Liska, Chamlin, and Reed, "Testing the Economic Production Model"; Stolzenberg, D'Allesio, and Eitle, "A Multilevel Test of Racial Threat Theory." A contrary finding is reported in Parker, Stults, and Rice, "Racial Threat."

69. Anderson, *Code of the Street*; Block, "Support for Civil Liberties"; Weitzer and Tuch, *Race and Policing in America*, p. 14.

70. Weitzer and Tuch, *Race and Policing in America*, chaps. 3 and 4.

71. Sherman, "After the Riots," p. 221.

72. Exceptions include Frank et al., "Reassessing the Impact of Race"; Howell, Perry, and Vile, "Black Cities, White Cities"; Murty, Roebuck, and Smith, "Image of the Police"; Weitzer, "White, Black, or Blue Cops?"; Weitzer, Tuch, and Skogan, "Police-Community Relations in a Majority-Black City"; Welch et al., *Race and Place.*

73. Decker and Smith, "Police Minority Recruitment."

74. Skogan, "Citizen Satisfaction with Police Services."

75. Smith, "Impact of Police Officer Diversity."

76. Saltzstein, "Black Mayors and Police Policies."

77. Jacobs and O'Brien, "Determinants of Deadly Force."

78. Weitzer, "Incidents of Police Misconduct."

79. Weitzer, "Incidents of Police Misconduct," p. 399.

80. Sigelman et al., "Police Brutality and Public Perceptions."

81. Kaminski and Jefferis, "Effect of a Violent Televised Arrest."

82. *Los Angeles Times* poll, unpublished, April 2000.

83. Weitzer, "Incidents of Police Misconduct," p. 400.

84. Chermak, McGarrell, and Gruenewald, "Media Coverage of Police Misconduct."

85. Weitzer and Tuch, *Race and Policing in America.*

86. Antonopoulos, "Ethnic and Racial Minorities and the Police"; Jackson and Lyon, "Policing After Ethnic Conflict."

87. Bayley, *Forces of Order*; Hinton, *The State on the Streets.*

88. Weitzer, "Policing a Divided Society"; Weitzer, *Policing Under Fire.*

89. Enloe, *Ethnic Soldiers*; Weitzer, *Transforming Settler States*; Ellison and Smyth, *The Crowned Harp.*

90. Hasisi and Weitzer, "Police Relations with Arabs and Jews in Israel"; Milton-Edwards, "Policing Palestinian Society."

91. Ethnically divided societies are not the only contexts where citizens are deeply alienated from the police. Estrangement is also evident in societies where the police have a predatory relationship with the public at large, as opposed to a particular ethnic or racial group. Such predatory policing is evident in many nations, including those with and without major ethnic or racial cleavages (Goldsmith, "Police Reform and the Problem of Trust"; Goldsmith, "Policing Weak States"; Hinton, *State on the Streets*; Marenin, "Police Performance and State Rule"; Gerber and Mendelson, "Public Experiences").

92. Cao and Zhao, "Confidence in the Police in Latin America."

93. Goldsmith, "Police Reform and the Problem of Trust"; Marenin, "Police Performance and State Rule."

94. Alexander, "Theorizing the Modes of Incorporation."

95. Weitzer and Tuch, *Race and Policing in America*.

96. Hebberecht, "Minorities, Crime, and Criminal Justice"; Hutterman, "Policing an Ethnically Divided Neighborhood"; Junger, "Studying Ethnic Minorities"; Vrij and Winkel, "Encounters Between Dutch Police and Minorities."

97. Miller, "I Can Stop and Search."

REFERENCES

Alexander, Jeffrey. 2001. Theorizing the modes of incorporation. *Sociological Theory* 19: 237–249.

Alpert, Geoffrey, John MacDonald, and Roger Dunham. 2005. Police suspicion and discretionary decision making during citizen stops. *Criminology* 43: 407–434.

Anderson, Elijah. 1999. *Code of the street*. New York: Norton.

Antonopoulos, Georgios. 2003. Ethnic and racial minorities and the police: A review of the literature. *Police Journal* 76: 222–245.

Apple, Nancy, and David O'Brien. 1983. Neighborhood racial composition and residents' evaluation of police performance. *Journal of Police Science and Administration* 11: 76–83.

Bayley, David. 1976. *Forces of order: Police behavior in Japan and the United States*. Berkeley and Los Angeles: University of California Press.

Blalock, Herbert. 1967. *Toward a theory of minority-group relations*. New York: John Wiley.

Block, Richard. 1970. Support for civil liberties and support for the police. *American Behavioral Scientist* 13: 781–796.

Bobo, Lawrence. 1999. Prejudice as group position. *Journal of Social Issues* 55: 445–472.

Brooks, Richard, and Haekyung Jeon-Slaughter. 2001. Race, income, and perceptions of the U.S. court system. *Behavioral Sciences and the Law* 19: 249–264.

Brown, Ben, and William Reed Benedict. 2002. Perceptions of the police. *Policing* 25: 543–580.

Brunson, Rod. 2007. "Police don't like black people": African American young men's accumulated police experiences. *Criminology and Public Policy* 6: 71–102.

Cao, Liqun, and Jihong Zhao. 2005. Confidence in the police in Latin America. *Journal of Criminal Justice* 33: 403–412.

Cao, Liqun, James Frank, and Francis Cullen. 1996. Race, community context, and confidence in the police. *American Journal of Police* 15: 3–21.

Chambliss, William, and Robert Seidman. 1971. *Law, order, and power*. Reading: Addison-Wesley.

Chermak, Steven, Edmund McGarrell, and Jeff Gruenewald. 2006. Media coverage of police misconduct and attitudes toward police. *Policing* 29: 261–281.

Cheurprakobkit, Sutham, and Robert Bartsch. 1999. Police work and the police profession: Assessing the attitudes of city officials, Spanish-speaking Hispanics, and their English-speaking counterparts. *Journal of Criminal Justice* 27: 87–100.

Chiricos, Ted, Michael Hogan, and Marc Gertz. 1997. Racial composition and neighborhood fear of crime. *Criminology* 35: 107–131.

Decker, Scott, and Russell Smith. 1980. Police minority recruitment. *Journal of Criminal Justice* 8: 387–393.

Ellison, Graham, and Jim Smyth. 2000. *The Crowned Harp: Policing Northern Ireland*. London: Pluto.

Enloe, Cynthia. 1980. *Ethnic Soldiers: State Security in Divided Societies*. Athens: University of Georgia Press.

Fagan, Jeffrey, and Garth Davies. 2000. Street stops and broken windows: *Terry*, race, and disorder in New York City. *Fordham Urban Law Journal* 28: 457–504.

Frank, James, Steven Brandl, Francis Cullen, and Amy Stichman. 1996. Reassessing the impact of race on citizens' attitudes toward the police. *Justice Quarterly* 13: 321–334.

Gelman, Andrew, Jeffrey Fagan, and Alex Kiss. 2007. An analysis of the New York City police department's "stop-and-frisk" policy in the context of claims of racial bias. *Journal of the American Statistical Association* 102: 813–823.

Gerber, Theodore, and Sarah Mendelson. 2008. Public experiences of police violence and corruption in contemporary Russia. *Law and Society Review* 42: 1–43.

Goldsmith, Andrew. 2003. Policing weak states. *Policing and Society* 13: 3–21.

———. 2005. Police reform and the problem of trust. *Theoretical Criminology* 9: 443–470.

Grinc, Randolph. 1994. Angels in marble: Problems in stimulating community involvement in community policing. *Crime and Delinquency* 40: 437–468.

Hagan, John, Carla Shedd, and Monique Payne. 2005. Race, ethnicity, and youth perceptions of criminal injustice. *American Sociological Review* 70: 381–407.

Hasisi, Badi, and Ronald Weitzer. 2007. Police relations with Arabs and Jews in Israel. *British Journal of Criminology* 47: 728–745.

Hebberecht, Patrick. 1997. Minorities, crime, and criminal justice in Belgium. In I. H. Marshall (ed.), *Minorities, migrants, and crime: Diversity and similarity across Europe and the United States*. London: Sage.

Hinton, Mercedes. 2006. *The state on the streets: Police and politics in Argentina and Brazil*. Boulder, CO: Lynne Rienner.

Hochschild, Jennifer. 1995. *Facing up to the American Dream: Race, class, and the souls of the nation*. Princeton: Princeton University Press.

Holmes, Malcolm. 1998. Perceptions of abusive police practices in a U.S.-Mexican border community. *Social Science Journal* 35: 107–118.

Howell, Susan, Huey Perry, and Matthew Vile. 2004. Black cities, white cities: Evaluating the police. *Political Behavior* 26: 45–68.

Human Rights Watch. 1998. *Shielded from justice: Police brutality and accountability in the United States*. New York: Human Rights Watch.

Hurst, Yolander, James Frank, and Sandra Browning. 2000. The attitudes of juveniles toward the police. *Policing* 23: 37–53.

Hutterman, Jorg. 2003. Policing an ethnically divided neighborhood in Germany. *Policing and Society* 13: 381–397.

Jackson, Arrick, and Alynna Lyon. 2002. Policing after ethnic conflict. *Policing* 25: 221–241.

Jackson, Pamela Irving. 1989. *Minority group threat, crime, and policing.* New York: Praeger.

Jacobs, David. 1979. Inequality and police strength: Conflict theory and social control in metropolitan areas. *American Sociological Review* 44: 913–925.

Jacobs, David, and David Britt. 1979. Inequality and police use of deadly force. *Social Problems* 26: 403–412.

Jacobs, David, and Robert O'Brien. 1998. The determinants of deadly force: A structural analysis of police violence. *American Journal of Sociology* 103: 837–862.

Jesilow, Paul, J'ona Meyer, and Nazi Namazzi. 1995. Public attitudes toward the police. *American Journal of Police* 14: 67–88.

Junger, Marianne. 1990. Studying ethnic minorities in relation to crime and police discrimination. *British Journal of Criminology* 30: 493–502.

Kaiser Foundation. 2000. Kaiser/*Washington Post*/Harvard University poll, May 2000.

Kaminski, Robert, and Eric Jefferis. 1998. The effect of a violent televised arrest on public perceptions of the police. *Policing* 21: 683–706.

Kane, Robert. 2002. The social ecology of police misconduct. *Criminology* 40: 867–896.

———. 2003. Social control in the metropolis: A community-level examination of the minority group-threat hypothesis. *Justice Quarterly* 20: 265–295.

Kent, Stephanie, and David Jacobs. 2005. Minority threat and police strength from 1980 to 2000. *Criminology* 43: 731–760.

Klinger, David. 1997. Negotiating order in police work: An ecological theory of police response to deviance. *Criminology* 35: 277–306.

Kubrin, Charis, and Ronald Weitzer. 2003. New directions in social disorganization theory. *Journal of Research in Crime and Delinquency* 40: 374–402.

Kusow, Abdi, Leon Wilson, and David Martin. 1997. Determinants of citizen satisfaction with the police: The effects of residential location. *Policing* 20: 655–664.

Leiber, Michael, Mahesh Nalla, and Margaret Farnworth. 1998. Explaining juveniles' attitudes toward the police. *Justice Quarterly* 15: 151–173.

Liska, Allen, and Mitchell Chamlin. 1984. Social structure and crime control among macrosocial units. *American Journal of Sociology* 90: 383–395.

Liska, Allen, and Jiang Yu. 1992. Specifying and testing the threat hypothesis: Police use of deadly force. In A. Liska (ed.), *Social threat and social control.* Albany: State University of New York Press.

Liska, Allen, Mitchell Chamlin, and Mark Reed. 1985. Testing the economic production and conflict models of crime control. *Social Forces* 64: 119–138.

Liska, Allen, Joseph Lawrence, and Michael Benson. 1981. Perspectives on the legal order: The capacity for social control. *American Journal of Sociology* 87: 412–426.

MacDonald, John, Robert Stokes, Greg Ridgeway, and K. Jack Riley. 2007. Race, neighborhood context, and perceptions of injustice by the police in Cincinnati. *Urban Studies* 13: 2567–2585.

Marenin, Otwin. 1985. Police performance and state rule. *Comparative Politics* 18: 101–122.

Mastrofski, Stephen, Michael Reisig, and John McCluskey. 2002. Police disrespect toward the public. *Criminology* 40: 519–51.

Meehan, Albert, and Michael Ponder. 2002. Race and place: The ecology of racial profiling African American motorists. *Justice Quarterly* 19: 399–429.

Messner, Steven, and Scott South. 1986. Economic deprivation, opportunity structure, and robbery victimization. *Social Forces* 64: 975–991.

Miller, Joel. 2007. *"I can stop and search whoever I want": Police stops of ethnic minorities in Bulgaria, Hungary, and Spain.* New York: Open Society Institute.

Milton-Edwards, Beverly. 1997. Policing Palestinian society. *Policing and Society* 7: 19–44.

Mollen Commission. 1994. *Report of the commission to investigate allegations of police corruption.* New York: Mollen Commission.

Murty, Komanduri, Julian Roebuck, and Joann Smith. 1990. The image of the police in black Atlanta communities. *Journal of Police Science and Administration* 17: 250–257.

National Research Council. 2004. *Fairness and effectiveness in policing: The evidence.* Washington, DC: National Academies Press.

Parker, Karen, Brian Stults, and Stephen Rice. 2005. Racial threat, concentrated disadvantage, and social control. *Criminology* 43: 1111–1134.

Quinnipiac. 2005. New Yorkers approve of NYPD 3 to 1. Quinnipiac University poll, June 23.

RAND. 2005. *Police-community relations in Cincinnati.* Santa Monica, CA: RAND.

Reisig, Michael, and Roger Parks. 2000. Experience, quality of life, and neighborhood context. *Justice Quarterly* 17: 607–29.

Rice, Stephen, John Reitzel, and Alex Piquero. 2005. Shades of brown: Perceptions of racial profiling and the intra-ethnic differential. *Journal of Ethnicity in Criminal Justice* 3: 47–70.

Saltzstein, Grace. 1989. Black mayors and police policies. *Journal of Politics* 51: 525–544.

Sampson, Robert, and Dawn Bartusch. 1998. Legal cynicism and (subcultural?) tolerance of deviance. *Law and Society Review* 32: 777–804.

Schafer, Joseph, Beth Huebner, and Timothy Bynum. 2003. Citizen perceptions of police services: Race, neighborhood context, and community policing. *Police Quarterly* 6: 440–468.

Schuck, Amie, Dennis Rosenbaum, and Darnell Hawkins. 2008. The influence of race/ethnicity, social class, and neighborhood context on resident's attitudes toward the police. *Police Quarterly* 11: 496–519.

Schuman, Howard, Charlotte Steeh, Lawrence Bobo, and Maria Krysan. 1997. *Racial attitudes in America.* Cambridge: Harvard University Press.

Sharp, Douglas, and Susie Atherton. 2007. To serve and protect? The experiences of policing in the community of young people from black and other ethnic minority groups. *British Journal of Criminology* 47: 746–763.

Sherman, Lawrence. 1978. *Scandal and reform: Controlling police corruption.* Berkeley and Los Angeles: University of California Press.

———. 1983. After the riots: Police and minorities in the United States. In N. Glazer and K. Young (eds.), *Ethnic pluralism and public policy.* Toronto: Lexington.

Sigelman, Lee, Susan Welch, Timothy Bledsoe, and Michael Combs. 1997. Police brutality and public perceptions of racial discrimination. *Political Research Quarterly* 50: 777–91.

Skogan, Wesley. 1979. Citizen satisfaction with police services. In R. Baker and F. Meyer (eds.), *Evaluating alternative law enforcement policies.* Lexington: Lexington Books.

———. 2006a. Asymmetry in the impact of encounters with police. *Policing and Society* 16: 99–126.

———. 2006b. *Police and community in Chicago: A tale of three cities.* New York: Oxford University Press.

Skolnick, Jerome, and David Bayley. 1986. *The new blue line: Police innovation in six American cities.* New York: The Free Press.

Smith, Brad. 2005. The impact of police officer diversity on police-caused homicides. *Policy Studies Journal* 31: 147–162.

Smith, Douglas. 1986. The neighborhood context of police behavior. In A. Reiss and M. Tonry (eds.), *Crime and Justice,* vol. 8. Chicago: University of Chicago Press.

Sorenson, Jonathan, James Marquart, and Deon Brock. 1993. Factors related to killings of felons by police officers. *Justice Quarterly* 10: 417–440.

South, Scott, and Richard Felson. 1990. The racial patterning of rape. *Social Forces* 69: 71–93.

Stolzenberg, Lisa, Steward D'Alessio, and David Eitle. 2004. A multilevel test of racial threat theory. *Criminology* 42: 673–698.

Stults, Brian, and Eric Baumer. 2007. Racial context and police force size. *American Journal of Sociology* 113: 507–546.

Taylor, Terrance, K. B. Turner, Finn-Aage Esbensen, and L. Thomas Winfree. 2001. Coppin' an attitude: Attitudinal differences among juveniles toward police. *Journal of Criminal Justice* 29: 295–305.

Terrill, William, and Michael Reisig. 2003. Neighborhood context and police use of force. *Journal of Research in Crime and Delinquency* 40: 291–321.

Terrill, William, and Stephen Mastrofski. 2004. Working the street: Does community policing matter? In W. Skogan (ed.), *Community policing: Can it work?* Belmont, CA: Wadsworth.

Velez, Maria. 2001. The role of public social control in urban neighborhoods. *Criminology* 39: 837–863.

Vrij, Albert, and F. Winkel. 1991. Encounters between Dutch police and minorities. *Police Studies* 14: 17–23.

Weitzer, Ronald. 1985. Policing a divided society: Obstacles to normalization in Northern Ireland. *Social Problems* 33: 41–55.

———. 1990. *Transforming settler states: Communal conflict and internal security in Northern Ireland and Zimbabwe.* Berkeley and Los Angeles: University of California Press.

———. 1995. *Policing under fire: Ethnic conflict and police-community relations in Northern Ireland.* Albany: State University of New York Press.

———. 1999. Citizens' perceptions of police misconduct: Race and neighborhood context. *Justice Quarterly* 16: 819–846.

———. 2000a. Racialized policing: Residents' perceptions in three neighborhoods. *Law and Society Review* 34: 129–155.

———. 2000b. White, black, or blue cops? Race and citizen assessments of police officers. *Journal of Criminal Justice* 28: 313–324.

———. 2002. Incidents of police misconduct and public opinion. *Journal of Criminal Justice* 30: 397–408.

Weitzer, Ronald, and Rod Brunson. 2009. Strategic responses to the police among inner-city youth. *Sociological Quarterly* 50: 235–256.

Weitzer, Ronald, and Steven Tuch. 1999. Race, class, and perceptions of discrimination by the police. *Crime and Delinquency* 45: 494–507.

———. 2002. Perceptions of racial profiling: Race, class, and personal experience. *Criminology* 40: 435–456.

———. 2006. *Race and policing in America: Conflict and reform.* New York: Cambridge University Press.

Weitzer, Ronald, Steven Tuch, and Wesley Skogan. 2008. Police-community relations in a majority-black city. *Journal of Research in Crime and Delinquency* 45: 398–428.

Welch, Susan, Lee Sigelman, Timothy Bledsoe, and Michael Coombs. 2001. *Race and place: Race relations in an American city.* New York: Cambridge University Press.

Williams, Brian. 1997. *Citizen perspectives on community policing.* Albany: State University of New York Press.

Wilson, James Q. 1968. *Varieties of police behavior: The management of law and order in eight communities.* Cambridge: Harvard University Press.

Wortley, Scot, John Hagan, and Ross Macmillan. 1997. Just deserts? The racial polarization of perceptions of criminal injustice. *Law and Society Review* 31: 637–676.

Wu, Yuning, Ivan Sun, and Ruth Triplett. 2009. Race, class or neighborhood context: Which matters more in measuring satisfaction with police? *Justice Quarterly* 26: 125–156.

Xu, Yili, Mora Fiedler, and Karl Flaming. 2005. Discovering the impact of community policing: The broken windows thesis, collective efficacy, and citizens' judgment. *Journal of Research in Crime and Delinquency* 42: 147–186.

|||||||||||||||||||||||||||||||||||||||||||||||||||||||||||||||||||||||||||||||

Chapter 6

Racially Biased Policing
A Review of the Judicial and Legislative Literature

Delores Jones-Brown and Brian A. Maule

The dealers and couriers are predominantly black males and black females.
—Criminal Intelligence Report, Maryland State Police, 1992

Today with this drug problem, the drug problem is cocaine or marijuana. It is most likely a minority group that's involved with that.
—Colonel Carl A. Williams, former superintendent,
New Jersey State Police, *Newark Star Ledger,* 1999

Introduction

One way in which the term racial profiling has been defined is: The practice of stopping and inspecting people who are passing through public places—such as drivers on public highways or pedestrians in airports or urban areas—where the reason for the stop is a statistical profile of the detainee's race or ethnicity.[1]

Though hotly debated in the attempts to empirically measure the existence (or not) of unwarranted use of race in law enforcement practices, such a definition, in operation, runs directly counter to the highly personal nature of constitutional rights embedded in the United States Constitution's Bill of Rights and Fourteenth Amendment.

In part, an individual's expectation of privacy and his or her right to be free from unreasonable governmental intrusion is secured in the Fourth Amendment, which provides, "the right of the people to be secure in their persons, houses, papers and effects, against unreasonable searches and seizures, shall not be violated, and no Warrants shall issue, but upon probable cause, supported by Oath or Affirmation, and *particularly* describing the place to be searched, and the person or things to be seized" (emphasis added). It is the violation of the particularity requirement, as it has been narrowly construed by the federal courts, that causes members of minority groups the most angst when hearing statements like those quoted at the beginning of this chapter—especially when they come from law enforcement officials. Such statements are problematic for at least two reasons. First, they suggest a negative characterization of the *group* to which *individual* minorities belong, and they fail to provide any objective evidence to support the "facts" asserted. Adherence to the beliefs that underlie such quotes means that, by virtue of racial identity (alone), regardless of individual character, members of the identified "class"[2] will suffer suspicion, even in the absence of *actual* offending behavior. Such suspicion is then arguably counter to notions of "equal protection under the law" guaranteed by the Fourteenth Amendment to the U.S. Constitution, in part because individuals who are not of the "suspected" class will not be suspected of wrongdoing, even when they are so engaged, simply because they do not fall within the identified racial category.[3] The opposite is also true: individual members of the suspect "class" will be presumptively seen as involved in criminality or potentially involved in criminality, even when no such criminality exists.[4]

More than thirty years ago, in the case of *U.S. v. Brignoni-Ponce*,[5] the United States Supreme Court struck down a conviction for transporting "illegally entering aliens" near the Mexican-American border, when the law enforcement officers' only justification for the stop was that fact that the "suspects" appeared to be of "Mexican ancestry." The Court found that "this factor alone would justify neither a reasonable belief that they were aliens, nor a reasonable belief that the car concealed other aliens who were illegally in the country."[6] The opinion went on to note that "the likelihood that any given person of Mexican ancestry is an alien is high enough to make Mexican appearance *a* relevant factor, but *standing alone it does not justify stopping all Mexican Americans to ask if they are aliens*"[7] (emphasis added).

In the thirty odd years since the *Brignoni-Ponce* decision, the Supreme Court of the United States has failed to make so clear a ruling regarding the role of race in police decision making. In this chapter, we contend that it is, in part, the Supreme Court's failure to make a clear statement regarding the permissible, or rather, impermissible, role of race (as opposed to ethnicity) in law enforcement practice that has kept the race and policing controversy alive. We also contend that, in fact, some of the Court's contemporary decisions actually buttress discriminatory police practices by expanding the scope of discretionary police authority, thereby making claims of racial profiling difficult to prove. Lastly, it is our contention that the cases we discuss here, which expand police discretionary authority, make racially biased policing legally invisible, in the absence of direct admissions or overt racial epithets by police during traffic or pedestrian stops (noting, however, that among the successfully litigated cases, there are ample examples of such damning police behavior).[8]

The cases we discuss here, with the exception of one state lower court decision (*State v. Soto*[9]), suggest that the federal, state, and local courts have become comfortable with subjugating the personal rights of individual minorities to perceived police efficiency in "fettering out crime"[10] (especially drug crime) and the alleged production of public safety. While striking the balance in this way may be acceptable to the mainstream,[11] among those in the affected class, like the authors here, the weight of the balance is morally unacceptable. Unfortunately, the space that we have been allotted does not allow for an exhaustive review of either the judicial or legislative landscape on this topic.

After our discussion of a select group of cases that, in our opinion, expand police discretionary authority in ways that, we contend, seriously affect the potential for racial minorities to become victims of racially biased policing, we turn to a brief discussion of the current proliferation of legislation that either prohibits racial profiling or requires data collection or special training by law enforcement to document and redress the possibility of such practices. Arguably, these legislative measures can provide effective checks on the expanded discretionary authority given to law enforcement agents by the judiciary. But, as we discuss, the enforcement of such measures requires a high level of integrity in an area that has been plagued by a racialized history, unwilling or inadequate supervisory controls,[12] and a steadfast belief in minority, especially black and Latino, criminality as expressed in the quotes that begin this chapter.[13]

We end with a discussion of some of the recent successful settlements of racial profiling lawsuits, mounted primarily by various divisions of the American Civil Liberties Union (ACLU), with the assistance of private law firms. The collaborative effort between advocacy groups, community organizations, and law enforcement agencies that these settlements entail, if implemented as designed, hold significant promise for addressing the moral and legal concerns raised by real and perceived racial bias in policing.

The Socio-Legal Background

Various sources trace the roots of modern policing in the United States to the formation of slave patrols in the South during the 1700s.[14] These informal groupings of "slave catchers" were given the authority to control and restrict the liberty of men and women based on race, in a developing land where others had come seeking freedom. The propriety of such freedom was later formally established as an edict of the country's professed moral and legal underpinning. From the outset, lawmaking in the United States, and therefore law enforcing in the United States, has had an overtly racialized bent. From slave patrols and slave codes to black codes and Jim Crow laws, racially biased formal legislation was legally enforceable and enforced for more than 250 years.[15] Policing agencies have had the unenviable position of enforcing formal laws that did not comport with moral standards of equal treatment. They were supported in their practices by judicial decisions that validated their authority and by the creation of numerous myths about race and criminality to justify overtly immoral practices.[16] Over time, many visibly identifiable "others"[17] were subjected to differential treatment under formal laws designed to maintain a white racial status quo based on notions of white racial superiority and propriety. It is against this historical backdrop that we come to examine the judicial and legislative literature on racially biased policing in contemporary times.

The racial history of policing (which includes significant acts of discrimination against its own members),[18] coupled with the nature of contemporary complaints, legitimately raise the following questions in police-civilian encounters: What do police notice first, the race of the individual or his alleged "suspicious" behavior? And how does what was first noticed contribute to the officer's decision to stop, question, frisk, or search individual "suspects"? These questions lie at the root of our understanding of the extent to which police action is influenced by race and may be determinative of a defendant's path through the criminal justice system.

In "Seeing Black: Race, Crime, and Visual Processing,"[19] Stanford University professor Jennifer Eberhardt and her colleagues confirm that both police and civilians associate images of black people with images of crime and vice versa. In fact, continuous findings by social psychologists confirm that both police agents and civilians harbor unconscious or implicit racial bias, especially against those they perceive as being of "black" racial identity.[20] And with the advent of neuro-imagining capability, these social psychologists have been able to accomplish the previously thought impossible task of reading people's minds. That is, by detecting changes in the fusiform face area (FFA) of the brain when research subjects are exposed to different racial cues, researchers like Professor Eberhardt have found remarkably consistent indications that police and civilians are more likely to "see" black faces as associated with crime and criminal objects, even when their responses on pen and paper tests reveal little or no overt racial biases.[21]

It has also been argued that the elastic nature of such legal terms as "probable cause" and the judicially created standard of "reasonable suspicion" give rise to, and support, racial bias in policing through their ambiguity and subjective determination.[22] Arguably, the less elastic of the two requirements, probable cause, should have a fixed legal standard and therefore be open to less interpretation than "reasonableness," a term that appears both in the Fourth Amendment and the case law that permits police to stop, question, and perhaps even "frisk" civilians for behavior that does not amount to "probable cause" to make a formal arrest.

The U.S. Supreme Court has said as much in holding that "a single, familiar standard is essential to . . . guide police officers . . . in the specific circumstances they confront."[23] Yet a concrete, objective, "single familiar standard" for guiding police practice has not been developed. The Court has opted instead to recognize a "totality of the circumstances" rule for the assessment of the existence of probable cause, while (in our opinion) finding it easier to identify, after-the-fact, unreasonable police practices, rather than establish a prospective "reasonableness" benchmark in cases that do not involve warrants.

In fact, with reference to probable cause, the legal concept from which "reasonable suspicion is a reduced analog," Lerner has noted that the legal standards for its determination have moved up and down the evidentiary poles ever since the term was enshrined in the Fourth Amendment in 1791. In a paper titled "Reasonable Suspicion and Mere Hunches," he notes that "[i]n the early years of the American republic, probable cause was a remarkably low (and therefore pro-government) evidentiary standard; it rose slightly (therefore tilting in a somewhat civil libertarian direction) in the early nineteenth century, only to retreat once more to a relatively low standard in the Prohibition era, only to become more stringent in the early years of the Warren Court, then to retreat in the early years of the Rehnquist Court, and then yet again to tilt in a civil libertarian direction in recent years, at least prior to the September 11, 2001 terrorist attacks."[24] It is within these murky waters that the judiciary must guide police agents and protect private citizens from governmental overreaching in the daily practice of law enforcement.

The Cases

For the past forty years the doctrinal framework provided by the U.S. Supreme Court in the landmark case of *Terry v. Ohio*[25] has been the standard that authorizes law enforcement agents, acting on their own individual discretion, to briefly detain, question, and, under appropriate circumstances (i.e., where there are reasonable indicators of potential physical danger), to perform a limited search—pat down or frisk—of the detainees' outer clothing for the purpose of discovering weapons that might be used against the officer or innocent others.[26] A recitation of the facts in *Terry* should help to illustrate the highly discretionary decision making that led to the arrest of two individuals who, to the untrained eye, could easily have been seen as engaged in nonsuspicious, innocent behavior.

On October 31, 1963, police detective Martin McFadden saw two black men, John W. Terry and Richard Chilton, pacing up and down a block of Huron Street in Cleveland, Ohio. One of the men would walk past a particular store, peer into the window, walk a short distance, turn back, and repeat his act of peering into the store. Several times after peering into the store window, he conversed with the other man and then continued his routine. Suspecting that they were casing the store for robbery, McFadden followed the two men, who were then joined by a third man. McFadden identified himself as a police officer and asked their names. When their responses were incoherent mumbles, McFadden patted them down and discovered that both Terry and Chilton were in possession of firearms. He confiscated the guns and arrested them for carrying concealed weapons.

Following the denial of his motion to suppress the weapon, Terry pleaded not guilty. He was found guilty and sentenced to one to three years in prison. On appeal, his conviction was affirmed by the Ohio Court of Appeals. The Ohio Supreme Court declined to hear the case. The U.S. Supreme Court granted certiorari.

The issue before the U.S. Supreme Court was not the propriety of the stop-and-frisk procedure itself, but whether evidence, such as the guns of defendants Terry and Chilton, discovered as a result of the stop-and frisk procedure should be excluded in accordance with the mandates of *Mapp v. Ohio*.[27] Presented with arguments that a lower standard of probable cause was needed by police officers to fight rising street crime, the *Terry* Court agreed and ruled that governmental interests in preventing and detecting crime, and ensuring a police officer's safety, outweigh the brief intrusion experienced by a citizen when stopped by a police officer.[28] In constitutional terms, it was decided that such detentions and outer garment pat downs do not amount to seizures or searches giving rise to full Fourth Amendment protection. Thus a stop and frisk, based on reasonable articulable suspicion, rather than probable cause, was sufficient for a valid investigative stop, and it was determined that a police officer is permitted to stop, and briefly detain for questioning, a citizen believed to be engaged in criminal activity, in the absence of both a warrant and probable cause.

But what is "articulable suspicion," and how can it be determined when it is reasonable for police to interfere with the liberty of presumptively innocent civilians during the course of their ordinary daily interactions?[29] Writing for the 8–1 majority, then Chief Justice Earl Warren, expressed the opinion that facts the officer can describe verbally, and rational inferences from those facts, of the nature normally required to obtain a warrant, are sufficient to support the reasonableness of the officer's suspicion and to legally justify his or her action.[30] In other words, the facts and the inferences that the police officer would have had to articulate to a judge to convince him or her to issue a search warrant must similarly be present for the officer to legally stop and question the detainee. Cases subsequent to *Terry* have confirmed that to justify the frisk, officers must articulate additional facts that give rise to a reasonable suspicion that the detainee presents a potential safety risk. While other decisions have helped to further define the operative meaning of "reasonable suspicion" by holding that although there is no bright line test that definitively establishes its existence (or not) in any one incident,[31] the facts and inferences must be more than just a vague feeling that criminal activity is afoot,[32] must take into account the totality of the circumstances, and must be specific and pertain specifically to the particular person stopped and frisked.[33]

Despite its legacy, much of the academic debate over the *Terry* Court's carving out of an exception to the Fourth Amendment's probable cause requirement has focused on the dichotomy between suspicion that is objectively based on articulable facts, and is therefore reasonable, and suspicion that is unreasonable because it is subjectively based on mere hunches, instinct, and other preconceptions. The literature is scant concerning the extent to which John Terry and Richard Chilton's race, being African American, contributed to white police officer Martin McFadden's suspicion that they were "casing" the store for possible robbery.[34]

Notwithstanding the fact that Terry and Chilton were armed and perhaps contemplating a robbery of the store, it seems appropriate to ask: What was the initial basis of McFadden's suspicion? Had Terry and Chilton been white and behaving similarly, would they have drawn McFadden's attention? Or might it have been presumed by McFadden that they were waiting for a friend who was inside the store? These questions are especially relevant in light of the fact that the Court acknowledged that there was "nothing unusual in two men standing together on a street corner."[35] Therefore, even though McFadden's thirty-five years of police experience was offered and accepted as a compelling basis for his suspicion, given the racialized history of American policing, in general, and the particularly acute racially biased climate of the time period, is it possible that two black men pacing outside of a store on Huron Street in 1963 Cleveland would be considered suspicious by a white police officer under any circumstances?[36]

In his lone dissent to the *Terry* decision, Justice William O. Douglas warned against expanding law enforcements discretionary authority in the manner endorsed by the majority of the Court. He noted that "[w]e hold today that the police have greater authority to make a 'seizure' and conduct a 'search' than a judge has to authorize such action. We have said precisely the opposite over and over again."[37] Justice Douglas continues with a characterization of probable cause that is contrary to our view of it, in terms of the precision of its determination, but that acknowledges, as we do, that it is a standard that affords the ordinary citizen greater protection against government intrusion than does reasonable suspicion. He notes that "the term 'probable cause' rings a bell of certainty [and perhaps neutrality] that is not sounded by phrases such as 'reasonable suspicion.'"[38] In his opinion, even if the creation of a "reasonable suspicion" standard for police intervention was seen as "a desirable step to cope with modern forms of lawlessness,"[39] to give police such "totalitarian" power required a constitutional amendment rather than a judicial decree. In his opinion, "the long prevailing standards [for probable cause] seek to safeguard citizens from rash and unreasonable interferences with privacy and from unfounded charges of crime."[40] And, while he does not mention race specifically, he notes further that "if the individual is no longer to be sovereign, if the police can pick him up when ever they do not like the cut of his jib, if they can 'seize' and 'search' him in their discretion, we have entered a new regime."[41]

We argue and attempt to illustrate, through our discussion of the following cases, that judicial decisions in the post-*Terry era*, even those that appear to be race-neutral, continue to expand rather than restrict police discretionary authority; that despite the implementation of legislative endeavors to combat racial profiling, these decisions work to support the "new regime" of Justice Douglas's fears and make possible the circumvention of the work of legislators in their attempts to combat the moral, legal, and ethical racial profiling problems mentioned in previous sections.

We see these cases as falling into two possible primary categories—(1) cases in which the courts are asked to specifically address the propriety of obvious or apparent racialized law enforcement practices; and (2) cases in which the arguments for and against relief and the consequent judicial decisions are, or can be perceived as, race-neutral, but serve to broaden police discretionary authority and function as a means of masking overt and implicit racial/ethnic bias in law enforcement practices.

Discussion and understanding of the latter category of cases is particularly important given: the volume of studies that have reached contradictory conclusions regarding whether racial disparity within statistics pertaining to traffic and pedestrian stops is evidence of improper or efficient (i.e., "good") police conduct;[42] that many criminological/criminal justice studies continue to treat the possibility of racial bias in policing as a null hypothesis, despite admissions by police (in New Jersey, for example), under oath, that they engaged in or were encouraged, commanded, or ordered to stop certain racial and ethnic minorities more frequently than members of other groups;[43] and despite personal accounts (many given under oath) by racial and ethnic minorities that during stops, police made verbal statements indicating that the stop was, at least in part, based on assumptions of criminality associated with the detainees' race.[44]

Although in the following sections reference will be made to some of them, we do not find it fruitful to continue or contribute to the debates as to whether the study of racial and ethnic disparities in police stops and other interactions is most efficacious when approached from a (purely) legalistic, criminological/criminal justice, normative, or economic perspective.[45] As members of the affected group, we see the issue of racially biased policing as primarily related to moral considerations and human and civil rights entitlements, and crucial to questions of legitimacy—not the legitimacy of the practices themselves, but the question of whether racial and ethnic minorities can ever consistently come to see and experience formal legal mechanisms, agents, and authorities as legitimate purveyors and protectors of the common good in a racially and ethnically heterogeneous society. As has been recognized by others,[46] this question of legitimacy has serious implications for whether racial and ethnic minorities will consistently accept formal law and its apparatus as meaningful dictators of appropriate normative values and behaviors (i.e., mechanism for social and self-control); whether members of such groups will cease to experience their moral, human, and civil rights as subordinate to the perceived needs and rights of the members of larger and more powerful groups; and whether the criminologist and other empiricist will become seriously interested in assessing and addressing the damage done to the psyche of individual members of the affected groups who recognize his or her own innate right to be free of governmental intrusion, in the absence of criminality, and yet are repeatedly the subject of law enforcement contact, whether racial/ethnic identity was one of several factors in the law enforcement agents decision to approach him or her.

Category 1: Overt Inclusion or Impact Based on Race/Ethnicity

Brignoni-Ponce Revisited

While the U.S. Supreme Court was willing to speak definitively on the issue of ethnicity and policing, in the 1975 case of *U.S. v. Brignoni-Ponce*, the Court may be validly criticized for failing to give the police adequate guidance or limits on how race may or may not legitimately factor into their work.[47] *Brignoni-Ponce* was among the first cases to present the issues of reasonable suspicion and ethnicity to the U.S. Supreme Court following the formulation and acceptance of that concept in *Terry*. As mentioned in our introduction, it involved the law enforcement practice of stopping motor vehicles near the Mexican border on the suspicion that the occupants, by appearing to be of Mexican ancestry, were illegal aliens.[48] The Court ruled that such stops were not reasonable under the Fourth Amendment since they lacked specific articulable facts beyond the occupants appearance and location to suspect them of being in violation of immigration laws.[49]

Although in subsequent years there has been some retreat from the breadth of the original ruling, the *Brignoni-Ponce* decision prohibited the use of broad ethnic descriptions (e.g., looking Hispanic) to suspect a particular individual of criminality. In fact the Court concluded that the officers' reliance on a "single factor to justify stopping respondent's car"—that is, the apparent Mexican ancestry of the occupants—"cannot furnish reasonable grounds to believe that the occupants were illegal aliens."[50] The Court also rejected law enforcement's probability argument that correlates proximity to the border and Mexican appearance with being an illegal alien by holding that "[t]he likelihood that any given person of Mexican ancestry is an illegal alien . . . does not justify stopping all Mexican-Americans to ask if they are aliens."[51]

Following the rationale articulated in *Brignoni-Ponce*, if it is unreasonable to stop a vehicle near the American-Mexican border simply on the suspicion that the occupants, by appearing to be of Mexican descent, are illegally in the United States, arguably it is also unreasonable to stop an African American on the suspicion that because of his skin color he may have committed or is committing a crime. After all, the suspicious association is appearance equals illegal alien in the first case and appearance equals generally criminal (but most often drug offender) in the second.

Recently, the creation and enforcement of municipal ordinances aimed at detecting and controlling the presence of undocumented persons (formerly referred to as illegal aliens) have come under judicial scrutiny. In the decided or settled cases,[52] these ordinances and the enforcement practices that accompanied them have failed to pass constitutional muster. For example, a federal lawsuit filed by the Puerto Rican Legal Defense Fund (PERLDF), on behalf of a group of Latino day laborers against Freehold Borough, in Monmouth County, New Jersey, enjoined the municipality from enforcing its loitering, traffic, and housing code regulations in ways that would interfere with the First, Fourth, Fifth, and Fourteenth Amendment rights of the laborers.[53] The success of ethnic minorities in such cases have served to exacerbate tensions between immigrants (both legal and illegal) of Latino ancestry and those of African ancestry, who see the Latinos as having triumphed in legal areas where their own efforts have failed or only enjoyed temporary success, despite years of continuous litigation. And, despite the victories, there is ample evidence to suggest that Latinos also suffer from being viewed as criminal, in conjunction with and separate and apart from preconceived notions about their immigration status.[54]

Brown v. the City of Oneonta

In *Brown et al. v. City of Oneonta*,[55] the U.S. Supreme Court upheld the legality of the police stopping and questioning every black male in Oneonta, New York, in connection with a single burglary investigation. On September 4, 1992, upon receiving information that a young black male had attacked a seventy-seven-year-old white woman, which resulted in an arm injury to the assailant, police in the City of Oneonta (population of fourteen thousand, including five hundred black residents) for the next three days rounded up every black male and one black female for questioning and physical examination. Although the victim's description of the perpetrator could be considered particularized, in that it was "a black man with a possible hand injury," in a city with five hundred African Americans it arguably should have been considered too general to meet the threshold of *Terry* and its progeny,[56] let alone the higher standard of probable cause required by the language in the Fourth Amendment.

In 1993 a group that included students at the State University of New York at Oneonta and other residents sued the City of Oneonta claiming that the police had violated their equal protection guarantee. In 1995 a federal district judge dismissed the claim and in 2000 the United States Court of Appeals for the Second Circuit affirmed the dismissal.[57] The Second Circuit affirmed the lower court ruling that the petitioners had no cause of action under the Equal Protection Clause because the police were acting on a racial description as provided by the victim and not on their own racial stereotypes or preferences. But was the description legally sufficient to protect the constitutional rights of the factually innocent blacks, and to comport with the particularity requirement embedded in the Fourth Amendment?[58]

The description given by the victim, who was attacked in the dark, was of a male that she thought was black based on what she could see of his arms. She also thought that he was young, based on the speed at which he moved. She also *thought* that he had cut his hand during the attack. In searching for "the" perpetrator, the police acted on the albeit-equivocal description as provided by the victim. When they decided to seize and search an entire segment of the community, however, it became questionable as to whether they were acting on their prejudices, because they failed to confine their inquiry to black males in the immediate vicinity of the crime and they failed to confine their inquiry to "suspects" who fit the other descriptors (i.e., young black men).[59] Arguably, the description of a relatively young black man with a possible hand injury was not sufficiently specific to narrow the field of potential suspects so as to protect the innocent from unwarranted police intrusion, and was sufficiently broad to allow police to act on their own racial biases. Despite the fact that the investigation of this one crime led to the search and seizure of all of Oneonta's black male residents, as well as one female,[60] on October 1, 2001, the U.S. Supreme Court denied certiorari.[61]

For the African Americans of the City of Oneonta, the Second Circuit decision to uphold the dismissal of the civil lawsuit, which even if technically consistent with some legal precedent, appears to be blatantly unjust, and the subsequent U.S. Supreme Court denial of certiorari accentuates the murky abyss that is part and parcel of the confluence of race and law enforcement investigative procedures.

In the case of *National Congress for Puerto Rican Rights v. City of New York*,[62] the plaintiffs' claims of violations of the equal protection guarantee were initially dismissed on the grounds that the plaintiffs had failed to show that similarly situated people of a different race were disparately treated.[63] In a twist of irony, however, the National Congress moved for reconsideration relying on rulings made during the appeals of *Brown v. City of Oneonta*. In *National Congress*, the trial court reversed itself, finding that the claims of equal protection violations were indeed sufficient. The court's reversal occurred because in *Brown v. City of Oneonta*: the Court of Appeals held that if the allegation of equal protection violation was that the police policy had an expressed racial classification, then plaintiffs need not identify similarly situated nonminorities who were not subjected to the same police conduct. In the case of *National Congress*, the plaintiffs made this very allegation.

State v. Soto

Even among the factually guilty, judicial questions have been raised about the propriety of targeting racial and ethnic minorities for the purpose of conducting drug interdiction efforts. After years of complaints around the country, arguably it was the trial court case of *State v. Soto*[64] and a shooting incident involving unarmed minority males by the New Jersey State Police on the New Jersey Turnpike[65] that brought the issue of racial profiling to national attention; which consequently resulted in a New Jersey Attorney General's report on racial profiling[66] and a consent decree requiring New Jersey State Police to maintain records of the race of persons stopped, searched, ticketed, or arrested.[67] Lawsuits in other locations have also led to settlements requiring similar record keeping measures.[68]

In *State v. Soto*, New Jersey Superior Court judge Robert Francis dismissed the cases of nineteen defendants based on claims of selective enforcement via racial profiling. Defendant Soto had filed a motion to suppress evidence found during the course of a traffic stop. Mr. Soto claimed that he and other minority motorists had been unfairly targeted for stops and searches along the New Jersey Turnpike. Judge Francis and Temple University professor John Lamberth found that black and Latino drivers were being stopped for speeding and arrested significantly out of proportion with their presence on the highway.[69] Though Lamberth's methodology has been criticized by other statisticians, he and Judge Francis were particularly struck by the finding that "troopers using radar tended to stop black drivers at near their rate in the highway population, while troopers on road patrol cruising without radar, who could more freely choose who to stop, arrested far more blacks."[70] Or as noted by Lamberth, "As they got more discretion, they stopped more blacks."[71]

Prior the 1996 *Soto* decision, the New Jersey State Police had consistently denied complaints of racial profiling that had been lodged against officers for years. In 1998, when two state troopers, John Hogan and James Kenna, shot eleven times at a van containing unarmed male occupants (three black and one Latino), during the resolution of criminal and disciplinary charges against them Hogan and Kenna testified that they had, in fact, engaged in racial profiling with the support and encouragement of superiors, and had falsified agency records to cover up the practice.[72]

Contemporaneous with the Hogan and Kenna testimony, minority troopers who had filed suit against the agency claiming personal discrimination and for having received orders that instructed them to engage in racial profiling, had their suits resolved in their favor.[73] Although the state had initially filed an appeal in the *Soto* case, that appeal was subsequently withdrawn. (Even in light of the successful claims in the aftermath of *Soto*, however, it is worth noting that in 1996, when black defendants made a claim of selective enforcement against Los Angeles County prosecutors in relation to cocaine sentencing, their claims were unsuccessful.)[74]

Kelly v. Paschall

The failure of case law to adequately set clear legal standards around the legitimate and illegitimate use of race in policing may be responsible for one of the worst cases of racially biased policing in post–Jim Crow history. In Tulia, Texas, population five thousand, the entire criminal justice system may have been complicit in giving legitimacy to what most would agree was a blatant case of racially biased policing[75] that resulted in the arrest and conviction of forty-six residents of color in and around the small town.

In January 1998 police launched Swisher County's first major drug sting, which after an eighteen-month investigation, culminated in the arrests of more than 10% of Tulia's African American population in July 1999.[76] Of the forty-three alleged drug traffickers arrested, forty were African American.[77] The arrests were based on over one hundred alleged drug buys made by detective Tom Coleman. "No drugs, money, or weapons were recovered" during the arrests, however.[78] More startling was the fact that no other police officers corroborated Detective Coleman's activities and no audio or video recordings of his alleged drug buys were made. Records of Coleman's buys consisted of notes written on scraps of paper or on his leg.[79] Still, Coleman's uncorroborated, unsubstantiated trial testimony was enough for convictions in the first set of trials, with sentences ranging from sixty to three hundred years.[80] The harshness of these sentences resulted in a rush by the remaining thirty-five defendants to plea bargain for lesser sentences ranging from probation to eighteen years.[81]

What is noteworthy about the Tulia arrests and convictions was that they were based solely on the undercover work of one individual, detective Tom Coleman, "a white man with a wretched work history, who routinely referred to black people as 'niggers' and who frequently found himself in trouble with the law."[82] In August 2003 Texas governor Rick Perry pardoned thirty-five of those convicted with the evidence provided by Tom Coleman, and eight months later the defendants agreed to a five-million-dollar settlement for the time spent in prison.[83] Tom Coleman was indicted and convicted of aggravated perjury in January 2005 and sentenced to ten years probation.[84]

As life-changing as the incident was in Swisher County, Texas, was for the individuals and their families, it can be argued that the criminal justice system corrected itself, even if only belatedly. What continues however is the greater issue of what flaw exists in the criminal justice system that allows its agents, not just the police, to tolerate and accept a belief that blacks are predisposed to criminality even in the absence of credible substantiating evidence?[85] More specifically, what would allow a single police officer, without serious inquiry, to negatively and falsely affect the lives of so many law-abiding African Americans?

What happened in Tulia is an extreme example of what is possible when the police are not adequately guided or monitored in the exercise of their duties. The degeneration of the U.S. Drug Enforcement Administration's "drug courier profile" into race-based profiling (as indicated by the Maryland State Police "intelligence" report) is indicative of the widely held association of race (i.e., blackness or brownness) and crime.[86] While the U.S. Supreme Court has upheld the legality of using courier profiles in drug investigations and prosecutions,[87] Johnson points out their self-fulfilling nature. He notes: "Proponents and opponents . . . argue over whether the profile results in differential enforcement of the law against people of color. Since the profile is a police initiated investigative strategy, the racist history of American law enforcement, the discriminatory social construction of the drug problem, and broad police legitimacy and discretion create a climate fraught with the potential for abuse."[88]

Category 2: Race-Neutral Holdings with Potential Racially Biased Impact

Terry v. Ohio Revisited

It will forever remain questionable whether the behavior of Terry and Chilton would have aroused Officer McFadden's suspicion if they had been two white men, and if it did, whether such suspicion, under the same circumstances, would have been considered reasonable by the U.S. Supreme Court. We ask again, what did Mc-Fadden notice first, the color of the men's skin or their behavior? If it was the color of their skin, even if it was thereafter followed by suspicious behavior, it can be argued that McFadden's suspicion was prejudicial and not reasonable because it was based on preconceived bias (whether overt or implicit) that presumptively "sees" black skin as an indicia of actual or potential criminality. In fact, the NAACP, in opposing the lower, reasonable suspicion standard advanced in the case, argued that the stop-and-frisk procedures were already unfairly and disproportionately practiced against minorities.[89] It seems that the drafters of the majority opinion in *Terry* not only ignored this contention, but also the reality of racism that underscores the nation's general and policing history. Empirical evidence of the endemic nature of racial bias in policing had already been made available through the results of a 1966 field study commissioned by the President's Commission on Law Enforcement and Administration of Justice.[90] According to the study's authors, 38% of police officers observed in Boston, Chicago, and Washington, D.C., expressed "extreme prejudice" toward blacks, while another 34% expressed "considerable prejudice" toward blacks.[91] Thus prejudice against blacks among police officers in 1966 (two years before the *Terry* decision) was found, by one government source, to exist within the minds of 72% of the police respondents.

Despite the apparent prevalence of police prejudice toward blacks at the time, all indications are that the *Terry* Court failed to seriously consider the role that race may have played in officer McFadden's decision. The Court placed considerable emphasis on Terry's and Chilton's behavior and on officer McFadden's policing experience, but indicated no appreciable attention to the question of whether Officer McFadden may have perceived the behavior as suspicious because of the color of the suspects' skin and the neighborhood in which the behavior occurred. Such questions have considerable contemporary relevance.[92]

On its face, a ruling that police may stop, question, and possibly frisk a person when there is reasonable suspicion to believe that that person may be engaged in or is about to engage in criminality is race-neutral. When, as noted in the chapter by Ronald Weitzer in this volume, neighborhood context is thrown into the mix, a series of Supreme Court cases appear to condone a reduced standard of "reasonable suspicion" and arguably even probable cause, when "suspects" are encountered by police in "high crime areas" or "high drug trafficking areas."[93] The holdings suggest that the Court is willing to give greater deference to the use of police discretion in such locations. We argue that such deference results in reduced constitutional protection for those who reside in such areas as compared to others.

Illinois v. Wardlow

Police testimony in the case of *Illinois v. Wardlow* details the flight of black defendant William Wardlow upon seeing a caravan of four police cars approaching his neighborhood.[94] According to the testimony, upon seeing the police cars, which were investigating drug trafficking in the "high-crime" neighborhood, Wardlow, with an opaque bag in his hand, looked in the direction of the approaching cars and then fled.[95] After a brief pursuit, the search of Wardlow uncovered a handgun.[96] At trial Wardlow's motion to suppress the weapon was denied and he was convicted. The state appellate court reversed the trial court's conviction and the Illinois Supreme Court affirmed the reversal, ruling that sudden flight in a high-crime area does not constitute reasonable suspicion.[97] The U.S. Supreme Court granted certiorari and reinstated the trial court's conviction in finding that although a neighborhood's characteristics (i.e., "high-crime") may provide suspicion for further investigation, and on its own the defendant's presence in a high-crime neighborhood is not enough to warrant reasonable particularized suspicion, when combined with Wardlow's (seemingly) unprovoked flight, a commonsense determination would lead to reasonable suspicion.[98] But of what? In *Terry*, at least Officer McFadden could articulate that he suspected that Terry and Chilton might be casing the jewelry store for a daytime robbery. In Wardlow's case, it has been suggested that rather than being engaged in crime, his conduct could easily have been an indication of the fear that he had of the police based on his accumulated negative experiences with them.[99]

In reaching the decision that it did, the U.S. Supreme Court has been accused of ignoring the role that race plays in police decision making. That is, by finding Wardlow's (seemingly) unprovoked flight, in an area known for crime, as a legally permissible indicator that he was engaged in some yet-unknown criminal behavior, the Court authorized the police to make legally significant inferences based on otherwise legally permissible and perhaps totally innocent behavior. The Court's willingness to sanction such a "commonsense" association, and in doing so provide more discretionary authority to law enforcement, results in a significant contraction of the Fourth and Fifth Amendment guarantees and a significant diminution of Fourteenth Amendment protection, in that "high-crime" areas are predominantly urban neighborhoods disproportionately populated by poor racial and ethnic minorities. Thus the *Wardlow* decision's expansion of the reasonable suspicion standard for investigatory stops has further increased the sphere of discretion in which racially biased policing may reside. Civil libertarians have dubbed Wardlow's case a documentation of the offense of "running while black."

Wilson, Whren, and Atwater

We contend that these three cases, among others, significantly expand the legally recognized discretionary authority of police when they conduct vehicle stops, and thereby increase the potential for racially biased abuse. While the initial stop of a vehicle requires probable cause to believe that the driver has committed, is committing, or is about to commit a crime or traffic violation, or that the car contains contra-band, in a series of cases extending from the late seventies to 2001 the U.S. Supreme Court has ruled that once stopped, law enforcement officers can order the driver[100] and other occupants[101] out of the vehicle pending completion of the stop; can search the passenger compartment,[102] including the belongings of a passenger,[103] without a warrant; and can make a custodial arrest rather than issue a summons for a violation or misdemeanor.[104] These rulings give police a wide range of discretion during traffic stops and thus are ripe for real or perceived racially biased policing practices.

In the case of *Maryland v. Wilson*, the Supreme Court's majority opinion gives law enforcement agents the right (at their discretion) to demand that innocent passengers exit vehicles whenever the driver is stopped for a traffic or other violation. While officer safety was cited by the majority as the rationale for issuing this opinion, the command to exit need not be accompanied by either probable cause or reasonable suspicion that the passengers present a risk of danger to the safety of the officer. Nor does it require that the officer hold any belief regarding the passengers' criminality. The order may be issued as a matter of routine, which means that patrol officers may pick and choose those passengers they will ask to get out, and those that they will allow to remain seated comfortably in the vehicle during the pendency of a stop.

In strongly worded dissents, two justices voiced their objection to the majority holding. Justice John Paul Stevens expressed his discontent with the notion that police were given the "unbridled" discretion to "order about . . . wholly innocent passengers" by virtue of the fact that the driver of a vehicle has been stopped. In the closing lines of his dissent, Justice Anthony Kennedy reminds his colleagues that "[l]iberty comes not from officials by grace, but from the Constitution by right."[105] It seems that the majority of justices did not fully appreciate the "totalitarian" nature of the power that they were bestowing on the police, or the potential for that power to be exercised in racially biased ways.

In *Atwater v. City of Largo Vista*, a Texas woman was arrested and jailed for a little over an hour for not having her two children secured in seat belts, although the regular police procedure under such circumstances was to issue a summons resulting in a fifty-dollar fine.[106] Much more than the oddity that is the U.S. Supreme Court's sanction of a custodial arrest for a misdemeanor of this nature is the judicial machi-nations and divisiveness that underlies the jurisdictional history of the case. The trial court granted summary judgment to the defendant, the City of Largo Vista, on Ms. Atwater's admission that she had violated Texas's seat belt law.[107] On appeal, a panel of the Fifth Circuit of the U.S. Court of Appeals reversed the trial court's grant of summary judgment, but a full Fifth Circuit, with three judges dissenting, overturned the decision of the panel and reinstated the trial court's decision. On granting certio-rari to determine whether the "Fourth Amendment . . . limits police officers' authority to arrest without warrant for minor criminal offenses," a five-to-four majority of the U.S. Supreme Court held that the Fourth Amendment did not prohibit peace officers from arresting citizens without a warrant for misdemeanors.[108] The holding validates the right of the police officer who arrested Ms. Atwater, acting on his own discretion, to either make a full-blown custodial arrest or issue a fifty-dollar summons.[109]

In its most elemental application, the *Atwater* decision grants unbridled discretion to law enforcement to make custodial arrests (or not) for relatively minor offenses, so long as there is probable cause to believe that some form of criminality (even minor) exists. Although the defendant in *Atwater* and the officer who stopped her were both white, in her dissent from the majority opinion Justice Sandra Day O'Connor points out that "[s]uch unbounded discretion carries with it grave potential for abuse . . . Indeed, as the recent debate over racial profiling demonstrates all too clearly, a relatively minor traffic infraction may often serve as an excuse for stopping and harassing an individual."[110]

A look at annual traffic stop statistics gives a better understanding of the breadth of the power granted by the Court. According to data collected by the U.S. Department of Justice, an estimated 19.3 million traffic stops were made in the United States in 1999; of these, 1.3 million drivers had their person or vehicle searched, and 578,000 of these drivers were arrested.[111] Beyond documenting the sheer number of stops, these estimates raise several questions. First, if only 6.7% of drivers stopped were frisked or had their vehicles searched, what was the original trigger for the 19.3 million stops? The answer should be the police officers' substantial factual belief (or probable cause) that the motorists stopped had committed or were committing particular crimes, presumably traffic offenses. Second, if of the vehicles and drivers searched only 578,000 were arrested, what supported the search of the other 722,000 cars and motorists who were not subsequently arrested? Again the answer should be that the police had probable cause that was "sufficient to warrant a prudent man in believing that the [suspect] had committed or was committing an offense."[112]

But the estimates also show that black drivers were twice as likely to be stopped than were white drivers, and were three times more likely to have their person or vehicles searched.[113] Substantiating these estimates are actual data collected by the Bureau of Justice Statistics, which show that, nationwide, criminal evidence is found in the possession of 17% of all white motorists searched, compared to 8% for African American motorists, yet African Americans were more than twice as likely to be searched than were white motorists (8% compared to 3.5%).[114]

Racial and ethnic minorities have often complained that law enforcement agents use pretextual stops to violate the privacy of their automobiles—that police stop minority motorists for some trivial and often ambiguous traffic violation in hopes that, during the course of the detention, they will discover more serious crimes. Despite the low hit rates, and evidence that police agencies were indeed using race as an indicator of who should be stopped, in 1996 the U.S. Supreme Court's decision in *Whren v. U.S.*[115] held that the underlying motivation of a police officer's decision to conduct a traffic stop is irrelevant to the sufficiency of the stop for purposes of probable cause and avoidance of the exclusionary rule.

The holding in *Whren* was in stark contrast to several lower court decisions dating back to 1968.[116] In those cases the lower courts had expressed a concern that "by allowing pretextual stops, police officers would be in a position to look for or manufacture 'grounds for an arrest for a minor offense in order to search for evidence of another suspected crime for which there was no probable cause.'"[117] In fact, although case law had held that vehicle owners, drivers, and passengers have a reduced expectation of privacy in automobiles as compared to their homes, up until the decision in *Whren* there was federal protection against police engaging in such "fishing" expeditions.

The U.S. Supreme Court made its decision in *Whren* despite the fact that, as persuasively argued in dissent, "even the most cautious driver would find it virtually impossible to drive for even a short distance without violating some traffic law."[118] While race-neutral in its wording, the Court's ruling allows police to hide racial bias within the realm of legitimate traffic law enforcement.

In *Whren*, plainclothes police officers in an unmarked car stopped a Nissan Pathfinder with two black occupants after the vehicle was observed stopped at a stop sign for what the officers described as an unusually long period of time (about twenty seconds). According to police testimony, upon seeing the police vehicle make a U-turn to come in its direction, the defendant's vehicle sped away and made a right turn without signaling.[119] Upon approaching the Pathfinder, one police officer observed two bags of crack cocaine in the hands of Whren, and additional drugs were discovered during the subsequent search of the vehicle. The occupants were charged and convicted of violating various federal drug laws. On appeal to the U.S. Court of Appeals for the D.C. Circuit, appellants argued that the stop was not justified by either a reasonable suspicion or probable cause to believe that they were engaged in illegal activity, and that the officers' stated grounds for the stop (a traffic violation) was pretextual. The D.C. Court of Appeals disagreed and affirmed the convictions.

The U.S. Supreme Court granted certiorari to "decide whether the temporary detention of a motorist who the police have probable cause to believe has committed a civil traffic violation is inconsistent with the Fourth Amendment's prohibition against unreasonable seizures."[120] Citing *U.S. v. Robinson*,[121] the majority opinion reiterated that the "Fourth Amendment's concerns with 'reasonableness' allows certain actions to be taken in certain circumstances, whatever the subjective intent," specifically that "ulterior motives cannot invalidate police conduct if that conduct is justified on the basis of probable cause."[122]

In essence, according to the *Whren* Court, not only is there no Fourth Amendment protection against racially biased policing if probable cause for a traffic violation exists,[123] but by refusing to take into account the subjective intention of the police officer, the *Whren* decision amounts to a license for police officers to use broad discretionary powers to enforce minor traffic infractions, even if the real motivation is to check to see if minority motorists are engaged in some other form of crime.[124] Arguably, if pretextual stops are valid when they are based on probable cause that a traffic violation has occurred, then it must be asked what if the pretext is the very "root" of the probable cause?[125] Research shows that police are more likely to be suspicious of, and stop and frisk, minorities based on nonbehavioral cues, while relying on behavioral cues to develop suspicion for nonminorities.[126] Under *Whren*, it is quite possible that a police officer, to effectuate his prejudice, could circumvent the probable cause requirement of the Fourth Amendment and engage in an after-the-fact justification for a racially biased stop. In fact, Justice Brennan warned of just such a possibility in his belief that pretextual stops violate the Fourth Amendment,[127] and, as urged by the defendants in *Whren*, that evidence found under such circumstances should be subject to exclusion.

If "the exclusionary rule was fashioned as a sanction to redress and deter over-reaching governmental conduct prohibited by the Fourth Amendment"[128] by closing the door to any exclusionary rule protection offered by the Fourth Amendment, the question for the citizen of color victimized by racially biased policing is where and how to get relief? According to the *Whren* Court, such a claim is properly raised under the Equal Protection Clause of the Fourteenth Amendment, whose goal is to prevent official conduct that discriminates on the basis of race.[129] The Equal Protection Clause is triggered if it can be shown that selective prosecution or enforcement had "a discriminatory effect . . . that was motivated by a discriminatory purpose."[130] In other words, not only must there be a disparate impact, but the impact must be as a result of intentional discrimination. This requirement presents an almost insurmountable barrier for the victim of racially-biased policing, as the history of such claims shows.[131] (But see also the more recent cases *People v. Roundtree*[132] and *People v. Rijo*,[133] which achieve a different result.)

The Legislation

Federal

The *Whren* and *Brown v. City of Oneonta* decisions specifically reflect the unsympathetic judicial territory where criminal defendants and civil plaintiffs may find themselves when raising federal police racial bias claims—a territory where racially biased policing may exist and thrive, masked by the appearance of legitimate discretionary police practice. As early as 1997, however, Rep. John Conyers (D-Mich.) introduced a federal bill (HR 118) to address the issue of racial profiling. The bill, which was approved by the House, required the U.S. attorney general to "conduct a study of traffic stops to determine whether police were targeting blacks or other racial and ethnic groups for harassment or selective enforcement." HR 118 became the Traffic Stops Statistics Study Act of 2000, introduced to the 106th Congress by Rep. Conyers.[134] As proposed, the law would authorize the U.S. attorney general to, inter alia, collect detailed traffic stop data recording:

(A) The traffic infraction alleged to have been committed that led to the stop.

(B) Identifying characteristics of the driver stopped, including the race, gender, ethnicity, and approximate age of the driver.

(C) Whether immigration status was questioned, immigration documents were requested, or an inquiry was made to the Immigration and Naturalization Service with regard to any person in the vehicle.

(D) The number of individuals in the stopped vehicle.

(E) Whether a search was instituted as a result of the stop and whether consent was requested for the search.

(F) Any alleged criminal behavior by the driver that justified the search.

(G) Any items seized, including contraband or money.

(H) Whether any warning or citation was issued as a result of the stop.

(I)   Whether an arrest was made as a result of either the stop or the search and the justification for the arrest.

(J)   The duration of the stop.[135]

Like the End Racial Profiling Act (ERPA)[136] that was introduced in 2001 and reintroduced in 2007, however, the Traffic Stops Statistics Study Act of 2000 has failed to garner the support it needs to become law.[137] This is so despite the fact that in his February 2001 address to Congress, President George W. Bush reported that he had asked then Attorney General John Ashcroft "to develop specific recommendations to end racial profiling." In his address to the joint session of Congress, President Bush noted that "[t]oo many of our citizens have cause to doubt our nation's justice, when the law points a finger of suspicion at groups, instead of individuals. All of our citizens are created equal and must be treated equal. It's wrong, and we will end it in America."[138]

Despite a memorandum from the president authorizing the attorney general's office to "develop methods or mechanisms to collect any relevant data" from federal law enforcement agencies, and directing the attorney general's office to work with state and local law enforcement in this same regard, by 2005 a senior statistician[139] from the Bureau of Justice Statistics claimed that he was forced out of his position when he complained that senior political officials were seeking to down play newly compiled data on the aggressive police treatment of black and Latino drivers. In addition, indications are that in the aftermath of the September 11, 2001, terrorist attacks, and in light of the conception of immigration as a "crisis," racial and ethnic profiling may be more prevalent than ever. (See the discussion of the lawsuits that appear later in this chapter.)

On December 13, 2007, the ERPA, also known as HR 4611 and which is identical to S 2481, was reintroduced. On January 4, 2008, it was referred to the Subcommittee on Crime, Terrorism, and Homeland Security, where it is awaiting action.

State and Local

Although the judiciary has been reluctant to provide adequate protection against racially biased policing, the American Civil Liberties Union (ACLU) has led efforts to address racially biased policing claims. Since roughly 1999, the ACLU has followed a two-prong approach of targeted litigation and legislation.[140] Targeted litigation, on the one hand, is aimed at chipping away at the pretextual block established in *Whren*, and on the other hand at convincing lower courts to allow racial profiling cases to proceed in the absence of a showing of similarly situated persons being disparately treated.

Rather than await the "right" set of circumstances to bring lawsuits and risk the uncertainty of litigation, the ACLU's legislative prong is aimed at lobbying legislatures across the nation to enact laws mandating law enforcement agencies to record the number of *Terry* stops made and some particulars, such as the race of the individual, for each stop. For example, in the late 1990s Connecticut, North Carolina,

Washington, and Missouri were the first states to enact legislation requiring their law enforcement departments to collect data on the race and other particulars of persons stopped and frisked.[141]

According to the Racial Profiling Data Collection Resource Center at Northeastern University, with the notable exceptions of North Dakota, Mississippi, Puerto Rico, Vermont, and Hawaii, hundreds of jurisdictions within the remaining forty-six states are collecting data because of court settlements, consent decrees, legislation, executive directives, or voluntary policy decisions by law enforcement agencies.[142] This number is a substantial increase over the thirty-two such states noted by federal reports in midyear 1999. With minor variations, most legislation is similar to the Traffic Stops Statistics Study Act of 2000.

In 2001 New Jersey became perhaps the first state to make racial profiling a criminal offense for which, upon conviction, government officials could receive up to five years in prison and be assessed up to a fifteen-thousand-dollar fine. First introduced as Assembly and Senate bills A-942 and S-856 respectively, the sponsors of the bill, assemblyman Leroy. J. Jones and state senator Shirley Turner, proposed the bill after reviewing the recommendations in an August 1999 report issued by the New Jersey Legislative Black and Latino Caucus. The caucus, which consisted of nineteen members of the New Jersey legislature, held hearings in multiple locations across the state before issuing its report, titled "Discriminatory Practices Within the New Jersey State Police."

In compiling its report, the caucus heard testimony from law enforcement experts, former state troopers, civil rights advocates, and private citizens. Persons claiming to be victims of racial profiling who testified before the caucus included, among others:

- a forty-two-year-old African American dentist who reported being stopped by the police more than eighty times between 1985 and 1989, while driving his BMW;
- a father of two children, both of whom were present during a stop, where the father was threatened and humiliated by state troopers;
- two human rights advocates (a male from Nigeria and a female from Egypt) who were physically assaulted during a traffic stop, including the female having a gun held to her head.

The stories told to the caucus were not new, and they were corroborated by former New Jersey state troopers.[143] Evidence of discriminatory practices within the agency had been reported as early as 1975, when its hiring practices were placed under federal monitoring and oversight.[144] Under the proposed legislation, racial profiling amounts to misconduct in office and abuse of office. The bills noted that "[a] law enforcement officer is guilty of racial profiling when the officer uses racial characteristics or color, either alone or in conjunction with other composite characteristics such as a generalized vehicle description or the age of the driver or passenger as the basis for initiating an investigative stop."[145] In 2003 the bills were signed into law by then Governor James McGreevey as a third-degree crime under chapter 30 of the criminal code.

Under the statute, racial profiling, as defined above, constitutes a deprivation of civil rights by public officials. In subsection 5(b) and (c) the statute points out the following:

(b) Such misconduct, and the corresponding damage to the public confidence, impairs the ability of government to function properly, fosters mistrust, and engenders disrespect for government and public servants.

(c) A particular concern arises when a law enforcement official, duty entrusted to protect the public safety and impartially enforce the laws, abuses that trust by unlawfully depriving persons of their civil rights, especially in the context of racial profiling.

The language quoted above became part of the "Misconduct in Office: Abuse of Office" chapter of the New Jersey criminal code effective March 14, 2003.

The question remains as to whether the statute has anything more than symbolic significance. Its enactment denotes that the government was responsive to serious concerns about the behavior of its agents. In testimony before the caucus, several former state troopers revealed that during their time with the police agency, they were trained and encouraged to make race/ethnicity-based stops. One Latino officer who was a ten-year veteran filed a federal discrimination suit against the agency with one of his primary claims being that he had been urged to make illegal stops of innocent black and Latino motorists.

An empirical question for criminologists and criminal justice scholars is whether a statute that makes racial profiling a crime can have the desired deterrent affect on police behavior. Rather than attempting to address this question, much criminology/criminal justice research focuses on whether statistics that show disparate racial impact within police stop data really mean that racially biased policing is taking place.[146] Some of that research suggests that the disparate figures reflect differences in offending patterns across race.[147] Other research suggests that racial profiling is an effective way to maximize limited police resources.[148] The New Jersey statute recognizes the danger in such attempts to deny or justify the existence of racial profiling as a police practice, but, by its wording, seems to limit criminal penalties to racial profiling in motor vehicle stops. What is not so clear is whether the statute is intended to also address race/ethnicity-based stops on the sidewalks.

The existence of the statute also gives rise to the question of whether state and local prosecutors, who work closely with police officers, will have the will and integrity to vigorously pursue racial profiling prosecutions against those same state and local police. To be effective, does the statute, of necessity, require the appointment of a special prosecutor in such cases?

The table at the end of this chapter summarizes the current information available about the state of racial profiling legislation in all fifty states. As of 2002, while thirty-eight states required some form of data collection for stops performed by the police, twenty-eight of the fifty states did not have legislation specifically prohibiting racial profiling of motorists or pedestrians; twenty-one states did. Early in 2000–2001, Eleanor Holmes Norton, the District of Columbia's nonvoting member of Congress, tried to introduce legislation that would withhold federal highway dollars from states that do not explicitly ban racial profiling. As proposed in May 2001, HR 1907, also known as the Racial Profiling Prohibition Act, would require states to enact racial profiling bans to be eligible for federal highway funds. The proposal gave states until 2003 to have their prohibition legislation in place. At the time of this writing, HR 1907 had still not been enacted.

Despite efforts to control unwarranted racial profiling through legislative enactments, incidents that suggest the use of such profiles and racially biased policing persist. For example, in New York City, where highly publicized incidents such as the torture of Abner Louima[149] and the shooting of Amadou Diallo[150] and Sean Bell[151] have all happened as a result of street encounters between males of African ancestry and the police, statistics reveal that over the years of record keeping and the express prohibition against racial profiling, as stated by the police commissioner, not only have the number of *Terry* stops increased, a greater percentage of minorities are being stopped and frisked. Figures released by the New York City Police Department (NYPD) show that in 2006 there were more than half a million of such stops. Statistics compiled by that agency indicate, specifically, that during 2006 there were 508,540 police stops. Among them, 52.8% of those stopped were African Americans, 29.2% were Hispanics, and 10.6% were Whites.[152] This means that 82% of those stopped were people of color, while it is estimated that people of color make up only 54% of New York City's population. The question is repeatedly asked: what accounts for these disparities in law enforcement's application of *Terry*'s stop and frisk procedures?

Researchers have attempted to unravel the underlying causes of these disparate figures (in New York and elsewhere) by using aggregate estimates of reported descriptions of suspects.[153] Such attempts miss the main point that Fourth Amendment protection is individualized in nature. The accumulation of data regarding the typical description called in to the police, in any given area, by law cannot serve as a basis for suspecting a particular person (or all persons who belong to the same racial identity group). As per the Fourth Amendment and most of the precedent case law, police intelligence coupled with the specificity of individual characteristics to that intelligence, along with personal conduct, are the only legitimate bases for police attention. Broad descriptions or presumptions based solely or primarily on racial assumptions are invalid (but see *Brown v. City of Oneonta*, discussed earlier in this chapter, to the contrary). Stops and frisks based on nonparticularized suspicion,[154] and traffic stops that target only certain law violators,[155] when prompted by visual cues such as race, arguably fall outside the permissible realm of even the relaxed Fourth Amendment standard—reasonable suspicion—announced in *Terry*.

The Lawsuits

As case law grants the police more and more discretion during police-citizen encounters, and statistics reveal racial disparities, there is little chance that racial bias can be definitively proved in the individual case, absent an admission by the officer[156] or other documentation that the law enforcement agents are operating on race-based assumptions. As recent data out of Los Angeles confirm,[157] racial profiling lawsuits

have been difficult but not impossible to win. One of the better-known early successful racial profiling cases involved the Criminal Intelligence Report of the Maryland
State Police quoted at the beginning of this chapter. In the 1995 lawsuit of *Wilkins v.
Maryland*,[158] a Maryland State Police confidential internal document revealed that
the department was operating on the belief that the majority of drug traffickers along
the I-95 corridor were black males and females. The memo provided no factual basis
for this claim.

When Robert Wilkins, a Washington, D.C. lawyer, was stopped for speeding by
Maryland state troopers, they apparently assumed that he was also potentially a drug
trafficker based on his appearance. When they asked to search the car in which he
was traveling with his family, he refused to give his permission. When he questioned
the troopers' probable cause for requesting a search, he was informed that he and his
family would not be permitted to leave without exiting the car. After roughly forty-
five minutes, Wilkins and his family were allowed to leave but only after they had
gotten out of the car and a drug sniffing dog had been brought to the scene. The
ACLU represented the Wilkins family in a suit against the Maryland State Police for
violation of their civil rights. Upon discovery of the intelligence report, the *Wilkins*
case was settled for just under one hundred thousand dollars and an agreement that
the agency would maintain computer records regarding all motorists stopped between 1995 and 1997. Statistics gathered as part of the settlement revealed that two of
the troopers in the Special Target Interdiction Force (STIF), a special unit for drug
interdiction, over a one-year period *only* stopped black motorists. Other sites of early
successful racial profiling lawsuits include Beverly Hills, California; Chicago, Illinois;
Eagle County, Colorado; Pittsburgh, Pennsylvania; Tinicum County, Pennsylvania;
Gloucester Township, New Jersey; and Volusia County, Florida. Their settlement
amounts total more than one million dollars.

In April 2008 the ACLU announced the settlement of a class action suit filed
against the Maryland State Police during the late nineties. The settlement totals more
than four hundred thousand dollars and includes a three-hundred-thousand-dollar
payment by the state of Maryland for damages and legal costs to the plaintiffs. It also
includes a commitment by the Maryland State Police (MSP) to pay up to one hundred thousand dollars to retain an independent police practices consultant. The consultant will assess how the MSP has implemented policy and practice changes that
address racial profiling concerns. This aspect of the settlement is related to a consent
decree reached in 2003. The consultant is expected to make recommendations to the
agency superintendent. Those recommendations cannot be rejected without reasonable cause.

In addition to the substantial funds provided as damages and attorneys' fees to the
individual plaintiffs, the settlement includes a joint statement condemning racial profiling, put forth by all parties involved in the suit (including the police). The statement
also highlights the importance of taking preventative action against the practice of
racial profiling in the future. This joint agreement by the ACLU, MSP, the individual
plaintiffs, and the Maryland National Association for the Advancement of Colored
People (NAACP) settles an ACLU federal lawsuit filed in 1998 on behalf of the Maryland NAACP and several private plaintiffs, based on accumulated evidence showing a

pattern and practice of discrimination. In contrast to commissioned studies that deny or attempt to justify racial profiling, this multifaceted settlement embodies a unique opportunity for law enforcement agencies, advocacy groups, and private citizens to work together to address a phenomenon that, despite legislative attempts at deterrence, is reported as an everyday occurrence in African American, Latino, and other ethnic-minority communities across the United States.[159]

TABLE 6.1

State	No law prohibiting racial profiling	Law prohibits racial profiling of motorists only	Law prohibits racial profiling of both pedestrians and motorists	No data collection	Data collection required by	Data collected at all stops	Data collected when citation issued	Data collected when arrest is made	Data collected when search made	Data collected when force is used
Alabama	✓				LAW		✓	✓	✓	✓
Alaska		✓			DPR*					
Arizona	✓			✓						
Arkansas			✓	✓						
California			✓		DPR	✓	✓	✓	✓	✓
Colorado			✓		LAW*		✓	✓		
Connecticut	✓				LAW	✓	✓	✓	✓	✓
Delaware	✓				AGR		✓	✓		✓
Florida			✓		LAW	✓	✓	✓	✓	✓
Georgia	✓									✓
Hawaii	✓									
Idaho	✓			✓						
Illinois			✓							
Indiana	✓				DPR		✓	✓		✓
Iowa	✓				DPR	✓	✓	✓	✓	✓
Kansas			✓		LAW		✓	✓		✓
Kentucky			✓		EOR		✓	✓	✓	✓
Louisiana	✓				LAW		✓	✓		✓
Maine	✓				DPR		✓	✓		
Maryland		✓			LAW*		✓	✓	✓	✓
Massachusetts			✓		LAW*	✓	✓	✓	✓	✓
Michigan	✓				DPR	✓	✓	✓	✓	✓
Minnesota		✓		✓						
Mississippi	✓				DPR		✓	✓		✓
Missouri		✓			LAW	✓	✓	✓	✓	
Montana			✓	✓						
Nebraska			✓		LAW		✓	✓	✓	✓
Nevada		✓			LAW		✓	✓		✓
New Hampshire	✓				DPR		✓	✓		
New Jersey			✓		CDR*	✓	✓	✓	✓	✓
New Mexico	✓			✓						
New York	✓				DPR			✓	✓	
North Carolina	✓				DPR	✓	✓	✓	✓	✓
North Dakota	✓			✓						
Ohio	✓				DPR	✓	✓	✓	✓	✓
Oklahoma			✓	✓						
Oregon	✓				DPR	✓	✓	✓	✓	✓
Pennsylvania	✓				DPR				✓	✓
Rhode Island	✓				DPR	✓	✓	✓	✓	✓
South Carolina	✓				DPR	✓	✓	✓		✓
South Dakota	✓				DPR			✓		
Tennessee					DPR*		✓	✓		✓
Texas			✓		LAW	✓	✓	✓	✓	✓
Utah			✓	✓						

(continued)

TABLE 6.1 (*continued*)

State	No law prohibiting racial profiling	Law prohibits racial profiling of motorists only	Law prohibits racial profiling of both pedestrians and motorists	No data collection	Data collection required by	Data collected at all stops	Data collected when citation issued	Data collected when arrest is made	Data collected when search made	Data collected when force is used
Vermont	✓				DPR			✓		
Virginia	✓				DPR	✓	✓	✓	✓	✓
Washington			✓		LAW	✓	✓	✓	✓	✓
West Virginia		✓			LAW*		✓	✓		✓
Wisconsin	✓				DPR		✓	✓	✓	✓
Wyoming	✓				DPR		✓	✓		

*A number of states collected data in the past during the years 2001–2007 but are not currently collecting. The particulars shown for these states are those that were recorded when collection was in effect.

Table constructed from data available at the Northeastern University's Racial Profiling Data Collection Resource Center (available at http://www.racialprofilinganalysis.neu.edu/), Amnesty International (available at http://www.amnestyusa.org/Racial _Profiling/Laws), and the U.S. Department of Justice Bureau of Justice Statistics (available at http://www.ojp.gov/bjs/abstract/ tsdcpo1.htm).

Key
LAW: Recording is required by law.
DPR: Recording is required by departmental policy.
AGR: Recording is required due to agreement between police officials and community.
CDR: Recording is required by consent decree.
EOR: Recording is required by executive order.

NOTES

1. Callahan and Anderson, "The Roots of Racial Profiling" at p. 2.

2. Ibid.

3. In social science this is the classic case of the false negative. See Engel, "A Critique of the 'Outcome Test.'"

4. This is the classic case of the false positive, or, as described by Callahan and Anderson, this amounts to class probability instead of case probability.

5. 422 U.S. 873 (1975).

6. Ibid., p. 886–887.

7. Ibid.

8. For example, in the companion cases to *Wilkins v. Maryland* against the Maryland State Police, when one plaintiff asked why he was being detained for three hours, he was told by the authorities that he "looked like a drug dealer." See Staples, "Why 'Racial Profiling' Will Be Hard to Fight." Also, in 2000 an internal memorandum to federal park rangers in California's Mendocino National Forest indicated "to develop probable cause for a stop . . . if a vehicle stop is conducted and no marijuana is located and the vehicle has Hispanics inside, *at a minimum*, we would like all individuals FI'd [field interrogated]" (emphasis added). See Callahan and Anderson, "The Roots of Racial Profiling," p. 2.

9. 324 N.J. Super 66 (1996).

10. See also the economic perspective on racial profiling discussed in Engel, "A Critique of the 'Outcome Test'"; and Harcourt, "Rethinking Racial Profiling."

11. Ibid.

12. A recently settled lawsuit between the ACLU, the Maryland NAACP, private individuals, and the Maryland State Police included deposition testimony by a senior trooper that supervisors thought nothing of the fact that two officers named in the class action suit stopped

only black motorists. There was no follow-up with the officers once the statistics were known —even though the agency had signed a consent decree to address racial profiling. See Staples, "Why 'Racial Profiling' Will Be Tough to Fight."

13. See also discussions regarding "hit rates" for black versus white detainees in Engel, "A Critique of the 'Outcome Test'"; and Harcourt, "Rethinking Racial Profiling."

14. Williams and Murphy, "Evolving Strategy of the Police."

15. McIntyre, "Criminalizing a Race."

16. Ibid.

17. See, for example, the Chinese Exclusion Act.

18. Williams and Murphy, "Evolving Strategy of the Police."

19. Eberhardt et al., "Seeing Black." See also Plant and Peruche, "The Consequences of Race"; Eberhardt and Goff, "The Morality of Associating Race and Crime"; and Dovidio et al., "Racial Stereotypes."

20. Ibid.

21. Eberhardt, "Imaging Race"; and Golby et al., "Differential Responses."

22. Lerner, "Reasonable Suspicion."

23. *Dunaway v. New York*, 442 U.S. 200, 213–214 (1979).

24. Lerner, "Reasonable Suspicion"

25. *Terry v. Ohio*, 392 U.S. 1 (1968).

26. Ibid.

27. *Mapp v. Ohio*, 367 U.S. 643 (1961).

28. It is noteworthy that the *Terry* decision coincided with the passage of the Omnibus Crime Control and Safe Streets Act of 1968, which, inter alia, aimed to prevent crime and insure the greater safety of U.S. citizens (P.L. 90-351, 82 Stat.197). One way of insuring this aim was article 2 of the act, which sought to overturn *Miranda v. Arizona*, 384 U.S. 436 (1966) by allowing the admission of voluntary admissions, even if the defendant was not informed of his Fifth Amendment rights.

29. As a relative term, it is safe to assume that "reasonableness" in 1791, when the Fourth Amendment was enacted, was quite different from today. For it can be argued that reasonableness pre–September 11, 2001, is quite different from post–September 11, 2001, as is evident in a post–September 11, 2001, statement by a U.S. Justice Department official who stated that persons suspected of terrorist involvement should be arrested for even the most minor offenses, including the act of spitting on the sidewalk. See Gearan, "U.S. Terror Tactics Detailed."

30. *Terry v. Ohio* at p. 21.

31. *Ohio v. Robinette*, 519 U.S. 33, 34 (1996).

32. *Brown v. Texas*, 443 U.S. 47, 57 (1979).

33. *United States v. Cortez*, 449 U.S. 411, 417 (1981).

34. See Schwartz, "Just Take Away Their Guns," which discusses the hidden racism of the *Terry* decision.

35. *Terry v. Ohio* at pp. 22–23.

36. According to Chief Justice Earl Warren, McFadden "was unable to say precisely what first drew his eye" to Terry and Chilton. *Terry v. Ohio*, 392 U.S. 1, 5 (1968).

37. *Terry v. Ohio*, p. 37.

38. Ibid., p. 38.

39. Ibid., p. 39.

40. Ibid., p. 38.

41. Ibid.

42. See the economic perspective discussed in Engel, "A Critique of the 'Outcome Test'"; and Harcourt, "Rethinking Racial Profiling."

43. Former New Jersey state troopers John Hogan and James Kenna testified to this effect in 1998, and other former troopers testified similarly to the New Jersey Black and Latino Legislative Caucus during hearings in 1999.

44. See note 12.

45. See Engel, "A Critique of the 'Outcome Test.'"

46. See New Jersey Criminal Law, 2C:30-5(b) and (c).

47. Jones-Brown, "Forever the Symbolic Assailant."

48. *U.S. v. Brignoni-Ponce*, 422 U.S. 873 (1975).

49. In *Almeida-Sanchez v. U.S.*, 413 U.S. 266 (1973), the issue was the use of roving patrols near the Mexican-American border to search cars whose occupants appeared to be of Mexican ancestry, whereas in *Brignoni-Ponce* the issue was the legality of the stop to question the occupants of the vehicle.

50. *U.S. v. Brignoni-Ponce*, pp. 885–886.

51. Ibid.

52. See *El Comite De Trabajadores Por El Progreso Y Bienestar Social et als v. Borough of Freehold*.

53. *El Comite De Trabajadores Por El Progreso Y Bienestar Social et al. v. Borough of Freehold*.

54. See quote in note 8 regarding the federal park ranger memorandum associating Latinos with marijuana possession.

55. 534 U.S. 816 (2001).

56. A similar fact pattern is presented in *Davis v. Mississippi*, 394 U.S. 721 (1969).

57. *Brown et al. v. City of Oneonta et al.*, 221 F. 3d 329 (2d Cir. 2000).

58. See Kennedy, "Race, Crime, and the Law"; Fagan and Davies, "Street Stops and Broken Windows"; Rice and Piquero, " Perceptions of Discrimination and Justice."

59. *U.S. v. Arvizu*, 534 U.S. 266 (2002).

60. In April 2001, charges against seventeen residents of Hearne, Texas, were dismissed because the drug task force had focused primarily on African Americans and the informant failed a polygraph test when questioned about tampering with evidence. See Drug Policy Alliance, "Recent Exoneration in Tulia, Texas."

61. *Brown et al. v. City of Oneonta et al.*, 534 U.S. 816 (2001).

62. 75 F. Supp 2d 154 (S.D.N.Y. 1999).

63. Ibid.

64. 324 N.J. Super 66 (1996).

65. On April 23, 1998, Danny Reyes, Keshon Moore, Rayshawn Brown, and Leroy Grant were shot at by New Jersey state troopers John Hogan and James Kenna during a stop for speeding. Reyes, Moore, Brown, and Grant were all unarmed and seated in a van. The troopers claimed that they feared for their lives as the van began to role backwards during the stop. In the subsequent investigation of the shooting, it was determined that the van had been stopped as part of a racial profiling scheme that the troopers had been engaged in for some time. Three of the vans occupants were struck by bullets. The shooting resulted in a thirteen-million-dollar settlement.

66. Farmer, Jr., and Zoubek, "Final Report of the State Police Review Team."

67. *State of New Jersey v. Pedro Soto et al.*, 324 N.J. Super 66 (1996).

68. For example, see *Robert L. Wilkins v. Maryland State Police, et al.*, Civil Action No. CCB-93-468 (1993).

69. The attorney general's "Final Report of the State Police Review Team" found that 46% of all drivers pulled over were African American, although African Americans constituted only 13.5% of drivers and 15% of speeders.

70. Kifner, "Van Shooting," p. 2.

71. Ibid.

72. Ibid.

73. One such plaintiff was a ten-year veteran of the force. He sued alleging personal discrimination and having been disciplined for failing to follow directives to stop Latinos and blacks.

74. *U.S. v. Armstrong*, 517 U.S. 456 (1996).

75. According to Jeff Blackburn, director of the Tulia Legal Defense Project, in an interview with NPR on June 17, 2003, "the sheriff, district attorney, and the judge were all complicit in this travesty."

76. The drug sting was the execution of a policy of mandatory drug testing adopted by the Tulia school board after one board member observed her child conversing with an African American child. To effectuate his drug sting, the local sheriff compiled a list of 60 "known drug dealers" and 246 African Americans. October 22, 2000 statement by Will Harris, executive director ACLU of Texas.

77. CNN.com, "Texas Drug Bust Raises Questions of Racial Prejudice."

78. Herbert, "Justice a Stranger."

79. Ibid.

80. In 2002 the Texas legislature passed a law "preventing a drug conviction based solely on the testimony of an informant." See Drug Policy Alliance, "Recent Exoneration in Tulia, Texas."

81. Herbert, "Justice a Stranger."

82. One of Coleman's buys was from Tonya White, who was able to prove that at the alleged time of the crime she had personally made a cash withdrawal at a bank in Oklahoma City. See ibid.

83. *Kelly v. Paschall*, Civ. 02-A-02-CA-702 JN, United States District Court for the Western District of Texas. See also Liptak, "$5 Million Settlement."

84. Barnes, "Ex-Narcotics Agent."

85. A 1999 study conducted by M/A/R/C Research for the American Bar Association found that 50% of respondents believed that law enforcement treats minorities different from white people, while 47% believed that the courts do. See Greenhouse, "47% in Poll View Legal System as Unfair."

Also, in a story for which they won the 1993 Pulitzer Prize for Investigative Reporting, Jeff Brazil and Steve Berry reported that in one week of videotaping traffic stops with cameras fitted to sheriff's cars in Volusia County, Florida, although only 5% of all users of a stretch of I-95 were minorities, 70% of drivers stopped were. See Brazil and Berry, "Color of Driver Is Key."

86. Eberhardt et al., "Seeing Black."

87. *U.S. v. Sokolow*, 490 U.S. 1 (1989).

88. Johnson, "The Self-Fulfilling Prophecy" at p. 93–94.

89. Amicus brief submitted by the NAACP Legal Defense and Education Fund Inc. in *Terry v. Ohio*, 392 U.S. 12, (1968) at p. 3 and note 79 at p. 45. For an in-depth discussion of the arguments presented to the U.S. Supreme Court for and against the probable cause exception, see Schwartz, "Just Take Away Their Guns."

90. "President's Commission on Law Enforcement."

91. Ibid., pp. 48–59.

92. See, for example, *Illinois v. Wardlow*, 528 U.S. 119 (2000); *U.S. v. Broadie*, 452 U.S. F.3d 875 (2006); and *California v. Hodari*, 499 U.S. 621 (1991).

93. Ibid.

94. *Illinois v. Wardlow.*

95. Ibid. at pp. 674–675.

96. Ibid. at pp. 675.

97. *Illinois v. Wardlow*, 183 Ill. App 2d 306.

98. Ibid. at p. 125.

99. See Brunson, "Police Don't Like Black People."

100. *Pennsylvania v. Mimms*, 434 U.S. 106, 111 (1977).

101. *Maryland v. Wilson*, 519 U.S. 408 (1997)

102. *Michigan v. Long*, 463 U.S. 1032 (1983).

103. *Wyoming v. Houghton*, 526 U.S. 295 (1999).

104. *Atwater et al., v. City of Largo Vista et al.*, 532 U.S. 318, 322 (2001).

105. *Maryland v. Wilson* at p. 891.

106. *Atwater et al., v. City of Largo Vista et al.* at p. 318.

107. Of interest is Justice Stewart's concurring opinion in *Gustafson v. Florida* stating that had the defendant not conceded that his arrest was constitutional he might have had "a persuasive claim . . . that [his] custodial arrest . . . for a minor traffic offense violated his rights under the Fourth and Fourteenth Amendments" at pp. 266–67.

108. *Atwater et al., v. City of Largo Vista et al.* at p. 341.

109. Ibid. at p. 354.

110. Ibid. at p. 372.

111. Schmitt et al., "Characteristics of Drivers Stopped," pp. 12–13.

112. *Beck v. Ohio*, p. 91. Although from some law enforcement agencies perspectives and the economic perspective put forth by academics, profiling (including racial), especially when utilized in reference to the interdiction of illegal drugs, was and continues to be "successful." Much research on racial profiling, however, shows its irrationality. For example, a high hit rate reported in the City of Indianapolis, over a three-month period, meant that police stopped 1,161 cars and made 104 arrests for a success rate of only 9%. Critics contend that hit rates are far lower, and even when reportedly high, they do not justify stopping law-abiding citizens because they match some theoretical paradigm, especially if they miss upwards of 90% of the time.

113. Schmitt et al., "Characteristics of Drivers Stopped By," p. 7.

114. Contacts between Police and the Public available at http://www.ojp.usdoj.gov/bjs.

115. 517 U.S. 806 (1996).

116. *U.S. v. Millio* (1984); *State v. Davis* (1983); the dissenting opinion in *People v. Holloway* (1982); and *Amador-Gonzalez v. U.S.* (1968).

117. *State v. Davis*, 35 WN App. 724 (1983) at p. 725.

118. Levit, "Pretextual Traffic Stops."

119. *Whren v. U.S*, 517 U.S. 806 (1996).

120. Ibid. at p. 808.

121. *U.S. v. Robinson*, 414 U.S. 218, 221 (1973).

122. *Whren v. U.S.* In *Brignoni-Ponce*, and again in *Prouse*, where the issue was reasonable suspicion, the Court weighed the public interest against the governmental interference with individual liberty in deciding the reasonableness of a police stop. The Court never explained why it is necessary to limit "reasonableness balancing" when the police use probable cause.

123. More than twenty-five years earlier, the *Terry* Court was likewise dismissive of Fourth Amendment claims based on racially biased policing in stating that the "wholesale harassment by . . . police . . . of which minority groups, particularly Negroes, frequently complain will not be stopped by the exclusion of any evidence from any criminal trial," *Terry v. Ohio*, 392 U.S. 1, 14–15 (1968).

124. *Atwater et al., v. City of Largo Vista et al.* at FN 32.

125. In *People v. Dickson* (1998), a New York trial court suppressed evidence after a police officer admitted to "pretextual motivation" for a traffic stop.

126. Alpert , MacDonald, and Dunham, "Police Suspicion."

127. *Horton v. California*, 496 U.S. 128 (1990).

128. *Davis v. Mississippi*, 394 U.S. 721, 724 (1969).

129. *Washington v. Davis*, 426 U.S. 229, 238 (1976); and *Whren v. U.S.* at p. 813.

130. *U.S. v. Bell*, 86 F. 3d 820, 823 (1998).

131. See *McCleskey v. Kemp*, 481 U.S. 279 (1987); and *U.S. v. Armstrong*.

132. 234 A.D.2d 612 (1996), 89 N.Y.2d 1040 (1997).

133. 220 A.D.2d 217 (1995).

134. It failed to gain sufficient support to become law in each of the previous years.

135. Union Calendar No. 287, 106th Congress, 2d Session, HR 1443.

136. The ERPA prohibits law enforcement agents from engaging in racial profiling, which it defines as "the practice of a law enforcement agent or agency relying to any degree, on race, ethnicity, national origin, or religion in selecting which individual to subject to routine or spontaneous investigatory activities or in deciding upon the scope and substance of law enforcement activity following the initial investigatory procedure." Among its other dictates, the ERPA requires that agencies maintain procedures and policies for eliminating racial profiling and calls for the cessation of any existing activities that allow racial profiling.

137. A similar bill, HR 258.IH, Traffic Stops Along the Border Statistics Study Act 2007, was proposed by Rep. Sheila Jackson-Lee. It would mandate the collection of the same data but restrict such collection to within twenty-five miles of the U.S. borders with Mexico and Canada.

138. Understanding Bias-Based Traffic Law Enforcement—Resources, retrieved October 28, 2008, http://nhtsa.gov/people/injury/enforce/biasbased03/resources.htm.

139. The official was Lawrence A. Greenfeld. See Lichtblau, "Profiling Report Leads to Demotion."

140. Harris, "Driving While Black."

141. In April 1996 North Carolina made it mandatory for state police to record the race, age, and gender of every motorist stopped. See Curry, "Profiling Cops" at p. 37.

142. Background and Current Data Collection Efforts: Jurisdictions Currently Collecting Data. The Racial Profiling Data Collection Resource Center at Northeastern University. Available at http://www.racialprofilinganalysis.neu.edu/index.php.

143. See New Jersey Legislative Black and Latino Caucus, "A Report on Discriminatory Practices."

144. Ibid at p. 4.

145. A-942 and S-856 and New Jersey Criminal code, 2C:30-5(d).

146. See studies that attempt to establish population baselines, benchmarks, or denominators: Engel and Calnon, "Comparing Benchmark Methodologies"; Walker, "Searching for the Denominator"; Knowles, Persico, and Todd, "Racial Bias in Motor Vehicle Searches."

147. This effort has included a study commissioned by the New Jersey attorney general's office that claimed to establish that blacks speed more than whites on the New Jersey

Turnpike. See also Engel, "A Critique of the 'Outcome Test'"; and Harcourt, "Rethinking Racial Profiling."

148. See, for example, Persico, "Racial Profiling, Fairness, and Effectiveness of Policing"; Borooah, "Racial Bias in Police Stops and Searches"; and Chakravarty, "Economic Analysis of Police Stops."

149. A Haitian immigrant violently attacked by NYPD officer Justin Volpe in 1997.

150. An unarmed West African immigrant killed by NYPD officers in a 1999 incident where the officers fired 41 bullets.

151. An unarmed groom killed on his wedding day in 2006 by police who had been conducting an undercover operation in the bar where the victim had held his bachelor party. Fifty bullets were fired at him and his companions while they were seated in a car.

152. Hamblett, "NYCLU Suit Claims Police Target Minorities for Stops," p. 1.

153. Ridgeway, "Analysis of Racial Disparities in New York."

154. See note 58.

155. See, for example, *State v. Soto* and *Wilkins v. Maryland State Police.*

156. See note 8.

157. While a report by the ACLU found racial disparity in police stops of blacks and whites in Los Angeles between July 1, 2003, and June 30, 2004, Police Chief William Bratton vehemently denied allegations of racial profiling and declared 252 out of 320 claims that officers confronted someone solely on the basis of race as either unfounded or lacking sufficient evidence. Another report covering 371 racial profiling complaints coming from nineteen agencies across the country, over a two-year period, found all but four to be unsubstantiated.

158. *Wilkins v. Maryland State Police.*

159. The ACLU has recently been involved with settling other cases against the California Highway Patrol ($875,000); the Transportation Security Administration (TSA); and the Rhode Island State Police. Note that ethnicity-based detentions in airports were a problem even before September 11, 2001.

REFERENCES

Alpert, Geoffrey, John MacDonald, and Roger Dunham. 2005. Police suspicion and discretionary decision making during citizen stops. *Criminology* 43:407–434.

Banks, R. Richard. 2001. Race-based suspect selection and colorblind equal protection doctrine and discourse. *UCLA Law Rev.* 48:1075–1124.

Banks, R. Richard. n.d. Beyond rights, irrationality, and racial profiling. Available at http://www.berkley.edu/institutes/csls/bankspaper.pdf.

Barnes, Steve. Ex-narcotics agent gets 10 years probation. *New York Times.* January 19, 2005.

Beck, Allen and Christopher Mumola. 1999. *Prisoners in 1998.* Washington, DC: U.S. Department of Justice, Bureau of Justice Statistics.

Blackburn, Jeff, director of the Tulia Legal Defense Project, interviewed by Terry Gross of National Public Radio on June 17, 2003.

Blacks law dictionary. 6th ed. 1990. St. Paul, MN: West Publishing.

Borooah, Vani. 2001. Racial bias in police stops and searches: An economic analysis. *European Journal of Political Economy* 17:17–37.

Bratton, William and Peter Knobler. 1998. *Turnaround.* New York: Random House.

Brazil, Jeff and Steve Berry. Color of driver is key to stops in I-95 videos. *Orlando Sentinel.* August 23, 1992, A1.

Brunson, Rod. 2007. Police don't like black people: African American young men's accumulated police experiences. *Criminology and Public Policy* 6:71–102.

Callahan, Gene and William Anderson. 2001. The roots of racial profiling. *Reason Magazine*. August–September.

Chakravarty, Shanti. 2002. Economic analysis of police stops and searches: a critique. *European Journal of Political Economy* 18:597–605.

CNN.com. Texas drug bust raises questions of racial prejudice. October 2, 2000.

Cole, David. 1999. *No equal justice: race and class in the American justice system*. New York: The New Press.

Curry, George E. 1999. Profiling cops: key to curbing police abuses. *Emerge* 10.

Davis, Marcia. 1999. Traffic violation. *Emerge* 10.

Dovidio, John, Nancy Evans, and Richard Tyler. 1986. Racial stereotypes: the contents of their cognitive representation. *Journal of Experimental Social Psychology* 22:22–37.

Dressler, Joshua. *Understanding criminal law*. 2d ed. 1997. New York: Mathew Bender.

Drug Policy Alliance. Recent Exoneration in Tulia, Texas. April 12, 2002.

Eberhardt, Jennifer. 2005. Imaging race. *American Psychologist* 60:181–190.

Eberhardt, Jennifer and Phillip Goff. 2004. The morality of associating race and crime. Unpublished raw data.

Eberhardt, Jennifer, Valerie Purdie, Phillip Goff, and Paul Davies. 2004. Seeing black: race, crime and visual processing. *Journal of Personality and Social Psychology* 87:876–893.

Engel, Robin. 2008. A critique of the "outcome test" in racial profiling research. *Justice Quarterly* 25:1–36.

Engel, Robin and Jennifer Calnon. 2004. Comparing benchmark methodologies for police-citizen contacts: stop data collection for the Pennsylvania state police. *Police Quarterly* 7: 97–125.

Fagan, Jeffrey and Garth Davies. 2000. Street stops and broken windows: *Terry*, race, and disorder in New York City. *Fordham Urb. L.J.* 28:457–504.

Farmer, Jr., John and Paul Zoubek. 1999. *Final report of the state police review team*. Trenton, NJ: Office of the Attorney General.

Gallup Organization. Poll of September 24, 1999. Public Opinion Online, November 16, 2001. Roper Center at the University of Connecticut, available at Lexis, News Library.

Gearan, Ann. U.S. terror tactics detailed. *Associated Press*. February 1, 2002.

Golby, Alexandra, John Gabrieli, Joan Chiao, and Jennifer Eberhardt. 2001. Differential responses in the fusiform region to same-race and other-race faces. *Nature Neuroscience* 4:845–850.

Greenhouse, Linda. Forty-seven percent in poll view legal system as unfair to poor and minorities. *New York Times*. February 24, 1999.

Gross, Samuel R. and Katherine Y. Barnes. 2002. Road work: racial profiling and drug interdiction on the highway. *U. of Michigan Law Rev.* 101:651–754.

Gross, Samuel R. and Debra Livingston. 2002. Racial profiling under attack. *Colum. L. Rev.* 102:1413–1438.

Hamblett, Mark. NYCLU suit claims police target minorities for stops. *New York Law Journal*. May 8, 2008.

Harcourt, Bernard. 2004. Rethinking racial profiling: a critique of the economics, civil liberties, and constitutional literature, and of criminal profiling more generally. *U. of Chicago Law Rev.* 71:1275–1381.

Harris, David A. 1997. "Driving while black" and all other offenses: the Supreme Court and pretextual traffic stops. *Crime and Criminology* 87:561–562.

Harris, David A. 1999. *Driving while black: racial profiling on our nation's highways.* American Civil Liberties Union special report. Available at http://www.aclu.org/racialjustice/racial profiling/15912pub19990607.html.

Harris, David A. 2002. *Profiles in injustice: why racial profiling cannot work.* New York: The New Press.

Harris, Will, executive director ACLU of Texas. October 22, 2000, statement.

Herbert, Bob. Justice a stranger in Tulia, Texas. *Virginia-Pilot.* July 30, 2002.

Johnson, Scott. 2000. The self-fulfilling prophecy of police profiles. In *The system in black and white: exploring the connections between race, crime and justice,* ed. Michael W. Markowitz and Delores D. Jones-Brown, 93–108. Westport, CT: Praeger.

Jones-Brown, Delores. 2007. Forever the symbolic assailant: the more things change the more they remain the same. *Criminology and Public Policy* 6:103–122.

Jones-Brown, Delores. 1999. *Maryland v. Wilson* revisited: combatting police use of racial and ethnic profiles. *Minorities in the Profession Section Newsletter.* New Brunswick, NJ: New Jersey State Bar Association.

Kelling, George and Catherine M. Coles. 1998. *Fixing broken windows: restoring order and reducing crime in our communities.* New York: Simon and Schuster.

Kennedy, Randall. 1997. *Race, crime, and the law.* New York: Pantheon.

Kicker, Charles. Legal system works in Tulia? *Amarillo Globe-News.* April 26, 2003.

Kifner, John. Van shooting revives charges of racial "profiling" by New Jersey state police. *New York Times.* May 10, 1998.

Knowles, John, Nicola Persico, and Petra Todd. 2001. Racial bias in motor vehicle searches: theory and evidence. *Journal of Political Economy* 109:203–299.

Lerner, Craig S. 2005. Reasonable suspicion and mere hunches. George Mason University School of Law, Working Paper Series, Paper 36, available at http://law.bepress.com/gmulwps/gmule/art36/.

Levit, Janet Koven. 1996. Pretextual traffic stops: *United States v. Whren* and the death of *Terry v. Ohio. Loy. U. Chi. L.J.* 28:145, 168–69.

Lichtblau, Eric. Profiling report leads to demotion. *New York Times.* August 24, 2005.

Liptak, Adam. $5 million settlement ends case of tainted Texas sting. *New York Times.* March 11, 2004.

Maclin, Tracy. 2001. The Fourth Amendment on the freeway. *Rutgers Race and L. Rev.* 3:117, 123.

McIntyre, Charshee. 1984. *Criminalizing a race: free blacks during slavery.* Queens, NY: Kayode.

NAACP Legal Defense and Education Fund. 1968. Amicus brief submitted in *Terry v. Ohio,* 392 U.S. 12.

New Jersey Legislative Black and Latino Caucus. 1999. A report on discriminatory practices within the New Jersey state police.

Persico, Nicola. 2002. Racial profiling, fairness, and effectiveness of policing. *American Economic Review* 92:1473–1497.

Plant, Ashby and B. Michelle Peruche. 2005. The consequences of race for police officers' responses to criminal suspects. *Psychological Science* 16:180–183.

President's Commission on Law Enforcement and Administration of Justice, 1966. 2006. *Criminology* 4:48–59.

Public Opinion Online, Roper Center at the University of Connecticut, Lexis.

Rice, Stephen and Alex Piquero. 2005. Perceptions of discrimination and justice in New York City. *Policing* 28:98–117.

Ridgeway, Greg. 2007. *Analysis of racial disparities in the New York Police Department's stop, question, and frisk practices*. Santa Monica, CA: RAND Corporation.

Robinson, Greg. 2001. *By order of the president: FDR and the interment of Japanese Americans*. Cambridge: Harvard University Press.

Schmit, Erica, Patrick Langan, and Matthew Durose. 2002. *Characteristics of drivers stopped by police, 1999*. Washington, DC: U.S. Department of Justice, Bureau of Justice Statistics.

Schwartz, Adina. 1996. "Just take away their guns": the hidden racism of *Terry v. Ohio*. *Fordham Urb. L.J.* 23:317–375.

Staples, Brent. Why "racial profiling" will be tough to fight. *New York Times*. May 24, 1999.

Taylor, Jr., Stuart. Politically incorrect profiling: a matter of life and death. *National Journal*. November 6, 2001.

Union Calendar No. 287, 106th Congress, 2d Session, HR 1443.

Walker, Samuel. 2001. Searching for the denominator: problems with police traffic stop data and an early warning system solution. *Justice Research and Policy* 3:63–96.

Williams, Hubert and Patrick Murphy. 1990. *The evolving strategy of the police: a minority view*. Washington, DC: National Institute of Justice.

Part II

The Methods

Introduction to Part II

Michael D. White

This section introduces the reader to the most common methods used to study issues related to race/ethnicity, bias, and policing. There are two overriding themes from the chapters in this section. First, there is no single best method to be used in the study of race/ethnicity, bias, and policing. The chapters by Ridgeway and MacDonald, and Paulhamus, Kane, and Piquero persuasively make this point, and they call for researchers to both understand the limits of their methods and use a range of approaches to compensate for those limitations. Second, while there may be no "magic bullet" when it comes to methodology, there are very clearly some techniques and approaches that outperform others. Several chapters take to task traditional benchmark measures such as population estimates via census data, arrest and crime data, and hit rates—the percentage of post-stop searches that produce contraband. Chapters by Brunson and Nobles offer viable alternatives to these traditional measures. Professor Brunson argues for an increased reliance on qualitative methodologies, in a way calling for a return to the observation- and narrative-based roots of police research. Nobles offers "cutting-edge" alternative techniques that center on the collection and analysis of police data through geographic information systems (GIS), best typified by the CompStat model. Each of the chapters is summarized briefly below.

In perhaps the most comprehensive review to date, Ridgeway and MacDonald's chapter serves as a must-read primer on methods for assessing racially biased policing. They note that the central issue in documenting the existence of racially biased policing is the identification of an appropriate benchmark, a task that is far more complicated than conventional wisdom suggests. Ridgeway and MacDonald present a detailed, cogent discussion of the entire range of external benchmarks, internal benchmarks, and post-stop outcomes that have been used in research on race/ethnicity, bias, and policing. Though the authors acknowledge that each measure has limitations and there "is no unifying method," they persuasively demonstrate that some measures are more useful than others. With regard to external benchmarking, Ridgeway and MacDonald note that the critical task is to identify the population at-risk of being stopped; most external measures—population data (via the census), licensed driver data, traffic accident data, researcher observation methods, and arrest/ crime suspect data—fall short in accomplishing this task. They highlight the use of instrumental variables analysis, which relies on naturally occurring randomization, as a potentially useful technique, but again, not without limitations. The authors give similar comprehensive treatment to internal benchmarks that focus on individual officer decision making, in particular highlighting the matching of peer officers via propensity score analysis and doubly robust estimation. Finally, the authors review a variety of post-stop outcome measures, including stop duration, search decisions, hit rates, and use of force. In the end, Ridgeway and MacDonald conclude that the appropriate benchmark "remains elusive" and "there is no clear way to establish the correct population at risk." As a result, researchers need to exercise caution in their work and avoid drawing conclusions that cannot be supported by the data.

In "Using Geographic Information Systems to Study Race, Crime, and Policing," Nobles offers a concise discussion of how geographic information systems have become indispensible in the study of policing. Nobles describes the long history of recognizing the importance of place and crime, and he effectively argues that GIS is a natural progression of that historical body of work, particularly in the study of race/ethnicity, bias, and policing. Nobles gives a brief tutorial on how to create and use maps with different types of software, and he presents a number of examples where both researchers and the police have utilized GIS in the study of racial profiling, including traffic stop studies in St. Louis, Cleveland, and Sacramento. Nobles concludes the chapter with a discussion of "open issues" related to GIS that clearly underscore the technique as a "relatively new and promising methodological approach to address old questions related to whether policing practice differs significantly and systematically from expectations based on the social and environmental conditions in a given area."

Like his cocontributors, Brunson highlights weaknesses with existing methodologies and data, but he makes a case for a different response to these weaknesses. Namely, he argues that researchers have failed to adequately employ qualitative methodologies, "which provide a unique opportunity to examine and better understand the range of experiences that may influence individuals' attitudes toward the police." Brunson further suggests that official statistics, such as traffic stop data, fail to account for the complexity of police–minority citizen interactions, and provides little insight into what actually occurs *during* the traffic stop. In response to these concerns, Brunson conducted in-depth interviews with forty African American young men from disadvantaged neighborhoods in St. Louis. Findings indicate that the vast majority of interviewees had personal experiences with police harassment and aggressive tactics. Many also detailed experiences that involved police violence and other forms of misconduct. Brunson highlights the implications of these experiences for citizen trust of the police, willingness to provide information to officers, and police-community relations more generally. The chapter concludes by underscoring the importance of capturing the "lived experiences" of individuals who are victims of racially biased policing, and Brunson suggests that there should be a continuing role for qualitative research in police departments' data collection efforts.

In the final chapter of the section, Paulhamus, Kane, and Piquero provide a succinct review of the substantive issues related to racially biased policing, and discuss how those issues have complicated the definition and measurement of the phenomena. In particular, they point to Skolnick's "symbolic assailant" and drug courier profiles associated with the "war on drugs" as early predecessors of the racial profiling problem. They also note that rulings by the Supreme Court—particularly the *Terry v. Ohio* and *Whren v. United States* decisions—have provided "the legislative foundations of police profiling." Paulhamus and colleagues effectively argue that these precursor events not only laid the foundation and justification for racially biased policing, they have also seriously complicated efforts to define and measure the problem. As a result, they advocate moving "beyond the question concerning whether minority overrepresentation in traffic stops is due to racial profiling by police or simply minorities differentially engaging in the sorts of behaviors that produce differentials in stops." Instead, they encourage a focus on how differences in participation and enforcement both contribute to racial profiling, as well as for better and more thorough data collection efforts to facilitate assessment of those differences. Last, Paulhamus, Kane, and Piquero state that we should move away from the term "racial profiling" in favor of the term "differential stops." They argue that "differential stops" allows researchers to begin from a neutral and objective position as the "term more squarely keeps the discussion centered around data rather than intent (of the officer), which is sure to be nearly impossible to ascertain."

|||||||||||||||||||||||||||||||||||||||||||||||||||||||||||||||||||||||||||||||

Chapter 7

Methods for Assessing Racially Biased Policing

Greg Ridgeway and John MacDonald

Introduction

Over the past ten years there has been a proliferation of research that has attempted to estimate the level of racial bias in police behavior. Many police agencies now mandate that their officers record official contacts made with citizens during routine traffic or pedestrian stops. These administrative data sources typically include a host of information on characteristics of the stops made by police officers, including: the race/ethnicity of the driver or pedestrian; reasons for the stop; and the actions that occurred after the stop, such as searches, contraband found, and citations or arrests made. These data have been the source for the majority of studies of racially biased police behavior. Analysts have sought to apply basic social science methods to assess whether police agencies as a whole, or in some cases individual police officers, are acting in a racially biased manner. A consistent theme in this research is the search for the appropriate benchmark[1] for which one can quantitatively assess whether police behavior is conducted in a racially biased manner. Studies have linked police administrative data on stops made by officers to a variety of data sources, including: police arrest data, population estimates collected by the Census Bureau, driver's license data, motor vehicle traffic accident data, moving violations data, systematic observations of drivers, and other sources. Analysts have also attempted to estimate racial bias from assessments of post-stop outcomes and examinations of the "hit rate" (contraband found) from searches. Post-stop outcomes have also focused on matching strategies to appropriately compare minorities and whites that were similarly situated. More recently, efforts have been made to assess individual police officer bias by peer-group officer comparisons.

In the following sections we outline the various methods that have been employed in studies of racially biased policing. We provide an overview of the use of external benchmarks, internal benchmarks, and post-stop outcomes analysis for assessing racial profiling. Our discussion is not an exhaustive review of the literature. Rather, we focus on assessing the methods, their appeal, and their substantive limitations. Developing an appropriate benchmark is more complicated than is presumed in media reports. All the methods we review for assessing racially biased policing have weaknesses, but some approaches are clearly stronger than others. There is no unifying method that can be applied to administrative data sources and definitively answer the question of whether the police are acting with racial bias. A key issue we address is the fact that the majority of approaches used do not meet the basic bedrock assumptions necessary for drawing a causal inference about the effect of race on police behavior. Yet over time the methods have improved and the policy discussions have inevitably become more nuanced and productive, leading to discussions about what the police should and should not be using as pretexts for their decisions on whom to stop and question.

External Benchmarks

There is a compulsion in media reports on racial disparities in police stops to compare the racial distribution of the stops to the racial distribution for the community's population as estimated by the U.S. Census. For example, in 2006 in New York City, 53% of stops police made of pedestrians involved black pedestrians while according to the U.S. Census they compose only 24% of the city's residential population. When the two racial distributions do not align, and they seem to do so rarely, such statistics promote the conclusion that there is evidence of racial bias in police decision making. Racial bias could be a factor in generating such disparities, but a basic introductory research methods course in the social sciences would argue that other explanations may be contributing factors. For example, differences by race in the exposure to the police or the rates of committing offenses may also contribute to racial disparities in police stop decisions. It is well documented, for example, that due to historical differences in racial segregation, housing tenure, poverty, and other sociopolitical factors, minorities in the United States are more likely to live in neighborhoods with higher rates of crime and disorder.[2] Police deployment in many cities also corresponds to differences in the demand for police services. Neighborhoods with higher volumes of calls to the police service typically have a higher presence of police.[3] Additionally, research indicates that racial minorities, and in particular blacks, are disproportionately involved in serious personal offenses as both victims and offenders.[4]

The crux of the external benchmarking analysis is to develop a benchmark that estimates the racial distribution of the individuals who would be stopped if the police were racially unbiased, and then compare that benchmark to the observed racial distribution of stopped citizens. The external benchmark can be thought of as the population at risk for official police contact. As we will see, estimating the appropriate population at risk is complicated. Crude approximations of the population at risk for police contact are poor substitutes and can hide evidence of racial bias or lead to exaggerated estimates of racial bias.

The likelihood of police stopping minority drivers involves some combination of police exposure to offending/suspicious activity, the racial distribution of the population involved in those activities, and the potential for racial bias. To provide some context, we use some hypothetical numbers and consider an unbiased officer on a foot post who makes stops only when a pedestrian matches a known-suspect description. This officer works in a precinct with forty blacks matching suspect descriptions and forty whites matching suspect descriptions. If we could somehow measure such numbers we would be inclined to propose a suspect-description benchmark of 50% black and 50% white. But if the routine daily activities of whites and blacks differ, then the officer will encounter different proportions of suspects by race. Say, for example, that the majority of the forty white suspects stay inside most of the day, travel only by car, or avoid the specific areas with high police presence; then this officer will stop only a small number of white suspects, deviating substantially from the 50% benchmark. Even the less extreme situation, in which half the white suspects are exposed to the officer, results in the officer stopping blacks in 67% of all their stops decisions. The suspect benchmark in this context is only valid if the police are equally exposed to suspects from the various racial groups. Therefore, even with unbiased officers, we cannot necessarily expect what seems like a reasonable external benchmark to match the racial distribution of stops. This example effectively demonstrates that any of the external benchmarks described in this section must be viewed with caution.

The primary reason for using U.S. Census data to form the benchmark is that it is inexpensive, quick, and readily available. A number of studies attempting to assess racial bias in police behavior use population data from the census, and some rely on estimates at local-area levels like neighborhood census tracts (see Parker and colleagues in this volume). For the reasons previously listed, however, benchmarking with census data does not help us isolate the effect of racial bias from differential exposure and differential offending. Even refinements to the residential census, such as focusing on subpopulations likeliest to be involved in crime (e.g., men or driving-age young adults) are not likely to eliminate differences in the exposure of officers to criminal suspects or provide a good approximation of the population at risk for official police action. Fridell[5] summarized the problem with using the census as a benchmark with regard to offender exposure by noting that "this method does not address the alternative hypothesis that racial/ethnic groups are not equivalent in the nature and extent of their . . . *law-violating behavior*" (p. 106, emphasis in original).

Census estimates provide only the racial distribution of residents and not how these numbers vary by time of day, business attractors such as shopping centers, daily traffic patterns involving commuters, and so forth. It is quite conceivable that the residential population in many neighborhoods has little resemblance to the patterns of people on the street during the day or night. Even if refinements in the census to the neighborhood or age-prone population at risk for police involvement could give a racially unbiased estimate, the differences between the residential population and the population at different times of the day and street segments are likely to overwhelm such a determination. Commuting patterns, for example, can easily exaggerate the racial disparities in traffic stops. Imagine that 20% of traffic stops in a neighborhood that is 95% nonwhite are made of white citizens. In this context we would suggest whites are stopped four times the rate of their composition of the neighborhood population (20/5 = 4) and are subjects of racially biased police behavior. But the stop rate may be a simple reflection of the fact that daily commuters reflect 20% of drivers in this neighborhood.

Dissatisfaction with the census as a benchmark has led some researchers to develop alternate external sets of benchmarks. Some studies of traffic stops attempt to acquire more precise estimates of the racial distribution of drivers on the road to serve as the external benchmark. Under such an approach, one should be able to compare the race distribution of traffic stops made by the police to the race distributions of drivers on the same roadways. Zingraff and colleagues,[6] for example, used the race distribution of licensed drivers rather than the residential population to estimate the race distribution of drivers at risk of being stopped by the police. Although this approach accounts for racial differences in the rate at which the population holds driver's licenses, it does not account for out-of-jurisdiction drivers or for potential racial differences in travel patterns, driving behavior, or exposure to police. To address the problem with out-of-jurisdiction drivers, Farrell and colleagues[7] borrowed driving population models from the transportation literature, which use an area's ability, based on employment or retail location, to pull drivers in from outside communities or to push residents outside the area. This certainly improves on the census benchmark. But it is widely documented that minorities (and even those who possess a driver's license) are more likely to take public transit to work and vary from whites in other important ways in their daily travel patterns. Therefore, a more accurate external benchmark would be one that could reliably take into account equivalent driving patterns and behavior between race groups.

Recognizing these limitations, Alpert and colleagues[8] used data on the location of traffic accidents and the race of the not-at-fault drivers to estimate the race distribution of the at-risk population. The logic of this approach is that the race distribution of not-at-fault drivers should approximate the racial distribution of the population of drivers. Although this approach may measure the race distribution of drivers on the road, it does not account for potential racial differences in driving behavior that may be important sources for police decision making, such as the likelihood of speeding, weaving through traffic, and driving slower than usual.

Other analysts have studied the race distribution of drivers flagged by photographic stoplight enforcement cameras[9] and by aerial patrols.[10] The advantage of these benchmarks is that they are truly race-blind and measure some form of traffic violation. One can question whether they capture race differences in other aspects of stop risk, such as seatbelt usage, equipment violations, and the other cues that police use in deciding whether or not to stop a citizen.[11]

Given that the police are not likely to stop people at random, comparisons of racial distribution of stops to the residential population or the driving population on the roadways tells one very little about the race neutrality of the police. Again, it is necessary to establish a benchmark for the population at risk for official police contact. This means that one needs an accurate estimate of the subpopulation that is likely to elicit reasonable suspicion by the police.

Observation Benchmarks

Observation benchmarks are a popular approach for attempting to estimate the subpopulation at risk for police behavior. Observation benchmarks typically involve fielding teams of observers to locations to tally the racial distribution of those observed driving and violating traffic laws. More than three decades ago Albert Reiss Jr.

advocated the use of systematic social observation as a key measurement strategy for studying the police and other social phenomena.[12] By systematic, he meant that the observation of behaviors and recordings are done according to explicit standardized rules that permit replication.

This methodology was pioneered to study racial bias in police traffic stops by Lamberth[13] in his study of the New Jersey Turnpike. Observation benchmarks' greatest potential occurs in its application to racial profiling on freeways, since vehicles have essentially the same exposure to the police, and speeding is the primary violation that highway patrol focuses on. Speeding, for example, accounted for 89% of the stop reasons in a subsequent study of New Jersey Turnpike traffic stops.[14] Measuring speeding through direct observations with radar guns, for example, provides a standardized approach that is easy to replicate and less subject to measurement error than accounting for other types of traffic violations that require observers to make judgments about infractions like weaving through traffic or making illegal turns. Lang and colleagues[15] and Alpert and colleagues provide two case studies using radar guns.[16] The main wrinkle in the analysis of benchmarks based on observation of speeding is determining the appropriate speed at which drivers should be considered "at risk" for being stopped in specific sections of the highway. For example, it is conceivable that in some areas the police are more vigilant with speeding. As long as this variation is not confounded with differences in the areas that minorities and whites travel then it can provide an unbiased assessment of racial disparities in highway traffic stops.

In urban environments, however, officers stop vehicles for a variety of reasons beyond simple moving violations. Exposure to police can vary widely across different geographic segments of the city.[17] In the current volume the reader will note that a number of authors attempt to take the intra-city variation in exposure to the police into account (see, e.g., Fagan and colleagues). Eck and colleagues[18] note that in Cincinnati, Ohio, the police allocate a greater share of officers to areas with a higher volume of crime incidents, and these areas happen to be composed predominantly of black residents. Relying on direct observations of traffic violations in different segments of Cincinnati would not provide an unbiased assessment of the population at risk for police exposure, because race is confounded with the areas that police are concentrated on. One would have to develop an observation method that appropriately balanced these differences in police resource allocation.

There are few examples where investigators have attempted to take the complexity of geographic areas of a city into account in using observation methods. Alpert and colleagues[19] provide one of the few published studies where trained observers recorded traffic violations (e.g., illegal turns, running stop lights, speeding) at sixteen high-volume intersections in Miami-Dade County in areas that were classified as predominately white, black, or racially mixed. A comparison of the racial distribution of observed traffic violators to actual police traffic stops in the same areas suggested little evidence of racial bias in stop decisions. Even if observers in this study did produce an accurate benchmark for individuals at risk for exposure to the police in these areas—a challenge in its own right—several issues remain. There is no reason to believe that police stops should be representative of those simply observed committing traffic violations in these areas. Officers target behaviors that they believe indicate drug transactions, stop individuals fitting suspect descriptions, and respond to calls for service. Once observers head down the path of trying to determine which vehicles or persons should be at risk for being stopped, the observations become more subjective and less systematic.[20] In fact, the variation between observers in such studies can exceed the estimate of the racial disparity. One observer may be more likely than others to measure some driving behavior as aggressive. Such variation in judgments in an observation study has to be taken into account, or observers have to be trained to near uniformity in judgments if one is going to produce a reliable estimate of the population at risk for police contact. Regardless, it is unclear that observational studies are relying on the same sets of markers that the police use in deciding who is suspicious and whom to stop. The courts have not consistently supported the use of observational benchmarks for this reason. In United States v. Alcaraz-Arellano[21] the court rejected the benchmark, since it was developed for a general population, not those violating the law.

Outside of traffic stop studies on speeding or moving violations on roadways, systematic observations of driving behavior are not likely to yield useful estimates for an external benchmark for an entire city. Recognizing these limitations, a number of investigators have turned to other approaches for establishing external benchmarks.

Arrest and Crime Suspect Benchmarks

Gelman, Fagan, and Kiss[22] quote then NYPD police commissioner Howard Safir: "The racial/ethnic distribution of the subjects of stop and frisk reports reflects the demographics of known violent crime suspects as reported by crime victims. Similarly, the demographics of arrestees in violent crimes also correspond with the demographics of known violent crime suspects." Safir is clearly suggesting that violent crime suspects or violent crime arrestees provide a reasonable benchmark from which the public can judge the department's racial distribution in stop percentages. This quote suggests that the arrestee population may serve as a useable benchmark for assessing racial bias in the police decision of whom to stop.

The arrestee benchmark, however, is also problematic because it is too narrow. For example, the police make stops for trespassing, vandalism, suspected drug sales, and a variety of other causes. Many stop decisions might be made for minor infractions, not serious crime incidents involving violence. The group of individuals stopped by the police in most large cities, therefore, far exceeds the group comprising the arrestee population. There are a variety of reasons that the racial distribution of individuals stopped by the police could have a racial distribution that differs greatly from that of arrestees. For one, arrests can often take place some distance away from where the crime actually occurred. Most problematic is that if officers are in fact racially biased, then we cannot use their arrests to represent what we would expect of an unbiased police force. Such a benchmark could actually hide bias. Investigators like Gelman and colleagues have attempted to control for this by using prior-year arrest decisions as an external benchmark. Again, there is no reason to expect that prior-year decisions are independent of current-year decisions—especially if, as research by Klinger[23] suggests, an established pattern of practices becomes ingrained in specific police precincts.

The criminal suspect benchmark may be a more plausible approach than the arrestee benchmark for establishing the population at risk for official police contact. It represents the public's reporting of those involved in suspicious activity and crime and would correspond more closely to racial distribution of criminals on the street.[24] Note that this benchmark is not a reasonable choice for traffic stops since police often have the intent to cite for a traffic violation without the expectation that it will lead to an arrest. Comparing the police to the public's reporting of suspicious activity at least answers the question of whether the police are finding suspicious individuals with features similar to those the public reports committing or attempting to commit crimes. Ridgeway, for example, found that in New York City black pedestrians were stopped at a rate 20 to 30% lower than their representation among the public's report of crime-suspect descriptions, and Hispanic pedestrians were stopped slightly more than their share of crime-suspect descriptions, by 5 to 10%.[25] The public may have their own racial biases, however, and they may also under- or overreport certain activities (e.g., drug market activity, suspicious individuals) depending on the area and the perceived problems that the police actively target.

Instrumental Variables

An ideal scientific method to estimate the extent of race bias in policing would be to use an experimental design and randomly assign police officers to be "race-blind" during certain periods. For example, for each officer and for each hour that an officer patrols the street, we flip a coin to determine whether that officer will be unable to perceive the race of a suspect. The difference between the percentage of stops involving minorities when the officers can perceive race and the percentage of stops involving minorities when the officers are race-blind gives us the effect of racial bias. If the officers were unbiased then the ability to perceive race should not matter in the selection of stopped individuals. If instead the officers are racially biased then we would observe more minority stops when the officers are not blinded to race.

Clearly such an experiment in the actual field is a fantasy, but instrumental variables (IV) analysis is an econometric approach that can sometimes solve such problems.[26] Instrumental variables analysis relies on the randomization that occurs in nature to replicate the classic randomized experimental design. The key hurdle is to identify an "instrument," in this case a variable that is predictive of the ability to perceive race,[27] that is not related to the actual race of suspects.[28] This is a generalization of the setup in the previous paragraph where our coin is the instrument, highly predictive of the ability to see race but unassociated with the race of potentially stopped individuals.

Grogger and Ridgeway[29] proposed as an instrument the natural variation in daylight and darkness that switches with the change in daylight savings. It is associated with the ability to perceive race but is not related to the race of drivers on the road. The randomization in nature that diminishes the ability of officers to view the actual race of suspects during specific times of the year may serve as an effective instrument for assessing racial bias in police traffic stops. Presumably the probability of race being visible is greater in daylight. Besides the logic of the statement, there is some evidence from the literature supporting this. Lamberth described a traffic survey in which the driver's race could be identified in 95% of the vehicles, but for which nighttime observations required auxiliary lighting.[30] Greenwald canceled plans for evening surveys after his observer could identify the race of only 6% of the drivers viewed around dusk.[31]

The logic of this approach goes back to the work of Neyman[32] in the 1920s and is a special case of more general instrumental variable methods. We first have to determine the percentage of black drivers among those stopped during daylight and the percentage of black drivers stopped during darkness. Second, to account for the fact that sometimes race is not visible during the day and can be visible at night, the difference in the percentage of blacks stopped needs to be divided by the difference in the probability of race being visible in daytime and darkness. Importantly, this estimate does not require complete race blindness at night and complete visibility during the day, only a substantive diminished capacity.

One of the difficulties that Grogger and Ridgeway faced when attempting to estimate this instrumental variable is that there is no direct measure of diminished capacity due to changes in daylight, the second step of the described IV estimator. A controlled scientific experiment could be conducted to estimate visibility by daylight and darkness, but this might not reflect the types of lighting situations that officers commonly experience on the streets, especially in parts of the city that are better lit than others. As a result Grogger and Ridgeway's analysis simply assumed, logically, that the denominator is positive, such that the probability of race being visible is greater in daylight.

The validity of this instrument also depends on race being independent of daylight/darkness visibility. But the race distribution of drivers on the road and exposed to the police may be quite different between daylight hours and nighttime hours. If there were mostly black drivers on the road at night then the analysis would indicate that officers stop an excessive fraction of black drivers during the night, but this would just be because there are a larger proportion of black drivers on the road at that time. To correct this potential problem, Grogger and Ridgeway controlled for clock time and compared stops occurring near the changes to and from daylight savings time. On one Monday stops at 6 pm occur in daylight and the following Monday stops at 6 pm occur in darkness. If we can assume that the race distribution of drivers on the road at 6 pm does not change with daylight savings time and that the police do not suddenly reallocate their officers, then this provides a valid instrument.

Figure 7.1 demonstrates the idea using data from Oakland, California. The horizontal axis indicates the clock time and the vertical axis indicates hours since dark. Throughout the analysis, we omit stops carried out during the roughly thirty-minute period between sunset and the end of civil twilight, since that period is difficult to classify as either daylight or dark. The solid points indicate stops of black drivers, whereas open circles represent stops of nonblack drivers. At any time between 5:19 pm and 9:06 pm, some stops are carried out when it is dark (gray shading) and some are carried out when it is light (no shading). The diagonal bands are a result of the natural

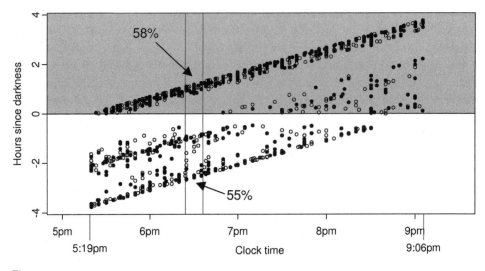

Figure 7.1

variation in daylight hours over the course of the study period. In particular, the large diagonal gap is a result of the shift from Pacific Daylight Time to Pacific Standard Time at the end of October. This shift is especially useful for our comparison since it creates extremes in visibility for fixed clock times. The vertical lines in figure 7.1 mark a period around 6:30 pm within which we can assess whether darkness influences the race of drivers stopped. During daylight hours, 55% of the stops involved black drivers, while stops after dark involved black drivers in 58% of the stops, a slight difference that, if anything, runs counter to the racial profiling hypothesis. Schell, Ridgeway, and colleagues provide a similar analysis of three years of traffic stops in Cincinnati and find similar null conclusions against racial bias in traffic stop decisions.[33]

The instrumental variables approach here, however, does have limitations. First, this method assumes that the variation in daylight/darkness gives enough of a diminished capacity to effectively remove the importance of a suspect's race in the decision of whom to stop. If the police use car profiles, such as stylistic rims or other features that are correlated with race and social class, as the primary proxy for race, then this approach will still yield an unbiased test of the race effect on police decisions but will be greatly underpowered because police will use these cues regardless of the level of daylight/darkness. Even if such proxies do not exist, the approach only measures the effect of race bias at those times of day that are sometimes light and sometimes dark. Since there is never daylight at 3 am, we cannot estimate an effect of race for stops that occur at that hour.

Internal Benchmarking

Recognizing the difficulty of assessing whether racial bias occurs on the aggregate in the decision to stop citizens has led some analysts to focus on the individual decision making of police officers. The decision to stop a citizen is only one stage in the traffic stop process, at each stage of which police officers can introduce race bias in their decisions. Highly publicized examples of racial bias in police behavior can give an impression of systemic bias, even if the source of bias is only a few problem officers[34] (see Weitzer in this volume).[35] The Christopher Commission in its assessment of abuse of police authority among the Los Angeles Police Department (LAPD), for example, noted that 10% of officers accounted for 27.5% of complaints of excessive force and 33% of all use-of-force incidents.[36] The methods described previously, which attempt to examine bias at the departmental level, are unlikely to detect the problem if the source is a small share of individual officers, and, even if somehow there are enough biased officers to create enough statistical power to detect the problem at the department level, these previous methods do not identify potential problem officers.

Walker[37] conceptualized the internal benchmark, a framework that compares officers' stop decisions with decisions made by other officers working in similar situational contexts. This method has been applied to department data in several localities and has been adopted as a part of several "early warning systems."[38] At the LAPD, the TEAMS II Risk Management Information System places officers in one of thirty-three peer groups.[39] Officers in the same peer group presumably are expected to conduct similar policing activities. If an officer exceeds certain thresholds for their peer group, such being in the top 1% on number of complaints or number of use-of-force incidents, the system generates an "action item" for follow-up. Officer roles in LAPD, however, are certainly more diverse than thirty-three groups can capture. Similar problems are likely in other audit systems that compute a "peer-officer-based formula" to flag officers[40] but do not fully take into account the variation in environments in which officers in the same peer group work. Sometimes the peer group construction may be reasonable. For example, Decker and Rojek[41] matched each St. Louis police officer to all other officers working in the same police districts. It is unclear whether matching by district alone was sufficient to ensure validity, although they argued that officers rotated shifts sufficiently so as not to warrant concern.

While this process is useful for flagging potential problem officers, it has some drawbacks. First, if officers in the entire precinct are equally biased, the method will not flag any officers as being problematic. We must rely on other analyses to assess that issue. Second, officers whom the method flags as outliers may have legitimate explanations for the observed differences. For example, a Spanish-speaking officer may appear to make an excessive number of stops of Hispanic suspects, when, in fact, the Spanish-speaking officer gets called in to handle and document those stops. Such situations should be detectable when supervisors review cases. Otherwise, the method eliminates possible explanations based on time or place, so the range of explanations is limited.

The fundamental goal of internal benchmarking is to compare the rate of nonwhite-pedestrian stops for a particular officer with the rate of nonwhite-pedestrian stops for other officers patrolling the same area at the same time. Matching in this way assures us that the target officer and the comparison officers are exposed to the same set of offenses and offenders.

Ridgeway and MacDonald[42] developed an internal benchmark methodology to

compare the racial distribution of pedestrians/drivers whom individual police officers have stopped with that of pedestrians/drivers whom other officers in the same
role have stopped at the same times and places. This method has been applied in case
studies in both Cincinnati[43] and New York City.[44] Utilizing an approach based on
propensity score weighting, doubly robust estimation, and false discovery rates, these
case studies attempt to customize the internal benchmark for each individual officer
to a set of officers working in similar environments exposed to similar suspects, and
to control the risk of too many officers being flagged as outliers (false positives). The

TABLE 7.1
Construction of an Internal Benchmark for a Sample Officer

Stop Characteristic	Officer A (%) (N = 392)	Internal Benchmark (%) (N = 3,676)
Month		
January	3	3
February	4	4
March	8	9
April	7	5
May	12	12
June	9	9
July	7	7
August	8	9
September	10	10
October	11	10
November	11	11
December	9	10
Day of the week		
Monday	13	13
Tuesday	11	10
Wednesday	14	15
Thursday	22	21
Friday	15	16
Saturday	10	11
Sunday	15	14
Time of day		
12–2 am	11	11
2–4 am	5	5
10 am–12 pm	0	1
12–2 pm	12	13
2–4 pm	13	12
4–6 pm	9	10
6–8 pm	8	8
8–10 pm	23	23
10 pm–12 am	17	17
Precinct		
A	0	0
B	98	98
C	1	1
D	1	0
Occurred inside?	4	6
Housing or transit		
Transit	0	0
Housing	0	0
Other	100	100
In uniform		
Yes	99	97
Radio run		
Yes	1	3

Note: The numbers in the table indicate the percentage of stops having that feature.

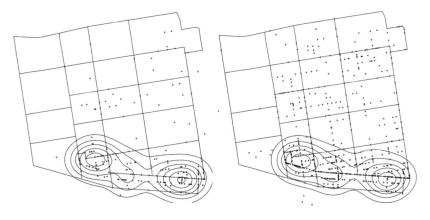

Figure 7.2

first of the three stages in this process is, for each officer, to reweight the stops made by other officers so that they have similar stop characteristics distributions.

Table 7.1 shows the results of this reweighting step for an example officer. Officer A made 392 stops. The method effectively identified 3,676 similarly situated stops made by other officers. These stops were selected as the benchmark group for Officer A because they were similar to Officer A's stops in terms of when they occurred (e.g., date, time of day), where they occurred (e.g., precinct, x-y coordinates), the assigned command of the officer making the stop, whether the officer making the stop was in uniform, and whether the stop was a result of a radio run. Figure 7.2 and table 7.1 demonstrate that this collection of 3,676 is nearly identical to the officer's stops in several respects. Furthermore, as shown in figure 7.2, the distribution of the locations of the stops can be aligned geographically so that regions of this officer's stops in 2006 can be compared to other officers making stops in the same region. An additional adjustment at this stage can improve the precision of this test. The second step of the process involves a regression model to further refine the benchmark, since some features are not perfectly matched between officers in table 7.1, such as the frequency of being in uniform and being on a radio run.

Combining propensity score analysis with a second stage regression model has recently been labeled "doubly robust estimation," since if either the propensity score weights construct a well-matched set of benchmark stops or the regression model is correctly specified, then the resulting estimate of the officer's effect on the race of those stopped can be consistently estimated.[45]

The z-statistic from these regression models is the commonly used statistical measure for assessing the magnitude of the difference between an officer's minority-stop fraction and the officer's internal benchmark group. The z-statistic scales the difference between the officer and his or her internal benchmark such that large differences based on a small number of stops are treated with greater uncertainty than large differences based on a large number of stops. Fridell[46] suggests 2.0 and Smith[47] suggests 1.645 as the appropriate z-scores to flag potentially problematic officers. But such cutoffs generate too many false positives to be useful and are one of the sources of problems for LAPD's system. In a department of one thousand officers we can expect fifty of them to have z-statistics in excess of 1.645 by chance alone.

Methods based on false discovery rates (fdr) helps address this kind of problem.[48] The fdr is the probability of no difference between the officer and the benchmark given the value of an observed test statistic, z. We should flag those officers who have values of z that suggest a low probability of being incorrectly flagged as a problem. When applied in Cincinnati this approach noted four potentially problematic officers, and in New York City fifteen potentially problematic officers.

Internal benchmark approaches provide a method for assessing individual officer bias. Again, the key to this approach is developing a reasonable peer group or comparison set of officers. This approach, however, is limited to departments with officers that make many stops. If officers make few stops (e.g., less than fifty), then chance differences from their benchmark are likely and the comparisons are underpowered. Accumulating stops across years can improve this. For departments with few officers (e.g., those with less than 100 officers), the fdr calculations become more unstable and more dependent on statistical assumptions.

Post-Stop Outcomes

The complexity of benchmarking for assessing bias in the decision to make a stop has in some cases caused analysts to abandon the endeavor in favor of assessing bias in post-stop outcomes, such as duration of the stop, decision to search, and use of force. This has its advantages, since for this analysis we have a better assessment of the race distribution of who is at risk. But substantial complexity remains.

Auditing Police-Citizen Interactions

An obstacle to understanding racial disparities in police decision making is that stopped drivers and pedestrians cannot observe how officers handle other stops, particularly those involving members of another race. They cannot answer the most pertinent question regarding racially bias policing: Would the same outcome have occurred if I had been a different race? While such counterfactual questions so far have not been answered, recordings of stops can provide some guidance to understanding the dynamics in police-citizen interactions.

Dixon and colleagues[49] used a stratified random sample of 313 vehicle-mounted video and audio recordings from Cincinnati Police Department (CPD) cars to study interactions between police and community members. The study described how the race of the driver and the race of the officer influenced the dynamics of stops, including stop features associated with "counterproductive or dissatisfying interactions," and described how typical police-motorist interactions occur as a function of race.

Among the results reported in this study is the finding that in interactions where the officer and driver are of the same race, officers are more likely to be interested in hearing the drivers' comments. The key problem that this creates in Cincinnati is that, since many more CPD officers are white, two-thirds of stops of black drivers involve a white officer while only one-third of stops of white drivers involve a black officer. Thus the impact of degraded communication due to interracial stops will be greatest for the black drivers.

Additional research by the same research team[50] found that white officers conducted more investigative stops (e.g., asking questions about guns or drugs, asking for the IDs of passengers) while black officers were more likely to focus on the traffic infractions alone. Importantly, these differences did not depend on the race of the driver. That is, white officers also closely investigated white drivers. Such differences between white and black officers, however, can exacerbate the perception of racially biased policing. The black driver in Cincinnati who experiences one stop with a black officer and another stop with a white officer is likely to attribute the white officer's more intense investigation to race bias, even though on average this white officer treats blacks and whites with a similar level of scrutiny.

The analysis of recorded interactions is useful at identifying problem interactions, factors that can contribute to the perceptions of race, and stops that could be useful in training. But such methods do not answer the question of whether the police use race as a factor in deciding whom to stop.

Hit Rates

Hit rates, the percentage of conducted searches that turn up contraband, have been a frequently discussed outcomes test for racial equity in searches. If the hit rate for searched nonwhite suspects is less than the hit rate for searched white suspects, police might be applying a lower standard of suspicion to nonwhite suspects when deciding whether to search.

A series of papers by Persico and Todd[51] provide the theory and empirical examples of the use of hit rates with police traffic stop data. Relying on the premise of a Nash equilibrium, these authors argue that hit rates provide a race-neutral test of bias in police decision making because police decisions about which suspects to search take into account the benefits of searching different suspects, and suspects take "into account the risk of getting searched" (p. 37).[52] If officers and criminals act as rational agents, then the outcome of stops should be race neutral. Following on the logic of a Nash equilibrium that officers want to maximize their ability to find illegal contraband in traffic stops, and suspects want to reduce their likelihood of being caught, then the probability of successful "hits" should be equal once one conditions on the race of who is stopped. If, for example, police officers want to find illicit drugs and suspects want to avoid detection, the results for searches among police officers who are intentionally biased toward blacks will be offset by a higher yield of searches among whites. In the long run the differences between races in hit rates should equalize. Persico and Todd's analysis of Maryland State Police traffic stop data in several publications reports findings that the fraction of blacks stopped exceeds the fraction of black motorists on the road, but that the hit rates across racial groups are statistically equivalent.

We, however, provide an example to demonstrate that a simple comparison of hit rates can distort the true racial differences. Assume that suspects are stopped for either burglary or robbery. Further assume that there is no racial difference in the rates at which suspects carry contraband and that police are racially neutral in making stop-and-frisk decisions (essentially blind to race). Last, consider the information shown in table 7.2. Within a crime category, hit rates are equal for black and white suspects. In this example, officers detain many more white suspects on suspicion of robbery, a crime with a higher hit rate, than they do black suspects, who are more likely to be stopped for burglary. In this example, though, those large differences in the rates of stops for burglary and robbery by race are due not to officer bias but are the result of racial differences in criminal participation. As a result, the total hit rate for white suspects is 4.6% ([1+45]/1,000), and for black suspects, 1.4% ([9+5]/1,000).

One could conclude from these two numbers (4.6% vs. 1.4%) that there is racial bias in the decision to search suspects, and that whites are not searched at sufficient rates. But officers in this hypothetical example are race-neutral by design. Hit rates are equal across races for suspected burglars and robbers. This is a reminder that failing to account for an important factor—suspected crime, in this example—can distort the conclusions. In practice, the only way for the Nash equilibrium as described by Persico and Todd to work would be if black burglars and white robbers adjusted their criminal behaviors to mirror each other because they had equal probability of being stopped by the police.

This example illustrates a statistical problem that Ayres[53] termed the subgroup validity problem, in which a particular relevant feature is more prevalent for certain racial groups. Other factors may affect the hit rate as well. Officers in some precincts may be likelier to frisk, due to crime in the area, recent surges in weapon recoveries, a series of recent shootings, or more hostile attitudes displayed by suspects. An elevated frisk rate in some precincts may not meet with the community's approval, but it would be premature to attribute this variation to racial bias by police officers without examining other relevant factors. Therefore, it is critical to account for factors correlated with race that might be associated with both suspect race and the rate of contraband recovery.

In Ridgeway's analysis of hit rates in New York City, shown in table 7.3, white and Hispanic suspects stopped in situations that were similar to the collection of black suspects had hit rates of 3.2 percent and 3.8 percent, respectively, compared with a hit rate of 3.3 percent for black suspects.[54] There was no statistical evidence for a difference between these recovery rates. Furthermore, there were no differences in the rates at which officers found weapons on suspects. The unadjusted hit rates, however, suggested evidence of bias—again showing that it is important to adjust for subgroup

TABLE 7.2
Hypothetical Example of a Hit-Rate Analysis

Race	Measure	Burglary	Robbery
White	Stopped and frisked	100	900
	Had contraband (%)	1	5
	Had contraband	1	45
Black	Stopped and frisked	900	100
	Had contraband (%)	1	5
	Had contraband	9	5

TABLE 7.3
Frisked or Searched Suspects Found Having Contraband or Weapons

	Black	Hispanic	White
Any contraband	3.3	3.2	3.8
Weapon	0.7	0.7	0.8

differences in the circumstances by which different racial groups are subjected to police authority.

It is plausible that the carry rates, the percentage of stopped suspects that have contraband, differ by race. If white suspects simply carry drugs more frequently, perhaps believing that officers are unlikely to search them, then the contraband recovery rates for white suspects will be higher. Persico and Todd theorized from the logic of a Nash equilibrium that criminals will assess their risk of being searched and adjust their frequency of carrying drugs and weapons accordingly, so that an outcome test will be race-neutral. It is difficult to confirm this in practice, and, as a result, conclusions drawn from table 7.3 must allow for the possibility that carry rates are not uniform across racial groups.

Analysis of Other Stop Outcomes

Other analysts have focused on developing appropriate benchmarks for studying the stop outcomes themselves. In Cincinnati, for example, Ridgeway[55] notes that 47% of stops involving black drivers lasted less than ten minutes while 56% of stops of nonblack drivers lasted less than ten minutes. On the surface this seems to be a rather large bias. But 18% of the stopped black drivers did not have valid driver's licenses while only 5% of nonblack drivers did not have valid licenses. As a result, we cannot discern whether the disparity in stop duration is attributable to the driver's race or to the additional time required to process a stop involving an unlicensed driver.

Social scientists recognize that adjusting for confounding variables is a critical step in all proper analyses, and there are clear examples in the current book where analysts attempt to make such adjustments (see Fagan et al., and Parker and colleagues in this volume). Particular to racial profiling analyses, police may approach vehicles more cautiously and conduct pat searches for weapons in high-crime neighborhoods during peak crime times (e.g., late evening on the weekends). These decisions may occur regardless of the driver's race, but may be confounded with race due to differences in the neighborhoods in which minorities and whites live. In high-crime neighborhoods police also may be more thorough in checking for vehicle registration and driver's license records, have a longer list of recent suspect descriptions that the stopped driver may match, and may be more likely to develop probable cause. In theory and practice, all these decisions could be independent of the driver's race. As a result, the stop location and time may influence all the measured post-stop activities even in the absence of a race bias. When the race distribution of drivers differs by time and neighborhood location, one should adjust for these differences when assessing racial bias in post-stop activity. The analysis also might adjust for other features occurring after the stop, such as whether the suspect had an open warrant or a suspended driver's license.

Location and time of the stop are two among a number of factors for which post-stop activity might vary that are confounded with race of drivers or pedestrians stopped by the police. While these differences may be structurally discriminatory based on racial differences in areas that individuals live, they may not be substantively discriminatory based on police decision making.

The common practice of "adjusting for" potentially confounding factors with multivariate regression is difficult to defend in the analysis of post-stop data. The regression adjustment is only effective if there is not a strong correlation between race and the other variables in the regression model. If in the case of citizen stops the distribution of stop features of blacks differs substantially from the distribution of stop features of whites by neighborhood, type of violation, time of day, and so forth, it is uncertain whether the estimate of the race effect on police post-stop outcomes sufficiently accounts for these potentially confounding variables. Unless stops of black and white suspects occur in similar circumstances, the regression model will be sensitive to the terms in the model, such as interactions between race and other predictors (e.g., race*location). Unfortunately, this situation is often overlooked in criminological studies of racial profiling.

Earlier we showed an example in which we could reweight the stops of other officers to match the features of stops of a particular officer. In the same manner, Ridgeway[56] showed that we can construct propensity score weights to reweight the stops of, for example, nonblack drivers or pedestrians to match the characteristics of the stops of black drivers or pedestrians. Table 7.4, from a Cincinnati Police Department study of racial profiling in traffic stops described in Schell, Ridgeway, and colleagues,[57] provides a demonstration. The second column displays the percentages for the black drivers; the third column displays the percentages for the weighted nonblack drivers.

The weighted percentages for the nonblack drivers are uniformly close to the percentages for the black drivers. Achieving this balance is the critical step when using propensity score techniques, and removes the problems of insufficient overlap between races and nonlinearity noted with regression models. Race, therefore, is the only factor differing between the groups by design. The fourth column in table 7.4 displays the raw percentages for the nonblack driver sample. These data indicate that very few nonblack drivers are involved in stops in Over-the-Rhine. Nonblack drivers are much more likely to be stopped on the freeways. Therefore, the weighted sample has been constructed to downweight nonblack drivers stopped on the freeways and upweight nonblack drivers stopped in Over-the-Rhine. Additionally, nonblack drivers with invalid driver's licenses are upweighted so that the rate of invalid driver's licenses in the comparison sample is closer to that of the black driver sample.

Aside from some statistical advantages, the method is also attractive because of the ease of establishing its face validity. Table 7.4 is easy to explain to a variety of policy audiences, and it is effective for arguing that the subsequent results are based on apples-to-apples comparisons.

The raw numbers indicated that black drivers were much less likely than nonblack drivers to have had a traffic stop last less than ten minutes, 47% versus 56%. After

TABLE 7.4
Comparison on a Subset of Stop Features of the Nonblack Driver Sample to Black Drivers

	% Black drivers N = 20,146	% Nonblack drivers (weighted) ESS = 5,365	% Nonblack drivers (unweighted) N = 24,383
Neighborhood			
Downtown	2.4	2.4	4.8
Over-the-Rhine	7.1	6.9	3.2
I-71	2.1	2.1	6.1
I-75	6.0	6.1	13.6
Time of day			
12–3 am	23.3	21.8	16.7
3–6 am	5.2	4.8	3.7
6–9 am	6.0	8.3	10.8
9 am–12 pm	6.8	7.8	12.7
12–3 pm	6.9	7.5	12.8
3–6 pm	16.9	17.8	15.2
6–9 pm	15.8	14.9	12.7
9 pm–12 am	19.0	17.0	15.4
Reason			
Equipment violation	24.0	22.6	12.7
Moving violation	66.1	69.7	83.4
Resident			
Cincinnati	91.8	90.8	63.2
Ohio (not Cincinnati)	3.8	4.3	18.8
Kentucky	1.9	2.6	11.7
Age			
Under 18	1.7	1.7	1.8
18–25	34.8	32.4	31.2
26–35	28.9	26.3	26.0
36–45	17.5	19.0	18.9
Invalid driver's license	18.0	13.2	5.3
Male	65.9	64.6	65.1

weighting, the nonwhite drivers stopped at similar times, places, and contexts had stops last less than ten minutes 47% of the time, the same as the black drivers. All the difference between the original numbers, 47% and 56%, can be attributable to the factors like time, place, and context.

As with the propensity score approach previously discussed, there are advantages and disadvantages to both hit rates and matching approaches. The hit rate approach has intuitive appeal, providing a clear thought experiment where all else should be equal once the police make the decision of whom to stop. The hit rates comparison assumes that selecting on whom police decide to stop equalizes the two groups so that whites and blacks should be equivalent. If blacks end up with lower hit rates than whites, then one can argue that the police are using a lower threshold in assessing suspicion for blacks. But is this reasonable? Actions transpire after the decision to stop that may be confounded with race. There is a body of research in criminology that suggests a variety of reasons for racial differences in stop outcomes. As we previously discussed, Dixon and colleagues found that black-white officer interactions in Cincinnati explained a substantial difference in the length of a stop and the decision to search a vehicle. These decisions, however, don't appear to be racially biased on the suspects but rather reflect racial differences in police officer practices. Engel and Tillyer[58] note the lengthy history of observation studies that find racial differences in suspect demeanor can affect outcomes in police-citizen interactions, such that all else but race is not equal once an officer has decided to stop a suspect.

By contrast, matching approaches try to make all the statistical adjustments available with observational data. If one has the right set of variables, then there is some confidence that a good test of the race effect in post-stop outcomes can be assessed with accuracy. White and black suspects can be compared to each other in similar situations. If the analyst does not have the right set of contextual variables, they can at least get better data and work on improving the matching strategy. There is no magic going on, no necessary thought experiment; one just wants to construct a feasible set of comparison groups.

Conclusions

The search for an appropriate method for assessing racial bias in police behavior has been a quest. Substantial improvements have been made as investigators have moved away from simple comparisons of police stop decisions to general populations estimates. The search for the appropriate benchmark, however, remains elusive. There is no clear way to establish the correct population at risk for police attention. All approaches have limitations. Clearly, the most feasible benchmarks are ones that attempt to remove as many factors that are potentially confounded with race as possible but are legally permissible on the part of the police. The key to drawing a causal inference about the importance of race is establishing a set of comparison conditions that are race-neutral. This is, however, a significant challenge because many factors are highly confounded with race. Census estimates are inappropriate benchmarks. Observations are difficult to collect in a systematic fashion, and require observers to note behaviors for which the police should consider someone suspicious. With enough training, effort, and time, observation methods can be an effective benchmark in studies that focus on traffic enforcement on highways where minorities and whites are exposed to similar circumstances, but they are less likely to be useful in highly stratified urban environments where the police focus on much more than traffic enforcement. Arrest data is too confounded with police stop decisions to be a useful benchmark. After all, arrests are often a consequence of the decision to stop and search someone. Instrumental variables offer some promise by relying on variations in nature that are independent of race, such as the switch from daylight to darkness. Here, too, instrumental variables are limited to drawing a causal inference from the conditions under which they are estimated. If, for example, the police behave systematically different toward minorities only in late night hours, variations in natural daylight won't be useful for detecting racial bias. Hit rates are attractive because of the idea that police want to maximize their ability to find contraband and make reasonable arrests, so selecting on who is stopped should provide a race-neutral test. Racial differences in the characteristics of criminal offenders, however, can make a focus on hit rates invalid. Approaches that compare like criminals will yield better hit rate assessments. Matching approaches that compare whites to minorities in similar circumstances offer promise because they attempt to make apple-to-apple comparisons.

A good matching approach, for example, could provide all relevant police factors net race. Omitted variables will always be a concern. What important variables are missing can, however, be a good subject of discussion. If the police cannot articulate a reasonable set of missing variables that are not recorded and are associated with racial differences in who is searched, the duration of stops, and so forth, then this provides at least circumstantial evidence of race bias.

Even if police decisions on whom to stop, search, and detain are not intentionally biased, they may be structurally discriminatory. Patrolling differently in high-crime neighborhoods may place a disparate burden on minorities but may not reflect actual bias in police decision making, especially when one compares whites and minorities in similarly situated circumstances. Blacks, for example, disproportionately live in neighborhoods plagued by crime and violence, and there are few large U.S. cities where whites live in comparable circumstances. Even when one does compare whites driving or walking through predominately minority neighborhoods and finds no difference in the probability of being stopped, searched, and so forth, the reality is that these individuals likely reflect only a small fraction of police actions in minority neighborhoods. So while the decisions by the police may not be intentionally biased, they may serve to affirm perceptions of bias because the level of police activity is greater in high crime-poverty areas disproportionately settled by minorities.

Unfortunately there is no unifying method that can establish the extent to which racially biased policing occurs. All approaches have weaknesses. Social scientists should therefore be measured in their assessments.

NOTES

1. This is sometimes referred to as the denominator from the standpoint that the proportion of minority stops should be divided by the population at risk (e.g., % black stops/ % blacks at risk for being stopped) to provide an appropriate adjustment for detecting racial disparities.

2. Sampson, R. and W. J. Wilson. Toward a theory of race, crime, and urban inequality, pp. 37–54.

3. Skogan. Disorder and decline: Crime and the spiral of decay in American neighborhoods.

4. Hindelang. Variations in sex-age-race incidence rates of offending, pp. 461–475.

5. Fridell. By the numbers: A guide for analyzing race data from vehicle stops.

6. Zingraff et al. Evaluating North Carolina State Highway Patrol data.

7. Farrell et al. Rhode Island Traffic Stop Statistics Act.

8. Alpert et al. Toward a better benchmark: Assessing the utility of not-at-fault traffic crash data in racial profiling research.

9. Montgomery County Department of Police. Traffic stop data collection analysis.

10. McConnell, E. H. and A. R. Scheidegger. Race and speeding citations: Comparing speeding citations issued by air traffic officers with those issued by ground traffic officers.

11. Alpert et al. Police suspicion and discretionary decision making during citizen stops, pp. 407–434.

12. Reiss. Systematic social observation of natural social phenomena, pp. 3–33.

13. Lamberth. Revised statistical analysis of the incidence of police stops and arrests of black drivers/travelers on the New Jersey Turnpike.

14. Maxfield, R. and G. Kelling. New Jersey State Police and stop data.

15. Lange et al. Speed violation survey of the New Jersey Turnpike.

16. Alpert et al. Investigating racial profiling by the Miami-Dade Police Department, pp. 25–56.

17. Smith. The neighborhood context of police behavior, pp. 313–341.

18. Eck et al. Vehicle police stops in Cincinnati.

19. Alpert et al. Investigating racial profiling by the Miami-Dade Police Department, pp. 25–56.

20. Ibid.

21. 302 F. Supp. 2d 1217, 1229–1232, D. Kan., 2004.

22. Gelman et al. An analysis of the New York City Police Department's "stop-and-frisk" policy in the context of claims of racial bias, pp. 813–823.

23. Klinger. Negotiating order in patrol work: An ecological theory of police response to deviance, pp. 277–306.

24. For a discussion of the benefits and limitations of citizens' calls for police service data see Klinger, D. and G. Bridges. Measurement error in calls-for-service as an indicator of crime, pp. 705–726.

25. Ridgeway. Analysis of racial disparities in the New York Police Department's stop, question, and frisk practices.

26. For technical details see Angrist et al. Identification of causal effects using instrumental variables, pp. 444–455.

27. This is known as the nonzero average causal effect of the instrument on actual treatment assignment.

28. This is known as the exclusion restriction.

29. Grogger, J. and G. Ridgeway. Testing for racial profiling in traffic stops from behind a veil of darkness, pp. 878–887.

30. Lamberth. Racial profiling data analysis study: Final report for the San Antonio Police Department.

31. Greenwald. Final report: Police vehicle stops in Sacramento, California.

32. Neyman. On the application of probability theory to agricultural experiments.

33. Schell et al. Police-community relations in Cincinnati: Year three evaluation report.

34. Jefferis et al. The effect of a videotaped arrest on public perceptions of police use of force, pp. 381–395.

35. Weitzer. Incidents of police misconduct and public opinion, pp. 397–408.

36. Christopher. Report of the Independent Commission on the Los Angeles Police Department.

37. See Walker. Searching for the denominator: Problems with police traffic stop data and an early warning system solution, pp. 63–95; Walker. The citizen's guide to interpreting traffic stop data: Un-raveling the racial profiling controversy; and Walker. Internal benchmarking for traffic stop data: An early intervention system approach.

38. Walker. Early intervention systems for law enforcement agencies: A planning and management guide.

39. Birotte. Training evaluation and management system (TEAMS) II audit, phase I (fiscal year 2007/2008).

40. Walker. Early intervention systems for law enforcement agencies: A planning and management guide.

41. Decker, S. and J. Rojek. Saint Louis Metropolitan Police Department traffic stop patterns.

42. Ridgeway, G. and J. MacDonald. Doubly robust internal benchmarking and false discovery rates for detecting racial bias in police stops.

43. Ridgeway, G. et al. Police-community relations in Cincinnati: Year two evaluation report.

44. Ridgeway, G. Analysis of racial disparities in the New York Police Department's stop, question, and frisk practices.

45. For technical details see Kang, J. and J. Schafer. Demystifying double robustness: A comparison of alternative strategies for estimating a population mean from incomplete data, pp. 523–580.

46. Fridell. By the numbers: A guide for analyzing race data from vehicle stops.

47. Smith, M. R. Depoliticizing racial profiling: Suggestions for the limited use and management of race in police decision-making, pp. 219–260.

48. Benjamini, Y. and Y. Hochberg. Controlling the false discovery rate: A practical and powerful approach to multiple testing.

49. Dixon, T. et al. The influence of race in police-civilian interactions: A content analysis of videotaped interactions taken during Cincinnati police traffic stops, pp. 530–549.

50. Schell, T. et al. Police-community relations in Cincinnati: Year three evaluation report.

51. See Knowles, J., N. Persico and P. Todd. Racial bias in motor vehicle searches, pp. 203–229; Persico, N. and P. Todd. Generalising the hit rates test for racial bias in law enforcement, with an application to vehicle searches in Wichita, pp. F351–F367; Persico, N. and P. Todd. The hit rates test for racial bias in motor-vehicle searches, pp. 37–53.

52. Persico, N. and P. Todd. The hit rates test for racial bias in motor-vehicle searches, pp. 37–53.

53. Ayres. Outcome tests of racial disparities in police practices, pp. 131–142.

54. Ridgeway, G. Analysis of racial disparities in the New York Police Department's stop, question, and frisk practices.

55. Schell et al. Police-community relations in Cincinnati: Year three evaluation report.

56. Ridgeway. Assessing the effect of race bias in post–traffic stop outcomes using propensity scores.

57. Schell et al. Police-community relations in Cincinnati: Year three evaluation report.

58. Engel, R. S. and R. Tillyer. Searching for equilibrium: The tenuous nature of the outcome test, pp. 54–71.

REFERENCES

Alpert, Geoffrey P., John M. MacDonald, and Roger G. Dunham. 2005. Police suspicion and discretionary decision making during citizen stops. *Criminology* 43: 407–434.

Alpert, Geoffrey P., Michael R. Smith, and Roger G. Dunham. 2004. Toward a better benchmark: Assessing the utility of not-at-fault traffic crash data in racial profiling research. *Justice Research and Policy* 6: 43–70.

———. 2007. Investigating racial profiling by the Miami-Dade Police Department: A multi-method approach. *Criminology and Public Policy* 6: 25–56.

Angrist, Joshua D., Guido W. Imbens, and Donald B. Rubin. 1996. Identification of causal effects using instrumental variables. *Journal of the American Statistical Association* 91: 444–455.

Ayres, Ian. 2002. Outcome tests of racial disparities in police practices. *Justice Research and Policy* 4: 131–142.

Benjamini, Yoav, and Yosef Hochberg. 1995. Controlling the false discovery rate: A practical and powerful approach to multiple testing. *Journal of the Royal Statistical Society, Series B* 57: 289–300.

Birotte, Andre. 2007. *Training evaluation and management system (TEAMS) II audit, phase I (fiscal year 2007/2008)*. Los Angeles: Office of the Inspector General, Los Angeles Police Department.

Christopher, Warren. 1991. *Report of the Independent Commission on the Los Angeles Police Department*. Los Angeles: Independent Commission on the Los Angeles Police Department.

Decker, Scott H., and Jeff Rojek. 2002. *Saint Louis Metropolitan Police Department traffic stop patterns*, St. Louis: University of Missouri.

Dixon, Travis L., Terry L. Schell, Howard Giles, and Kristin L. Drogos. 2008. The influence of race in police–civilian interactions: A content analysis of videotaped interactions taken during Cincinnati police traffic stops. *Journal of Communication* 58: 530–549.

Eck, John E., Lin Liu, and Lisa G. Bostaph. 2003. *Police vehicle stops in Cincinnati: July 1–December 31, 2001*. Cincinnati: University of Cincinnati.

Efron, Bradley. 2004. Large-scale simultaneous hypothesis testing: The choice of a null hypothesis. *Journal of the American Statistical Association* 99: 96–104.

———. 2007. Correlation and large-scale simultaneous significance testing. *Journal of the American Statistical Association* 102: 93–103.

Engel, Robin S., and Tillyer, Rob. 2008. Searching for equilibrium: The tenuous nature of the outcome test. *Justice Quarterly* 25: 54–71.

Farrell, Amy, Dean Jack McDevitt, Shea Cronin, and Erica Pierce. 2003. *Rhode Island traffic stop statistics act final report*. Boston: Northeastern University.

Fridell, Lorie A. 2004. *By the numbers: A guide for analyzing race data from vehicle stops*. Washington, D.C.: Police Executive Research Forum.

Gelman, Andrew, Jeffrey Fagan, and Alex Kiss. 2007. An analysis of the New York City Police Department's "stop-and-frisk" policy in the context of claims of racial bias. *Journal of the American Statistical Association* 102: 813–823.

Greenwald, Howard P. 2001. *Final Report: Police vehicle stops in Sacramento, California*. Sacramento: Sacramento Police Department.

Grogger, Jeffrey, and Greg Ridgeway. 2006. Testing for racial profiling in traffic stops from behind a veil of darkness. *Journal of the American Statistical Association* 101: 878–887.

Imbens, Guido. 2003. *Nonparametric estimation of average treatment effects under exogeneity: A review. Technical Working Paper 294*. Cambridge: National Bureau of Economic Research.

Hindelang, Michael. 1981 Variations in sex-age-race incidence rates of offending. *American Sociological Review* 46: 461–474.

Jefferis, Eric S., Robert J. Kaminski, Stephen Holmes, and Dena E. Hanley. 1997. The effect of a videotaped arrest on public perceptions of police use of force. *Journal of Criminal Justice* 25: 381–395.

Kang, Joseph D. Y., and Joseph L. Schafer. 2007. Demystifying double robustness: A comparison of alternative strategies for estimating a population mean from incomplete data. *Statistical Science* 22: 523–580.

Klinger, David A. 1994. Demeanor or crime? Why "hostile" citizens are more likely to be arrested. *Criminology* 32: 475–494.

———. 1997. Negotiating order in patrol work: An ecological theory of police response to deviance. *Criminology* 35: 277–306.

Klinger, David A., and George Bridges. 1997. Measurement error in calls-for-service as an indicator of crime. *Criminology* 35: 705–726.

Knowles, John, Nicola Persico, and Petra Todd. 2001. Racial bias in motor vehicle searches: Theory and evidence. *Journal of Political Economy* 109: 203–229.

Lamberth, John. 1994. *Revised statistical analysis of the incidence of police stops and arrests of black drivers/travelers on the New Jersey Turnpike between exits or interchanges 1 and 3 from the years 1988 through 1991.* Philadelphia: Temple University, Department of Psychology.

Lamberth, John. 2003. *Racial profiling data analysis study: Final report for the San Antonio Police Department.* San Antonio: SAPD.

Lange, James E., Kenneth O. Blackman, and Mark B. Johnson. 2001. *Speed violation survey of the New Jersey Turnpike: Final report.* New Jersey: Office of the Attorney General of New Jersey.

Maxfield, Michael, and George L. Kelling 2005. *New Jersey State Police and stop data: What do we know, what should we know, and what should we do?* Newark: The Police Institute at Rutgers-Newark, School of Criminal Justice, Rutgers University.

McConnell, E. H., and A. R. Scheidegger. 2001. Race and speeding citations: Comparing speeding citations issued by air traffic officers with those issued by ground traffic officers. Paper presented at the annual meeting of the Academy of Criminal Justice Sciences, April 4–8, in Washington, D.C.

Montgomery County Department of Police. 2002. *Traffic stop data collection analysis, 3rd report.* Maryland: Montgomery County Department of Police.

Neyman, Jerzy 1923. On the application of probability theory to agricultural experiments: Essay on principles, Section 9. Translated in *Statistical Science* 5: 465–480, 1990.

Persico, Nicola, and Petra Todd. 2006. Generalising the hit rates test for racial bias in law enforcement, with an application to vehicle searches in Wichita. *The Economic Journal* 116: 351–367.

———. 2008. The hit rates test for racial bias in motor-vehicle searches. *Justice Quarterly* 25: 37–53.

Reiss, Albert J. 1971. Systematic observation of natural social phenomena. *Sociological Methodology* 3: 3–33.

Ridgeway, Greg. 2006. Assessing the effect of race bias in post–traffic stop outcomes using propensity scores. *Journal of Quantitative Criminology* 22: 1–26.

Ridgeway, Greg. 2007. *Analysis of racial disparities in the New York Police Department's stop, question, and frisk practices.* Santa Monica: RAND Corporation.

Ridgeway, Greg, and John M. MacDonald. 2008. Doubly robust internal benchmarking and false discovery rates for detecting racial bias in police stops. *Unpublished Manuscript.*

Ridgeway, Greg, Terry L. Schell, K. Jack Riley, Susan Turner, and Travis L. Dixon. 2006. *Police-community relations in Cincinnati: Year two evaluation report.* Santa Monica: RAND Corporation.

Sampson, Robert J., and William Julius Wilson. 1995. Toward a theory of race, crime, and urban inequality. In *Crime and Inequality*, ed. John Hagan and Ruth D. Peterson, 37–54. Stanford: Stanford University Press.

Schell, Terry L., Greg Ridgeway, Travis L. Dixon, Susan Turner, and K. Jack Riley. 2007. *Police-community relations in Cincinnati: Year three evaluation report.* Santa Monica: RAND Corporation.

Skogan, Wesley G. 1990. *Disorder and decline: Crime and the spiral of decay in American neighborhoods.* Berkeley and Los Angeles: University of California Press.

Smith, Douglas A. 1986. The neighborhood context of police behavior. In *Communities and*

Crime, ed. Albert J. Reiss and Michael H. Tonry, 313–341. Chicago: University of Chicago Press.

Smith, Michael. R. 2005. Depoliticizing racial profiling: Suggestions for the limited use and management of race in police decision-making. *George Mason University Civil Rights Law Journal* 15: 219–260.

Walker, Samuel. 2001. Searching for the denominator: Problems with police traffic stop data and an early warning system solution. *Justice Research and Policy* 3: 63–95.

———. 2002. The citizen's guide to interpreting traffic stop data: Un-raveling the racial profiling controversy. *Unpublished manuscript.*

———. 2003a. *Early intervention systems for law enforcement agencies: A planning and management guide.* Washington, D.C.: U.S. Department of Justice, Office of Community Oriented Policing Services.

———. 2003b. *Internal benchmarking for traffic stop data: An early intervention system approach.* Washington, D.C.: Police Executive Research Forum.

Weitzer, Ronald. 2002. Incidents of police misconduct and public opinion. *Journal of Criminal Justice* 30: 397–408.

Zingraff, Matthew T., Mary Mason, William Smith, Donald Tomaskovic-Devey, Patricia Warren, Harvey L. McMurray, and C. Robert Fenlon. 2000. *Evaluating North Carolina State Highway Patrol data: Citation, warnings, and searches in 1998.* North Carolina: North Carolina Department of Crime Control and Public Safety and North Carolina State Highway Patrol.

Chapter 8

Using Geographic Information Systems to Study Race, Crime, and Policing

Matt R. Nobles

Introduction

Recently, the relationships between space (in the ecological or geographical sense) and other social phenomena have benefitted from advancements of powerful technologies that put new analytical methods into the hands of researchers and practitioners alike. In particular, GIS (Geographic Information Systems) has become indispensible in the study of policing, where it is relied on to help identify patterns in offending, guide resource deployment and targeted interventions, increase awareness of police-community relations, and a host of other roles. Although many examples of the application of GIS technology to policing may be available in the field, one highly visible model is the use of CompStat, a GIS-focused approach to investigation, problem solving, resource management, and accountability in routine police patrol. CompStat represents not only an adoption of new technological tools in the fight against crime, but also a shift in strategic and tactical decision making that puts crime data and geographical information at the forefront of proactive policy. This chapter briefly acknowledges the extensive and diverse literature connecting geography, race, and policing to the study of crime before turning to a discussion of the methodological advantages of using GIS to visualize these relationships. Several case studies involving the use of GIS in the study of race, crime, and policing are presented, followed by a discussion of GIS as a less obvious tool for identifying and combating social problems.

Literature Review

Perspectives on Place, Race, and Crime

Scholars in criminology, sociology, and related fields have long embraced the idea that crime is related to geography. This concept is readily identified in some of the most influential criminological theories,[1] beginning with the Chicago School emphasizing human ecology and social disorganization,[2] and later extending to more literal interpretations and implications for urban design and crime prevention policy.[3]

Further, many important constructs related to geography, such as physical disorder and racial/ethnic composition, are routinely borrowed from these theories in neighborhood or community-level studies of crime. Though findings vary in important ways, these studies collectively represent a rich and diverse literature on the relationship between space and crime.

The precise role of geography in understanding crime varies according to theoretical perspectives, type and level of analysis, and outcome of interest. Critically, they also present challenges in determining the relationships (if any) between race and crime. For example, some researchers state that there is an explicit link between criminal decision making and spatial patterns of individual-level offending, perhaps involving rational processes that evaluate factors such as target attractiveness and spatial opportunity in the urban context.[4] Others imply that space and crime are related but function in an indirect and structural fashion, perhaps in association with the conditioning effects of disadvantage, which frequently vary between black and white communities.[5] Research on structural causes of violent crime suggests that those causes (e.g., concentrated disadvantage) do not vary across racial groups, at least when blacks and whites are similarly situated.[6] But some evidence indicates that substantial racial disparities exist between whites and non-whites regardless of social class, and that even affluent blacks are concentrated in areas with higher rates of violent crime than are poor whites.[7] Still others show evidence for the effects of spatial proximity to other crime exerting an independent effect even when other neighborhood-level characteristics are controlled.[8] These examples illustrate just a few of the ways in which crime and geography are theoretically and empirically linked.

Issues of geography, crime, and race are always focal concerns for police, from the strategic level down to the beat cop. For example, recent research on this topic shows that police use-of-force decisions for officers from a large Southeastern municipality are consistently and independently influenced by neighborhood threat levels and by the percentage of non-white residents in a given area.[9] This finding has implications that range from officer safety to community relations to legal liability, all of which could have serious ramifications for the way that the agency as a whole operates. In short, the nexus among space, crime, race, and policing have important, real-world consequences. Thus methods for disentangling the relationships among race, crime, and policing are of paramount value to researchers and practitioners alike.

Race and Policing

Throughout history, police have served different functions in the community, ranging from fire fighting to operating soup kitchens. But police organizations have an especially difficult and contentious history relating to the black community. By some accounts, from the antebellum South through the civil rights movement the police were tasked primarily with maintaining racial dominance by recapturing escaped slaves, suppressing black demonstrations and riots, and pursuing "high risk" minority drug offenders.[10] Over the past forty years, however, institutional racism has become a more subtle and elusive phenomenon. The modern equivalents of overt, historical racial bias in policing center on differential enforcement for minorities compared to whites. The majority of empirical studies on this topic rely on data and analysis of traffic stops to infer the prevalence of racial profiling (also see Ridgeway and Mac-Donald, this volume). Unfortunately, while considerable scholarship has been devoted to racial profiling or "race-based policing," very few studies have approached the problem using GIS as a methodological tool.

The apparent relationships among place, race, crime, and policing appear reflexive and reciprocal. For their part, police have been shown to exert an effect on localized crime rates even in highly concentrated minority areas. Proactive patrol policies have been shown to have a direct and inverse effect on rates of robbery after controlling for several structural covariates, and this effect is largest for black adult offenders.[11] Even the racial composition of a municipal police force may affect crime-related outcomes differentially according to race. An analysis of racial composition of city police forces and racial patterns of arrest revealed that increases in minority officers were associated with increases in arrests for whites but not non-whites, while increases in white officers were associated with increases in arrests for non-whites but not whites.[12] Conversely, evidence from the field strongly suggests that context matters to police. In a broad sense, several studies suggest that neighborhood context affects police discretion and behavior, both in terms of attitudes and outcomes.[13]

Although specific definitions of the practice vary between researchers, state statutes, and the relevant case law, one operational definition of racial profiling is the "use of race as a key factor in police decisions to stop and interrogate citizens."[14] In general, empirical research on racial profiling in police traffic stops might be characterized as mixed. For example, one study analyzing traffic stops in Richmond, VA, showed that minorities, especially blacks, were stopped at disproportionately higher rates compared to the driving-eligible population; the authors note, however, that whites were significantly more likely than minorities to be searched, ticketed, and arrested.[15] Gaines[16] reported minority overrepresentation in some traffic stops in Riverside, CA, but those differences were not statistically significant; further, there were no major differences in searches or dispositions across race. Withrow[17] conducted an analysis of traffic stops in Wichita, KS, and concluded that some evidence supports the existence of race-based policing, but that "the issue does not appear to be driving while Black. Instead, it appears that the issue is more like driving while different."[18] Several studies explicitly consider ecology and geography while analyzing racial profiling in police traffic stops. One such study concludes that there is evidence for racial profiling based on disproportionate surveillance and stopping of minority drivers in a white suburban community, and thus that profiling is a function of not just race but also geographical context.[19] Conversely, another study concludes that crime rates at the census-tract level were the only significant factor that predicted police traffic stops.[20]

Like the apparent contradictions in direct examinations of racial profiling, indirect support is also somewhat contradictory. Many studies examine racial profiling through traditional survey methods, as citizen opinions, attitudes, and personal histories may play a role in understanding not just the objective reality but also the perception of police profiling. Findings from this part of the literature hold that opinions on the practice are largely, and perhaps unsurprisingly, related to race and perceptions of personal experience as well as general support for police, while some evidence supports findings for class and media exposure.[21]

In sum, the changing and expanding role played by police in the delivery of social services, order maintenance, community development, and public safety has not been without challenges and conflict in the realm of race relations. Many issues surrounding the existence, nature, and severity of racial bias in policing also carry an implicit linkage to geography. To the extent that researchers, policymakers, and police themselves can utilize spatial policing data that is faster to acquire, more precise, and more readily analyzed, investigators will also be in a better position to understand and react to evidence of bias at the individual or agency level.

GIS and Policing

Broadly defined, a Geographic Information System (GIS) is a collection of computer-based visualization and statistical tools used to manage, display, and analyze spatial data. Visualization of spatial data permits the geographical association of features or properties on a map, while the supporting tools permit manipulation of sample data to display trends or attributes that are not readily apparent, such as common patterns in burglaries within a neighborhood. Importantly, these techniques offer advantages to social scientists studying crime and crime-related phenomena as well as to practitioners doing applied work for police agencies.[22] Crime analysis using maps has a long and interesting history, by some accounts dating back to the early 1800s.[23] Undoubtedly crime mapping capability has advanced very substantially since those early days, but at a fundamental level GIS can be used to provide essentially the same information as pin maps did two centuries ago. Conversely, the popularization and proliferation of personal computers has pushed GIS to ever-greater levels of sophistication. This trend largely mirrors the development of desktop GIS applications, originating with descriptive mapping objectives and evolving over time to incorporate temporal, statistical, and other progressively more powerful analytical tools.[24]

One of the greatest challenges to making GIS truly functional for police agencies is determining what specific questions or objectives need to be answered. Obviously, the greatest technology available is unlikely to be leveraged without the need or ability to do so, and as a result some critics observe that GIS is an expensive gimmick that accomplishes the same things that paper maps could. This is to say that some GIS crime "analysis" is no more than a superficial examination of static points. But the real capabilities lie in the potential to make complex calculations, statistical tests, and logical queries quickly and easily accessible to police and civilian analysts, thus enhancing the study of social phenomena in the spatial context.[25] To that end, the practice of policing can be shaped in many ways by GIS. Crime analysis featuring mapping capabilities varies greatly in terms of implementation between jurisdictions, but the potential for application for all types of crimes and for agencies of all sizes is well documented, ranging from patrolling borders for counter-drug operations to tracking murder suspects to hidden grave sites.[26] A common theme across all implementations is that GIS is an evolving tool that offers several advantages over lower-tech alternatives, including the ability to dynamically analyze spatial proximity by adding new data layers, to explore potentially valuable social data not created or maintained directly by police (e.g., census data), and to sub-classify spatial data by specific attributes that may be relevant to crime patterns.[27] Any or all of these features may pertain to police agencies' strategic partnerships, tactical management, or operational objectives depending on the availability of data, personnel, and interpretation of analysis results.

The utility of the analysis of spatial crime data may be illustrated on many levels and in many novel ways, depending on the research question or outcome of interest. For instance, LeBeau[28] demonstrates an application of GIS technology to identify areas considered "most hazardous" to police. Hazard in this study is operationalized as any of five different types of police service calls considered to involve risk to officers, including emergency response, gun-related incidents, officer use of force, officer injury, and calls requesting immediate officer help. LeBeau's technique utilizes a countywide gridded map to calculate the number of each type of incident. Those grid cells that exceed a predetermined threshold level are labeled "most hazardous," and the resulting maps provide an illustration of which geographic areas have the highest densities of police hazard (though hazard density is not equivalent to risk). The author observes that training and policy adjustments could be used to enhance occupational safety for patrol officers. In this example, occupational risk (a complex and nuanced concept shaped by many extraneous factors) is the phenomenon under investigation, but the ability to localize such an abstract notion to specific geographic areas is a very powerful device indeed.

From a separate and more progressive perspective that extends beyond police, GIS may help community service agencies begin to address underlying structural correlates of crime. One way that this can be accomplished is using GIS to provide an indirect but insightful tool for long-term strategic planning related to general social problems, including visualizing the availability of social services like public transportation, or identifying the spatial distribution of child care subsidies,[29] the homeless population,[30] or to crime victims themselves,[31] potentially making outreach for at-risk groups more effective. Another peripherally related GIS study identified geographic characteristics of ambulance runs to suspected drug overdose victims, offering opportunities to target anti-drug interventions to specific geographic areas or focus more heavily on "street level" intelligence about trafficking patterns.[32] By facilitating aid to those who are most in need, the technology has the potential to help improve quality of life and perhaps inoculate against some citizens' perception of inequity when dealing with police, government services, and other official agencies.

Visualizing Race and Crime with GIS

GIS applications related to race, crime, and policing are highly data-dependent. More specifically, GIS systems utilize data that feature geographic or spatial identifiers, such as police arrest records that include attributes of the arrestee (sex, race, etc.), the arrest charge (specific offenses, name of victim, etc.), and the location where the individual was arrested. Although all crime data is "spatial" in the sense that every crime physically occurs somewhere, GIS data requires very specific location attributes, such as GPS coordinates or a complete and properly formatted street address, to be functional. Data that feature good geographic attributes are essential to any GIS-related task. While crime data itself may originate from within the agency, most municipal police departments are not equipped to create or maintain data that offers indicators of social context, thus visualizing these phenomena may require the sharing of data between agencies. Some tasks for researchers and practitioners alike may require social context variables from the U.S. census, which tracks structural variables such as median income, racial composition, family structure (female-headed households), the percentage of owner-occupied dwellings, and so forth. Many trained analysts and crime mapping experts are familiar with ESRI's ArcGIS suite for creating descriptive and analytical maps, but relatively few may be familiar with the free GeoDa software package.[33] GeoDa features exploratory spatial data analysis tools that can aid in identifying non-random spatial patterns and distributions, in addition to estimating multivariate spatial regression models that correctly account for spatial autocorrelation in crime data.

A first step toward understanding a complex social phenomenon such as racial profiling is establishing benchmarks for environmental conditions that describe or illustrate how attributes are associated in space. In particular, researchers and analysts may be interested in whether the percentages of minority drivers in police traffic stops differs significantly from the overall percentage of minorities in a given area, or whether proportions of minorities involved in traffic stops to minorities in a given area indicate bias. To this end, it is useful to visualize spatial associations of social facts such as racial composition. Anselin and Bera[34] characterize these associations between social factors as the clustering of similar values (however the variables may be operationalized) in space, or as locations that are surrounded by neighbors with similar or dissimilar values.[35] Therefore spatial association may involve several adjacent census block groups that all possess a high (or low) value for a given variable, such as median family income or the percentage of black residents.[36]

Anselin[37] also demonstrates the use of local indicators of spatial association (LISA), a method of representing levels of a given variable, such as the percentage of individuals within a census block that identify themselves as black, across geographic areas.[38] For example, a county consisting of several individual census tracts would be evaluated by comparing the value for a given variable, such as median income, in each census tract to the value of median income in all neighboring census tracts. LISA analysis, therefore, provides not only an indication of high or low values for a given variable within particular tracts, but also illustrates the *concentration* of values among spatially related units. Every individual in this example may be non-significant (indicating no spatial association) or significant, depending on the comparison between the individual tract and all neighboring tracts. Statistically significant LISA values result in one of four categories of spatial association: high-high, low-low, high-low, and low-high. In this example, the high-high case shows that the median income value for a given tract is high and that that individual tract is surrounded by other tracts that are similarly high.

Figure 8.1 shows an example LISA cluster map created using GeoDa 0.9.5i. In this map, the spatial concentration of median family income measured at the census

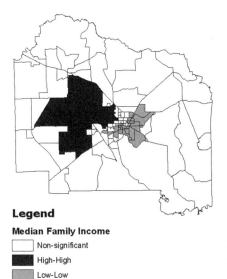

Legend

Median Family Income

☐	Non-significant
■	High-High
▨	Low-Low

Figure 8.1. Example LISA cluster map of median family income for Alachua County, Florida. (2000 U.S. Census)

block group level is dramatic, with concentrated (high-high) family income to the west and concentrated (low-low) family income to the east. This technique may be easily adapted for any existing census variables, or adapted to use a newly calculated proportion or index of dissimilarity[39] that serves as a proxy for inferring police bias. LISA maps not only allow for ordinary comparisons between aggregated geographic areas but also show statistically significant spatial concentration. As an exploratory tool this permits researchers and analysts to state not only whether a problem exists, but also where and to what extent it exists—capabilities lacking in non-spatial analysis.

An alternative technique for mapping concentrations of events or attributes is kernel density estimation in ArcGIS. A "kernel" is a graphical pattern on a GIS map that represents a concentration of points. The creation of density maps in ArcGIS involves aggregation of point data (e.g., arrests) within a user-defined boundary. The aggregated values are then used to create a smoothed surface with visual patterns of color or shading indicating variability over space within the defined search radius.[40] Although kernel density maps are preferred for some police crime analysis tasks, they lack the advantage of incorporating preexisting census variables and spatial units (e.g., block groups). Thus social scientists may find this method less conducive to the use of quantifiable spatial statistics and hypothesis testing, and therefore less appealing for the exploration of their research questions.

Figure 8.2 shows an example kernel density map created with ArcGIS 9.2. In this map, the spatial concentration of municipal police department arrests (measured by aggregating discrete point data) is clear, with the highest concentration shown in the northeast quadrant and tapering off at different rates depending on direction. This map also displays two additional "high density" spots due west and toward the south, though some location densities appear stronger and better defined than others.[41]

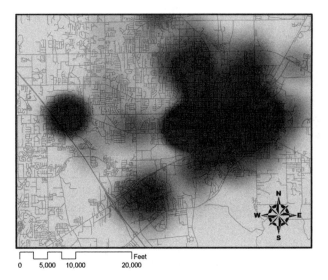

Figure 8.2. Example kernal density map showing concentration of municipal police arrests.

Given that agencies, communities, public officials, and others are all aware of and concerned by the potential for racial bias in policing, leveraging new methods to establish the context of police activity and identify whether patterns fall outside of normal expectations is a natural evolution. Below are three pertinent case studies from the criminology literature that illustrate the use of GIS in testing racial profiling by police.

CASE STUDY #1: ST. LOUIS TRAFFIC STOPS

Rojek, Rosenfeld, and Decker[42] make use of GIS as a tool to aid in more accurate multivariate analysis of police traffic stops. They selected as their unit of analysis 92 Missouri municipalities with driving-age populations of five thousand or greater, representing more than two-thirds of all traffic stops in the state for the four-month observation period. Their measure of interest, a disproportionality index, was computed by dividing the proportion of traffic stops accounted for by a given group by that group's proportion of the population.[43] The critical relationship in their analysis is the relationship between minority traffic stops and the inherent demographic characteristics of the municipalities.[44] The authors conclude that differences in the probability of being stopped are small but persistent between groups, with larger racial differences in probability of driver search and arrest.

CASE STUDY #2: CLEVELAND TRAFFIC STOPS

Engel and colleagues[45] utilize GIS to study racial bias in traffic stops for the Cleveland Division of Police (CDP). Their extensive analysis includes comparisons between traffic stop data, which is collected at the police zone level, and residential census data, which is used to approximate population and racial composition within each of the CDP zones. The authors calculate "expected" rates of traffic stops for each racial group based on the racial composition of each area used in the analysis, and then compare these rates to the actual rates observed.[46] They conclude that black motorists overall are 1.5 times more likely to be stopped by CDP officers than white drivers, while racial disparities are more severe, with blacks more than four times more likely than whites to be stopped in two specific CDP zones during the observational period.

CASE STUDY #3: SACRAMENTO TRAFFIC STOPS

Greenwald[47] performs an analysis of traffic stops in Sacramento, CA, as part of a multi-year study of racial profiling carried out by Sacramento Police Department (SPD) patrol officers. The author opts to employ a different type of GIS analysis to visualize Sacramento's traffic stop and neighborhood-level data. Specifically, he supplements his analyses with GIS density maps[48] displaying patterns of police vehicle stops compared to frequencies of citizen calls for service, reported crimes, residential locations for probationers, and residential locations for parolees. Greenwald concludes that the density maps show consistent spatial relationships between police traffic stops and areas of Sacramento having high concentrations of crime and people with criminal histories. He also states that the available evidence generally suggests that patterns of police traffic stops in Sacramento are "consistent with both population and crime suspect characteristics,"[49] thus advancing a police responsiveness view along with the general conclusion that black drivers are overrepresented in SPD traffic stops. The author also notes that several factors suggest evidence against the racial profiling argument, including no apparent systematic disparity between the race of the officer and the race of the driver, and no apparent effect of surveillance cameras on the rates at which drivers of particular races were stopped.

Each of these examples illustrates the potential for GIS techniques to expand our body of knowledge about the relationships among place, race, crime, and policing. In each case, researchers were able to leverage spatial data and GIS tools to exceed the limits of aspatial analysis, whether through augmentation of traditional statistical techniques (like calculating populations using inverse distance weights) or visualizing the spatial patterning of variables of interest. To the extent that all social phenomena are associated (whether explicitly or implicitly) with context and geography, GIS analysis is an essential method for visualizing spatial relationships, identifying trends over time and space, and performing statistical tests that quantify patterns as non-random.

Discussion

The results presented here suggest that GIS is unlikely to diminish in service to researchers and practitioners studying relationships among place, race, crime, and policing. The tools are already being widely utilized in a problem-oriented policing role to identify police/crime problems, develop interventions, and assess the impact of those interventions.[50] These findings articulate with previous (non-GIS) work examining factors related to serious assaults on police officers at the neighborhood level, which concludes with strong associations between police assault and block groups with high arrestee density, known criminogenic conditions, and propensity for violence.[51]

As crime data and the tools with which to study it become both more plentiful and more accessible to agencies and researchers, several implications emerge with respect to GIS. Maltz,[52] for example, states that the full realization of the FBI's National Incident-Based Reporting System (NIBRS) vastly expands the quantity and richness of data related to the details of crimes reported to police, thus requiring new methodologies to handle, analyze, and interpret data. The author also notes that traditional statistical testing procedures "will be absolutely meaningless"[53] when data sets are extremely large, requiring adjustments to the social science toolbox to discern meaning in amassed crime data. These observations have several implications for the use of GIS. First, GIS is a complement to traditional social science methods that can aid in data reduction. While statistical testing with large data sets may be untenable, maps need not be overly complex—symbology can express information related to social processes that would not be possible with other approaches (e.g., expansion of arrest patterns over time). Second, graphically depicting spatial concentrations provides information that non-spatial data cannot provide. While traditional data may be able to capture the presence or absence of a social variable, the expression of concentrations requires mathematical consideration of geographic area. Similarly, maps can help to identify "threshold" areas for phenomena where non-spatial statistics cannot. Finally, as spatial crime data becomes commonplace, it is increasingly likely that the field of criminology will adapt to incorporate more explicitly spatial relationships in the development, revision, and integration of theoretical frameworks. As a result, not only will crime mapping be routine in practice, but it may play a role in shaping how crime is defined and operationalized in the abstract sense.

Maltz, Gordon, and Friedman[54] pose several "open" issues with respect to mapping crime data that, by extension, are also relevant to data and maps dealing with race and policing. First, the authors state that institutionalizing the cooperative use of technology (between the police and the community, for example) is as important as developing the capability in the first place. This cooperation fosters trust, communication, and the sense that both community and police concerns are taken seriously. Second, widespread use of GIS at the agency level has important implications for training, from superior officers responsible for allocating resources to rank-and-file officers who may resist the suggestion because "a good cop knows his beat."[55] Greater awareness comes through training and recognition of patterns that may be elusive at the street level. Third, the authors observe that other police data, such as calls for service, could readily or dynamically be mapped and analyzed to create new intelligence related to community problems that usually do not warrant the same urgency as criminal incidents. Collectively, these ideas demonstrate progressive thinking about the ways that GIS may be utilized to proactively address issues that could be associated with greater operational effectiveness as well as combating institutional racism. For example, active and cooperative alliances with community organizations and resident groups that involve maps and the sharing of certain intelligence could work counter to the "us versus them" mentality that police and some citizens harbor. Also, the opportunity for retraining and integration of new crime data sources may offer evidence of genuine explanations for crime and delinquency that serve as a counterpoint to entrenched bias. If prejudiced police officers can be shown "proof" that some crime is associated with factors other than race, there may be long-term dividends.

Various scholars have offered suggestions on dealing with racial bias and profiling in policing. Most of these recommendations address the needs of agencies and researchers related to detecting evidence of the practice and its surrounding circumstances rather than offering direct solutions. Jefferson,[56] for example, suggests that methodological implications such as representative sampling, case studies, and historical documentation may shape contemporary understanding of the state of police-minority relations. GIS can help to accomplish these goals by making data more accessible to researchers and analysts, including through various sampling strategies, and by providing "case studies" describing the geography of race and police traffic stops from individual jurisdictions. Additionally, several initiatives championed by federal agencies and directed at state and local police departments endeavor to improve data collection efforts related to studying the extent of police racial profiling, now required under state law in some jurisdictions.[57] Improvements in these areas will allow academics, auditors, and investigators to make a clearer and more compelling case for the existence of racial profiling.

Conclusion

Empirical evidence for and against the existence of racial bias in policing may support both sides of the issue. Nevertheless, Webster[58] states, "Police processes and activities, from the most routine to the use of deadly force, show a consistent pattern in the relationship between the police and racial and ethnic minorities that suggests the existence of police racism." This view seems to characterize not only the consensus academic view of policing practice, especially post-9/11, but also a systematic trend in racial disparities throughout the criminal justice system. GIS is one relatively new and promising methodological approach to address questions related to whether policing practice differs significantly and systematically from expectations based on the social and environmental conditions in a given area. As racial profiling continues to dominate public discourse, mixed methods for exploring this topic, including GIS, are sure to gain additional exposure and popularity as scholars from all backgrounds grapple with answers.

NOTES

1. See Eck & Weisburd, 1995 for a full review.
2. See Park, Burgess, & McKenzie, 1925; Shaw & McKay, 1942.

3. For examples, see Newman, 1972; Jeffery, 1971; Jacobs, 1961.

4. Capone & Nichols, 1976; Brantingham & Brantingham, 1984.

5. Krivo & Peterson, 2000.

6. Ibid.

7. Logan & Stults, 1999; McNulty, 1999.

8. Morenoff, Sampson, & Raudenbush, 2001.

9. Lersch et al., 2008.

10. Hawkins & Thomas, 1991; Bass, 2001.

11. Sampson & Cohen, 1988.

12. Donohue & Levitt, 2001.

13. For a full discussion, see Smith & Klein, 1984; Smith, 1986; Worden, 1989; Terrill & Reisig, 2003; Lersch et al., 2008.

14. Weitzer & Tuch, 2002, p. 435.

15. Smith & Petrocelli, 2001.

16. Gaines, 2006.

17. Withrow (2004a, 2004b).

18. Withrow, 2004b, p. 361.

19. Meehan & Ponder, 2002.

20. Petrocelli, Piquero, & Smith, 2003.

21. See Weitzer & Tuch, 1999; Weitzer & Tuch, 2002; Weitzer & Tuch, 2005; Brunson & Miller, 2006; Reitzel & Piquero, 2006.

22. Vann & Garson, 2001.

23. Weisburd & McEwen, 1998.

24. La Vigne & Groff, 2001; Lersch, 2004.

25. Wong, 1996.

26. See Leipnik & Albert, 2003 for several examples.

27. Murray et al., 2001.

28. LeBeau, 2001.

29. Queralt & Witte, 1998.

30. Rock, 2005.

31. Stoe et al., 2003.

32. Merchant et al., 2006.

33. Anselin, Syabri, & Kho, 2006.

34. Anselin & Bera, 1998.

35. Statistically speaking, geographic association or clustering of a given variable is termed "spatial autocorrelation," to indicate the geographic relationship ("spatial," indicating relative proximity in Cartesian space) among a group of cases for a single factor or attribute ("autocorrelation," indicating that a variable is empirically associated with itself in a group of cases).

36. A test statistic, Moran's I, is a measure of spatial autocorrelation that indicates the extent to which the spatial pattern of the data is consistent with a null hypothesis of spatial randomness. A significant value for Moran's I indicates non-random spatial autocorrelation. While visualizing spatial autocorrelation may be useful as an exploratory tool, it may also be regarded as a "nuisance" in multivariate analyses because it violates traditional assumptions of OLS regression and may result in biased coefficient estimates.

37. Anselin, 1995.

38. Statistically, the LISA technique permits assessment of the null hypothesis of spatial randomness by comparing values in each unit to values in neighboring units. A "significant"

value on a LISA map indicates that the level of a variable of interest in one area is significantly higher or lower than the levels of that variable in surrounding areas.

39. See Wong, 1996.

40. Chainey, Tompson, & Uhlig, 2008.

41. This technique may be easily adapted for any existing areal point data, such as the residences of registered sex offenders or the locations where illegal guns are confiscated. Kernel density maps allow for some inference about spatial concentration, subject to user-defined settings such as the search radius.

42. Rojek, Rosenfeld, & Decker, 2004.

43. Ibid., p. 135.

44. Distances in this case are calculated using ArcGIS and consist of measurements between the geographic centers of the ninety-two municipalities in the analysis, according to the authors (Rojek, Rosenfeld, & Decker, 2004, p. 136). They further estimate driving population for each unit using an inverse distance weights matrix, whereby more weight is assigned to units that are near in proximity, with a distance cutoff of twenty miles; these weights were then multiplied by populations of white, black, and Hispanic residents. The resulting spatial weighting scheme and imputation of populations is largely accurate in representing racial composition of drivers in the area under study, according to the authors; they also state, however, that for most jurisdictions under analysis it "makes little difference whether the residential population or the imputed population is used to determine the degree of racial disproportionality in traffic stops" (p. 143).

45. Engel et al., 2006.

46. Specifically, census variable values used by Engel and colleagues for CDP zones that contained multiple block groups used the sum of values from all block groups that were completely within the zone. Zones that bisected one or more block groups were apportioned based on the weighted value of the overlapping surface area. In this way, the authors were able to assign values from census variables to each of the CDP zones even when those zones were generally incongruent with census block groups. From these values, they were able to calculate a disproportionality index for each police zone by dividing the number of stops for one racial/ethnic group by the expected value of stops based on the racial composition and total population values from the census block groups. The authors note that this method requires the assumption that individuals are randomly distributed within a given block group; thus an overlap of 75% of the surface area would be weighted at 0.75 times the value for each demographic variable of interest (e.g., population or racial composition). The authors state that this assumption is questionable but that this technique is the best available given the constraints of the data.

47. Greenwald, 2001.

48. See Vann & Garson, 2001.

49. Greenwald, 2001, p. 27.

50. La Vigne, 1999.

51. Kaminski, Jefferis, & Gu, 2003.

52. Maltz, 1998.

53. Ibid., p. 398.

54. Maltz, Gordon, & Friedman, 1990.

55. Ibid., p. 135.

56. Jefferson, 1988.

57. Fridell, 2004; McMahon et al., 2006.

58. Webster, 2007, p. 99

REFERENCES

Anselin, Luc. 1995. Local indicators of spatial association—LISA. *Geographical Analysis* 27: 93–115.

Anselin, Luc, and Anil Bera. 1998. Spatial dependence in linear models with an introduction to spatial econometrics. In H. Ullah & D. Giles (Eds.), *Handbook of Applied Econometrics Statistics*. New York: Marcel Dekker, 237–290.

Anselin, Luc, Ibnu Syabri, and Youngihn Kho. 2006. GeoDa: An introduction to spatial data analysis. *Geographical Analysis* 38: 28–35.

Bass, Sandra. 2001. Policing space, policing race: Social control imperatives and police discretionary decisions. *Social Justice* 28: 156–176.

Brantingham, Patricia L., and Paul J. Brantingham. 1984. *Patterns in Crime*. New York: Macmillan.

Brunson, Rod K., and Jody Miller. 2006. Young black men and urban policing in the United States. *British Journal of Criminology* 46: 613–640.

Capone, Donald L., and Woodrow W. Nichols. 1976. Urban structure and criminal mobility. *American Behavioral Scientist* 20: 199–213.

Chainey, Spencer, Lisa Tompson, and Sebastian Uhlig. 2008. The utility of hotspot mapping for predicting spatial patterns of crime. *Security Journal* 21: 4–28.

Donohue, John J., and Steven D. Levitt. 2001. The impact of race on policing and arrests. *Journal of Law and Economics* 44: 367–394.

Eck, John E., and David Weisburd. 1995. Crime places in crime theory. In J. E. Eck & D. Weisburd (Eds.), *Crime and Place*. Monsey, NY: Criminal Justice Press; and Washington, DC: Police Executive Research Forum, 1–33.

Engel, Robin S., James Frank, Charles Klahm, and Rob Tillyer. Understanding police decision making during traffic stops: Results from the Cleveland division of police traffic stop study. Paper presented at the annual meeting of the American Society of Criminology (ASC). 2006-10-09 from http://www.allacademic.com/meta/p127254_index.html.

Fridell, Lorrie A. 2004. *By the Numbers: A Guide for Analyzing Race Data from Vehicle Stops*. Washington, DC: Police Executive Research Forum.

Gaines, Larry K. 2006. An analysis of traffic stop data in Riverside, California. *Police Quarterly* 9: 210–233.

Greenwald, Howard P. 2001. *Final Report: Police Vehicle Stops in Sacramento, California*. Sacramento, CA: City of Sacramento.

Jacobs, Jane. 1961. *The Death and Life of Great American Cities*. New York: Vintage.

Jefferson, Tony. 1988. Race, crime, and policing: Empirical, theoretical, and methodological issues. *International Journal of the Sociology of Law* 16: 521–539.

Jeffery, C. Ray. 1971. *Crime Prevention Through Environmental Design*. Beverly Hills, CA: Sage.

Hawkins, Homer, and Richard Thomas. 1991. White policing of black populations: A history of race and social control in America. In E. Cashmore & E. McLaughlin (Eds.), *Out of Order? Policing Black People*. New York: Routledge, 65–86.

Kaminski, Robert J., Eric Jefferis, and Joann Gu. 2003. Community correlates of serious assaults on police. *Police Quarterly* 6: 119–149.

Krivo, Lauren J., and Ruth D. Peterson. 2000. The structural context of homicide: Accounting for racial differences in process. *American Sociological Review* 65: 547–559.

La Vigne, Nancy G. 1999. Computerized mapping as a tool for problem-oriented policing. *Crime Mapping News* 1: 1.

La Vigne, Nancy G., and Elizabeth R. Groff. 2001. The evolution of crime mapping in the

United States: From the descriptive to the analytic. In A. Hirschfield & K. Bowers (Eds.), *Mapping and Analysing Crime Data: Lessons from Research and Practice.* London: Taylor and Francis, 203–222.

LeBeau, James L. 2001. Mapping out hazardous space for police work. In A. Hirschfield & K. Bowers (Eds.), *Mapping and Analysing Crime Data: Lessons from Research and Practice.* London: Taylor and Francis, 139–155.

Leipnik, Mark R., and Donald P. Albert, eds. 2003. *GIS in Law Enforcement: Implementation Issues and Case Studies.* London: Taylor and Francis.

Lersch, Kim M. 2004. *Space, Time, and Crime.* Durham, NC: Carolina Academic Press.

Lersch, Kim M., Thomas Bazley, Thomas Mieczkowski, and Kristina Childs. 2008. Police use of force and neighbourhood characteristics: An examination of structural disadvantage, crime, and resistance. *Policing and Society* 18: 282–300.

Logan, John R., and Brian J. Stults. 1999. Racial differences in exposure to crime: The city and suburbs of Cleveland in 1990. *Criminology* 37: 251–276.

Maltz, Michael D. 1998. Visualizing homicide: A research note. *Journal of Quantitative Criminology* 14: 397–410.

Maltz, Michael D., Andrew C. Gordon, and Warren Friedman. 1990. *Mapping Crime in Its Community Setting: Event Geography Analysis.* New York: Springer Verlag.

McMahon, Joyce, Joel Garner, Ronald Davis, and Amanda Kraus. 2006. *How to Correctly Collect and Analyze Racial Profiling Data: Your Reputation Depends on It!* Washington, DC: U.S. Government Printing Office.

McNulty, Thomas L. 1999. The residential process and the ecological concentration of race, poverty, and violent crime in New York City. *Sociological Focus* 32: 25–42.

Meehan, Albert J., and Michael C. Ponder. 2002. Race and place: The ecology of racial profiling African American motorists. *Justice Quarterly* 19: 14–55.

Merchant, Roland C., Beth L. Schwartzapfel, Francis A. Wolf, Wenjun Li, Lynn Carlson, and Josiah D. Rich. 2006. Demographic, geographic, and temporal patterns of ambulance runs for suspected opiate overdose in Rhode Island, 1997–2002. *Substance Use and Misuse* 41: 1209–1226.

Morenoff, Jeffrey D., Robert J. Sampson, and Stephen W. Raudenbush. 2001. Neighborhood inequality, collective efficacy, and the spatial dynamics of urban violence. *Criminology* 39: 517–560.

Murray, Alan T., Ingrid McGuffog, John S. Western, and Patrick Mullins. 2001. Exploratory spatial data analysis techniques for examining urban crime. *British Journal of Criminology* 41: 309–329.

Newman, Oscar. 1972. *Defensible Space: Crime Prevention Through Urban Design.* New York: Macmillan.

Park, Robert E., Ernest W. Burgess, and Roderick D. McKenzie. 1925. *The City.* Chicago: University of Chicago Press.

Petrocelli, Matthew, Alex R. Piquero, and Michael R. Smith. 2003. Conflict theory and racial profiling: An empirical analysis of police traffic stop data. *Journal of Criminal Justice* 31: 1–11.

Queralt, Magaly, and Ann D. Witte. 1998. A map for you? Geographic information systems in the social sciences. *Social Work* 43: 455–469.

Reitzel, John, and Alex R. Piquero. 2006. Does it exist? Studying citizens' attitudes of racial profiling. *Police Quarterly* 9: 161–183.

Rock, Amy E. 2005. Identifying the spatial distribution of homelessness in Summit County, Ohio, using GIS. Unpublished master's thesis, Ohio University, Athens, OH.

Rojek, Jeff, Richard Rosenfeld, and Scott Decker. 2004. The influence of driver's race on traffic stops in Missouri. *Police Quarterly* 7: 126–147.

Sampson, Robert J., and Jacqueline Cohen. 1988. Deterrent effects of the police on crime: A replication and theoretical extension. *Law and Society Review* 22: 163–189.

Shaw, Clifford R., and Henry D. McKay. 1942. *Juvenile Delinquency and Urban Areas.* Chicago: University of Chicago Press.

Smith, Douglas A. 1986. The neighborhood context of police behavior. *Crime and Justice* 8: 313–341.

Smith, Douglas A., and Jody R. Klein. 1984. Police control of interpersonal disputes. *Social Problems* 31: 468–481.

Smith, Michael R., and Matthew Petrocelli. 2001. Racial profiling? A multivariate analysis of police traffic stop data. *Police Quarterly* 4: 4–27.

Stoe, Debra A., Carol R. Watkins, Jeffrey Kerr, Linda Rost, and Theodosia Craig. 2003. *Using Geographic Information Systems to Map Crime Victim Services: A Guide for State Victims of Crime Act Administrators and Victim Service Providers.* NCJ 191877. Washington, DC: National Institute of Justice. http://www.ojp.usdoj.gov/ovc/publications/infores/geoinfosys 2003/.

Terrill, William, and Michael Reisig. 2003. Neighborhood context and police use of force. *Journal of Research in Crime and Delinquency* 40: 291–321.

Vann, Irvin B., and G. David Garson. 2001. Crime mapping and its extension to social science analysis. *Social Science Computer Review* 19: 471–479.

Webster, Colin. 2007. *Understanding Race and Crime.* London: Open University Press.

Weisburd, David, and Tom McEwen, eds. 1998. *Crime Mapping and Crime Prevention.* New York: Criminal Justice Press.

Weitzer, Ronald, and Steven A Tuch. 1999. Race, class, and perceptions of discrimination by the police. *Crime and Delinquency* 45: 494–507.

Weitzer, Ronald, and Steven A Tuch. 2002. Perceptions of racial profiling: Race, class, and personal experience. *Criminology* 40: 435–456.

Weitzer, Ronald, and Steven A Tuch. 2005. Racially biased policing: Determinants of citizen perceptions. *Social Forces* 83: 1009–1030.

Withrow, Brian L. 2004a. Race-based policing: A descriptive analysis of the Wichita stop study. *Police Practice and Research* 5: 223–240.

Withrow, Brian L. 2004b. Driving while different: A potential theoretical explanation for race-based policing. *Criminal Justice Policy Review* 15: 344–364.

Wong, David. 1996. Enhancing segregation studies using GIS. *Computers, Environment, and Urban Systems* 20: 99–109.

Worden, Robert. 1989. Situational and attitudinal explanations of police behavior: A theoretical reappraisal and empirical assessment. *Law and Society Review* 23: 667–711.

Chapter 9

Beyond Stop Rates

Using Qualitative Methods to Examine
Racially Biased Policing

Rod K. Brunson

Most of the research on citizens' perceptions of and experiences with police has been based on surveys or official data. In addition, these studies have typically focused on discrete, one-time encounters rather than cumulative measures of police-citizen contacts. And while these investigations have highlighted the importance of race and age differences, they have not elicited the kind of information that would allow researchers to acquire deeper understandings of meanings for study participants. On the other hand, qualitative research methods provide a unique opportunity to examine and better understand the range of experiences that may influence individuals' attitudes toward the police. The research presented in this chapter draws from in-depth interviews with forty African American adolescent males in a disadvantaged urban community and seeks to investigate their personal experiences with aggressive policing. In addition, the current study highlights the benefits of utilizing comprehensive and nuanced qualitative measures of police–minority citizen encounters.

Disenfranchised citizens of color have routinely protested being unjustly targeted, detained, questioned, and searched by the police for several decades. The news media and law enforcement administrators began to take the matter seriously, however, after a host of high-profile minorities, who were not accustomed to these aggressive police practices, complained of similar treatment.[1] Policing scholars and policymakers also have recently begun to examine the nature and extent of racially biased policing in several locales across the country.[2] Much of this research suggests that discriminatory policing is a problem, at least in some jurisdictions. The U.S. government along with a growing number of state and local law enforcement agencies has vehemently denounced the practice. While strong condemnations and sweeping policy changes are fitting responses, they are perhaps not enough to adequately insulate minority citizens from discriminatory policing practices.

Although public interest in racial profiling research has increased considerably, the vast majority of studies have relied on survey or official data to document the frequency of stops experienced by members of various racial groups.[3] Thus, many researchers have faced difficulty in determining whether minority citizens are being stopped in proportion to a particular baseline measure (e.g., the number of licensed drivers, motorists involved in traffic accidents, registered voters, or vehicle owners).[4] While these studies have highlighted important race differences, examining the racial composition of individuals stopped by the police tells only part of the story. In particular, traffic stop statistics themselves are not capable of capturing the complexity of police–minority citizen interactions, and prevent scholars from obtaining a thorough understanding of what actually takes place *during* involuntary police encounters. This limitation is especially important for residents of poor minority communities because, regardless of their accuracy, claims of racially biased policing have the potential to be dismissed out of hand if stop rates reflect the racial composition of the neighborhood or precinct.

In addition, the systematic gathering and analyses of vehicle stop data does little to alleviate the fears of individuals routinely at the receiving end of discriminatory policing practices in the United States: young minority males.[5] Thus I offer that a wide range of insights might be attained by focusing specifically, and qualitatively, on their personal experiences with the police. Such an approach has the potential to greatly contribute to our understanding of these citizens' perspectives and life experiences. In particular, in-depth interview techniques provide a unique opportunity for researchers to acquire deeper understandings of the situational contexts of events and their meanings for those involved.

Race, Place, and Aggressive Policing

One of the most consistent findings in research on attitudes toward the police is that citizen distrust and dissatisfaction is more prevalent among African Americans than whites.[6] Further, studies examining the relationship between perceptions and the nature of citizens' encounters with police indicate that negative views of the police stem from unpleasant (voluntary and involuntary) police encounters.[7] For instance, Weitzer and Tuch observed that "net of other factors, race and personal experience with racial profiling are among the strongest and most consistent predictors of attitudes toward the police."[8] In particular, they find that direct experience with racial discrimination "can have lasting, adverse effects" on individuals' evaluations of the police.[9]

Residents of disadvantaged neighborhoods have a substantial risk of experiencing frequent, unwelcome contact with police because of the aggressive crime-suppression tactics to which they are exposed. Specifically, a number of scholars propose that black citizens' consistent unfavorable evaluations of law enforcement personnel can best be understood by considering the nature of policing in their communities, and their views regarding their own interactions with the police.[10] One investigation[11] noted that legal cynicism and dissatisfaction with the police were both strongly correlated with neighborhood concentrated disadvantage.[12] In fact, after controlling for concentrated disadvantage and neighborhoods' violent crime rates, racial differences in dissatisfaction with the police disappeared in their model.[13]

A considerable body of research has examined the social ecology of policing and the disproportionate effects of police practices and misconduct on black citizens.[14] These studies document a wide range of harms to residents of disadvantaged neighborhoods, including unparalleled experiences with being suspected and stopped,[15] irreverence,[16] arrests,[17] the unjustified use of physical and deadly force,[18] officer misconduct,[19] as well as slower response times and fewer police services.[20] Moreover, it is specifically young black men who are disproportionately encumbered by these adverse experiences.[21]

Why Qualitative Methods?

Qualitative research methods are well suited for better understanding the social world from the points of view of study participants.[22] Specifically, rigorous examination of respondents' accounts offers a means of "arriving at meanings or culturally embedded normative explanations [for behavior, because they] represent ways in which people organize views of themselves, of others, and of their social worlds."[23] This approach is especially important for understanding the experiences of urban young black men—a group that is consistently the disproportionate target of aggressive policing tactics, but whose perspectives are rarely included in scholarly examinations of police-citizen encounters.[24] Therefore, in the research presented later in this chapter, I sought to investigate their personal experiences with what they considered unjustified police stops and physically intrusive searches.[25]

This study draws from in-depth interviews with forty African American young men living in disadvantaged neighborhoods, and is based on the belief that an improved understanding of the relationship between the police and black male youth can be realized by attending to the views of those who are most likely to experience unwelcome police attention in the United States. This study has the potential to make an important contribution to the racial profiling literature by examining in detail the accounts of those who are disproportionately watched and detained by the police. Finally, this qualitative investigation highlights the benefits of using comprehensive and nuanced measures to examine police–minority citizen encounters.

Methodology

Data for this examination are drawn from a larger study of African American youths' experiences with community violence. The present investigation is based on information obtained from in-depth interviews with forty black males residing in St. Louis, Missouri.[26] Study participants range in age from thirteen to nineteen, with a mean age of sixteen. The interviews were conducted between spring 1999 and spring 2000. Participation in the study was voluntary, and respondents were paid twenty dollars and assured confidentiality.[27]

Organizations working with both "at-risk" and delinquent adolescents helped the research team recruit young men to participate in the project. These consisted of two alternative St. Louis public high schools and one community agency. Approximately equal numbers of respondents were obtained from each study site. The community agency was a neighborhood-based recreation center on St. Louis's north side where youths were allowed to gather and socialize. The two alternative schools were attended by students who had been expelled from traditional St. Louis public schools for a variety of transgressions (e.g., absenteeism, fighting, insubordination, and property damage). School counselors were asked to identify and approach young men for participation in the study who were known to live in distressed St. Louis neighborhoods. All interviews were conducted in vacant classrooms or private offices.

I limit my focus here to African American male adolescents because research has identified them as the group for whom unwelcome police interactions are most frequent and salient in the United States.[28] As explained earlier, "racial differences in attitudes toward police have been among the most robust findings in criminal justice research."[29] Research has also demonstrated that youths' assessments of police are less positive than those of adults,[30] and has supported the view that this is related to the pervasiveness of their police contacts.[31] Few studies, however, have offered an in-depth examination of the nature of black male adolescents' personal experiences with the police, or their perceptions of these encounters. The present research strategy allows for a systematic examination of these issues.

Study Setting

St. Louis' socioeconomic character and the policing efforts operating within its distressed neighborhoods made it an ideal setting to engage in this type of study. For example, St. Louis is characteristic of the highly distressed urban city in the United States, and includes large concentrations of extreme disadvantage that result in high crime rates, limited resources, and social isolation. Table 9.1 demonstrates census data comparing young men's neighborhoods, the City of St. Louis, and St. Louis County.[32] As illustrated, study participants lived in neighborhoods distinguished by severe racial segregation, as well as disproportionate rates of female-headed families, unemployment, and poverty. These are exactly the types of neighborhood conditions that scholars have associated with both aggressive policing and police misconduct.[33]

Similar to police-minority community relations in urban cities of similar size, the relationship between black community members and the St. Louis police department is tenuous.[34] Further, each is distrustful of the other and allegations of police wrongdoing against black citizens routinely intensify those feelings.[35] In addition, the president of the St. Louis Police Officers' Association has been openly skeptical of African American community leaders' motives for attempting to create a civilian review board.[36] The St. Louis police department is one of several law enforcement agencies that have adopted community policing in the hope of reducing crime and improving their relationships with the public. While the department is led by a philosophy that includes community-oriented policing strategies, in terms of policy this means that a public affairs officer is assigned to each of the nine police districts and is expected to attend neighborhood meetings. On the other hand, study participants reported that policing efforts in their communities largely consisted of frequent pedestrian and vehicle stops by uniformed personnel, detectives, as well as by members of specialized

TABLE 9.1
Select Neighborhood Characteristics

	Respondents' Neighborhoods	St. Louis City	St. Louis County
Percent African American	82.6%	51.2%	18.9%
Percent Poverty	33.8%	24.6%	6.9%
Percent Unemployment	18.0%	11.3%	4.6%
Percent Female-Headed Families with Children	43.1%	28.8%	10.7%

Source: U.S. Census, 2000.

TABLE 9.2
Exposure to Police Harassment and Select Respondent Characteristics

	N	Percent
Survey Responses to Questions Regarding Police Harassment		
Harassed or mistreated by the police	33	83%
Survey Responses to Questions Regarding Delinquency and Arrest		
*Delinquency ever	29	75%
*Delinquency within past six months	16	40%
Arrest ever	26	65%
Arrest within past year	20	50%

*Serious delinquency consisted of stealing over fifty dollars, stealing a motor vehicle, attacking someone with a weapon with the intent to seriously hurt them, robbery, and selling marijuana or other drugs.

units and task forces. At the same time that the young men understood that this approach was in response to particular neighborhood problems such as drug and gang activity, these techniques were also the basis on which study participants described their interactions with the police as often constituting harassment.

Sampling was purposive in nature. That is, the goal was to interview youths who were at-risk or involved in delinquent activities, as these individuals would reasonably have more involuntary police contact. Young men known to have negative experiences with the police or who had expressed bias against them were not targeted. As table 9.2 demonstrates, all the study participants reported having engaged in some form of delinquency in their lifetime. In fact, 75 percent reported having engaged in serious delinquency, while 40 percent reported involvement in serious delinquency in the last six months. Further, half of the young men reported having been arrested in the last year, and 65 percent reported ever having been arrested at some point in their lives. Thus the sample reflects variation in both delinquent involvement and official contact with the criminal justice system.

Study respondents were asked to participate in an audiotaped in-depth interview. The tapes from those interviews were later transcribed and those records serve as the data for this contextual examination. During the interviews, the youths were asked whether they had been harassed or mistreated by the police. The goal was to collect data that could provide a relatively holistic assessment of young men's experiences with and perceptions of police harassment and mistreatment. Thus the interviews were semi-structured, with open-ended questions that allowed for considerable probing. Respondents who reported having experienced unfavorable treatment by the police were asked to provide detailed descriptions of the circumstances leading up to these events, the events themselves, their consequences, and the youths' interpretation of what happened and why. They also were asked to describe and explain their perceptions of the police in their neighborhoods.

In the analysis, care was taken to ensure that the concepts developed and illustrations provided typified the most common themes in young men's accounts. This was accomplished using grounded theory methods, including the search for, and explication of, deviant cases.[37] Reliability was strengthened through a triangulated data collection technique, by asking study participants about their experiences at multiple points, and asking for detailed accounts during the in-depth interviews.

Study Findings

The vast majority (83 percent) of study participants reported having personal experiences with police harassment (see table 9.2). This is not surprising given that respondents consistently identified frequent pedestrian and vehicle stops as the foundation of neighborhood policing strategies. Further, for respondents these tactics exemplified police harassment. In addition, it was not simply that young men objected to being routinely stopped, but they took particular exception to the way officers spoke to them during these encounters.[38] For instance, several study participants expressed grave concern about being ordered to sit or lie on the ground while enduring physically intrusive searches.

Next, I examine in detail young men's direct experiences with aggressive crime control strategies along with their perceptions of how race and neighborhood together structured their encounters with the police.

Aggressive Policing

Many young men were particularly frustrated when they were stopped in situations in which they believed there was no basis for suspicion, and ten respondents (about a quarter of the sample) described experiences that exceeded what they considered harassment, to include assault and other forms of police misconduct. The most frequent kind of wrongdoing reported were allegations of physical abuse. But respondents also reported other types of wrongdoing, such as officers taking money and abandoning suspects in rival neighborhoods.

Study participants' views about the police resulted mostly from aggressive policing strategies. These tactics were seemingly insidious to respondents and formed the basis of their direct negative experiences. While study participants understood that such efforts at times produced modest, short-lived successes, they considered the police an occupying force. For example, William commented, "If [the police] see us every five minutes go around or in a different part of the neighborhood, they think we selling drugs or something, and they'll stop us like five, six times a day. Just to pat us down and ask questions." Likewise, Shaun noted, "[The police are] a trip, we be sitting on the front [porch] or something, they'll pull up just 'cuz we sitting there. Or we be chillin' in front of the store, [they] get out checking everybody." And Terence explained:

On certain days, [the police] might do a sweep through the neighborhood. They'll come in like, three or four cars deep, two paddy wagons, and they'll just roll down every block that they think mainly sellin' drugs or whatever. And anybody outside, if they think you got something, they gon' check you. Just everybody that happen to be on the block. If you look like you got something or look like you do something, so they say, then they just come up to you, tell you to assume the position or whatever. [Tell you to] put your hands on the hood [and they] check you. If you do got something, you in the paddy wagon and they take you downtown. If not, they gon' check you, talk bad to you for a lil' minute and then tell you to go on about your business.

Due to the pervasiveness of aggressive policing in respondents' neighborhoods, they doubted whether the police were genuinely interested in combating crime, or were merely interested in harassing people. The majority of study participants concluded it was the latter. For example, Darnell said, "Police over there by me, they stop you just to mess with you for real. That's what they do. Sometimes they'll pull up and be like, 'Get that damn crack out your mouth boy!' and keep going."

Respondents came to recognize that certain settings and seemingly innocuous items had the potential to increase police suspicion of them.[39] And while they acknowledged this reality, they nonetheless found it unfair. For example, Jamal explained how certain symbols of affluence might subject black males to negative police attention: "It's like, because the clothes that the teenagers wear, [police] feel that if you have fancy clothes or you have a lot [of] money, you selling drugs. They can't see a black male these days having a good job. They always want to pull you over or search you to find something." In agreement, Gary noted, "They see you out there, black, with gold in your mouth, and they think you out there *selling dope or something.*"

Ricky explained how hanging out on the street with other young men usually attracted unwelcome police attention, regardless of whether anyone in the group was involved in illegal behaviors. He commented, "The police will ride up on a group of guys, they'll get out, they'll make you lay on the ground, they'll pull your clothes all off you. Or they make you take your shoes and socks off. I mean, just unnecessary stuff." Likewise, Leon observed:

I was sittin' on the front [steps] and two police they pulled over or whatever and got to askin' me all the [usual] questions like, "Where the dope at?" and all this kinda stuff and I said, "Aw, man, I don't know what y'all talking about." [The police said,] "Come on man, you know what we talkin' about." [One officer] tried to get [out of the car] and he wanted to search me and I asked him why and he said he just *wanted* to. So I said, "I feel [like] you harassing me 'cuz *every* time you see us you out here you stop[ping] somebody and checkin' 'em." He said he was gon' show me what harassment was and locked me up.

Leon's description draws attention to the injury that can result from routine negative, involuntary police contacts. Specifically, he perceived being frequently stopped and searched by the same officers as harassment. Further, study participants reported that the police acted as if their criminal involvement was a forgone conclusion and they merely needed to locate the supporting evidence to make an arrest. As did many other respondents, Leon discovered that there were often negative consequences associated with questioning the legality of officers' actions.

Consistent with research on the relationship between race and place, respondents came to expect poor treatment from the police, as they believed it was the combination of being black and living in a distressed neighborhood that put them at greater risk for abuse. For example, Lamont noted, "[The police] they crooked. I mean they try to do anything [to you]. I ain't tryin' to be prejudice[d] but I think the police don't like black people. You know like all the crooked cops always be in the ghettos, where all the black people at and they try to get as many black people off the street as they can." The majority of young men shared Lamont's view that the urban policing mission disproportionately focuses on poor blacks. His remarks also demonstrate that perceptions of discriminatory policing practices have the potential to undermine police legitimacy by reducing officers' moral authority in the eyes of community residents. Finally, respondents' detailed descriptions of aggressive policing suggest how commonplace the behaviors were for all young black men in their neighborhoods.

Police Misconduct

In addition to objecting to aggressive policing strategies, a few respondents also complained about direct experiences with various forms of misconduct, such as theft and being left stranded in potentially dangerous neighborhoods. Maurice concluded that officers' presumption that young black males were criminals seemingly allowed them to disregard the law themselves. He explained, "If you ain't got no proof of where your money coming from, then they automatically suspect that it's drug money and they take as much as you got. It don't matter if you say, 'I got that for a birthday present,' they still can take it. That's messed up."

Several respondents also reported that when officers lacked the physical evidence to arrest them, they would put them in their patrol cars and drive to another neighborhood before forcing them to get out. For instance, Kevin recalled, "When I used to live downtown, what the police used to do was like, when they lock you up or they arrest you, instead of taking you to the station they'll take you somewhere like the north side or something [and] let you go. [You'll] have to walk home and might walk to the wrong place." Similarly, Doug described how officers treated him shortly after he moved into a new neighborhood:

When I first move[d] over there, I was walking down the street one day, me and my friend and [the police] picked us up. They asked us our name[s]. We told 'em our names and stuff, they was still [acting] like they didn't believe us for some reason, so they took us to the station. Well, that's where we thought we was goin' to the station, but they took us somewhere far, I didn't even know where I was at. I still don't know to this day. And they dropped us off. Told us to get out there and that was it. I called someone and they knew where I was at. [They] shouldn't be police if they gotta do all that. What's the point? You supposed to protect and serve, not put us in a place where you know we don't know where we at. [There] could be gangs over there. We might get jumped, killed, anything. It's like you tryin' to make us find trouble when we're not tryin' to.

Doug not only questioned the appropriateness of the officers' actions but, more important, their fitness as law enforcement personnel. Moreover, while young men suspected that police used this tactic mostly to inconvenience them, they were fully aware that being abandoned in rival neighborhoods had potentially dangerous consequences.

Though young men considered aggressive policing practices and the various forms of misconduct that sometimes ensued troubling, study participants came to view them as *normal* features of police–urban black male youth interactions. Despite their being routine, however, respondents viewed aggressive policing strategies as repressive, and this belief helped shape their general views of officers. Young men were specifically asked how they felt about policing strategies in their neighborhoods. Raymond quipped, "I don't trip off the police 'cuz I know they ignorant." Jermaine answered, "It make me feel mad that just *looking* suspicious will get you pulled over." And Andrew explained, "I start feeling violated sometimes, but then I think, nah, that's something I should expect 'cuz that's just the police. I figure since they got some authority and can do whatever they want to do, they gonna do it."

Police Violence

Although involuntary police contacts usually began with some type of aggressive, bodily contact (i.e., forcibly undressing suspects, pushing, rifling through pockets), the majority of young men's interactions with officers did not result in any serious physical harm. Respondents expressed grave concern, however, regarding what they considered more serious forms of police misconduct—specifically, the excessive use of force. The most common forms of police violence that young men reported included kicking, punching, pushing, shoving, and the use of Mace. I present young men's descriptions of their personal experiences with police violence below.

Some respondents reported many direct experiences with police violence, and for them this was an unfortunate but routine aspect of neighborhood life. For example, Ricky commented, "I been thrown on the ground, I been kicked [laughs], I been choked, man I could go on forever." And Lamont explained, "Sometimes they'll beat you up and let you go. Sometimes they'll beat you up and take you to jail." Travis described how an undercover officer who incorrectly believed he was hiding drugs in his mouth choked him in an effort to obtain the evidence. He explained:

I was standing on the corner and we got these police we call the jump out boys. They the police [that be] riding them regular cars and look like regular people. They like, "What you doing on this corner?" And I'm just steady talking to 'em and they thought I had some dope in my mouth. So this one cop grabbed me and just started squeezing [my throat]. I was coughing and spitting up stuff and I'm like, "What you all doing this for?" and they kept on like, "Don't swallow it, son." I'm like, "Swallow, I ain't got no dope!" I opened up my mouth after they let go. I was showing them and everything. I mean that's they job to make sure dope isn't on the street but I mean I don't think it is their job to literally squeeze someone's Adam's apple.

Young men expressed feeling particular outrage when they were aggressively confronted in situations that clearly did not carry contextual suspicion. Whereas respondents understood that law-abiding status did not guarantee immunity from aggressive policing strategies, they also discovered that it did not shield them from physical assault. While study participants did not claim that violence at the hands of the police was an everyday occurrence, it occurred enough to convince them that it was possible during *any* contact with police officers.

Although some study participants reported being assaulted when they where in law-abiding contexts, respondents also experienced police violence when they were caught committing crimes. Young men explained that in this context, police typically used physical force to gain compliance from uncooperative suspects or when they sought evidence in an investigation. For instance, Wayne described being roughed up by the police as they questioned him about an object he had thrown after observing them:

> I was real young at the time, I was twelve years old. I learned a lot from that mistake I made. I was carrying a pistol for somebody. It was about twelve o'clock in the morning. I was walking up an alley and I'd seen [the police] ride past the alley first and I tossed the gun or whatever. And they came back up the alley. They pretty much threatened me that they would lock me up for something I didn't do if I didn't tell them what it was [that I threw]. . . . So I was saying, "I didn't throw nothing, I didn't throw nothing." And they like, "We know you threw something," and holding my arms real hard, like cramping them up a little bit. They're like, "We know you threw something." . . . [Then] he kind of like pushed me down on the car, put the cuffs on me like pretty rough, but not beating me or nothing like that.

Frank provided an account of a more serious assault that occurred after he and another suspect refused to tell police where their accomplices in an auto theft were hiding. He explained:

> [The police] was like, "Where the rest of 'em at, where the rest of 'em?" I'm like, "Where the rest of who at?" They like, "Oh you wanna play?" [The] Po-Po, white police hit the reverse, he drives out to the dark, stops and pow, pow, pow, pow, pow, got to hittin' hard, he hittin' us with a stick, hurting us. [I'm like,] "Dang, I don't know where anybody at." He like, "You lying." Pow, hit me again in my face. Next thing I know I'm just going to sleep. I wake up in a little cell, like up in the county [jail] cell.

And Carlos said that the police sprayed him with Mace because following his arrest, he repeatedly complained that the handcuffs were too tight. He reported, "Fuck, they Mace[d] me 'cuz I kept talking. They wouldn't let me out the handcuffs, they were too tight." While respondents who were physically assaulted while engaged in crime readily acknowledged their guilt, they did not dismiss the inappropriateness of the arresting officers' actions. Specifically, young men said that in spite of their wrongdoing, they expected that officers would perform their duties in accordance with the law.

Discussion

An abundant body of research concerning citizens' attitudes toward the police has consistently found that black adults and adolescents report more dissatisfaction and distrust than their counterparts from other racial groups.[40] Most studies, however, have relied on surveys and have not been able fully to capture the complexities of police–minority citizen relations. This methodological approach recognizes the importance of focusing specifically, and qualitatively, on the accumulated experiences of young black males—who are often studied as offenders and considered troublemakers in their neighborhoods but rarely have their own viewpoints used as a credible starting point for social inquiry. Thus the goal of the current study was to use in-depth interviewing techniques to examine their personal police experiences in an effort to better understand how these encounters shaped their views of the police in their communities.

Unwelcome police-citizen interactions are more likely to take place in distressed neighborhoods where aggressive policing efforts are disproportionately employed. For instance, study participants reported that most of their encounters with police were the result of officer-initiated contacts, and characterized officers' demeanor as combative, hostile, and threatening. Frequent, involuntary police contacts, coupled with what study participants considered poor treatment due to their race, contributed to a body of negative experiences that ultimately influenced young men's views of police. Feagin and Sikes explain that "experiences with serious discrimination not only are very painful and stressful in the immediate situation and aftermath but also have a *cumulative* impact on particular individuals, their families and their communities."[41]

Repeated harassment and discourteous treatment were the most common forms of police misconduct respondents reported. And young men directly linked these behaviors to aggressive policing strategies. Study participants also made allegations of other forms of police malfeasance. For example, they described incidents where officers stole pocketed money because they believed it came from drug sales. Further, respondents said that some officers engaged in the potentially dangerous practice of leaving them stranded in unfamiliar neighborhoods when they were unable to find sufficient grounds to justify an arrest. Finally, young men reasoned that these and other kinds of misconduct served to undermine officers' legitimacy.

Reports of brutality were prominent features of respondents' police interactions. In fact, young men came to view being physically attacked by the police as a common feature of urban law enforcement. For instance, study participants explained that police often used or threatened to use violence against them both to gain compliance and as an investigative tool. Further, young men offered that officers routinely filed resisting-arrest charges against suspects to fend off allegations of abuse. While the majority did not report serious cases of police violence in their police encounters, most described incidents in which officers needlessly "put their hands on" them. For example, young men reported that many of their interactions with police began with some kind of aggressive physical contact by officers.

Whereas young men's law-abiding status failed to adequately insulate them from general police harassment, it also did not protect them from police violence. According to study participants, being innocent could increase young men's chances of being assaulted, as they were more likely to challenge the inappropriateness of officers' actions. At the same time, despite their strong negative feelings about police violence, respondents understood that there were circumstances when officers' use of force was justified. They believed, however, that the amount of force often used, even against guilty persons, was typically unwarranted.

The findings presented here are consistent with prior research regarding the relationship between involuntary, negative police experiences and unfavorable attitudes toward the police. In addition, the current study draws attention to key issues that may guide future studies concerning police–minority citizen interactions. In particular, the qualitative approach used in this study underscores that police–minority citizen relations are multifaceted and that a myriad of experiences ultimately help to shape individuals' experiences with and perceptions of the police. Finally, whereas research analyzing survey and traffic stop data has advanced our understanding of discriminatory policing practices, young men's detailed accounts make clear how these statistics translate into lived experiences.

Policy Implications

Citizen trust of the police is an important topic that has serious implications for effective police-community relations. For example, police agencies often rely on community members to assist in their crime-control efforts. Residents, however, may be reluctant to come forward with information if they view the police negatively.[42] Additional research on this topic reveals that avoidance of the police is among young men's strategic responses to what they consider routine police harassment and mistreatment.[43] Along with their desire to elude overly aggressive officers, study participants were determined to steer clear of the "snitch" label that neighborhood residents often applied to anyone observed voluntarily speaking with police. Thus young men went to great lengths to avoid being called a snitch, and their preoccupation with doing so highlights the impact of recent "stop snitching" campaigns.[44] Whereas informal rules against snitching seemingly thwarted police efforts to secure witnesses, it also prevented respondents from reporting their own victimization.

Policy Recommendations

The current research suggests that it is important for scholars and police executives to look beyond official stop data when trying to evaluate whether officers under their command are involved in discriminatory police practices. Whereas several law enforcement agencies have begun to compile statistics on vehicle and pedestrian stops, police administrators could broaden the scope of their data collection efforts. For example, patrol officers could be required to issue "contact" cards to citizens following *every* interaction (calls for service and self-initiated contacts). These cards could be stamped with unique identifiers linking them to individual officers. In addition, the cards could contain a brief statement advising citizens that the department is interested in hearing from them concerning their perceptions of the recent encounter. Finally, the cards could provide a toll-free telephone number or website where citizens could share their detailed accounts with a research partner who would be responsible for analyzing the data and preparing periodic, public reports. This strategy might improve citizen perceptions of police legitimacy and simultaneously allow us to gain a better understanding of police-citizen encounters.

NOTES

1. Meeks, Driving while black: Highways, shopping malls, taxi cabs, sidewalks: How to fight back if you are a victim of racial profiling; Harris, Profiles in injustice: Why racial profiling cannot work.

2. Alpert et al., "Police suspicion and discretionary decision making during citizen stops"; Rojek et al., "The influence of driver's race on traffic stops in Missouri"; Warren et al., "Driving while black: Bias processes and racial disparity in police stops."

3. Smith and Petrocelli, "Racial profiling? A multivariate analysis of police traffic stop data"; Engel, "Citizens' perceptions of distributive and procedural injustice during traffic stops with police."

4. Walker, "Searching for the denominator: Problems with police traffic stop data and an early warning system solution."

5. Brunson and Miller, "Young black men and urban policing in the United States."

6. Hagan and Albonetti, "Race, class, and the perception of criminal injustice in America"; Sampson and Bartusch, "Legal cynicism and (subcultural?) tolerance of deviance: The neighborhood context of racial differences"; Webb and Marshall, "The relative importance of race and ethnicity on citizen attitudes toward the police"; Weitzer, "Citizen perceptions of police misconduct: Race and neighborhood context"; Weitzer, "Racializing policing: Residents' perceptions in three neighborhoods"; Weitzer, "Incidents of police misconduct and public opinion"; Weisburd et al., Police attitudes toward abuse of authority: Findings from a national study; Barlow and Barlow, "Racial profiling: A survey of African American police officers"; Weitzer and Tuch, "Race, class, and perceptions of discrimination by the police"; Engel, "Citizens' perceptions of distributive and procedural injustice during traffic stops with police"; Frank et al., "Reassessing the impact of race on citizens' attitudes toward the police: A research note."

7. Decker, "Citizen attitudes toward the police: A review of past findings and suggestions for future policy"; Huebner et al., "African American and white perceptions of police service: Within- and between-group variation"; Murty et al., "The image of the police in black Atlanta communities"; Webb and Marshall, "The relative importance of race and ethnicity on citizen attitudes toward the police"; Brandl et al., "Global and specific attitudes toward the police."

8. Weitzer and Tuch, "Race, class, and perceptions of discrimination by the police," p. 445.

9. Weitzer and Tuch, "Race, class, and perceptions of discrimination by the police," p. 452.

10. Anderson, Streetwise: Race, class, and change in an urban community; Anderson, Code of the street: Decency, violence, and the moral life of the inner city; Fagan and Davies, "Street stops and broken windows: *Terry*, race, and disorder in New York City"; Leitzel, "Race and policing"; Sampson and Bartusch, "Legal cynicism and (subcultural?) tolerance of deviance: The

neighborhood context of racial differences"; Tyler and Wakslak, "Profiling and police legitimacy: Procedural justice, attributions of motive, and acceptance of police authority"; Weitzer, "Racializing policing: Residents' perceptions in three neighborhoods"; Weitzer and Tuch, "Race, class, and perceptions of discrimination by the police"; Weitzer and Tuch, "Perceptions of racial profiling: Race, class, and personal experience."

11. Sampson and Bartusch, "Legal cynicism and (subcultural?) tolerance of deviance: The neighborhood context of racial differences."

12. Anderson, Code of the street: Decency, violence, and the moral life of the inner city.

13. Sampson and Bartusch, "Legal cynicism and (subcultural?) tolerance of deviance: The neighborhood context of racial differences"; Hagan and Albonetti, "Race, class, and the perception of criminal injustice in America"; Weitzer and Tuch, "Race, class, and perceptions of discrimination by the police."

14. Bass, "Policing space, policing race: Social control imperatives and police discretionary decisions"; Meehan and Ponder, "Race and place: The ecology of racial profiling African American motorists"; Phillips and Smith, "Police violence occasioning citizen complaint: An empirical analysis of time-space dynamics."

15. Browning et al., "Race and getting hassled by the police: A research note"; Fagan and Davies, "Street stops and broken windows: *Terry*, race, and disorder in New York City"; Hurst et al., "The attitudes of juveniles toward the police: A comparison of black and white youth"; Jones-Brown, "Debunking the myth of Officer Friendly: How African American males experience community policing"; Kennedy, Race, crime, and the law; Weitzer, "Citizen perceptions of police misconduct: Race and neighborhood context."

16. Mastrofski et al., "Police disrespect toward the public: An encounter-based analysis"; Weitzer, "Citizen perceptions of police misconduct: Race and neighborhood context."

17. Smith and Visher, "Street-level justice: Situational determinants of police arrest decisions."

18. Jacobs and O'Brien, "The determinants of deadly force: A structural analysis of police violence"; Smith and Holmes, "Community accountability, minority threat, and police brutality: An examination of civil rights criminal complaints"; Terrill et al., "Police culture and coercion"; Terrill and Reisig, "Neighborhood context and police use of force"; Weitzer, "Citizen perceptions of police misconduct: Race and neighborhood context"; Worden, "The causes of police brutality: Theory and evidence on police use of force."

19. Kane, "The social ecology of police misconduct."

20. Anderson, Streetwise: Race, class, and change in an urban community; Klinger, "Negotiating order in patrol work: An ecological theory of police response to deviance"; Smith and Klein, "Police control of interpersonal disputes."

21. Brunson and Miller, "Young black men and urban policing in the United States," "Gender, race, and urban policing: The experience of African American youths"; Hurst et al., "The attitudes of juveniles toward the police: A comparison of black and white youth"; Weitzer and Brunson, "Strategic responses to the police among inner-city youth."

22. Miller, One of the guys: Girls, gangs, and gender; Getting played: African American girls, urban inequality, and gendered violence.

23. Orbuch, "People's accounts count: The sociology of accounts," p. 455.

24. Phillips and Bowling, "Racism, ethnicity, and criminology: Developing minority perspectives."

25. The complete findings were published in Brunson, "'Police don't like Black people': African American young men's accumulated police experiences."

26. A primary focus of the larger project, however, is violence against women, and there-

fore it includes interviews with thirty-five female study participants. For more on the study methodology and data collection process, see Miller, Getting played: African American girls, urban inequality, and gendered violence.

27. Pseudonyms are used throughout the paper, both for young men and for the streets they occasionally name.

28. Hurst et al., "The attitudes of juveniles toward the police: A comparison of black and white youth."

29. Taylor et al., "Coppin' an attitude: Attitudinal differences among juveniles toward the police," p. 302.

30. Taylor et al., "Coppin' an attitude: Attitudinal differences among juveniles toward the police"; Hurst et al., "The attitudes of juveniles toward the police: A comparison of black and white youth."

31. Fine et al., "'Anything can happen with police around': Urban youth evaluate strategies of surveillance in public places"; Leiber et al., "Explaining juveniles' attitudes toward the police"; Snyder and Sickmund, Juvenile offenders and victims: A national report.

32. To ensure anonymity, young men's addresses were not solicited; instead, they were asked to provide the names of two cross streets near where they lived. Data presented in table 9.1 comes from census block data from these cross streets. Thus it is not a precise measure, but it does provide a rough match for their neighborhoods. This information was unavailable for four young men in the sample because the street names they provided were parallel. In two of these cases, census data at the zip code level was not verifiable. This data is not included in table 9.1, though it was comparable to the block-level characteristics. One additional note on table 9.1: the figures for St. Louis County do not include those of the city, as the city is its own county.

33. Fagan and Davies, "Street stops and broken windows: *Terry*, race, and disorder in New York City"; Kane, "The social ecology of police misconduct."

34. The U.S. Census Bureau reported the population of St. Louis city as 396,685 in 1990 and 348,189 in 2000.

35. St. Louis does not have a civilian complaint review panel, despite the efforts of several African American community groups (see http://stlcin.missouri.org/alderman/bbDetail.cfm?BBId=384). Instead, the department's Internal Affairs Division investigates and adjudicates allegations of police misconduct.

36. Ahlbrand, "From the president" (2006a), "From the president" (2006b).

37. Strauss, Qualitative analysis for social scientists.

38. Mastrofski et al., "Police disrespect toward the public: An encounter-based analysis"; Tyler and Wakslak, "Profiling and police legitimacy: Procedural justice, attributions of motive, and acceptance of police authority."

39. Weitzer and Tuch, "Perceptions of racial profiling: Race, class, and personal experience."

40. Hurst and Frank, "How kids view cops: The nature of juvenile attitudes toward the police"; Hurst et al., "The attitudes of juveniles toward the police: A comparison of black and white youth"; Leiber et al., "Explaining juveniles' attitudes toward the police"; Taylor et al., "Coppin' an attitude: Attitudinal differences among juveniles toward the police."

41. Feagin and Sikes, Living with racism: The black middle-class experience, p. 16.

42. Decker, "Citizen attitudes toward the police: A review of past findings and suggestions for future policy."

43. Weitzer and Brunson, "Strategic responses to the police among inner-city youth."

44. Hampson, "Anti-snitch campaign riles police, prosecutors."

REFERENCES

Ahlbrand, Kevin. 2006a. From the president. *Gendarme* 36: 1, 2–3.

———. 2006b. From the president. *Gendarme* 36: 2, 2–3.

Alpert, Geoffrey P., John M. MacDonald, and Roger G. Dunham. 2005. Police suspicion and discretionary decision making during citizen stops. *Criminology* 43: 407–434.

Anderson, Elijah. 1990. *Streetwise: Race, class, and change in an urban community.* Chicago: University of Chicago Press.

———. 1999. *Code of the street: Decency, violence, and the moral life of the inner city.* New York: Norton .

Barlow, David E., and Melissa Hickman Barlow. 2002. Racial profiling: A survey of African American police officers. *Police Quarterly* 5: 334–358.

Bass, Sandra. 2001. Policing space, policing race: Social control imperatives and police discretionary decisions. *Social Justice* 28: 156–176.

Brandl, Steven, James Frank, Robert Worden, and Timothy Bynum. 1994. Global and specific attitudes toward the police. *Justice Quarterly* 11: 119–134.

Browning, Sandra Lee, Frank Cullen, Liquin Cao, Renee Kopache, and Thomas J. Stevenson. 1994. Race and getting hassled by the police: A research note. *Police Studies* 17: 1–11.

Brunson, R. K. "Police don't like Black people": African American young men's accumulated police experiences." *Criminology and Public Policy* 6: 71–102.

Brunson, Rod K., and Jody Miller. 2006a. Young black men and urban policing in the United States. *British Journal of Criminology* 46: 613–640.

———. 2006b. Gender, race, and urban policing: The experience of African American youths. *Gender and Society* 20: 531–552.

Decker, Scott H. 1981. Citizen attitudes toward the police: A review of past findings and suggestions for future policy. *Journal of Police Science and Administration* 9: 81–87.

Engel, Robin S. 2005. Citizens' perceptions of distributive and procedural injustice during traffic stops with police. *Journal of Research in Crime and Delinquency* 42: 445–481.

Fagan, Jeffrey, and Garth Davies. 2000. Street stops and broken windows: *Terry*, race, and disorder in New York City. *Fordham Urban Law Journal* 28: 457.

Feagin, Joe R. 1991. The continuing significance of race: Antiblack discrimination in public places. *American Sociological Review* 56: 101–116.

Feagin, Joe R., and Melvin P. Sikes. 1994. *Living with racism: The black middle-class experience.* Boston: Beacon Press.

Fine, Michelle, Nicholas Freudenberg, Yasser Payne, Tiffany Perkins, Kersha Smith, and Katya Wanzer. 2003. "Anything can happen with police around": Urban youth evaluate strategies of surveillance in public places. *Journal of Social Issues* 59: 141–158.

Frank, James, Steven G. Brandl, Francis T. Cullen, and Amy Stichman. 1996. Reassessing the impact of race on citizens' attitudes toward the police: A research note. *Justice Quarterly* 13: 321–334.

Hagan, John, and Celesta Albonetti. 1982. Race, class, and the perception of criminal injustice in America. *American Journal of Sociology* 88: 329–355.

Hampson, Rick. 2006. Anti-snitch campaign riles police, prosecutors. *USA Today*, March 28.

Harris, David A. 2002. *Profiles in injustice: Why racial profiling cannot work.* New York: The New Press.

Huebner, Beth M., Joseph A. Schafer, and Timothy S. Bynum. 2004. African American and white perceptions of police service: Within- and between-group variation. *Journal of Criminal Justice* 32: 123–135.

Hurst, Yolander G., and James Frank. 2000. How kids view cops: The nature of juvenile attitudes toward the police. *Journal of Criminal Justice* 28:189–202.

Hurst, Yolander G., James Frank, and Sandra Lee Browning. 2000. The attitudes of juveniles toward the police: A comparison of black and white youth. *Policing* 23: 37–53.

Jacobs, David, and Robert M. O'Brien. 1998. The determinants of deadly force: A structural analysis of police violence. *American Journal of Sociology* 103: 837–862.

Jones-Brown, Delores D. 2000. Debunking the myth of Officer Friendly: How African American males experience community policing. *Journal of Contemporary Criminal Justice* 16: 209–229.

Kane, Robert J. 2002. The social ecology of police misconduct. *Criminology* 40: 867–896.

Kennedy, Randall. 1997. *Race, crime, and the law.* New York: Vintage.

Klinger, David A. 1997. Negotiating order in patrol work: An ecological theory of police response to deviance. *Criminology* 35: 277–306.

Leiber, Michael J., Mahesh K. Nalla, and Margaret Farnworth. 1998. Explaining juveniles' attitudes toward the police. *Justice Quarterly* 15: 151–174.

Leitzel, Jim. 2001. Race and policing. *Society* 38: 38–42.

Mastrofski, Stephen D., Michael D. Reisig, and John D. McCluskey. 2002. Police disrespect toward the public: An encounter-based analysis. *Criminology* 40: 515–551.

Meehan, Albert J., and Michael C. Ponder. 2002. Race and place: The ecology of racial profiling African American motorists. *Justice Quarterly* 19: 399–430.

Meeks, Kenneth. 2000. *Driving while black: Highways, shopping malls, taxi cabs, sidewalks: How to fight back if you are a victim of racial profiling.* New York: Broadway Books.

Miller, Jody. 2001. *One of the guys: Girls, gangs, and gender.* New York: Oxford University Press.

———. 2008. *Getting Played: African American Girls, Urban Inequality, and Gendered Violence.* New York: New York University Press.

Murty, Komandri S., Julian B. Roebuck, and Joann D. Smith. 1990. The image of the police in black Atlanta communities. *Journal of Police Science and Administration* 17: 250–257.

Orbuch, Terri L. 1997. People's accounts count: The sociology of accounts. *Annual Review of Sociology* 23: 455–478.

Phillips, Coretta, and Benjamin Bowling. 2003. Racism, ethnicity, and criminology: Developing minority perspectives. *British Journal of Criminology* 43: 269–290.

Phillips, Tim, and Philip Smith. 2000. Police violence occasioning citizen complaint: An empirical analysis of time-space dynamics. *British Journal of Criminology* 40: 480–496.

Rojek, Jeff, Richard Rosenfeld, and Scott H. Decker. 2004. The influence of driver's race on traffic stops in Missouri. *Police Quarterly* 7: 126–147.

Sampson, Robert J., and Dawn Jeglum Bartusch. 1998. Legal cynicism and (subcultural?) tolerance of deviance: The neighborhood context of racial differences. *Law and Society Review* 32: 777–804.

Smith, Brad W., and Malcolm D. Holmes. 2003. Community accountability, minority threat, and police brutality: An examination of civil rights criminal complaints. *Criminology* 41: 1035–1064.

Smith, Douglas A., and Christy A. Visher. 1981. Street-level justice: Situational determinants of police arrest decisions. *Social Problems* 29: 167–177.

Smith, Douglas A., and Jody R. Klein. 1984. Police control of interpersonal disputes. *Social Problems* 31: 468–481.

Smith, Michael R., and Matthew Petrocelli. 2001. Racial profiling? A multivariate analysis of police traffic stop data. *Police Quarterly* 4: 4–27.

Snyder, Howard N., and Melissa Sickmund. 1996. *Juvenile offenders and victims: A national report*. Washington, DC: Office of Juvenile Justice and Delinquency Prevention.

Strauss, Anselm L. 1987. *Qualitative Analysis for Social Scientists*. Cambridge: Cambridge University Press.

Taylor, Terrance J., Kelly B. Turner, Finn-Aage Esbensen, and L. Thomas Winfree, Jr. 2001. Coppin' an attitude: Attitudinal differences among juveniles toward the police. *Journal of Criminal Justice* 29: 295–305.

Terrill, William, Eugene A. Paoline III, and Peter K. Manning. 2003. Police culture and coercion. *Criminology* 41: 1003–1034.

Terrill, William, and Michael D. Reisig. 2003. Neighborhood context and police use of force. *Journal of Research in Crime and Delinquency* 40: 291–321.

Tyler, Tom R., and Cheryl J. Wakslak. 2004. Profiling and police legitimacy: Procedural justice, attributions of motive, and acceptance of police authority. *Criminology* 42: 253–281.

Walker, Samuel. 2001. Searching for the denominator: Problems with police traffic stop data and an early warning system solution. *Justice Research and Policy* 3: 63–95.

Warren, Patricia, Donald Tomaskovic-Devey, William Smith, Matthew Zingraff, and Marcinda Mason. 2006. Driving while black: Bias processes and racial disparity in police stops. *Criminology* 44: 709–738.

Webb, Vincent J., and Chris E. Marshall. 1995. The relative importance of race and ethnicity on citizen attitudes toward the police. *American Journal of Police* 14: 45–66.

Weisburd, David, Rosann Greenspan, and Edwin E. Hamilton. 2000. *Police attitudes toward abuse of authority: Findings from a national study*. Washington, DC: National Institute of Justice.

Weitzer, Ronald. 1999. Citizen perceptions of police misconduct: Race and neighborhood context. *Justice Quarterly* 16: 819–846.

———. 2000. Racializing policing: Residents' perceptions in three neighborhoods. *Law and Society Review* 34: 129–155.

———. 2002. Incidents of police misconduct and public opinion. *Journal of Criminal Justice* 30: 397–408.

Weitzer, Ronald, and Rod K. Brunson. 2009. Strategic responses to the police among inner-city youth. *The Sociological Quarterly* 50: 235–256.

Weitzer, Ronald, and Steven A. Tuch. 1999. Race, class, and perceptions of discrimination by the police. *Crime and Delinquency* 45: 494–507.

———. 2002. Perceptions of racial profiling: Race, class and personal experience. *Criminology* 40: 435–457.

Worden, Robert E. 1996. The causes of police brutality: Theory and evidence on police use of force. In *Police violence: Understanding and controlling police abuse of force*, ed. William A. Geller and Hans Toch. New Haven: Yale University Press.

Chapter 10

||||||||||||||||||||||||||||||||||||||||||||||||||||||||||||||||||||||||||||||

State of the Science in Racial Profiling Research
Substantive and Methodological Considerations

Meaghan Paulhamus, Robert J. Kane, and Alex R. Piquero

Within the academic conceptualization of racial profiling, there are myriad nuanced ambiguities, such as "hard profiling" (the use of only race or ethnicity in a decision to stop a citizen) and "soft profiling" (the use of race or ethnicity as one of several factors in the decision to stop a citizen).[1] Ramirez and colleagues[2] offered an integrated definition of racial profiling, operationalizing it as "the inappropriate use of race, ethnicity, or national origin rather than behavior or individualized suspicion to focus on an individual for additional investigation." As with many conceptualizations of racial profiling, Ramirez and colleagues' definition highlights two vexing methodological dilemmas that remain unresolved. The first is the more obvious: how to properly standardize police-citizen contacts in ways that allow for the objective assessment of factors associated with any observed racial disparities. In Ramirez and colleagues' terms, this relates to how to infer the "inappropriate use of race" (commonly referred to as the "denominator problem"). The second dilemma is less mechanical and more conceptual: how to contextualize racial profiling in ways that distinguish it from other theoretical perspectives that also explain why police might use race as a proxy for criminal involvement—that is, as if racial profiling is not part of the broader enforcement paradigm of American policing.

The present chapter examines the methodological implications of studying racial profiling, focusing first on the *concept* of profiling to gain better insight into why police would be motivated a priori to associate race with crime. Next we focus on several specific methodological issues (e.g., the so-called "denominator" problem, as well as other limitations) to assess the state of the science in profiling research. We describe the roots of "racialized" policing in the urban United States, some of the legal constraints placed on police authority with respect to the use of race as an indicator of probable cause, and the public's expectations of the police function as it relates to crime control.

The Foundations of Racial Profiling

In his now-classic volume *Justice Without Trial*, Skolnick[3] observed that the occupational elements of danger and authority led police officers to develop a "working personality" that ostensibly helped them efficiently identify "symbolic assailants": suspects most likely to commit violence against the police.[4] More generally, Skolnick noted that "policemen [*sic*] are trained to view departures from the 'normal.' They are called on in many aspects of their work to make 'hunch' judgments, based on loose correlations." These judgments about "departures from normal" theoretically help police to identify criminal (i.e., felony) suspects. Moreover, according to both Skolnick[5] and Van Maanen,[6] officers and departments often justify profiling practices as effective policing, providing officers the predictive capacity to detain those who commit the majority of crimes.[7] As Jones-Brown[8] contends, the police have an almost-Pavlovian reaction to a suspected offender's minority status—a legacy of guided reactions common in police departments that is, as Buerger and Farrell[9] write, "the latest manifestation of old problems."

Much of the discussion of the origins, efficacy, and perpetuation of racially biased policing is rooted (whether explicitly or not) in the original function of American police: to manage or control the "dangerous" classes.[10] In the rural South throughout the nineteenth century, controlling the dangerous classes often meant deploying slave patrols. In the urban North (and upper Midwest) controlling the dangerous classes was often synonymous with breaking strikes, protecting union jobs, and maintaining social stratification boundaries. Indeed, particularly in the North throughout the Industrial Revolution, a primary function of the police was to ensure that those who were not contributing to the division of labor[11] did not interfere with those who worked in the mass-production sector of the urban economy.

Although the concept of the dangerous class (and more recently the underclass) has remained fairly static since the Industrial Revolution, the groups identified as members of such classes have changed.[12] As William Julius Wilson[13] has observed, it was in the wake of the Civil Rights Movement, the de-industrialization of U.S. urban centers, and the increased racially concentrated poverty, crime, and other social pathologies in cities that led to the "young black male" becoming the archetype of urban criminal offender; and consistent with their role in society, the police concomitantly shifted their focus from managing "disorderly" white/European ethnic group members to attempting to control African Americans.[14]

More recently, researchers have identified the development of the (second) war on drugs as a renewal of racial profiling tactics in many police departments.[15] Michael Tonry[16] writes that prior to President Reagan's 1986 declaration of a "war," drug abuse had already begun to decline, setting the stage for an inevitable victory as declared by President Bush in 1990 and a legacy of unnecessary racially motivated legislative and social programs. As a result of the federal government's "war" on drug sales and trafficking during the mid-1980s, many local, state, and federal police agencies created extensive profiles of likely drug couriers expected to traverse state highways. Although these profiles contained a host of descriptive factors, some form of race, ethnicity, or nationality was usually included as possible indication of narcotic activity.

A salient question for racial profiling researchers is, *Why would police departments create drug courier profiles that relied heavily on race?* Large-scale drug arrests carry significant occupational capital for arresting officers and departments, and MacDonald[17] attributes any eagerness to collar drug traffickers and sellers as a response to such career incentives. Officers are continually reviewed for advancement based on successful collars and their ability to meet department standards and goals for arrests.[18] The notoriety and achievement garnered by officers who arrest traffickers and confiscate large amounts of uncut drugs serve as quantifiable measures of competence, providing police with a tangible incentive to collar drug offenders.[19] Employing drug courier profiles that rest largely on race seems substantively equivalent to the police developing other occupational templates, such as Skolnick's "symbolic assailant," to *efficiently* identify persons of interest. In terms of the symbolic assailant, persons of interest are those who might wish to do harm to police officers; in terms of drug couriers, persons of interest are people trafficking in illegal drugs.

Research identifying the police practice of using race to help officers identify persons of interest pre-dates Skolnick.[20] In his examination of police violence, William Westley[21] identified the process officers used while on the "hunt" for the "felon." As Westley observed, the felony arrest generated the most professional currency for officers as compared to all other police outputs. It was the goal of virtually every officer in Westley's study to make as many felony arrests as possible; and because most officers associated black males with criminal offending, they often used race as a proximate indicator of criminal involvement. Indeed, what researchers now call racial profiling seems substantively equivalent to Westley's "hunt for the felon" and Skolnick's "symbolic assailant." As such—and as with the felon and the symbolic assailant—it is likely more useful (both conceptually and methodologically) to discuss racial profiling more as a *process* than as an *outcome*.

Apart from the organizational incentives that may encourage racial profiling, some researchers hold that the practice of profiling is historically ingrained and culturally pervasive in U.S. society. Thus its roots are more systemic and institutionalized in nature, not simply a response to an emphasis on felony or drug arrests.[22] Scholars argue that this systemic feature can be attributed to the antebellum slave codes and post–Civil War Jim Crow laws of the South, periods of particularly racialized policing in which minority stature (specifically blackness) became equated with criminality.[23] Meehan and Ponder[24] acknowledge this historical tradition of race and class bias, but contend that catalysts for racial profiling in the past few decades may rest in heightened population mobility due to increased automobile ownership and a shift in economic zones of metropolitan areas. They contend that minorities are more mobile and travel through or to "white" neighborhoods for work, shopping, or leisure activities, thus increasing visibility of minority citizens in traditionally white enclaves.[25] Hence, from a methodological standpoint, is it possible to examine the process of racial profiling without isolating the cultural and organizational incentives that may drive virtually *all* racially biased policing practices?

The "Legalities" of Racial Profiling

The legislative foundations of police profiling are rooted primarily in two Supreme Court cases implicating a citizen's protection under the Fourth Amendment. In 1968 the Court's ruling in the case of *Terry v. Ohio* gave a police officer discretion to stop and search an individual for a weapon without a search warrant when that officer suspects the citizen of engaging or attempting to engage in criminal activity. Thereafter, the *Terry* decision was used as justification for routine stop-and-search procedures in primarily street-based interactions between officers and citizens.

The 1996 decision in *Whren v. United States* upheld the practice of using race as a factor in officer decisions to stop and search a suspect, and furthered the work of *Terry* to apply explicitly to interactions between an officer and a motorist.[26] *Whren* upheld the practice of stopping a vehicle under the pretext of a traffic violation but with the intent to investigate for other, perhaps non-related, law violations; since all drivers commit some amount of minor traffic violations, *Whren* more importantly affirmed the practice of using race in the decision to stop a motorist for a minor violation with the purpose of gaining permission to search a vehicle.[27] As Harris[28] writes, once a motorist has violated traffic laws in some capacity, the true intent of the officer making the stop is irrelevant. Over time, the impact of *Whren* on officer practice was an allowance of a form of "soft profiling," deeming that stops made in part on the basis of a suspect's race are not a violation of the Fourth Amendment. Although some critics view *Terry* as a precursor to racial profiling, it is the *Whren* case that is most often mentioned as solidifying the practice of racial profiling in modern police departments.[29]

If the aforementioned cases provide legal support for the implementation of racial profiling practices, we look to two similarly foundational cases to help establish the existence and limits of racial profiling. Representation for the plaintiffs in both *Wilkins v. Maryland State Police* and *State of New Jersey v. Pedro Soto et al.* employed research from John Lamberth regarding incidence and prevalence of traffic stops along two interstate highways.[30]

Wilkins, a class action lawsuit filed in 1993 against the Maryland State Police by the National Association for the Advancement of Colored People (NAACP) and a group of individual motorists, resulted in a civil settlement in 1996 due in large part to the data collected and presented at trial by Lamberth. Robert Wilkins, an attorney on the case and the original plaintiff, had been traveling with his family en route from a funeral in Chicago when he was pulled over and he and his family were forced to wait outside his rented vehicle in the rain for the arrival of a drug-sniffing dog. When the dog arrived and did not alert to the presence of any illegal substances, Wilkins was issued a citation and let go. Shortly thereafter he called the American Civil Liberties Union (ACLU) to state that his civil liberties had been violated.

Soto, a class action case brought by sixteen black and Hispanic plaintiffs, also utilized Lamberth to provide demographic and traffic-stop data indexing a trend of racial profiling practices along the New Jersey Turnpike. The 1996 decision by a state superior court judge suppressed drug evidence seized during a series of stops, ruling that the stops were made on the basis of motorist race and thus alleging selective enforcement of the state's drug laws.

The body of case law that has developed from the Court's interpretations of how the police may use race to establish probable cause is virtually identical in tone to the body of case law established to define the boundaries of police interrogations. In *Brown v. Mississippi* (1936) the Supreme Court banned police use of physical coercion during interrogations, leading (as some scholars suggest) the police to rely on psychological coercion as a means of obtaining confessions. When the Court officially ended the use of "intense psychological" coercion of suspects in police custody,[31] the police began to use "trickery" to obtain confessions.[32] In *Frazier v. Cupp* the Court ruled that the use of "trickery" was generally acceptable, but that it amounted to a custodial interrogation. Thus, if the police were going to attempt to trick suspects into confessing, they were required to advise suspects of their so-called Miranda warnings (specifically the right to counsel and the right to remain silent).

The sole reason this body of case law developed was because, despite the emergence of sophisticated forensic investigative techniques, the police still rely on the confession as their primary evidentiary tool when building cases against suspects. Similarly, despite public rhetoric about the inappropriateness of using race as a primary factor in establishing probable cause, the police still use "shorthand" techniques for identifying persons of interest. Until the police and the public stop equating the young black male with urban criminal offender, racially biased policing will likely continue, despite court interventions.

Operationalizing Public and Official Expectations of the Police

Just as worthy of note is the way in which laws are integrated into society's everyday practice, a process Donald Black[33] terms "legal mobilization." He contends this is a conjunction at which little attention is focused, with the larger academic populace preferring to focus on rules and their application as two relatively separate circumstances rather than an interaction of legal and social dynamics.[34] An interesting counterpoint to this common logic is Shearing and Ericson's[35] assertion that officers seem to take pride in the fact that good police work is not prescribed but rather a series of guttural and experiential reactions to situations. These reactions are an extension of an officer's "sensibility," a type of personality developed within departmental parameters of behavioral norms.[36] Thus any discussion of racial profiling must focus not only on the "legalities" of racially motivated contacts between police and citizens but also on the way in which departments and individual officers choose to interpret the few guidelines meted out by the courts.

Engel and colleagues[37] identify aspects of this process as meeting the tenets of expectancy theory in that, at both the macro (department) and micro (officer) levels, work output is dependent on output expectations by supervising agencies. In the case of the individual officer, output is designed to meet supervisor expectations, while in the case of the department, output is directed toward meeting public expectations of racial sensitivity and uniform application of law.[38] As Miller[39] contends, this reporting of race in traffic stops furthers a department's "image management" and symbolizes the agency's attempt to meet public expectations of a departmental response to racial profiling.

Despite the recent and current focus on racial profiling practices and the numerous public repudiations of its use, a search of major U.S. police department websites yields no explicit or even vague definition of "racial profiling." The International Association of Chiefs of Police (IACP) includes a resolution against "biased policing," a term defined as an act where the basis of police action is an individual's race, ethnicity, sexual orientation, gender, age, socioeconomic status, or religious affiliation.[40] The U.S. Department of Justice, for its part, only indirectly defines racial profiling as "race based assumptions in law enforcement" in a 2003 "fact sheet" avowing the erroneous practice. Ironically, under the subheading of "Defining the Problem: Racial Profiling Is Wrong and Will Not Be Tolerated," we only read that it is, indeed, wrong and will not be tolerated.[41]

The gap that may exist between officer and public expectations of racial profiling and "good" policing may be best informed by Manning's[42] integration of police theory and Goffman's[43] thesis on sociological dramaturgy. Manning not only highlights the role conflicts inherent to defining the police mandate, but also identifies the ways in which officers and departments seek to remedy this conflict with carefully generated actions and behaviors. Manning argues that police administrators who are successful at controlling the "message" sent to the policing audience (i.e., the public) are able to successfully reinforce the need for a police force and obscure the less desirable department practices.[44]

At the heart of the policing mandate is its dependence on enforcement of the normative social order, by definition divisive and discriminatory against at least one faction of society.[45] In the case of racial profiling, officers and departments are faced with the task of buttressing the normative social order and satisfying their majority white constituency, but at the same time this regulation veers into the precarious territory of selective enforcement. The special nature of police work dictates that officers be invested with legitimacy to define those at-times ambiguous terms describing violation and social norms, but not without conflicting and inconsistent messages from citizens.[46] We see this in the aforementioned problems with the mere definition of racial profiling, and perhaps it is this inconsistency in expectation parameters that causes departments to purposefully *not* publicize or declare definitive measures of racial profiling practices. Policing is highly symbolic in nature, and Manning[47] posits that the "realities" of policing are disguised by a veil of moral representation of the state; as such, officers and departments have become adept at impression management, illustrating efficiency, impartiality, and uniformity through a campaign of social presentation. This negotiation of imagery thus becomes an imperative as it serves as a form of social currency that then helps officers defend and reinforce the police mandate. Accordingly, any challenge to the potentially racially motivated practices of officers or police departments frees these agencies of the accusation that they have violated their own self-described standards for enforcement.

Assessing the Effectiveness of Racial Profiling

As a practice, racial profiling and the academic tests of its robustness have produced little evidence as to its effectiveness as a policing tool.[48] Widespread societal recognition of its use by the police, however, has contributed new vocabulary to the English language, namely Driving While Black (DWB); and although popular polls often cite an overwhelming public opposition to racial profiling, perceptions of its prevalence vary.[49] In their series of tests assessing the relationship between perceptions of profiling and confidence in police authority and legitimacy, Tyler and Wakslak[50] found that minorities were more likely to believe in the prevalence of profiling and thus were less trustful of the police. These findings were suggestive of a variation in perceptions of profiling quite possibly representative, as Tyler and Wakslak[51] and later Russell-Brown[52] note, of the fact that those who are not profiled or regularly exposed to profiling anecdotes do not recognize its pervasiveness. Further, a series of attitudinal studies comparing white, black, and Hispanic perceptions associated with research profiling serve to underscore these findings. For example, in a series of studies using data from New York City residents, important differences were identified across the three groups with respect to perceptions associated with whether racial profiling is widespread, whether it is justified, and whether respondents believed that they had ever been profiled.[53]

The policy implications of racial profiling and its potential for significant impact on perceptions of police legitimacy and subsequent police-citizen interactions hinge on the ability of scholars to effectively measure its value as a tool of offender identification.[54] We know black and Hispanic interactions with officers and perceptions of being profiled by police lead to a diminished perception of officer legitimacy, and we know these interactions are shared within communities as anecdotes that then produce both personal and vicarious experiences with racial profiling.[55] Indeed, much of the recent scholarship on racial profiling documents incidents of profiling. Some of these cases are anecdotal and serve purposes only within close social networks, but others are more widely publicized due to the popularity of the profiled citizen, or to the highly controversial behavior of those involved. Weitzer and Tuch[56] found blacks more likely than Hispanics to perceive police injustice, and found both groups more likely than whites to perceive police injustice. Feagin and Sikes[57] identified a cumulative effect of frequent police-initiated interaction and perceptions of unfair treatment by officers as affecting the views of police as reported by respondents and acquaintances, and Russell[58] identified behavioral management strategies as taught and operationalized within black communities to minimize or avoid risks of race-based police stops. According to Brunson,[59] African Americans tend to have the poorest attitudes toward police, a conclusion he reaches based on the finding that minorities typically experience racial injustice through word of mouth and vicarious experiences, while whites learn of racial injustice through the media.[60]

In short, cautionary tales of perceived racial profiling by police are disseminated throughout minority communities. Furthermore, others report, for both whites and minorities, that stories and testimonies of race-based interactions perpetuate the "contemporary racial order."[61] Thus, although the methods of dissemination vary, reports of race-based interactions can serve an almost-regulatory function.

Data Collection and More Specific Methodological Issues

Central to the ethical, legal, and utilitarian issues associated with racial profiling is the question of representation: does the disproportionate representation of blacks and Hispanics in the criminal justice system represent higher rates of criminality (i.e., different participation) or higher rates of interaction with police and criminal justice system (i.e., differential enforcement), or some combination thereof?[62] The debate initiated by this question strongly implicates the importance of accurate and consistent measurement in racial profiling studies. This question of data collection, specifically the definition, identification, and consistent collection of racial profiling data, is at the center of scholarly discourse.[63] Admittedly, this is produced by society's slow recognition of racial profiling as an issue, though it has long been recognized within minority communities.[64] Because of this newness and the varied nature of policing, definitions of racial profiling vary among policing agencies and academics, yielding no consistently operationalized definition of racial profiling; data that are often incomplete or susceptible to social and organizational influences;[65] and little legislative or judicial guidance as to a definition of racial profiling.[66] Further, Russell contends that the genesis of measurement discrepancies can be found in the disproportionate focus on formal stages of the criminal justice system rather than the subtler, informal stages. She acknowledges that formal stages are more conducive to empirical and unequivocal records, but posits that is the proverbial "gray" area of the informal stages at which racial discrimination might be most prevalent.

Despite the breadth of racial profiling contexts and activities, most recent analyses of racially biased policing have been limited to traffic stop data originally collected in conjunction with lawsuits.[67,68] These retrospective examinations have been made possible, in part, by mandates in some states that require documentation of demographic statistics for all traffic stops, as well as the increasing prevalence of computers and video surveillance in patrol cars. As such, much of what is known about racial profiling is shaped by landmark motorist-profiling cases in Ohio, Colorado, New Jersey, Maryland, and Florida. And yet, these cases hinged largely on gross circumstances of officer misconduct and not the more common and frequent methods of racial profiling.[69] Furthermore, most of these data are procured from the government and policing agencies that, until very recently, did not employ impartial supervision in data collection practices. Meehan and Ponder[70] point to this interior data collection as a specific threat to obtaining complete and accurate information; they contend that officers are adept at "off the record" interactions and, given the discretion understood in an officer's job, can omit information otherwise collected (see Kane[71] for a discussion of the limitations of the collection and distribution of police department data). Other researchers have also expressed concern about the data's accuracy, generalizability, and comparability to other studies, as well its ability to account for other race-neutral variables.[72]

Although traffic stop data lend easily to statistical analysis and are increasingly common to obtain, the question of data fit frequently arises. Since large concentrations of minorities reside in urban centers—zones in which residents often walk or use public transportation and seldom frequent interstates—are researchers who employ interstate traffic stop data risking measurement validity?[73] In fact, researchers have had some success in identifying class-based rather than race-based distinctions in cases of racial profiling, finding that class is rarely a determinant in the decision to stop but identifying race as a mediating variable in stop outcome.[74]

Several considerations as to the quality of data collection also bear mention. Chief among them is determination of the "base rate" of drivers who would be stopped by officers absent any racial prejudice.[75] Herein lies the crux of what is commonly known as the "denominator problem."[76] As there is no way to measure which drivers are not stopped because of their race, many statisticians have attempted to use population statistics or driver's license records to estimate the demographic composition of interstate highways, but these measures are seen as weak estimations of highway populations.[77] Additionally, there is some discourse regarding which measurements to use as a benchmark, those drivers who are speed-limit violators or any drivers.[78] To date, John Lamberth's[79] attempts to address these weaknesses in two separate analyses of police stops along New Jersey and Maryland interstate systems have been credited with advancing measurement of interstate racial composition and interstate criminality, and are seen as some of the most accurate measures available.[80] On each interstate in question, Lamberth's team indexed the racial representation of drivers at a series of randomly chosen times during the day to create a distribution of interstate population, and then coupled this with observed racial representation and proportion of motorists violating speeding regulations. With this latter measure, he developed an index of criminality, which compares stops and actual law violations—or, more specifically, compares *who* is stopped to *who* more frequently violates laws.

Meehan and Ponder[81] later implemented a similar model of a highway composition measurement through the use of observation and randomized motorist selection, improving on Lamberth's estimation with their linkage of motorist location and time of day. In their multimethod approach to measuring racial profiling, Alpert and colleagues[82] also compared individual officer stop and arrest behavior with the larger, aggregate-level data and reported a higher arrest rate—3.7%—for blacks compared to the combined 2% arrest rate for whites and Hispanics. Lamberth's[83] findings in both studies indicated an overwhelmingly biased response to race; in New Jersey, vehicles with black motorists or passengers made up 13.5% of the turnpike population and yet blacks constituted 34.9% of stops and 73.2% of the arrests made from these stops. In his Maryland observations, Lamberth[84] found 74.7% speed-limit violators to be white and 17.5% black, but blacks made up 28.8% of the drivers stopped and 71.3% of those searched.

Another response to the question of highway population and such large-scale measurements has been an emphasis on neighborhood and contextual studies of traffic stops.[85] Petrocelli and colleagues[86] found some support for this avenue of measurement, noting in their Richmond data that, although suspect race indicated an officer's likelihood to search a vehicle, neighborhood crime rates—not race—predicted an officer's decision to stop a vehicle. Similarly, Engel and Calnon[87] found that suspect race predicted outcome of a traffic stop but had less of an impact on an officer's initial decision to stop a vehicle.

Meehan and Ponder[88] found support for this contextual space argument, reporting a profiling sensitivity toward blacks in wealthy white areas. They argue that this specific profiling could be born out of a combined sense of duty to monitor community boundaries and a recognition of community segregation practices, and thus is more dependent on community character than suspect race.[89] Glover[90] noted similar findings and developed an "out of place" doctrine reminiscent of Weitzer and Tuch's[91] notion of a "red flag" and the "reverse discrimination" argument outlined by Bonilla-Silva and colleagues.[92] As Glover[93] found, officers identify whites as being "out of place" when observed in minority neighborhoods; further investigation therefore frees an officer of any accusation of profiling blacks and supports the argument that an officer is concerned only with the criminality of the neighborhood. Through this semantic sidestep, Glover[94] writes, an officer believes any accusation of profiling the criminal black man or criminalized minority space is avoided in the decision to stop a white suspect. Russell[95] contends, however, that this practice is inherently biased and conducive of de facto guilt as there are more white neighborhoods than black neighborhoods, and she identifies the "out of place" doctrine as dangerous when given the parameters provided by the case of *Whren v. United States*.

Other critiques of measurement in racial profiling studies center around reliance on "outcome tests"[96] and the importance of "hit rates."[97] This is one of the newest methodological attempts to address the denominator issue in testing for racial profiling, one in which researchers focus not on the bench marks, geographic scale, and officer/department delineations but rather on an outcome measure. Such tests are reminiscent of an economic measure of stop success in police stops, one in which success is defined as the discovery of illegal activity or substances during one such stop and which has been popularly received by practitioners for their tangible answers to often-polluted research questions and simple measurements.[98] Essentially, if the practice of profiling yields equitable "hit rates" of criminal apprehension and drug seizures, profiling is then statistically based and not racially motivated.[99] This argument echoes similar arguments for spatial and community profiling in that the focus of and basis for the profiling is officially lifted from the demographic variables of race and placed on related but less controversial variables.

Although "outcome tests" are relatively new in practice, academics have identified specific concerns about their use, most of which center on assumptions specific to these studies. Chief among those concerns is the assumption that all vehicle searches are made under the full purview and discretion of the officer.[100] Often, a stop may be discretionary, but the decision to search may be mandatory or motivated by other factors. An additional concern is an officer's use of discretion; "outcome tests" assume a uniformity in reaction to a set of suspect characteristics and often do not allow for variability in officer response and interpretation of suspect characteristics.[101] Consequently, another criticism of outcome tests is the ignorance of other mediating factors that might supercede race in the decision to stop and search.[102] Among these variables are those identified by Scolnick[103] and Van Maanen[104] as intervening and suspicious behavior variables or other demographic variables.

Going Forward

Similar to the debate regarding minority overrepresentation in institutionalization (i.e., is it due to differences in offending, enforcement, or some combination), now is a good time to move beyond the question concerning whether minority overrepresentation in traffic stops is due to racial profiling by police or simply minorities differentially engaging in the sorts of behaviors that produce differentials in stops. Instead, research and policy is more likely to advance to the extent that two avenues are simultaneously transversed.

In the first, we should abandon the quest to sort between the amount of variance explained in traffic stops due to differential participation and differential enforcement, as both are surely involved (60% for one, 40% for the other, or whatever the amounts really are). Going forward, we should follow the lead of the juvenile justice processing area and focus instead on how differences in participation and enforcement contribute to racial profiling.[105] The second avenue that will be important is geared around data collection efforts. Here the laundry list is long but important, as improving the methods that researchers use to collect data—as well as the types of data that are collected—bear directly on matters of policy. We envision an important set of efforts designed around triangulation of methods and sources that will provide a much firmer database than currently exists to study the profiling issue. For example, data are sorely needed across different types of communities, police agencies, and sample compositions, as crime and its reaction are local problems and differentials in traffic stops may be a function of these characteristics. Also, the collection of race/ethnicity data from driver's licenses, information on driving-eligible populations, traffic patterns, and police deployment issues are all important inputs into how stops are made, and how they may (or may not) vary across race/ethnic lines. In short, a sustained, systematic research program will offer the only input necessary for policy-makers to arrive at important decisions regarding police practices and the outcomes and consequences associated with those practices. Injecting some rationality into the discussion of racial profiling would do wonders for moving research and policy ahead.

The above suggestions are likely to not generate much controversy, as researchers typically speak with one voice about gathering more and better data, but we also wish to recommend what will likely be a more controversial statement: the movement away from the term "racial profiling" and a replacement with the term "differential stops." This term more squarely keeps the discussion centered around data rather than intent (of the officer), which is sure to be nearly impossible to ascertain. We believe that this change will generate a fuller appreciation of these issues, and not assume, a priori, that the police are profiling certain people solely because they possess certain observable characteristics.

Finally, and relatedly, considering the difficulty of isolating racial profiling outcomes from the larger social and organizational processes that likely drive much of the racial disparities observed in policing outputs, it seems artificial and theoretically simplistic to examine racial profiling as if it exists in a contextual vacuum. Apart from the specific problems discussed above, it may be that racial profiling research is methodologically limited because of improper comparison groups. Researchers conducting inquiries into racially biased police practices might compare patterns of traffic stops to other police processes. It may be that police organizations that experience high rates of racial disparities in traffic stops might experience similar disparities in rates of non-compliance to police requests, assaults against officers, use of force by officers, and misdemeanor arrests by officers. Such findings would suggest that what researchers often call "racial profiling" is really part of a larger process of racial conflict produced perhaps by public expectations of crime control and order maintenance, as well as organizational value systems that encourage enforcement outputs. Thus, to effectively study and assess racial profiling outcomes, it seems necessary to understand the processes that lead to the conditions that produce the racial conflict in the first place.

NOTES

1. MacDonald, "The Myth of Racial Profiling."
2. Ramirez, Hoopes et al., "Defining Racial Profiling in a Post–September 11 World."
3. Skolnick, *Justice Without Trial.*
4. See Skolnick in this volume.
5. Skolnick, *Justice Without Trial.*
6. Van Maanen, "The Asshole."
7. Harris, "The Stories, the Statistics, and the Law: Why 'Driving While Black' Matters"; Taylor and Whitney, "Crime and Racial Profiling by U.S. Police: Is There an Empirical Basis?"; Callahan and Anderson, "The Roots of Racial Profiling"; Meehan and Ponder, "Race and Place: The Ecology of Racial Profiling African American Motorists"; Alpert, Dunham et al., "Investigating Racial Profiling by the Miami-Dade Police Department: A Multimethod Approach."
8. Jones-Brown, "Forever the Symbolic Assailant: The More Things Change, the More They Remain the Same."
9. Buerger and Farrell, "The Evidence Of Racial Profiling: Interpreting Documented and Unofficial Sources."
10. Shelden, *Controlling of the Dangerous Classes.*
11. Giddens, *The Nation-State and Violence.*
12. Kane, "Social Control in the Metropolis."
13. Wilson, *The Truly Disadvantaged*; Wilson, *When Work Disappears.*
14. An exception to the presumed post-modern origins of racially biased law enforcement comes from the first U.S. War on Drugs, which began in the second decade of the 20th century. By the time the Harrison Act passed in 1914, giving Congress (among other powers) the authority to regulate opium and coca leaf derivatives, most middle- and upper-class whites who previously used controlled substances had broken their addictions to heroin, cocaine, and opium, turning instead to alcoholic beverages. Most black narcotics addicts could not afford drug treatment or to pay physicians to prescribe them narcotics, leaving them legally

susceptible to arrest and prosecution under the Harrison Act. As a result, by 1923 African Americans represented 31% of the national prison population, while making up only 9% of the U.S. population. See Courtwright, *Dark Paradise: Opiate Addiction in America Before 1940*; Kennedy, "Drug Wars in Black and White."

15. Tonry, *Malign Neglect—Race, Crime, and Punishment in America*; Callahan and Anderson, "The Roots of Racial Profiling"; MacDonald, "The Myth of Racial Profiling"; Cordner, Williams, et al., "Vehicle Stops in San Diego"; Engel, Calnon et al., "Theory and Racial Profiling: Shortcomings and Future Directions in Research"; Meehan and Ponder, "Race and Place: The Ecology of Racial Profiling African American Motorists"; Ramirez, Hoopes et al., "Defining Racial Profiling in a Post–September 11 World"; Engel and Calnon, "Examining the Influence of Drivers' Characteristics on Traffic Stops with Police: Results from a National Survey."

16. Tonry, *Malign Neglect—Race, Crime, and Punishment in America*.

17. MacDonald, "The Myth of Racial Profiling."

18. Lamberth, "Driving While Black; A Statistician Proves That Prejudice Still Rules the Road."

19. MacDonald, "The Myth of Racial Profiling."

20. Skolnick, *Justice Without Trial*.

21. Westely, *Violence and the Police*. Although published in 1970, Westely conducted the research and collected the data for the project in 1950—sixteen years in advance of the publication of Skolnick's *Justice Without Trial*.

22. Engel, Calnon et al., "Theory and Racial Profiling: Shortcomings and Future Directions in Research"; Bonilla-Silva, Lewis et al., "'I Did Not Get That Job Because of a Black Man . . .': The Story Lines and Testimonies of Color-Blind Racism"; Engel and Calnon, "Examining the Influence of Drivers' Characteristics on Traffic Stops with Police: Results from a National Survey"; Stokes, "Legislative and Court Decisions that Promulgated Racial Profiling: A Sociohistorical Perspective."

23. Buerger and Farrell, "The Evidence of Racial Profiling: Interpreting Documented and Unofficial Sources"; Jones-Brown, "Forever the Symbolic Assailant: The More Things Change, the More they Remain the Same."

24. Meehan and Ponder, "How Roadway Composition Matters in Analyzing Police Data on Racial Profiling."

25. Weitzer and Tuch, "Perceptions of Racial Profiling: Race, Class, and Personal Experience."

26. Meehan and Ponder, "Race and Place: The Ecology of Racial Profiling African American Motorists."

27. Russell, "'Driving While Black': Corollary Phenomena and Collateral Consequences."

28. Harris, "'Driving While Black' and All Other Traffic Offenses: The Supreme Court and Pretextual Traffic Stops."

29. Harris, "The Stories, the Statistics, and the Law: Why 'Driving While Black' Matters"; Weitzer and Tuch, "Perceptions of Racial Profiling: Race, Class, and Personal Experience."

30. See Lamberth, "Driving While Black; A Statistician Proves That Prejudice Still Rules the Road."

31. *Spano v. New York*.

32. del Carmen, *Civil Liabilities in American Policing*.

33. Black, "The Mobilization of Law."

34. Black, "The Mobilization of Law."

35. Shearing and Ericson, "Culture as Figurative Action."

36. Shearing and Ericson, "Culture as Figurative Action."

37. Engel, Calnon et al., "Theory and Racial Profiling: Shortcomings and Future Directions in Research."

38. Engel, Calnon et al., "Theory and Racial Profiling: Shortcomings and Future Directions in Research."

39. Miller, "Racial Profiling and Postmodern Society: Police Responsiveness, Image Maintenance, and the Left Flank of Police Legitimacy."

40. IACP, "Civil Rights/Diversity."

41. USDOJ, "Fact Sheet: Racial Profiling."

42. Manning, *Police Work: The Social Organization of Policing.*

43. Goffman, *The Presentation of Self in Everyday Life.*

44. Manning, *Police Work: The Social Organization of Policing.*

45. Manning, *Police Work: The Social Organization of Policing.*

46. Manning, *Police Work: The Social Organization of Policing.*

47. Manning, *Police Work: The Social Organization of Policing.*

48. Harris, "'Driving While Black' and All Other Traffic Offenses: The Supreme Court and Pretextual Traffic Stops"; Harris, "The Stories, the Statistics, and the Law: Why 'Driving While Black' Matters"; Ramirez, Hoopes et al., "Defining Racial Profiling in a Post–September 11 World"; Engel and Calnon, "Examining the Influence of Drivers' Characteristics on Traffic Stops with Police: Results From a National Survey"; Tyler and Wakslak, "Profiling and Police Legitimacy: Procedural Justice, Attributions of Motive, and Acceptance of Police Authority"; Harris, "The Importance of Research on Race and Policing: Making Race Salient to Individuals and Institutions Within Criminal Justice."

49. Harris, "'Driving While Black' and All Other Traffic Offenses: The Supreme Court and Pretextual Traffic Stops"; Harris, "The Stories, the Statistics, and the Law: Why 'Driving While Black' Matters"; Russell, *The Color of Crime: Racial Hoaxes, White Fear, Black Protectionism, Police Harassment, and Other Macroagressions*; Carlson, "Racial Profiling Seen as Pervasive, Unjust"; Engel and Calnon, "Examining the Influence of Drivers' Characteristics on Traffic Stops with Police: Results From a National Survey."

50. Tyler and Wakslak, "Profiling and Police Legitimacy: Procedural Justice, Attributions of Motive, and Acceptance of Police Authority."

51. Tyler and Wakslak, "Profiling and Police Legitimacy: Procedural Justice, Attributions of Motive, and Acceptance of Police Authority."

52. Russell-Brown, *Protecting Our Own: Race, Crime, and African Americans.*

53. Rice and Piquero, "Perceptions of Discrimination and Justice in New York City"; Rice, Piquero et al., "Shades of Brown: Perceptions of Racial Profiling and the Intra-ethnic Differential"; Reitzel, Rice et al., "Lines and Shadows: Perceptions of Racial Profiling and the Hispanic Experience"; Reitzel and Piquero, "Does It Exist? Studying Citizen's Attitudes of Racial Profiling."

54. Harris, "The Stories, the Statistics, and the Law: Why 'Driving While Black' Matters"; Weitzer, "Racialized Policing: Residents' Perceptions in Three Neighborhoods"; MacDonald, "The Myth of Racial Profiling"; Weitzer and Tuch, "Perceptions of Racial Profiling: Race, Class, and Personal Experience"; Engel and Calnon, "Examining the Influence of Drivers' Characteristics on Traffic Stops with Police: Results from a National Survey"; Weitzer and Tuch, "Race and Perceptions of Police Misconduct"; Miller, "Racial Profiling and Postmodern Society: Police Responsiveness, Image Maintenance, and the Left Flank of Police Legitimacy."

55. Russell, *The Color of Crime: Racial Hoaxes, White Fear, Black Protectionism, Police Harassment, and Other Macroagressions*; Weitzer and Tuch, "Race, Class, and Perceptions of Discrimination by the Police"; Weitzer, "Racialized Policing: Residents' Perceptions in Three Neighborhoods"; Websdale, *Policing the Poor: From Slave Plantation to Public Housing*;

Buerger and Farrell, "The Evidence of Racial Profiling: Interpreting Documented and Unofficial Sources"; Weitzer and Tuch, "Race and Perceptions of Police Misconduct"; Weitzer and Tuch, "Racially Biased Policing: Determinants of Citizen Perceptions."

56. Weitzer and Tuch, "Race, Class, and Perceptions of Discrimination by the Police"; "Racially Biased Policing: Determinants of Citizen Perceptions."

57. Feagin and Sikes, *Living with Racism: The Black Middle-Class Experience.*

58. Russell, "'Driving While Black': Corollary Phenomena and Collateral Consequences."

59. Brunson, "'Police Don't Like Black People': African American Young Men's Accumulated Police Experiences."

60. See Brunson in this volume.

61. Hurwitz and Peffley, "Public Perceptions of Race and Crime: The Role of Racial Stereotypes"; Russell, *The Color of Crime: Racial Hoaxes, White Fear, Black Protectionism, Police Harassment, and Other Macroagressions*; Websdale, *Policing the Poor: From Slave Plantation to Public Housing*; Bonilla-Silva, Lewis et al., "'I Did Not Get That Job Because of a Black Man . . .': The Story Lines and Testimonies of Color-Blind Racism."

62. MacDonald, "The Myth of Racial Profiling"; Piquero and Brame, "Assessing the Race-/Ethnicity-Crime Relationship in a Sample of Serious Adolescent Delinquents."

63. Harris, "The Stories, the Statistics, and the Law: Why 'Driving While Black' Matters"; MacDonald, "The Myth of Racial Profiling"; Cordner, Williams et al., "Vehicle Stops in San Diego"; Engel and Calnon, "Examining the Influence of Drivers' Characteristics on Traffic Stops with Police: Results from a National Survey."

64. Harris, "The Stories, the Statistics, and the Law: Why 'Driving While Black' Matters"; Russell, "'Driving While Black': Corollary Phenomena and Collateral Consequences."

65. Harris, "The Stories, the Statistics, and the Law: Why 'Driving While Black' Matters"; Buerger and Farrell, "The Evidence of Racial Profiling: Interpreting Documented and Unofficial Sources"; Meehan and Ponder, "Race and Place: The Ecology of Racial Profiling African American Motorists"; Ramirez, Hoopes et al., "Defining Racial Profiling in a Post–September 11 World"; Parker, MacDonald et al., "A Contextual Study of Racial Profiling: Assessing the Theoretical Rationale for the Study of Racial Profiling at the Local Level"; Miller, "Racial Profiling and Postmodern Society: Police Responsiveness, Image Maintenance, and the Left Flank of Police Legitimacy."

66. Russell, "Racial Profiling: A Status Report of the Legal, Legislative, and Empirical Literature."

67. MacDonald, "The Myth of Racial Profiling"; Meehan and Ponder, "Race and Place: The Ecology of Racial Profiling African American Motorists"; Weitzer and Tuch, "Perceptions of Racial Profiling: Race, Class, and Personal Experience"; Petrocelli, Piquero et al., "Conflict Theory and Racial Profiling: An Empirical Analysis of Police Traffic Stop Data"; Parker, MacDonald et al., "A Contextual Study of Racial Profiling: Assessing the Theoretical Rationale for the Study of Racial Profiling at the Local Level."

68. As Kane noted, one of the primary methods by which police scholars gain access to police department data is through civil litigation—that is, participating as an expert witness in lawsuits against the police. Ironically, "police agencies in greatest need of transparency are (often) those compelled to offer it only in light of a public scandal" (Kane, "Collect and Release Data on Coercive Police Actions," 778).

69. Buerger and Farrell, "The Evidence of Racial Profiling: Interpreting Documented and Unofficial Sources."

70. Meehan and Ponder, "How Roadway Composition Matters in Analyzing Police Data on Racial Profiling."

71. Kane, "Collect and Release Data on Coercive Police Actions."

72. Ramirez, McDevitt et al., "A Resource Guide on Racial Profiling Data Collection Systems: Promising Practices and Lessons Learned"; Engel, Calnon et al., "Theory and Racial Profiling: Shortcomings and Future Directions in Research."

73. Buerger and Farrell, "The Evidence of Racial Profiling: Interpreting Documented and Unofficial Sources."

74. Weitzer and Tuch, "Race, Class, and Perceptions of Discrimination by the Police"; Weitzer, "Racialized Policing: Residents' Perceptions in Three Neighborhoods"; Weitzer and Tuch, "Perceptions of Racial Profiling: Race, Class, and Personal Experience."

75. MacDonald, "The Myth of Racial Profiling"; Engel and Calnon, "Theory and Racial Profiling: Shortcomings and Future Directions in Research."

76. Walker, "Searching for the Denominator: Problems with Police Traffic Stop Data and an Early Warning System Solution"; see also Ridgeway and McDonald in this volume.

77. MacDonald, "The Myth of Racial Profiling"; Engel and Calnon, "Theory and Racial Profiling: Shortcomings and Future Directions in Research."

78. Alpert, Dunham et al., "Investigating Racial Profiling by the Miami-Dade Police Department: A Multimethod Approach."

79. Lamberth, "Revised Statistical Analysis of the Incidence of Police Stops and Arrests of Black Drivers/Travelers on the New Jersey Turnpike Between Exits or Interchanges 1 And 3 from the Years 1988 Through 1991"; "Driving While Black; A Statistician Proves That Prejudice Still Rules the Road."

80. Harris, "The Stories, the Statistics, and the Law: Why 'Driving While Black' Matters."

81. Meehan and Ponder, "How Roadway Composition Matters in Analyzing Police Data on Racial Profiling."

82. Alpert, Dunham et al., "Investigating Racial Profiling by the Miami-Dade Police Department: A Multimethod Approach."

83. Lamberth, "Revised Statistical Analysis of the Incidence of Police Stops and Arrests of Black Drivers/Travelers on the New Jersey Turnpike Between Exits or Interchanges 1 And 3 from the Years 1988 Through 1991"; "Driving While Black; A Statistician Proves That Prejudice Still Rules the Road."

84. Lamberth, "Driving While Black; A Statistician Proves That Prejudice Still Rules the Road."

85. Weitzer, "Racialized Policing: Residents' Perceptions in Three Neighborhoods"; Smith and Petrocelli, "Racial Profiling? A Multivariate Analysis of Police Traffic Stop Data"; Engel, Calnon et al., "Theory and Racial Profiling: Shortcomings and Future Directions in Research"; Petrocelli, Piquero et al., "Conflict Theory and Racial Profiling: An Empirical Analysis of Police Traffic Stop Data"; Parker, MacDonald et al., "A Contextual Study of Racial Profiling: Assessing the Theoretical Rationale for the Study of Racial Profiling at the Local Level."

86. Petrocelli, Piquero et al., "Conflict Theory and Racial Profiling: An Empirical Analysis of Police Traffic Stop Data"

87. Engel and Calnon, "Examining the Influence of Drivers' Characteristics on Traffic Stops with Police: Results from a National Survey."

88. Meehan and Ponder, "How Roadway Composition Matters in Analyzing Police Data on Racial Profiling"; "Race and Place: The Ecology of Racial Profiling African American Motorists."

89. Meehan and Ponder, "How Roadway Composition Matters in Analyzing Police Data on Racial Profiling"; "Race and Place: The Ecology of Racial Profiling African American Motorists."

90. Glover, "Police Discourse on Racial Profiling."

91. Weitzer and Tuch, "Perceptions of Racial Profiling: Race, Class, and Personal Experience."

92. Bonilla-Silva, Lewis et al., " 'I Did Not Get That Job Because of a Black Man . . .': The Story Lines and Testimonies of Color-Blind Racism."

93. Glover, "Police Discourse on Racial Profiling."

94. Glover, "Police Discourse on Racial Profiling."

95. Russell, *The Color of Crime: Racial Hoaxes, White Fear, Black Protectionism, Police Harassment, and Other Macroagressions.*

96. Engel and Calnon, "Examining the Influence of Drivers' Characteristics on Traffic Stops with Police: Results from a National Survey"; Engel, "A Critique of the 'Outcome Test' in Racial Profiling Research."

97. Ramirez, Hoopes et al., "Defining Racial Profiling in a Post–September 11 World."

98. Engel, "A Critique of the 'Outcome Test' in Racial Profiling Research."

99. Engel, "A Critique of the 'Outcome Test' in Racial Profiling Research."

100. Engel, "A Critique of the 'Outcome Test' in Racial Profiling Research."

101. Engel, "A Critique of the 'Outcome Test' in Racial Profiling Research."

102. Engel, "A Critique of the 'Outcome Test' in Racial Profiling Research."

103. Scolnick, *Justice Without Trial.*

104. Van Maanen, "The Asshole."

105. Piquero, "Disproportionate Minority Contact."

REFERENCES

Alpert, G. P., R. Dunham, et al. 2007. "Investigating racial profiling by the Miami-Dade Police Department: A multimethod approach." *Criminology and Public Policy* 61: 25–56.

Black, D. J. 1978. "The mobilization of law." *Policing: A view from the street.* P. K. Manning and J. Van Maanen. Santa Monica, CA: Goodyear Publishing.

Bonilla-Silva, E., A. Lewis, et al. 2004. " 'I did not get that job because of a black man . . .': The story lines and testimonies of color-blind racism." *Sociological Forum* 194: 555–581.

Brown v. Mississippi, 297 U.S. 278 1936.

Brunson, R. K. 2007. " 'Police don't like black people': African American young men's accumulated police experiences." *Criminology and Public Policy* 61: 71–102.

Buerger, M. E. and A. Farrell. 2002. "The evidence of racial profiling: Interpreting documented and unofficial sources." *Police Quarterly* 53: 272–305.

Callahan, G. and W. Anderson. 2001. "The roots of racial profiling." *Reason* (August-September): 37–43.

Carlson, D. K. 2004. "Racial profiling seen as pervasive, unjust." Gallup.

Cordner, G., B. Williams, et al. 2002. "Vehicle stops in San Diego." Eastern Kentucky University, Vanderbilt University, San Diego State University: 1–45.

Courtwright, D. 1982. *Dark paradise: Opiate addiction in America before 1940.* Cambridge, MA: Harvard University Press.

del Carmen, R. 1991. *Civil liabilities in American policing : A text for law enforcement personnel.* Englewood Cliffs, NJ: Brady.

Engel, R. S. 2008. "A critique of the 'outcome test' in racial profiling research." *Justice Quarterly* 251: 1–36.

Engel, R. S. and J. M. Calnon 2004. "Examining the influence of drivers' characteristics on traffic stops with police: Results from a national survey." *Justice Quarterly* 211: 49–90.

Engel, R. S., J. M. Calnon, et al. 2002. "Theory and racial profiling: Shortcomings and future directions in research." *Justice Quarterly* 192: 249–271.

Feagin, J. R. and M. P. Sikes 1994. *Living with racism: The black middle-class experience.* Boston: Beacon Press.

Frazier v. Cupp, 394 U.S. 731 1969.

Giddens, A. 1987. *The nation-state and violence.* Berkeley and Los Angeles: University of California Press.

Glover, K. S. 2007. "Police discourse on racial profiling." *Journal of Contemporary Criminal Justice* 233: 239–247.

Goffman, E. 1959. *The presentation of self in everyday life.* Garden City, NY: Doubleday Anchor.

Harris, D. A. 1997. "'Driving while black' and all other traffic offenses: The Supreme Court and pretextual traffic stops." *The Journal of Criminal Law and Criminology* 872: 544–581.

Harris, D. A. 1999. "The stories, the statistics, and the law: Why 'driving while black' matters." *Minnesota Law Review* 84: 1–50.

Harris, D. A. 2007. "The importance of research on race and policing: Making race salient to individuals and institutions within criminal justice." *Criminology and Public Policy* 61: 5–24.

Hurwitz, J. and M. Peffley 1997. "Public perceptions of race and crime: The role of racial stereotypes." *American Journal of Political Science* 412: 375–401.

IACP. 2008. "Civil rights/diversity." *Resolutions.* Retrieved September 2, 2008, from http://www.theiacp.org/resolution/.

Jones-Brown, D. 2007. "Forever the symbolic assailant: The more things change, the more they remain the same." *Criminology and Public Policy* 61: 103–122.

Kane, R. 2007. "Collect and release data on coercive police actions." *Criminology and Public Policy* 6: 773–780.

Kane, R. 2003. "Social control in the metropolis: A community-level examination of the minority group–threat hypothesis." *Justice Quarterly* 20: 265–296.

Kennedy, J. 2003. "Drug wars in black and white." *Law and Contemporary Problems* 66: 153–173.

Lamberth, J. 1994. "Revised statistical analysis of the incidence of police stops and arrests of black drivers/travelers on the New Jersey Turnpike between exits or interchanges 1 and 3 from the years 1988 through 1991." Temple University: 1–29.

Lamberth, J. 1998. "Driving while black; A statistician proves that prejudice still rules the road." *Washington Post*, August 16.

MacDonald, H. 2001. "The myth of racial profiling." *City Journal* 112: 14–27.

Manning, P. K. 1977. *Police work: The social organization of policing.* Prospect Heights, IL: Waveland Press.

Meehan, A. J. and M. C. Ponder 2002. "How roadway composition matters in analyzing police data on racial profiling." *Police Quarterly* 53: 306–333.

Meehan, A. J. and M. C. Ponder 2002. "Race and place: The ecology of racial profiling African American motorists." *Justice Quarterly* 193: 399–429.

Miller, K. 2007. "Racial profiling and postmodern society: Police responsiveness, image maintenance, and the left flank of police legitimacy." *Journal of Contemporary Criminal Justice* 233: 248–262.

Parker, K. F., J. M. MacDonald, et al. 2004. "A contextual study of racial profiling: Assessing the theoretical rationale for the study of racial profiling at the local level." *American Behavioral Scientist* 47: 943–964.

Petrocelli, M., A. R. Piquero, et al. 2003. "Conflict theory and racial profiling: An empirical analysis of police traffic stop data." *Journal of Criminal Justice* 31: 1–11.

Piquero, A. R. 2008. "Disproportionate minority contact." *The Future of Children* 182: 59–79.

Piquero, A. R. and R. Brame. 2008. "Assessing the Race-/Ethnicity-Crime Relationship in a Sample of Serious Adolescent Delinquents." *Crime and Delinquency* 54: 390–422.

Ramirez, D. A., J. Hoopes, et al. 2003. "Defining racial profiling in a post–September 11 world." *American Criminal Law Review* 40: 1195–1235.

Ramirez, D. A., J. McDevitt, et al. 2000. "A resource guide on racial profiling data collection systems: Promising practices and lessons learned." Department of Justice, Washington, DC.

Reitzel, J. and A. R. Piquero. 2006. "Does it exist? Studying citizen's attitudes of racial profiling." *Police Quarterly* 9:161–183.

Reitzel, J., S. Rice, and A.R. Piquero. 2004. "Lines and shadows: Perceptions of racial profiling and the Hispanic experience." *Journal of Criminal Justice* 32: 607–616.

Rice, S. and A. R. Piquero. 2005. "Perceptions of discrimination and justice in New York City." *Policing: An International Journal of Police Strategies and Management* 28: 8–117.

Rice, S. A.R. Piquero, and J. Reitzel. 2005. "Shades of brown: Perceptions of racial profiling and the intra-ethnic differential." *Journal of Ethnicity in Criminal Justice* 3: 47–70.

Russell, K. K. 1998. *The color of crime: Racial hoaxes, white fear, black protectionism, police harassment, and other macroaggressions.* New York: New York University Press.

Russell, K. K. 1999. "'Driving while black': Corollary phenomena and collateral consequences." *Boston College Law Review* 40: 717–732.

Russell, K. K. 2001. "Racial profiling: A status report of the legal, legislative, and empirical literature." *Rutgers Race and the Law Review* 613: 1–19.

Russell, K. K. 2001. "Racing crime: Definitions and dilemmas." *What is crime? Controversies over the nature of crime and what to do about it.* S. Henry and M. Lanier. Lanham, MD: Rowman and Littlefield.

Russell-Brown, K. 2006. *Protecting our own: Race, crime, and African Americans.* Lanham, MD: Rowman and Littlefield.

Shearing, C. and R. Ericson 2005. Culture as figurative action. *Policing: Key readings.* T. Newburn. Portland, OR: Willan Publishing.

Shelden, R. G. 2007. *Controlling the dangerous classes.* Boston: Allyn and Bacon.

Sherman, L. W. 2004. Fair and effective policing. *Crime: Public policies for crime control.* J. Q. Wilson and J. Petersilia. Oakland, CA: Institute for Contemporary Studies.

Smith, M. R. and M. Petrocelli 2001. "Racial profiling? A multivariate analysis of police traffic stop data." *Police Quarterly* 4: 4–27.

Spano v. New York, 360 U.S. 315 1959.

Stokes, L. D. 2007. "Legislative and court decisions that promulgated racial profiling: A sociohistorical perspective." *Journal of Contemporary Criminal Justice* 23: 263–275.

Taylor, J. and G. Whitney 1999. "Crime and racial profiling by U.S. police: Is there an empirical basis?" *The Journal of Social, Political, and Economic Studies* 244: 485–511.

Tonry, M. 1995. *Malign neglect—Race, crime, and punishment in America.* Oxford: Oxford University Press.

Tyler, T. R. and C. J. Wakslak 2004. "Profiling and police legitimacy: Procedural justice, attributions of motive, and acceptance of police authority." *Criminology* 422: 253–283.

USDOJ. 2003. "Fact sheet: Racial profiling." Retrieved September 2, 2008, from http://www.usdoj.gov/opa/pr/2003/June/racial_profiling_fact_sheet.pdf.

Van Maanen, J. "The Asshole." *Policing: A view from the street.* P. Manning and J. Van Maanen. Santa Monica, CA: Goodyear.

Walker, S. 2001. "Searching for the denominator: Problems with police traffic stop data and an early warning system solution." *Justice Research Policy* 3: 1–33.

Websdale, N. 2001. *Policing the poor: From slave plantation to public housing.* Boston: Northeastern University Press.

Weitzer, R. 2000. "Racialized policing: Residents' perceptions in three neighborhoods." *Law and Society Review* 341: 129–155.

Weitzer, R. and S. A. Tuch. 1999. "Race, class, and perceptions of discrimination by the police." *Crime and Delinquency* 45: 494–507.

Weitzer, R. and S. A. Tuch. 2002. "Perceptions of racial profiling: Race, class, and personal experience." *Criminology* 402: 435–457.

Weitzer, R. and S. A. Tuch 2004. "Race and perceptions of police misconduct." *Social Problems* 513: 305–325.

Weitzer, R. and S. A. Tuch. 2005. "Racially biased policing: Determinants of citizen perceptions." *Social Forces* 833: 1009–1030.

Welch, K. 2007. "Black criminal stereotypes and racial profiling." *Journal of Contemporary Criminal Justice* 233: 276–288.

Westely, W. 1970. *Violence and the police.* Cambridge: MIT Press.

Wilson, W. J. 1987. *The truly disadvantaged.* Chicago: University of Chicago Press.

Wilson, W. J. 1996. *When work disappears: The world of the new urban poor.* New York: Knopf.

The Research

Introduction to Part III

Michael D. White

The primary objective of this section is to immerse the reader in the state-of-the-art research on race/ethnicity, bias, and policing. The section includes original contributions from the top experts in the country describing their latest work in this important area. There are three persistent themes in the collection of chapters presented here. The first theme is methodological, as the research clearly demonstrates a need to collect data from multiple sources, and to examine relationships among key variables at multiple levels of analysis. Chapters by Warren and colleagues, Engel and colleagues, Parker and colleagues, and White and Saunders, in particular, capture this theme. The second theme is definitional and relates to the need to expand our conception of race/ethnicity beyond the traditional black/white dichotomy. Chapters by Fagan and colleagues and Parker and colleagues deal specifically with broadened definitions of race/ethnicity and bias. The third theme involves police behavior itself and addresses the importance of expanding the range of police activities that warrant examination. More specifically, the chapter from Fagan and colleagues expands the study of "traffic" stops to include "stop and frisk" activities by police. Also, after being overshadowed by concerns of profiling in traffic stops, questions over race and police use of force have now reemerged. The classic chapter by Fyfe, and White and Saunders's study of race and TASERs, highlight the importance of this theme. Each of the chapters in this section is described in more detail below.

Warren and colleagues examine the impact of race on the likelihood of being stopped by both the North Carolina Highway Patrol and local police in the state. This study resonates with the methodological theme, as the authors use citizen survey data that allows them to capture a range of contextual variables that often are missing in traffic stop studies—most notably, measures of self-reported driving behavior. Warren and colleagues find that race is a significant predictor of traffic stops in the data involving local police, but not in the Highway Patrol data. They suggest that race may be less important for Highway Patrol because officers in that agency are less likely to do routine patrol work, and because race is often difficult to discern when patrolling highways (i.e., given the speed at which vehicles travel). The authors conclude by suggesting that research should be tailored based on the agency under study, and that future research should also focus on officer decision making after the stop has been made.

Engel and colleagues respond to this call in their contribution as they examine the post-stop arrest decision in traffic stops conducted by Cleveland police officers. The authors note that since data collection involving traffic stops has occurred in response to concerns over racial profiling, there has been much less interest in understanding why racial disparities might exist. As a consequence, traffic stop studies have rarely included factors known from prior research to influence police behavior, most notably citizen demeanor. Engel and colleagues examine more than forty-two thousand traffic stops by Cleveland police, and as part of their study, officers were asked to rate citizen demeanor on a scale with values ranging from civil to physically resistant. Although bivariate analysis indicate that minority motorists are more likely to be arrested, multivariate analysis shows that race/ethnicity is no longer a significant predictor of arrest when controlling for other legal and extra-legal variables—including citizen demeanor. Moreover, Engel and colleagues do find that demeanor is a predictor of arrest, and they suggest that failure to account for this influential extra-legal variable represents a serious limitation in prior traffic stop studies.

Fagan et al. build on the earlier work of Fagan and Davies (2000) and offer an updated examination of the development of "order maintenance policing" in New York City. Reflecting the spirit of the third theme—a broadened conception of police behavior—Fagan and colleagues study stop-and-frisk activity by New York City police officers by examining temporal and spatial patterns of stops from 1999, 2003, and 2006. The authors report that stop rates have increased by 500 percent since 1999, despite little change in crime rates during that time. Like the earlier Fagan and Davies (2000) study, Fagan and colleagues also find that stop activity is greatest in poor and minority communities, and that stop patterns are more closely tied to demographic and social conditions than to disorder or crime. Last, the authors report that the efficiency of stops has dropped considerably (measured as "hit rates"), and again, that the sharpest declines have occurred in minority neighborhoods. The authors conclude that "the racial-spatial concentration of excess stop activity threatens to undermine police legitimacy and diminish the social good of policing, while doing little to reduce crime or disorder."

Parker and colleagues' chapter reflects all three of the persistent themes in this section. Using data from more than sixty-one thousand traffic stops in Miami-Dade County, the authors examine the impact of community-level indicators (theme #1) on police search decisions (theme #2) among traffic stops involving white, black, and Hispanic motorists (theme #3). In particular, Parker and colleagues explore the role of growth in ethnic diversity, concentrated disadvantage, and residential characteristics on search decisions by police while also controlling for other legal and extra-legal factors known to influence police behavior. They find that community-level characteristics such as concentrated disadvantage are significant predictors of increased search rates for whites and Hispanics, but not for blacks. Parker and colleagues suggest that this finding may reflect a benign-neglect argument whereby the high levels of disadvantage and isolation in black neighborhoods make these areas less threatening. Just as important, the study finds that growth in the Hispanic immigrant population does not influence search rates, while increases in foreign born residents serve to *decrease* search rates. The authors note that these findings raise interesting questions for the study of immigration and crime, requiring that researchers "move beyond traditional explanations and incorporate other race and ethnic groups in their research agendas."

The final two chapters in this section reflect the third theme, a broader view of police activities as they relate to race and potential bias. Both chapters address police use of force, though the first examines an old question and the second examines a new question. The old question involves race and police use of deadly force. The chapter by Jim Fyfe seeks to identify factors that explain the disproportionate number of black males who are victims of police shootings. Using a hazard-based typology of shootings and data from New York City and Memphis, Fyfe demonstrates that the difference in shooting rates between the two cities is explained by the greater frequency with which Memphis officers shot fleeing property crime suspects in non-life-threatening encounters. Moreover, an examination of the types of shootings by suspect race indicates that this deadly force practice disproportionately involved black suspects, leading Fyfe to conclude that "the data strongly support the assertion that police there did differentiate racially with trigger fingers, by shooting blacks in circumstances less threatening than those in which they shot whites."

The last chapter in this section, by White and Saunders, continues this line of research on police use of force, but they examine available data on race and police use of the TASER. Consistent with the methodological theme, the authors investigate six different data sources, including official police data and reports, media reports, industry data, human and civil rights data, and civil litigation. White and Saunders seek to assess the availability of data on race and the TASER, as well as to determine whether there is any indication of racial bias in use of the device. They conclude that there is a "virtual absence" of data to explore these questions, perhaps because of the larger, more pressing concerns over risk of death associated with the device. Nevertheless, White and Saunders found several news stories claiming disproportionate use against minority suspects, and they suggest that these stories "may signal that questions regarding racial bias and the TASER are on the horizon for police departments in the United States."

Chapter 11

|||||||||||||||||||||||||||||||||||||||||||||||||||||||||||||||||||||||||||||||||

Driving While Black
Bias Processes and Racial Disparity in Police Stops

Patricia Warren, Donald Tomaskovic-Devey,
William R. Smith, Matthew Zingraff,
and Marcinda Mason

Minority citizens have long suspected that their risk of a traffic stop is not proportionate to either their driving infractions or presence on our nation's roads and highways (ACLU, 1999; Weitzer and Tuch, 2002). A national survey suggests that this belief is shared by a majority of white citizens as well (Newport, 1999). Indeed, some scholars have argued that this practice is so pervasive that it should be referred to as the crime of "Driving While Black" (Gates, 1995). Media accounts (see Adams, 2000; Antonelli, 1996; Bell, 1992; Goldberg, 1999), racial profiling litigation in New Jersey and Maryland (see Lamberth, 1996), and the interim report on racial profiling completed by the New Jersey Attorney General (Verniero and Zoubek, 1999), as well as some early empirical research (Browning et al., 1994; Norris et al., 1992), all suggest that the targeting of minority motorists is quite real, at least in some police jurisdictions. Although these studies identify levels of disparity in stop and poststop outcomes, they are mostly at aggregate levels and fail to conceptualize the mechanisms, either racially biased or not, that may produce the observed race differences in stops (see the discussion in Engel, Calnon, and Bernard, 2002).

Recent research, with greater attention to and sophistication in design and measurement, generally provides evidence in support of differential enforcement of traffic laws by race (see Gaines, 2002; Lundman and Kaufman, 2003; Parker, 2001; Smith and Pettrocelli, 2001). Of these studies Lundman and Kaufman (2003) were the first to use survey data rather than police records to produce estimates of race-ethnic disparity in police vehicle stops.

Understanding the extent to which race is an important factor in criminal justice outcomes has been an issue in criminal justice research for the last 30 years. Although research has demonstrated that minority citizens are policed, searched, and arrested at much higher rates than their white counterparts, much of this research has failed to theoretically identify the reasons for the disparity. Engel and Calnon (2004) maintain that the lack of theoretical development has inhibited this research

From *Criminology* 44: 709–738. © *Criminology* 2006. Reprinted with permission of *Criminology*.

from identifying the causal mechanisms that give rise to racial disparity in criminal justice outcomes while also limiting the methodological designs. They further argue that, though the lack of theory is a problem for criminal justice research in general, it is particularly salient to the racial profiling literature, which has primarily been reactive to allegations launched against various police departments in the United States.

This research seeks to build on earlier studies, particularly the work of Lundman and Kaufman (2003). We do this by first, reporting survey based estimates of racial disparity in police stops for two types of police agencies. In doing so, we highlight the idea that racial bias is a variable product of police organization and not a constant across all police forces. Second, our estimates are based on a more extensive and appropriate set of contextual and control variables than were available to Lundman and Kaufman. For example, none of their analyses included measures of driving behaviors or factors that might make drivers more or less at risk for police stops. In our analyses, we adjust estimates of racial disparity in stops with self-reported driving behavior and status attributes of drivers and their cars, as well as unobserved driver behavior and spatial heterogeneity. Finally, we introduce a set of theoretical mechanisms that might lead to racial bias in stop decisions. Although we do not examine these mechanisms empirically, we offer them as useful guides for the design of future research. By identifying possible sources of police bias as well as employing a more targeted survey design and modeling strategy than used in past research, this study makes a strong theoretical and empirical case for the presence of racially biased policing in some organizational contexts and for weak or no racial bias in other policing contexts.

Background

Are minority drivers disproportionately targeted by police officers? Although extant research has demonstrated that minority citizens believe that they are unfairly targeted by police (Smith et al., 2003; Weitzer, 1999; Weitzer and Tuch, 1999), only recently have researchers systematically examined official police data to determine the extent to which racial profiling does exist (Langan et al., 2001; Parker, 2001; Smith et al., 2003). Findings indicate that minority citizens, particularly African Americans, are disproportionately stopped by police relative to their baseline populations (Browning et al., 1994; Lamberth, 1996; Meehan and Ponder, 2002; Smith and Pettrocelli, 2001). The magnitude of racial disparity, however, varies across studies. For example, Gaines' (2002) Riverside Police study found that blacks are 25 percent more likely than whites to be stopped. In an analysis of San Diego Police Department data, Berejarano (2001) found that African Americans in that city are 50 percent more likely to be stopped than any other drivers. Much more modestly, Smith and colleagues (2003) report that African American drivers were 17 percent more likely than white drivers to be ticketed by the North Carolina Highway Patrol. These results suggest that the degree of racial disparity can vary dramatically across jurisdictions.

Most of the recent research on race bias in police stops uses official police records to assess levels of racial disparity in stops (see the discussion in Ramirez, McDevitt, and Farrell, 2000). Official data have many advantages, including large sample sizes, accurate information on the geographic and organizational context of stops, low data collection costs to the research community, and the basic legitimacy that comes from official records. However, there are several shortcomings to using official police reports. First, no information on driver behavior is available other than police records of what precipitated the stop. Second, no comparison can be made between those who are stopped and those who are not. Third, drivers who receive verbal warnings are often not captured in official records. Fourth, official data can potentially be biased if officers falsify or incompletely record traffic stop information (Donohue, 2000; Smith et al., 2003; Verniero and Zoubuck, 1999).

Surveys offer an alternative to official records. They allow for data that are unlikely to be available in official reports to be collected and analyzed. For example, we use information about self-reported driving behavior and past vehicle stops to statistically control for law-breaking behavior when predicting the probability of a stop. Finally, in situations where police organizations resist collecting race-ethnic identifiers in official stop records, surveys may be the only source of data on potential racial disparity in police stops.

Lundman and Kaufman (2003) were among the first researchers to use the *Contacts between Police and the Public* component of the 1999 National Crime Victimization Survey to estimate models of racial disparity in self-reported police vehicle stops. Their models adjust for sample selection in the probability of driving, social class, city size, and age. Net of these statistical adjustments, they find that African Americans, Latinos, and males are more likely to report being stopped by the police. African Americans and Latinos are also less likely to report being stopped for a legitimate reason. Last, African American and Latino drivers are both more likely to report being treated improperly by the police.

There are, of course, nonbias mechanisms that may also produce the appearance of racial disparity in stops. These would include race differences in driving behavior, race differences in the number of miles driven, police patrolling patterns only coincidentally associated with the race distribution of drivers, and other bases for police stop discretion that may be associated with race, such as class, gender, or age. Racial differences in driving behavior and driving location may be important nonbias mechanisms that produce observed disparities in police stop patterns (see Engel and Calnon, 2004). For example, Smith and his colleagues (2003) argue that there are fairly large racial and ethnic differences in driving patterns that reflect differences in driving locations. Because in most regions of the country, African American and white citizens live in segregated neighborhoods and work in different organizations, the racial composition of drivers will be highly variable. Because police do not patrol streets randomly or proportional to citizen populations, police stops may simply reflect the racial compositions of the roads police patrol.

The 1995 Nationwide Transportation Survey found that African American and white drivers on average do have different driving patterns. For example, African American drivers are significantly more likely to travel during the late-night hours. Therefore, significantly increased night patrolling or police stops may contribute to racial disparities in stops and citations. In North Carolina, the highway patrol reports more aggressive patrolling of areas and highway segments that have higher incidences of accidents, and African American drivers are more likely to drive through these areas, primarily because the roads run through the parts of the state with higher minority populations (Smith et al., 2003).

In this study we model nonbias mechanisms that might produce racial disparities in stops. We include measures of self-reported driving behavior, previous driving convictions (to control for unobserved driver lawbreaking behavior), and a control for spatial variation in police stop intensity. Thus, our statistical models are clear improvements over previous research. We expect our models to have lower specification error, and thus expect to have more trustworthy estimates of the race gap. We now turn to a discussion of the mechanisms that might produce racial bias.[1]

Racial Profiling

Profiling refers to police organizations' creating and acting on a set of characteristics, which can include race, used to describe a typical offender or offending population (Harris, 2002). The policing literature has identified two types of racial profiling as potential organizational practices: the use of race in drug interdiction profiles and out-of-place profiling (Smith et al., 2003). The first became widespread in the United States during the 1990s, when it was developed and disseminated to state police forces by the U.S. Department of Justice (Harris, 2002). By 1998 more than 25,000 police officers from forty-eight states were trained to use drug courier profiles that either implicitly or explicitly encouraged the targeting of race and ethnicity, which singled out cars to be stopped and subsequently searched for drugs (ACLU, 1999; Allen-Bell, 1997).

During the 1990s, the Department of Justice maintained that using race as part of an explicit profile produced more efficient crime control than did random stops (Engel, Calnon, and Bernard, 2002). Opponents to this policy have challenged the use of racial profiles, arguing that using race as a signal for making pretextual stops (those with some legal pretext, such as an illegal lane change) leads to a disproportionate number of minority drivers being stopped and searched. Research suggests, however, that increasing the number of stops and searches among minority citizens has not led to more drug seizures than traffic stops and searches among white drivers (Antonelli, 1996; Kociewiewski, 2002; Lamberth, 1996). Therefore, racial profiling has really become a tool for criminalizing certain segments of the population.

The second type of racial profiling is termed *out-of-place* profiling (Fagan, Dumanovsky, and Gelman, 1999). Minorities traveling through white—particularly white upper-class—neighborhoods are at increased risk of being stopped by the police. Because their race does not match the typical race of the neighborhood, police assume that they are not residents. Meehan and Ponder (2002) show a clear pattern of increased police investigation and stops of minority drivers in predominately white and more well-to-do neighborhoods. Thus minorities who are out of place are viewed as symbols of danger in majority communities.

Racial profiling is unlikely, for two reasons, to be a mechanism in the initiation of a routine speeding stop by a highway patrol officer. One, it is often difficult to identify the race of the driver when cars are traveling at fairly high speeds. Two, stops are typically initiated by speed detector technologies (Smith et al., 2003). This is particularly salient because if highway patrol officers are unable to identify the race of the driver before the stop, to the extent that racial disparity actually exists, the magnitude of the disparity is likely to be underestimated. If racial profiling is likely to exist within this organization, it is therefore likely to operate during the citizen-officer interaction after the stop has been made.

Deployment

Police are seldom deployed evenly across communities. Police administrators are well aware that the majority of crimes occur in or around certain "hot spots" (Sherman, Gartin, and Buerger, 1989). Such areas thus tend to receive a disproportionate share of police attention. In addition to differences in deployment across communities, policing styles also vary across communities. Policing tends to be more proactive and aggressive in areas with higher crime rates (Smith, Visher, and Davidson, 1984; Weitzer, 1999).

Because crime rates tend to be higher in lower-class communities where African Americans disproportionately reside, these communities are more likely to be subjected to aggressive policing (Krivo and Peterson, 1996; Peeples and Loeber, 1994). Because of this, the people who live in these communities are often subjected to higher levels of police suspicion, stops, interrogations, and searches (Groves, 1968; Smith, Visher, and Davidson, 1984). In addition, some research suggests that police are more likely to threaten or to actually use force in poor and minority areas than in other neighborhoods (Smith, 1986; Smith and Visher, 1981; Smith, Visher, and Davidson, 1984).

Although higher police deployment in minority neighborhoods is not necessarily a result of a racial bias process, it may produce an unintentional race bias in police vehicle stops because of the heightened activity in these neighborhoods. Deployment patterns are thus potentially biased in that they increase the odds of minority stops relative to stops of white drivers for reasons unrelated to race difference in traffic law violation behavior.

Cognitive Bias and Stereotyping

Cognitive bias is a third mechanism that might produce a disproportionate number of stops among minority drivers. Social cognition theorists suggest that the primary way people simplify and manage complex flows of information is by reducing it into social categories (Allport, 1954; Bodenhausen, 1990; Hamilton and Trolier, 1986). People tend to categorize themselves and others into groups automatically (Bower and Karlin, 1974; McArthur and Baron, 1983). When we lack unique identifying information about people, we tend to focus on obvious status characteristics such as sex, race, or age (Brewer, 1988). Once people are categorized, racial (and other) stereo-types automatically and often unconsciously become activated and influence behav-ior (Bargh, Chen, and Burrows, 1996; Devine, 1989).

When patrolling, police officers often must quickly process large amounts of infor-mation with few unique descriptors. They observe people doing many things in a va-riety of dynamic settings. Assuming police officers process information the same way other people do, racial categorization and the associated stereotypes of dangerousness and criminality may influence their determination of who seems suspicious or other-wise worthy of special attention. Therefore, when an officer is making discretionary decisions about who to pull over and who to cite, cognitive bias processes may make the misbehavior observed seem slightly more suspicious or dangerous when a car is driven by a minority citizen. Although we have focused on race, the cognitive bias mechanism can be extended to any status characteristic (for example, young, male, lower-class) that might invoke a stereotype of dangerousness.

Kennedy (1997) suggests that the symbol of dangerousness that is often attributed to minorities increases police surveillance of them. It seems likely that this symbol might play out in all types of police encounters, but will be particularly heightened in circumstances in which minority citizens appear to be out of place (see also Skol-nick, 1966). In their observational study of police, Alpert, MacDonald, and Dunham (2005) found that police are more likely to be suspicious of minority citizens. They suggest that this suspicion is a reflection of the cognitive schemas that categorize mi-nority citizens as criminal or dangerous.

Prejudice and Racial Animus

Prejudice and racial animus refer to active racism. Conscious racial prejudice or active dislike of minorities can encourage individual actors to discriminate. In dis-cussions of police bias, this is often referred to as the search for bad apples. We sus-pect that most police forces formally proscribe active racist behavior, so the actual expression of racist tastes in police stops or search decisions should be rarer than the incidence of racial prejudice or animus among officers. We anticipate this because opinion research in general has shown that racial animus has significantly decreased in the United States across the last 40 years. For example, 10 percent of white re-spondents in the 1996 General Social Survey (GSS) reported the belief that racial differences in jobs, income, and housing arise "because most minorities have less in-born ability to learn" down from 26 percent in 1972 (Schuman, Steeh, and Bobo, 1997: 159).

It is possible, of course, for some organizations to have more bad apples than oth-ers. This might be the case if recruitment or training processes encourage the devel-opment or expression of racial animus (Kappeler, Sluder, and Alpert, 1998). It might also be expected if the prohibition of racist behavior was not or was only symboli-cally enforced in a particular police agency.

The distinction between racial prejudice and cognitive bias mechanisms is poten-tially arbitrary. We view the central difference between them as whether the officer is self-consciously discriminating on the basis of race or unconsciously processing information (as described by cognitive bias theory).

These four bias mechanisms point to different police contexts or actors producing racially biased police stops. Racial profiling should produce racial disparity in police stops when a police organization uses an explicit profile.[2] The literature points to drug interdiction and out-of-place neighborhood stops as the most likely organizational practices to employ the racial profiling mechanism. Deployment is most likely associated with more intensive policing of minority or high-crime neighborhoods. Cognitive bias is likely to be widespread across officers, but is most influential when officers lack individuating information and must quickly process high volumes of information. Finally, racial prejudice is a likely mechanism when officers are actively biased and work in a management context that tolerates acting on such prejudices.

We do not presume to know how widespread these mechanisms are across and within the many police organizations that patrol U.S. neighborhoods and highways. It seems likely that cognitive bias would be the most widespread but also the weakest, given that it is largely unconscious. The other three seem more likely to be found in specific kinds of organizational settings. For example, if a police force did not routinely search cars for drugs, patrol neighborhoods, or tolerate active racial prejudice we might expect low levels of racial disparity in vehicle stops, reflecting only the cognitive bias mechanism. On the other hand, if a police force did more of the work associated with these four bias mechanisms we might expect higher rates of racial disparity in police stops.

Although the mechanisms articulated here are not empirically observed in the analyses that follow, we do observe differences in the magnitude of stops and the processes that generate them in two different organizational contexts. Therefore, this research will answer three questions. Is there racial disparity in police stops in North Carolina? Do differences in nonbias mechanisms account for the variation in the number of police stops reported by African Americans and whites? Does the disparity vary across policing organizations?

Data and Methods

The data for this project are taken from the North Carolina Highway Traffic Study's (NCHTS) driver survey. Data were collected between June 22, 2000 and March 20, 2001 in a telephone survey of a weighted stratified random sample of 2,920 North Carolina licensed drivers. The sample was stratified by race in order to have sufficient sample sizes to compare the experiences of white and African American drivers. The sampling frame included only those drivers who had applied for or renewed their licenses in the previous six months.[3] Table 11.1 presents comparisons of our final sample to the actual race-gender-age distribution of licensed drivers in North Carolina and shows that our final sample is a very good match to the state distributions. For all four race-gender groups, young adults between the ages of 30 and 39

TABLE 11.1
*Age, Gender, and Racial Distribution of Survey Respondents and
North Carolina Licensed Drivers*

| | African American Drivers | | White Drivers | |
Gender-Age	Survey Percent	DMV Percent	Survey Percent	DMV Percent
Males 18–29	12.4	13.3	9.3	10.2
Males 30–39	9.4	11.8	8.7	10.7
Males 40–49	11.5	10.3	10.9	10.2
Males 50–59	7.2	6.2	9.1	8.1
Males 60+	6.6	6.0	10.4	10.3
Females 18–29	14.3	13.5	10.2	9.8
Females 30–39	8.6	12.6	9.1	10.4
Females 40–49	13.7	11.5	11.8	10.2
Females 50–59	8.2	7.1	8.9	8.3
Females 60+	9.3	7.6	11.9	11.6

are somewhat underrepresented. In the descriptive table we weight the data to correspond to the North Carolina Division of Motor Vehicles known race, gender, and age distributions of licensed drivers within the two race strata. The multivariate analyses are not weighted because the respondents' race, age, and gender are all included in our models.

We were concerned about potential reporting errors in response to our questions about police stops because being stopped by the police for speeding or any other violation is potentially embarrassing for some people. It is well known in survey research that respondents tend to underreport embarrassing behaviors (Tomaskovic-Devey et al., 2006; Turner, 1987). We conducted a separate record check survey of almost 600 drivers with known speeding stops in the last year to ascertain the degree of underreporting of stops we could expect in the larger driver survey. This revealed that 76.7 percent of whites and 70.8 percent of African Americans admitted to having been stopped in the last year.

These results suggest that in the larger driver survey quite a few respondents claimed not to have been stopped, but in fact were. And, though both groups underreport traffic stops for speeding, African Americans do so at a slightly higher rate. Thus, blacks have lower validity on reporting law violating behavior than white respondents because of their greater tendency to respond in socially acceptable ways. Accordingly, the North Carolina survey data will underestimate the number of stops for both blacks and whites, and slightly underestimate the magnitude of the racial disparity.

Organizational and Spatial Context

In this study the survey data are reported from the point of view of the driver who has been stopped, not the officer who makes the stop decision. We know from the data the residence location of the respondents as well as whether they were stopped by the North Carolina State Highway Patrol (NCSHP) or by local police. We make use of this spatial information and the distinction between the NCSHP and local police to inform our data analyses.

Officers of the NCSHP are primarily responsible for traffic safety. The vast majority of their work is stopping cars that violate traffic laws and responding to traffic accidents. The NCSHP does not do the type of routine law enforcement traditionally associated with local police, such as neighborhood patrolling and routine calls for service. In general, the NCSHP does not routinely patrol highways and roads within the jurisdictions of municipal police (see discussion in Smith et al., 2003). Although some evidence indicates that the NCSHP may have used racial profiling in its drug interdiction strategy in the mid 1990s, it is clear that by the survey year this practice had eroded considerably and that the vast majority of officers never searched a single car (Smith et al., 2003). We know that the NCSHP is deployed more heavily in parts of the state with higher African American populations. We control for this spatial source of race differences in stops in our statistical models.

Measurement and Descriptive Analyses

Dependent Variable

We measure the number of stops in the last year by asking the respondent about up to three stops that occurred in the past year. Respondents were then asked to report whether they were stopped by a state trooper, county sheriff, or local police officer. We focus on two dependent variables—stops by state troopers and stops by the local police.[4] Although we could make distinctions between county sheriff and local police officers, we did not feel confident that we had enough organizational information to make a clear distinction in the type of police work these two kinds of officers routinely engage in. Thus we decided to analyze local police as a heterogeneous group. In contrast to the highway patrol, local police forces typically have both crime control and investigative responsibility, in addition to traffic patrol responsibilities.

Descriptive Analyses

Table 11.2 reports the gender-specific race-age distribution of stops from the North Carolina driver survey for African American and white drivers. The data are weighted to correspond to the 2000 North Carolina DMV race-age-gender distributions. We use the age categories to highlight the experiences of younger drivers or those who the police might place under greater scrutiny. We were specifically interested in examining whether stop disparity was limited to certain status characteristics, such as young black male. In general, we find that race matters, regardless of the age category.

The top panel describes the stop experiences of male drivers. Young men report more stops than older drivers, and African American males tend to be stopped more

TABLE 11.2
Race, Age, and Gender Distribution of the Number of Stops in North Carolina

	18–22			23–49			50+		
	AA	White	Odds Ratio	AA	White	Odds Ratio	AA	White	Odds Ratio
Males									
Mean Stops	1.24	.68		.51	.33		.26	.17	
(S.D.)	(2.41)	(1.41)		(9.95)	(.79)		(.59)	(.61)	
Any Stop	42.10%	32.10%	1.31	32.60%	24.00%	1.36	18.80%	12.50%	1.50
Local Officer Stop	35.10%	25.90%	1.36	23.40%	14.90%	1.57	13.3%	7.00%	1.90
Highway Patrol Stop	17.00%	15.50%	1.10	13.80%	10.40%	1.33	6.00%	5.90%	1.02
Sample Size	101	80		401	385		170	271	
Females									
Mean Stops	.40	.31		.33	.23		.26	.09	
(S.D.)	(.63)	(.60)		(.87)	(.51)		(1.10)	(.30)	
Any Stop	32.70%	25.90%	1.26	24.60%	19.20%	1.28	13.20%	8.20%	1.61
Local Officer Stop	22.20%	16.00%	1.39	16.80%	11.90%	1.41	9.60%	3.70%	2.60
Highway Patrol Stop	10.20%	12.30%	.83	8.80%	8.40%	1.05	4.50%	4.10%	1.10
Sample Size	97	81		418	370		198	294	

often than white drivers. Young African American male drivers report an average of 1.24 stops in the past year, almost twice as many as their white counterparts (.68). The majority of racial disparity in stops among male drivers is attributable to local police. Highway patrol stops of young African American male drivers (17 percent) and young white male drivers (15.5 percent) are very similar. This pattern holds up for older male drivers as well. In all cases there are racial disparities in stops, but these are much larger for the local police than for the NCSHP. The absolute probability of being stopped drops for both black and white males as they age.

The bottom panel of table 11.2 displays race differences in stop experiences among women. Women, both African American and white, tend to be stopped less often than men at all ages. Black women between the ages of 18 and 22 report about a third as many stops as black men within the same age range. Young white women report about half as many stops as young white men. Among women, police stop experiences decrease with age. Similar to the results found among men, the racial disparity in stops is larger among the local police than among the NCSHP. In fact, young white women report slightly more stops by the highway patrol than their African American counterparts do. Although older black women report relatively more stops by the highway patrol than older white women do, the race disparity is very small.

Table 11.3 reports race comparisons in stops, driving behaviors, and demographic background, again weighted to correspond to the 2000 age-gender-race distribution of North Carolina drivers. In panel 1 we further examine stop experiences. Approximately 22 percent of the sample reported a stop in the last year. The local police have a higher mean number of stops (.19) relative to the NCSHP (.11). More than a quarter (26.4 percent) of African American drivers reported a stop in the last year. Only 18.1 percent of whites reported a stop in the last year. Blacks also report 4 percent more stops per year of driving than white drivers.

TABLE 11.3
Race Differences in Stops, Driving Behavior, and Demographic Background (N = 2,830)

	Total Population (S.D)	African American (S.D)	White (S.D)	Significant Difference?
Stop Events				
Any Stop in Last Year	22.0%	26.40%	18.10%	Yes
Number of Stops by Local Police in Last Year	.19	.25	.13	Yes
Number of Stops by Highway Patrol in Last Year	.11	.12	.10	No
Prior Lifetime Stops/Years of Driving	.25 (.48)	.27 (.54)	.23 (.44)	Yes
Driving Behaviors				
Driving Ten MPH over the Speed Limit	7.30%	7.40%	6.70%	No
(LN) Miles Driven Last Year	1.93 (1.49)	1.54 (1.63)	2.23 (1.25)	Yes
Frequency of Interstate Travel				
No Interstate Travel	4.70%	6.90%	3.00%	Yes
Once or Twice a Year	11.70%	14.30%	9.40%	Yes
Every Few Months	9.80%	9.80%	9.80%	No
Few Times per Month	18.80%	17.90%	19.80%	No
Once per Week	10.90%	8.20%	13.10%	Yes
Few Times per week	19.90%	18.40%	21.40%	Yes
Every Day	24.20%	24.50%	23.50%	No
Risky Driving Behavior				
Speeding	7.30%	8.0%	6.80%	No
Does Not Wear Seatbelt	9.30%	8.0%	11.00%	Yes
Does Not Signal before Changing Lanes/Turning	21.60%	15.0%	28.00%	Yes
Frequently Changes Lanes to Drive Faster	44.00%	44.2%	44.90%	No
Frequently Passes Slow Drivers	24.00%	25.4%	23.00%	No
Frequently Rolls through Stop Signs	29.40%	24.0%	34.00%	Yes
Frequently Drives through Yellow Light	57.00%	52.0%	62.00%	Yes
Frequency of Methods Used to Avoid Speeding Tickets	3.64 (.39)	3.67 (.94)	3.77 (1.02)	Yes
Demographic Background				
Gender				
Male	49.00%	48.00%	51.00%	—
Female	51.00%	52.00%	49.00%	—
Age	43 (15.70)	41 (15.30)	45 (15.80)	Yes
Education	3.91 (1.92)	3.67 (1.85)	4.14 (1.94)	No
Residence				
City	42.00%	52.10%	33.80%	Yes
Suburb	18.00%	17.00%	18.00%	No
Town	10.00%	8.20%	12.30%	Yes
Country	30.00%	23.00%	36.00%	Yes
Model Year of Car Typically Driven	94 (5.19)	93.02 (5.35)	94.01 (5.01)	Yes

Explanatory Variables

RISKY DRIVING BEHAVIORS

Respondents were asked to report characteristics of their driving behavior. They were specifically asked to report whether they engage in risky driving behaviors such as frequently changing lanes to drive faster, frequently changing lanes to pass slower drivers, failing to wear seatbelts, speeding (10 miles per hour over the speed limit), failing to signal before changing lanes or turning, rolling through stop signs, and driving through yellow lights. As can be seen in table 11.3, African Americans are slightly more likely to report driving 10 miles per hour above the speed limit and frequently passing slow drivers. The differences, however, are not statistically significant.

White drivers, on the other hand, are significantly more likely to report failing to wear seatbelts, failing to signal before changing lanes, frequently rolling through stop signs, and frequently driving through yellow lights.

MILES DRIVEN

We also asked respondents to estimate the number of miles driven in the last year as well as how frequently they drive on the interstate. It seems reasonable to expect that people who drive more frequently are at greater risk of being stopped by the police. Miles driven, however, cannot explain the race gap in stops in North Carolina because white drivers report driving more miles per year.[5] In the multivariate analyses that follow, the log transformation of this variable is used.

INTERSTATE FREQUENCY

We measured where respondents typically drive to see whether they have higher baseline exposure to the local police or to the NCSHP. Interstate frequency is coded as 7 = every day, 6 = few times a week, 5 = once a week, 4 = few times a month, 3 = every few months, 2 = once or twice a year, and 1 = don't drive on interstates. In general, whites are significantly more likely than blacks to drive on interstate highways, thus increasing their exposure to the NCSHP. Correspondingly, blacks probably have a higher baseline exposure to local police because a higher proportion of their driving is not on the interstate. To maximize potential explanatory power, dummy variables were created for each category, with driving on the highway every day as the reference category.

METHODS TO AVOID SPEEDING TICKETS

We asked respondents to report how often they use cruise control, use a radar detector, listen to a citizens band radio, and watch and follow trucks to avoid being stopped by the police. The response categories are 1 = don't use, 2 = occasionally, 3 = often, 4 = all the time. None of these methods are used frequently, although many people reported using at least one method. For example, drivers who use radar detectors might be less likely to use a citizens band radio to avoid police attention. We created an additive scale with these items and then divided by the number 4 to maintain the variables original metric. White drivers (3.77) report using methods to avoid a police stop more often than black drivers (3.67). If these methods reduce the risk of being stopped they may also account for some of the race disparity in police stops observed in these data.

AVERAGE LIFETIME STOPS

The average lifetime stops variable is used to account for otherwise unobserved individual heterogeneity in the probability of being stopped by the police. It was created by dividing the total number of stops across the respondent's driving career by total driving years. We reason that drivers who have received more tickets in the past are more likely to be stopped by the police in the future. This variable is treated as a control for unobserved driver differences in law violation. Because this approach also controls for prior differences in racially biased police stops, it is a conservative approach to the estimation of contemporary racial disparity in police stops. As we have already seen in the top panel of table 11.3, African Americans have significantly higher rates of self-reported stops per year of driving.

DEMOGRAPHIC CHARACTERISTICS

In addition to race, we observed age, gender, educational attainment, whether the respondent lives in a city, in a suburb, in a town, or in the country, and the model year of the car most often driven. The race variable is coded as 0 = white or 1 = African American. Age is measured in years and gender is coded as 0 = male or 1 = female. Respondents were also asked their educational attainment, which represents a crude measure of social class. Responses were coded as 1 = some high school to 7 = graduate school or degree. Respondents also reported the model year of the car they most often drive, which is coded in years. Last, we asked respondents to report whether they live in a 1 = city, 2 = suburb, 3 = town, or 4 = country. Dummy variables were created for place of residence, with living in the city as the reference category.

Panel 3 of table 11.3 compares the demographic backgrounds of African American and white drivers. The differences are substantial. African Americans are on average younger, more likely to live in the city, and more likely to drive slightly older cars. They are also less educated and more apt to report speeding, though these differences are not significant.

These demographic differences are potentially important explanations of the racial disparity in police stops. The public concern on this issue implies that police discretion coupled with police reaction to driver attributes combine to produce racial bias in the pattern of stops. If this is a reasonable model of the causal process, then we would expect that other status attributes associated with police perceptions of driver risk or dangerousness will also be associated with the decision to stop. In particular, we would expect that male, younger, and poorer drivers are more likely to be stopped. We use the age of car as an indicator of economic disadvantage, because of its visibility to the police.

Overall, the comparisons in table 11.3 suggest that in North Carolina blacks report driving fewer miles than white drivers. Whites, on the other hand, report using more methods to avoid being pulled over by the police. Because white drivers also report driving more frequently and have significantly higher reports of driving through stop signs, controlling for driving behavior is likely to increase the estimated size of the race gap in stops in the multivariate models. On the other hand, African American drivers are younger, more likely to be male, and more likely to drive older cars. Each of these attributes might also explain some of the higher African American probability of police stops presented in tables 11.2 and 11.3.

Modeling Stops in a Multivariate Context

Although the vast majority of drivers in this study who reported being stopped were pulled over only once in the previous year, some respondents reported up to three stops. Because of this, we use negative binomial regression to predict the number of stops. To ensure that this is the most appropriate statistical tool for our study, we tested the models for overdispersion, which tests the hypothesis that the mean dispersion parameter is equal to zero (H_0: $K=0$) against the alternative hypothesis that the mean dispersion parameter is greater than zero (H_a: $K>0$). In all the models presented here we can reject the null hypothesis, which assumes the variance and the mean are equal ($K=0$). Negative binomial regression, then, is indeed the preferred approach for these data. In the tables that follow we display exponential coefficients. The models were estimated using only cases with no missing values. There is very little missing data in this survey. We dropped approximately ninety cases, less than 4 percent of the original sample. To ensure that dropping the missing cases introduced no bias, we estimated models that included all cases. We then compared the coefficients to those presented in tables 11.4 and 11.5. The coefficients did not significantly change, suggesting that sample selection bias is not a problem in these data. The sample size for the multivariate analyses is 2,830.

The logic of the analysis is to establish the size of racial disparity in stops, net of a series of demographic and behavioral control variables. We begin with a model that includes, along with the heterogeneity measure, race and other status characteristics that might be associated with police stops. Because indicators of driving behavior may contain measurement error and have limited coverage, these models are open to the threat of unobserved heterogeneity in the propensity of police to make a legitimate stop. We use a report of lifetime stops before the study year, divided by total years of driving experience, to account for otherwise unmeasured individual heterogeneity in the probability of being stopped. We believe this is a strong, even conservative, control against omitted variable bias.[6] We include this control in model 1 to produce a more accurate estimate of race and other status differences in the number of stops in the last year, net of previous stops.

In the second model we include self-reported driving behaviors. To the extent that they influence police stop decisions they should be significantly associated with stop outcomes. In addition, if status characteristics are simply associated with different driving behaviors, the most important nonbias mechanism for eliciting a police stop, adding driving behaviors to the models should erode the coefficients associated with demographic status characteristics. Significant coefficients after adjusting for driving behavior and prior stops suggests that police may be reacting to drivers' status characteristics rather than their typical driving behavior. All analyses are repeated for stops by the local police and by the NCSHP.

We see two additional sources of omitted variable bias—variation in police organizational practice and community context. Substantial variation in organizational practices across various local police forces is likely. Drug interdiction and neighborhood policing are likely to be more prevalent in some communities than others. We have no way to know which local police forces are more likely to use any of these spatially linked mechanisms. We are, however, fairly confident that as a function of the work they do, the NCSHP is not being deployed to intensively police minority neighborhoods, though they are more likely to be deployed to highways where African Americans are more likely to drive (see discussion in Smith et al., 2003). Variation in police patrolling can also have a significant impact on racial disparity in stops.

For example, the state police in North Carolina patrol Interstate 95 more intensively than Interstate 40 because I-95 is less safe and more accidents occur on it. There are more African Americans traveling along I-95 than along I-40, reflecting their higher population densities along the East Coast (Smith et al., 2003).

We use fixed effects models of spatial heterogeneity to investigate the degree to which organizational and spatial variation in police functions or management orientation might produce observed racial disparities in the number of vehicle stops. We suspect that police practices might vary with community racial norms, the type of neighborhood, the degree of professionalization of the police force, and the intensity of policing. All of these are tied to a geographical or community context. We use a community context fixed effect to control for such processes. This is equivalent to entering a dummy variable for each community context and estimating within-place models of racial disparity. This provides a strong test of the generality of the processes being modeled and essentially limits our focus to race disparity in the number of police stops within places. This essentially controls for any unmeasured between-place spatial correlates of police practice, such as the more intensive policing of I-95 than of I-40.

Unfortunately, we do not know the precise locations of the reported stops. We use the residence of the driver as a proxy under the assumption that most stops, like most driving, occur fairly close to home. Smith and colleagues (2003) maintain that where people drive is closely related to the locations of their residence and their likely destination (such as workplace or stores). Thus we use place of residence as a proxy for stop location. For the NCSHP we used the fifty-three multicounty districts in which the officers work as the community units within which we modeled fixed effects. This is a good match to the real organizational variation in police activity within this state-level police force. If race disparity is reduced in a fixed effect context, it suggests that some spatial variation in the level of highway patrol activity is associated with the race composition of localities.

We use county as the community context for the local police analyses. Although this is a good match to the actual patrol areas for the county sheriff, it is not for the numerous city and town police forces, because they typically patrol much smaller geographical units. Thus the fixed effect strategy is not as strong a modeling strategy for the local police analyses as for the highway patrol. Sample size limitations preclude use of any smaller geographical distinction.

Multivariate Analyses

Table 11.4 displays the multivariate analyses of local police stops. In it, we first assess the extent to which being African American and having certain other status characteristics increases or decreases the number of stops by the local police. In model 1, African Americans (1.69) and those with more education report more stops by local police. The education result is unexpected, because education is not a status characteristic typically visible to police. Women, older respondents, and those driving newer cars all report fewer stops. These findings are similar to those of Lundman and

TABLE 11.4
Negative Binomial Regression Models of Total Stops by the Local Police [a]
(N = 2,830)

	Model 1	Model 2	Model 3
Race (1 = AA)	1.686***	1.775***	1.701***
Gender (1 = Female)	.758**	.808	.803*
Education	1.084**	1.073*	1.057
Age	.979***	.979***	.978***
Model Year of Car	.974**	.975**	.969**
Suburb	.933	.877	.852
Town	.787	.811	.848
Country	.902	.903	1.019
Speeding		1.084	1.106
Seatbelt		1.120	1.135
Signal		1.035	1.105
Change Lanes		.790*	.861
Passing		.870	.814
Roll through Stop Sign		1.063	1.04
Drive through Yellow Light		1.309**	1.341*
Log of Miles Driven in Last Year		1.042	1.045
Methods to Avoid Ticket		.932	1.040
Never Drive on Interstate		1.363	1.153
Drive on Interstate Once or Twice a Year		.793	.719
Drive on Interstate Every Few Months		.976	.876
Drive on Interstate a Few Times/Month		.615**	.607*
Drive on Interstate Once a Week		.825	.781
Drive on Interstate a Few Times/Week		.976	.951
Lifetime Stops (Heterogeneity)	1.656***	1.588**	1.464***
Chi-Square	212.34***	229.81***	253.78***
Log-Likelihood	−1276.243	−1215.154	−1041.580

[a] The estimates are presented as exponentiated coefficients.
* $p \leq .05$.
** $p \leq .01$.
*** $p \leq .001$.

Kaufman (2003). In that analysis, minority drivers consistently reported more police stops and older and female drivers reported fewer.

Model 2 includes the respondent's self-reported driving behaviors. The race coefficient compared to model 1, increases in this model. African American drivers, those who report more years of education, younger drivers, drivers of older cars and drivers who drive through yellow lights report more stops by the local police. Having more lifetime stops also significantly increases stops by the local police. However, drivers who frequently change lanes and drive on the interstate a few times per month report fewer stops by the local police.

Model 3 is the fixed effect model. If a neighborhood or community-level process produces the observed race disparity in earlier models, the effect should significantly decrease in the fixed effect model. To the extent that it does not suggests that the processes that produce racial disparity in police stops are more generic across places. In model 3, the race coefficient drops from 1.77 to 1.70. Thus very little of the observed racial disparity in the number of local police stops can be attributed to between-county variation in the intensity of policing. The vast majority of race disparities in local police stops happen within the county units we are using to model spatial heterogeneity. The likelihood ratio for the model declines dramatically in model 3 relative to model 1, suggesting substantial variation across counties in the

TABLE 11.5
Negative Binomial Regression Models of Total Stops by the NCSHP[a] (N = 2,830)

	Model 1	Model 2	Model 3 Fixed Effect
Race (1 = AA)	1.173	1.456**	1.306
Gender (1 = Female)	.778	1.020	.986
Education	1.058	1.032	1.042
Age	.980***	.986**	.987**
Model Year of Car	.999	.986	.989
Suburb	1.279	1.117	1.028
Town	.892	.775	.816
Country	1.275	1.204	1.058
Speeding		1.280	1.233
Seatbelt		1.432*	1.190
Signal		1.166	1.159
Change Lanes		1.256	1.276
Passing		.818	.893
Roll through Stop Sign		1.146	1.113
Drive through Yellow Light		1.159	1.230
Log of Miles Driven in Last Year		1.271***	1.251***
Methods to Avoid Ticket		.584***	.631**
Never Drive on Interstate		1.267	1.056
Drive on Interstate Once or Twice a Year		1.494	1.057
Drive on Interstate Every Few Months		1.760*	1.082
Drive on Interstate a Few Times/Month		1.214	.872
Drive on Interstate Once a Week		1.231	1.096
Drive on Interstate a Few Times/Week		1.134	1.018
Lifetime Stops (Heterogeneity)	1.769***	1.571***	1.607***
Chi-Square	108.44***	172.84***	184.20***
Log-Likelihood	−887.809	−824.634	−666.901

[a] The estimates are presented as the exponentiated coefficients.
* $p \leq .05$.
** $p < .01$.
*** $p \leq .001$.

probability of a local police stop. It is only weakly associated with the race compositions of counties.

Table 11.5 reports our analyses of NCSHP stops. In model 1, younger drivers as well as those with more lifetime stops report more stops by the NCSHP. Race is not a significant predictor. After controlling for self-reported driving behavior in model 2, race becomes significantly associated with stops by the highway patrol. Younger drivers, those who fail to wear their seatbelts, those who have driven more miles in the last year report more stops. Respondents who report driving on the interstate every few months as well as those with more lifetime stops, also report significantly more stops by the highway patrol. Drivers who frequently use methods to avoid a speeding ticket report fewer stops.

Model 3 estimates racial disparity in highway patrol stops using a fixed effect for the fifty-three organizational units within the NCSHP. The race coefficient declines slightly and is no longer statistically significant. As in previous models, age is the only characteristic that significantly influences the number of highway patrol stops. Miles driven, methods to avoid a stop, and prior stops all remain significantly associated. In general, these findings suggest that when making stops the highway patrol tends to react to illegal behavior rather than to the characteristics of drivers or their cars.

The models all suggest that there is no or very little race bias in NCSHP stops. This does not mean that there are no officers in the NCSHP who are racially biased in their stop decisions, but that the average officer is not. In addition, because we do not observe treatment after a stop, it might be that race disparity in how drivers are treated occurs after the stop. It might take the form of differences in officer demeanor, ticketing, or search behavior. This point is particularly important because on the highway cars generally move at very high speeds, which makes detecting race difficult and might reduce the degree of racial disparity observed in stops. This observation should discourage future research from overrelying on racial disparity in stops in policing agencies like the highway patrol, and encourage it to examine racial disparity in treatment after the stop.

Summary

Overall, the estimates presented in the highway patrol and local police models are very different. Status characteristics appear to influence stop decisions made by local police. In all local police models, race, age, and age of the vehicle are significant predictors. Highway patrol officers' stop decisions, on the other hand, appear to be influenced more by driving behaviors than status characteristics. This is not to suggest that highway patrol officers never use race or other status characteristics as a cue to decide whether to stop a driver. It suggests instead simply that at least in North Carolina in 2000, they were more likely to stop a driver on the basis of driving behavior than status characteristics.

The observed race difference in NCSHP stops before adjusting for driving behaviors is so small that it would be surprising if any racial disparity were even visible to patrol officers or their superiors. In the fixed effects model, race is no longer a significant predictor of NCSHP stops. This suggests that the significant race differences in NCSHP stops are potentially a product of two weak processes: a tendency for the NCSHP to stop more cars in places with more African American drivers, and a statistically nonsignificant tendency within places to stop blacks more often than whites net of driving behavior (Smith et al., 2003).

Conclusions

This research compares stops by local police to those by the highway patrol in North Carolina in 2000. In general, we find a fairly large race disparity in local police officer stops and a very small one in highway patrol stops. We expected this, for two reasons. First is that the NCSHP generally does not do the type of routine police work traditionally associated with the local police. Second is that it is difficult for the highway patrol to identify the race of drivers because cars are moving at fairly high speeds. This is not to suggest that highway patrol officers are never racially biased in their enforcement strategies. Rather, it is to suggest that stops might not be the best mechanism for identifying such bias when it exists. Examining racial disparity in treatment after the stop might be the better approach for this policing organization. In other research we are developing, race disparity is evident in how African American and white respondents believe they are treated by NCSHP officers during a stop (see Warren and Tomaskovic-Devey, 2006) and in the late 1990s race differences in the probability a car would be searched were significant.

Our data were not ideal for isolating the distinctions between specific mechanisms that produce racial disparity in stops. We strongly suspect that study designs using official data might be particularly useful in investigating the out-of-place variant of the racial profiling mechanism and in documenting which communities are policed more intensively. Although our sampling design endeavored to represent an entire state, more geographically focused surveys might do a better job at identifying where a stop took place. In any case, once specific bias mechanisms that might produce racial disparity are identified, it becomes easier to prospectively design studies to observe the presence or absence of those mechanisms.

Generalizability issues flow from both our empirical results and our theoretical discussion. North Carolina appears to be a heavily policed state in terms of vehicle stops, at least compared to the national average. When more cars are stopped, a constant rate of racial disparity will accumulate into more minority disadvantage. Compared to Lundman and Kaufman's (2003) estimates, North Carolina may also have a higher rate of racial bias in police stops, at least among local police officers, than the national average.

We did not theorize a mechanism for racial bias in vehicle stops that might be tied to these larger regional comparisons. Given that past research is fairly clear that racial employment disparity varies across communities (Beggs, Villemex, and Arnold, 1997; Tomaskovic-Devey and Roscigno, 1996), it should be no surprise if racial bias in police stops does as well. In the employment literature the bias mechanism is typically described as racial threat derived from competition for political, social, and economic power (Blalock, 1967). It might be the case that this racial threat process exacerbates the bias mechanisms we described by heightening stereotypes, producing more active bigots, increasing police monitoring of minority neighborhoods, or heightening suspicion of minorities in white neighborhoods (Anderson, 1990; Sampson and Bartusch, 1998; Smith, 1986).

Although survey reports of police stops and driving behavior are a good potential methodology for examining the magnitude and prevalence of racial disparity in stops, the accuracy of results may be compromised if the self-reports differ by race. We conducted a reverse record check survey in which we directly assessed the degree, and consequences of, race differences in self-reports of police stops. In our sample of drivers who had been cited for speeding in the preceding year, we found that 77 percent of white and 71 percent of African American respondents admitted to being stopped. Although both groups underreported stops, more African American drivers did so, suggesting that the survey estimates will underestimate the magnitude of the racial disparity. This has important implications for this research because, given the results presented here, we suspect that the magnitude of racial disparity in police stops for both the local police and the NCSHP are potentially underestimated.

One of the main goals of this research was to provide a theoretical framework for future research that might explain why racial disparity in police stops might exist. In fact, some researchers, such as Engel and Calnon (2004), maintain that one of the major shortcomings of the racial profiling research is the lack of a clearly articulated theoretical framework. This is in part due to the absence of available data that would allow researchers to test specific mechanisms. For example, to date no data available allow researchers to empirically test the mechanisms we have identified in this study. It has also impeded the development of more sophisticated methodological designs that might further explain race disparity in stops.

Lundman and Kaufman (2003) suggest that triangulated data will significantly improve Driving While Black research. Triangulated data allows researchers to use multiple data sources that complement each other. The analysis of police stops would include self-reports of police stops, a comparison between those drivers who are stopped for traffic violations and those who break the law but whom police choose not to bother. This is an important agenda for future Driving While Black research—using multiple sources of data to isolate the extent to which the Driving While Black phenomenon exists, and assisting law enforcement agencies in understanding why such bias processes exist. We also suspect that the next step is to use explicit theory about mechanisms, such as those we proposed in this paper, to help design future studies. One of the simplest design innovations is to pay attention to the large variation across police organizations in observed racial disparity in police vehicle stops.

NOTES

1. The discussion of bias mechanisms is elaborated on and an outline of observational strategies presented in Tomaskovic-Devey, Mason, and Zingraff (2004).

2. It is possible that a single officer might use a racial profile, but this seems to us to be more indicative of active racial prejudice rather than of organizational policy.

3. Using this method we had expected to get phone numbers and addresses that were relatively current. Unfortunately, it turns out that North Carolina Department of Motor Vehicles personnel rarely ask for or record telephone numbers, nor do they require proof of home address for license renewals. Thus we had to use a telephone match based on surname and address to develop useful contact information for our sample frame. The return on the telephone match was 48.6 percent, lowest for black females at 39.0 percent and highest for white males at 62.8 percent. Cooperation rates on the survey were much better at 59.1 percent, with a high for African American females of 61.8 percent and a low for white males of 56.5 percent. The final sample closely matched the actual race-gender-age distribution of drivers.

4. This question turned out to be remarkably easy for respondents to answer. There were no missing data on the recall of police type.

5. In North Carolina, black drivers report driving approximately 32,681 miles before they are stopped by the police but whites more than twice that many (68,944).

6. It is a good control for unmeasured driver characteristics. If, because of social desirability effects, equivalent African Americans report fewer lifetime stops than whites, this control

for unmeasured heterogeneity might still be an overestimate of the racial disparity in stops. On the other hand, the practice of controlling for previous stops may also incorporate any temporally stable race bias processes that the driver has previously encountered.

REFERENCES

Adams, Jim. 2000. Study: Police stopped blacks twice as often as whites. *The Courier-Journal*, October 29, A11.

Allen-Bell, Angela. A. 1997. The birth of the crime: Driving while black (DWB). *Southern University Law Review* 25:195–225.

Allport, George. W. 1954. *The Nature of Prejudice*. Garden City, NY: Doubleday Anchor.

Alpert, Geoffrey P., John M. MacDonald, and Roger G. Dunham. 2005. Police suspicion and discretionary decision making during citizen stops. *Criminology* 34(2): 407–34.

American Civil Liberties Union (ACLU). 1999. *Driving While Black: Racial Profiling on Our Nation's Highways*. New York: American Civil Liberties Union.

Anderson, Elijah. 1990. *Street Wise: Race, Class, and Change in an Urban Community*. Chicago: University of Chicago Press.

Antonelli, Kris. 1996. Profiles lose favor in drug interdiction: Legal challenges say checklists target racial groups. *The Baltimore Sun*, December 10, 1B.

Bargh, John. A., Mark Chen, and Lara Burrows. 1996. Automaticity of social behavior: Direct effects of trait construct and stereotype activation on action. *Journal of Personality and Social Psychology* 71:230–44.

Beggs, John J., Wayne Villemex, and Ruth Arnold. 1997. Black population concentration and black-white inequality: Expanding the consideration of place and space effects. *Social Forces* 76:65–91.

Bell, Kim. 1992. Police target I-44 for drug couriers: Profile used, some lawyers say. *St. Louis Post-Dispatch*, June 7, 1A.

Berejarano, David. 2001. *Vehicle Stop Study Year End Report: 2000*. San Diego, CA: San Diego Police Department.

Blalock, Hubert M. 1967. *Toward a Theory of Minority-Group Relations*. New York: John Wiley and Sons.

Bodenhausen, Galen V. 1990. Second-guessing the jury: Stereotypic and hindsight biases in perceptions of court cases. *Journal of Applied Social Psychology* 20:1112–121.

Bower, Gordon H., and Martin B. Karlin. 1974. Depth of processing pictures of faces and recognition memory. *Journal of Experimental Psychology* 4:751–57.

Brewer, Marilyn B. 1988. A dual process model of impression formation. In *Advances in Social Cognition*, eds. Robert Wyer and Thomas Srull. Hillsdale, NJ: Lawrence Erlbaum.

Browning, Sandra Lee, Francis T. Cullen, Liquan Cao, Renee Kopache, and Thomas J. Stevenson. 1994. Race and getting hassled by the police: A research note. *Police Studies* 17:1–11.

Devine, Patricia G. 1989. Stereotypes and prejudice: Their automatic and controlled components. *Journal of Personality and Social Psychology* 56:5–18.

Donohue, Brian. 2000. 10 troopers cleared of charges as Dunbar sees profiling end. *The Star Ledger*, April 15, A1.

Engel, Robin, and Jennifer Calnon. 2004. Examining the influence of drivers' characteristics during traffic stops with police: Results from a national survey. *Justice Quarterly* 21(1): 49–90.

Engel, Robin Shepard, Jennifer M. Calnon, and Thomas J. Bernard. 2002. Theory and racial profiling: Shortcomings and future directions in research. *Justice Quarterly* 19:249–73.

Fagan, Jeffrey A., Tamara Dumanovsky, and Andrew Gelman. 1999. *Analysis of NYPD "Stop and Frisk Practices."* Albany, NY: Office of the Attorney General.

Gaines, Larry K. 2002. *An Analysis of Traffic Stop Data in the City of Riverside.* Riverside, CA: City of Riverside.

Gates, Henry Louis. 1995. Thirteen ways of looking at a black man. *New Yorker,* October 23, 59.

Goldberg, Jeffrey. 1999. The color of suspicion. *New York Times Magazine,* June 20, 50.

Groves, W. Eugene. 1968. Police in the ghetto. In *Supplemental Studies for the National Advisory Commission on Civil Disorders.* Washington, DC: U.S. Government Printing Office.

Hamilton, Dugan L., and Thomas K. Trolier. 1986. Stereotypes and stereotyping: An overview of the cognitive approach. In *Prejudice and Discrimination,* eds. John F. Dovidio and Samuel L. Gaertner. Orlando, FL: Academic Press.

Harris, David A. 2002. *Profiles of Injustice: Why Racial Profiling Cannot Work.* New York: The New Press.

Kappeler, Victor E., Richard D. Sluder, and Geoffrey P. Alpert. 1998. *Forces of Deviance: Understanding the Dark Side of Policing.* Long Grove, IL: Waveland Press.

Kennedy, Randall. 1997. *Race, Crime, and the Law.* New York: Pantheon Books.

Kociewiewski, David. 2002. Study suggests racial gap in speeding in New Jersey. *New York Times,* March 21, B1.

Krivo, Lauren, and Ruth Peterson. 1996. Extremely disadvantaged neighborhoods and urban crime. *Social Forces* 75(4): 619–48.

Lamberth, John. 1996. *A Report to the ACLU.* New York: American Civil Liberties Union.

Langan, Patrick A., Lawrence A. Greenfeld, Steven K. Smith, Matthew R. Durose, and David J. Levin. 2001. *Contacts Between Police and the Public: Findings from the 1999 National Survey.* NCJ 184957. Washington, DC: U.S. Department of Justice, Bureau of Justice Statistics.

Lundman, Richard J., and Robert L. Kaufman. 2003. Driving while black and male: Effects of race, ethnicity, and gender on citizen self-reports of traffic stops and police actions. *Criminology* 41(1): 195–220.

McArthur, Leslie Z., and Reuben Baron. 1983. Toward an ecological theory of social perception. *Psychological Review* 90:215–38.

McFadden, Robert D. 1996. Police singled out Black drivers in drug crackdown, judge says. *New York Times,* March 10, 33.

Meehan, Albert, and Michael Ponder. 2002. The ecology of racial profiling African American motorists. *Justice Quarterly* 19:399–430.

Newport, Frank. 1999. Racial profiling seen as widespread, particularly among young black men. Gallup Poll Release, December 9. Washington, DC: The Gallup Organization.

Norris, Clive, Neigel Fielding, Charles Kemp, and Jane Fielding. 1992. Black and blue: An analysis of the influence of race on being stopped by the police. *British Journal of Sociology* 43: 207–24.

Parker, Robert Nash. 2001. *Traffic Tickets, Ethnicity, and Patrol in Riverside, 1998: Evidence for Racial Profiling in Patterns of Traffic Enforcement.* Riverside, CA: The Press Enterprise.

Peeples, Faith, and Rolf Loeber. 1994. Do individual factors and neighborhood context explain ethnic differences in juvenile delinquency? *Journal of Quantitative Criminology* 10(2): 141–57.

Ramirez, Deborah, Jack McDevitt, and Amy Farrell. 2000. *A Resource Guide on Racial Profiling Data Collection Systems: Promising Practices and Lessons Learned.* NCJ 184768. Washington, DC: U.S. Department of Justice.

Sampson, Robert, and Dawn Bartusch. 1998. Legal cynicism and subcultural tolerance of deviance. *Law and Society Review* 32(4): 777–804.

Schuman, Howard, Charlotte Steeh, and Lawrence Bobo. 1997. *Racial Attitudes in America.* Cambridge, MA: Harvard University Press.

Sherman, Lawrence, Patrick Gartin, and Michael Buerger. 1989. Hot spots of predatory crime: Routine activities and the criminology of place. *Criminology* 27(1): 27–55.

Skolnick, Jerome H. 1966. *Justice Without Trial: Law Enforcement in Democratic Society.* New York: John Wiley & Sons.

Smith, Douglas A. 1986. The neighborhood context of police behavior. In *Ethnicity, Race, and Crime: Perspectives Across Time and Place*, ed. Darnell F. Hawkins. Albany: State University of New York Press.

Smith, Douglas A., and Christy A. Visher. 1981. Street-level justice: Situational determinants of police arrest decisions. *Social Problems* 29:167–77.

Smith, Douglas A., Christy A. Visher, and Laura Davidson. 1984. Equity and discretionary justice: The influence of race on police arrest decisions. *Journal of Criminal Law and Criminology* 75: 234–49.

Smith, Michael R., and Matthew Petrocelli. 2001. Racial profiling: A multivariate analysis of police traffic stop data. *Police Quarterly* 4(1): 4–27.

Smith, William R., Donald Tomaskovic-Devey, Matthew Zingraff, H. Marcinda Mason, Patricia Y. Warren, Cynthia Pfaff Wright, Harvey McMurray, and C. Robert Felon. 2003. *The North Carolina Highway Traffic Study. Final Report to the National Institute of Justice.* Washington, DC: U.S. Department of Justice.

Tomaskovic-Devey, Donald, Marcinda Mason, and Matthew Zingraff. 2004. Looking for the driving while black phenomenon: Conceptualizing racial bias processes and their associated distributions. *Police Quarterly* 7(10): 3–29.

Tomaskovic-Devey, Donald, Cynthia Pfaff-Wright, Ronald Czaja, and Kirk Miller. 2006. Self-reports of police speeding stops by race: Results from the North Carolina reverse record check survey. *Journal of Quantitative Criminology* 22(4): 279–97.

Tomaskovic-Devey, Donald, and Vincent Roscigno. 1996. Racial economic subordination and white gain in the U.S. south. *American Sociological Review* 61:565–89.

Turner, J. C. 1987. *Rediscovering the Social Group: A Self-Categorization Theory.* New York: Basil Blackwell.

Verniero, Peter, and Paul H. Zoubek. 1999. *Interim Report of the State Police Review Team Regarding Allegations of Racial Profiling.* Newark: New Jersey Office of the Attorney General.

Warren, Patricia Y., and Donald Tomaskovic-Devey. 2006. Race and trust in the police: Are belief in racial profiling and network stories the missing links? Unpublished manuscript.

Weitzer, Ronald. 1999. Citizens' perceptions of police misconduct: Race and neighborhood context. *Justice Quarterly* 16:819–46.

Weitzer, Ronald, and Steven Tuch. 1999. Race, class, and perceptions of discrimination by the police. *Crime & Delinquency* 45:494–507.

Weitzer, Ronald, and Steven Tuch. 2002. Perceptions of racial profiling: Race, class, and personal experience. *Criminology* 40(2): 435–57.

‖‖‖

Chapter 12

Citizens' Demeanor, Race, and Traffic Stops

Robin S. Engel, Charles F. Klahm IV, and Rob Tillyer,

Introduction

Since the 1960s, a body of academic literature has developed that seeks to explain police decision making during police-citizen encounters.[1] This body of research began with rich, ethnographic descriptions of police work, followed by more quantitative analyses designed to test hypotheses about extra-legal influences over police decision making. Collectively, this research has consistently demonstrated that legal factors have the strongest influence over the outcomes citizens receive during police-citizen encounters.[2] Of great importance, however, are findings from a handful of studies that suggest that extra-legal factors, including citizens' characteristics, continue to influence police decision making even after other legal factors are considered. Although the findings regarding the influence of extra-legal factors are substantively weaker and more inconsistent across studies compared to the reported link between legal factors and police decision making, they have fueled the continuing interest in documenting and understanding outcomes resulting from police-citizen encounters. As a result, this body of research has continued to grow, making significant theoretical, methodological, and statistical advances in the field.

Researchers studying police behavior have recently narrowed the focus of their inquiries regarding police decision making to specifically examining racial/ethnic disparities during traffic stops. This attention was fueled by perceptions of racial discrimination at the hands of police as they sought "profiles" of drug couriers for criminal interdiction purposes on interstates and highways across the country.[3] These claims of racial/ethnic profiling resulted in the collection of official data during traffic and pedestrian stops by police agencies across the country, and analyses of these data designed to determine the impact of citizens' race/ethnicity on the likelihood of being stopped and subsequent coercive outcomes.[4] Numerous studies have confirmed the existence of racial/ethnic disparities in traffic stops and traffic stop outcomes.[5] Unlike the larger body of research examining police decision making, however, traffic stop studies have not considered many of the legal and extra-legal factors known to affect officers' behavior. One factor in particular—citizens' behavior—has consistently been shown in previous research to influence police behavior, but has not been systematically considered in traffic stop studies.

The current study offers an initial exploration of the impact of some forms of citizens' behavior, including their demeanor and compliance, over police decision making during traffic stops. Unlike previous research that has relied on *observers' perceptions* of citizens' demeanor and compliance, this research measures *officers' perceptions* and estimates their impact on arrest decisions. The data examined are based on traffic stops initiated by the Cleveland Division of Police during an eight-month period in 2005–06. It is believed to be the only study utilizing official data that also considers officers' perceptions of citizens' behaviors during traffic stops. This study specifically examines the relationship between driver's race/ethnicity and the likelihood of arrest while controlling for citizens' demeanor and compliance.

The findings demonstrate that consistent with prior research examining police behavior, citizen displays of disrespect and noncompliance or resistance significantly increases the likelihood of arrest during traffic stops. These findings demonstrate that citizens' behaviors, which are currently unmeasured in most traffic stops studies, are important considerations for future research. Further, the findings demonstrate the need to consider racial/ethnic differences in citizens' behaviors during police-citizen encounters to best understand the oft-reported racial/ethnic disparities in traffic stop outcomes.

Racial Profiling and Explaining Police Discretion: Two Diverging Bodies of Research

The practice of targeting racial minorities for routine traffic and pedestrian stops originated with the war on drugs and promoted profiling as an effective policing tactic to detect drug offenders.[6] It was believed by some law enforcement officials that significant quantities of drugs were being trafficked by minority groups; thus race/ethnicity was considered a valid tool for police to use to interrupt this activity.[7] As knowledge of this approach spread, in part through formal police training curricula, several academics and civil rights groups raised concerns that the use of citizens' race or ethnicity by police officers was inappropriate.[8] This attention was fueled by concerns that the racial/ethnic disparities in traffic stops were based on police discrimination.[9] By the mid-1990s, law enforcement agencies faced severe criticism for these practices, and in some locales, legal challenges were raised against the use of race/ethnicity as a factor in disrupting criminal activity.

In addition to mounting societal and political pressure, the use of race/ethnicity was initially legally challenged in Maryland and New Jersey by those claiming constitutional violations based on selective enforcement.[10] Other jurisdictions have also been the focus of criminal and civil proceedings associated with the use of race/ethnicity. One of the resolutions to these legal challenges was to initiate data collection on all traffic stops to identify any patterns of racial/ethnic bias and to assess the extent to which race/ethnicity was affecting officer behavior.[11] Moreover, data collection was supported by legislators who viewed the practice as a reasonable response to these claims, and by the academic community who saw it as an opportunity to gather quantitative information on the issue.[12]

Law enforcement agencies reacted to these societal concerns and legal challenges in a variety of ways. Some agencies developed official policies against the use of race/ethnicity prior to or during a traffic stop, others re-focused or initiated training to emphasize not using race/ethnicity as a tool, and some began data collection.[13] The response to this movement was widespread data collection efforts by law enforcement agencies.[14] The most common data collection method became official data collected by police officers conducting traffic and pedestrian stops.[15] These data collection efforts were initiated voluntarily by law enforcement agencies, mandated by court orders or legal settlements, or required by law.[16]

The general result patterns from these studies demonstrated a fairly consistent trend of racial/ethnic disparities in traffic stops and traffic stop outcomes.[17] These data collections and analyses however, have been fraught with methodological and statistical limitations, particularly with regard to comparing traffic stops to an appropriate benchmark.[18] Although other data sources, including citizen surveys, have also been explored to assess the reported patterns of racial/ethnic disparities in traffic stops,[19] the most common information source used to examine racial/ethnic disparities in traffic stops is official data.

The impetus for this research agenda, however, is not driven by an interest in understanding police decision making, as in the case of citizens' demeanor, but rather is based on concerns regarding allegations of racial profiling.[20] As a result, research on traffic stops is focused primarily on identifying patterns of racial/ethnic disparity. The selection of the data collection mechanism, the variables measured, and the analysis conducted all inform conclusions as to the existence of racial/ethnic disparities in traffic stops or traffic stop outcomes. What is absent from this literature, however, is a concern with understanding why there are racial/ethnic disparities in police stops.[21] Unfortunately, research focusing on traffic stops has generally failed to examine factors known from other research to influence police behavior. Although researchers have moved the field forward with both theoretical and methodological advances, a glaring deficiency in this research remains the inability to examine citizen behaviors that previous research has demonstrated to influence other forms of officer decision making.

In regard to understanding police discretion, the study of police-citizen interactions has a research history of over fifty years. Initially, the 1957–58 American Bar Foundation Survey of criminal justice agencies highlighted the extensive use of discretion within the criminal justice system, and in particular by police officers.[22] The result of this in-depth inquiry into the criminal justice system was the identification of potential extralegal factors that might influence criminal justice actors' behaviors. Reaction to this series of studies initiated a body of research that emerged to understand more thoroughly why and how police officers use their discretion. While early studies were often qualitative in nature,[23] the research has become heavily quantitative over the past forty years.[24]

Examinations of police behavior most often focus on the issuance of citations, arrests, and the use of force. The factors that explain police behavior generally include situational factors (e.g., legal, suspect, victim, and encounter characteristics), individual factors (i.e., officers' characteristics), police organizational factors, and community factors. Summaries of this substantial body of research have generally indicated that legal variables demonstrate the most consistent and strongest influence on officer behavior.[25] Although extra-legal variables typically explain a relatively small portion of the variance in police behavior when compared to legally relevant variables, they have been the focus of an overwhelming number of studies of police behavior.

In contrast to the larger body of research on police decision making, "racial profiling" research was prompted by high-profile litigation, political pressure, widespread public disapproval of policing tactics, and recommendations from social scientists. Unfortunately, the initial result was a growing body of research that generally failed to ask the proper questions, is often methodologically weak, and has findings that have been misinterpreted by social scientists, the media, politicians, and the courts.[26] As evidenced by the studies and discussions within the chapters of this book, these shortcomings are being addressed. One of the biggest hurdles is applying what social scientists have learned from the larger body of research examining police discretion to current research exploring racial/ethnic disparities in traffic stops.

Citizens' Demeanor

One extra-legal factor that has generated much research attention in the larger literature examining police discretion is the impact of suspects' demeanor over outcomes resulting from police-citizen encounters. Studies have employed citizens' demeanor as a predictor to explain various forms of police behavior, including arrest,[27] use of force,[28] ticket and citation writing,[29] and searches.[30] The majority of these studies have reported that citizens who display disrespect or noncompliance toward police are more likely to be subjected to these types of police actions compared to their more respectful and compliant counterparts. While some studies do report a null effect for citizen demeanor,[31] the overwhelming majority of empirical evidence suggests a strong and relatively consistent relationship between citizen demeanor and certain police officer actions, including arrest and use of force.

The study of citizens' demeanor was reconsidered when David Klinger noted that the conceptual and operational definitions of citizens' demeanor were not consistent throughout the literature.[32] Specifically, Klinger reported that citizens' demeanor had been previously conceptualized as legally permissible behaviors in extant research, yet measures of demeanor often included actions that constituted criminal behavior. As a result of this discrepancy, Klinger suggested that existing research findings might be flawed because measures of citizens' demeanor had confounded legally permissible behaviors and criminal actions. When criminal actions were examined separate from measures of disrespect, Klinger reported that "hostile" suspects were not significantly more likely to be arrested in Metro-Dade, Florida, in 1985.

Following Klinger's challenge to conventional wisdom about the impact of displays of disrespect over officer decision making, several researchers reexamined previous research to separate disrespect from measures of criminal behavior.[33] In each study, some measures of citizens' demeanor (including disrespect in some cases) still exhibited a significant influence on whether a suspect was arrested. The forms of demeanor that exhibited the strongest impact over police decision making were measures of citizens' noncompliance and resistance.

Given the overall strength and general consistency of the findings regarding citizens' demeanor over police behavior, consideration of these factors seems important for research examining traffic stops. One of the most frequent police-citizen encounters occurs as a result of traffic stops.[34] Despite the frequency of these interactions, less is known about the effect that citizens' demeanor has over traffic stop outcomes, including citations, searches, and arrests. Only six studies (using four data sources) have measured the impact of citizens' demeanor over police behavior during traffic stops.[35] In 1994 Lundman reexamined data collected from the Midwest City data set in the 1970s to examine how citizen behavior might influence ticketing using five different measures of the demeanor. In these analyses, only one of the five measures of demeanor significantly influenced the likelihood of receiving a ticket (i.e., impolite). Using the same data source, in 1996 Lundman also explored the relationship between citizen demeanor and arrest during traffic stops initiated for suspected drunk driving. In contrast, these analyses demonstrated that three of the five measures of citizen demeanor increased the probability of arrest while controlling for other relevant factors (i.e., impolite, dummy impolite, and hostile demeanor measure). In 1996 Worden and Shepard's reanalysis of the Police Services Study from 1977 examined how citizens' demeanor influenced officers' decisions to issue verbal warnings, written warnings, citations, and to invoke an arrest during traffic stops. Their results indicated that hostile and verbally resistant citizens were more likely to experience a negative sanction than their compliant counterparts. Brown and Frank (2005) examined factors that influence issuing citations during traffic stops by Cincinnati police officers in 1997. They reported that citizens' displays of disrespect did not influence whether a ticket was issued in the sample they analyzed, and did not consider measures of citizens' noncompliance or resistance. Finally, Paoline and Terrill in 2005 examined the Project on Policing Neighborhoods (POPN) data collected in 1996–97 to examine the impact citizen demeanor had over officers' decisions to conduct a vehicle search during traffic stops. They determined that disrespectful citizens were not significantly more likely to have their vehicle searched, but citizens that displayed resistance were 4.2 times more likely to be searched.

It is important to note that these studies that have examined the impact of citizens' demeanor over police behavior during traffic stops all relied on data collected by observers through social systematic observation. Despite the importance of these findings, studies that examine racial/ethnic disparities in traffic stops using official data sources have not included measures of citizens' behavior—including disrespect, noncompliance, and resistance—in their analyses. The issues surrounding the measurement of citizen behavior through official data sources are described in detail below.

Research Issues

Numerous studies have indicated that citizens' behaviors—including disrespect, noncompliance, and resistance—have a relatively strong and consistent influence over police behavior. Although some studies have found citizens' race/ethnicity to be a significant factor in coercive police action (e.g., citations, arrests, and use of force), the majority of studies that have reported race effects also note that these effects are relatively small and account for little of the explained variance in the statistical models.[36] Alternatively, some research has suggested that there are racial/ethnic differences in citizen behavior—including displays of disrespect, noncompliance, and resistance—during police-citizen encounters.[37] Therefore, examinations of traffic stop data that have failed to measure citizens' behavior, while simultaneously indicating racial/ethnic disparities in outcomes, are likely misspecified. This is likely due to the limitations inherent in using data collected by police officials during traffic stops. Often these data sources do not include any information about the behavior of the motorists during traffic stops.

Each of the previous studies examining citizens' demeanor during traffic stops was based on data collected through systematic social observation and not official traffic stop data. Systematic social observation involves placing trained observers in the field with officers and requires them to document various dimensions of an officer's entire shift. This method of data collection is desirable because it is systematic and replicable across research sites.[38] Moreover, this method provides very rich information regarding multiple aspects of the police-citizen encounter. But there may be variation in the amount of detail observers capture on the various data collection instruments as well as their interpretation of events, and officer reactivity may affect the quality of the data.[39] This is especially true with observers' perceptions of citizens' demeanor. The reliability and validity of observers' reports regarding citizens' demeanor is unknown. Further, it is unknown if observers' perceptions accurately reflect the perceptions of the officer.[40] Ultimately, it is the officers' perceptions of demeanor—not the observers'—that should be measured to examine any potential relationships between citizen demeanor and officer behavior. In 2006, Smith, Makarios, and Alpert suggested that script theory best explains factors that may influence officers' perception of suspicion toward citizens. Script theory suggests that people construct cognitive road maps through engagement with repeated situations, and that cognitive schematics inform their perceptions of these situations and guide their behavior in subsequent encounters. Thus an officer who consistently interacts with disrespectful people might, over time, consider that behavior status quo and disregard it as a negative experience. What is status quo for the officer might be interpreted as disrespectful by the observer because there is a lower threshold for such behaviors, ultimately biasing the data collected by observers.

These data limitations affect the ability of researchers to fully understand the relationship between citizen demeanor and police officer decision-making processes. It is clear that policing research is lacking reliable measures of citizens' demeanor from officers' perspectives. Existing measures use observer perceptions, post hoc assessment, and hypothetical scenarios as means of measuring citizen demeanor. None of these tap into how officers perceive citizens are behaving during actual police-citizen encounters. The inability to assess citizens' demeanor from officers' perspectives has impeded the ability to determine which citizen actions influence officer decision making. The current study is a first step toward merging the larger policing literature explaining police behavior with the relatively newer research examining police decision making during traffic stops. In the research described below, drivers' behaviors—specifically disrespect, noncompliance, and resistance—are measured directly based on officers' perceptions of citizens' behavior during traffic stops conducted by the Cleveland Division of Police.

Cleveland Traffic Stop Study

The traffic stops examined in this study occurred in Cleveland, Ohio. Based on the 2000 Census, the population of Cleveland is slightly less than 500,000 with 51% Black, 42% White, and 7% Hispanic.[41] In 2003 the Cleveland Division of Police (CDP) had slightly more than 1,800 sworn officers, of which roughly 80% were male. Caucasian officers made up approximately 65% of all sworn officers and Black officers represented roughly 30% of the force.

Through a federal grant, the Cleveland Division of Police (CDP) received funding to study officer decision making during traffic stops. Specifically, the grant provided for an independent, external evaluation of policing practices during traffic stops conducted by the CDP. A research team from the University of Cincinnati (UC) was awarded the contract to perform this evaluation. The initial purpose of the study was to aid CDP administrators in determining if racial or ethnic disparities in traffic stops and post-stop outcomes existed, and if evident, the possible sources of these disparities. Four different types of data were collected as part of the larger project: (1) traffic stop data collected by CDP officers, (2) observations of traffic patterns collected at ten locations in the city by UC undergraduate and graduate students, (3) Census data for the City of Cleveland, and (4) geographic information systems (GIS) data for the City of Cleveland, collected by the CDP. This chapter reports only those relevant analyses using the traffic stop data collected by the CDP.

A traffic stop form was developed to collect information for *all* officer-initiated traffic stops conducted by the Cleveland Division of Police, regardless of the disposition of the traffic stop. Specifically, the traffic stop form collected information on the following: (1) the stop (e.g., date/time, location, type of roadway, reasons for the stop, and the duration of the stop), (2) the driver (e.g., gender, age, race/ethnicity, zip code of residency, demeanor), (3) the vehicle (e.g., condition of the vehicle, modifications, state of registration, number of passengers), (4) the outcome of the stop (e.g., citation, written warning, arrest, search, property seized during the search), and (5) identification information (e.g., location of the stop by zone, and officers' badge number, unit number, and district number). Officers collected this information on Scantron forms that were sent directly to the UC research team for compilation. This form was initially pilot tested during a one-month period with all officers from the traffic unit. Based on this pilot test, adjustments were made to the form and the training provided to officers. A second pilot test was conducted for two-months with the full department. Based on biweekly reports provided to district commanders regarding the accuracy of the data, additional training was conducted, and the traffic stop data utilized for this research began July 1, 2005.[42]

Data

Data analyzed represented information recorded during officer-initiated traffic stops from July 1, 2005, to February 28, 2006.[43] During the eight-month study period, the Cleveland Division of Police reported traffic stops of 43,707 drivers. One of the most important findings of the larger study was that in 96.7% of the traffic stops reported, at least one citation was issued to the driver. In the remaining 3.3% of traffic stops, nearly all involved some other form of official action taken by the police, including a written warning, search or arrest of the driver, or a written warning, citation, search, or arrest of one or more passengers in the vehicle.[44] This finding suggests that the purpose and design of the research study (to capture information on all traffic stops, regardless of formal dispositions) was compromised. It is unlikely that information was collected on all the drivers stopped by CDP officers during the eight-month study period. Specifically, no information is available for those motorists who were stopped but were not officially sanctioned. Therefore, the study is better described as an examination of more serious traffic stops that rise to the level of citations or arrests, rather than a study of *all* traffic stops.[45]

Measures

Of the 43,707 traffic stops that were recorded, 42,570 (97.4%) contained valid information on all data fields of interest. The range, frequency, and standard deviation of the variables included in the analyses are reported in table 12.1. A custodial arrest of the driver was reported in 4.8% of the traffic stops. The racial/ethnic characteristics of drivers stopped were determined through officers' perceptions; drivers were not asked to identify their race or ethnicity.[46] Of the 42,570 motorists stopped by CDP officers, the majority (62.6%) were Black, 31.0% Caucasian, 4.7% Hispanic, and 1.6% other races/ethnicities.[47]

The likelihood of arrest varied across racial/ethnic groups. Of the Caucasian motorists stopped by CDP officers, 3.3% were arrested, compared to 5.7% of Black motorists and 4.7% of Hispanic motorists. Chi-square tests confirm that Black and Hispanic motorists were statistically significantly *more* likely than Caucasian motorists to be arrested during these recorded traffic stops.[48] As noted in multiple sources, however, the interpretation of these bivariate findings must be couched with additional information. The racial/ethnic differences detected in post-stop outcomes may exist due to legal and extralegal factors other than motorists' race/ethnicity. To explore this possibility, multivariate statistical modeling was performed to statistically control for other factors that might influence officers' decisions to arrest motorists, including other driver characteristics, vehicle characteristics, stop characteristics, reason for the stop, and other legal factors.

Driver Characteristics

The average age of drivers stopped by CDP officers was 36.3 years, and 66.6% of the stopped drivers were male. Almost all drivers were Ohio residents (97.8%), while

TABLE 12.1
Traffic Stop Descriptives (N = 42,570)

	Min.	Max.	Mean	S.D.
Driver Arrested	0	1	0.048	0.214
Driver Characteristics				
Caucasian	0	1	0.310	0.463
Black	0	1	0.626	0.484
Hispanic	0	1	0.047	0.212
Other	0	1	0.016	0.127
Male	0	1	0.666	0.471
Age	7	106	36.342	12.863
In Zone	0	1	0.292	0.455
Vehicle Characteristics				
No Registration	0	1	0.048	0.213
Modifications	0	1	0.018	0.132
Poor Condition	0	1	0.079	0.269
Number of Passengers	0	5	0.702	0.963
Stop Characteristics				
Daytime	0	1	0.552	0.497
Rush Hour	0	1	0.336	0.472
Weekend	0	1	0.193	0.395
Interstate/Main Roadway	0	1	0.792	0.406
Reason for the Stop				
Speeding/Moving Felony	0	1	0.257	0.437
Moving Misdemeanor	0	1	0.532	0.499
Equipment	0	1	0.062	0.242
License/Registration	0	1	0.076	0.264
Preexisting Information	0	1	0.015	0.121
Other	0	1	0.053	0.225
Other Legal Variables				
Number of Reasons for the Stop	1	6	1.093	0.360
Contraband Seized	0	1	0.053	0.225
Demeanor Variables				
Disrespect	0	1	0.041	0.198
Noncompliant/Resistant	0	1	0.035	0.185

many were also Cleveland residents (62.3%). As indicated in table 12.1, 29.2% of the stopped drivers were residents of the police zone in which they were stopped.

CDP officers were asked to indicate on the traffic stop form whether the driver was civil, disrespectful, noncompliant, verbally resistant or physically resistant, and the officer could mark all that applied. Drivers were considered civil if they complied with the officer's requests and deferred to their authority. Following Worden and Shepard (1996), officers recorded that drivers were disrespectful if they demonstrated any behavior (verbal or nonverbal) that was discourteous, rude, or indicated an unwillingness to defer to the officer's authority. Noncompliant drivers were defined as those who refused to comply with officers' requests or refused to answer officers' questions. Verbally resistant drivers were verbally abusive, including cursing at or threatening the officer. Finally, officers recorded drivers as physically resistant if they attempted to flee, or physically threatened or physically assaulted officers. Officers were provided training on completion of the form, and the above-listed definitions of the demeanor categories were available to officers as part of this training. During the pilot test, there were no known concerns raised by officers regarding the definition of these categories. Likewise, throughout the course of the project, no questions were raised to the research team regarding the traffic stop form or the information collected on it.

This is the first traffic stop study known to the authors that attempted to collect officers' perceptions of citizens' demeanor during traffic stops. Across the department a substantial majority of drivers (93.2%) were reported to be civil, compared to 4.1% of drivers reported as disrespectful, 1.9% noncompliant, 1.8% verbally resistant, and 0.3% physically resistant. These measures were not mutually exclusive (e.g., a driver could be recorded as both disrespectful and noncompliant). For the multivariate analyses reported below, the categories of noncompliant, verbally resistant, and physically resistant are combined into a single measure of noncompliant/resistant (3.5%).

Vehicle Characteristics

In addition to driver attributes, CDP officers also gathered information on certain vehicle characteristics. For example, officers recorded whether the vehicle had a valid registration sticker displayed at the time the stop was initiated; 4.8% involved vehicles without proper registration. Officers also noted whether the vehicle involved in the traffic stop had any aftermarket modifications, such as tinted windows, high performance exhaust systems, or aftermarket rims. Approximately 2% of traffic stops involved a vehicle with some type of aftermarket modification. The condition of the vehicle was also a characteristic officers assessed during the traffic stop. Officers described 7.9% of the vehicles they stopped as being in poor condition if they had visible cosmetic defects to the exterior of the vehicle including broken head or taillight(s), mirror(s), muffler, window(s), or severe body damage.

Stop Characteristics

A majority of traffic stops initiated by CDP (55.2%) occurred during daylight hours between 7 A.M. and 7 P.M. Morning and afternoon rush hours (7:00 A.M. to 9:30 A.M. and 4:00 P.M. to 6:30 P.M. respectively) accounted for 33.6% of all traffic stops. The majority of traffic stops occurred during weekdays (80.7%) and on main roadways or interstate highways (79.2%).[49] The majority of traffic stops did not involve passengers; the average number of passengers (excluding the driver) was 0.7.

Legal Factors

Officers documented the reason they initiated the traffic stop, which included speeding, felony and misdemeanor moving violations, equipment inspection, traffic enforcement, and registration/license check. Across the department, the most frequent violations observed prior to a traffic stop were moving misdemeanor violations (53.2%), followed by speeding or other moving felonies (25.7%). The number of infractions documented during a traffic stop ranged from 1 to 6, with a mean of 1.1. To account for post-stop outcomes, officers recorded whether a search was conducted and if contraband was seized. Department wide 8.9% of stops resulted in vehicle searches and contraband was seized in 5.3% of all stops.

Findings

Table 12.2 reports results for the logistic regression models predicting arrest for the 42,570 traffic stops analyzed (97.4% of the total number of traffic stops recorded). This model is substantively strong, explaining 35.1% of the variance in the likelihood of arrest. The findings demonstrates that drivers' race/ethnicity does not significantly influence whether drivers are arrested once other legal and extralegal factors, including disrespect and noncompliance/resistance, are considered. Of the drivers' characteristics that significantly predict an arrest, drivers' displays of disrespect and

TABLE 12.2
Logistic Regression Analyses Predicting Arrests (N = 42,570)

	Coefficient	Standard Error	Odds Ratio
Intercept	−4.68*	0.16	0.01
Driver Characteristics			
Black	0.19	0.06	—
Hispanic	0.02	0.13	—
Other	−0.80	0.32	—
Male	0.98*	0.07	2.65
Age	−0.02*	0.00	0.99
In Zone	0.26*	0.06	1.30
Vehicle Characteristics			
No Registration	0.88*	0.10	2.40
Modifications	−0.13	0.16	—
Poor Condition	0.55*	0.07	1.73
Number of Passengers	−0.01	0.03	—
Stop Characteristics			
Daytime	−0.55*	0.08	0.58
Rush Hour	0.14	0.09	—
Weekend	0.31*	0.06	1.36
Interstate/Main Roadway	−0.19	0.06	—
Reason for the Stop			
Moving Misdemeanor	0.35*	0.08	1.42
Equipment	0.21	0.12	—
License/Registration	0.78*	0.10	2.18
Preexisting Information	1.09*	0.18	2.99
Other	1.10*	0.11	3.01
Other Legal Variables			
Number of Reasons for the Stop	0.24*	0.06	1.27
Contraband Seized	3.08*	0.06	21.68
Demeanor Variables			
Disrespect	0.87*	0.09	2.38
Noncompliant/Resistant	1.32*	0.09	3.74
Chi-Square	5,078.79*		
Nagelkerke R-Square	0.351		

*= $p < .001$

noncompliance/resistance were the most substantively important predictors of arrest. Specifically, drivers that were described by police officers as disrespectful were 2.4 times more likely to be arrested compared to those described as civil. Likewise, drivers who were described by police officers as noncompliant, verbally resistant, or physically resistant were 3.7 times more likely to be arrested compared to drivers who complied with police.

Some drivers' characteristics other than demeanor also had a significant influence over whether an arrest is made during traffic stops. Male drivers, younger drivers, and drivers who are stopped in the police zone where they reside are significantly *more* likely to be arrested compared to female drivers, older drivers, and drivers who reside outside of the police zone in which they are stopped.

Some characteristics of the vehicle also had a significant influence over the likelihood of drivers being arrested during traffic stops. Drivers of vehicles that had no registration and drivers of vehicles in poor condition were significantly more likely to be arrested compared to drivers of vehicles that were registered and drivers of vehicles in fair or good condition. Specifically, drivers of vehicles with no registration were 2.4 times more likely to be arrested and drivers of vehicles in poor condition were 1.7 times more likely to be arrested, compared to drivers of registered vehicles and vehicles in better condition. Two stop characteristics were significant predictors of arrest—time of day and day of the week. Drivers stopped during nondaylight hours and drivers stopped on a weekend day (i.e., Saturday or Sunday) were significantly more likely to be arrested compared to drivers stopped during daylight hours or on a weekday.

Likewise, the reason for the stop was a significant predictor of arrest. All the reasons for the stop except one (equipment) significantly predicted the likelihood of arrest. Drivers who were stopped for a moving misdemeanor, license or registration violation, preexisting information, or some other (unknown) reason were significantly more likely to be arrested compared to drivers stopped for speeding or a felony moving violation. Finally, both of the additional legal variables included in the model significantly predicted arrest. Drivers who were stopped for more reasons and drivers with contraband found during a search were significantly more likely to be arrested compared to drivers stopped for fewer reasons and those without contraband found. As one would expect, the discovery of contraband was by far the most substantively important predictor of arrest. Drivers with contraband discovered were 21.7 times more likely to be arrested compared to drivers without the discovery of contraband. While this finding is intuitive, it is important to include this type of legal variable in the model predicting arrest so that the effect of other extralegal variables can be examined after this legal variable is statistically controlled for.

Conclusion

Findings from the multivariate statistical models estimating arrest indicated that Black and Hispanic motorists were *not* significantly more likely than Caucasians to be arrested during traffic stops when other legal and extralegal factors are considered.

Instead, these analyses suggest that a number of situational and officer-level factors accounted for the variance in arrest rates across racial/ethnic groups (e.g., being male, disrespectful, driving a vehicle in poor working condition, being stopped at night, etc.). Of particular importance in this study is the need to consider officers' perceptions of motorists' disrespect and noncompliance/resistance to better understand traffic stop outcomes. Motorists described by police as disrespectful were 2.4 times more likely to be arrested compared to those who were not disrespectful. Likewise, motorists who were noncompliant, verbally resistant, or physically resistant were 3.7 times more likely to be arrested compared to those who were compliant.

The strength of these findings suggests that the failure to consider citizens' demeanor in previous examinations of traffic stop outcomes is a significant limitation of this body of research. Previous research has demonstrated racial/ethnic differences in citizens' behaviors that are relevant to consider during police-citizen encounters. For example, research that examines criminal interdiction traffic stops suggests that racial and ethnic differences may exist in cues of suspicion that officers are trained to identify when determining who to search.[50] Social psychology and cross-cultural communications research suggests that normal (i.e., noncriminal), nonverbal communication styles among African Americans are more likely to be identified as "suspicious" by both laypersons and police officers.[51] Research on consumerism and marketing has revealed cultural differences in style of dress, vehicle preferences, and recreational travel practices that could cause noncriminal behaviors by minority drivers to be interpreted as indicators of drug smuggling.[52] Finally, demographic research indicates that patterns of residence and vehicle ownership for minorities could cause them to unwittingly fit the characteristics police officers are trained to look for when identifying drug smugglers.[53] Considering the issue of citizens' demeanor specifically, some research has demonstrated that citizens' demeanor during police-citizen encounters differs across racial/ethnic groups. Engel (2003) found that non-White suspects were significantly less likely to be compliant toward White officers (e.g., refuse to answer questions or comply with officer requests), but were not more likely than White suspects to show more aggressive forms of resistance (e.g., verbal aggression, physical aggression, or disrespect). If there are racial/ethnic differences in demeanor and compliance, it is plausible that some of the racial/ethnic disparities reported in traffic stop research may at least partially be explained by citizens' behavior.

The next step in this line of research is to examine racial/ethnic differences in displays of disrespect, noncompliance, and resistance. In these data, Black motorists were significantly more likely to be perceived by CDP officers as acting in a disrespectful manner and noncompliant manner compared to White motorists. It is also important to note other characteristics that were previously unmeasured in other studies but shown here to significantly influence arrest decisions (e.g., condition of the vehicle and vehicle aftermarket modifications) also differ across race. Black suspects were significantly more likely to drive vehicles in poor condition and that had aftermarket modifications compared to White motorists. Therefore, it appears that previously unmeasured citizen behaviors—demeanor and the types of vehicles driven —not only have a direct impact on police decisions to arrest during traffic stops, but also are correlated strongly with race. The failure to measure these behaviors in previous research may have produced spurious findings of racial/ethnic differences in traffic stop outcomes.

It is also important to consider that officers' *perceptions* of citizens' demeanor may themselves be racially biased. That is, officers may be more likely to perceive particular behaviors displayed by Black motorists as disrespectful or noncompliant while similar behaviors displayed by White motorists would not be considered as such. Alternatively, officers may perceive particular behaviors displayed by White motorists as disrespectful or noncompliant that would not be interpreted in the same manner if displayed by Black motorists. An additional possibility is that the officers' race/ethnicity influences their perceptions of citizens' disrespect across racial groups. For example, analyses of videotapes of traffic stops in Cincinnati have demonstrated that police-citizen encounters with the same race officers and suspects (i.e., Black officer and Black suspect, or White officer and White suspect) tend to be more civil and polite compared to encounters between officers and suspect of different races.[54] These findings lead to a larger consideration of race relations in American society.

Smith and Alpert have suggested that racial/ethnic disparities in traffic stop outcomes result from unconscious stereotypes.[55] These unconscious stereotypes are formed through repeated contacts with particular demographic groups often involved in criminal activity, and are reinforced through officers' personal and vicarious experiences or media exposure to messages regarding these groups. These stereotypes reflect the categorization of individuals into groups identified by demographic characteristics, specifically race/ethnicity. It is possible that these same unconscious stereotypes may shape officers' perceptions of behavior across racial/ethnic groups. If this were true, we would expect that officers would be more likely to view particular behaviors displayed by Black motorists as disrespectful, noncompliant, or resistant compared to the same behaviors displayed by White motorists. Alternatively, disrespectful behaviors that might be considered by some officers as "typical" for certain racial groups may be less likely to affect police behavior compared to the same behaviors displayed by individuals of a different race where such behavior may be more shocking, or at least less expected. Both possibilities suggest a need for further examination of how, when, and why officers interpret behaviors as disrespectful.

It is important to note, however, that although interesting, determining the accuracy of officers' perceptions about citizens' demeanor is not necessary for this research study. As previously argued in 2001 by Engel and Silver in their examination of arrest decisions based on citizens' mental status, "If the goal is to understand officers' decision making, then officers' perceptions of mental disorder are more relevant than classifications based on clinical criteria. Therefore, an advantage of the current study is that mental disorder was not measured using a clinical checklist but rather was based on officers' perceptions."[56] The same logic applies to this research examining citizens' demeanor and traffic stop outcomes. If the goal is to understand police arrest decisions during traffic stops, then officers' perceptions of citizens' demeanor are the appropriate measures, regardless of whether independent observers would classify those same motorists as disrespectful or noncompliant.

One important limitation of these findings is the difficulty in disentangling causal order. It is possible that drivers do not become disrespectful, noncompliant, or resistant until after a custodial arrest is made. In these situations, demeanor does not predict arrest, but rather arrest may predict demeanor. Following the pilot test for this data collection effort, CPD was instructed by the research team to advise officers that the recording of citizens' demeanor was to occur at the beginning and during the traffic stop, but not after an arrest. It is unknown, however, if this coding instruction was distributed to all officers. The findings reported here are based on the assumption that all officers were made aware of and adhered to this coding procedure.

To further develop this area of study, researchers should continue to rigorously explore the influence of citizens' demeanor on police decision making. It is also prudent to expand the focus and examine how citizens' demeanor differs across racial/ethnic groups, and whether these differences affect police behavior. Further, it is critical to the understanding of police decision making to examine whether officers differentially interpret the same behavior across different types of citizens as disrespectful, noncompliant, or resistant. Most important, however, these findings demonstrate the need for researchers to expand their focus beyond the original items recommended for collection on traffic stop forms. An entire body of research examining police behavior clearly demonstrates the importance of considering citizens' behavior when attempting to explain officer decision making. This need clearly transcends traffic stops studies. Currently, police agencies across the country are collecting superficial information about traffic stops, citizens' race/ethnicity, and outcomes generated during those stops. The result has been study after study that reports racial/ethnic disparities in traffic stops outcomes without a clear understanding of why these outcomes exist. If the goal is ultimately to reduce these racial/ethnic disparities, then social scientists need to better understand the factors that likely affect officer decision making, including the detailed interactions between police and citizens during traffic stops.

Unfortunately, based on the current data collected by many police agencies during traffic stops, our ability to clearly understand the causes of the oft-reported racial/ethnic disparities is at a standstill. Regardless of the numerous statistical advances in the field, more meaningful data is necessary. This may require examinations of multiple sources, and particularly a consideration of unconventional data, including qualitative information. Recent research using qualitative data analysis to examine summaries of focus groups with police officers heavily engaged in criminal interdiction work has demonstrated a host of factors that influence police decision making during traffic stops that are not captured through official data sources.[57] For example, these qualitative analyses have demonstrated that officers' decisions to search or request consent to search are largely affected by the presence of pre-stop and during-the-stop indicators of suspicion (e.g., changes in driving behavior, physical displays of nervousness, vehicle condition or modifications, etc.) as well as the totality of circumstances within the context of each individual situation (e.g., driver demeanor, inconsistent stories). None of these factors are measured in official data sources.

In summary, it appears that the collection of official data during traffic stops was not the panacea that some researchers, politicians, and citizens declared in the mid-1990s. Simply collecting cursory information during traffic stops does provide evidence of racial/ethnic disparities in traffic stop outcomes, but it does not provide much in the way of explanation. We need to move beyond this simplistic model by expanding our current official data inquiries, and embracing new methods of information gathering, including some qualitative techniques. It is only when we better understand police decision making as a whole that we can work to reduce racial/ethnic disparities during police-citizen contacts.

NOTES

1. Walker, 1993.
2. For review, see National Research Council, 2004; Riksheim & Chermak, 1993.
3. Harris, 1999, 2002.
4. Ramirez, McDevitt, & Farrell, 2000.
5. Alpert Group, 2004; Alpert et al., 2006; Engel, Cherkauskas, & Tillyer, 2007; Farrell et al., 2004; Ingram, 2007; Lamberth, 2003; Lovrich et al., 2005; Ridgeway et al, 2006.
6. Harris, 2002; Tonry, 1995.
7. Harris, 1999.
8. Harris, 2002.
9. Buerger & Farrell, 2002; GAO, 2000; Harris, 2002, 2006.
10. E.g., *Wilkins v. Maryland State Police*, 1993; *State of New Jersey v. Soto*, 1996.
11. Engel & Calnon, 2004a.
12. GAO, 2000; Ramirez, McDevitt, & Farrell, 2000.
13. Tillyer, Engel, & Wooldredge, 2008.
14. Fridell et al., 2001; Fridell, 2005; Hickman, 2005; Institute on Race and Poverty, 2001; Strom, Brien, & Smith, 2001.
15. Barlow & Barlow, 2002; Birzer & Birzer, 2006; Kowalski & Lundman, 2007; Walker, 2001.
16. Engel, Tillyer, & Cherkauskas, 2007.
17. E.g., Alpert Group, 2004; Alpert et al., 2006; Engel, Tillyer, & Cherkauskas, 2007; Farrell et al., 2004; Ingram, 2007; Lamberth, 2003; Lovrich et al., 2005; Ridgeway et al., 2006.
18. Engel & Calnon, 2004b; Fridell et al., 2001; Fridell, 2004; Fridell, 2005; Ramirez, McDevitt, & Farrell, 2000.
19. Engel, Tillyer, & Cherkauskas, 2007; Lundman, 2004; Tomaskovic-Devey et al., 2006.
20. Engel, Calnon, & Bernard, 2002.
21. Ibid.
22. Walker, 1993.
23. Bittner, 1970; Rubinstein, 1973; Skolnick, 1966; Van Maanen, 1974.
24. For review, see National Research Council, 2004; Riksheim & Chermak, 1993.
25. National Research Council, 2004; Riksheim & Chermark, 1993; Sherman, 1980.
26. Engel, Calnon, & Bernard, 2002; Smith & Alpert, 2002; Tillyer et al., 2008.
27. E.g., Smith and Visher, 1981; Worden and Shepard, 1996; Engel, Sobol, & Worden, 2000.
28. E.g., Westley, 1953; Engel, Sobol, & Worden, 2000; Garner, Maxwell, & Heraux, 2002; Terrill and Mastrofski, 2002.
29. E.g., Brown and Frank, 2005; Lundman, 1994, Schafer, 2005.
30. E.g., Paoline and Terrill, 2005.
31. E.g., Mastrofski et al., 2000; McClusky, Terrill, & Paoline, 2005; Terrill and Mastrofski, 2002.
32. Klinger, 1994.

33. E.g., Lundman, 1994, 1996; Worden & Shepard, 1996; Worden, Shepard, & Mastrofski, 1996.

34. Durose, Smith, & Langan, 2007.

35. Brown & Frank, 2005; Lundman, 1994, 1996; Paoline & Terrill, 2005; Worden & Shepard, 1996; Worden, 1989.

36. E.g., Engel & Silver, 2001; Novak et al., 2002; Riksheim & Chermak, 1993; Terrill & Mastrofski, 2002; Worden, 1989; for review, see National Research Council, 2004.

37. Engel, 2003; Greenleaf & Lanza-Kaduce 1995; Lanza-Kaduce & Greenleaf, 2000; Mastrofski, Snipes, & Supina 1996; McCluskey, Mastrofski, & Parks, 1999.

38. Sampson and Raudenbush, 1999.

39. Alpert and Smith, 1999; Lersch and Mieczkowski, 2004; Spano, 2006.

40. Engel & Silver, 2001.

41. U.S. Census, 2000.

42. See Engel et al., 2006, for additional details regarding the data collection process.

43. CDP officers were instructed to fill out these forms after *every officer-initiated* traffic stop. Traffic stops based on citizens' initiation or as the result of police checkpoints (e.g., registration, DUI, seat belts, etc.) were not included in the data. In addition, contact with citizens resulting from traffic accidents was also excluded from the data collection effort.

44. Engel et al., 2006.

45. This had a number of important implications on the analyses, findings, and conclusions of the larger study, which are fully reported in ibid.

46. The use of officers' perceptions of drivers' race/ethnicity is an acceptable method for examining racially based policing. Officers may incorrectly perceive drivers' actual race or ethnicity. This possible misperception, however, is irrelevant for data collection analyses that seek to explain officer decision making. Accusations of racial profiling are based on the presumption that officers treat minority citizens differently. Therefore, proper data collection efforts must identify officers' *perceptions* of the race/ethnicity of the driver, not the driver's actual race/ethnicity. Other information about the driver (year of birth and residential zip code) was gathered from drivers' licenses.

47. Originally, the traffic stop form captured officers' perceptions of drivers' race/ethnicity in one of seven categories, but due to the infrequent occurrence of Native American, Asian/Pacific Islander, and Middle Eastern drivers these categories were combined with the unknown/missing category to form a category labeled as "Other" drivers.

48. Engel et al., 2006.

49. Main city roadways are defined as any main thoroughfare that is heavily populated with traffic on which vehicular traffic is given preferential right-of-way, and at the entrances to which vehicles from intersecting roadways are required to stop or yield by law. They may include divided highways, four-lane roads, or two-lane roads.

50. Engel & Johnson, 2006.

51. Fuertes, Potere, & Ramirez, 2002; Fugita, Wexley, & Hillery, 1974; Garratt, Baxter, & Rozelle, 1981; Ickes, 1984; LaFrance & Mayo, 1976; Smith, 1983; Vrij, Dragt, & Koppelaar, 1992; Vrij & Winkel, 1991, 1994; Winkel & Vrij, 1990; for review, see Engel & Johnson, 2006.

52. Brown & Washton, 2002; Connors & Nugent, 1990; Harris, 1999; Remsberg, 1997; for review, see Engel & Johnson, 2006.

53. Connors & Nugent, 1990; Harris, 1999, Remsberg, 1997; for review, see Engel & Johnson, 2006.

54. Ridgeway et al, 2006.

55. Smith and Alpert, 2002.

56. Engel & Silver, 2001, 236.
57. Engel, Cherkauskas, & Smith, 2008; Engel, Tillyer, & Cherkauskas, 2007.

REFERENCES

Alpert, Geoffrey, Elizabeth Becker, Mark Gustafson, Alan Meister, Michael Smith, and Bruce A. Strombom. 2006. *Pedestrian and motor vehicle post-stop data analysis report.* Los Angeles: Analysis Group. Available: http://www.analysisgroup.com/uploadedFiles/Publishing/Articles/LAPD_Data_Analysis_Report_07-5-06.pdf.

Alpert, Geoffrey and Roger Dunham. 2004. *Understanding police use of force: Officers, suspects, and reciprocity.* Cambridge, UK: Cambridge University Press.

Alpert, Geoffrey and Michael Smith. 1999. Police use-of-force data: Where we are and where we should be going. *Police Quarterly 2*: 57–78.

Alpert Group. 2004. *Miami-Dade Police Department Racial Profiling Study.* Available: http://www.aclufl.org/pdfs/Miami-Dade%20Police%20Department%20%20Racial%20Profiling%20Study%20-%20The%20Alpert%20Group.pdf.

Barlow, David and Melissa Hickman Barlow. 2002. Racial profiling: A survey of African American police officers. *Policing Quarterly 5*: 334–358.

Birzer, Michael and Gwynne Harris Birzer. 2006. Race matters: A critical look at racial profiling, it's a matter for the courts. *Journal of Criminal Justice 34*: 643–651.

Bittner, Egon. 1970. *The functions of police in modern society.* Washington, DC: U.S. Government Printing Office.

Brown, Robert and James Frank. 2005. Police-citizen encounters and field citations: Do encounter characteristics influence ticketing? *Policing: An International Journal of Police Strategies and Management 28*: 435–454.

Brown, Robert and Ruth Washton. (Eds.). 2002. *The U.S. African American market.* New York: Market Research Inc.

Buerger, Michael and Amy Farrell. 2002. The evidence of racial profiling: Interpreting documented and unofficial sources. *Police Quarterly 5*: 272–305.

Connors, Edward and Hugh Nugent. 1990. *Street-level narcotics enforcement.* Washington, DC: U.S. Bureau of Justice Assistance.

Durose, Matthew, Erica Smith, and Patrick Langan. 2007. *Contacts between police and the public, 2005.* Washington, DC: Bureau of Justice Statistics, U.S. Department of Justice.

Engel, Robin. 2003. Explaining suspects' resistance and disrespect toward police. *Journal of Criminal Justice 31*: 475–492.

Engel, Robin and Jennifer Calnon. 2004a. Examining the influence of drivers' characteristics during traffic stops with police: Results from a national survey. *Justice Quarterly 21*: 49–90.

Engel, Robin and Jennifer Calnon. 2004b. Comparing benchmark methodologies for police-citizen contacts: Traffic stop data collection for the Pennsylvania State Police. *Police Quarterly 7*: 97–125.

Engel, Robin, Jennifer Calnon, and Thomas Bernard. 2002. Theory and racial profiling: Shortcomings and future directions in research. *Justice Quarterly 19*: 249–273.

Engel, Robin, Jennifer Cherkauskas, and Michael Smith. 2008. *Identifying best practices in criminal interdiction activities for the Arizona Department of Public Safety.* University of Cincinnati Policing Institute: Cincinnati, OH. Submitted to the Arizona Department of Public Safety, Phoenix, AZ.

Engel, Robin, Jennifer Cherkauskas, and Rob Tillyer. 2007. *Traffic stop data analysis study report: Final literature review and review of other jurisdictions.* University of Cincinnati

Policing Institute: Cincinnati, OH. Submitted to the Arizona Department of Public Safety, Phoenix, AZ.

Engel, Robin, James Frank, Rob Tillyer, and Charles Klahm. 2006. *Cleveland Division of Police traffic stop study: Final Report.* University of Cincinnati Policing Institute: Cincinnati, OH. Submitted to the City of Cleveland, Division of Police, Office of the Chief, Cleveland, OH.

Engel, Robin and Richard Johnson. 2006. Toward a better understanding of racial and ethnic disparities in search and seizure rates. *Journal of Criminal Justice 34:* 605–617.

Engel, Robin, James Sobol, and Robert Worden. 2000. Further exploration of the demeanor hypothesis: The interaction effects of suspects' characteristics and demeanor on police behavior. *Justice Quarterly 17:* 235–258.

Engel, Robin and Eric Silver. 2001. Policing mentally disordered subjects: A reexamination of the criminalization hypothesis. *Criminology 39:* 225–252.

Engel, Robin, Rob Tillyer, and Jennifer Cherkauskas. 2007. *Understanding best search and seizure practices: Final report.* University of Cincinnati Policing Institute: Cincinnati, OH. Submitted to the Ohio State Highway Patrol, Columbus, OH.

Farrell, Amy, Jack McDevitt, Lisa Bailey, Carsten Andresen, and Erica Pierce. 2004. *Massachusetts racial and gender profiling study.* Institute on Race and Justice: Northeastern University. Available: http://www.racialprofilinganalysis.neu.edu/IRJsite_docs/finalreport.pdf

Fridell, Lori. 2005. *Understanding race data from vehicle stops: A stakeholder's guide.* Washington, DC: Police Executive Research Forum.

Fridell, Lori. 2004. *By the numbers: A guide for analyzing race data from vehicle stops.* Washington, DC: Police Executive Research Forum.

Fridell, Lori, Robert Lunney, Drew Diamond, and Bruce Kubu. 2001. *Racially biased policing: A principled response.* Washington, DC: Police Executive Research Forum.

Fuertes, Jairo, Jodi Potere, and Karen Y. Ramirez. 2002. Effects of speech accents on interpersonal evaluations: Implications for counseling practice and research. *Cultural Diversity and Ethnic Minority Psychology 8:* 346–356.

Fugita, Steven, Kenneth Wexley and Joseph Hillery. 1974. Black-White differences in nonverbal behavior in an interview setting. *Journal of Applied Social Psychology 4:* 343–350.

Fugita, Steven, Mark Hogrebe, and Kenneth Wexley. 1980. Perceptions of deception: Perceived expertise in detecting deception, successfulness of deception and nonverbal cues. *Personality and Social Psychology Bulletin 6:* 637–643.

Garner, Joel, Christopher Maxwell, and Cedric Heraux. 2002. Characteristics associated with the prevalence and severity of force used by the police. *Justice Quarterly 19:* 705–746.

Garratt, Gail, James Baxter, and Richard Rozelle. 1981. Training university police in Black-American nonverbal behaviors. *Journal of Social Psychology 113:* 217–229.

General Accounting Office. 2000, March. *Better targeting of airline passengers for personal searches could produce better results (Publication No. GAO/GGD-00-38).* Washington, DC: General Accounting Office, U.S. Customs Service.

Greenleaf, Richard and Lonn Lanza-Kaduce. 1995. Sophistication, organization, and authority-subject conflict: Rediscovering and unraveling Turk's theory of norm resistance. *Criminology 33:* 565–585.

Harris, David. 2006. U.S. experiences with racial and ethnic profiling: History, current issues, and the future. *Critical Criminology 14:* 213–239.

Harris, David. 2002. *Profiles in injustice: Why racial profiling cannot work.* New York: The New Press.

Harris, David. 1999. *Driving while Black: Racial profiling on our nation's highways.* Available: http://www.aclu.org/racialjustice/racialprofiling/15912pub19990607.html.

Hickman, Matthew. 2005. *Traffic stop data collection policies for State Police, 2004* (NCJ 209156). Washington, DC: Bureau of Justice Statistics, U.S. Department of Justice.

Ickes, William. 1984. Compositions in Black and White: Determinants of interaction in interracial dyads. *Journal of Personality and Social Psychology 47*: 497–512.

Ingram, Jason. 2007. The effect of neighborhood characteristics on traffic citation practices of the police. *Police Quarterly 10*: 371–393.

Institute on Race and Poverty. 2001. *Saint Paul traffic stops data analysis.* Minneapolis, MN: University of Minnesota.

Klinger, David. 1994. Demeanor or crime? Why "hostile" citizens are more likely to be arrested. *Criminology 32*: 475–493.

Kowalski, Brian and Richard Lundman. 2007. Vehicle stops by police for driving while Black: Common problems and some tentative solutions. *Journal of Criminal Justice 35*: 165–181.

LaFrance, Marianne and Clara Mayo. 1976. Racial differences in gaze behavior during conversations: Two systematic observational studies. *Journal of Personality and Social Psychology 33*: 547–552.

Lamberth, John. 2003. *Racial profiling study and services: A multijurisdictional assessment of traffic enforcement and data collection in Kansas.* Available: http://www.racialprofilinganalysis .neu.edu/IRJ_docs/KS_2003.pdf.

Lanza-Kaduce, Lonn and Richard Greenleaf. 2000. Age and race deference reversals: Extending Turk on police-citizen conflict. *Journal of Research in Crime and Delinquency 37*: 221–236.

Lersch, Kim and Thomas Mieczkowski. 2004. Violent police behavior: Past, present, and future research directions. *Aggression and Violent Behavior 10*: 552–568.

Lovrich, Nicholas, Michael Gaffney, Clayton Mosher, Mitchell Pickerill, and Travis Pratt. 2005. *Analysis of traffic stop data collected by the Washington State Patrol: Assessment of racial and ethnic equity and bias in stops, citations, and searches using multivariate quantitative and multi-method qualitative research techniques.* University of Washington: Seattle, WA. Submitted to the Washington State Police, Olympia, WA.

Lundman, Richard. 2004. Driver race, ethnicity, and gender and citizen reports of vehicle searches by police and vehicle search hits: Towards a triangulated scholarly understanding. *Journal of Criminal Law and Criminology 94*: 309–350.

Lundman, Richard. 1996. Demeanor and arrest: Additional evidence from previously unpublished data. *Journal of Research in Crime and Delinquency 33*: 306–323.

Lundman, Richard. 1994. Demeanor or crime? The Midwest City police-citizen encounters study. *Criminology 32*: 631–656.

Mastrofski, Stephen, Jeffery Snipes, and Anne Supina. 1996. Compliance on demand: The public's response to specific police requests. *Journal of Research on Crime and Delinquency 33*: 269–305.

Mastrofski, Stephen, Jeffery Snipes, Roger Parks, and Christopher Maxwell. 2000. The helping hand of the law: Police control of citizens on request. *Criminology 38*: 307–342.

Mastrofski, Stephen, Robert Worden, and Jeffery Snipes. 1995. Law enforcement in a time of community policing. *Criminology 33*: 539–563.

McCluskey, John, Steven Mastrofski, and Roger Parks. 1999. To acquiesce or rebel: Predicting citizen compliance with police requests. *Police Quarterly 2*: 389–416.

McCluskey, John, William Terrill, and Eugene Paoline III. 2005. Peer group aggressiveness and the use of coercion in police-suspect encounters. *Police Practice and Research: An International Journal 6*: 19–37.

National Research Council. 2004. *Fairness and effectiveness in policing: The evidence.* Washington, DC: National Academies Press.

Novak, Kenneth. 2004. Disparity and racial profiling in traffic enforcement. *Police Quarterly* 7: 65–96.

Novak, Kenneth, James Frank, Brad Smith, and Robin Engel. 2002. Revisiting the decision to arrest: Comparing beat and community officers. *Crime and Delinquency 48*: 70–98.

Paoline, Eugene, III, and William Terrill. 2005. The impact of police culture on traffic stop searches: An analysis of attitudes and behaviors. *Policing: An International Journal of Police Strategies and Management 28*: 455–472.

Ramirez, Deborah, Jack McDevitt and Amy Farrell. 2000. *A resource guide on racial profiling data collection systems: Promising practices and lessons learned.* Washington, DC: U.S. Department of Justice.

Remsberg, Charles. 1997. *Tactics for criminal patrol: Vehicle stops, drug discovery, and officer survival.* Northbrook, IL: Calibre Press.

Ridgeway, Greg, Terry Schell, K. Jack Riley, Susan Turner, and Travis Dixon. 2006. *Police-community relations in Cincinnati: Year two evaluation report.* RAND Corporation: Santa Monica, CA. Submitted to the City of Cincinnati, OH.

Riksheim, Eric and Steven Chermak. 1993. Causes of police behavior revisited. *Journal of Criminal Justice 21*: 353–382.

Rubinstein, Jonathan. 1973. *City police.* New York: Ballantine.

Sampson, Robert and Steven Raudenbush. 1999. Systematic social observation of public spaces: A new look at disorder in urban neighborhoods. *American Journal of Sociology 105*: 603–651.

Schafer, Joseph. 2005. Negotiating order in the policing of youth drinking. *Policing: An International Journal of Police Strategies and Management 28*: 279–300.

Sherman, Lawrence. 1980. Causes of police behavior: The current state of quantitative research. *Journal of Research in Crime and Delinquency 1*: 69–100.

Skolnick, Jerome. 1966. *Justice without trial: Law enforcement in democratic society.* New York: Wiley.

Smith, Althea. 1983. Nonverbal communication among Black female dyads: An assessment of intimacy, gender, and race. *Journal of Social Issues 39*: 55–67.

Smith, Douglas and Christy Visher. 1981. Street-level justice: Situational determinants of police arrest decisions. *Social Problems 29*: 167–177.

Smith, Michael and Geoffrey Alpert. 2002. Searching for direction: Courts, social science, and the adjudication of racial profiling claims. *Justice Quarterly 19*: 673–703.

Smith, Michael, Matthew Makarios, and Geoffrey Alpert. 2006. Differential suspicion: Theory specification and gender effects in the traffic stop context. *Justice Quarterly 23*: 271–295.

Spano, Richard. 2006. Observer behavior as a potential source of reactivity: Describing and quantifying observer effects in a large-scale observational study of police. *Sociological Methods and Research 30*: 521–553.

Strom, Kevin, Peter Brien, and Stephen Smith. 2001. *Traffic stop data collection policies for state police, 2001 (NCJ 191158).* Washington, DC: Bureau of Justice Statistics, U.S. Department of Justice.

Terrill, William and Steven Mastrofski. 2002. Situational and officer based determinants of police coercion. *Justice Quarterly 19*: 215–248.

Tillyer, Rob, Robin Engel, and John Wooldredge. 2008. The intersection of racial profiling and the law. *Journal of Criminal Justice 36*: 138–153.

Tomaskovic-Devey, Donald, Cynthia Wright, Ronald Czaja, and Kirk Miller. 2006. Self-reports of police speeding stops by race: Results from the North Carolina reverse record check survey. *Journal of Quantitative Criminology 22*: 279–297.

Tonry, Michael. 1995. *Malign neglect.* New York: Oxford University Press.

U.S. Census. 2000. Available: http://www.census.gov/.

Van Maanen, John. 1974. A developmental view of police behavior. In H. Jacob (Ed.), *The Potential for Reform of Criminal Justice*. Beverly Hills, CA: Sage Publications.

Vrij, Aldert, August Dragt, and Leendert Koppelaar. 1992. Interviews with ethnic interviewees: Nonverbal communication errors in impression formation. *Journal of Community and Applied Social Psychology* 2: 199–208.

Vrij, Aldert and Frans Winkel. 1994. Perceptual distortions in cross-cultural interrogations: The impact of skin color, accent, speech, style, and spoken fluency on impression formation. *Journal of Cross-Cultural Psychology* 25: 284–295.

Vrij, Aldert and Frans Winkel. 1991. Cultural patterns in Dutch and Surinam nonverbal behavior: An analysis of simulated police citizen encounters. *Journal of Nonverbal Behavior* 5: 169–184.

Walker, Samuel. 2001. Searching for the denominator: Problems with police traffic stop data and an early warning system solution. *Justice Research and Policy* 3: 63–95.

Walker, Samuel. 1993. *Taming the system: The control of discretion in Criminal Justice, 1950–1990*. New York: Oxford University Press.

Westley, William. 1953. Violence and the police. *American Journal of Sociology* 59: 34–41.

Winkel, Frans and Aldert Vrij. 1990. Interaction and impression formation in a cross-cultural dyad: Frequency and meaning of culturally determined gaze behavior in a police interview setting. *Social Behavior* 5: 335–350.

Worden, Robert. 1989. Situational and attitudinal explanations of police behavior: A theoretical reappraisal and empirical assessment. *Law and Society Review* 23: 667–771.

Worden, Robert and Robin Shepard. 1996. Demeanor, crime, and police behavior: A reexamination of the police services study data. *Criminology* 34: 83–105.

Worden, Robert Shepard, and Stephen Mastrofski. 1996. On the meaning and measurement of suspect's demeanor toward the police: A comment on "demeanor and arrest." *Journal of Research in Crime and Delinquency* 33: 324–332.

CASES CITED

State of New Jersey v. Soto et al., 734 A. 2d 350 (N.J. Super. 1996).

Wilkins v. Maryland State Police et al., Civ. No. MJG-93-468 (D.Md. 1993).

Chapter 13

||||||||||||||||||||||||||||||||||||||||||||||||||||||||||||||||||||||||||||||||||||

Street Stops and Broken Windows Revisited
The Demography and Logic of Proactive Policing in a Safe and Changing City

Jeffrey A. Fagan, Amanda Geller, Garth Davies, and Valerie West

I. Introduction

The role of policing in New York City's crime decline has been the subject of contentious debate for well over a decade. Violent crime reached its modern peak in New York City in 1991, followed by a 10 percent decline in 1992–93 (Fagan, Zimring, and Kim, 1998). This initial crime decline was spurred by the hiring and quick deployment in 1991 of five thousand additional officers under the Safe Streets Program (McCall, 1997; Greene, 1999; Waldeck, 2000; Karmen, 2000). During this initial decline, police tactics remained largely unchanged from the preceding years. Following the mayoral election in 1993, newly appointed police commissioner William Bratton implemented a regime of "order-maintenance policing" (OMP), which—together with other management reforms and innovations—dramatically and suddenly changed both the strategy and tactics of policing across the City. The new strategy was grounded in *Broken Windows* theory (Wilson and Kelling, 1982; Kelling and Cole, 1996) and focused on the connection between physical and social disorder and violence (Greene, 1999; Livingston, 1997; Spitzer, 1999; Sampson and Raudenbush, 1999; Duneier, 1999; Waldeck, 2000; Fagan and Davies, 2000; Taylor, 2001; Harcourt, 2001).

In the new policing model, police tactics, resources, and attention were redirected toward removal of visible signs of social disorder—"broken windows"—by using police resources both for vigorous enforcement of laws on minor "quality of life" offenses, while aggressively interdicting citizens in an intensive and widespread search for weapons (Kelling and Cole, 1996; Bratton and Knobler, 1998; Silverman, 1999). Tactically, policing in this era had several faces, from frequent arrests for low-level crimes such as public drinking, graffiti, and marijuana possession (Golub, Johnson, and Dunlap, 2007; Harcourt and Ludwig, 2007; Levine and Small, 2008), to aggressive street-level interdictions and searches of citizens whose behaviors signaled their potential for any of several types of crime, but most notably carrying weapons (Harcourt, 1998; Fagan and Davies, 2000; Gelman, Fagan, and Kiss, 2007). Using aggressive "stop and frisk" tactics, this brand of OMP was designed to reduce violence and weapons possession (Spitzer, 1999; Waldeck, 2000; Fagan and Davies, 2000; Harcourt, 2001).

The origins of the tactical shift are revealed in strategy documents issued by the New York City Police Department (NYPD) in 1994. First, Police Strategy No. 5, *Reclaiming the Public Spaces of New York*, articulated a reconstructed version of *Broken Windows* theory (Wilson and Kelling, 1982) as the driving force in the development of policing policy. It stated that the NYPD would apply its enforcement efforts to "reclaim the streets" by systematically and aggressively enforcing laws against low-level *social* disorder: graffiti, aggressive panhandling, fare beating, public drunkenness, unlicensed vending, public drinking, public urination, and other misdemeanor offenses. Second, Police Strategy No. 1, *Getting Guns Off the Streets of New York*, formalized the strategic focus on the eradication of gun violence through the tactical measure of intensifying efforts to seize illegal firearms. Homicide trends in New York City since 1985 provided strong empirical support for emphasizing gun violence in enforcement policy (Davis and Matea-Gelabert, 1999). Nearly all the increases in homicides, robberies, and assaults from 1985 to 1991 were attributable to gun violence (Fagan et al., 1998). The homicide crisis was a critical theme in the mayoral election campaign of 1993, and focused the attention of the incoming Giuliani administration's crime-control policy on gun violence (Silverman, 1999).

By the end of the decade, stops and frisks of persons suspected of crimes had become a flashpoint for grievances by the City's minority communities, who came under the closest surveillance of the police and were most often stopped and frisked (Spitzer, 1999; Kocieniewski, 1999; Roane, 1999; Jackson, 2000). In a fifteen-month period from January 1998 through March 1999, non-Hispanic Black, Hispanic Black, and Hispanic White New Yorkers were three times more likely than their White counterparts to be stopped and frisked on suspicion of weapons or violent crimes relative to each group's participation in each of those two types of crimes (Gelman et al., 2007). These excess stops—stops beyond the rate that one would predict from the race-specific crime rates—could be explained neither by the crime rates in those areas in the City's poorest areas, nor by signs and manifestations of social disorder, nor by the presence of physical disorder in the form of actual "broken windows" or building or neighborhood decay. Instead, Fagan and Davies (2000) reported that policing was disproportionately concentrated in the City's poorest neighborhoods with the highest concentrations of minority citizens, even after controlling for rates of crime and physical disorder in those places (see also Gelman et al., 2007).

Despite its racial disproportionality, the harsh spotlight of a federal court order enjoining the NYPD from racially selective enforcement (*Daniels et al. v. City of New York*, 2003), and arrest rates of less than 15 percent resulting from stops (Spitzer, 1999; Gelman et al., 2007), the OMP policy continued far into the next decade (Baker, 2009). Yet New York City had changed dramatically during this period, even after rates of crime and disorder had fallen. Housing prices had soared for more than a decade in all neighborhoods, including those that had the highest violence rates in the preceding decade (Fagan and Davies, 2007), and new housing replaced abandoned lots and decaying buildings across the City (Schwartz, 1999). Welfare rolls thinned, the number of immigrants landing in the City's poorest neighborhoods rose sharply, and populations of African Americans declined by more than 10 percent (U.S. Census Bureau, 2006). With minor and random ticks up and down, crime remained nearly flat and low since 2000 (Levine and Small, 2008).

Yet, in a safe and thriving city, the number of citizen stops grew by 500 percent between 2003 and 2008 (Baker, 2008, 2009; Ridgeway, 2007), long after crime had precipitously declined to and remained at historic lows. The efficiency of these stops —that is, the rate at which crime was detected leading to an arrest—declined from about 15 percent in 1998–99 (Gelman et al., 2007) to 7.8 percent in 2003 to less than 4.1 percent in 2006 (table 13.1 infra; Ridgeway, 2007).

As we show in this chapter, street stops continue to be disproportionately concentrated in the City's poorest areas, not unlike a decade earlier. The logic of a sharp rise in street stops and a corresponding sharp decline in their efficiency, in an era of flat crime rates, demands analysis and explanation. In this chapter, we examine the exponential rise in street stops in an era of stable crime rates and look to the community contexts of these stops to identify the predictors of stops and their outcomes.

The everyday routines of New Yorkers of different ethnic and racial groups take place in vastly different local contexts, and it is in these contexts that the heterogeneity and disparate impact of policing practices are most observable. Accordingly, we identify local area characteristics of crime, disorder, and social structure that predict race-specific police stop activity. We extend the work of Fagan and Davies (2000) from 1999 to two time periods in the current decade, across an extended era of declining and then stably low crime rates. We find that the dramatic increase in stop activity in recent years is concentrated predominantly in minority neighborhoods, and that minority residents are likely to be disproportionately subjected to law enforcement contact based on the neighborhoods in which they live rather than the crime problems in those areas. Moreover, this disproportionate contact is based on more than the level of neighborhood crime and disorder; demographic makeup predicts stop activity above and beyond what local crime conditions suggest is necessary and justifiable.

We also test the efficiency of street stops to detect wrongdoing and sanction offenders, and find it to be low and declining over time: as stops have become more prevalent in recent years, they are substantially less likely to lead to arrests. These limitations are particularly pronounced in neighborhoods with high Black populations, suggesting that Black citizens are not only at an elevated risk of police contact compared to non-Hispanic Whites and Hispanics, but that the standards used to justify stops in their neighborhoods may be lower than those in neighborhoods with higher White populations. Finally, we examine and compare specific age-race-cohort impacts of policing to illustrate the extraordinary concentration of policing along racial and ethnic lines.

Our analysis begins with a brief history of the constitutional and theoretical frameworks for New York's OMP strategy, with attention to the racial dimensions of modern policing. We then discuss the data, models, and results, followed by discussion and conclusions.

II. Background

A. Race, Neighborhoods, and Police Stops

Nearly a century of legal and social trends set the stage for the current debate on race and policing. Historically, close surveillance by police has been a part of everyday life for African Americans and other minority groups (see, for example, Musto, 1973; Kennedy, 1997; Cole, 1999; Loury, 2002; Weitzer and Tuch, 2006). In recent decades, the U.S. Supreme Court has sanctioned border interdictions of persons of Mexican or Hispanic ethnicity to halt illegal immigration (*U.S. v. Martinez-Fuerte*, 1976), as well as the racial components of drug courier profiling by airlines (*U.S. v. Harvey*, 1992). In *U.S. v. Whren* (1996), the Supreme Court allowed the use of race as a basis for a police stop as long as there were other factors that motivated the stop, and in *Brown v. Oneonta* (2000), a federal district court permitted the use of race as a search criterion if there was an explicit racial description of the suspect.

The legal standard to regulate the constitutionality of police conduct in citizen stops derives from *Terry v. Ohio* (1968), which involved a pedestrian stop that established the parameters of the "reasonable suspicion" standard for police conduct in detaining citizens for purposes of search or arrest. Recently, the courts have expanded the concept of "reasonable suspicion" to include location as well as the individual's behavior. In fact, the Court has articulated and refined this "high-crime area" doctrine, in cases from *Adams v. Williams* (1972) to *Illinois v. Wardlow* (2000). This line of cases allows police to consider the character of a neighborhood as a factor justifying a standard lower than the constitutionally defined threshold in individualized "reasonable" suspicion articulated in *Terry v. Ohio* (1968) (Ferguson and Bernache, 2008). For example, in *Wardlow*, the Supreme Court noted that although an individual's presence in a "high-crime area" does not meet the standard for a particularized suspicion of criminal activity, a location's characteristics are relevant to determining whether a behavior is sufficiently suspicious to warrant further investigation. Since "high-crime areas" and social disadvantage often are conflated both perceptually and statistically with concentrations of minority citizens (Massey and Denton, 1993; Sampson and Lauritsen, 1994; Loury, 2002; Fagan, 2008; Sampson and Raudenbush, 1999, 2004; Alpert et al., 2005; Ferguson and Bernache, 2008; Massey, 2007), this logic places minority neighborhoods at risk for elevating the suspiciousness of their residents in the eyes of the police.

But in connecting race and policing, the Court was only formalizing what criminologists had known for decades. Early studies on police selection of citizens for stops suggested that both the racial characteristics of the suspect and the racial composition of the suspect's neighborhood influence police decisions to stop, search, or arrest a suspect (Reiss, 1971, Bittner, 1970). Particularly in urban areas, suspect race interacts with neighborhood characteristics to animate the formation of suspicion among police officers (Smith, 1986; Thompson, 1999; Smith et al., 2006). For example, Alpert and colleagues (2005) showed that police are more likely to view a minority citizen as suspicious—leading to a police stop—based on nonbehavioral cues while relying on behavioral cues to develop suspicion for White citizens.

Individuals—including police and political leaders—also may substitute racial characteristics of communities for racial characteristics of individuals in their cognitive schema of suspicion, and, more important, act on them. Quillan and Pager (2001) find that urban residents' perceptions of crime in their neighborhoods are significantly predicted by the prevalence of young Black men, even after crime levels and other neighborhood characteristics are controlled for. Police perceptions may be similarly skewed, resulting in elevated stop rates in neighborhoods with high concentrations of minority populations, and the pathway is through the translation of perceptions into neighborhood stigma. For example, in a study of police practices in three cities, Smith (1986) showed that suspects in poor neighborhoods were more likely to be arrested, after controlling for suspect behavior and the type of crime. Suspects' race and the racial composition of the suspect's neighborhood were also significant predictors of police response. It seems that social psychological mechanisms interact with cultural processes (patterns of behavior) and structural features of neighborhoods (poverty, concentrations of minority citizens) to produce perceptions of disorder that perpetuate urban inequality (Sampson and Raudenbush, 2004) through several forms of discrimination, including policing intensity and tactics (Fagan and Davies, 2000). Recall that Fagan and Davies showed that street stops in New York were predicted not by disorder but by race and poverty, despite policing theories that emphasized disorder as a pathway to elevated crime. Poor neighborhoods are stigmatized in this way, and people both within these areas as well as those who reside elsewhere—including those with administrative authority to withhold or allocate various services—are likely to act on their perceptions.

Alternatively, these coercive police responses may relate to the perception that poor neighborhoods may have limited capacity for social control and self-regulation. This strategy was formalized in the influential "broken windows" essay of Wilson and Kelling (1982). They argued that police responses to disorder were critical to communicate intolerance for crime and to halt its contagious spread. *Broken Windows* called for the targeting of police resources to neighborhoods where public order was deteriorating, with the expectation that stopping disorderly behavior would stem the "developmental sequence" to more serious crime. In the original essay, Wilson and Kelling worried about "criminal invasion" of disorderly neighborhoods. Neighborhood disorder has explicitly been used as a criterion for allocating police resources in New York City since 1994, when commissioner William Bratton set policies to focus on minor offenses such as subway fare evasion and aggressive panhandling, in addition to felonies and other serious crime (Kelling and Cole, 1996). The policy also called for aggressive responses to social disorder that was endogenous to neighborhoods, in contrast to the "criminal invasion" concern in the theory's pristine form.

This order-maintenance approach also has been disputed, however, as critics question the causal link between disorder and more serious crime (compare Harcourt, 1998, 2001; Sampson and Raudenbush, 1999, 2004; and Taylor, 2001; with Skogan, 1990; Corman and Mocan, 2000; Rosenfeld, Fornango, and Rengifo, 2007). Moreover, these studies suggest that a focus on disorder might have a disparate impact on citizens of different races. A study of Chicago neighborhoods finds that city residents' perceptions of disorder conflate systematically observable conditions with their neighborhoods' racial and socioeconomic makeup (Sampson and Raudenbush, 2004). The association between race, poverty, and perceived disorder is significant in residents of all racial and ethnic backgrounds; race and concentrated poverty predict both residents' and outsiders' perceptions of disorder even more strongly than does systematically observed disorder. And the effect grows stronger as the concentration of poverty and minority groups increase.

So the concentration of "order maintenance" policing in poor places with high concentrations of poor residents should come as no surprise: order-maintenance policing strategies ostensibly targeted at "disorderly" neighborhoods were in fact focused on minority neighborhoods, characterized by social and economic disadvantage (Fagan and Davies, 2000). This racial bait and switch with disorder is fundamental to understanding the broad spatial and social patterns of policing in New York in the past decade. Most interesting and important is the persistence of these policies even as the objective indicia of poverty and disorder fade in what we show below is a steadily improving and safe City.

B. Approaches to Studying Police Stops

Recent empirical evidence on police stops supports perceptions among minority citizens that police disproportionately stop African American and Hispanic motorists, and that once stopped, these citizens are more likely to be searched or arrested (Cole, 1999; Veneiro and Zoubeck, 1999; Harris, 1999; Zingraff et al., 2000; Gross and Barnes, 2002; Weitzer and Tuch, 2006; Ayres, 2008). For example, two surveys with nationwide probability samples, completed in 1999 and in 2002, showed that African Americans were far more likely than other Americans to report being stopped on the highways by police (Langan et al., 2001; Durose et al., 2005). Both surveys showed that minority drivers also were more likely to report being ticketed, arrested, handcuffed, or searched by police, and that they more often were threatened with force or had force used against them. These disparities in stop rates exact high social costs that, according to Loury (2002), animate culturally meaningful forms of stigma that reinforce racial inequalities, especially in the practice of law enforcement. These stigma translate into withdrawal of minority populations from cooperation with the police and other legal authorities in the coproduction of security (Tyler and Huo, 2002; Tyler and Fagan, 2008).

Traffic violations often serve as the rationale or pretext for stops of motorists (Walker, 2001; Harris, 2002), just as "suspicious behavior" is the spark for both pedestrian and traffic stops (Alpert et al., 2005; Ayres, 2008). As with traffic violations, the range of suspicious behaviors is broad enough to challenge efforts to identify an appropriate baseline against which to compare race-specific stop rates (see Miller, 2000; Smith and Alpert, 2002; Gould and Mastrofski, 2004). Pedestrian stops are at the very core of policing, used to enforce narcotics and weapons laws, to identify fugitives or other persons for whom warrants may be outstanding, to investigate reported crimes and "suspicious" behavior, and to improve community quality of life. For the NYPD, a "stop" provides an occasion for the police to have contact with persons presumably involved in low-level criminality without having to effect a formal arrest, and under the lower constitutional standard of "reasonable suspicion" (Spitzer, 1999). Indeed, because low-level "quality of life" and misdemeanor offenses were more likely to be committed in the open, the "reasonable suspicion" standard is more easily satisfied in these sorts of crimes (Rudovsky, 2001, 2007).

Two distinct approaches characterize recent efforts to model and understand racial disparities in police stops. Each focuses less on identifying racial bias than on understanding the role of race in explaining patterns of police behavior. Attributing bias is difficult: causal claims about discrimination would require far more information than the typical administrative (observational) data sets can supply. For example, when Officer McFadden stopped suspect Terry in the events leading to the landmark 1968 U.S. Supreme Court decision in *Terry v. Ohio*, he used his law enforcement "experience" to interpret Terry's behavior in front of the jewelry store.[1] Were McFadden's notions of "suspicious" behavior skewed by his longtime work in poor and minority neighborhoods? Was the timing of the event (shortly after the closing of the store) or the location (a deserted part of the downtown area) influential? What role did Terry's and McFadden's race play? Would Terry's actions have been interpreted differently if he were White? If McFadden were Black? If the store was in a residential neighborhood instead of downtown? In a minority neighborhood or a predominantly White one? The multiplicity of interacting factors complicated the identification of the role of race in the decision to detain Terry (Kennedy, 1997), but several analyses of the facts and jurisprudence of *Terry* suggest that the Supreme Court opinion discounted the influence of race in the opinion (Thompson, 1999; Carbado, 2002; Carbado and Gulati, 2000; Roberts, 1999; Rudovsky, 2007).

In *Terry*, it would be difficult to identify race alone, apart from the context in which race was observed, as the factor that animated McFadden's decision to stop and frisk suspect Terry. Instead, reliable evidence of ethnic or racial bias in these instances would require experimental designs that control for these competing and interacting factors—situational context, demeanor of suspect—so as to isolate differences in outcomes that could only be attributed to race or ethnicity. Such experiments are routinely used in tests of discrimination in housing and employment (see, for example, Pager, 2003, 2007; Thacher, 2008). But observational studies that lack such controls are often embarrassed by omitted variable biases: few studies can control for all the variables that police consider in deciding whether to stop or search someone, much less their several combinations or permutations. Research in situ that relies on direct observation of police behavior (e.g., Gould and Mastrofski, 2004; Alpert et al., 2005) requires officers to articulate the reasons for their actions, a task that is vulnerable to numerous validity threats. Sampling considerations, as well as the presence of the researchers in the context of the decision, also challenge the validity of observational studies.

The first approach to studying racial disparities bypasses the question of whether police intend to discriminate on the basis of ethnicity or race, and instead focuses on disparate impacts of police stop strategies. This strategy is prevalent in studies of decisions in the context of highways stops. In this approach, comparisons of "hit rates," or efficiencies in the proportion of stops that yield positive results, serve as evidence of disparate impacts of police stops. This type of analysis has been used in several studies, including Knowles, Persico, and Todd (2001); Ayres (2002a,b); Gross and Barnes (2002); and many other studies of police behaviors on highways (see, e.g., Durlauf, 2006b). This approach bypasses the supply-side question of who is stopped (and for what reason), and instead looks only at disparate impacts or outcomes for different groups.

Outcome tests are agnostic with respect to race-based motivations for stops or frisks versus a search for efficiency and deterrence (Ayres, 2002b; Dominitz and Knowles, 2006). They can show when a particular policy or decision-making outcome has a disparate impact whose racial disproportionality is not justified by heightened institutional productivity. In the context of profiling, outcome tests assume that the ex post probability that a police search will uncover drugs or other contraband is a function of the degree of probable cause that police use in deciding to stop and search a suspect (Ayres, 2002a). If searches of minorities are less productive than searches of Whites, this could be evidence that police have a lower threshold of probable cause when searching minorities. At the very least, it is a sign of differential treatment of minorities that in turn produces a disparate impact.

Knowles, Persico, and Todd (2001) consider this "hit rate" approach theoretically as well as empirically in a study finding that, of the drivers on Interstate 95 in Maryland stopped by police on suspicion of drug trafficking, African Americans were as likely as Whites to have drugs in their cars. Their theoretical analysis posits a dynamic process that considers the behaviors of police and citizens of different races, and integrates their decisions in equilibrium where police calibrate their behavior to the probabilities of detecting illegal behavior, and citizens in different racial groups adjust their propensities to accommodate the likelihood of detection. They concluded that the search for drugs was an efficient allocation of police resources, despite the disparate impacts of these stops on minority citizens (Lamberth, 1997; Ayres, 2002a; Gross and Barnes, 2002; but see Sanga, 2009, for different conclusions).

Outcome tests can be constructed as quasi experiments, with race as a treatment, to identify the role of race in the selection of citizens for searches. Ridgeway (2007) matched suspects within officers to compare the post-stop outcomes of White suspects to those of minority suspects in similar locations, stopped at similar times and for the same reasons. He reports no differences in post-stop arrests ("hit rates") despite the greater number of stops of non-Whites. But this approach seeks to explain away contextual variables, especially neighborhood context, rather than explicitly incorporate these factors in an identification strategy. Close and Mason (2007) construct a disparate outcome quasi experiment to identify the role of race in police searches by comparing the preferences of officers of different races to search motorists, controlling for the motorist's race. They use both an outcomes-based nonparametric (quasi-experimental) analysis and a standard benchmarking parametric (regression) approach, and report both personal biases and police cultural bias in their propensity to search African American and Latino drivers.

These are useful but limited strategies. The robustness of these designs is compromised by the omission of several factors—some unobservable and others usually absent from administrative data—that might bias their claims, such as racial differences in the attributes that police consider when deciding which motorists or pedestrians to stop, search, or arrest (see, for example, Alpert et al., 2005; Smith et al., 2006), or differences in police behavior in neighborhoods or other social contexts with different racial makeup (Smith, 1986; Fagan and Davies, 2000; Alpert et al., 2005). For example, Ridgeway (2007) estimated the racial proportionality of police stops of citizens based on victim reports of suspect race. This is a sound strategy, but only for the approximately 20 percent of stops based on a rationale of "fits suspect description" (see, for example, Spitzer, 1999), and only if we are confident in the accuracy of victim identification of the suspect(s) and the accompanying classification of race.[2]

The omission of neighborhood context also biases estimates of the proportionality of police stops of citizens. The randomizing equilibrium assumptions in the Persico and colleagues approach—that both police and potential offenders adjust their behavior in response to the joint probabilities of carrying contraband and being stopped—tend to average across broad heterogeneous conditions both in police decision making and offenders' propensities to crime (Dharmapala and Ross, 2004; Durlauf, 2006a, 2006b), and discount the effects of race-specific sensitivities toward crime decisions under varying conditions of detection risk via police stop (Alpert et al., 2005; Dominitz and Knowles, 2006). When these two concerns are addressed, Dharmapala and Ross (2004) identify different types of equilibria that lead to different conclusions about racial prejudice in police stops and searches.

Accordingly, the nature and extent of racial bias in the policing of motorists and pedestrians remains unsettled empirically (Persico and Todd, 2005; Antonovics and Knight, 2004; Bjerk, 2007; Donohue and Levitt, 2001; Close and Mason, 2007). Supply-side issues, both in the number and characteristics of the persons available for stops by virtue of law violation or even suspicious behavior, complicate the search game paradigm by perceptually skewing the population of stopped drivers according to the *ex ante* probabilities of criminality that police officers assign to different racial groups. Institutional or individual differences in the goals of law enforcement may also create heterogeneity both in the selection of individuals to be stopped and the decisions to engage them in searches for drugs, weapons, or other contraband. Officers may pursue one set of law enforcement goals for one group (maximizing arrests) while pursuing a different set of goals (minimizing crime) for another. Racial nepotism or antagonism may lead to differences in police stop-and-search behaviors when officers of one race face choices of whether to stop or search a driver of the same or a different racial or ethnic group (Close and Mason, 2007).

These complexities illustrate the difficulty of identifying the role of race in producing racial disparities in stops and searches, and suggest a second approach that incorporates the contexts in which individual officers consider race in their everyday interactions with citizens. Gelman and colleagues (2007) and Alpert and colleagues (2005) show how neighborhood context influences both the attribution of suspicion that animates an encounter and the outcomes of police-citizen encounters. The institutional context of policing also may influence individual officers' decisions by stigmatizing neighborhoods as "high-crime" or disorderly, skewing how officers perceive and interpret the actions of citizens. Institutional cultures also may implicitly tolerate such perceptual or cognitive schema and internalize them into policy preferences and strategic decisions, as well as internal preferences for reward, promotion, or discipline. These contextual concerns, informed by crime plus social and demographic dimensions of neighborhoods, suggest the second approach, one that explicitly incorporates either a multilevel approach that examines officer-place interactions, or shifts the focus from the actions of individual officers and individual suspects to the behaviors of cohorts of officers who collectively patrol neighborhoods with measurable attributes that incorporate race and ethnicity, and where aggregation biases from racial concentration may shape officers' preferences about crime and thresholds of suspicion.

These issues inform several features of the analyses reported in this chapter. First, to explain the distribution and predictors of street stops and then of arrests ("hit rates"), we focus on neighborhoods, not individual officers. Neighborhoods are the focal point of the underlying theories of order-maintenance policing. Place also is the unit of analysis for the allocation and deployment of police resources, and neighborhood crime rates are the metrics by which the resources of the police are managed and evaluated. Place also imparts meaning to the interpretation of routine actions and movements of citizens, whether local residents or outsiders whose appearance may evoke special attention. And the benchmark of the social composition of place, in conjunction with actual crime, is sensitive to the actual allocation of police resources as well as tactical decisions by the NYPD, and is widely used in research on selective enforcement in policing (Alpert et al., 2005; Fagan, 2002; Fridell, 2004; Skogan and Frydl, 2004).

Next we address supply-side and omitted-variable problems by controlling for the prevalence of the targeted behaviors in patrolled areas, assessing whether stop-and-search rates exceed what we would predict from knowledge of local criminal activity. This responds to the benchmark problem in research on selective enforcement. This approach requires estimates of the supply of individuals engaged in the targeted behaviors, and the extent of racial disproportionality is likely to depend on the benchmark used to measure criminal behavior (see Miller, 2000; Fagan and Davies, 2000; Walker, 2001; Smith and Alpert, 2002; Ayres, 2008; Durlauf, 2006a, 2006b; Ridgeway and MacDonald, this volume). Ideally, we would know race-specific crime rates in each social area to disaggregate benchmarks by race and ethnicity. But we observed practical problems in this approach. For example, clearance rates vary by crime type, and so the race of suspects is often unknown. Fewer than one in four stops in 2007 were based on a match between the person detained and a suspect description known to the police (Ridgeway, 2007). And suspected crimes that animate a large share of stops, such as weapons or drug possession, often do not follow from crime reports that identify the race of a suspect, so these base rates of offending are unknown.

Accordingly, we use homicide arrests as a measure of reported crime. Homicide victimization and arrests are stably measured over time, limiting measurement error. In New York, its racial distribution—both offending and victimization—is highly correlated with the demography of the neighborhood where the crime takes place (Fagan and Davies, 2004; Fagan et al., 2007). In New York City, the site of this research, homicide records are both a strong lag and lead indicator of crime, correlated at .75 or more with reported crimes for other Part I felonies for the seventeen years from 1984 to 2000. Homicides also are the most stably and reliably measured indicator of crime over time and through police administrations, whereas other violent crimes (e.g., aggravated assault) are subject to classifications biases that vary over time and place (Zimring and Hawkins, 1997).

Following Gelman and colleagues (2007), we estimate whether the stop rate and "hit rate" within neighborhoods is predicted by local crime conditions, the physical and social composition of the neighborhood, or its racial composition. Since race is correlated with neighborhood composition and crime, we expect that race will not be a significant predictor either of stop patterns or of efficiency (the rate at which stops produce arrests), once we account for crime and other neighborhood conditions. But as we show below, race does predict stop rates and hit rates, after controlling for crime and local conditions. Is this evidence of racial animus, targeted collectively by officers in a neighborhood or through institutional and administrative levers that mark neighborhoods characterized by their racial or ethnic composition as worthy of heightened suspicion? The fact that police are stopping minorities, and others in minority neighborhoods, at a higher rate than is justified by local crime conditions does not require that we infer that police engaged in disparate treatment—but, at a minimum, it is evidence that whatever criteria the police employed produced an unjustified racially disparate impact.

III. Data and Methods

A. Data

We examine changes in OMP enforcement patterns beginning with the period examined by Spitzer (1999), Fagan and Davies (2000), and Gelman and colleagues (2007). Including that period (1998–99), we examine three distinct periods, termed the "early" (1998–1999), "middle" (2002–2004), and "recent" (2005–2006) periods. In each period, data on stop activity are based on records from the New York Police Department. The department has a policy of keeping records on stops (on "UF-250 forms") (see Spitzer, 1999; *Daniels et al. v. City of New York*, 2003); this information was collated for all stops from January 1998 through March 1999, and the 2003 and 2006 calendar years. Stops are recorded and aggregated for each precinct. Appendix A discusses the legal requirements for a stop, frisk, and arrest pursuant to a stop. Data on stops, frisks, and arrests from 2003 to 2007 were made publicly available by the NYPD following a Freedom of Information Law (FOIL) request and subsequent court order (NYCLU, 2008). Data from the "early" period were published in Spitzer (1999) and Fagan and Davies (2000).

Stop rates are analyzed in the context of citywide crime, demographic, and socioeconomic conditions. We use total stop rates (undifferentiated by suspected crime) and stop rates disaggregated by the race of person stopped. We use two measures of crime in the preceding year. First, in the figures, we use reported homicides in the police precinct in the preceding year as the measure of crime. This lagged function allows us to avoid simultaneity concerns from using contemporaneous measures of crime and police actions. Second, in the multivariate models, we use homicide arrests as the marker of crime.

We measure homicides for the "early" period using the NYPD's arrest-and-complaint file, and the city's COMPSTAT records for the "middle" and "recent" periods. In the multivariate estimates in tables 13.2 and 13.3, we use lagged homicide arrests in each neighborhood as the benchmark for estimating the proportionality of police stops and frisks. There are obvious strengths and weaknesses in this measure. Arrests are subject to police preferences for resource allocation, and also to police skills in identifying and capturing offenders. Homicide arrests also may vary by neighborhood based on externalities such as the extent of citizen cooperation with police investigations. Arrests also are vulnerable to measurement error: they often are reduced to other charges when evidence is too inconclusive to sustain a greater charge. But arrests also have strengths as a measure of crime. Reported homicides and homicide arrests are highly correlated over time across police precincts in New York: the partial correlation by month and precinct from 1989 through 2001 was .952.[3] This endogeneity of crime and policing within neighborhoods captures the preferences of police to allocate resources to particular areas in the search for offenders. Also, homicide arrests are a strong indicator of both arrests and complaints for other serious crimes.[4] To the extent that crime in the prior year is influenced *both* by crime and the policing that it attracts, the use of arrests as a measure of both the presence of police and of local crime conditions avoids omitted-variable problems when using only measures of reported crimes. Finally, arrest trends in preceding periods incorporate the priors of both individual officers and their supervisors as well as neighborhood characteristics, and in fact may capture officers' propensities to stop citizens based on the joint influence of individual and neighborhood racial markers.

We also incorporate demographic and socioeconomic variables in each area that might compete with or moderate crime as influences on stop activity: concentrated neighborhood disadvantage, residential turnover, and ethnic heterogeneity have each been associated with low levels of neighborhood collective efficacy and informal social control. These are both indicia of perceived disorder (Sampson and Raudenbush, 1999) and risk factors for crime (Fagan and Davies, 2004). More important, Fagan and Davies (2000) showed that these were salient predictors of stop activities in the "early" period, and we examine their influences over time as time-varying predictors. Areas in which these phenomena are concentrated might therefore be unable to informally regulate local residents, requiring law enforcement agencies to impose formal social control instead and leading to greater search activity.

Demographic and socioeconomic data for each period is based on the New York City Housing and Vacancy Survey (HVS), a survey completed every three years by the City's Department of Housing Preservation and Development, in cooperation with the U.S. Bureau of the Census (http://www.census.gov/hhes/www/housing/nychvs/nychvs.html). We analyze the 1999, 2002, and 2005 waves of the survey to generate baseline estimates of neighborhood social and economic status. Each wave covers approximately eighteen thousand housing units, classified into fifty-five "subboros," based on the Public Use Microdata Areas (PUMAs) for New York City (Community Studies of New York, 2007). We used shape files provided by the New York City Department of City Planning to reconcile the subboro boundaries with the police precincts (see Fagan and Davies, 2000). In the small number of precincts where there was overlap in the boundaries, precincts were assigned to the subboro that contained the majority of its population.

B. Base Rates and Citywide Trends

A quick look at the data on New York City neighborhoods suggests that the social and demographic makeup of the City has changed significantly since 1999. Table 13.1 shows that the city's racial and ethnic makeup has become more diverse. The bulk of the city's population growth has come from racial and ethnic minorities, plus

TABLE 13.1
Stop Activity and Neighborhood Socioeconomic Conditions

	1999 Stops per 1,000 persons		2002–2003 Stops per 1,000 persons		2005–2006 Stops per 1,000 persons		% change (99–05)
Citywide Stop Rates							
Stops per 1,000 Population							
Total Stops	12.5		19.4		60.2		381.6%
Blacks	26.6		37.7		130.8		391.7%
Whites	3.5		6.0		17.9		411.4%
Hispanics	15.1		19.5		63.9		323.2%
	Mean	SD	Mean	SD	Mean	SD	
Neighborhood Stop Activity							
Number of Stops	1813.4	1098.9	2922.5	1670.5	9208.9	6480.4	407.8%
Stops of Blacks	988.1	864.3	1411.9	1368.6	4863.0	5479.1	392.2%
Stops of Whites	187.0	145.3	320.1	273.8	972.7	860.8	420.2%
Stops of Hispanics	583.9	559.9	810.2	599.5	2688.4	2173.9	360.5%
Physical Disorder							
Exterior Walls	3.09%	0.03	2.63%	0.02	2.83%	0.02	−8.5%
Exterior Windows	3.36%	0.03	3.45%	0.03	2.36%	0.02	−29.8%
Stairways	5.25%	0.04	5.29%	0.04	4.24%	0.03	−19.3%
Floors	5.08%	0.04	4.75%	0.04	4.06%	0.03	−20.1%
Structural Characteristics							
Public Assistance	18.24%	0.13	15.17%	0.10	16.41%	0.11	−10.0%
Foreign-Born	46.19%	0.16	43.56%	0.14	49.61%	0.16	7.4%
Immigrant (different in HVS)	36.34%	0.16	43.56%	0.14	41.18%	0.16	13.3%
Entropy	89.02%	0.24	93.64%	0.25	95.48%	0.22	7.3%
Mobility (% Living < 5 years)	40.26%	0.05	35.88%	0.05	36.08%	0.05	−10.4%
Vacancy Rate	5.62%	0.03	6.87%	0.04	6.68%	0.03	18.8%
Households							
Total	52153	19305	54642	16552	55236	16803	5.9%
Black	12150	11930	13115	13382	12570	12603	3.5%
White	24112	23404	24359	22015	24191	21426	0.3%
Hispanic	11682	9155	12200	9063	12881	9206	10.3%

Sources: Socioeconomic and Household Data from New York City Housing and Vacancy Surveys, 1999, 2002, 2005, Stop data from NYPD, Population data from U.S. Census Bureau.

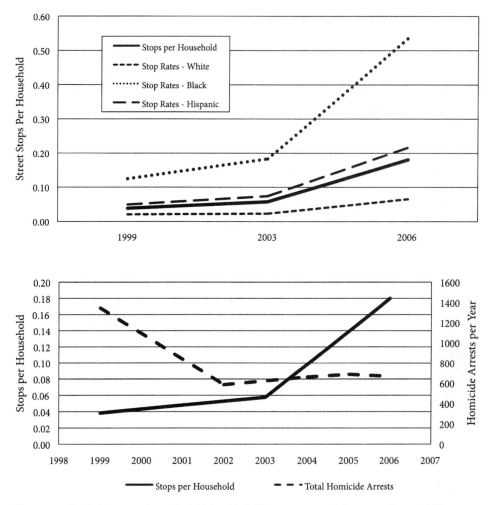

Figure 13.1 (*top*). Stops per household, New York City, 1999–2006. Sources: (Stops) NYS, Office of the Attorney General, 1999; NYC Police Department, Stop Frisks and Search Data, 2003–2007, (Households) NYC Housing and Vacancy Survey.

Figure 13.2 (*bottom*). Stops per household and total homicide arrests, New York City, 1999–2006. Sources: (Stops) NYS, Office of the Attorney General, 1999; NYC Police Department, Stop Frisks and Search Data, 2003–2007, (Households) NYC Housing and Vacancy Survey, (Arrests) NYS Division of Criminal Justice Services.

a notable increase among immigrants. Individual neighborhoods have also become more integrated, as shown by the increase in neighborhood entropy. At the same time, socioeconomic conditions have improved, with a decline in both public assistance receipt and neighborhood levels of physical disorder.

Even as the city has changed demographically and improved socioeconomically, stops and searches have become far more prevalent. Figure 13.1 shows the average neighborhood—subboro—stop rate, computed as stops per household. We use household because this is the population parameter in the HVS in each analysis period. While city residents of all races have become increasingly likely to be stopped by the police, stop rates vary dramatically by race; by 2006, Blacks were more than twice as likely to be stopped as either Whites or Hispanics. The increase in stop activity is particularly striking when considering that New York City crime rates fell dramatically between 1999 and 2006. As shown in figure 13.2, homicide arrests in the City fell by more than 50 percent between 1999 and 2002, and, albeit with a slight increase, remained low through 2006.

Following the examples of Knowles and colleagues (2001), Ayres (2002a,b), Gross and Barnes (2002), Gelman and colleagues (2007), and Ridgeway (2007), we measure the effectiveness of street stops by their "hit rates," the rate at which stops result in arrests. Figures 13.3a–c, like figure 13.1, present average neighborhood stop rates per household in each of the three time periods of interest, disaggregated by race, with average hit rates overlaid onto the graph. And since crime rates remained relatively stable across the period, there is no evidence that the increase in stops contributes to crime minimization. While not as pronounced as the differences in stop rates, hit rates also suggest substantial racial disparities. Figure 13.3b shows that even as stop rates have increased dramatically for Blacks from 2003 to 2006, hit rates have fallen steadily, suggesting that the increase in stop activity has added little value in maximizing efficiency via generating arrests. Stops of Whites appear more likely than stops of Blacks to lead to arrest, suggesting that Blacks are disproportionately subjected to stops, with little public safety payoff.

C. Stop Activity by Neighborhood

Stop rates have not only increased dramatically, but between-neighborhood differences in stop rates have become far more pronounced. Figure 13.4 displays one data point for each of the fifty-five HVS subboros in each period, each representing the average neighborhood stop rate per household in each year. We also show the count of homicides citywide over the same period. While earlier studies have identified neighborhoods that have the greatest racial disparity in stop-and-frisk practices, figure 13.4 shows that the dramatic growth in average stop rates from 2003 to 2006 is explained by extreme increases in a subset of neighborhoods with high rates of African American and Latino residents: Brownsville, East New York, Central Harlem, East Harlem, Bedford-Stuyvesant, and Mott Haven. Although some of this increase may be due to improved reporting, it is curious that all the improved reporting has been in neighborhoods with the highest non-White populations in the City. These neighborhoods are predominantly African American, according to the Department of City Planning.[5]

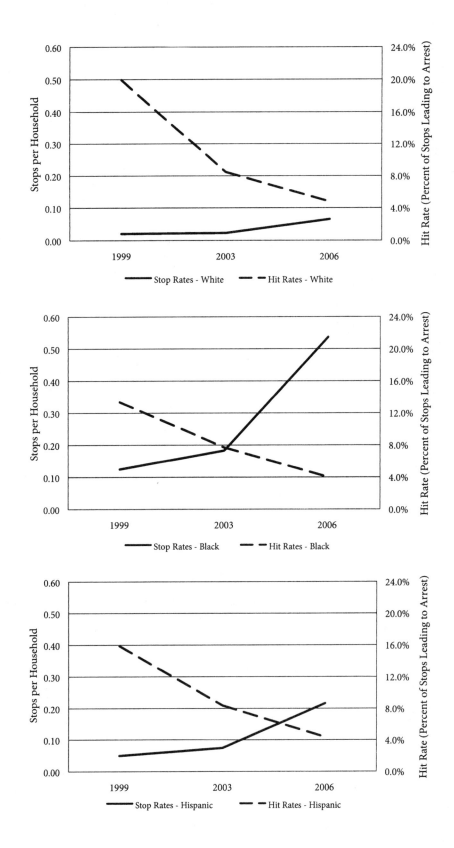

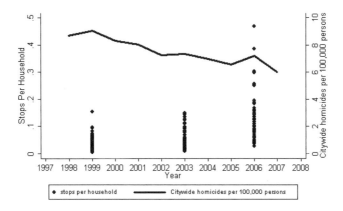

Figure 13.4. Street stops per neighborhood, selected years, 1999–2006.

Given the degree of racial segregation across New York City neighborhoods, we address this disparity below by examining neighborhood-level drivers of stop activity.

Figures 13.5a–c suggest that neighborhood racial composition explains not only stop activity but also hit rates and stop efficacy. Each figure shows, for 1999, 2003, and 2006, respectively, a LOWESS-smoothed estimate of the relationship between hit rates and the percentage of Blacks in each of the fifty-five neighborhoods for each period of time. As in figure 13.3 (a,b,c), these graphs suggest that hit rates are falling over time in stops of all racial groups. Particularly in 2006, however, the year when between-neighborhood differences are most pronounced (see figure 13.4), there is a visible difference in neighborhoods with the highest concentrations of Black households. In neighborhoods where 60 percent of households (or more) are Black, stops are not only less effective than in more mixed or White neighborhoods, but hit rates are particularly low in stops of Black and Hispanic individuals.

Opposite page:

Figure 13.3a (*top*). Stops per household and arrests per stop, White suspects, New York City, 1999–2006. Source: (Stops and Arrests) New York State, Office of the Attorney General, 1999; New York City Police Department, Stop Frisks and Search Data, 2003–2007, (Households) NYC Housing and Vacancy Survey.

Figure 13.3b (*middle*). Stops per household and arrests per stop, Black suspects, New York City, 1999–2006. Source: (Stops and Arrests) New York State, Office of the Attorney General, 1999; New York City Police Department, Stop Frisks and Search Data, 2003–2007, (Households) NYC Housing and Vacancy Survey.

Figure 13.3c (*bottom*). Stops per household and arrests per stop, Hispanic suspects, New York City, 1999–2006. Source: (Stops and Arrests) New York State, Office of the Attorney General, 1999; New York City Police Department, Stop Frisks and Search Data, 2003–2007, (Households) NYC Housing and Vacancy Survey.

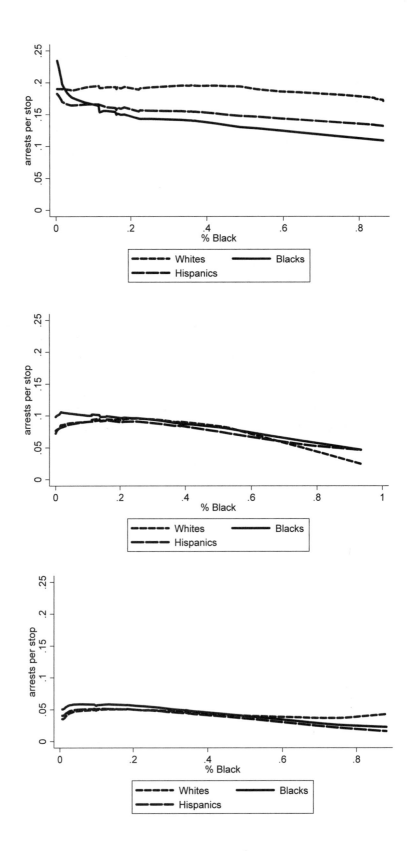

D. Modeling Strategy

1. PREDICTING STOP ACTIVITY

Given the between-neighborhood disparities shown in figure 13.4, we examine stop activity at the neighborhood level to identify factors that explain between-neighborhood differences both within periods and over time. Following Gelman and colleagues (2007), we estimate a series of Poisson regressions to predict the number of stops conducted in each neighborhood in each time period. The racial disparities shown in figures 13.1 and 13.3 may be driven not by race, but rather by differences in neighborhood social conditions where Blacks, Whites, and Hispanics are concentrated, or by differences in their *ex ante* crime conditions. If, for example, the police make more stops in high-crime areas, but treat individuals similarly within similarly situated localities, racial disparities in stop rates could be explained entirely by neighborhood crime conditions. Or the NYPD's focus on "broken windows" and order-maintenance policing might lead stop activity to be most prevalent in neighborhoods with disorderly conditions (Wilson and Kelling, 1982; Kelling and Cole, 1996). We therefore estimate a model where the stop count y_i in neighborhood i is distributed based on predictors X, with an expected value of:

$$E[y_i|X_i] = e^{X\beta}$$

The vector X includes a measure of neighborhood crime (homicide arrests, lagged), and several socioeconomic characteristics we expect to be correlated with crime rates and policing practices. First, we explicitly control for crime conditions in the previous year, using the number of homicide arrests in each neighborhood. To reflect the NYPD focus on disorder in the 1990s and early 2000s, we estimate and control for a single principal components factor (computed for each year) that summarizes the physical condition ("broken windows," literally) of local residences (based on the percentage of buildings whose windows, walls, floors, and stairways have problems visible to outside observers). The disorder theories animating OMP strategies considered both physical and social disorder as cues of weak informal social control and low guardianship of neighborhoods. We consider only physical disorder since some elements of social disorder—such as fighting, visible drug use—are in fact crimes and would be correlated with stop activity.[6] Also, physical disorder tends to be highly correlated with social disorder, and its component behaviors, including public intoxication, loitering, and fighting (Sampson and Raudenbush, 1999). These are targeted in OMP as a wedge to reduce crime opportunities and to identify persistent criminals. To reflect the likelihood that police activity is higher in more populated areas, we control for the logged number of households in each neighborhood.

Opposite page:

Figure 13.5a (*top*). Lowess-smoothed arrest rates by neighborhood racial composition, 1999.

Figure 13.5b (*middle*). Lowess-smoothed arrest rates by neighborhood racial composition, 2003.

Figure 13.5c (*bottom*). Lowess-smoothed arrest rates by neighborhood racial composition, 2006.

We also control for traditional and temporally stable predictors of neighborhood crime (Shaw and McKay, 1942; Sampson and Lauritsen, 1994; Land et al., 1990; Fagan and Davies, 2004, Fagan, 2008; Kirk and Laub, in press): concentrated disadvantage (measured by the percentage of households receiving public assistance), residential instability (measured by the percentage of families who have moved to the their current residence within five years, and by the residential vacancy rates), ethnic diversity (measured by the percent of residents who are Black or Hispanic, the percentage who are foreign-born, and a measure of entropy, which captures the degree of ethnic heterogeneity in the neighborhood). We expect, however, that these factors will be correlated with police activity only to the extent that they predict crime; once crime conditions are controlled for, there should be no marginal relationship between social structure and stop activity. Variables (with the exception of logged population) are standardized to a mean of zero and variance of one, and neighborhood observations are weighted based on the number of households in each.

To assess the extent to which neighborhood conditions, and their influence on policing, change over time, we first estimate three separate cross-sectional models, one for each time period of interest. We then combine the observations into a pooled cross section (model 4), and add controls for year fixed effects in Model 5. Model 6 contains year fixed effects and random intercepts with standard errors clustered by neighborhood to account for neighborhood differences.

Although the City has changed for the better over the period of analysis, and stop activity has increased dramatically over time, the crime, disorder, and socioeconomic predictors vary far more between neighborhoods than they do within neighborhoods over time, and these differences—at least in ordinal position—are stable over time (see Sampson and Morenoff, 2006). Accordingly, we rejected the option to control for neighborhood fixed effects in Model 6, preferring instead to focus on differences between neighborhoods. Controlling for neighborhood fixed effects identifies the relationship between crime and stop activity, and social structure and stop activity, solely from within-neighborhood variation. Because we acknowledge that the allocation of police resources is determined by differences between neighborhoods, model 6 is specified to reflect between-neighborhood differences, with random intercepts and standard errors clustered by neighborhood.

2. PREDICTING STOP EFFECTIVENESS

We next examine the crime and socioeconomic conditions predicting stop effectiveness, the "hit rate" at which stops lead to arrests. We expect that this rate might be tied to the same conditions of crime and disorder that predict stop activity, since "excess stops" above the crime rate are likely to be concentrated in poor neighborhoods with concentrations of minority population. Accordingly, we estimate a series of linear probability models using the predictors detailed above. As we hypothesize with stop activity, however, in the case of race-neutral policing hit rates should not be significantly related to neighborhood social structure. For these analyses, we estimate the effects of neighborhood racial composition on stop rates using both neighborhood fixed effects and, also, as above, using random intercepts.

IV. Results

A. Explaining Neighborhood Differences in Stop Rates

Table 13.2 shows the relationship between neighborhood conditions and the incidence of street stops. Models 1–3 show results for each year. As expected, stops are more frequent in neighborhoods in which crime is more prevalent for all years, but in larger neighborhoods only in 1999. Controlling for homicides, stops are more frequent in neighborhoods with higher Black populations. The effect size is fairly stable across years, even as the overall number of stops rose over time. Model 4 is a pooled cross-sectional model for all years, with no controls for time. Standard errors are clustered by neighborhoods. The effect for Black population remains significant, and population is again significant when the three time periods are pooled.

TABLE 13.2
*Poisson Regressions of Stops per Neighborhood, Controlling for
Social Structure and Crime, 1998–2006*

Sample Year	Model					
	(1) 1999	(2) 2003	(3) 2006	(4) All Years	(5) All Years	(6) All Years
Homicide Arrests (lagged)	.202**	.163*	.182**	.172**	.183**	.027*
	[.074]	[.069]	[.067]	[.084]	[.055]	[.052]
% Receiving Public Assistance	.106	.056	.169	.257*	.159	.198*
	[.127]	[.089]	[.099]	[.131]	[.086]	[.082]
% Foreign-Born	−.011	.006	−.045	−.056	−.032	−.076
	[.079]	[.062]	[.083]	[.072]	[.060]	[.065]
Racial Entropy	.186*	.007	.091	.090	.082	.085
	[.086]	[.060]	[.064]	[.066]	[.050]	[.059]
% Black	.216*	.198**	.262**	.260**	.237**	.279***
	[.109]	[.072]	[.068]	[.068]	[.060]	[.064]
% Hispanic	.053	.002	.054	−.023	.021	.031
	[.113]	[.078]	[.083]	[.072]	[.063]	[.074]
% Moved Within 5 years	.005	−.056	−.012	−.007	−.006	.008
	[.098]	[.065]	[.098]	[.082]	[.069]	[.064]
Vacancy Rate	.038	−.074	.090	−.007	.050	.026
	[.090]	[.076]	[.076]	[.074]	[.044]	[.042]
Physical Disorder	.028	.152	−.109	−.011	−.053	−.048
	[.081]	[.074]*	[.105]	[.114]	[.071]	[.064]
Log Population	.505*	.438	.451**	.769**	.445**	.407**
	[.231]	[.230]	[.173]	[.212]	[.157]	[.065]
2003 FE					.460**	.451**
					[.060]	[.065]
2006 FE					1.590**	1.585**
					[.078]	[.083]
Constant	1.953	3.140	4.115	−.003	2.600	1.002
	[2.523]	[2.521]	[1.911]	[2.323]	[1.727]	[1.729]
Observations	55	55	55	165	165	165
Wald Chi-squared	114.76	64.32	119.12	156.3	1081.5	832.1
Neighborhood FE?	No	No	No	No	No	No[a]
Year FE?	No	No	No	No	Yes	Yes

Socioeconomic predictors are standardized to a mean of 0 and variance of 1.
Observations weighted by the number of households per neighborhood.
Robust standard errors in brackets; models 4–6 cluster standard errors by neighborhood.
[a] Model 6 includes random intercepts for neighborhoods and AR(1) covariance.
* $p < .05$; ** $p < .01$.

Model 5 includes year fixed effects, but not neighborhood fixed effects, and the standard errors are clustered by neighborhood. The results are unchanged from model 4. The year fixed effects for 2003 and 2006 are significant, reflecting the increase in the stops in the subboros in those periods relative to the 1999 rate. Physical disorder is not significant, nor are the majority of other covariates that characterize neighborhoods. But stops are more frequent in areas with higher concentrations of public assistance receipt, and with higher Black populations, after controlling for homicides and physical disorder. Since homicide rates in New York and physical disorder are correlated with Black population concentration (Fagan and Davies, 2000, 2004), we estimated models including interaction terms for percentage of Black residents and local disorder conditions (physical disorder). The relationship of Black population and the stop rate is robust to the inclusion of either interaction term (data available from authors).

Thus far, model 5 shows a strong and significant relationship between neighborhood racial composition and stop activity; police stop significantly more people in neighborhoods with more Black households. Given that all predictors are standardized, with the exception of the logged number of households, the coefficient magnitudes suggest a particularly strong relationship; racial composition is as important as local crime conditions in predicting police stop activity.

For Model 6, we also included two types of sensitivity analyses. First, we estimated the models including interactions of percent black by lagged crime and percent Hispanic by lagged crime. The results were unchanged. Next, recognizing the potential endogeneity of crime, disorder, neighborhood social and racial composition and stop rates, we estimated propensity scores for the racial composition measures and included them as predictors (results available from the authors). We estimated propensity scores to predict separately the Hispanic and Black concentrations in each neighborhood, and fixed effects for year. We then re-estimated Model 6 to include these propensity scores together with the main racial composition predictor. Following Bang and Robins (2005), we included a predictor that expressed the propensity scores for each racial composition variable in two ways:

$$(1)\ X_{i,j} = 1\ /\ PS_{i,j}$$
$$(2)\ X_{i,j} = 1\ /\ (1\text{-}PS_{i,j})$$

In equations 1 and 2, X is the expression of the transformed propensity score PS_i, the estimated (predicted) racial composition for each race i and in neighborhood j. We repeated this procedure using the standardized residuals from the propensity score estimation, creating two additional propensity scores expressions. Again, the results using these estimators were unchanged (results available from the authors). Accordingly, the results in Table 13.2 are robust with respect to a variety of controls and specifications of the local crime and social conditions that might influence stop rates.

We also estimated Model 6 using both neighborhood and year fixed effects, but the model fits were unacceptably poor and the results uninterpretable. Which modeling strategy produces the most accurate and reliable accounting for the relationship among neighborhood, crime, and stop activity? Which is a more accurate identification strategy for estimating the effects of policing on neighborhoods? We are confident in the results in models 5 and 6, and reject the unstable results for the neighborhood fixed effects model, for four reasons. First, as mentioned earlier, while there were strong within-neighborhood changes over time, the relative position of neighborhoods in terms of both crime and concentrated socioeconomic disadvantage over time was largely unchanged. In other words, the worst places still are the worst places—the places with the highest homicide rates still are the places with the highest homicide rates, the places with the highest concentration of physical disorder are still the places with the most bad housing, even as the extent of disorder in those places dissipates over time. Neighborhood fixed effects are somewhat helpful in identifying differences between places, but such differences are likely to be unimportant in this analysis. Inclusion of fixed effects for neighborhoods in this context would overdetermine the model, explaining everything and nothing at the same time.

Second, the neighborhoods are changing over time, but the rates of change are dissimilar. The social, economic, and crime conditions in poorer neighborhoods changed more than in wealthier neighborhoods (Fagan, 2008). The assumptions of stable between-unit rates of change in fixed effects models are challenged under these conditions. Third, fixed effects estimators are quite limited when the possibility exists of dynamic selection, or changes in the circumstances or preferences that would affect the assignment of the intervention—police stops, in this case—over time (Bjerk, 2008). Dynamic selection is intrinsic to the policy preferences in the allocation of police resources and tactics in the OMP model (Bratton and Knobler, 1998; Silverman, 1999). This in turn leads to our fourth concern: we think that fixed effects models in this context ask the wrong question. Our interest here is estimating the probabilities of being stopped in neighborhoods of different racial makeup and crime conditions, not with differentials by race of persons within neighborhoods. In other words, ours is a within-neighborhood design, and we seek to explain differences in stop probabilities that are quite dramatic across places and over time.

B. The Efficiency of Street Stops in Detecting Crime

Table 13.3 presents the relationship between neighborhood conditions and "hit rates," or the percent of stops that lead to arrests. As suggested earlier, by figures 13.3a–3c and 13.5a–5c, stop efficacy has declined over the period of analysis, a trend underscored by the year fixed effects in models 5 and 6. We would expect that neighborhood hit rates, driven by the likelihood of stopped residents to be engaged in illegal activity, would not be tied to neighborhood social structure; models 1–5, however, show that arrests per stop are lower in neighborhoods whose populations are predominantly Black: over time, stops in predominantly Black neighborhoods are significantly less productive in yielding arrests than in other parts of the City. Table 13.2 shows that stops are far more prevalent in these areas, to a degree beyond

TABLE 13.3

OLS Regression of Arrrests per Stop, Controlling for Social Structure and Crime, 1998–2006

Sample Year	(1) 1999	(2) 2003	(3) 2006	(4) All Years	(5) All Years	(6) All Years
Homicide Arrests (lagged)	.010	.002	.008*	.010*	.007*	.003
	[.010]	[.005]	[.003]	[.004]	[.003]	[.007]
% Receiving Public Assistance	−.010	.000	.006	−.002	.003	−.018
	[.012]	[.007]	[.004]	[.006]	[.004]	[.012]
% Foreign-Born	.000	.002	−.003	.001	−.001	.013
	[.011]	[.005]	[.004]	[.005]	[.004]	[.016]
Racial Entropy	−.007	.000	.007	.003	.004	.011
	[.010]	[.004]	[.004]	[.004]	[.003]	[.016]
% Black	−.029*	−.009	−.012**	−.018**	−.014**	−.013
	[.011]	[.006]	[.004]	[.006]	[.004]	[.039]
% Hispanic	.007	.009	−.004	.001	.001	−.010
	[.014]	[.008]	[.005]	[.006]	[.005]	[.029]
% Moved Within 5 years	−.008	.000	.001	−.004	−.003	−.007
	[.010]	[.004]	[.003]	[.004]	[.002]	[.006]
Vacancy Rate	−.003	.011**	.001	.006	.005	.009
	[.012]	[.003]	[.004]	[.005]	[.003]	[.005]
Physical Disorder	.001	−.009	−.007	−.005	−.006	−.007
	[.011]	[.005]	[.005]	[.006]	[.004]	[.006]
Log Population	−.024	.047*	.016	−.010	.017	.080
	[.031]	[.019]	[.013]	[.014]	[.011]	[.102]
2003 FE					−.070**	−.074**
					[.009]	[.012]
2006 FE					−.108**	−.109**
					[.007]	[.011]
Constant	.412	−.433	−.131	.170	−.035	−.602
	[.339]	[.205]*	[.146]	[.156]	[.125]	[1.085]
Observations	55	55	55	165	165	165
R-squared	.280	.380	.410	.130	.690	.830
Log Likelihood (model)	92.91	119.83	143.11	278.03	363.02	412.01
BIC	−141.7	−195.6	−242.1	−499.9	−659.7	−762.8
Year FE?	No	No	No	No	Yes	Yes
Neighborhood FE?	No	No	No	No	No	Yes

Socioeconomic predictors are standardized to a mean of 0 and variance of 1.

Observations weighted by the number of stops made.

Robust standard errors in brackets; models 4–6 cluster standard errors by neighborhood.

* p < .05; ** p < .01.

what differential criminal activity would suggest; the models in Table 13.3 suggest that there is little public safety payoff. The results in model 6, however, suggest that race is no longer a significant predictor of hit rates when we treat neighborhoods as fixed effects. But when we estimate Model 6 using random intercepts and population-averaged models, we obtain the same results as in Model 5: arrest rates are significantly lower in neighborhoods with greater black population (for percent black, b = .13, s.e. = .005, p = .017). Again, we face the same issues in interpretation with respect to the neighborhood fixed effects models, and for the same reasons as discussed earlier, we reject the neighborhood fixed effects model in favor of other identification strategies that rely on clustering of standard errors by neighborhood.

Finally, to put the hit rate analysis in perspective of gains and losses, we computed the number of firearms obtained from stops. In 2003, a total of 633 firearms were seized pursuant to stops, a rate of 3.9 firearms per 1,000 stops. More than 90 percent of the firearms seized were pistols. By 2006, following a 300 percent increase in the number of stops, the seizure rate fell to 1.4 firearms seized per 1,000 stops. The firearm seizure rates for Blacks, who were stopped more than ten times the rate per person compared to whites, were slightly higher: 4.6 firearms seized per 1,000 stops in 2003, and 1.6 seizures per stop in 2006. The seven hundred firearms seized in 2006 through stops accounted for about 10 percent of the total number of firearm seizures in New York City that were traced in the nationwide firearm trace system. On the surface, the expenditure of police resources to seize only a fraction of seizures made by other means seems inefficient, to say the least. Since removal of guns from the street was the animating goal of OMP, the low seizure rate is further evidence of the inefficiency if not futility of the strategy.

C. How Much Is Too Much? How Much Is Enough?

The burden of OMP policing in the decade since the Spitzer (1999) report has fallen disproportionately on African Americans, and, to a lesser extent, on Latinos. The strategic goal of OMP has principally been one of law enforcement—maximization of arrests and punishment. This was evident in the policy memoranda that were issued at that the outset of the OMP experiment in 1994. Crime minimization goals were path-dependent on the law enforcement goals, rooted in the putative benefits of increased stops and arrests of citizens for both minor crimes plus the detection of weapons and other contraband. Through careful allocation of police resources, the focus was on "high-crime" areas, which—in the logic of OMP—were those places with the highest concentrations of poor, non-White citizens. The high-crime area concept has proven to be elastic, though, and has expanded now to include public housing developments, despite equivocal evidence that crime in public housing is higher than in the adjacent areas (Fagan and Davies, 2000; Fagan et al., 2006). The result has been a dramatic increase in street stops since 2003, with nearly five hundred thousand New Yorkers stopped in both 2006 and 2007. In addition, tens of thousands of misdemeanor marijuana arrests (Golub et al., 2007; Levine and Small, 2008) are part of the totality of enforcement that nearly blankets some parts of the City.

Crime rates, though, have remained relatively stable in the years since 2003 as stops have increased. Figure 13.4 shows that homicide rates have remained stable after 1999, rising and falling randomly over an eight-year period. One might have expected crime rates to plunge further with the mobilization of OMP tactics, especially with the increase beginning in 2003, but that hasn't been the case. After all, a secondary benefit of maximizing punishment through street stops would be to raise the risk of detection and arrest for carrying weapons, increasing the deterrent threats of OMP tactics. But we are hard-pressed to detect such trends, given the stability of crime rates. Nor have marijuana arrests declined, despite the sharp rise in the likelihood of detection and arrest, so New Yorkers continue to use marijuana, often openly, flouting the law and discounting or ignoring the risks and consequences of arrests.

The inelasticity of crime relative to street stops raises two related questions. First, if crime minimization is the goal of OMP, rather than maximizing punishment without tangible linkages to crime reduction, how many stops are enough to maintain or lower the crime rate? Economists and criminologists have long sought algorithms that would create an optimal level of law enforcement (see Garoupa, 1997; Polinsky and Shavell, 2000, 2007; Curtin et al., 2007) or incarceration (Blumstein and Nagin, 1978) to control crime. For example, Persico and colleagues (2001) suggest that an optimal level of police searches of motorists can achieve an equilibrium across racial groups in the propensities of motorists to transport drugs or other contraband. So are five hundred thousand stops too many? Not enough to control crime? These are important questions, but we do not address them in this chapter.

The second question, though, is a first step in the process of answering the first question. Under current OMP tactics, what is the likelihood of police contact for citizens of specific racial and ethnic groups? Knowing the exposure of different population groups to detection and enforcement is a necessary antecedent to discerning whether there is leverage in these contact rates that can influence crime rates for any population group, or even for the areas where specific groups are concentrated. And if race, neighborhood, and crime are conflated to shape perceptions of "high-crime areas" that merit intensive patrol and enforcement, we would expect the exposure to be highest for non-Whites, and, as we see in figure 13.4, for African Americans in particular.

Accordingly, we estimated the probability of contact during 2006 for non-Hispanic African American males ages eighteen and nineteen, a group that has been the focus of criminal justice policy debate and research attention for nearly two decades (Fagan and Wilkinson, 1998; Cook and Laub, 1998; Loury, 2002; Feld, 1999). There were 28,945 stops of this group during 2006. The total population in 2006, according to the U.S. Bureau of the Census (U.S. Census Bureau, 2006), was 30,999. Accordingly, the point estimate for contact is .93, a figure that on its face is shocking. We reestimated this probability excluding stops made in police precincts in the City's central business districts and park areas: lower Manhattan, Midtown (including Times Square), and Central Park. With these restrictions, we reestimated the probability of contact at .92 (28,539 stops).[7] This compares to estimates of less than .20 for eighteen- and nineteen-year-old White males and .50 for Hispanic males (both Black and White Hispanics).

The stop totals are likely to include persons stopped more than once, so we reestimated these probabilities under varying assumptions about the number of persons stopped more than once and the total number of stops that were repeat stops. Table 13.4a shows that if 10 percent of the African American males ages eighteen and nineteen were stopped more than once, and these repeaters accounted for 25 percent of all stops, the probability of being stopped by the police of anyone in this age cohort is now .79. For example, if 10 percent of the population of Black men aged eighteen and nineteen (approximately 3,100 individuals) are considered "high-stop individuals," and this group makes up 25 percent of all stops within this demographic bracket, then these 3,100 people were stopped a combined 7,135 times. These men were stopped an average of 2.3 times over the course of the year, rather than the 0.92 suggested by the raw numbers. Assuming that the remaining stops (21,404) are distributed one-per-person, the total number of people stopped over the course of the year would be 24,504. Although the raw ratio of stops to people in this demographic bracket is 0.92, the actual percentage of the population stopped by the police is lower, 0.79, shown in the upper-left cell of table 13.4a. If 25 percent of the persons were stopped more than once and they accounted for 50 percent of all stops, the probability declines to .71. Note that in table 13.4a, some cells could not be computed because the total number of stops would exceed the population in that group.[8]

We next expand the age boundaries for these estimates to include males ages eighteen to twenty-four. This age group was disproportionately involved in lethal violence throughout the 1990s in New York (Fagan and Wilkinson, 1998; Fagan et al., 1998) and elsewhere in the United States (Cook and Laub, 1998; Zimring and Hawkins, 1997). Also, desistance from crime increases substantially as persons reach their mid-twenties (Farrington, 1998). The unadjusted probability of being stopped in 2006, before accounting for repeaters, is .14 for non-Hispanic Whites, .78 for African Americans, and .39 for Hispanics.

Tables 13.4b–d show the rates accounting for different assumptions about the number of repeaters and the number of repeat stops. Given the lower stop rates of Whites and Hispanics, we rescaled the probabilities in tables 13.4c and 13.4d, hence the comparisons reflect distributions that are unique for each racial or ethnic group. Under the most likely scenarios, tables 13.4b–d show that when 10 percent of the persons account for 25 percent of the stops, the probability that an African American male is stopped (.69) is still far greater than the probability that a White or Hispanic male is stopped. Under more restrictive and conservative assumptions—that 50 percent of the persons account for 75 percent of the stops, we still estimate rates for African Americans that are twice the rate of Hispanics.

The important context in which to view these numbers is whether they are productive; by any reasonable standard, however, they are not. Figure 13.3 (a,b,c) shows two important features of hit rates: there are only negligible differences between hit rates for Whites, African Americans, and Hispanics, and the rates themselves are approximately 5 percent. Beyond the evidence of racial disparity, we are also concerned that these extraordinary stop rates of African Americans include a high volume of excess stops, stops that express unwarranted blanket suspicion that may have little marginal deterrent or law enforcement returns. But with stop rates this high and inefficiencies running at 96 percent, claims of a general deterrent effect from these stops are empirically strained by the scarcity of sanctions. So deterrence or crime control may be a secondary goal to maximization of punishment. And efficiency concerns are only one side of the social and public good of policing: equity, fairness, and distributive considerations co-occupy another dimension of policing (Moore, 2002). Even if we thought that there were crime control returns, it seems unlikely that most citizens would condone trading in the private harm of excess stops of African Americans, not to mention the stigma and internalized psychological costs, against putatively lower susceptibility to crime for the majority group. The costs of this regime lie in the harm to the 95 percent who are innocent in these excess stops.

TABLE 13.4A

Probability of Stops for African American Males, Ages 18–19, 2006

	% Repeat Stops		
	25%	50%	75%
% Stopped More Than Once			
10%	0.79	0.56	0.33
25%		0.71	0.48
50%			0.73

Note: Excludes stops that were made in 1st, 14th, 22d, and 18th precincts.
Population: 30,999. Stops: 28,539.

TABLE 13.4B

Probability of Stops for African American Males, Ages 18–24, 2006

	% Repeat Stops		
	25%	50%	75%
% Stopped More Than Once			
10%	0.69	0.49	0.30
25%		0.64	0.45
50%			0.70

Note: Excludes stops that were made in 1st, 14th, 22d, and 18th precincts.
Population: 104,880. Stops: 82,125.

TABLE 13.4C

Probability of Stops for Hispanic Males, Ages 18–24, 2006

	% Repeat Stops		
	25%	50%	75%
% Stopped More Than Once			
10%		0.29	0.20
20%			0.30
25%			0.35

Note: Excludes stops that were made in 1st, 14th, 22d, and 18th precincts.
Population: 127,128. Stops: 48,968.

TABLE 13.4D

Probability of Stops for Non-Hispanic White Males, Ages 18–24, 2006

	% Repeat Stops		
	25%	50%	75%
% Stopped More Than Once			
2%	0.12	0.09	0.05
5%		0.12	0.08
10%			0.13

Note: Excludes stops that were made in 1st, 14th, 22d, and 18th precincts.
Population: 107,936. Stops: 15,065.

V. Discussion

For nearly a decade, through a prolonged era of stably low crime rates and improving social and economic health across the City's neighborhoods, the number and rate of stops of citizens has increased by more than 500 percent while the efficiency of those stops has declined by nearly 50 percent. The burdens and benefits of these stops are disproportionately concentrated in the City's poorest neighborhoods, the places with both the highest crime rates and the highest proportions of non-White households. Our focus in this chapter is not on the race or ethnicity of individual stops of citizens, but on the rates of stops in neighborhoods with the highest concentrations of Black residents. We focus on neighborhoods because place, not individuals, has been most closely linked to the logic of policing under OMP since its inception fifteen years ago. It is place that is the focal point of the underlying theories of order-maintenance policing, place is the unit of analysis for the allocation and deployment of police resources, and the indicia of crime in places are the metrics by which the resources of the police are managed and evaluated. And the benchmark of place, in conjunction with crime, is sensitive to the actual allocation of police resources as well as tactical decisions by the NYPD, and is widely used in research on selective enforcement in policing (Alpert et al., 2005; Fagan, 2002; Fridell, 2004; Skogan and Frydl, 2004).

The effects we observe in these analyses are notable in three ways. First, stops within neighborhoods take place at rates in excess of what would be predicted from the separate and combined effects of population demography, physical and social conditions, and the crime rate. This excess seems to be concentrated in predominantly Black neighborhoods. Second, the excess stops in these neighborhoods persist over time, even as the Black population declines, crime rates remain low and effectively unchanged, the City's overall social and economic health improves, and housing and other investments increase across the City's neighborhoods, including its poorest and most segregated neighborhoods. Third, there appears to be a declining return in crime detection from marginal increases in enforcement, and this efficiency gap seems to grow over time. Like the stops that supply the arrests, the declining number of arrests that take place pursuant to stops are disproportionately concentrated in neighborhoods with higher Black populations, after controlling for crime, poverty, and disorder in those places.

The preferences for neighborhood selection for intensified stops seems to be inelastic to changes in crime rates or to the limited payoffs in arrest efficiencies from marginal increases in stops. This inelasticity is difficult to understand as either individual preferences of police officers, or as a rational tactical or management decision. As the rank and file of police in New York become more diverse and reflective of the City's demography, it is unlikely that individual preferences or subjective assessments of suspiciousness by individual officers would continue to be racially skewed over time and through changes in the social contexts of the areas they patrol.

Institutionally, the declining returns to crime control from marginal increases in stop activity is the opposite of economics. We assume, from the policy statements of police in New York, that the goal of stops is to minimize and deter crime rather than to maximize the hit rate of stops. An elastic policy sensitive to crime rates might seek to locate an optimal level of stop activity within each neighborhood or patrol area and adjust in real time. Dominitz and Knowles (2006) suggest that such a crime minimization approach works only if the priors of illegal behavior are known to vary across groups in specific ways. Perhaps the absence of assumptions or knowledge of specific variation in between-group (and by extension, between-neighborhood) crime preferences explains the persistence of these stop patterns. But we doubt that the NYPD is flying blind, since the allocation of police to neighborhoods and smaller areas is driven by real-time data about group- or area-specific crime rates.

So there is no simple explanation for the exponential growth over time in stops in the face of broad, long-term secular declines in crimes across all population groups in all places, and in the face of declining yields of legally sustainable arrests (Weiser, 2008). What then can explain the durability of a policy whose utility is weakening over time? Two possibilities come to mind. The first is that these patterns over time reflect a durable institutionalized preference to maintain these tactics even as their necessity and value is less apparent, and even as the practice's political costs mount. The practice has persisted through sharp political and legal criticism (Spitzer, 1999) and civil rights litigation against the NYPD that resulted in injunctive relief and oversight by private legal groups (*Daniels et al. v. City of New York*, 2003).

Beyond political costs, the persistence of policing tactics with disparate neighborhood impacts has salient social costs. Normative considerations—the absence of tangible returns from the policy and practice in the face of high social costs to citizens that are unevenly distributed by race and by place—suggest that the policy diminishes the social good of policing and weakens its welfarist ideology (Durlauf, 2006b), while making the job of the police harder (Skogan and Frydl, 2004; Harris, 2002). The dissipation of the social good itself has one-off costs—the withdrawal of citizens' cooperation with the police in the civic project of the coproduction of security (Tyler and Fagan, 2008; Fagan and Meares, 2007), or, in the worst case, defiance of legal and social norms (Fagan and Meares, 2007; Paternoster et al., 1997; Sherman, 1993). But such external criteria are beside the point if the preference is internalized; it need only be justified within the internal logic of the organization. Whether habit or something more, the maintenance of this policy responds to internalized incentives that remain invisible to outside observers. Its persistence requires a form of "racial blindsight" (Taslitz, 2007) to deracialize institutional recognition and acknowledgement of its consequences.

The second possibility is more mundane, and has two faces. Stops and searches of citizens are simple productivity measures for the police. Generating accurate and detailed information about stops conducted by police provides a numerical measure of police activity and outputs that is easily conveyed to citizens and oversight entities. This is especially important as crime rates decline and the traditional metrics of police productivity—arrests, crimes—no longer are sufficiently sensitive to gauge the efforts of a large and complex organization (Moore, 2002). If policing is a public good, the stop numbers provide a valuable measure of the services that produce that good.

Stops also generate a cheap form of intelligence. Intelligence was the traditional utility of the data generated in the course of stops and searches of citizens (Spitzer,

1999).[9] For years, the reports generated by stops of citizens sat in file drawers in precincts and were examined as police searched for suspects when crime patterns emerged. The information was entered into databases starting in the late 1990s, in part as a response to external investigations in reaction to political conflict following a sequence of violent, tragic, and well-publicized deaths of two citizens during encounters with the police (Spitzer, 1999). This rudimentary neural network of information was automated in the late 1990s, and has evolved into a systematic database that is one of the primary sources of information on police activity.

These institutionalized preferences, which endure in the face of persistent utility, serve the bureaucratic interests of the police hierarchy. Normative concerns over racial impacts take a backseat to the institutional interests that are indifferent to the potential for externalized costs and racial inequalities that ensue from a sustained policy with declining returns. Yet everyone has a stake in a safe society, and so security—which is primarily the province of the police—is a public good (Loader and Walker, 2007). Policing is not a discretionary service, nor is it nontrivial in the sense that it is cost-free. In New York, the cost burden of this safety—which largely accrues to White New Yorkers—is shifted to the 95 percent of African American citizens who are stopped but innocent of whatever suspected crime triggered the action. The benefits of policing—safety, calling offenders to account, conflict resolution, order, information—are social goods that are available to everyone at a low social cost, or at least at a cost that is equitably distributed. The production of this social good is not well served by the patterns we observe over the past decade of order-maintenance policing in New York.

Appendix A: Specific Police Conduct Permitted under DeBour

A. What Is a Stop?

Police stop-and-frisk procedures have been ruled constitutional under specific conditions articulated in *Terry v. Ohio* (1968). Under *Terry*, Fourth Amendment restrictions on unreasonable searches and seizures allow a police officer to stop a suspect on the street and search him or her without probable cause if the police officer has a reasonable suspicion that the person has committed, is committing, or is about to commit a crime. For their own protection, police may perform a quick surface search of the person's outer clothing for weapons if they have reasonable suspicion that the person stopped is armed. This reasonable suspicion must be based on "specific and articulable facts" and not merely on an officer's hunch.

B. Permissible Behaviors

New York law regulates police conduct more thoroughly than does *Terry*. The state law articulates a four-step analysis articulated in *People v. DeBour* (1976) and *People v. Holmes* (1996). Stops are governed by N.Y. Crim. Proc. Law § 140.50(1) (2007):

"In addition to the authority provided by this article for making an arrest without a warrant, a police officer may stop a person in a public place located within the geographical area of such officer's employment when he reasonably suspects that such person is committing, has committed or is about to commit either (a) a felony or (b) a misdemeanor defined in the penal law, and may demand of him his name, address and an explanation of his conduct."

"Stops" and "frisks" are considered separately under New York statutes. A police officer may stop a suspect but not to frisk him given the circumstances. Frisks and

TABLE 13.A1
DeBour's Four Levels of Street Encounters[a]

Predicate	Permissible Response
Level 1	Objective Credible Reason Approach to Request Information
Level 2	Founded Suspicion—Common Law Right of Inquiry
Level 3	Reasonable Suspicion Stop and (If Fear of Weapon) Frisk
Level 4	Probable Cause Arrest and Full Search Incident

[a] *People v. DeBour*, 40 N.Y. 2d 210 (1976).

TABLE 13.A2
Permissible Actions by Police Officers during Stops

Predicate	Permissible Response
Level 1	PO can ask nonthreatening questions regarding name, address, destination, and, if person carrying something unusual, police officer can ask about that. Encounter should be brief and nonthreatening. There should be an absence of harassment and intimidation. PO can: • say "STOP" (if not "forceful") • approach a stopped car • touch holster. PO cannot: • request permission to search • cause people to reasonably believe they're suspected of crime, no matter how calm and polite the tone of the questions.
Level 2	PO can ask pointed questions that would reasonably lead one to believe that he/she is suspected of a crime. Questions can be more extended and accusatory, and focus on possible criminality. PO can: • request permission to search. PO cannot: • pursue • forcibly detain.
Level 3	PO can: • forcibly detain • frisk for weapons if in fear • pull car out of traffic flow • order defendant to lie on the ground • handcuff (for good reason) • pursue.
Level 4	PO can: • arrest and search suspect.

searches are governed by N.Y. Crim. Proc. Law § 140.50(3), which requires a legitimate "stop" as a predicate to any frisk.[10] In many cases, reasonable suspicion that a person is engaging in violent or dangerous crime (such as murder, burglary, assault, etc.) will justify both a stop *and* a frisk. Table 13.A1 shows the circumstances that are necessary for a stop to escalate to a frisk and ultimately to an arrest. Table 13.A2 shows the specific police actions that are permitted at each level of a *Terry/DeBour* stop in New York.

NOTES

1. The facts of the case and its doctrinal implications have been the subject of intense interest in both constitutional criminal procedure, case law, and legal scholarship. On October 31, 1963, Cleveland police detective Martin McFadden saw two men (John W. Terry and Richard Chilton) standing on a street corner and acting suspiciously. One man would walk past a certain store window, stare in, walk on a short distance, turn back, stare in the store window again, and walk back to the other man and converse for a short period of time. The two men repeated this ritual alternately between five and six times apiece—in all, roughly a dozen trips. Each completion of the route was followed by a conference between the two on a corner, at one of which they were joined by a third man, who subsequently left swiftly. Suspecting the two men of casing the store for a robbery, McFadden followed them and saw them rejoin the third man a couple of blocks away. The officer approached the three men, identified himself as a police officer, and asked their names. When they "mumbled something" in response, McFadden patted them down for weapons and discovered that Terry and Chilton were armed. He removed their guns and arrested them for carrying concealed weapons. When the trial court denied his motion to suppress, Terry pleaded not guilty, but the Court found him guilty and sentenced him to one to three years in prison.

2. The procedure to generate a stop rationale takes place pursuant to the stop, not before, and therefore may be endogenous to the stop. Except in "radio runs," where officers are dispatched to a crime scene or location based on a citizen report or a report by another officer, and where a suspect description is provided by the dispatcher, the classification of a stop as being motivated by the match between a citizen and a "suspect description" is determined after the stop is concluded and the UF-250 form is completed. There is no method to verify the basis for the formation of suspicion for the stop. And since many stops are generated simply because the suspect "looked like a perp" (Bacon, 2009), there is considerable potential for error and theoretical misspecification. To put it less politely or scientifically, the stated rationale for the stop may in fact be either racialized, highly conditional on the conditions where the stop takes place, or simply a fiction.

3. We preferred to use both homicide arrests and homicides to test the robustness of our estimates, as well as a wider range of localized crime rates. Unfortunately, we were not privileged by the NYPD with access to its data of reported crimes that could be disaggregated to precincts, neighborhoods, and subboros. Those data were not published by the NYPD in summary form after 2001.

4. The partial correlations by year and precinct from 1984 to 2000 between homicide arrests and arrests for other Part I felony crimes was .633, and .711 for all felony crimes. For crime complaints, the partial correlation by year and precinct from 1984 to 2000 between homicide arrests and crime-specific complaints were .810 for murder, .704 for rape, .629 for robbery, and .791 for assault.

5. The stop rate and racial and ethnic distribution in these areas are:

TABLE 13.N1

Neighborhood	Stops per Household 2006	Percent African American	Percent Latino
Brownsville/Ocean Hill	.68	78	15
East New York	.65	45	38
Central Harlem	.52	71	14
East Harlem	.51	36	45
Bedford Stuyvesant	.49	72	16
Mott Haven/Hunts Point	.44	21	76

Source: New York City, Department of City Planning.

6. When arrests are made by the police upon observation of a crime, such as smoking marijuana, a stop report is completed to back-fill the case record. Accordingly, some portion of both crime complaints and stops reflect arrest-generated activity rather than independent police events.

7. In these estimates, we include Black Hispanics among Hispanics, not among African Americans.

8. Table cells are left blank in cases where the hypothesized population/stop allocations do not correspond to a "high-stop" population stopped multiple times per year. For example, in table 13.4a, the lower-left cell posits a distribution where 50 percent of the population accounts for 25 percent of the stops. If 25 percent of stops (7,135) were evenly distributed over 50 percent of the population (14,270 people), this would roughly correspond to only one-half of a stop per person. Since police stops are discrete events, an average stop rate of less than one stop per person suggests that either the "high-stop" population is overestimated, or that the portion of stops allocated to this group is underestimated. In either case, the cell is left blank, since the combination does not represent a scenario where a portion of the population is stopped repeatedly.

9. For juveniles, the parallel intelligence-gathering mechanism is the issuance of so-called YD cards to minors who are stopped by the police but not arrested. YD (for Youth Division) cards are not entered into electronic databases.

10. "When upon stopping a person under circumstances prescribed in subdivisions one and two a police officer or court officer, as the case may be, reasonably suspects that he is in danger of physical injury, he may search such person for a deadly weapon or any instrument, article or substance readily capable of causing serious physical injury and of a sort not ordinarily carried in public places by law-abiding persons. If he finds such a weapon or instrument, or any other property possession of which he reasonably believes may constitute the commission of a crime, he may take it and keep it until the completion of the questioning, at which time he shall either return it, if lawfully possessed, or arrest such person." N.Y. Crim. Proc. Law § 140.50(3).

REFERENCES

Alpert, Geoffrey, John H. MacDonald, and Roger G. Dunham (2005). "Police Suspicion and Discretionary Decision Making During Citizen Stops," *Criminology* 43(2): 407–434.

Antonovics, Kate L. and Brian G. Knight (2004). "A New Look at Racial Profiling: Evidence from the Boston Police Department," NBER Working Papers 10634, National Bureau of Economic Research, Inc.

Ayres, Ian (2002a). "Outcome Tests of Racial Disparities in Police Practices," *Justice Research and Policy*, 4, 131–142.

Ayres, Ian (2002b). *Pervasive Prejudice: Unconventional Evidence of Race and Gender Discrimination*. Chicago: University of Chicago Press.

Ayres, Ian (2008). *Racial Profiling and the LAPD: A Study of Racially Disparate Outcomes in the Los Angeles Police Department*. Los Angeles: American Civil Liberties Union of Southern California; available at http://www.aclu-sc.org/documents/view/47.

Bacon, Paul C. (2009). *Bad Cop: New York's Least Likely Police Officer Tells All*. New York: Bloomsbury.

Baker, Al (2008). "Police Data Shows Increase in Street Stops," *New York Times*, May 6; available at http://www.nytimes.com/2008/05/06/nyregion/06frisk.html.

Baker, Al (2009). "Police Stops on City Streets Rose Significantly Last Year," *New York Times*, February 10, at A29.

Bittner, E. (1970). *Functions of the Police in Modern Society: A Review of Background Factors, Current Practices, and Possible Role Models*. Rockville, MD: National Institute of Mental Health.

Bjerk, David (2007). "Racial Profiling, Statistical Discrimination, and the Effect of a Colorblind Policy on the Crime Rate," *Journal of Public Economic Theory* 9(3): 543–567.

Bjerk, David (2008). "How Much Can We Trust Causal Interpretations of Fixed-Effects Estimators in the Context of Criminality?" Working Paper 2008-4, Robert Day School of Economics and Finance; available at http://ssrn.com/abstract=1144201.

Blumstein, Alfred and Daniel Nagin (1978). "On the Optimal Use of Incarceration for Crime Control," *Operations Research* 26(3): 381–405.

Bowling, Ben (2007). "Fair and Effective Policing Methods: Towards 'Good Enough' Policing," *Journal of Scandinavian Studies in Criminology and Crime Prevention* 8 (S1): 17–32.

Bratton, William and Peter Knobler (1998). *The Turnaround: How America's Top Cop Reversed the Crime Epidemic*. New York: Random House.

Carbado, Devon W. (2002). "(E)racing the Fourth Amendment," *Michigan Law Review* 100: 946–1044.

Carbado, Devon W. and Mitu Gulati (2000). "Working Identity," *Cornell Law Review* 85: 1259, 1280–1283.

Close, Billy R. and Patrick L. Mason (2007). "Searching for Efficient Enforcement: Officer Characteristics and Racially Biased Policing," *Review of Law and Economics* 3(2): 263–321.

Cole, David (1999). *No Equal Justice: Race and Class in the Criminal Justice System*. New York: The New Press.

Community Studies of New York (2007). "Guide to Infoshare Online." Retrieved February 14, 2007, from http://www.infoshare.org.

Cook, Philip J. and John H. Laub (1998). "The Unprecedented Epidemic of Youth Violence," *Crime and Justice: A Review of Research* 24: 27–64.

Cook, Philip J. and John H. Laub (2001). "After the Epidemic: Recent Trends in Youth Violence in the United States." Pp. 1–37 in *Crime and Justice: A Review of Research* (M. Tonry, ed.). Chicago: University of Chicago Press.

Corman, Hope and Naci Mocan (2000). "A Time-Series Analysis of Crime, Deterrence, and Drug Abuse in New York City," *American Economic Review* 90(3): 584–604.

Curtin, Kevin M., Karen Hayslett-McCall, and Fang Qiu (2007). "Determining Optimal Police Patrol Areas with Maximal Covering and Backup Covering Location Models." *Network and Spatial Economics*, online only; available at http://www.gmu.edu/departments/geog/People/Curtin/NETSOnlineFirst.pdf.

Davis, Robert C. and Pedro Matea-Gelabert (1999). *Respectful and Effective Policing: Two Examples in the South Bronx*. New York: Vera Institute of Justice.

Dharmapala, D. and S. L. Ross (2004). "Racial Bias in Motor Vehicle Searches: Additional Theory and Evidence," *Contributions to Economic Policy and Analysis* 3(1); available at http://www.bepress.com/bejeap/contributions/vol3/iss1/art12.

Dominitz, Jeffrey and John Knowles (2006). "Crime Minimization and Racial Bias: What Can We Learn from Police Search Data?" *Economic Journal* 116 (November): F368–F384.

Donohue, John and Steven Levitt (2001). "The Impact of Race on Policing, Arrest Patterns, and Crime," *Journal of Law and Economics* 44(2): 367–394.

Duneier, Mitchell (1999). *Sidewalk*. New York: Farrar, Straus and Giroux.

Durlauf, Steven N. (2006a). "Assessing Racial Profiling," *Economic Journal* 116 (November): F402–F426.

Durlauf, Steven N. (2006b). "Racial Profiling as a Public Policy Question: Efficiency, Equity, and Ambiguity," *American Economic Review* 92(2): 132–136.

Durose, Matthew. R., Erica L. Schmitt, and Patrick A. Langan (2005). "Contacts Between Police and the Public: Findings from the 2002 National Survey," NCJ 207845, Bureau of Justice Statistics, U.S. Department of Justice.

Fagan, Jeffrey (2002). "Law, Social Science, and Racial Profiling," *Justice Research and Policy* 4 (December): 104–129.

Fagan, Jeffrey (2008). "Crime and Neighborhood Change," Pp. 81–126 in *Understanding Crime Trends* (A. Goldberger and R. Rosenfeld, eds.). Washington, DC: National Academy of Sciences, National Academies Press.

Fagan, Jeffrey and Garth Davies (2000). "Street Stops and Broken Windows: *Terry*, Race, and Disorder in New York City," *Fordham Urban Law Journal* 28: 457–504.

Fagan, Jeffrey and Garth Davies (2004). "The Natural History of Neighborhood Violence," *Journal of Contemporary Criminal Justice* 20 (2): 127–147.

Fagan Jeffrey and Garth Davies (2007). "The Political Economy of the Crime Decline in New York City." Presented at the Annual Meeting of the American Association for the Advancement of Science, San Francisco, February.

Fagan, Jeffrey, Garth Davies, and Jan Holland (2006). "The Paradox of the Drug Elimination Program in New York City Public Housing," *Georgetown Journal of Poverty, Law, and Policy* 13 (September): 415–60.

Fagan, Jeffrey and Tracey L. Meares (2008). "Punishment, Deterrence, and Social Control: The Paradox of Punishment in Minority Communities," *Ohio State Journal of Criminal Law* 6: 173–229.

Fagan, Jeffrey and Deanna L. Wilkinson (1998). "Guns, Youth Violence, and Social Identity," *Crime and Justice: A Review of Research* 24: 373–456.

Fagan, Jeffrey, Deanna L. Wilkinson, and Garth Davies (2007). "Social Contagion of Violence." Pp. 688–723 in *The Cambridge Handbook of Violent Behavior* (D. Flannery, A. Vazsonyi, and I. Waldman, eds.). Cambridge: Cambridge University Press.

Fagan, Jeffrey, Franklin E. Zimring, and June Kim (1998). "Declining Homicide in New York: A Tale of Two Trends," *Journal of Criminal Law and Criminology* 88: 1277–1324.

Farrington, David P. (1998). "Predictors, Causes, and Correlates of Male Youth Violence," *Crime and Justice: A Review of Research* 24: 421–476.

Feld, Barry C. (1999). *Bad Kids: Race and the Transformation of the Juvenile Court*. New York: Oxford University Press.

Ferguson, Andrew Guthrie and Damien Bernache (2008). "The 'High Crime' Question: Requiring Verifiable and Quantifiable Evidence for Fourth Amendment Reasonable Suspicion Analysis," *American University Law Review* 57: 1587–1644.

Fridell, Lorie (2004). *By the Numbers: A Guide for Analyzing Race Data from Vehicle Stops.* Washington, DC: The Police Executive Research Forum.

Garoupa, Nuno (1997). "The Theory of Optimal Law Enforcement," *Journal of Economic Surveys* 11(3): 267–295.

Gelman, Andrew, Jeffrey Fagan, and Alex Kiss (2007). "An Analysis of the New York City Police Department's 'Stop-and-Frisk' Policy in the Context of Claims of Racial Bias." *Journal of the American Statistical Association* 102(479): 813–823.

Golub, Andrew, Bruce D. Johnson, and Eloise Dunlap (2007). "The Race/Ethnic Disparities in Marijuana Arrests in New York City," *Criminology and Public Policy* 6(1): 131–164

Gould, Jon and Stephen Mastrofski (2004). "Suspect Searches: Assess Police Behavior Under the U.S. Constitution," *Criminology and Public Policy* 3: 315–361.

Greene, Judith A. (1999). "Zero Tolerance: A Case Study of Police Policies and Practices in New York City," *Crime and Delinquency* 45(2): 171–199.

Gross, Samuel R. and Katherine Y. Barnes (2002). "Road Work: Racial Profiling and Drug Interdiction on the Highway," *Michigan Law Review* 101: 653–754.

Harcourt, Bernard E. (1998). "Reflecting on the Subject: A Critique of the Social Influence Conception of Deterrence, the Broken Windows Theory, and Order-Maintenance Policing New York Style," *Michigan Law Review* 97: 291.

Harcourt, Bernard E. (2001). *Illusion of Order: The False Promise of Broken Windows Policing.* Cambridge, MA: Harvard University Press.

Harcourt, Bernard and Jens Ludwig (2007). "Reefer Madness: Broken Windows Policing and Misdemeanor Marijuana Arrests in New York City, 1989–2000," *Criminology and Public Policy* 6(1): 165–182.

Harris, David A. (1999). "The Stories, the Statistics, and the Law: Why 'Driving While Black' Matters," *Minnesota Law Review* 84: 265–326.

Harris, David A. (2002). *Profiles in Injustice: Why Racial Profiling Cannot Work.* New York: New Press.

Jackson, David (2000). "Winning War on Crime has a Price: Giuliani Alienates Many in New York City's Black and Hispanic Communities," *Denver Post*, Aril 20, at A23.

Karmen, Andrew (2000). *New York Murder Mystery.* New York: New York University Press.

Kelling, George and Catherine Cole (1996). *Fixing Broken Windows.* New York: The Free Press.

Kennedy, Randall (1997). *Race, Crime, and Law.* Cambridge, MA: Harvard University Press.

Kirk, David and John Laub (in press). "Neighborhood Change and Crime in the Modern Metropolis," *Crime and Justice: A Review of Research.*

Knowles, John, Nicola Persico, and Petra Todd (2001). "Racial Bias in Motor Vehicle Searches: Theory and Evidence," *Journal of Political Economy* 109: 203–229.

Kocieniewski, David (1999). "Success of Elite Police Unit Exacts a Toll on the Streets," *New York Times*, February 15, at A1.

Lamberth, John (1997). "Report of John Lamberth, Ph.D.," American Civil Liberties Union; available at http://www.aclu.org/court/lamberth.html.

Land, Kenneth C., Patricia L. McCall, and Lawrence E. Cohen (1990). "Structural Covariates of Homicide Rates: Are There Any Invariances Across Time and Social Space?" *American Journal of Sociology* 95: 922–963.

Langan, Patrick, Lawrence A. Greenfeld, S. K. Smith, Matthew R. Durose, and D. J. Levin (2001). "Contacts Between Police and the Public: Findings From the 1999 National Survey," NCJ 194957, Bureau of Justice Statistics, U. S. Department of Justice.

Levine, Harry G., and Debra Peterson Small (2008). *Marijuana Arrest Crusade: Racial Bias and Police Policy in New York City, 1997–2007.* New York: New York Civil Liberties Union; available at http://www.nyclu.org/files/MARIJUANA-ARREST-CRUSADE_Final.pdf.

Livingston, Debra (1997). "Police Discretion and the Quality of Life in Public Places: Courts, Communities, and the New Policing," *Columbia Law Review* 97: 551–625.

Loader, Ian and Nigel Walker (2007). *Civilizing Security*. Cambridge: Cambridge University Press.

Loury, Glenn (2002). *The Anatomy of Racial Equality*. Cambridge, MA: Harvard University Press.

Manning, Peter K. (2001). "Theorizing Policing: The Drama and Myth of Crime Control in the NYPD," *Theoretical Criminology* 5(3): 315–344.

Massey, Douglas S. (2007). *Categorically Unequal: The American Stratification System*. New York: Russell Sage Foundation Press.

Massey, Douglas S. and Nancy Denton (1993). *American Apartheid: Segregation and the Making of the Underclass*. Cambridge, MA: Harvard University Press.

McCall, H. Carl (1997). *Report on the Safe Streets Program of the New York City Police Department, Re: Report 96-F-40*. Albany: Office of the State Comptroller of New York State; available at http://www.osc.state.ny.us/audits/allaudits/093097/96f40.htm.

Miller, Jeffrey (2000). "Profiling Populations Available for Stops and Searches," Police Research Series Paper 121, Home Office Research, Development and Statistics Directorate, UK.

Moore, Mark H. (2002). *Recognizing Value in Policing*. Washington, DC: Police Executive Research Forum.

Musto, David (1973). *The American Disease*. New Haven, CT: Yale University Press.

New York Civil Liberties Union v. New York City Police Department (Seeking Access to NYPD Stop-and-Frisk Database Under FOIL), New York Supreme Court, Index No. 07/115154 (Direct) (2008).

Pager, Devah (2003). "The Mark of a Criminal Record," *American Journal of Sociology* 108: 937–975.

Pager, Devah (2007). *Marked: Race, Crime, and Finding Work in an Era of Mass Incarceration*. Chicago: University of Chicago Press.

Paternoster, Raymond, Robert Brame, Ronet Bachman, and Lawrence W. Sherman (1997). "Do Fair Procedures Matter? The Effect of Procedural Justice on Spouse Assault," *Law and Society Review* 31: 163–204.

Persico, Nicola and Petra Todd (2005). "Passenger Profiling, Imperfect Screening, and Airport Security," *The American Economic Association Papers and Proceedings*, 127–131.

Persico, Nicola, John Knowles, and Petra Todd (2001). "Racial Bias in Motor-Vehicle Searches: Theory and Evidence," *Journal of Political Economy* 109(1): 203–229.

Polinsky, A. Mitchell and Steven Shavell (2000). "The Economic Theory of Public Enforcement of Law," *Journal of Economic Literature, American Economic Association* 38(1): 45–76.

Polinsky, A. Mitchell and Steven Shavell (2007). "The Theory of Public Enforcement of Law." Pp. 403–454f in *Handbook of Law and Economics* (A. Mitchell Polinsky and Steven Shavell, eds.). Amsterdam: Elsevier Science Publishing.

Quillan, Lincoln and Devah Pager (2001). "Black Neighbors, Higher Crime? The Role of Racial Stereotypes in Evaluations of Neighborhood Crime," *American Journal of Sociology* 107: 717–767.

Reiss, A. (1971). *The Police and the Public*. New Haven, CT: Yale University Press.

Ridgeway, Greg (2007). "Analysis of Racial Disparities in the New York Police Department's Stop, Question, and Frisk Practices," RAND Corporation, TR-534; available at http://www.rand.org/pubs/technical_reports/2007/RAND_TR534.pdf.

Roane, Kit R. (1999). "Minority Private-School Students Claim Police Harassment," *New York Times*, March 26, at B5.

Roberts, Dorothy E. (1999). "Race, Vagueness, and the Social Meaning of Order-Maintenance Policing," *Journal of Criminal Law and Criminology* 89: 775–836.

Rosenfeld, Richard, Robert Fornango, and Andres F. Rengifo (2007). "The Impact of Order-Maintenance Policing on New York City Homicide and Robbery Rates: 1988–2001," *Criminology* 45(2): 355–384.

Rudovsky, David (2001). "Law Enforcement by Stereotypes and Serendipity: Racial Profiling and Stops and Searches Without Cause," *University of Pennsylvania Journal of Constitutional Law* 3: 296–366.

Rudovsky, David (2007). "Litigating Civil Rights Cases To Reform Racially Biased Criminal Justice Practices," *Columbia Human Rights Law Review* 39(1): 97–123.

Sampson, Robert J. and Janet L. Lauritsen (1994). "Violent Victimization and Offending: Individual-, Situational-, and Community-Level Risk Factors." Pp. 1–99 in *Understanding and Preventing Violence* (Albert J. Reiss, Jr., and Jeffrey A. Roth, eds.). Washington, DC: National Academy Press.

Sampson, Robert J. and Jeffrey Morenoff (2006). "Durable Inequality: Spatial Dynamics, Social Processes, and the Persistence of Poverty in Chicago Neighborhoods." Pp. 176–203 in *Poverty Traps* (Samuel Bowles, Steve Durlauf, and Karla Hoff, eds.). Princeton, NJ: Princeton University Press.

Sampson, Robert J. and Stephen W. Raudenbush (1999). "Systematic Social Observation of Public Spaces: A New Look at Disorder in Urban Neighborhoods," *American Journal of Sociology* 105: 622–630.

Sampson, Robert J. and Stephen W. Raudenbush (2004). "Seeing Disorder: Neighborhood Stigma and the Social Construction of 'Broken Windows,'" *Social Psychology Quarterly* 67: 319–342.

Sanga, Sarath (2009). "Reconsidering Racial Bias in Motor Vehicle Searches: Theory and Evidence." *Journal of Political Economy* 16(6), in press.

Schwartz, Alex (1999). "New York City and Subsidized Housing: Impacts and Lessons of New York City's $4 Billion Capital Budget Housing Plan," *Housing Policy Debate* 10(4): 839–877.

Shaw, Clifford R. and Henry D. McKay (1942). *Juvenile Delinquency in Urban Areas.* Chicago: University of Chicago Press.

Sherman, Lawrence W. (1993). "Defiance, Deterrence, and Irrelevance: A Theory of Criminal Sanctions," *Journal of Research in Crime and Delinquency* 30(4): 4445–4473

Silverman, Eli (1999). *The NYPD Battles Crime: Innovative Ideas in Policing.* Boston: Northeastern University Press.

Skogan, Wesley G. (1990). *Disorder and Decline: Crime and the Spiral of Decay in American Cities.* New York: The Free Press.

Skogan, Wesley G. and Kathryn Frydl (eds.) (2004). *The Evidence on Policing: Fairness and Effectiveness in Law Enforcement.* Washington, DC: National Academy Press.

Smith, Douglas A. (1986). "The Neighborhood Context of Police Behavior." Pp. 313–342 in *Communities and Crime: Crime and Justice: An Annual Review of Research* (A. J. Reiss and M. Tonry, eds.). Chicago: University of Chicago Press.

Smith, Michael and Geoffrey Alpert (2002). "Searching for Direction: Courts, Social Science, and the Adjudication of Racial Profiling Claims," *Justice Quarterly* 19: 673–704.

Smith, Michael R., M. Makarios, and Geoffrey P. Alpert (2006). "Differential Suspicion: Theory Specification and Gender Effects in the Traffic Stop Context," *Justice Quarterly* 23: 271–295.

Spitzer, Elliott (1999). *The New York City Police Department's "Stop and Frisk" Practices.* Albany: Office of the New York State Attorney General; available at http://www.oag.state.ny.us/bureaus/civil_rights/pdfs/stp_frsk.pdf.

Taslitz, Andrew C. (2007). "Racial Blindsight: The Absurdity of Color-Blind Criminal Justice." *Ohio State Journal of Criminal Law* 5(1): 1–17.

Taylor, Ralph B. (2001). *Breaking Away From Broken Windows: Baltimore Neighborhoods and the Nationwide Fight Against Crime, Grime, Fear, and Decline.* Boulder, CO: Westview Press.

Thacher, David (2008). "The Rise of Criminal Background Screening in Rental Housing," *Law and Social Inquiry* 33(1): 5–30.

Thompson, Anthony (1999). "Stopping the Usual Suspects: Race and the Fourth Amendment," *New York University Law Review* 74: 956–1013.

Tyler, Tom R. and Jeffrey Fagan (2008). "Legitimacy, Compliance and Cooperation: Procedural Justice and Citizen Ties to the Law," *Ohio State Journal of Criminal Law* 6(1): 231–275.

Tyler, Tom R. and Yuen J. Huo (2002). *Trust in the Law: Encouraging Public Cooperation with the Police and Courts.* New York: Russell Sage Foundation Press.

U.S. Census Bureau (2006). "2006 American Community Survey: Overview"; available at http://www.census.gov/acs/www/Products/users_guide/ACS_2006_Overview.pdf.

Veneiro, Peter and P. H. Zoubeck (1999). "Interim Report of the State Police Review Team Regarding Allegations of Racial Profiling," Office of the New Jersey State Attorney General.

Waldeck, Sarah (2000). "Cops, Community Policing, and the Social Norms Approach to Crime Control: Should One Make Us More Comfortable with the Others?" *Georgia Law Review* 34: 1253–1297.

Walker, Samuel (2001). "Searching for the Denominator: Problems with Police Traffic Stop Data and an Early Warning System Solution," *Justice Research and Policy* 3: 63–95.

Weiser, Benjamin (2008). "Police in Gun Searches Face Disbelief in Court," *New York Times,* May 12, at B1.

Weitzer, Ronald and Steven A. Tuch (2006). *Race and Policing in America.* New York: Cambridge University Press.

Wilson, James Q. and George L. Kelling (1982). "Broken Windows: The Police and Neighborhood Safety," *Atlantic Monthly,* March, 29–38.

Zimring, Franklin E. and Gordon Hawkins (1997). *Crime Is Not the Problem: Lethal Violence in America.* New York: Oxford University Press.

Zingraff, Matthew, H. M. Mason, William R. Smith, D. Tomaskovic-Devey, Patricia Warren, H. L. McMurray, C. R. Fenlon, et al. (2000). *Evaluating North Carolina State Highway Patrol Data: Citations, Warnings, and Searches in 1998.* Raleigh: North Carolina Department of Crime Control and Public Safety.

CASES CITED

Adams v. Williams, 407 U.S. 143 (1972).

Brown v. Oneonta, 221 F.3d 329 (2000).

Daniels et al. v. City of New York, Stipulation of Settlement, 99 Civ 1695 (SAS) (2003).

Illinois v. Wardlow, 528 U.S. 119 (2000).

People v. DeBour, 40 NY 2d 210 (1976).

Terry v. Ohio, 392 U.S. 1 (1968).

U.S. v. Harvey, 961 F.2d 1361 (1992).

U.S. v. Martinez-Fuerte, 428 U.S. 543 (1976).

U.S. v. Whren, 517 U.S. 806 (1996).

Chapter 14

Community Characteristics and Police Search Rates

Accounting for the Ethnic Diversity of Urban Areas in the Study of Black, White, and Hispanic Searches

Karen F. Parker, Erin C. Lane, and Geoffrey P. Alpert

Police officers' decisions to conduct searches subsequent to traffic stops are based on a number of factors including, but not limited to, their own discretion.[1] Criminologists have long explored racial disparities in police behavior, ranging from arrest to incarceration.[2] More recently researchers have suggested that race plays a role in the determination to search beyond other relevant legal factors.[3] But other studies have found no significant evidence of racial disparities in searches when taking into account hit rates[4] or the constitutionality of the search.[5] The role of race in the decision making of police officers continues to elude us.

A growing body of research is interested in understanding the link between community characteristics and police behavior at the macro level.[6] Studies have identified differential treatment of suspects by police officers relative to ecological conditions.[7] According to Terrill and Mastrofski[8] and Smith,[9] neighborhood characteristics such as concentrated disadvantage, high crime rates, and racial composition increase the likelihood that police will handle suspects more coercively. Other studies have found that officers may equate neighborhood characteristics with the populations residing in them,[10] and may use the ecological characteristics of areas as cues in decision making.[11] Unfortunately, many of these studies focus on police use of force, coercive behavior, and, only recently, traffic stops.[12] Few studies examine the relationship between the ecological conditions of neighborhoods and police search rates.[13] Because this literature is limited, it remains unclear how and to what degree community characteristics contribute to search rates of distinct groups. The lack of research is increasingly troublesome in light of the growing race and ethnicity diversity of urban communities, such as the rise in Hispanic immigration and the percentage of foreign-born residents in American cities. Hispanics are a largely understudied group, and this void is particularly noticeable in the area of police searches.[14]

In an attempt to explore the linkages between community characteristics and police behavior, this chapter examines the influence of structural characteristics on race- and ethnic-specific search rates at the community level. Our research utilizes citizen contact and officer data from more than sixty-one thousand traffic stops in Miami-Dade County, collected by the Miami-Dade Police Department over a six-month period in 2001. Because of its ethnic and economic diversity, the Miami-Dade area is a particularly important geographic location in which to conduct a study of race, ethnicity, and policing. Our work adds to the existing research by incorporating indicators common to community-level studies, such as concentrated disadvantage and residential characteristics, in addition to tapping the growing levels of ethnic diversity in Miami-Dade communities, when examining police search rates of blacks, whites, and Hispanics.

Police and Ecological Context

As stated above, research on searches is less frequent than for other forms of police behavior. Among those studies produced, inconsistent evidence has been found in terms of the significance of race at the individual level.[15] Like others, we argue that race alone is less relevant to police behavior without consideration of the ecological context in which that behavior occurs.[16] Specifically, structural forces that concentrate race and ethnic groups in disadvantaged communities are likely contributors to search rates, rather than race alone. That is, because blacks, whites, and Hispanics reside in areas that are often spatially dissimilar, racial variation in the rate of searches across communities is highly probable. Below we review literature that specifically links ecological characteristics to police behaviors.[17]

In one of the most cited studies of its kind, Smith[18] examined the relationship between police behavior and community characteristics, such as racial composition and levels of disadvantage. The author found that police officers were significantly more likely to use coercive behavior in both nonwhite areas as well as areas characterized by racial heterogeneity. Racial composition was also relevant to police behavior, whereby police officers were more likely to act coercively toward blacks in primarily black neighborhoods.

Terrill and Reisig[19] examined the impact of neighborhood context on police use of force in two U.S. cities. Consistent with other research findings in this vein, the results indicated that officers were more likely to treat young, male, lower-class suspects with more force. Moreover they found that officers were significantly more likely to use force in neighborhoods characterized by high levels of crime and concentrated disadvantage. These findings remained statistically significant after controlling for suspect behavior.[20] And in one of the few studies examining police search practices based on ecological context, Fagan and Davies[21] found that measures of social disorganization and related structural characteristics were the most significant predictors of race-specific "stop and frisk" practices by police. "Stop and frisk" practices were concentrated in poor neighborhoods with large minority populations. Noting the racial composition of poverty in the United States, blacks and Hispanics were overrepresented in police "stop and frisk" practices.[22] Finally, Kane[23] examined the influence of social ecological characteristics on changes in police misconduct in New York City police precincts and division from 1975 to 1996. He concluded that indicators associated with social disorganization and racial conflict perspectives explained the changes in police misconduct, such as bribery and excessive force, over time.

Community Characteristics

The above studies find that police officers are significantly influenced by the ecological context in which police-citizen contacts occur. Officers make distinctions between communities and, to some degree, treat residents differentially across locales,[24] a process Werthman and Piliavin called "ecological contamination."[25] We seek to understand race and ethnic variation in search rates within the multiethnic context of Miami-Dade neighborhoods. We begin by reviewing some of the literature on ethnic diversity and Hispanic immigration.

Ethnic Diversity and Hispanic Immigration

Research on the potential link between immigration and crime has grown, yet this research remains largely narrow, maybe even sparse.[26] Early studies examined how restrictive legislation designed to slow immigration into the United States, as well as the negative stereotypes of immigrants as "criminals" dominant in the popular press, influence rising incarceration rates of these groups.[27] Recent scholars have found that urban economies are rebounding with growing immigrant populations, which reduce crime.[28] When incorporating criminological theories, others articulate how immigration increases crime, particularly when drawing from opportunity and social disorganization theories.[29] Consequentially, there is no agreement in the literature as to whether immigration will increase or decrease crime.[30] Reid and colleagues argue that these inconsistencies are largely due to the fact that the immigration and crime relationship is dependent on a mixture of factors, such as what obstacles the group will face once they enter the United States (e.g., discrimination, unemployment) and the type of acculturation that occurs.[31] That is, the link between immigration and crime will be positive or negative depending on a set of characteristics and conditions.

Research does show that recent immigrants face higher levels of poverty[32] and difficulty establishing themselves in the labor market.[33] Additionally, recent immigrants tend to be young and male,[34] and face potential communication barriers with the police and neighboring residents, which also increase the potential for criminal behavior and police contact (e.g., stops and searches). Sociological theories, then, would propose that recent immigrants would engage in greater levels of crime as a result of blocked opportunities.[35] Moreover, a higher proportion of foreign-born residents and recent immigrants in the community could lessen community ties that maintain social control (via social disorganization theory) or face greater barriers to employment (via blocked opportunities), which have been found to influence both criminal offending and police behavior in previous community-based studies.

On the other hand, an equally convincing literature shows that immigration will have no impact on crime.[36] For example, the assumption that immigrants enter the United States economically disadvantaged and with low educational attainment may be erroneous.[37] As Zhou states, "The image of the poor, uneducated, and unskilled 'huddled masses,' used to depict the turn-of-the-century European immigrants, does not apply to today's newcomers."[38] Rather, many immigrating groups enter the United States with college degrees and corresponding economic resources. Even those immigrants with less education and skills may not face the same level of racial discrimination and economic difficulties known to African American workers. That is, the formation of ethnic enclaves within larger cities and ability to create niches in the labor market provide avenues to employment, business ownership, as well as other opportunities,[39] even among the most recent immigrants.[40] Hence, the assumption found within criminological theories concerning fragile community ties and blocked opportunities might not be applicable to the more recent and larger immigrant populations entering the United States today.

Concentrated Disadvantage and Community Disorder

In his book *The Truly Disadvantaged,* Wilson discussed the rising levels of concentrated poverty in American cities since the 1970s, which largely affected black communities due to industrial changes that removed low-skilled jobs in the inner city. Massey and colleagues[41] add that racial discrimination in housing played a central role in the sharp rise in poverty concentration. For example, racial residential segregation combined with income disparities produced a spatial concentration of extreme disadvantage in black neighborhoods more so than in areas comprising other race and ethnic groups.[42] Researchers have linked the concentration of disadvantage to rates of urban crime and violence.[43]

Key to this literature is that blacks are much more likely to live in areas of extreme deprivation and disadvantage, while only 2% of whites live in areas of similar disadvantage.[44] Importantly, police are also concentrated disproportionately in poor black neighborhoods,[45] and not coincidentally, researchers have documented a rise in arrest and incarceration rates over time, particularly among black males.[46] But researchers have also found that Hispanics face high levels of disadvantage,[47] even though they tend to be less segregated and isolated residentially than blacks[48] and have lower levels of family disruption.[49] Therefore, given the heightened disadvantages among blacks and Hispanics in communities with increased police presence, search rates tend to be higher among these groups, relative to whites.

Not only do these communities face disadvantage, but the lack of available jobs require residents to travel outside the community for work or face unemployment as jobs are relocated outside city boundaries.[50] Disorganized areas characterized by vacant buildings, graffiti, trash on the streets, and the presence of panhandlers and prostitutes act to create and intensify police suspicion of local residents.[51] Residents living in disadvantaged areas are less capable of realizing common goals and initiatives that reduce crime, leading to greater dependency on formal agents of social control (such as the police) to fill the void.[52] Taken together, ecological areas characterized by disadvantage and disorder, separate from the ethnic composition and diversity of these areas, increase officers' suspicion and the likelihood of searches.

In sum, as the above literatures suggest, there is every reason to believe that community characteristics influence police behavior, including search rates. While studies have explored population composition and structural conditions on police use of force and stops rates, few studies have incorporated factors associated with the growing ethnic diversity of urban communities and concentrated disadvantage on police search rates particularly. Further, community-based studies establish differences across race and ethnic groups, largely based on differential levels of concentrated disadvantage faced by these groups in their communities. Below we outline the methodological considerations and analytical strategy we used to explore the potential relationship between these characteristics and police search behavior in Miami-Dade communities.

Data and Methods

Given the focus on community characteristics, all data included are aggregated to the community or census-tract level. While the census tract does not explicitly represent the geographical boundaries of communities, census tracts have been used in extant community research as the unit of analysis because they are more likely to correspond to actual community boundaries.[53] The Census Bureau reports that Miami-Dade County comprises 348 census tracts. Because data on searches involve a recent study of police officers from the Miami-Dade Police Department (MDPD), who were not assigned to all areas in the county, however, the number of census tracts included in the analysis is reduced.[54] Additionally, we further restrict our analysis to all tracts that contain a population of at least 50 persons for the specific group being examined in the multivariate model. This strategy increases the generalizability of our results, and avoids the issue of unstable parameters often associated with low residential populations.

Data Sources and Measures

The data were compiled by the MDPD in cooperation with academic researchers in an effort to detect and identify patterns of racial bias in police behaviors. Data collection involved all stops that occurred in Miami census tracts between April 1, 2001, and October 31, 2001. As the MDPD does not require information to be collected on each stop, input from an appointed advisory board was used to develop citizen contact cards to be filled out upon each police stop by the officer. Examples of information collected include: the reason for making the stop, driver race, driver age, driver sex, driver residence, stop location, events that transpired after the initial stop, and numerous other details pertinent to the detection of racial bias. This study yielded data on 66,109 traffic stops, out of which 1,989 searches were performed, as described below.

The three dependent variables are the number of searches involving (non-Hispanic) whites, blacks, and Hispanic persons. To get a clear indication of search behaviors, our measures combine all forms of searches in the analysis, including search of person, search by consent, inventory search, search of vehicle, search of driver, and search of passenger.[55]

Census Bureau data in 2000 are used to estimate social, economic, and demographic measures at the census-tract level, which are used to reflect community characteristics.[56] Multiple indicators are included. To capture ethnic diversity of Miami neighborhoods we included two measures: the percentage of Hispanic persons who migrated into the United States within the past five years, and the percent of foreign-born residents. The first measure allows us to tap the potential influence of recent Hispanic immigrants into the urban community on police search behavior, while the second measure captures the overall level of ethnic diversity in Miami communities, including but not limited to Latino populations.

Measures commonly used to reflect concentrated disadvantage in previous studies are also included here, such as poverty, joblessness (number of persons aged sixteen and older not employed out of the total persons aged sixteen and older), and the presence of female-headed households with children under the age of eighteen. Each measure is race (non-Hispanic in the case of whites) and ethnic specific.[57] Residential mobility captures instability in the population for the specific race and ethnic groups included in this study. That is, it is a race- and ethnic-specific measure of the percentage of persons with a different residence within the past five years. Percent of vacant housing units is based on the number of vacant units out of the total number of housing units. Finally, the percentage of persons who journey to work twenty-five minutes or more accounts for the lack of available local employment.[58]

The MDPD provided information on officers employed by the Miami-Dade Police Department during the time of the study. Specifically, information was obtained on each of the 1,659 officers in the citizen contact database, including officer's race, age, rank, sex, and the like. The Professional Compliance Bureau provided data on disciplinary actions, including complaints and use-of-force reports, for a four-year time period (1997–2000). In this study we include use of force reports, defined as the rate of use of force per ten thousand residents within the past four years. We include this measure to tap variation in officer conduct across communities. Importantly, it was necessary to transform the use-of-force rate to its natural log due to significant variation about the mean.

In terms of other control measures, crime statistics for the geographic area of Miami-Dade were obtained for five years from 1997 to 2001 (N = 121,765 cases). Using these data, we calculated race-specific homicide rates per ten thousand persons to take into account variation in crime rates across neighborhoods.[59] Because a count of Hispanic homicides was not available in the crime data provided to us, the total homicide rate was used in the Hispanic model.

Because previous studies have confirmed that measures associated with concentrated disadvantage are highly correlated, principal components analysis was used to reduce this methodological problem.[60] Essentially the three measures of (1) the percentage of persons living below poverty, (2) the percentage of persons not employed (jobless), and (3) the percentage of female-headed households with children present load together to form the composite measure called the *concentrated disadvantage index*. The factor loadings do not vary across the race- and ethnic-specific groups.

Miami-Dade offers a particularly ideal domain in which to study race-based policing because of the area's divergent ethnic and economic makeup. Table 14.1 displays the descriptive statistics for measures included in our models, as well as information on the demographic makeup of Miami-Dade County. As can be seen at the bottom of this table, the Miami-Dade population is composed of approximately 68% white residents and 22% black residents; further, approximately 54% of all residents are of Hispanic origin. Although the ethnic diversity of this area has been discussed in the literature,[61] Miami-Dade is an understudied area in policing research.[62] Miami-Dade has a large race and ethnic mix, such as the relatively large size of Cuban and Haitian populations in the area. As revealed in table 14.1, approximately 11 percent of the Miami-Dade area is composed of Hispanics who recently migrated into the United States from abroad (minimum value of zero, maximum value of 45.9% across Miami-Dade communities). The mean percentage of foreign-born residents is 49 percent, with a range from 0 to 89.3%.

In terms of economic characteristics, the level of concentrated disadvantage among blacks is nearly two times that of whites, a condition observed in a majority of large U.S. cities.[63] The level of concentrated disadvantage among Hispanics is sizable as well, yet Hispanics have a lower level of concentrated disadvantage when compared

TABLE 14.1
Descriptive Statistics: Means (and Standard Deviations) for Variables in Race-Specific Search Models

	Black	Hispanic	White
Dependent Variable			
Search Count	4.09 (7.64)	9.27 (12.80)	6.09 (9.22)
Community Characteristics			
Recent Hispanic Immigration	11.46 (6.24)	11.35 (6.69)	11.44 (6.65)
Foreign-Born	48.56 (19.96)	48.97 (20.07)	49.60 (19.52)
Concentrated Disadvantage Index	50.48 (30.09)	38.90 (19.38)	27.27 (17.66)
Residential Mobility	55.13 (21.54)	53.62 (14.59)	42.18 (18.39)
Vacant Housing Units	7.57 (7.48)	7.67 (8.04)	7.56 (7.97)
Percent Persons Who Travel to Work			
25 Minutes or More	52.02 (10.47)	51.46 (10.66)	51.45 (10.73)
Controls			
Officer Use of Force Reports	4.11 (1.99)	4.12 (2.00)	4.09 (2.00)
Homicide Rate Per 10,000	0.78 (3.84)	1.72[a] (6.09)	0.32 (1.94)
N	249	327	320
Population Composition of Miami-Dade County (N = 348 tracts)			
% White Population	67.53 (30.12)		
% Black Population	22.34 (29.87)		
% Hispanic Population	54.36 (29.11)		

[a] Total homicide rate is used in the Hispanic model; otherwise, race-specific.

to blacks. Residential mobility is notable among blacks (approximately 55%) and Hispanics (approximate 54%), yet whites exhibit lower levels of residential instability (approximately 42%). As for police searches, police search Hispanic persons more than whites and blacks (9.3, 6.1, 4.1, respectively). Based on the raw counts or the actual number of searches, blacks are the least likely group to be searched by police. Also evident in the means and standard deviations for the search counts reported here is over-dispersion (mean/variance inequality). This methodological issue will be addressed below.

Multivariate Analysis

Police searches are rare events, resulting in low counts, which is a methodological issue that Poisson regression can more appropriately address as compared to OLS techniques.[64] Poisson regression, however, assumes that the conditional variance is equal to the conditional mean. This assumption is often violated in count data when the model reveals that the conditional variance is either larger (over-dispersion) or smaller (under-dispersion) than the mean.[65] An examination of these data and statistical tests performed show evidence of over-dispersion. To control for over-dispersion we estimated a negative binomial version of Poisson model that contains a dispersion parameter.[66,67] The model findings are presented in table 14.2.[68] Importantly, we offset the group-specific driving population (that is, persons fifteen or older) in the models, thereby essentially creating a rate of the dependent variables.[69] The results will also include an interpretation whereby we multiply the coefficient by a value of exp (bx_k).[70]

In table 14.2 we examine the influence of community characteristics on search rates; the table reveals coefficients varied, exhibiting evidence of differences in the effects of these predictors on searches rates involving distinct groups. But we find some

TABLE 14.2
Negative Binomial Regression Coefficients (and Standard Errors)

	Black	Hispanic	White
Community Characteristics			
Recent Hispanic Immigration	.076 (.042)	−.001 (.014)	−.010 (.014)
Foreign-Born	−.063** (.011)	−.040** (.004)	−.016** (.005)
Concentrated Disadvantage Index[a]	−.023** (.006)	.015** (.003)	.014** (.005)
Residential Mobility[a]	−.019 (.010)	−.006 (.005)	.008* (.005)
Vacant Units	−.088** (.029)	−.004 (.007)	−.028* (.012)
Percent Persons Who Travel to Work			
25 Minutes or More	−.045** (.022)	−.004 (.007)	−.019** (.008)
Controls			
Officer Use of Force Reports (log)	.117 (.163)	.701** (.047)	.786** (.054)
Homicide Rate Per 10,000[a]	.028 (.030)	.028* (.015)	.047 (.039)
Constant	1.967	−7.192	−8.79
Log Likelihood	−620.13	−904.35	−771.08
Pseudo R²	0.078	0.214	0.161
Maximum Likelihood R²	0.342	0.778	0.603
N	249	327	320

*p < 0.05; **p < 0.01
[a] Denotes a race or ethnic specific indicator, except total homicide rate in Hispanic model.

similarities as well. First, concerning the recent Hispanic immigration indicator, we find that communities with recent Hispanic immigrants do not have higher rates of searches, regardless of the race and ethnicity of the driver. This finding is consistent with other studies, which find that Hispanic immigration is not related to crime rates.[71] Yet, by examining police behavior in this study, we find that communities with higher level of recent Hispanic immigrants do not differ significantly from other areas in terms of police search rates. The percentage of the population that is foreign-born has a statistically significant, inverse relationship with police search rates in all three models. That is, a one standard deviation increase in the foreign-born population results in a 71.6% decrease in the black search rate (exp [−.063 × 19.96] = 0.2844), while Hispanic searches decrease by 55.2% (exp [−.040 × 20.07] = 0.4481) and white search rates decrease by 26.8% in Miami-Dade communities (exp [−.016 × 19.52] = 0.7317).

The remaining community characteristics are more commonly used indicators in the criminological literature. Like crime rates, these indicators have varied effects on police behavior, particularly across race and ethnic models. Concentrated disadvantage contributes to police search rates in all three models. But we find that areas with high levels of black concentrated disadvantage have fewer black searches, while disadvantage among whites and Hispanics contributes to higher search rates. That is, as the level of concentrated disadvantage increases among whites and Hispanics, the rate at which they are searched in these areas also increases. Residential mobility has a negligible influence on black and Hispanic search rates, but instability in the white residential population exhibits a positive influence on police search rates. The final indicators, vacant units and the percentage of persons traveling to work for twenty-five minutes or longer, are negatively related to searches involving whites and Blacks only.

Finally, in terms of control indicators, the police use-of-force measure reached statistical significance in two of the three search models. That is, in areas where police use-of-force reports increase, so too do search rates of whites and Hispanics, which is largely consistent with extant literature.[72] The crime rate (via homicide rate) was positively related to Hispanic search rates only. Recall that the total homicide rate was used in the Hispanic model because of a lack of ethnic-specific crime data in the official record. Overall these findings highlight the influence of community characteristics on rates of police searches at the community level, while controlling for crime rates and other factors relevant to police behavior in these areas. Below we provide a more detailed discussion of these results and offer some conclusions concerning police searches within the community context.

Discussion and Conclusions

The goal of this research was to determine if the indicators associated with ethnic diversity and structural characteristics influenced race- and ethnic-specific search rates at the community level. To achieve this goal, we offered an empirical test of linkages among ethnic diversity, concentrated disadvantage, and search rates involving whites, blacks, and Hispanics within the Miami-Dade area, while taking into account factors relevant to police behavior, such as police use of force and crime rates in these areas. The results suggest that police officers, such as the MDPD officers in this study, are influenced by community characteristics when making decisions to search. This research supports the claims made by other scholars that officers make distinctions between communities, contributing to officers' differential treatment of groups within these locales.[73] Moreover, community characteristics are relevant to police research,[74] expanding this literature beyond the study of urban crime and violence. We discuss our findings in detail below.

First, when it comes to police response to the ethnic diversity of Miami-Dade communities, we find that the increased numbers of recent Hispanic immigrants in this locale does not influence police searches, while the presence of foreign-born residents works to decrease rates of searches across race and ethnic groups. The negative association observed between the proportion of the foreign-born population and search rates of whites, blacks, and Hispanics might suggest that police officers do not equate immigrants (particularly Hispanics, who are the majority-population group) with those responsible for criminal activity in those areas. Recent research shows that immigrants are less violent[75] and that immigration tends to reduce crime.[76] In this way, police activity (i.e., searches) is less frequent in communities where foreign-born residents are found in larger numbers. While studies have documented the propensity for police officers to identify cues based on the characteristics of urban communities, including the number of police searches,[77] recent Hispanic immigrants may not serve as a cue within Miami communities.

Concentrated disadvantage (via racial residential segregation and limited economic opportunities) contributes to crime in urban communities. Studies have also found disproportionate dispatching of police to areas characterized by high levels of disadvantage.[78] Our findings reveal that the level of concentrated disadvantage in urban communities is relevant to the search rates of blacks, whites, and Hispanics. Specifically, as disadvantages become increasingly concentrated in Miami communities, search rates among Hispanics and whites increase as expected. On the other hand, we unexpectedly found a negative relationship between concentrated disadvantage and black search rates. This finding may reflect benign-neglect arguments, in that areas where social isolation and disadvantage are imposed on blacks at high levels become less of a threat, resulting in less police activity.[79] But extreme levels of disadvantage are not known to the other groups, because even the poorest whites do not live in neighborhoods with levels of concentrated poverty experienced by the majority of blacks;[80] therefore, disadvantage increases search rates in white communities. A similar pattern is found among Hispanics, in that an increase in Hispanic searches occurs in more disadvantaged areas. Overall, the dissimilarity in the geographic concentration of disadvantage among blacks, relative to whites and Hispanics, may be the key difference in search rates for this group. Simply stated, the inability of these data to produce similar effects in search rates involving blacks when compared to whites and Hispanics reflects the very different neighborhood conditions faced by this group in the Miami-Dade area.

Community perspectives also hold that the degree of attachment to the community, communication barriers, and signs of disorder will inhibit informal social control, resulting in increased rates of crime within these neighborhoods. Scholars have argued that residents within disorganized areas are less able to maintain informal control or to organize against unfair police treatment.[81] Policing literature tells us that police officers respond to community context, increasing the level of suspicion and causing officers to act punitively and coercively toward suspects encountered in these areas.

While community disorder and disadvantage might increase crime rates, our findings suggest a different relationship with police search rates, which was unexpected. For example, when linking travel time to crime rates, the social disorganization perspective proposes a positive relationship, whereby those who travel a great distance to work are home less often, contributing less to the supervision of youth or other at-risk groups in these neighborhoods, and therefore are less able to provide informal social control necessary to reduce crime. The influence of this indicator works differently on police decision making, however, where a negative relationship is found in the black and white search models. That is, an increase in travel time to work means residents are home less often, reducing time in their communities, thus decreasing the potential for contact with police. This association may exemplify the removal of low-skilled jobs in urban communities and the suburbanization of work. Specifically, deindustrialization changed the economic landscape of urban areas, resulting in potential employers moving farther away from workers.[82] Perhaps future research should consider the spatial location of labor market opportunities and its potential effect on police behavior. Further, it would be particularly important to incorporate race and ethnic differences in labor market experiences, such as the location and availability of ethnic-owned businesses, into macro-level research of policing and urban crime. Similarly, we find that the presence of vacant units also decreases police search rates of blacks and whites. This finding is also contradictory to our expectation based on community-based studies of criminal behavior.

The potential contributions of this research are many. Our study is one of only a small number on race-specific search rates conducted using such extensive and detailed data. The data were gathered using a combination of sources, including 2000 census indicators, the Uniform Crime Report, data on officer conduct, and information on citizen-police contacts, thus allowing for a more thorough investigation of the research question.[83] Obtaining such data is never possible without the cooperation of, and collaboration between, scholars and practitioners. This research is also guided by the community literature, which often are applied to crime rates but rarely to police behavior.[84] In this way this study moves beyond extant research, which neglects theory prior to statistical analysis.[85] As we draw on community-based perspectives concerning disadvantage and disorder, this study contributes to the macro-level or aggregate research on police behavior, rather than research that estimates individual factors. Finally, this study considered the growing levels of Hispanic immigrants and the percentage of foreign-born residents when investigating the relationship between community characteristics and police search behavior. As research moves beyond black-white comparisons and attempts to capture the multiethnic nature of American cities today, it appears that the influence of growing ethnic diversity within urban communities are positive and numerous. Clearly these findings contradict popular

press and some assumptions of criminological theories concerning the negative influence of immigration on crime and communities. A paradox, then, exists concerning
the influence of Hispanic immigration,[86] which will require researchers to move beyond traditional explanations and incorporate other race and ethnic groups into their
research agendas.

NOTES

1. We would like to thank Brian Stults and Alex Piquero for comments made on an earlier draft of this chapter. We also acknowledge the Miami-Dade Police Department for their
role in this research, although the opinions and comments made here are solely those of the
authors.

2. Walker, Spohn, and DeLone, "*The color of justice*"; Weitzer, and Tuch, "*Race and policing
in America.*"

3. Alpert, Dunham, and Smith, "Investigating racial profiling"; Fagan, and Davies, "Street
stops and broken windows"; Harcourt, "Unconstitutional police searches"; Zingraff, Marcinda,
Smith, Tomaskovic-Devey, Warren, McMurray, and Fenlon., "*Evaluating North Carolina state
highway patrol data.*"

4. Becker, "Assessing the use of profiling"; Knowles, Persico, and Todd, "Racial bias in motor vehicle searches"; Smith, and Petrocelli, "Racial profiling?"

5. Gould, and Mastrofski, "Suspect searches"

6. Gould, and Mastrofski, "Suspect searches"; Klinger, "Negotiating order in patrol
work"; Terrill, and Reisig, "Neighborhood context"; Weitzer, and Tuch, "*Race and policing in
America.*"

7. Kane, "The social ecology of police misconduct"; Smith, "The neighborhood context of
police behavior"; Chambliss, "Policing the ghetto underclass"; Meehan, and Ponder, "Race and
place"; Lundman, "Driver race, ethnicity, and gender."

8. Terrill, and Mastrofski, "Situational and officer-based determinants."

9. Smith, "The neighborhood context of police behavior."

10. Engel, and Calnon, "Examining the influence of drivers' characteristics"; Lundman,
"Driver race, ethnicity, and gender"; Meehan, and Ponder, "Race and place"; Werthman, and
Piliavin, "Gang members and the police."

11. Smith, Makarios, and Alpert, "Differential suspicion."

12. Gould, and Mastrofski, "Suspect searches"; Klinger, "Negotiating order in patrol work";
Zingraff, Marcinda, Smith, Tomaskovic-Devey, Warren, McMurray, and Fenlon, "*Evaluating
North Carolina state highway patrol data.*"

13. For exception, see Fagan, and Davies, "Street stops and broken windows."

14. Martinez, "Incorporating Latinos and immigrants into policing research."

15. Becker, "Assessing the use of profiling"; Fagan, and Davies, "Street stops and broken
windows"; Terrill, and Reisig, "Neighborhood context."

16. Kane, "The social ecology of police misconduct"; Sampson, and Wilson, "Toward a
theory of race, crime, and urban inequality"; Sampson, and Bean, "Cultural mechanisms and
killing fields."

17. Fagan, and Davies, "Street stops and broken windows"; Kane, "The social ecology of
police misconduct"; Smith, "The neighborhood context of police behavior"; Terrill, and Mastrofski, "Situational and officer-based determinants of police coercion"; Terrill, and Reisig,
"Neighborhood context."

18. Smith, "The neighborhood context of police behavior."

19. Terrill, and Reisig, "Neighborhood context."

20. Terrill, and Reisig, "Neighborhood context."

21. Fagan, and Davies, "Street stops and broken windows."

22. Fagan, and Davies, "Street stops and broken windows."

23. Kane, "The social ecology of police misconduct."

24. Weitzer, and Tuch, *"Race and policing in America"*; Smith, Visher, and Davidson, "Equity and discretionary justice."

25. Werthman, and Piliavin, "Gang members."

26. Reid, Weiss, Adelman, and Jaret, "The immigration-crime relationship."

27. Hagan, and Palloni, "Sociological criminology."

28. See Lee, Martinez, Rosenfeld, et al., "Does immigration increase homicide?"; Portes, and Mooney, "Social capital and community development."

29. Bankston, "Youth gangs"; Martinez, *Latino homicide.*"

30. Reid, Weiss, Adelman, and Jaret, "The immigration-crime relationship."

31. Reid, Weiss, Adelman, and Jaret, "The immigration-crime relationship."

32. Clark, "Mass migration and local outcomes."

33. Waldinger, "The ethnic enclave debate revisited."

34. Waters, *"Crime and immigrant youth."*

35. Lee, Martinez, Rosenfeld, et al., "Does immigration increase homicide?"; Reid, Weiss, Adelman, and Jaret, "The immigration-crime relationship."

36. Lee, Martinez, Rosenfeld, et al., "Does immigration increase homicide?"

37. Zhou, "Contemporary immigration."

38. Zhou, "Contemporary immigration," 206.

39. Logan, Alba, and McNulty, "Ethnic economies in metropolitan regions"; Waldinger, "The ethnic enclave debate revisited"; Wilson, *When work disappears."*

40. Wilson, *When work disappears."*

41. Massey, and Denton, *"American apartheid";* Massey and Eggers, "The ecology of inequality."

42. Massey, Eggers, and Denton, "Disentangling the causes of concentrated urban poverty."

43. See Krivo and Peterson, "Extremely disadvantaged neighborhoods," "The structural context of homicide"; Parker and McCall, "Structural conditions and racial homicide patterns"; Velez, Krivo, and Peterson, "Structural inequality and homicide."

44. Krivo, and Peterson, "Extremely disadvantaged neighborhoods," "The structural context of homicide"; Sampson, and Wilson, "Toward a theory of race, crime, and urban inequality."

45. See Chambliss, "Policing the ghetto underclass"; Jackson and Carroll, "Race and the war on crime"; Liska, Lawrence, and Benson, "Perspectives on the legal order."

46. Bureau of Justice Statistics, *"Correctional population in the U.S., 1994";* Lynch, and Sabol, *"Did getting tougher on crime pay?";* Rose, and Clear, "Incarceration, social capital, and crime."

47. Martinez, *"Latino homicide."*

48. Alba, Logan, and Stults, "The changing neighborhood contexts"; Massey, and Denton, *"American apartheid."*

49. Martinez, *"Latino homicide."*

50. See Morenoff, Sampson, and Raudenbush, "Neighborhood inequality, collective efficacy"; Triplett, Gainey, and Sun, "Institutional strength, social control, and neighborhood crime rates"; Wilson, *The truly disadvantaged."*

51. Klinger, "Negotiating order in patrol work," "Environment and organization"; Meehan,

and Ponder, "Race and place"; Sampson, and Raudenbush, "Systematic social observation of public spaces."

52. Manning, "The police."

53. Land, McCall, and Cohen, "Structural covariates of homicide rates"; Morenoff, Sampson, and Raudenbush, "Neighborhood inequality, collective efficacy."

54. See Alpert, Dunham, and Smith, "Investigating racial profiling."

55. Because inventory searches are less likely to involve police decision making, as they are considered mandatory protocol upon arrest, we computed search measures that exclude inventory searches and re-estimated our multivariate models. Our results did not change; thus inventory searches are included in the results presented here.

56. Krivo, and Peterson, "Extremely disadvantaged neighborhoods," "The structural context of homicide"; Meehan, and Ponder, "Race and place"; Parker, and McCall, "Structural conditions and racial homicide patterns"; Sampson, and Raudenbush, "Neighborhood inequality, collective efficacy."

57. Land, McCall, and Cohen, "Structural covariates of homicide rates"; Ousey, "Homicide, structural factors"; Parker, and McCall, "Structural conditions and racial homicide patterns"; Stretesky, Schuck, and Hogan, "Space matters."

58. See Morenoff, Sampson, and Raudenbush, "Neighborhood inequality, collective efficacy"; Triplett, Gainey, and Sun, "Institutional strength, social control, and neighborhood crime rates"; Wilson, "The truly disadvantaged."

59. Werthman, and Piliavin, "Gang members and the police."

60. Land, McCall, and Cohen, "Structural covariates of homicide rates"; Parker, and McCall, "Structural conditions and racial homicide patterns"; Stretesky, Schuck, and Hogan, "Space matters."

61. Alpert, and Dunham, "Policing multi-ethnic neighborhoods"; Martinez, "Latino homicide"; Parker, MacDonald, Alpert, Smith, and Piquero, "A contextual study of racial profiling."

62. Martinez, "Incorporating Latinos and immigrants into policing research."

63. Sampson, and Bean, "Cultural mechanisms and killing fields."

64. Gardner, Mulvey, and Shaw, "Regression analyses of counts and rates"; Greene, "Econometric"; Osgood, "Poisson-based regression analysis."

65. Agresti, "Negative binomial regression."

66. Cameron, and Trivedi, "Regression analysis of count data."

67. Spatial analytic methods are commonly used in community-level studies because of methodological concerns, such as spatial autocorrelation and spatial interdependency of proximal neighborhoods (Anselin, "GeoDa 0.9 user's guide"). Using GeoDa, a statistical software program developed by Anselin, our regression diagnostics did not reveal spatial interdependence issues. The Lagrange Multiplier statistics indicated that neither spatial lag nor spatial error were problematic in our models (see also Morenoff, Sampson, and Raudenbush, "Neighborhood inequality, collective efficacy," for detailed discussion of spatial modeling).

68. Collinearity diagnostics were performed, including variance inflation factors (VIFs) to assess the amount of collinearity among the regressors included in the models. None of the VIFs exceeded a value of 4.0, which is commonly used as a cutoff value for evidence of collinearity. The bivariate correlation between recent Hispanic immigration and the percentage of foreign-born resident is .3765.

69. In a set of negative binominal models we offset the group-specific population, instead of the group-specific driving age population, to make sure this criterion did not affect our results. Our findings remained the same.

70. See Osgood, "Poisson-based regression analysis."

71. Lee, Martinez, Rosenfeld, et al., "Does immigration increase homicide?"; Lee, and Martinez, "Social disorganization revisited"; Martinez, "*Latino homicide*"; Zhou, "Contemporary immigration."

72. Smith, "The neighborhood context of police behavior"; Smith, and Holmes, "Community accountability, minority threat, and police brutality"; Terrill, and Mastrofski, "Situational and officer-based determinants of police coercion"; Terrill, and Reisig, "Neighborhood context."

73. Smith, "The neighborhood context of police behavior"; Smith, Visher, and Davidson, "Equity and discretionary justice."

74. See also Kane, "The social ecology of police misconduct."

75. Martinez, "*Latino homicide*."

76. Lee Martinez, Rosenfeld, et al., "Does immigration increase homicide?"; Lee, and Martinez, "Social disorganization revisited"; Martinez, "*Latino homicide*."

77. See Smith, Makarios, and Alpert, "Differential suspicion."

78. Jackson, and Carroll, "Race and the war on crime"; Liska, Lawrence, and Benson, "Perspectives on the legal order."

79. Liska, and Chamlin, "Social structures and crime control"; Parker, Stults, and Rice, "Racial threat, concentrated disadvantage, and social control"; Terrill, and Mastrofski, "Situational and officer-based determinants of police coercion."

80. Sampson, and Wilson, "Toward a theory of race, crime, and urban inequality"; Wilson, "*The truly disadvantaged*."

81. See Kane, "The social ecology of police misconduct."

82. Massey, and Denton, "*American apartheid*"; Wilson, "*The truly disadvantaged*."

83. Lundman, "Driver race, ethnicity, and gender."

84. Schuck, and Rosenbaum, "Promoting safe and healthy neighborhoods."

85. Engel, Calnon, and Bernard, "Theory and racial profiling."

86. Kubrin, Wadsworth, and DiPietro, "Deindustrialization, disadvantage, and suicide among young black males"; Martinez, "*Latino homicide*"; Wadsworth, and Kubrin, "Hispanic suicide in U.S. metropolitan areas."

REFERENCES

Agresti, Alan. 2002. "Negative binomial regression." In *Categorical data analysis*, 2nd Edition. New York: Wiley.

Alba, Richard D., John R. Logan, and Brian J. Stults. 2000. The changing neighborhood contexts of the immigrant metropolis. *Social Forces* 79: 587–621.

Alpert, Geoffrey, and Roger Dunham. 1988. *Policing multi-ethnic neighborhoods: The Miami study and findings for law enforcement in the United States*. New York: Greenwood Press.

Alpert, Geoffrey, Roger Dunham, and Michael R. Smith. 2007. Investigating racial profiling by the Miami-Dade Police Department: A multimethod approach. *Criminology and Public Policy* 6: 201–232.

Anselin, Luc. 2003. *GeoDa 0.9 user's guide. Spatial analysis laboratory*. Urbana-Champaign, IL: University of Illinois.

Bankston, C. L. 1998. Youth gangs and the new second generation: A review essay. *Aggression and Violent Behavior* 3: 35–45.

Becker, Stan. 2004. Assessing the use of profiling in searches by law enforcement personnel. *Journal of Criminal Justice* 32: 183–193.

Bureau of Justice Statistics. 1996. *Correctional population in the U.S., 1994.* Executive Summary. Washington, DC.

Cameron, A. Colin, and Pravin K. Trivedi. 1998. *Regression analysis of count data.* Cambridge, UK: Cambridge University Press.

Chambliss, William. 1994. Policing the ghetto underclass: The politics of law and law enforcement. *Social Problems* 41: 177–194.

Clark, W. 1998. Mass migration and local outcomes: Is international migration to the United States creating a new urban underclass? *Urban Studies* 35: 371–383.

Clear, Todd R., Dina R. Rose, and Elin Waring. 2003. Coercive mobility and crime: A preliminary examination of concentrated incarceration and social disorganization. *Justice Quarterly* 20: 33–64.

Engel, Robin S., and Jennifer M. Calnon. 2004. Examining the influence of drivers' characteristics during traffic stops with police: Results from a national survey. *Justice Quarterly* 21: 49–90.

Engel, Robin S., Jennifer M. Calnon, and Thomas J. Bernard. 2002. Theory and racial profiling: Shortcomings and future directions in research. *Justice Quarterly* 19: 249–274.

Fagan, Jeffrey, and Garth Davies. 2000. Street stops and broken windows: *Terry*, race, and disorder in New York City. *Fordham Urban Law Journal* 28: 457–504.

Gardner, William, Edward P. Mulvey, and Esther C. Shaw. 1995. Regression analyses of counts and rates: Poisson, overdispersed poisson, and negative binomial models. *Psychological Bulletin* 118: 392–404.

Gould, Jon, and Stephen Mastrofski. 2004. Suspect searches: Assessing police behavior under the U.S. Constitution. *Criminology and Public Policy* 3: 315–362.

Greene, William H. *Econometric analysis.* Upper Saddle River, NJ: Prentice Hall, 2000.

Hagan, J., and A. Palloni. 1999. Sociological criminology and the mythology of Hispanic immigration and crime. *Social Problems* 46: 617–632.

Harcourt, Bernard. 2004. Unconstitutional police searches and collective responsibility. *Criminology and Public Policy* 3: 363–378.

Jackson, Pamela I., and Leo Carroll. 1981. Race and the war on crime: The sociopolitical determinants of municipal police expenditures in 90 non-southern U.S. cities. *American Sociological Review* 46: 290–305.

Kane, Robert. 2002. The social ecology of police misconduct. *Criminology* 40: 867–896.

Klinger, David. 1997. Negotiating order in patrol work: An ecological theory of police response to deviance. *Criminology* 35: 277–306.

———. 2004. Environment and organization: Reviving a perspective on the police. *The Annals of the American Academy of Political and Social Science* 593: 119–136.

Knowles, John, Nicola Persico, and Petra Todd. 2001. Racial bias in motor vehicle searches: Theory and evidence. *Journal of Political Economy* 109: 203–229.

Krivo, Lauren J., and Ruth D. Peterson. 1996. Extremely disadvantaged neighborhoods and urban crime. *Social Forces* 75: 619–650.

———. 2000. The structural context of homicide: Accounting for racial differences in process. *American Sociological Review* 65: 547–559.

Kubrin, Charis, Tim Wadsworth, and Stephanie DiPietro. 2006. Deindustrialization, disadvantage, and suicide among young black males. *Social Problems* 84: 1559–1579.

Land, Kenneth C., Patricia L. McCall, and Lawrence E. Cohen. 1990. Structural covariates of homicide rates: Are there any invariances across time and social space? *American Journal of Sociology* 95: 922–963.

Lee, Matthew T., and Ramiro Martinez. 2002. Social disorganization revisited: Mapping the recent immigration and black homicide relationship in northern Miami. *Sociological Focus* 35: 363–380.

Lee, Matthew T., Ramiro Martinez, Richard Rosenfeld, et al. 2001. Does immigration increase homicide? Negative evidence from three border cities. *Sociological Quarterly* 42: 559–580.

Liska, Allen E., and Mitchell B. Chamlin. 1984. Social structures and crime control among macrosocial units. *American Journal of Sociology* 90: 388–95.

Liska, Allen E., Joseph J. Lawrence, and Michael Benson. 1981. Perspectives on the legal order: The capacity for social control. *American Journal of Sociology* 87: 413–26.

Logan, J. R., R. Alba, and T. L. McNulty. 1994. Ethnic economies in metropolitan regions: Miami and beyond. *Social Forces* 72: 691–724.

Lundman, Richard. 2004. Driver race, ethnicity, and gender and citizen reports of vehicle searches by police and vehicle search hits: Toward a triangulated scholarly understanding. *Journal of Criminal Law and Criminology* 94: 309–349.

Lynch, James, and William Sabol. 1997. *Did getting tougher on crime pay? Crime Policy Report.* Washington, DC.: Urban Institute State Policy Center.

Manning, Peter. 1978. "The police: Mandate, strategies, and appearances." In *Policing: A view from the street*, eds. Peter Manning and John van Maanen, 7–31. Santa Monica, CA: Goodyear.

Martinez, Jr., Ramiro. 2002. *Latino homicide: Immigration, violence, and community.* New York: Routledge.

———. 2007. Incorporating Latinos and immigrants into policing research. *Criminology and Public Policy* 6: 601–609.

Massey, Douglas S., and Nancy A. Denton. 1993. *American apartheid: Segregation and the making of the underclass.* Cambridge, MA: Harvard University Press.

Massey, Douglas S., and Mitchell L. Eggers. 1990. The ecology of inequality: Minorities and the concentration of poverty, 1970–1980. *American Journal of Sociology* 96: 1153–1188.

Massey, Douglas S., Mitchell L. Eggers, and Nancy A. Denton. 1994. Disentangling the causes of concentrated urban poverty. *International Journal of Group Tensions* 24: 267–316.

Meehan, Albert J., and Michael C. Ponder. 2002. Race and place: The ecology of racial profiling African American motorists. *Justice Quarterly* 19: 399–430.

Morenoff, Jeffrey D., Robert J. Sampson, and Stephen W. Raudenbush. 2001. Neighborhood inequality, collective efficacy, and the spatial dynamics of urban *violence. Criminology* 39: 517–558.

Osgood, D. W. 2000. Poisson-based regression analysis of aggregate crime rates. *Journal of Quantitative Criminology* 16: 21–43.

Ousey, Graham. 1999. Homicide, structural factors, and the racial invariance assumption. *Criminology* 37: 405–426.

Parker, Karen F., and Patricia L. McCall. 1999. Structural conditions and racial homicide patterns: A look at the multiple disadvantages in urban areas. *Criminology* 37: 447–477.

Parker, Karen F., John MacDonald, Geoffrey P. Alpert, Michael R. Smith, and Alex Piquero. 2004. A contextual study of racial profiling: Assessing the theoretical rationale for the study of racial profiling at the local level. *American Behavioral Scientist* 47: 943–962.

Parker, Karen F., Brian J. Stults, and Stephen K. Rice. 2005. Racial threat, concentrated disadvantage, and social control: Considering the macro-level sources of variation in arrests. *Criminology* 43: 1111–1134.

Portes, A and M. Mooney. 2002. Social capital and community development. In *The new economic sociology: Developments in an emerging field*, eds. Guillen, Collings and England, 303–329. New York: Russell Sage.

Reid, Lesley W., Harald Weiss, Robert Adelman, and Charles Jaret. 2005. The immigration-crime relationship: Evidence across U.S. metropolitan areas. *Social Science Research* 34: 757–780.

Rose, Dina R., and Todd R. Clear. 1998. Incarceration, social capital, and crime: Implications for social disorganization theory. *Criminology* 36: 441–479.

Sampson, Robert J., and Lydia Bean. 2006. Cultural mechanisms and killing fields: A revised theory of community-level racial inequality. In *The many colors of crime: Inequalities of race, ethnicity, and crime in America*, eds. Ruth Peterson, Lauren Krivo, and John Hagan, 8–38. New York: New York University Press.

Sampson, Robert J., and Stephen W. Raudenbush. 1999. Systematic social observation of public spaces: A new look at disorder in urban neighborhoods. *American Journal of Sociology* 105: 603–651.

Sampson, Robert J. and William J. Wilson. 1995. Toward a theory of race, crime, and urban inequality. In *Crime and inequality*, eds. John Hagan and Ruth Peterson, 37–54. Stanford: Stanford University Press.

Schuck, Amie, and Dennis Rosenbaum. 2006. Promoting safe and healthy neighborhoods: What research tells us about intervention. In *Community Change: Theories, Practice, and Evidence*, eds. K. Fulbright-Anderson and P. Auspos, 61–140. Washington, DC: Aspen Institute.

Smith, Brad W., and Malcolm D. Holmes. 2003. Community accountability, minority threat, and police brutality: An examination of civil rights criminal complaints. *Criminology* 41: 1035–1063.

Smith, Douglas A. 1986. The neighborhood context of police behavior. In *Communities and crime*, eds. Albert J. Reiss and Michael Tonry, 313–341. Chicago: University of Chicago Press.

Smith, Douglas, Christy Visher, and Laura Davidson. 1984. Equity and discretionary justice: The influence of race on police arrest decisions. *Journal of Criminal Law and Criminology* 75: 234–249.

Smith, Michael R., Matthew Makarios, and Geoffrey P. Alpert. 2006. Differential suspicion: Theory and gender effects in the traffic stop context. *Justice Quarterly* 23: 271–295.

Smith, Michael R., and Matthew Petrocelli. 2001. Racial profiling? A multivariate analysis of police traffic stop data. *Police Quarterly* 4: 4–27.

Stretesky, Paul B., Amie M. Schuck, and Michael J. Hogan. 2004. Space matters: An analysis of poverty, poverty clustering, and violent crime. *Justice Quarterly* 21: 817–841.

Terrill, William, and Stephen D. Mastrofski. 2002. Situational and officer-based determinants of police coercion. *Justice Quarterly* 19: 215–248.

Terrill, William, and Michael D. Reisig. 2003. Neighborhood context and police use of force. *Journal of Research in Crime and Delinquency* 40: 291–321.

Triplett, Ruth, Randy Gainey, and Ivan Sun. 2003. Institutional strength, social control, and neighborhood crime rates. *Theoretical Criminology* 7: 439–467.

Velez, Maria, B., Lauren J. Krivo, and Ruth D. Peterson. 2003. Structural inequality and homicide: An assessment of the black-white gap in killings. *Criminology* 41: 645–672.

Wadsworth, Tim, and Charis Kubrin. 2007. Hispanic suicide in U.S. metropolitan areas: Examining the effects of immigration, assimilation, affluence, and disadvantage. *American Journal of Sociology* 6: 1848–1885.

Waldinger, R. 1993. The ethnic enclave debate revisited. *International Journal of Urban and Regional Research* 17: 444–452.

Walker, Samuel, Cassia Spohn, and Miriam DeLone. 2001. *The color of justice: Race, ethnicity, and crime in America,* 2nd Edition. Florence, KY: Wadsworth.

Waters, T. 1999. *Crime and immigrant youth.* Thousand Oaks, CA: Sage.

Weitzer, Ronald, and Steven Tuch. 2006. *Race and policing in America: Conflict and reform.* Cambridge, UK: Cambridge University Press.

Werthman, Carl, and Irving M. Piliavin. 1967. Gang members and the police. In *The police: Six sociological essays,* ed. D. Brodura, 56–98. New York: John Wiley.

Wilson, William J. 1987. *The truly disadvantaged: The inner city, the underclass, and public policy.* Chicago: University of Chicago Press.

———. 1996. *When work disappears: The world of the new urban poor.* New York: Knopf.

Zhou, M. 2001. Contemporary immigration and the dynamics of race and ethnicity. In *America becoming: Racial trends and their consequences,* eds. Neil Smelser, William Julius Wilson, and Faith Mitchell, 200–242. Washington, DC: National Academy Press.

Zingraff, Matthew, Mason H. Marcinda, William R. Smith, Donald Tomaskovic-Devey, P. Warren, H. McMurray, and C. R. Fenlon. 2000. *Evaluating North Carolina state highway patrol data: Citations, warnings, and searches in 1998.* Raleigh, NC: North Carolina State University.

Chapter 15

Blind Justice
Police Shootings in Memphis

James J. Fyfe

The literature on police use of deadly force[1] has produced two major findings. First, researchers report extreme variation in rates of police shooting among American jurisdictions.[2] Second, regardless of its geographic scope, the research invariably reports that the percentage of police shootings involving black victims far exceeds the percentage of blacks in the population.[3] This chapter examines factors affecting both of these findings.

I. Interjurisdictional Variations

Attempts to identify sources of interjurisdictional shooting rate variation have produced mixed results. Milton suggests that differences among shooting rates are associated with differences in levels of community violence and risk to officers.[4] Kania and Mackey, in an attempt to test two related hypotheses, report strong associations between fatal police shooting rates and public homicide and arrest rates over the 50 states.[5] Despite flaws in the data employed by Kania and Mackey,[6] their thesis, that shootings are associated with community violence and risk to officers, is supported by Fyfe. He reports close associations between police shooting rates and arrest and homicide rates across the geographic subdivisions of a single large police jurisdiction, where internal organizational policies and practices which might influence shooting rates are presumably constant.[7] The relative influence upon police shooting rates of such internal policies and practices is suggested by Kiernan, who found that police shooting rates among nine American cities vary by as much as 1500% even when controlling for a measure of community violence and police exposure to shootings (arrests for violent felonies).[8]

Kiernan's suggestion that police internal organizational variables also affect shooting rates is reinforced by Uelman, who reports that the major determinants of the levels of police shooting in the California agencies he studied were the "personal philosophies" of police chiefs and the administrative controls they devised.[9] Thus, varia-

From *Journal of Criminal Law and Criminology* 73: 707–722. © 1982 *Journal of Criminal Law and Criminology*. Reprinted with permission of *Journal of Criminal Law and Criminology*.

tions in the shooting rates of American police jurisdictions apparently are associated both with "external" variables (e.g., community violence; threats to officer safety) and with "internal" variables (e.g., administrative philosophies; adequacy of training; restrictiveness of police shooting policies; intensity of shooting incident review).

II. Black Disproportion

Goldkamp's survey of the literature of police deadly force offers a similar and useful construct of researchers' theories regarding minority disproportion among those shot and shot at by police.[10] Those who have studied deadly force, he states, subscribe to one of two "Belief Perspectives." Belief Perspective I holds that minority overrepresentation among shooting victims is a result of differential police practices: that "police have one trigger finger for whites, and another for blacks."[11] This perspective, therefore, attributes black disproportion among shooting victims to variables internal to police organizations (e.g., racism by officers and by the administrators who encourage or allow them to express it by shooting blacks in situations in which they would refrain from shooting whites). Belief Perspective II views black shooting victim disproportion as a consequence of variables external to police organizations. From this perspective, black shooting victim disproportion is seen as a consequence of justifiable police responses to the relatively great involvement of blacks in violent crime and other activities likely to precipitate shooting.[12]

Since the formulation of Goldkamp's two Belief Perspectives, there has been considerable research into the relationship of race and police shootings. Fyfe found that black disproportion among New York City police shooting victims was closely associated with the representation of blacks among violent crime arrestees and among homicide victims.[13] Belief Perspective II is also supported by Blumberg's study of police shootings in Atlanta and Kansas City, which, like Fyfe's work, reports little variation in the degree of danger confronted by police officers involved in shootings of citizens of different racial groups.[14]

Despite these apparent confirmations of Belief Perspective II, it is possible that the relationships between high rates of police shooting victimization and indications of black violence are artifacts of differential police enforcement and reporting practices. In other words, it may be that the relationship between black shooting rates and black arrest rates is a result of arbitrariness in arrest and crime reporting practices, as well as in shooting practices. Further, given great interjurisdictional variation in police shooting rates, it is also possible that the validity of either of Goldkamp's two Belief Perspectives is place dependent.

In jurisdictions where police shooting is infrequent and closely controlled by stringent policies and incident review procedures conducted by administrators whose personal philosophies mitigate against arbitrary shootings, black disproportion may be explained by Belief Perspective II. In such places, it may be that internal organizational strategies have minimized officer arbitrariness, and that external variables (e.g., crime rate differentials among the races) do account for black shooting victim disproportion. Conversely, in jurisdictions characterized by high police shooting rates and loose or non-existent training, shooting policies, and review procedures, it may be that officers are exercising their broad discretion in a manner that validates Belief Perspective I. In such places, it may be true that officers shoot blacks in situations in which they would refrain from shooting whites, and that their actions are congruent with the personal philosophies of their supervisors. In view of the wide range in restrictiveness of police shooting policies and other internal organizational variables across jurisdictions,[15] therefore, it would be surprising if either Belief Perspective I or Belief Perspective II was universally valid among American police agencies. Indeed, it may be that the empirical support for Belief Perspective II exists because research access has been granted by only those police agencies that have attempted to control shooting discretion in a manner that minimizes the opportunity for officers to exercise "differential trigger fingers," and which, consequently, have little fear that researchers will publish embarrassing findings.

III. A Model for Analysis

Blumberg has commented that without "baseline data with regard to the situational characteristics of all police-citizen encounters . . . , it is not possible to definitively refute the contention that the police are not more likely to shoot blacks than whites under the same circumstances."[16] Such an observation applies equally to interjurisdictional variation. Without data on situations characteristic of all police-citizen encounters, it may not be possible to identify definitively the sources of interjurisdictional shooting variations.

Data regarding all police-citizen encounters are not likely to become available in the foreseeable future, but this author has argued that a useful surrogate may be found in data related to the situational characteristics of police shootings.[17]

At the most basic level, police shootings may be dichotomized into "elective" shootings (those in which the officer involved may elect to shoot or not to shoot at little or no risk to himself or others), and "nonelective" shootings (those in which the officer has little real choice but to shoot or to risk death or serious injury to himself or others). Like elective surgery, elective shootings—those involving unarmed fleeing property criminals, for example—are real exercises in discretion. Thus, they are subject to reduction by internal police policies and practices designed to limit officer discretion. The chief can direct his officers not to shoot at the backs of unarmed fleeing property crime suspects without increasing risk to officers caused by encounters with such suspects. Nonelective shootings, by contrast, are largely a consequence of influences external to the police agency, and are less subject to administrative control strategies. The police chief has little direct control over the number or ethnic groups of armed robbers in his jurisdiction, nor can he direct officers not to resort to firearms when they come face to face with them in life-threatening circumstances.

Stated most simply, elective shooting rates are most greatly influenced by factors internal to police organizations, and nonelective shooting rates are most greatly influenced by factors external to police organizations.[18]

From this perspective, it is clear that aggregate shooting rates—either among police jurisdictions or among victim racial distributions—are of minimal informational value. If one is to know whether the police are "more trigger happy" in some jurisdictions than others, one must know something about the situations in which officers in those jurisdictions shoot at other human beings. To know whether police differentiate along racial lines with their trigger fingers, one must know something about the situations in which police shoot at members of different racial groups.

Thus, this author suggested the utility of a typology of police shooting based on a "scale of immediate hazard" to the officer.[19] Using "degree of officer injury" as a criterion, such a scale (with eleven separate shooting types, which varied from clearly elective events to clearly nonelective events) was constructed and used in this author's analysis of New York City police shootings; it was found that the situations in which officers shot blacks threatened life relatively more often and more seriously (and, thus were more often nonelective) than those in which they shot whites.[20] Blumberg employed a similar typology with similar results in his study of Atlanta and Kansas City police shootings.[21] This chapter employs such a hazard based typology to examine comparative shooting rates in Memphis and New York City, and to examine black shooting disproportion in Memphis.

A. Data Sources

The New York City shooting data used in this research are part of a data set which includes all reported incidents in which members of that agency discharged firearms and/or were seriously assaulted or killed between January 1, 1971, and December 31, 1975. For the purposes of this analysis, only those reports involving shootings were employed.

The Memphis shooting data employed herein cover slightly different time periods, and were provided by the NAACP Legal Defense Fund, which had obtained them in connection with a civil suit resulting from a police shooting in that city.[22] They consist of a Memphis Police Department condensation of the circumstances in which officers in that agency employed deadly force against property crime suspects, as well as summary data on other uses of firearms during the years 1969–74. In addition, this research employs data on all fatal police shootings in Memphis during 1969–76, except for those occurring between January 16 and December 31, 1972, a period for which no information is available.[23] In neither city was any attempt made to reconcile these official versions of shootings with other accounts.

IV. Analysis

A. Interjurisdictional Variations: Memphis and New York City

Table 15.1 presents the aggregate data for New York City and Memphis police shootings, along with mean annual rates of shooting per 1,000 officers. The table

TABLE 15.1
Police Shooting Incidents in Memphis and New York City

Measure	Memphis 1969–74	New York City 1971–75
Number of Police Shootings	225	2,926
Mean Annual Police Shooting Rate per 1,000 Officers	33.5	19.6

TABLE 15.2
Measures of Public Violence, Police Hazard and Police Shooting in Memphis And New York City

Measure	Memphis 1969–74	New York City 1971–75
Mean Annual Murder/Non-Negligent Manslaughter Rate per 100,000 Population	2.97	2.75
Mean Annual Violent Felony Arrest Rate per 1,000 Officers*	587.12	1172.95
Police Shooting Rate per 1,000 Violent Felony Arrests	56.98	16.71

*Includes arrests for murder/nonnegligent manslaughter, rape, robbery, aggravated assault.

shows that between 1969 and 1974, firearms were discharged by one or more Memphis police officers on 225 separate occasions, producing a mean annual rate of 33.5 shootings per 1,000 officers. In New York City during 1971–75, there were 2,926 such incidents, producing a mean annual rate of 19.2 shootings per 1,000 officers.

These aggregate rates indicate that Memphis police use their guns considerably more often than their New York City counterparts. They tell us little, however, of the variations in violence and police hazard generally in those cities. Nor are they informative on the questions of percentages or rates of elective and nonelective shootings in Memphis and New York. Indeed, as explained below, not all of the shootings described in table 15.1 involve shootings at other persons.

Table 15.2 presents surrogate measures of general police hazard in Memphis and New York City. As noted earlier, these were found by this author to be closely associated with police shooting rates over New York's 20 police subjurisdictions where internal influences (policy, training, etc.) presumably were held relatively constant.[24] In that study, strong relationships between police shooting rates and the external influences of community violence (shooting rate per 1,000 officers and murder/nonnegligent manslaughter rate per 100,000 population, where $r = +.78$) and police confrontations with violent suspects (shooting rate and rate of arrest for violent felonies, where $r = +.62$) were reported.[25] Table 15.2 suggests, however, that these external influences are not associated with the differences in shooting rates between Memphis and New York. The table indicates that F.B.I. Uniform Crime Reports derived murder rates per 100,000 population were relatively similar in those cities during the periods studied (Memphis = 2.97; New York = 2.75), and that New York City police annually effected approximately twice as many violent felony arrests per 1,000 officers (1172.95) as Memphis officers (587.12). Further, the table's rates of police shootings per 1,000 violent felony arrests effected indicate that Memphis officers were more than three times as likely to have used their guns in relation to this measure of police hazard than were New York officers (rates = 56.98 and 16.71, respectively).

The absence of association between variations in these measures and variations in Memphis and New York City police shooting rates suggests that varying internal police organizational influences may be operative. In table 15.3, the reasons for shooting given by the officers involved in the incidents in each city are presented. Before any attempt is made to interpret the table, however, several caveats are in order. The Memphis data include shootings to "apprehend violent suspects" within the "Defend Life" category, regardless of whether the officers or others were in imminent danger at the time shots were fired or whether the "violent suspect" was fleeing from a violent crime that had already been completed. Thus, the Memphis "Defend Life" cell includes both elective and nonelective shootings. Conversely, only nonelective shootings in which officers reported that they or others were subjects of attempted, threatened, or successfully completed deadly assaults at the instant of shooting are included in the New York City cell for the "Defend Life" category. Consequently, the Memphis "Apprehend Suspects" cell includes only shootings to apprehend property crime suspects, while the New York City "Apprehend Suspects" cell includes shootings to apprehend persons suspected of both property crimes and crimes of personal violence. Thus, the table understates the differences between Memphis and New York City in both the nonelective "Defend Life" and elective "Apprehend Suspects" categories. Finally, the aggregate Memphis figures upon which this table is based permit no

TABLE 15.3
Officer's Reason for Shooting in Memphis and New York City

Measure	Memphis 1969–74	New York City 1971–75
Defend Life[a]	28.0% (n = 63)	60.2% (1760)
rate[b]	9.4	11.8
Apprehend Suspects[c]	50.7% (114)	6.1% (179)
rate	16.9	1.2
Accidental	4.9% (11)	8.5% (249)
rate	1.6	1.7
Destroy Animal	5.8% (13)	9.2% (270)
rate	1.9	1.8
Warning Shots	4.4% (10)	11.1% (326)
rate	2.1	2.2
Miscellaneous[d]	4.4% (10)	4.9% (142)
rate	1.5	1.0
TOTAL	100.0% (225)	100.0% (2926)
rate	33.5[e]	19.6

chi-square = 414.18, df 5, p < .001

[a] Memphis "Defend Life" includes apprehensions of "violent suspects"; New York does not.
[b] Rate = mean annual rate per 1,000 officers.
[c] Memphis "Apprehend Suspects" includes only apprehensions of property crime suspects; New York includes apprehensions of property crime and personal violence crime suspects.
[d] Memphis = not ascertained; New York = suicides, criminal shootings, etc.
[e] Subcell rates may not equal totals due to rounding.

analysis of the severity of threats to life precipitating shooting in that city; no data regarding suspect's weapon, etc., are available.

Given those limitations, the table shows great differences in the reasons given for shooting by officers in Memphis and New York City (p .001). Three fifths (60.2%) of the New York City shootings reportedly occurred in defense of the lives of officers or others, while only slightly more than one fourth of the Memphis shootings involved either the defense of life or the apprehension of persons suspected of crimes of violence. Conversely, half (50.7%) of the Memphis shootings involved apprehensions of property crime suspects, while only one in seventeen (6.1%) of the New York shootings was precipitated by attempts to apprehend persons suspected of either property crimes or crimes of violence.

Even more striking than these percentage differences are the variations in annual shooting rates per 1,000 officers. Memphis officers were less likely than New York officers to shoot in defense of life (rates=9.4 and 11.8, respectively), especially given that the Memphis shootings in this category include an unknown number of "violent suspect apprehensions" which were presumably elective in that the lives of officers or others were not in imminent danger. On the other hand, Memphis officers were at least fourteen times as likely as New York City officers to have fired in order to apprehend property crime suspects (Memphis property crime apprehension rate=16.9; New York property and violent crime apprehension rate=1.2). Interestingly, rates in the remainder of the table's cells—which generally do not involve authorized intentional shootings at other persons—are remarkably consistent between Memphis and New York City.

Before concluding that the variation in shooting rates between Memphis and New York is attributable to the great frequency with which Memphis officers engage in elective shootings of fleeing property crime suspects, an alternative explanation of these differences should be considered. Because the data analyzed in this study are based upon officers' reports of shootings rather than upon direct observations of such incidents, it is possible that any differences found are attributable to differential police reporting practices rather than to differential police shooting practices. Several considerations, however, suggest that this is not the case.

First, the Memphis–New York difference in Apprehend Suspects shooting rates (16.9–1.2=15.7) is greater than the total shooting rate difference between Memphis and New York (33.5–19.2=14.3). A difference of such magnitude amid the relative constancy of the other categories in table 15.3 suggests that it could not be accounted for by differential reporting practices absent a massive conspiracy of report falsification and disposal of dead and wounded citizens by New York police officers and their superiors. If the New York rate for the Apprehend Suspects category were, in fact, identical to the Memphis rate, the number of such incidents in New York City during the period studied would have exceeded 2,500. Both logic and experience (the author was a member of the New York City Police Department for 16 years during which time he collected the New York data analyzed in this paper) suggest that, even in that large city, 2,500 police shootings cannot be concealed from the public, the media, and researchers.

Given the implausibility of this alternate explanation, the table provides strong evidence that the variation in shooting rates between Memphis and New York is largely attributable to the great frequency with which Memphis officers engaged in elective shootings of fleeing property crime suspects in the years studied in this chapter. As indicated earlier, such relatively unrestrained use of firearms in elective shootings at fleeing property crime suspects suggests that internal agency controls in policy shooting are loose or nonexistent. In other work, this author has reported that the 1972 imposition of restrictive shooting policy guidelines and accompanying internal review procedures were associated with a 75 percent decrease in New York City shootings at fleeing suspects.[26] Those guidelines describe the New York City officer's weapon as an instrument to be carried "for personal protection against persons feloniously attacking an officer or another at close range,"[27] and are enforced stringently. During the period after which the guidelines become operative, fewer than one fourth of the New York City officers who fired at unarmed persons escaped departmental censure or arrest.[28]

Thus, it is useful to examine the shooting guidelines operative in Memphis at the time the shootings analyzed in this study occurred. The 1975 Memphis Police department regulations, the most contemporaneous available, state in their entirety:

Use of force: Officers are confronted daily with situations where control must be exercised to effect arrests and to protect the public safety. Control may be achieved through advice, warnings, and persuasion, or by the use of physical force. While the use of reasonable physical force may be necessary in situations which cannot be otherwise controlled, force may not be resorted to unless other reasonable alternatives have been exhausted or would clearly be ineffective under the particular circumstances. Officers are permitted to use whatever force is reasonable and necessary to protect others or themselves from bodily harm.[29]

Self Defense and Defense of Others: The law of justifiable homicide authorizes an officer to use deadly force when it is necessary to protect himself or others from what reasonably appears as an immediate threat of great bodily harm or from imminent peril of death. The policy of the Department does not limit that law. Under certain specified conditions, deadly force may be exercised against a fleeing felon.[30]

Of these guidelines, the Tennessee Advisory Committee to the United States Commission on Civil Rights observes that:

Nowhere in the department's Policies and Regulations are those "certain specified conditions" written. It might assume conditions cited in the first paragraph, "Use of Force," apply. But that is not stated. The results of such broad State law and departmental policies appear to have been the frequent use of deadly force by Memphis police officers; use primarily employed against black Memphians.[31]

Thus, the committee suggests that black disproportion among Memphis police shooting victims is a consequence of the absence of clear shooting guidelines.[32] If that assertion is correct, it may also be true that Goldkamp's Belief Perspective I

—that police shoot blacks in situations less threatening than those in which they shoot whites[33]—was also valid in Memphis during 1969–74.

B. Black Disproportion in Memphis

As noted earlier, research that reports that blacks were shot or shot at by police in circumstances at least as life-threatening as those in which whites were shot was conducted in cities (Atlanta, Kansas City, and New York City) where stringent shooting guidelines had been in place for some time.[34] Thus, it is useful to examine black shooting victim disproportion in Memphis, a city in which police shooting guidelines were very loose during the years studied and in which the pattern and frequency of shooting varied so much from at least one such city, in order to see whether similar results will be obtained.

Table 15.4 presents a crosstabulation of the races and injuries of property crime suspects shot at by Memphis police during 1969–74 (race data on persons shot at in other incidents were not available). The table shows that 85.7% of those shot at were black, and that 14.3% were white, with similar racial distributions among all injury categories. Again, however, these aggregate percentages tell little about the relative presence of blacks in either the general population or the Memphis property-crime population. Thus, several rates were constructed to put these percentages in better perspective.

First, the rate per 1,000 officers shows that, between 1969 and 1974, Memphis police were six times as likely to have shot at and missed black property crime suspects as they were for whites (noninjured rates = 10.4 and 1.6 per 1,000 officers annually), that they were 13 times more likely to have wounded blacks than whites under such circumstances (rounded black rate = 1.9; rounded white rate = 0.1), and that they were

TABLE 15.4

Race and Injury of Property Crime Suspects Shot at by Memphis Police, 1969–1974

Suspect's race	Suspect injury			
	None	Wounded	Killed	Totals
White	13.6% (11)	7.1% (1)	23.5% (4)	14.3% (16)
rate per 1,000 officers[a]	1.6	0.1	0.6	2.4
rate per 100,000 population[b]	2.9	0.3	1.0	4.2
rate per 1,000 arrests[c]	1.2	0.1	0.5	1.8
Black	86.4% (70)	92.9% (13)	76.5% (13)	85.7% (96)
rate per 1,000 officers	10.4	1.9	1.9	14.3
rate per 100,000 population	28.9	5.4	5.4	39.6
rate per 1,000 arrests	3.2	0.6	0.6	4.3
TOTALS[d]	72.3% (81)	12.5% (14)	15.2% (17)	100.0 (112)
rate per 1,000 officers	12.0	2.1	2.5	16.9
rate per 100,000 population	13.0	2.2	2.7	18.0
rate per 1,000 arrests	2.6	0.5	0.5	3.6

n/a = 2
[a] Mean annual rate per 1,000 officers.
[b] Rate per 100,000 population.
[c] Rate per 1,000 arrests for burglary, larceny, auto larceny.
[d] Subcell rates may not equal totals due to rounding.

TABLE 15.5
Actions of Persons Shot Fatally by Memphis Police, 1969–1976

Victims' actions	Victims' races		
	White	Black	Totals
Assaultive—armed with gun	62.5% (5)	26.9% (7)	35.3% (12)
rate[a]	1.3	2.9	1.9
Assaultive—not armed with gun	25.0% (2)	23.1% (6)	23.5% (8)
rate	0.5	2.5	1.3
Non-assaultive—unarmed	12.5% (1)	50.0% (13)	41.2% (14)
rate	0.3	5.4	2.2
TOTALS	23.5% (8)	76.5% (26)	100.0% (34)
rate	2.1	10.7	5.4

n/a = 5
[a] Rate per 100,000 population.

three times more likely to have killed blacks than whites at scenes of property crimes (rates = 1.9 and 0.6).

The second set of rates shows that black Memphians were nearly ten times as likely as whites to have been shot at in such circumstances (rates per 100,000 population = 39.6 and 4.2). Further, standardizing the table's raw figures on each racial group's population in this way shows that blacks were 18 times more likely to have been wounded (black wounded rate = 5.4; white = 0.3), and more than five times as likely to have been killed in these situations than were their fellow white citizens (black killed rate = 5.4; white = 1.0).

Neither of these rates, of course, gives a precise measure of the degree to which blacks disproportionately may expose themselves to the risk of being shot while fleeing from officers at scenes of property crimes. Thus, the third set of rates presents the number of persons shot at for each category per 1,000 property criminals of that same category arrested by Memphis police. Here again, one finds great disproportion. During the years studied, 4.3 black property crime suspects were shot at for each 1,000 black property crime arrestees; the comparable white rate is 1.8. The table also indicates that the black wounded rate (0.6) is six times higher than the white rate (0.1), and that the black non-injured rate (3.2) is nearly three times higher than the white rate (1.2).

This last rate may hide other sources of this variation (e.g., the legal categories used to define "property crimes" include many divergent activities; blacks may run from property crimes, while whites surrender). Even given this possibility, however, the table suggests that Memphis blacks were in far greater risk of being shot or shot at in these circumstances than can be explained by either their presence in the general population or the arrestee population.

Similar inferences may be drawn from table 15.5, which crosstabulates the actions and races of persons fatally shot by Memphis police during 1969–76 (less the period January 15 to December 31, 1972). The table shows that more than three fourths (26) of the 34 persons whose race is known were black. Half of these blacks (13) were reportedly unarmed and nonassaultive at the time of their death. Only one of the eight whites shot and killed died in such an elective event. This disparity yields a black death rate from police shootings while unarmed and nonassaultive (5.4 per 100,000) that is 18 times higher than the comparable white rate (0.3). Looking into shootings involving situations which are more life threatening, we find assaultive blacks not armed with guns dying at a rate (2.5) five times higher than whites (0.5). Finally, black representation among those reportedly armed with guns and presumably leaving officers few alternatives to shooting (2.9 per 100,000) is slightly more than twice as high as the comparable white rate (1.3).

Taken together, table 15.5's percentages and rates clearly indicate black disproportion among shooting victims but they also indicate that this disproportion is greatest where elective shootings of nonassaultive, unarmed people are concerned. Unless Memphis officers differentially reported the circumstances of shootings of black and white citizens during the period studied, the data suggest also that the difference between the shooting rates of Memphis and New York was not an artifact of reporting practices, but was, in fact, a reflection of the great frequency with which Memphis police shot unarmed blacks. In addition, the table suggests that the Tennessee Advisory Committee was correct in its assessment of the negative impact upon Memphis blacks of the absence of clear shooting guidelines. Finally, they suggest that Goldkamp's Belief Perspective I was valid in Memphis during 1969–76. The data strongly support the assertion that police there did differentiate racially with their trigger fingers, by shooting blacks in circumstances less threatening than those in which they shot whites.

V. Conclusions

This analysis has demonstrated that one cannot generalize readily about police shooting rate disparities. Hopefully, it also provides some direction for future examinations of shooting rate variation among jurisdictions and among races. Intensive analyses of those phenomena are required so that policing in this democratic society can occur with minimal bloodshed. Police shootings are a consequence of violence in the community and the number of times members of various population subgroups expose themselves to the danger of being shot at by police; but levels of police shootings are also greatly affected by organizational variables. Thus, analysis of the circumstances under which shootings occur can point the way to police administrative action to reduce elective shootings. It may also suggest broader social action to change the conditions which spawn the nonelective shootings over which police chiefs and police officers have very limited direct control.

Administrative action to reduce elective shootings in Memphis has occurred since the end of the period studied in this report. In 1979, for example, that department instituted a more stringent shooting policy and incident review procedure than had existed.[35] It has also recently initiated an "officer survival" training program designed to help police more safely respond to the potentially violent situations which often precipitate nonelective shootings. In short, apparently the Memphis Police Department has acted responsibly to address major problems in the use of deadly force by its officers.[36]

Hopefully, future research conducted on the use of deadly force in Memphis subsequent to the implementation of these measures will find both reductions in the frequency of shootings and changes in the patterns of shootings. Hopefully also, the future research will encourage other jurisdictions in which Goldkamp's Belief Perspective I is valid to follow the example of Memphis by taking measures to reduce officer shooting discretion and, consequently, to reduce the rate of elective police shootings.

NOTES

1. "Deadly Force" generally is defined as force likely to kill or capable of killing. Since police deadly force most often occurs when police point and fire their guns at other human beings, and since such actions do not always result in death, "police deadly force" will be defined in this chapter to include all police shootings at others.

2. See C. MILTON, POLICE USE OF DEADLY FORCE (1977); Kania & Mackey, Police Violence as a Function of Community Characteristics, 15 CRIMINOLOGY 27 (1977); Kiernan, Shooting by Policemen in District Declines, Wash. Star, Sept. 2, 1979, ? B, at 1, col. 2; Sherman & Langworthy, Measuring Homicide by Police Officers, 70 J. CRIM. L. & C. 546 (1979).

3. See C. MILTON, supra note 2, at 22; Fyfe, Race and Extreme Police-Citizen Violence, in RACE, CRIME, AND CRIMINAL JUSTICE 89 (C.E. Pope & R. McNeely eds. 1981); Harding & Fahey, Killings by Chicago Police, 1969–70: An Empirical Study, 46 S. CAL. L. REV. 284 (1973); Kobler, Police Homicide in a Democracy, 31 J. SOC. ISSUES 163 (1975); Meyer, Police Shootings at Minorities: The Case of Los Angeles, in 452 ANNALS 98 (1980); Takagi, A Garrison State in "Democratic" Society, in POLICE-COMMUNITY RELATIONS 357–71 (A. Cohn & E. Viano eds. 1976).

4. C. MILTON, supra note 2, at 144.

5. Kania & Mackey, supra note 2.

6. Kania and Mackey necessarily included in their analysis only data on fatal police shootings, thus excluding many nonfatal exercises of police deadly force. Further, their data on fatal shootings were obtained from the United States Vital Statistics' annual reports on Causes of Mortality, a source subsequently found highly unreliable by Sherman & Langworthy, supra note 2, at 559.

7. Fyfe, Geographic Correlates of Police Shooting. A Microanalysis, 17 J. RESEARCH CRIME & DELINQUENCY 101 (1980).

8. Kiernan, supra note 2.

9. Uelman, Varieties of Police Policy. A Study of Police Policy Regarding the Use of Deadly Force in Los Angeles County, 6 LOY. L.A. L. REV. 1 (1973). See also Fyfe, Administrative Interventions on Police Shooting Discretion. An Empirical Examination, 7 J. CRIM. JUST. 309 (1979); Sherman & Langworthy, supra note 2.

10. Goldkamp, Minorities as Victims of Police Shootings. Interpretations of Racial Disproportionality and Police Use of Deadly Force, 2 JUST. SYS. J. 169 (1976).

11. Id at 170 (quoting Takagi, supra note 3).

12. Id at 173.

13. Fyfe, supra note 3, at 93–94.

14. M. Blumberg, Race and Police Shootings: An Analysis in Two Cities, (1980) (paper presented to the Annual Meeting of the American Society of Criminology). See also W. GELLER & K. KARALES, SPLIT SECOND DECISION: SHOOTINGS OF AND BY CHICAGO POLICE (1981).

15. See Uelman, supra note 9.

16. M. Blumberg, supra note 14, at i.

17. Fyfe, Toward a Typology of Police Shootings in CONTEMPORARY ISSUES IN LAW EN-FORCEMENT 136–151 (Fyfe, ed. 1981).

18. The elective/nonelective dichotomy proposed here is an attempt to simplify very complex phenomena. It should not be interpreted as a suggestion that nonelective shootings do not vary in degree of immediacy of hazard to the officers involved, or as a suggestion that nonelective shooting rates are not affected at all by internal police organizational variables. Two officers attacked by a lone man with a knife, for example, probably face less danger and have more alternatives to shooting than a lone officer who is fired upon without warning by several bankrobbers armed with shotguns. Indeed, if the officers in the knife situation are trained and equipped to employ nonlethal means of subduing their assailant without endangering themselves (e.g., evasive or self-defense tactics; electronic "stun-guns"; chemical sprays; nets, etc.), any resulting shooting should be classified as elective. Conversely, if the officers are poorly trained and equipped, they may find themselves without alternatives to shooting, so that such an event would most accurately be classified as nonelective shooting. It is doubtful, however, that any existing training program or technology would provide the officer in the bank robbery situation with alternatives to shooting. Thus, a more detailed alternative to the elective/nonelective dichotomy would be a continuum which classified shootings along a scale ranging from elective to nonelective on the basis of gravity and hazard to officers and others, and availability of alternatives to shootings. Such a continuum (modified to fit data limitations) is employed in the remainder of this article.

19. Fyfe, supra note 17.

20. Fyfe, Shots Fired: An Examination of New York City Police Firearms Discharges 921 (1978) (unpublished Ph.D. dissertation, State University of New York at Albany).

21. M. Blumberg, supra note 14, at i.

22. Garner v. Memphis, No. 77–1089 (6th Cir. 1979). The author is grateful to Steve Winter of the NAACP Legal Defense Fund for making the data available.

23. TENNESSEE ADVISORY COMMITTEE TO THE U.S. COMM. ON CIVIL RIGHTS, CIVIL CRISIS-CIVIC CHALLENGE: POLICE COMMUNITY RELATIONS IN MEMPHIS (1978) [hereinafter cited as TENNESSEE ADVISORY COMMITTEE].

24. Fyfe, supra note 7.

25. Id at 107.

26. Fyfe, supra note 9, at 318.

27. New York City Police Department, Temporary Operating Procedure 237 (1972).

28. J. Fyfe, Police Shootings in Philadelphia, 1975–1978: A System Model Analysis 43 (1980) (unpublished consultant paper presented to U.S. Department of Justice, Civil Rights Division).

29. Memphis Police Department, Policies and Regulations 5 (1975).

30. Id at 9 (emphasis added)

31. TENNESSEE ADVISORY COMMITTEE, supra note 23, at 80.

32. Memphis police officers are also limited in their use of deadly force by Tennessee state law. In addition to allowing officers to shoot in order to defend their lives or the lives of other innocent persons, the Tennessee statute defining officers' power to use deadly force in felony arrest situations states, "[i]f, after notice of the intention to arrest the defendant, he either flee or forcibly resist, the officer may use all the necessary means to effect the arrest. TENN. CODE ANN. ch. 40, 808.

33. See Goldkamp, supra note 10.

34. Fyfe, supra note 3, at 102; M. Blumberg, supra note 14, at 10.

35. Memphis Police Department, Training Academy, General Order #5-79, Deadly Force Policy 1–2 (1979), states that officers may use deadly force in arrest situations only as a last resort in order "(t)o apprehend a suspect fleeing from the commission of a dangerous felony when an officer has witnessed the offense or has sufficient information to know as a virtual certainty that the suspect committed the offense." General Order #5-79 defines as "dangerous felonies" kidnapping, murder in the 1st or 2nd degree, manslaughter, arson, criminal sexual assault, 1st, 2nd, or 3rd degree (rape and attempted rape), aggravated assault, robbery, burglary 1st, 2nd or 3rd degree, or any attempt to commit these crimes. The order also establishes an internal shooting review procedure.

36. See Memphis Police Made Own Films on Deadly Force, 6 TRAINING AIDS DIGEST 1 (Feb. 1981).

||||||||||||||||||||||||||||||||||||||||||||||||||||||||||||||||||||||||||||||

Chapter 16

Race, Bias, and Police Use of the TASER
Exploring the Available Evidence

Michael D. White and Jessica Saunders

Although local police forces generally regard themselves as public servants with the responsibility of maintaining law and order, they tend to minimize this attitude when they are patrolling areas that are heavily populated with Negro citizens. There, they tend to view each person on the streets as a potential criminal or enemy, and all too often that attitude is reciprocated. Indeed, hostility between the Negro communities in our large cities and the police departments, is the major problem of law enforcement in this decade. It has been a major cause of all recent race riots.[1]

. . . the *war model* [emphasis in original] of policing encourages police violence of the type that victimized Rodney King. When any soldiers go to war, they must have enemies. When cops go to war against crime, their enemies are found in inner cities and among our minority populations.[2]

Last year, 45 percent of the people struck with Tasers were black, while 42 percent were white. Some call those statistics alarming, since the 2000 U.S. Census found that blacks make up 8 percent of the city's population while whites make up 68 percent.[3]

Introduction

The first two quotes above, the first from the late 1960s and the second from the mid-1990s, underscore the long history of tension and violence between police departments and minority communities in the United States. This history is perhaps best illustrated by the over-representation of blacks as victims of police use of force. For example, results from the Police-Public Contact Survey indicated that, in 2002, blacks represented 9.7 percent of persons who had contact with police, but they accounted for 26.3 percent of cases where police used force.[4] Minority over-representation in use of force by police has been a long-standing and serious source of tension between many police departments and their constituents. As a result, over the last several decades police researchers have devoted considerable attention to the issue, producing a sizeable body of work. This research, reviewed below, suggests that police decisions to use force are complex and are likely influenced by a range of key variables associated with the suspect, the officer, the incident itself, the police organization, and the social environment in which the encounter occurs.

The third quote that opens this chapter deals with one of the most controversial issues surrounding police use of force today—the TASER. Over the last decade, conducted energy devices (CEDs) have been widely adopted by law enforcement agencies across the United States. TASER International, the manufacturer of the TASER, estimates that more than ten thousand law enforcement agencies in the United States have purchased its weapons as a less-lethal force alternative.[5] Serious questions have been raised concerning the weapon's use and effectiveness, however, as well as its potential to cause serious injury or death; and the ongoing debate has been widely publicized, drawing both national media attention and public scrutiny.

This chapter explores the nexus of these two prevailing themes in police decisions to use of force: minority over-representation and use of the TASER. Unfortunately, despite its increasing popularity and the controversies surrounding the device, there is very little empirical research examining police use of the TASER. As a result, basic questions about race and the device remain unanswered. For example, how often is the device used against white and minority suspects? Is there is evidence of disproportionality? Are there differences in the circumstances in which the TASER is used against white and minority suspects? Or in other words, is there evidence of racial bias in police use of the TASER?

This chapter explores these questions through an examination of a range of available data sources: (1) official police department data examined in independent studies (most notably the New York Police Department, 2002–2007); (2) Internal police reports that are publicly available; (3) Conducted energy device (CED) industry data (TASER International), (4) civil and human rights group reports and data (Amnesty International and the American Civil Liberties Union); (5) media data (searches on LexisNexis and the *New York Times'* TimesSelect for all newspaper articles on the TASER from 2002 to 2006); and (6) civil litigation against officers and departments for improper use of CEDs. Our primary objective is to provide an exploratory assessment of the availability of data regarding suspect race and the TASER, as well as to explore whether the available data suggests racial bias in use of the device by police. The chapter concludes with a discussion of the implications of the findings for the literature on race and policing, as well as the ongoing debate regarding police use of the TASER.

Prior Research

The Context: Police and the Use of Force

Police have legal authority to use force in a wide range of situations, including physical force, less-lethal weapons (e.g., CEDs), and, as a last resort, the firearm.[6]

Despite its central role in policing,[7] research indicates that police use of force is statistically rare, occurring in only about 1 percent of all police-citizen encounters.[8] In addition, there are constitutionally derived mandates that govern police use of force, requiring that officers use only the minimum force necessary to accomplish their objective (any force beyond the minimum required is considered excessive—the reasonableness standard established in *Graham v. Connor* [1989], 490 U.S. 386). Police departments closely monitor use of force and provide policy guidance and training to officers through a "force continuum," which describes verbal and physical actions an officer can take in response to different levels of suspect resistance.

Regardless of whether it is excessive, the application of physical force can have serious, long-term consequences for the suspect and the officer, as well as for the police agency and the community.[9] Recent examples include the Los Angeles riots following the acquittal of the four officers who beat Rodney King, and the strained community relations in New York City following the shootings of Amadou Diallo in 1999 and Sean Bell in 2006.

Race and Use of Force

Over a period of several decades, research has consistently shown that police use force disproportionately against minorities. For example, Reiss found that police officers used more coercive approaches with black suspects.[10] Early studies of police use of deadly force indicated that the shooting rate for black suspects was six to seven times higher than the shooting rate for white suspects.[11] Recent data from the Bureau of Justice Statistics indicates that this over-representation extends to lesser degrees of force and is still persistent today.[12]

Explanations for disproportionate use of force against minorities have focused on four levels of analysis: sociological, psychological, organizational, and ecological.[13] The first two levels were the primary focus of much of the early work on police use of force. Research examining the sociological level has tended to focus on the social status of the citizen, suggesting that those with lower status (poor, minorities, mentally ill, etc.) are perceived as being more deserving of punishment (i.e., force) because they routinely violate society's norms.[14] Research at the psychological level, however, has focused on personal characteristics of police officers, suggesting that "officers with certain traits, experiences, or attitudes will respond differently in similar situations."[15] That is, an officer's background, attitudes (including prejudices), and experiences influence the decision to use force (or not).[16]

Recognition that sociological and psychological explanations fail to account for larger, contextual influences on police decision making has led to an emphasis on the organizational and, most recently, ecological levels. At the organizational level, research has suggested that departmental characteristics—both formal and informal—can shape police field practices. Wilson argued that formal organizational structure and political atmosphere help determine patterns of police behavior, such as use of force.[17] Klinger later argued that workgroup dynamics and the rules that govern those workgroups play an important role in guiding street behavior.[18] Last, building on early work by Werthman and Piliavin, and Smith, much of the recent research on causes of police use of force has taken an ecological perspective, highlighting the influence of neighborhood context, crime, and racial composition on police decision making.[19] For example, a number of recent studies have found evidence supporting conflict theory, whereby levels of force and misconduct are greatest in communities with the highest levels of disadvantage and minority representation.[20] Terrill and Reisig concluded that "officers are significantly more likely to use higher levels of force when encountering criminal suspects in high-crime areas and neighborhoods with high levels of concentrated disadvantage independent of suspect behavior and other statistical controls."[21]

Development of the TASER

Because of the potential consequences of use of force by their officers, police agencies have sought to expand their alternatives for resolving encounters with resistant suspects. As a result, CEDs such as the TASER have become an increasingly visible feature in American policing. The TASER fires two small probes at a rate of 180 feet per second and, upon striking the subject, delivers a fifty-thousand-volt shock over a five-second cycle.[22] According to Vilke and Chan, "CEDs directly stimulate motor nerve and muscle tissue, overriding the central nervous system control and causing incapacitation regardless of the subject's mental focus, training, size, or drug intoxication state. . . . This effect terminates as soon as the electrical discharge is halted. Immediately after the TASER shock, subjects are usually able to perform at their physical baseline."[23] The TASER's rapid growth in policing and researchers' failure to keep pace has led to serious questions in three areas: use, effectiveness, and physiological impact.

WHEN IS IT APPROPRIATE TO USE THE TASER?

Police departments have varied considerably in terms of where they place the TASER on the force continuum, and more specifically, whether they allow the device to be used against suspects who fail to follow verbal commands or who are passively resisting police efforts.[24] The International Association of Chiefs of Police (IACP) and the Police Executive Research Forum (PERF) have both issued model policies to offer guidance to agencies, and both suggest that CEDs only be used against those who are actively resisting.[25]

DOES THE TASER WORK EFFECTIVELY?

Research examining the effectiveness of the TASER has focused on two general questions: (1) does the device terminate suspect resistance? and (2) does the device decrease the prevalence of suspect and officer injuries? Several police agencies have reported reductions in injuries sustained during police-citizen contacts following adoption of the TASER.[26] With regard to suspect resistance, CED industry and police data place the effectiveness rate of the TASER at 80–94 percent.[27] In their study of the New York City Police Department (NYPD), White and Ready reported an effectiveness rate of 89 percent, but they found that the TASER's impact on suspect resistance was mitigated by suspect weight, intoxication, and distance between suspect and officer.[28]

DOES THE TASER INCREASE THE RISK OF SUSPECT DEATH?

Amnesty International began raising concerns regarding the potential physiological risks of the TASER in 2001. These concerns have led to a wealth of recent research, including reviews of coroner reports in death cases, literature reviews of available research, and bio-medical laboratory research on animals and healthy human volunteers.[29] The research examining the physiological impact of the TASER has failed to identify a causal link between the device and death.[30] In October 2007 the Wake Forest University Medical Center released results from its field study (the first of its kind), which involved physician review of one thousand real-world TASER incidents, and found that 99.7 percent of suspects had minor or no injuries.[31] The National Institute of Justice published a special report in June 2008 examining deaths following "electro muscular disruption" and stated that "there is no conclusive medical evidence within the state of current research that indicates a high risk of serious injury or death from the direct effects of CED exposure."[32]

Summary

There is a large body of literature documenting racial disproportionality in police use of force, and the explanations for this disproportionality are complex, with influential factors at multiple levels. Alternatively, the emergence of the TASER on the American policing landscape over the last decade has been the subject of little study by researchers. As a result, there are still a number of unanswered questions regarding the TASER—including whether there is evidence of minority over-representation or racial bias in use of the device. Though the body of research on police use of force would seem to suggest that the TASER may be used primarily against minority suspects, there has been virtually no inquiry into this question. This chapter seeks to fill this void by exploring available data sources to investigate questions about race and police use of the TASER.

Data and Methods

Ideally, this chapter would draw on a national archive of incident-level data detailing police-citizen encounters involving the TASER. Unfortunately there is no such archive. To address our research questions, we identified six available sources of data on police use of the TASER, and each is described below.

Objective, Empirical Studies

There are several empirical studies of police use of the TASER that have been completed by independent researchers. Two are described in this chapter. First, White and Ready have published several articles examining TASER data from the NYPD.[33] Their data include all reported cases of TASER use by NYPD personnel during a five-year period, from January 1, 2002, through May 15, 2007 (n = 820). The results of these studies are described briefly, with emphasis on findings related to suspect race. Also, additional analyses with the NYPD data are carried out to explore whether there are racial differences in TASER-use patterns.

Second, Smith and colleagues published an article in 2007 examining use-of-force data from the Miami-Dade Police Department (MDPD) and Richland County Sheriff's Department (RCSD).[34] The data include 467 use-of-force incidents involving RCSD officers from January 2005 to July 2006; and 1,178 use-of-force incidents involving MDPD officers from January 2002 to May 2006. The authors sought to identify the nature of the relationship between TASER use and injuries among officers and suspects when controlling for other relevant variables, including suspect race. The findings from their study are summarized below.[35]

Internal Police Reports

Several police departments have published reports that provide descriptive information on TASER-related incidents. In some cases, these reports have also been made available on the website of TASER International. Fourteen of these internal police department reports were examined here, with special emphasis on suspect race.

Industry Reports and Data

TASER International has made available on their website a variety of reports/data from police departments and other sources addressing issues surrounding use and effectiveness. The company has also created a *TASER Research Compendium*—available on hard copy and CD—which includes hundreds of articles and reports (encompassing several thousand pages) focusing on a range of issues. Finally, TASER International has compiled a database of TASER incidents, based on reports submitted by police departments from around the country. These data were the basis for a study carried out by Jenkinson and colleagues. All of these data were explored for race-related information.

Human and Civil Rights Groups

Both Amnesty International (AI) and the American Civil Liberties Union (ACLU) have been active in the debate over police use of the TASER, and both have produced reports and data on the issue. We explored the websites of the groups and content analyzed available reports, press releases, and data. Significant attention was placed on two AI documents. The first is a 2004 report where AI outlines its concerns regarding the TASER and provides summary information on more than seventy cases where the suspect/citizen died after being struck with the TASER. The report concludes with a call for a moratorium on use of the device by police until more research is conducted. The second document is written testimony given in September 2007 by

AI to the chief medical panel in charge of the U.S. Department of Justice inquiry into in-custody deaths following use of conducted energy devices.

Media Reports

We also explored media data by conducting keyword searches on LexisNexis and TimesSelect to identify all print media articles involving police use of the TASER from January 2002 through December 2006 (n = 691). Information for up to 68 variables relating to officer and suspect information, and the circumstances in which police used the TASER, were recorded.[36] We then explored the prevalence of race as reported in these media data.

Civil Litigation

The final source of data involves civil litigation against the police resulting for inappropriate TASER use. Smith, Petrocelli, and Scheer conducted a comprehensive search of ALLSTATES and ALLFEDS databases through Westlaw and identified 630 federal and state cases in which "TASER" appeared in print.[37] The authors limited their focus to cases where: a TASER was used by a law enforcement officer; the device was used during the course of an arrest or to control a citizen; the victim filed a constitutional claim of excessive use of force against the officer or other entities; and the claim was adjudicated in court. With these criteria, the authors content analyzed fifty-three cases, and we summarize their findings here, again with specific focus on race.

Limitations

Before exploring these sources, there are several important data-related caveats that warrant discussion. First, given the exploratory nature of the study, we have set aside concerns regarding the objectivity of the data sources. In effect, we have simply sought to assess the extent to which data regarding race and police use of the TASER are available, and to characterize that data. Second, given the chapter's emphasis on covering multiple data sources, our treatment of the various sources is necessarily superficial, with specific emphasis on the research questions at hand. We urge the reader to seek out the original reports and papers for more complete coverage of the research and data described in brief here.

Third, although our search for data and reports was extensive, it would be ill-advised to claim that we have uncovered every existing report (or data set). Instead, we simply state that we focused our efforts on the most likely outlets for such reports/data, and in doing so, feel reasonably confident that we have captured the majority of publicly available information on the issue. Last, given the controversial nature of this topic, there are likely a number of ongoing and planned studies across the country that will add to the literature on police use of the TASER. Consequently, by the time this chapter is in print it will be, at least to some extent, out-of-date. The reader should bear in mind that this study explores available data from six disparate sources as of June 2008.

Results

Official Police Data: White and Ready's NYPD Studies

White and Ready have published two studies examining the NYPD's use of the TASER.[38] The first study is a primarily descriptive analysis of 243 incidents from 2002 to 2004, highlighting officer-, suspect-, and incident-related characteristics. The study's primary findings include: nearly all suspects were emotionally disturbed and violent; just under one-half were armed; few were intoxicated; backup and supervisors were almost always present; and the TASER immediately stopped suspect resistance in 86 percent of cases.[39] White and Ready's second study added another year of data (2002–2005; n=375), and the authors used a variety of multivariate techniques to identify predictors of weapon effectiveness. The authors found that a number of factors reduced weapon effectiveness, including close proximity between the participants (three feet or less), suspect weight (more than two hundred pounds), suspect's drug and alcohol use, and problems with weapon operation (e.g., misfire, one or both prongs miss, etc.).[40]

In their work, White and Ready reported that just over half of suspects were black, and 27 percent were Hispanic (19 percent were white). In the second study, suspect race was not related to any of the effectiveness measures examined.[41] To address the disproportionality question, we compared White and Ready's racial breakdown of TASER incidents to NYPD data from the RAND study, which examined more than five hundred thousand stop, question, and frisk (SQF) incidents from 2006.[42] RAND found that 53 percent of suspects in those SQF incidents were black and 27 percent were Hispanic. RAND's analysis of NYPD arrestee data from 2006 also showed that blacks and Hispanics made up about one-half and one-quarter of all arrestees, respectively.

The New York City TASER deployment data mirror the SQF and arrestee data in terms of suspect race. However, all of these data indicate over-representation for blacks, who, according to 2000 U.S. Census data, make up only about 25 percent of the New York City population (Hispanics also make up 25 percent of the city population, in line with their proportion of the TASER, SQF, and arrestee data). To explore this disproportionality further, RAND used an additional benchmark that is independent of the police: the racial breakdown of criminal suspects identified by victims and witnesses. In those data, 75 percent of individuals identified as criminal suspects were black, while just 15 percent were Hispanic.[43] These independent data do not support the argument that racial bias among police explains the over-representation of blacks in TASER, arrest, and SQF data.

ADDITIONAL ANALYSIS OF THE NYPD TASER DATA

We expanded White and Ready's data to include all incidents from January 1, 2002, through May 15, 2007 (n=820). The racial breakdown of suspects remains consistent with their earlier studies: 53 percent black, 26 percent Hispanic, and 16 percent white. The TASER data were then disaggregated by race and ethnicity, and table 16.1 shows that there were some notable differences among black, Hispanic, and white suspects.

While the majority of suspects were classified as emotionally disturbed, white suspects were significantly more likely than minority suspects to be assigned that classification (93.5 percent of white suspects, compared to 81.3 percent for blacks and 84.9 percent for Hispanics). Alternatively, while few incidents involved intoxicated individuals, Hispanic suspects were nearly twice as likely as white or black suspects to be labeled as such (21.3 percent for Hispanics, compared to 13.1 percent for whites and 10.5 percent for blacks). Table 16.1 also shows a combined intoxication/mental illness measure, and a significantly larger percentage of black suspects—nearly one-quarter—were neither "high" nor emotionally disturbed, compared to white (7.8 percent) and Hispanic suspects (17.8 percent). At the same time, however, black suspects were more likely than white or Hispanic suspects to direct physical violence at the officer—64.5 percent for blacks compared to 47.5 percent for whites and 60.1 percent for Hispanics.

In short, there are notable racial differences in the characteristics of suspects that bring them to the attention of the police and lead to TASER use. There are a number of potential explanations for these differences, including differential prevalence rates among white and minorities in terms of mental illness and substance abuse, different reporting patterns by race (e.g., how police find out about the call), and differential TASER deployment patterns by police (i.e., racial bias; police "tase" black suspects in situations where they do not "tase" white suspects). One method for investigating the racial bias explanation is to explore measures of TASER use and effectiveness across race categories and determine whether variation also exists in how the device is deployed (i.e., is the device used in different circumstances based on race).

TABLE 16.1
Suspect Characteristics by Race/Ethnicity

Characteristic	White	Black	Hispanic
Gender			
Male	89.1%	86.6%	92.5%
Female	10.9%	13.4%	7.5%
Age**	36.66	33.07	33.43
Weight*	200.08	198.10	188.23
Emotionally Disturbed**	93.5%	81.3%	84.9%
Intoxication**			
None	86.9%	89.5%	78.7%
Drugs	4.1%	4.3%	9.6%
Alcohol	5.7%	4.5%	10.2%
Both	3.3%	1.8%	1.5%
Emotional Disturbance or Intoxicated***	92.2%	76.7%	82.2%
Weapon			
None	66.9%	73.4%	71.8%
Knife	24.8%	20.2%	20.3%
Gun	0%	.8%	1.6%
Other	8.3%	5.6%	6.3%
Violence*			
None	7.4%	2.8%	2.0%
Self-Directed	18.9%	10.7%	15.2%
Officer-Directed	47.5%	64.5%	60.1%
Other-Directed	1.6%	3.3%	3.5%
Multiple Directed	24.6%	18.8%	19.2%

* p < .05; ** p < .01; *** p < .001.

TABLE 16.2
TASER Efficiency and Effectiveness by Race/Ethnicity

Characteristic	White	Black	Hispanic
Distance from Suspect (feet)	4.7	4.8	4.4
Contact Penetrated Skin	69.7%	66.3%	67.2%
Missed Suspect			
No	89.2%	86.7%	92.2%
One Contact	7.5%	6.2%	4.8%
Both Contacts	0%	3.1%	1.2%
Fall Off Clothing	3.2%	4.0%	1.8%
Number of Dart Contacts	1.63	1.55	1.56
Need for Additional Shots	15.8%	18.6%	12.0%
Time to Incapacitate (seconds)	9.5	8.1	7.0
Continued Resistance	30.8%	27.1%	31.1%
Supervisor Present	92.2%	89.5%	86.4%
Backup Present	94.6%	92.0%	89.9%
Multiple Officers Deploying TASER	7.0%	6.5%	8.9%
Other Less-than-Lethal Weapons Used			
Mace	5.0%	3.5%	2.5%
Other Stun Device	11.6%	10.9%	14.6%
Other Weapon	1.7%	4.3%	4.5%
Devise Performed Satisfactorily	74.6%	80.1%	81.2%
Conformed with Policy	94.3%	92.7%	93.4%

Table 16.2 shows a number of different measures of TASER use and effectiveness, including distance between officer and suspect, dart contact and penetration, multiple deployments, time to incapacitation, use of other non-lethal devices, presence of supervisors and backup, continued resistance, officer satisfaction, and whether the incident conformed with department policy. Importantly, all these measures are virtually identical across suspect race categories. This consistency strongly suggests that the racial differences in behavior that initiated the incidents (mental illness, intoxication, violence—as reported in table 16.1) are, in fact, individual-level variation among suspects, rather than a consequence of racial bias in TASER use by NYPD officers.

Official Police Data: Smith and Colleagues

With the exception of the White and Ready papers, Smith and colleagues' study of the Richland County Sheriff's Department and the Miami-Dade Police Department represents the only other published independent study of TASER use by police (as of June 2008).[44] The purpose of their study was to "examine the effect of police use of conducted energy devices (CEDs) on officer and suspect injuries while controlling for other types of force and resistance."[45] Although the authors attempted to conduct similar analyses across sites, differences in department policy, practice, and data collection made this difficult. Notably, the key variable for this chapter—suspect race—was available for inclusion in the MDPD analyses but not in the RCSD analyses.

The findings from the MDPD analyses indicate that use of a CEDs significantly reduced the odds of both officer and suspect injury. Suspect race was included as a predictor in the MDPD analyses and it emerged as significant in the suspect injury model: "The odds of injury were significantly lower for nonwhite suspects than for white suspects."[46] The authors note that this significant finding occurred with minor injuries only—race was not significantly related to more serious injuries. Unfortunately, the authors do not explore this race finding in greater detail as it is not a primary focus of their study and it is not a part of the RCSD findings.

Internal Police Reports and Data

We reviewed a selection of reports, press releases, and letters produced by law enforcement agencies regarding the TASER, identified through searches on the internet and through the TASER International website. The reviewed documents were in no way intended to represent the population of existing reports, or even a random sample of such reports. Rather, the authors simply sought to review a small number of documents to get a sense of this data source, and to assess the degree to which suspect race and issues of racial bias are discussed. The reviewed documents (all in electronic format) include:

- City of Boise/Boise (ID) Police Department: 2006 report from the community ombudsman;[47]
- Cincinnati (OH) Police Department: 2005 memo on how the department uses the TASER;[48]
- Columbus (OH) Police Department: undated memo from the defensive tactics unit to the chief of police describing a six-month TASER study;[49]
- Granite City (IL) Police Department: 2004 memo from the office of the chief to TASER International describing the impact of TASERs on risk reduction;[50]
- Green Bay (WI) Police Department: 2006 report describing TASER deployments in 2004 and 2005;[51]
- Madison (WI) Police Department: memo to the chief describing TASER incidents through the end of 2005;[52]
- Michigan Municipal Risk Management Authority: 2005 report describing policy recommendations for adoption of less-lethal weapons;[53]
- Mobile (AL) Police Department: 2005 press release on use of the TASER;[54]
- Oakland (CA) Police Department: 2006 PowerPoint presentation on the department's history with the TASER;[55]
- Orange County (CA) Sheriff's Office TASER Task Force: 2007 report from the task force on adoption and use of the TASER;[56]
- Phoenix (AZ) Police Department: 2004 press release on the dramatic decrease in officer-involved shootings;[57]
- Putnam County (FL) Sheriff's Office: 2005 annual report;[58]
- Seattle (WA) Police Department: 2002 report describing a one-year pilot project with the TASER M26;[59]
- Toronto (Canada) Police Department: 2006 annual report on TASER use.[60]

For each document, we used the search function to find the keywords "race," "racial bias," and "discrimination." None of the documents include any discussion of racial bias or discrimination. Two documents include discussions of suspect race: the

Green Bay and Madison police department reports. Both reports review just under one hundred TASER incidents, and suspect race is described. In Green Bay, 25 percent of suspects in TASER incidents were black, 23 percent were American Indian, and 3 percent were Hispanic.[61] In the Madison report, 41 percent of suspects were black and 6 percent were Hispanic.[62] Neither report makes mention of bias or discrimination claims, though the Madison report states that the racial breakdown of TASER and arrest incidents is similar. In short, this data source offered little insight regarding race and the TASER.

CED Industry Reports and Data

We conducted extensive reviews of the TASER International website (http://www .taser.com/), the *TASER Research Compendium*, as well as an article by Jenkinson and colleagues that uses TASER International's field deployment database. The TASER International website is organized into six different sections: company information, products (for consumers, law enforcement and corrections, and military), "shop" (where to buy), research, training (academy and events), and support (customer support and product activation) (as of June 2008). We focused primarily on the research section. This section is composed of five sub-sections: technology, science and medical research, legal research, statistics and papers, and frequently asked questions (FAQs).

The statistics and papers section was composed of several field-use reports from law enforcement agencies—each of which was reviewed in the previous section. Though there is some variation, the general content of each report focuses on a case review of field deployments, officer and suspect injuries, effectiveness, and outcomes. These reports make little mention of suspect race, and there is no discussion of racial bias. There is also a TASER International presentation in PowerPoint that presents information on reductions in officer and suspect injuries, shootings, and workers' compensation claims for more than fifty law enforcement agencies in the United States and abroad. Suspect race and racial bias are not mentioned in this presentation either.[63]

We also reviewed the *TASER Research Compendium* (5th edition), a collection of articles, letters, and documents presenting TASER-related research.[64] The *Compendium*, more than two thousand pages in length, is available in hard copy and on CD, and presents research in the following categories: general, government-funded, international, municipalities and law enforcement agencies, and safety and use statistics. We used the search function to find mentions of "race," "racial bias," and "discrimination" throughout the entire *Compendium*. Searches of "racial bias" and "discrimination" produced no returns. The "race" search produced eight returns. The first three were sample use-of-force reports that had sections for officers to record suspect race. The other five returns came from a Lakeland (FL) Police Department report that presented arrest and TASER deployment data by race across its several police districts. The information is presented in tabular format with no discussion of bias or discrimination.

Last, TASER International maintains a field deployment database composed of incident-level data from law enforcement agencies around the world. Submission of data is voluntary, and access to the database is granted to any agency that is licensed for TASER use. In 2006, Jenkinson and colleagues published a chapter in the *Journal of Clinical Forensic Medicine* that examined field use data from the TASER database (n = 2,050), as well as data from the Northamptonshire Police Force in Great Britain.[65] The article compares injury rates for the TASER, CS spray, baton, and police dogs, and reports the lowest injury rates for the TASER. There is no mention of suspect race or racial bias in the article, and given our inability to access the TASER database, we cannot comment on the reporting of race in those data.

Human and Civil Rights Group Reports/Data

AMNESTY INTERNATIONAL

In 2004 Amnesty International issued a ninety-page report outlining its primary concerns with police use of the TASER. The report is broken down into three sections. The first section describes AI's general concerns, highlighting the lack of consensus regarding where on the use-of-force continuum the TASER should be placed. The report details a number of incidents where the device was used against nonviolent or passive persons. AI also singled out use of the device against vulnerable populations including children, the elderly, pregnant women, and prisoner/suspects who were physically restrained. In total, this section of the report provides brief descriptions of approximately 55 TASER incidents, and in these descriptions, the race of the suspect was mentioned only four times (three African Americans, one Latino). This suggests that AI did not perceive the citizen's race to be relevant to the issues they were addressing in this section.

The second section of the report highlights more than seventy cases in which citizens died after being struck with the TASER. The report states, "The deceased were males aged 18 to 59 years of age, of varying racial and ethnic origin, with the exception of one case involving the death of a female fetus after the pregnant mother was tasered."[66] The report also provides summaries of approximately twenty death cases, but none of the summaries include the victim's race. There is a more inclusive table in the appendix of the AI report that provides descriptive information for all seventy-four death cases, including name and age, data source (newspaper or autopsy), police agency, cause of death, number of TASER activations, other restraint used, and time between TASER deployment and death. The race of the victim is indicated in twenty-three of the seventy-four cases, and fourteen were minority victims—ten black and four Hispanic. Finally, the last section of the report details specific recommendations, including the call for a moratorium on use of the TASER, and additional training in line with the United Nations Code of Conduct for Law Enforcement Officials. None of the report's nineteen recommendations make any mention of race, or express any concerns about disproportionate use of the TASER against minority citizens.

On September 27, 2007, representatives from AI gave testimony before the chief medical panel leading a U.S. Department of Justice inquiry into in-custody deaths involving the TASER. AI reiterated many of their ongoing concerns, including use of the device against passively resistant suspects, use in the "drive stun" or direct contact mode, subjecting persons to multiple or prolonged shocks, use of the TASER in conjunction with other less-than-lethal devices (i.e., pepper spray), as well as the number of deaths that occurred following a TASER deployment (estimated at 290). Again, however, there is no mention of citizen race/ethnicity, nor is there any discussion of concerns regarding racial bias or disproportionate use against minority citizens.

The authors also reviewed the Amnesty International (USA) website. A search of the keyword "TASER" produced both the 2004 report and the 2007 testimony described above. AI also issued an update of the 2004 report in late 2006. The search also returned two United Nations documents—both related to principles of good policing—and nine video clips of TASER incidents. Last, there are five audio recording clips from an activist radio show called *Law and Disorder*. None of these additional data sources discuss race or racial bias.

AMERICAN CIVIL LIBERTIES UNION

We entered "TASER" in the search engine on the main page of the ACLU website, and the search produced forty-five documents. None of these documents specifically discuss TASER use against minority citizens. There were approximately a dozen press releases from local ACLU offices in Wisconsin, San Francisco, Denver, Providence (RI), Boston, and Miami that discuss specific TASER incidents resulting in death, make claims of excessive force (in prisons and jails, as well as in public), and advocate for increased regulation or limited use against suspects. Finally, there were several blogs in which ACLU representatives lamented about the United States' continuing violations of the United Nations Torture Treaty, and police use of the TASER is cited as an example of such violations. There was one blog stating that in San Diego, African Americans and Latinos are twice as likely as whites to be struck with a TASER. There is no link to a more detailed report, however, and no evidence to support the claim.

Media Reports

Through searches on LexisNexis and TimesSelect, we identified all newspaper articles describing incidents where police used a TASER on a suspect from January 2002 through December 2006 (n = 691). The articles were then content analyzed for details about the race/ethnicity of the parties involved.[67] Surprisingly, just 7 percent of the articles identified the suspect's race or ethnicity (n = 51). Among those fifty-one articles, sixteen involved black suspects; twenty-one involved Hispanic suspects; and thirteen involved white suspects. The failure to report race/ethnicity did not extend to other demographic characteristics, as three-quarters of the articles identified the suspect's gender and over 60 percent discussed the suspect's age.

Although the primary finding from the media data is that suspect race is rarely reported, there are some interesting patterns among the fifty-one articles in which race is mentioned. First, media reports were much more likely to mention mental illness when the suspect is white. Among the thirteen articles involving white suspects, ten described the suspect as mentally ill. In the sixteen articles involving black suspects, none are described as mentally ill; and just six of the twenty-one articles describing Hispanic suspects make mention of mental illness. Alternatively, articles involving minority suspects were much more likely to state that the suspect was intoxicated; this occurs in 38 percent of the articles involving black suspects (six of sixteen) and 48 percent of the articles involving Hispanic suspects (ten of twenty-one). Notably, none of the articles involving white suspects mention intoxication. While these findings are clearly secondary to the larger, more important "non-reporting" finding, it is interesting that these racial differences in behavior that initiate the incident parallel findings reported earlier in White and Ready's NYPD data.

Last, our review of media reports uncovered a small number of newspaper articles that deal specifically with minority over-representation and the TASER. In February 2004 the *Seattle Post-Intelligencer* reported that 45 percent of the people struck with TASERS were black, while census data indicate that blacks make up less than 10 percent of the city's population. In December 2006 the *Houston Chronicle* published an article concerning the Houston Police Department's (HPD) use of the TASER, stating that the police have used the TASER "indiscriminately" against black suspects: "Of the 969 times police used a TASER last year, more than 60 percent of the victims were black. Twenty-three percent of the city's population is black."[68] Two weeks later, a similar article appeared in the *Washington Post* focusing on questions of racial bias and TASER use by the HPD.[69] Houston Police Department officials responded to the over-representation claims by highlighting the racial characteristics in arrest statistics from 2005—in which blacks represent more than half of arrestees.

Evidence from Civil Trials against Police

A final source of data that may inform the discussion of suspect race and police use of the TASER is civil litigation brought against police departments for their officers' use of the device. In a recent study, Smith, Petrocelli, and Scheer examined fifty-three court rulings in civil cases brought against police because of use of the TASER.[70] The authors identified three separate types of cases: those that involved municipalities or supervisors as defendants; those that involved individual officers that federal courts decided on motions to dismiss; and those that involved individual officers that courts decided on motions for summary judgment. Claims brought against officers, departments, and municipalities have focused on a number of key issues, including the custom and practice of allowing officers to carry TASERs un-holstered,[71] use of a TASER on a suspect without justification,[72] use of a TASER to avoid a physical struggle,[73] and failure to equip officers with the TASER.[74]

This case review is highly informative and offers considerable insight into key issues surrounding courts' interpretations of when it is appropriate for police to use the TASER.[75] The authors note that courts have clearly stated that use of the TASER must comport with the reasonableness standard established in *Graham v. Connor* (1989), 490 U.S. 386. Courts have also addressed specific issues such as the inappropriateness of using the TASER without provocation against non-resistant citizens; the importance of using verbal commands first; and the importance of being able to articulate that there was a potential or real physical threat before using the device.[76] None of the fifty-three court cases highlighted in this study, however, address issues of race in police use of the TASER. In particular, table A1 at the end of Smith and colleagues' article describes the key allegations in each case—all dealing with section 1983 claims of excessive force.[77] None of those allegations raised the issue of discrimination or racial bias. As a result, this data source offers little insight into questions of race, bias, and use of the TASER.

Discussion

This chapter explores the intersection of two prevailing themes in police use of force: minority over-representation as victims, and officers' increasing reliance on the TASER. While there is a large body of research examining use of force by police, particularly against minority citizens, there has been very little research on use of the TASER. Consequently, we know little about who the TASER is used against, under what circumstances it is used, and whether there is any evidence of racial bias. This chapter sought to investigate basic questions regarding race and police use of the TASER through an exploration of a range of available data sources. While by no means exhaustive, the breadth and scope of the data reviewed here was considerable, offering a contemporary picture of the available evidence on the nexus of the two themes. The primary findings and their implications are described below.

The Virtual Absence of Discussions of Race in TASER Data

The most important finding from the review of available data is the absence of virtually any discussion of race. The persistence of this finding across data sources could be a consequence of the relative novelty of the TASER, as well as the lack of data documenting its use. Also, questions of race, bias, and disproportionality may be overshadowed by larger questions regarding physiological impact and the potential for death. Nevertheless, the nearly absolute silence on issues of race and the TASER is remarkable. Consider the following. An exhaustive review of the websites, reports, and press releases of both Amnesty International and the American Civil Liberties Union—perhaps the two most active watchdogs of police use of force in the world—produced no substantive discussions of race or racial bias in TASER use. Both groups have focused considerable attention on the potential for death and for misuse of the device by police, but neither has raised concerns about differential use against minorities.

Perhaps most surprising is the media's failure to report on race in articles describing TASER incidents. We reviewed nearly seven hundred news articles from across the United States describing incidents where police used the TASER, and the race of the suspect is reported in just 7 percent of those news articles. The media has a long history of monitoring and questioning police actions—especially use of force—and this past reporting has often focused on racial bias and discrimination. But this has simply not been the case in reporting of TASER incidents. Like the ACLU and AI, the media has focused considerable attention on incidents resulting in death, again perhaps overshadowing the race issue.

Less surprising is the absence of race discussions in police data and reports, and in available data from the CED industry. Quite simply, police in general typically take a reactive stance in responding to controversial issues, particularly those involving race. That is, police departments are usually put on the defensive when their officers' field behavior is questioned by citizens, the media, or activist groups. Police then respond to their critics regarding the issue at hand. The failure of the three primary monitors of the police—AI, ACLU, and the media—to raise questions about race and the TASER has, in turn, driven the silence among police and the CED industry.

Secondary Findings: Themes from the Available Evidence

With the larger "virtual absence" finding as a backdrop, our analysis did produce a few noteworthy results involving race and police use of the TASER. The most compelling findings were derived from the White and Ready studies of the NYPD, and our secondary analyses of those data. Importantly, White and Ready reported that approximately half of citizens/suspects in TASER incidents were black and one-quarter were Hispanic.[78] We compared these findings with the results from the recent RAND study on the NYPD and found that the racial breakdown of suspects in TASER incidents matched the race of suspects in both arrest and stop, question, and frisk (SQF) data.[79] Moreover, RAND examined the race of criminal suspects from victim and witness data and found a *higher* percentage of blacks than in the TASER, SQF, and arrest data (75 percent, though Hispanics were under-represented at 15 percent).

The secondary analysis of the NYPD data investigated whether there were incident-level differences in TASER deployments across categories of suspect race. We identified differences in how individuals came to the attention of police: white suspects were more likely to be classified as emotionally disturbed; Hispanic suspects were more likely to be classified as intoxicated; and black suspects were more likely to be neither mentally ill nor intoxicated, but were more likely to be violent toward police. But TASER use, deployment, and effectiveness characteristics across racial categories were nearly identical, suggesting that the individual-level patterns in suspect behavior were not a consequence of differential TASER use patterns. In simple terms, there is no evidence of racial bias in the NYPD's use of the TASER.

Next Steps

There is a clear need for more independent, empirical research on police use of the TASER, particularly incident-level studies that would allow for investigation of issues related to race and racial bias. It is unclear whether the "virtual absence" of discussions of race and the TASER will continue. Notably, the emergence of the TASER in American law enforcement has mirrored the introduction of oleoresin capsicum (OC) spray (i.e., pepper spray) in the early 1990s. During that time, similar concerns were raised regarding OC spray, particularly the potential for misuse and serious physiological side effects. Interestingly, concerns over racial bias and police use of OC spray never really emerged. If the TASER continues to follow the trends of its "predecessor," claims of racial bias in TASER use may never materialize. Our analysis of media reports, however, uncovered a small number of articles that specifically address claims of racial disproportionality in police use of the TASER. In particular, news reports in Seattle and Houston have documented disproportionate TASER use against minorities, using census population data as a benchmark. Numerous other chapters in this book address problems with using appropriate benchmarks—including census data—for documenting minority over-representation. Nevertheless, the identification of these articles may signal that questions regarding racial bias and the TASER are on the horizon for police departments in the United States. Importantly, our analysis here shows that there is little in the way of available data to effectively respond to those questions.

NOTES

1. This quote is from the testimony of George Edwards before the National Advisory Commission on Civil Disorder (Kerner Commission) (1968). Edwards was the commissioner of the Detroit Police Department from 1961 to 1963, and served as a judge of the United States Court of Appeals for the Sixth Circuit (1967).

2. Skolnick and Fyfe, *Above the Law.*

3. Castro, "Less Lethal Weapons Still Pack a Big Punch."

4. Bureau of Justice Statistics, *Contacts Between Police and the Public.* See also Hickman in this volume.

5. http://www.taser.com/ (retrieved September 1, 2008).

6. Walker and Katz, *The Police in America.*

7. See Bittner, *The Functions of Police in Modern Society.*

8. Bureau of Justice Statistics, *Contacts Between Police and the Public.* This estimate becomes much greater if handcuffing and verbal commands are included as use of force.

9. Fyfe, "Police Use of Deadly Force"; Geller and Scott, *Deadly Force.*

10. Reiss, *The Police and the Public.*

11. Robin, "Justifiable Homicides by Police Officers"; Fyfe, "Blind Justice."

12. Bureau of Justice Statistics, *Contacts Between Police and the Public.*

13. Terrill and Reisig, "Neighborhood Context and Police Use of Force."

14. Chevigny, *Police Power;* Reiss, "Police Brutality"; Black, *The Behavior of Law;* Van Maanen, "Working the Street."

15. Terrill and Reisig, "Neighborhood Context and Police Use of Force," p. 293.

16. Muir, *Police;* Brown, *Working the Street;* Worden, "The 'Causes' of Police Brutality."

17. Wilson, *Varieties of Police Behavior.*

18. Klinger, "Negotiating Order in Patrol Work."

19. Werthman and Piliavan, "Gang Members and the Police"; Smith, "The Neighborhood Context of Police Behavior."

20. Jacobs and O'Brien, "The Determinants of Deadly Force"; Kane, "The Social Ecology of Police Misconduct."

21. Terrill and Reisig, "Neighborhood Context and Use of Force," p. 307.

22. Vilke and Chan, "Less Lethal Technology."

23. Vilke and Chan, "Less Lethal Technology," p. 349.

24. There are other questions surrounding appropriate use against vulnerable persons, such as children, pregnant women, and the elderly.

25. International Association of Chiefs of Police, *Electro-Muscular Disruption Technology (EMDT)*; Police Executive Research Forum, *PERF Conducted Energy Device Policy and Training Guidelines for Consideration*.

26. Jenkinson et al., "The Relative Risk of Police Use-of-Force Options"; Smith et al., "The Impact of Conducted Energy Devices and Other Types of Force and Resistance on Officer and Suspect Injuries."

27. See, for example, Seattle Police Department, *Seattle Police Department TASER Use and Deployment Fact Sheet*; TASER International, *TASER Non-lethal Weapons*.

28. White and Ready, "The Impact of the TASER on Suspect Resistance."

29. See Vilke and Chan, "Less Lethal Technology" for a complete review of this research.

30. Vilke and Chan, "Less Lethal Technology," p. 353.

31. Wake Forest University Baptist Medical Center. Two suspects died, but neither death occurred as a result of the TASER.

32. National Institute of Justice, *Study of Deaths Following Electro Muscular Disruption*, p. 3.

33. White and Ready, "The TASER as a Less-Lethal Force Alternative"; "The Impact of the TASER on Suspect Resistance"; Ready et al., "Shock Value."

34. Smith et al., "The Impact of Conducted Energy Devices and Other Types of Force and Resistance on Officer and Suspect Injuries."

35. There is growing body of literature that has examined the physiological side effects of the TASER, particularly whether it increases the risk of death. This literature includes reviews of coroner reports, biomedical studies with animals and healthy human volunteers, and reviews of available research. Though many of these studies have been conducted by independent researchers, this literature is outside the scope of this study—with its focus on race—and is not reviewed here. See Vilke and Chan, "Less Lethal Technology," for a succinct review of this body of research.

36. Originally, nearly seven hundred articles were located, but several categories of articles were limited. First, the focus of this study is on police use of the device, so articles describing other aspects of the device or company (e.g., stock and business reports) were eliminated. Duplicate cases were also excluded to prevent certain articles from being over-represented in the comparative analysis. Duplicate cases were defined as any news reports that contained the same information as another report (typically published on the same date) describing a specific incident in which police used the TASER on a suspect. The duplicates were identified by cross-referencing the articles using the author or suspect's name and the newspaper in which the article was published. Researchers also removed news reports in which the TASER was referred to incidentally but was not the primary focus of the narrative. A portion of these data were also used in previous work by Ready et al., "Shock Value."

37. Smith et al., "Excessive Force, Civil Liability, and the TASER in the Nation's Courts."

38. A third study by Ready et al., "Shock Value," compared NYPD data to media data drawn from LexisNexis and TimesSelect.

39. White and Ready, "The TASER as a Less-Lethal Force Alternative." Notably, suspects began active resistance again at some later point in about 20 percent of cases, highlighting the temporary effect of the TASER.

40. White and Ready, "The Impact of the TASER on Suspect Resistance." Weapon effectiveness was measured as terminating suspect resistance and officer satisfaction with the device.

41. White and Ready, "The Impact of the TASER on Suspect Resistance."

42. RAND, *Do NYPD's Pedestrian Stop Data Indicate Racial Bias?*

43. RAND, *Do NYPD's Pedestrian Stop Data Indicate Racial Bias?*

44. Lawton, in "Levels of Non-lethal Force," examines all uses of non-lethal force by Philadelphia police officers in 2002. While he found that 30 percent of incidents involved OC spray or the TASER, there is no independent analysis of TASER incidents. Lawton does report overrepresentation of African Americans among use of force victims, but again, there is no specific discussion of TASER events. He also finds that citizen race is unrelated to type of force used.

45. Smith et al., "The Impact of Conducted Energy Devices and Other Types of Force and Resistance on Officer and Suspect Injuries."

46. Smith et al., "The Impact of Conducted Energy Devices and Other Types of Force and Resistance on Officer and Suspect Injuries."

47. Boise Ombudsman, *Ombudsman Special Report.*

48. Cincinnati Police Department, *Cincinnati Police Department Report to the Community.*

49. Columbus Police Department, *Six Month TASER Study.*

50. Granite City Police Department, *Granite City Police Department Risk Reduction.*

51. Green Bay Police Department, *TASER Report.*

52. Madison Police Department, *TASER Report.*

53. Michigan Municipal Risk Management Authority, *Less-Lethal Weapons.*

54. Mobile Police Department, *Police Use TASER for Last-Minute Rescues.*

55. Oakland Police Department, *You Can Make a Difference.*

56. Orange County Sheriff's Office, *Annual Use of Force Report, 2006.*

57. Phoenix Police Department, *Police-Involved Shootings Lowest in 14 Years.*

58. Putnam County Sheriff's Office, *2005 Annual Report.*

59. Seattle Police Department, *The M26 Taser.*

60. Toronto Police Department, *2006 Annual Report.*

61. Green Bay Police Department, *TASER Report.*

62. Madison Police Department, *TASER Report.*

63. We also used the search engine on the TASER International website, entering "race," "racial bias," and "discrimination" as keywords. The search of "racial bias" and "discrimination" produced no documents. The "race" search produced five documents, including the Green Bay and Madison police department reports. The other three documents were not relevant to this study.

64. TASER International, *TASER Research Compendium.* The authors also reviewed the *Sudden In-Custody Death Research* collection and found no relevant discussion of race, racial bias, or discrimination.

65. Jenkinson et al., "The Relative Risk of Police Use-of-Force Options."

66. Amnesty International, *Excessive and Lethal Force?*, p. 43.

67. See Ready et al., *Shock Value*, for a detailed discussion of the media reports.

68. Villafranca, "HPD."

69. Moreno, "In Houston, Questions of Bias over TASERs."

70. Smith et al., "Excessive Force, Civil Liability, and the TASER in the Nation's Courts." See the earlier discussion of their methodology.

71. *McKenzie v. City of Milpitas*, 1990.

72. *Batiste v. City of Beaumont*, 2006.

73. *Stanley v. City of Baytown*, 2005.

74. *Plakas v. Drinski*, 1994.

75. Smith et al., "Excessive Force, Civil Liability and the TASER in the Nation's Courts."

76. Smith et al., "Excessive Force, Civil Liability and the TASER in the Nation's Courts."
77. Smith et al., "Excessive Force, Civil Liability and the TASER in the Nation's Courts."
78. White and Ready, "The Impact of the TASER on Suspect Resistance."
79. RAND, *Do NYPD's Pedestrian Stop Data Indicate Racial Bias?*

REFERENCES

Amnesty International. 2004. Excessive and lethal force? Amnesty International's concerns about deaths and ill treatment involving police use of tasers. Amnesty International: London.

Batiste v. City of Beaumont, 2006a, 421 F. Supp 2d 1000 (Tex).

Bittner, Egon. 1970. The functions of police in modern society. Washington, DC: U.S. Government Printing Office.

Black, Donald. 1976. The behavior of law. New York: Academic Press.

Brown, Michael. K. 1981. Working the street: Police discretion and the dilemma of reform. New York: Russell Sage Foundation.

Bureau of Justice Statistics. 2005. Contacts between police and the public: Findings from the 2002 national survey. Washington, DC: U.S. Department of Justice.

Castro, Hector. 2004. Less lethal weapons still pack a big punch. New police guns not as deadly, but require lots of extra training. Seattle Post Intelligencer, February 2.

Chevigny, Paul. 1969. Police power: Police abuses in New York City. New York: Pantheon.

Cincinnati Police Department. 2005. Cincinnati Police Department report to the community. Cincinnati: Cincinnati Police Department.

Columbus Police Department. undated. Six-month TASER study. Memo from defensive tactics unit to chief James Jackson. Columbus, OH: Columbus Police Department.

Fyfe, James. J. 1982. Blind justice: Police shootings in Memphis. Journal of Criminal Law and Criminology 73: 702–722.

Fyfe, James. J. 1988. Police use of deadly force: Research and reform. Justice Quarterly 5: 165–205.

Geller, William., and Michael. S. Scott. 1992. Deadly force: What we know. Washington, DC: Police Executive Research Forum.

Granite City Police Department. 2004. Granite City Police Department risk reduction. Letter from Office of the Chief to TASER International. Granite City, IL: Granite City Police Department.

Green Bay Police Department. 2006. TASER report. Green Bay: Green Bay Police Department.

International Association of Chiefs of Police. 2005. Electro-muscular disruption technology (EMDT): A nine-step strategy for effective deployment. Alexandria: International Association of Chiefs of Police.

Jacobs, David., and Robert M. O'Brien. 1998. The determinants of deadly force: A structural analysis of police violence. American Journal of Sociology 103: 837–862.

Jenkinson, Emma, Clare Neeson, and Anthony Bleetman. 2006. The relative risk of police use-of-force options: Evaluating the potential for deployment of electronic weaponry. Journal of Clinical Forensic Medicine 13: 229–241.

Lawton, Brian. 2007. Levels of non-lethal force: An examination of individual, situational, and contextual factors. Journal of Research in Crime and Delinquency 44: 163–184.

Kane, Robert J. 2002. The social ecology of police misconduct. Criminology 40: 867–896.

Klinger, David A. 1997. Negotiating order in patrol work: An ecological theory of police response to deviance. Criminology 35: 277–306.

Madison Police Department. 2006. TASER report. Madison, WI: Madison Police Department.

McKenzie v. City of Milpitas, 1992, 953 F. 2d 1387 (9th Cir).

Michigan Municipal Risk Management Authority. 2005. Less-lethal weapons. Michigan: Michigan Municipal Risk Management Authority.

Mobile Police Department. 2005. Police use TASER for last-minute rescues. Press release. Mobile, AL: Mobile Police Department.

Moreno, Sylvia. 2006. In Houston, questions of bias over TASERs; police use on black suspects is criticized. Washington Post, December 18.

Muir, William K. 1977. Police: Streetcorner politicians. Chicago: University of Chicago Press.

Murphy, Pierce. 2006. Ombudsman's special report. Boise, ID: City of Boise.

National Advisory Commission on Civil Disorder. 1968. Report of the national advisory commission on civil disorder. Washington, DC: U.S. Government Printing Office.

National Institute of Justice. 2008. Study of deaths following electro-muscular disruption: Interim report. Washington, DC: U.S. Department of Justice.

Oakland Police Department. 2006. You can make a difference. Oakland: Oakland Police Department.

Orange County Sheriff's Office. 2007. Annual use of force report, 2006. Orange County, CA: Orange County Sheriff's Office.

Phoenix Police Department. 2004. Police-involved shootings lowest in 14 years. Phoenix: Phoenix Police Department.

Plakas v. Drinski, 1994, 19 F. 3d 1143 (7th Cir).

Police Executive Research Forum (PERF). 2005. PERF conducted energy device policy and training guidelines for consideration. Washington, DC: PERF Center on Force and Accountability.

Putnam County Sheriff's Office. 2006. 2005 Annual report. Putnam County, FL: Putnam County Sheriff's Office.

RAND. 2008. Do NYPD's pedestrian stop data indicate racial bias? Santa Monica, CA: RAND.

Ready, Justin, Michael D. White, and Christopher Fisher. 2007. Shock value: A comparative analysis of news reports and official police records on TASER deployments. Policing: An International Journal of Police Strategies and Management 31: 148–170.

Reiss, Albert J., Jr. 1968. Police brutality: Answers to key questions. Trans-Action, 10–19.

Reiss, Albert J., Jr. 1971. The police and the public. New Haven: Yale University Press.

Robin, Gerald D. 1963. Justifiable homicide by police officers. Journal of Criminal Law, Criminology, and Police Science 52: 225–231.

Seattle Police Department. 2002. The M26 Taser: Year one implementation. Seattle: Seattle Police Department

Seattle Police Department. 2004. Seattle Police Department TASER use and deployment fact sheet. Seattle: Seattle Police Department.

Skolnick, Jerome H., and James J. Fyfe. 1993. Above the law: Police and the excessive use of force. New York: Free Press.

Smith, Douglas A. 1986. The neighborhood context of police behavior. In Crime and Justice: Annual Review of Research, ed. Albert Reiss and Michael Tonry, 8:313–341. Chicago: University of Chicago Press.

Smith, Michael R., Robert J. Kaminski, Jeffrey Rojek, Geoffrey P. Alpert, and Jason Mathis. 2007. The impact of conducted energy devices and other types of force and resistance on officer and suspect injuries. Policing: An International Journal of Police Strategies and Management 30: 423–446.

Smith, Michael R., Matthew Petrocelli, and Charlie Scheer. 2007. Excessive force, civil liability, and the TASER in the nation's courts. Policing: An International Journal of Police Strategies and Management 30: 398–422.

Stanley v. City of Baytown, 2005, WL 2757370 (Tex).

TASER International. 2006a. TASER Research Compendium. Scottsdale: TASER International.

TASER International. 2006b. TASER non-lethal weapons: Field data as of July 2006. Scottsdale: TASER International.

Terrill, William, and Michael D. Reisig. 2003. Neighborhood context and police use force. Journal of Research in Crime and Delinquency 40: 291–321.

Toronto Police Department. 2007. 2006 annual report: Use of TASERS. Toronto: Toronto Police Department.

Van Maanen, John. 1974. Working the street: A developmental view of police. In The potential for reform in criminal justice, ed. H. Jacob, 93–130. Beverly Hills: Sage.

Vilke, Gary M., and Theodore C. Chan. 2007. Less lethal technology: Medical issues. Policing: An International Journal of Police Strategies and Management 30: 341–357.

Villafranca, Armando. 2006. HPD: TASER claims "unfair," police attribute high number of black victims to '05 arrest statistics. Houston Chronicle, December 5.

Wake Forest University Baptist Medical Center. 2007. Nationwide independent TASER study results suggest devices are safe. Winston-Salem: Wake Forest University.

Walker, Samuel, and Charles M. Katz. 2002. The police in America: An introduction. New York: McGraw-Hill.

Werthman, Carl, and Irving Piliavin. 1967. Gang members and the police. In The police: Six sociological issues, ed. D. Bordua, 56–98. New York: John Wiley.

White, Michael D., and Justin Ready. 2007. The TASER as a less-lethal force alternative: Findings on use and effectiveness in a large metropolitan police agency. Police Quarterly 10: 170–191.

White, Michael D., and Justin Ready. 2009. The impact of the TASER on suspect resistance: Identifying predictors of effectiveness. Crime and Delinquency. Pre-published in Onlinefirst, February 26, 2008, DOI: 10.1177/0011128707308099.

Wilson, James Q. 1968. Varieties of police behavior. Cambridge: Harvard University Press.

Worden, Robert E. 1995. The "causes" of police brutality: Theory and evidence on police use of force. In And justice for all: Understanding and controlling police abuse of force, ed. William A. Geller and Hans Toch, 31–60. Washington, DC: Police Executive Research Forum.

Part IV

The Future

Introduction to Part IV

Stephen K. Rice

Two goals of *Race, Ethnicity, and Policing* have been to outline the multidisciplinary theoretical foundations of the study of race, ethnicity, and policing and to provide heuristics for the empirical assessment of a relationship (the police/minority community) which has faced great challenge. The final section in the volume, "The Future," attempts to offer a way forward by examining the experiences of previously understudied populations (e.g., Hispanics/Latinos, immigrants, Muslim Americans), specifying innovative analytical strategies (e.g., coupling neighborhood context with spatial dynamics), offering alternatives to actuarial (predictive) methods in policing, and outlining how police departments can stem future incidents of racially and ethnically biased policing through the realization of the democratic ideals of accountability, transparency, and fairness.

In the section's first chapter, Stults and colleagues offer the first known examination of the role of spatial dynamics and neighborhood characteristics on police stop rates, and do so by incorporating the experiences of not only white and black motorists but also those of Hispanics—an underdeveloped area of focus (see Martínez, Weitzer, this volume). Utilizing census data and information to include crime reports, officers' demographic and behavioral indicators, and police-citizen contacts from the Miami-Dade Police Department (e.g., driver race and residence, reasons for stops, geo-coding of stops), the authors set out to assess macro-level, structural predictors of stops (e.g., racial composition, disadvantage, social disorder), to understand the spatial clustering of stops in relation to neighborhood characteristics, and to explore the influence of nearby (proximate) areas on the potential for police-citizen interactions in Miami-Dade communities. The study includes several major findings. In possible support of the racial threat hypothesis (i.e., formal social control being mobilized against minority groups when such groups come to be seen as threats to majority interests), the rate of black stops were found to increase in areas with higher percentages of whites, while rates of white and Hispanic stops decreased. With regard to this clustering, Stults and colleagues proffer, "This pattern may well be the result of formal social control being implemented in the form of police stops when blacks travel to white neighborhoods." Consistent with this trend, black stop rates were also found to be low in areas where the white population was low. With regard to the intriguing finding of reduced stop rates for Hispanics in areas with sizable percentages of whites, the authors point to a possible contact effect, or a reduction in inter-group conflict, as a result of increased contact between racial/ethnic groups—a dynamic that takes special shape in South Florida vis-à-vis its distinct intersections of race and ethnicity. Hypotheses related to the impact of disorganization (community disorder) on stop rates are also assessed, suggesting important differences in the influence of disorder relative to race and ethnicity. In total, the chapter provides a compelling example of the methodological and theoretical utility of space in the study of race, ethnicity, and policing.

The next two chapters in the section aim to provide the deep context necessary to better understand the relationships between understudied populations and the police generally, and to also provide guidance for finer theoretical and methodological "cuts" to social groupings to illuminate idiosyncratic perceptions and experiences (e.g., those of immigrants versus native-born residents). The first chapter, by Martínez, is grounded in a premise that the relative lack of research on Latinos and policing is "one of the most enduring shortcomings in the development of race/ethnicity and the criminal justice scholarship," a trend that Martínez finds surprising given early attention to immigrants and crime by the Wickersham Commission (1931), scholarship by voices to include Mexican anthropologist/sociologist Manuel Gamio (1883–1960), and historical evidence that Latinos, like blacks, have come to be cast as symbolic assailants (see Skolnick, this volume) by some federal, state, and local personnel (e.g., incidents with Border Patrol, LAPD). Yet despite this, Martínez argues, systematic research remains scarce, a void that is surprising given Latinos' ascension as the United States' largest racial/ethnic minority group. Like Weitzer, Parker, and colleagues, and Stults and colleagues (this volume), the chapter outlines areas for study to include the impact of raids on businesses in search of "illegal" immigrants, the potential roles of concentrated disadvantage, legal cynicism, history, culture, demography, and intra-ethnic variation on police-Latino interactions, and, harking to the Los Angeles "zoot suit" riots of 1943, whether there has been evidence of differential enforcement of the law across major categories of race and ethnicity.

Complementing other chapters that provide guidance for better understanding the experiences of understudied populations, Rice and Parkin couple the structural, sociopolitical, and codal perspectives that have dominated discourse related to Muslim Americans with social psychological principles (e.g., perceived procedural/distributive injustice) and explain how such principles must come to hold a more prominent position in explaining deference, defiance, and the effective rule of law. In effect, Rice and Parkin argue that law enforcement scholars and practitioners must transcend what *New York Times* columnist Thomas Friedman calls "the United States of Fighting Terrorism"—an orientation that blinds the system from seeing how the interpersonal and intrapsychic processes that have received considerable support in explaining trust in the law among whites, blacks, and Hispanics (e.g., Tyler and Fagan, this volume) must come to also be applied to a population of 2.4 million people who have experienced differential treatment in the years since 9/11 (e.g., in their communities, on mass transit). In support of this mandate, Rice and Parkin outline Muslim Americans' shared histories and social locations and offer ways forward.

The next two chapters outline how police accountability, transparency, and fairness can act as hedges against racially- and ethnically biased policing. White's chapter focuses on the adoption of internal and external controls as means toward departmental accountability—steps that, through their reduction in police misconduct (of which demonstrated bias is one form)—serve to reduce civil litigation, reduce criminal prosecution, and improve police-community relations. While recognizing that there is no "magic bullet" that will ensure each of these outcomes, White provides evidence regarding the efficacy of internal mechanisms such as careful recruitment of personnel, effective training and supervision, administrative guidance (e.g., polices, rules, regulations), internal affairs, and early warning systems (i.e., information systems that afford indicators of problematic officer behavior). To this the chapter adds external controls such as criminal and civil prosecution of misconduct, judicial intervention (e.g., injunctions), special commissions, consent decrees, and citizen/media oversight. The strengths and weaknesses of the varied controls are outlined, with White recommending context-specific, comprehensive accountability packages that best speak to specific community needs.

Hickman, like White, calls for more rigorous monitoring of the manner in which police conduct themselves and serve the public, with Hickman tying such an effort to the fundamental precepts of democratic policing—an orientation that requires the ready flow and capture of information related to police accountability, transparency, and fairness (e.g., objectivity, nonbias, dignity, respect). Further, in Hickman's view a paradox has taken shape: while "we (the United States) are strong advocates of democratic policing abroad . . . our country is not presently in a position to be able to speak to any of these ideals; we simply don't have the necessary information." With regard to the former, the chapter provides evidence of global expenditures that have been estimated to be as high as nearly one billion dollars (FY 2004). These sizable foreign investments are often framed and budgeted as facilitators of police accountability, openness, and fairness—the paradox that Hickman seeks to address: "It would be interesting to turn this kind of a model on ourselves . . . we might be surprised by what we find in our own country." The remainder of the chapter provides specifics for applying this model inward by outlining the national indicators of policing that exist at present (e.g., the Bureau of Justice Statistics' PPCS, LEMAS, SILJ), which are especially critical to aspirations of democratic policing (e.g., those dealing with public perceptions of police-citizen interactions), politics that can be involved in such endeavors (note: Hickman once served as a BJS statistician), how "place-based policing" may provide an important first step toward these goals, and how meaningful change will best be ensured through the explicit demonstration (reportage) of fundamental fairness between police and the public they serve.

The final chapter in the volume, Harcourt's "Moving Beyond Profiling," is notable for its seeming audacity: he argues that actuarial tools common to criminal justice in predicting future dangerousness/violations (e.g., among parolees, or candidates for terror events) are counterproductive because through their use of strategies such as racial profiling, they produce racial distortion in the prison system, diverge from effective crime prevention philosophies, and bias the public's conception of fair and just punishment. The primary means through which racial distortion emanates, Harcourt explains, is when a profiled group is less elastic (essentially, less responsive) to policing: "If minorities are less responsive to policing than whites, then their decrease in offending will be outweighed, in absolute numbers, by the more elastic responsiveness of whites—that is, by the increased offending of whites in response to the fact that they are being policed less. This is true despite the fact that the overall number of successful police interventions *increases*—despite the fact that the police are detecting and punishing *more* crime." Instead, Harcourt calls for an embrace of *randomization* by making justice determinations independent (blind) to predictions of future dangerousness. This orientation, he asserts, would not mean searching without probable cause or "pulling prison sentences out of a hat"—it simply means that criminal justice would get out of the business of making decisions based on (highly imperfect, and counterproductive) predictions of future dangerousness, and would instead (for example) randomly sample from among suspects where there is probable cause. Harcourt closes by locating the merits and anticipated outcomes of randomization in policing within broader issues of punishment (e.g., criminal sentencing).

Chapter 17

Space, Place, and Immigration
New Directions for Research on Police Stops

Brian J. Stults, Karen F. Parker, and Erin C. Lane

A report from the U.S. Department of Justice on incarceration trends shows that the incarceration rate of blacks is six times the rate of whites (2,209 vs. 366 per 100,000 residents), while Hispanics are twice as likely to be incarcerated as whites (759 vs. 336 per 100,000).[1] While researchers offer a number of different perspectives on the high rates of crime and arrests among blacks,[2] other scholars consider the cause to stem from law enforcement officers' use of race as a determinant for stopping, searching, or arresting black individuals.[3] In light of this research, the study of race, ethnicity, and policing has taken on a more prominent role in criminology. Still, little is known about police stops of Hispanics specifically, and even fewer studies take into account the spatial context of neighborhood boundaries when assessing the relationship between race, ethnicity, and police behavior. The neglect of these two issues persists, though recent research clearly implies the relevance of community to police behavior.[4]

In this chapter we attempt to make both substantive and methodological contributions to the macro-level study of race, ethnicity, and policing. Our research takes into account two important yet neglected considerations in criminological literature. First, we assess the influence of structural conditions not only on police stops of white and black drivers, but also on police stops of Hispanic drivers in the Miami-Dade area. This is particularly important for a study set in Miami-Dade County, where over 50% of the population is Hispanic, but the inclusion of Hispanics in criminological research is becoming increasingly essential across all regions of the United States. Indeed, the U.S. Census shows that there were eighteen cities with a Hispanic population of more than 50% in the year 2000, ranging from Paterson, NJ, to Laredo, TX, and the Hispanic population continues to grow. Based on a 2005 Census release, the percentage of persons of Hispanic origin reached 14.5% nationally, a 16% increase since the 2000 Census estimates taken just five years earlier, making Hispanics the largest minority group in the United States.[5] While research on the relationship between Hispanic immigration and criminal activity is conflicting, if not dominated by myths,[6] recent research finds that Hispanics are stopped, frisked, and searched at rates higher than whites.[7] Moreover, Hispanics tend to face high levels of concentrated disadvantage in addition to blocked opportunities (such as employment) due to communication barriers.[8] By examining stop rates of Hispanic drivers, along with rates for white and black drivers, our theoretically guided study allows for a systematic examination of race, ethnicity, and police stop rates beyond the black and white analysis that is typical in prior research.

Second, residential patterns of racial groups and concentrated disadvantage characterize many U.S. cities, concentrating blacks and Hispanic immigrants into poor, disorganized urban communities. We examine the relationship between the spatial and contextual characteristics of neighborhoods and police stop rates for different racial and ethnic groups using spatial statistical methods. By conducting a contextual analysis, we are able to examine whether police stop rates are influenced by the characteristics of neighborhoods, and whether those effects are different depending on the race and ethnicity of the driver. Spatial methods also allow us to take into account the likelihood that neighborhoods in close proximity to one another share characteristics that may influence the extent to which white, black, and Hispanic drivers are stopped by police. As prior research suggests, the likelihood of being stopped by the police may be related to characteristics in a given neighborhood, as well as the characteristics of geographically proximate areas.[9] Thus we advance the literature by directly addressing the role of spatial dependence.

Race, Ethnicity, and Policing: The Spatial and Theoretical Issues

Racial profiling by police officers, defined as the process by which law enforcement agents use race as a key factor in determining whether to stop, search, cite, or arrest minority group members, has recently become a prominent focus within the field of criminology.[10] Recent findings from studies on the differential treatment of minorities by police officers illustrate the importance of further research in this area.[11] The phrase "driving while black" was coined in the early 1990s as the United States began to see a rise in public awareness and disapproval of discriminatory practices by police officers.[12] But such a phrase neglects to consider the differential treatment of Hispanics, even though a handful of recent studies suggest that Hispanics are stopped and searched at higher rates than whites.[13] For example, Fagan and Davies' study of "stop and frisk" practices of NYPD officers revealed that blacks are six times more likely to be searched than whites, and Hispanics were four times more likely to be searched than whites.[14] The researchers also found that blacks and Hispanics were significantly more likely to be stopped—two to three times more likely than whites on average. Langan and colleagues also found that blacks and Hispanics were more likely to report that they had been ticketed, arrested, handcuffed, or searched by police.[15]

Few studies have examined police officers' decisions to conduct stops within the spatial and ecological context of neighborhoods. Of those works, many find that police officers' decision-making processes are affected by neighborhood conditions.[16] For example, Smith examined the effects of various community characteristics on police behaviors, including crime rates, racial composition, poverty levels, and other socioeconomic factors.[17] He found that individuals were three times more likely to be arrested if encountered within poor and minority neighborhoods. Fagan and Davies, discussed briefly above, also focused on the impact of structural indicators on police behavior.[18] They found that structural characteristics associated with social disorganization were the most significant predictors of race-specific "stop and frisk" practices by NYPD officers. Because blacks and Hispanics are more likely to live in disadvantaged areas, their exposure to, and contact with police is greater than for whites, who are far less likely to live in areas of extreme disadvantage.[19]

The above literature provides evidence of disparities in police contact for racial and ethnic groups, and ties police-citizen encounters to the ecological context in which the contact occurs. That is, police officers are likely to make distinctions between communities,[20] or what Werthman and Piliavin called "ecological contamination."[21] However, studies often fail to offer multiple constructs based on community-level theories or employ statistical techniques that account for spatial interdependence. We outline the relevance of these two considerations below.

Spatial Dimensions

An impressive list of studies have found that "neighborhoods matter" to crime rates.[22] Increasingly, researchers are also recognizing the importance of not only the context of a neighborhood itself, but also the broader geographic context within which it is situated.[23] The movement toward incorporating spatial analytic methods into the criminological study of communities is motivated by both methodological and theoretical concerns. First, one persistent methodological concern of community-based research has been the selection of an appropriate set of boundaries for delineating neighborhoods in a meaningful way. The majority of research has settled on the use of census tracts, in large part because more data are readily available for this geographical approximation of neighborhoods than for any other. However, the social processes and interactions that are of interest to criminologists are likely to transcend these, or any other, artificial boundaries. To the extent that this is true, levels of any unmeasured predictors are likely to be similar among proximal neighborhoods resulting in a condition called spatial autocorrelation.[24] The typical consequence of this statistical problem is an artificially increased likelihood of finding factors that significantly influence the outcome of interest. The spatial methods used in this study are able to mitigate concerns about the artificiality of administratively imposed boundaries by explicitly modeling the spatial interdependence of proximal neighborhoods.

Beyond their methodological importance, spatial models also allow researchers to account empirically for the theoretical likelihood that what occurs in one neighborhood is directly influenced by what occurs in nearby neighborhoods. While prior research indicates that police officers are influenced by contextual factors of the neighborhoods where they encounter citizens, these previous studies did not utilize spatial analytic methods to explicitly identify the impact of *surrounding* neighborhood characteristics on the likelihood of police-citizen contacts and officers' decisions to conduct race-specific stops. That is, surrounding neighborhoods—in terms of their structural characteristics or potential impact on the level of exposure in citizen/police encounters—are crucial to understanding rates of police stops.

Theoretical Considerations and Hypotheses

Because ecological studies of crime have long argued that neighborhood character-istics shape the social interactions of those persons found within the geographical space, spatial interdependence is as theoretically relevant as it is methodologically. Our interest in the ecological concentration of police stops for racial and ethnic groups leads us to include two perspectives that have been consistently used in the study of communities and crime—concentrated disadvantage and social disorganiza-tion.[25] That is, while these perspectives have been used to explain the linkages be-tween structural characteristics and crime, we build on these insights to provide a rationale for incorporating community-based theories into the study of race, ethnic-ity, and policing.

Racial Composition, and Concentrated Disadvantage

In his book *The Truly Disadvantaged*, Wilson describes how the changing structure of the urban economy of the 1970s contributed to rising poverty and its concentra-tion among minority groups in the inner city.[26] While Wilson argued that the rise in the concentration of poverty was largely due to the relocation of manufacturing jobs, Massey and colleagues document the role that racial residential segregation patterns play in this process.[27] The impact of urban disadvantage has been found in studies of property crime,[28] drug arrest rates,[29] and urban violence.[30]

When linking concentrated disadvantage to police action, a key component is that the geographical concentration of disadvantage is more pronounced among minority groups (blacks and Hispanics) as compared to whites. Even the poorest whites are significantly less likely to live in areas of concentrated disadvantage.[31] On the other hand, where blacks and whites increasingly share residential space, racial antagonism and conflicts between racial groups can result, which contributes to the use of social control against minority groups.[32] Consequently, police officers will be more likely to use race as a factor in their decisions to conduct stops.[33] To address the possibil-ity that the racial composition of a given area may differentially influence the rate at which police stop race and ethnic groups, we hypothesize that:

> H1: In areas where the proportion of whites is higher, we expect to see higher rates of stops of black and Hispanic drivers, and lower rates of stops for white drivers.

Research has shown that as disadvantage increases, levels of political disloca-tion also increase, which can have the effect of creating strained relationships be-tween blacks and police officers. Much literature demonstrates that police relations with black communities have long been strained.[34] This effect may also be true for Hispanics; a Bureau of Justice Statistics study showed that Hispanics were far less likely to call the police, yet far more likely to have police-initiated contact with offi-cers than are whites or blacks.[35] Because police officers are influenced by community characteristics, particularly in regard to the racial and economic characteristics of the community,[36] high levels of unemployment and disadvantage will increase the likelihood of citizen contact with police, thus increasing the likelihood of police stops.[37] That is, indicators of disadvantage are likely to contribute to the stops of blacks and Hispanics as compared to whites due to the overrepresentation of these groups in areas of concentrated disadvantage. We therefore hypothesize that:

H2: As levels of concentrated disadvantage increase, the rates of stops involving black and Hispanic drivers will also increase.

Social Disorganization Theory

Based on the work of Shaw and McKay, the social disorganization perspective argues that ecological conditions in urban areas contribute to crime indirectly through ineffective social control.[38] Research by Sampson, for example, suggests that family dissolution and joblessness weaken informal social control networks within a community, which in turn leads to higher rates of crime and urban violence.[39] Previous studies have linked social disorganization indicators to urban rates of crime or violence.[40]

In terms of the current study, we argue that police respond to the breakdown in informal social control, which occurs when urban neighborhoods face residential instability, ethnic diversity, and signs of disorder such as the presence of vacant housing units. Neighborhood residents in such areas must rely on formal social control, which translates into greater police presence, thus increasing the likelihood of police-citizen encounters and, subsequently, traffic stops. Officers' perceptions of neighborhoods characterized by social disorganization may also influence stop behavior, independent of crime rates. For example, areas characterized by vacant housing units and unsupervised youth "hanging out" on street corners may cause officer suspicion of community residents. Importantly, these indicators should lead to an increase in traffic stops, regardless of race or ethnicity. Therefore, while we theorize that measures of social disorganization increase police-initiated traffic stops, we expect to observe no significant racial differences in the effect of social disorganization on stop rates:[41]

H3: As indicators of social disorganization increase, we expect to find an increase in traffic stops in general, regardless of race or ethnicity of the driver.

Data and Methods

In our attempt to assess the spatial dynamics of race, ethnicity, and policing in the context of Miami communities, we merged a series of different data sources, including information on police-citizen contacts involving officers from the Miami-Dade Police Department, census data (including race-specific measures of theoretical predictors), crime reports from the Miami-Dade Police Department, and demographic and behavioral indicators of police officers who were involved in police-citizen stops.

All data sources were carefully merged and aggregated to the census-tract level to allow for neighborhood-level analysis. While the census tract is not explicitly considered a neighborhood, census tracts have been used in extant research as the unit of analysis that corresponds to actual community boundaries.[42]

The police-citizen contact data file was compiled by the Miami-Dade Police Department (MDPD) in cooperation with a team of academic researchers. The data file used in this study was part of a larger funded project to detect and identify patterns of racial bias in police behaviors (see http://www.miamidade.gov/irp/racial_profiling_reports.asp). One component of the research was to collect stop data, which required MDPD police officers to complete Citizen Contact Forms after each traffic stop from February 1, 2001, to October 31, 2001. As a part of the research design, MDPD officers were trained on how to fill out the citizen contact cards. During training sessions, issues that they experienced were taken into account in the contact card design.[43] While officers were trained on how to use the contact cards, the information provided on the card was left for the officer to determine at the time of the stop. That is, the officer's identification of the driver's race or ethnicity was based on the officer's perceptions and information collected by the officer at the time of the stop. Thus officers were to use their own judgments based on visual/verbal interaction. To illustrate, if an officer believes the person he is stopping is white, but on approach hears him speak with a Hispanic accent and sees a Hispanic newspaper in the car, the officer would then determine that the person is Hispanic. Types of information collected on the contact card included the reason for the stop, driver race, driver age, driver residence, and numerous other details such as the time and duration of the stop and vehicle description. Composed of 66,109 traffic stops, the data set also includes geocoding of stop locations, aggregated to the census tract. Due to the inability to geocode some incidents, however, the original sample is reduced by 7.3% to a total of 61,255 stops.[44]

Dependent Variables

The dependent variables are based on the number of traffic stops by police officers involving blacks, Hispanics, and (non-Hispanic) whites. Specifically, computation of the dependent variables involved dividing race- and ethnic-specific police stops by the number of each group in the census tract, multiplied by ten thousand. While we are interested in assessing the variation in race and ethnic stop rates across neighborhoods, it is important to note that the racial distribution of drivers within an area may differ from the racial distribution of the residential population of that area, partially due to differences in car ownership by race, travel patterns, and out-of-area drivers.[45] We used the natural log of the rates in the spatial multivariate analysis.

Independent and Control Variables

Explanatory and control measures were retrieved from multiple sources, including the 2000 Census, crime statistics, and detailed police officer data provided to us by the Miami-Dade Police Department. We begin by operationalizing the theoretical indicators derived by relevant census data.

Variables used to reflect disadvantage include race- and ethnic-specific measures of poverty, joblessness (persons not employed age sixteen and older), and female-headed households with children. Each of these measures has been included in analyses of disadvantage and crime in extant research.[46]

Indicators of social disorganization were also selected based on existing literature and our efforts to tap the level of ethnic diversity in Miami-Dade communities. To capture Hispanic presence, we include two indicators: the percentage of Spanish-speaking population speaking English "not well" or "not at all," age five and above, and the percentage of Hispanics in the total population.[47] More commonly used indicators of social disorganization were also included, such as residential mobility and percentage of vacant housing units.

In terms of control indicators, policing research has shown racial differences in officers' use of force, particularly involving blacks, which lead us to control for incidents of police use of force in our study.[48] The Miami-Dade Police Department provided discipline reports on each of the 1,659 officers in the database over a five-year period (1997–2000), which we used to calculate the rate of use of force within the past five years.[49] The natural log of this rate was used in our multivariate models. We also control for the level of criminal activity in a given area via the violent crime rate per ten thousand residents, as well as the percentage males of driving age (fifteen or older) in the population.

Statistical Analysis

It is typical in macro-level research involving units such as neighborhood, cities, and counties for the independent variables to be strongly associated with one another. For example, neighborhoods characterized by high levels of poverty often also have high rates of unemployment and female-headed households. This leads to a potential statistical problem referred to as multicollinearity, which can make it difficult to detect significant effects and can lead to overall instability in the results. After computing the indicators described above and performing collinearity diagnostics, we found that a number of our indicators were highly correlated, particularly among the disadvantage and Hispanic measures. One way to avoid problems with multicollinearity, and the approach that we follow here, is to combine empirically and conceptually similar indicators into composite indexes.[50] Using the technique of principal components analysis, we found that the indicators of disadvantage and social disorganization can be combined to produce separate, theoretically distinct indices of *concentrated disadvantage* and *Hispanic presence*.

The disadvantage index includes three measures of disadvantage that are consistent with extant literature as indicators of urban disadvantage, disaggregated by race.[51] The measures of the percentage of persons living below poverty level, percentage jobless, and the percentage of female-headed households with children under eighteen were highly correlated, and thus loaded together, creating the race- and ethnic-specific dis-advantage indices. The Hispanic index reflects a combination of the percentage of Hispanics in the total population and percentage of the Spanish-speaking population age five and older that speaks English "not well" or "not at all." These two conceptu-ally distinct indices emerged from the factor analysis and are treated as independent variables in the multivariate models. After incorporating these two indices, further tests indicated that collinearity is not problematic in the models. Detailed descriptive statistical information on our dependent and independent indicators is provided in the appendix.

Spatial Analysis

Neighborhoods are not isolated entities, but exhibit interdependency where events that occur in one area affect events that occur in spatially proximate areas. While previous studies have found support for this claim, particularly when revealing that homicide events are not randomly distributed across space, the spatial proximity of police behavior has yet to be examined.[52] Much like criminal behavior, police stops are not randomly distributed. Rather, as hypothesized above, we would expect a spa-tial clustering of police stops in areas where certain theoretically defined neighbor-hood characteristics are also present.

To explore this possibility, we begin our analysis by visually illustrating the geo-graphic clustering of police stops and the percentage of whites in the residential population. We suspect that the racial composition of a neighborhood will influence the rate at which each group is stopped by the police, but we also suspect that the composition of *surrounding* neighborhoods will matter. If this is the case, we would expect to find, for example, that clusters of neighborhoods with particularly high percentages of whites coincide geographically with clusters of neighborhoods with high rates of black police stops. To examine this possibility for each racial and ethnic group, we present a series of maps that draw on a statistic referred to as a Local Indi-cator of Spatial Association (LISA maps).[53]

To generate the maps, we first used localized Moran scatter plots to classify neighborhoods into one of the following five categories of spatial autocorrelation: (1) low-low, for neighborhoods that have a low percentage of whites and are also in close proximity to neighborhoods with low percentages of whites; (2) low-high, for neighborhoods that have low percentages of whites in the population, yet are in close proximity to neighborhoods with high percentages; (3) high-low, for neighborhoods with high percentages of whites in the population but are proximate to neighbor-hoods with low levels; (4) high-high, for areas with high percentages of whites in the population that are also in close proximity to areas with high levels; and (5) not significant, for areas where there was not significant geographic clustering.[54] These categories are represented in the maps by different fill patterns. For example, neigh-borhoods that have a large percentage of whites and are surrounded by similarly white neighborhoods are described as "high-high" and are indicated by a light gray background.

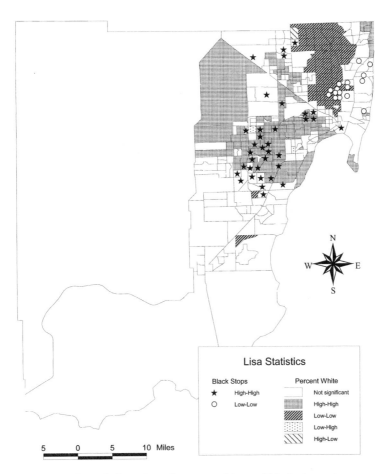

Figure 17.1. Spatial clustering of percent white and black stop rate

We then generate the same spatial typology for racial and ethnic police stop rates and use symbols to represent significant clusters, where stars indicate significant high-high values (e.g., neighborhoods that have high rates of race-specific stops, which are in close proximity to other neighborhoods with high stop rates of that race or ethnic group) and circles reflect low-low values.

The role of spatial proximity in police stops is clear in each of the figures, in that there is a high degree of spatial clustering of police stop rates for all racial and ethnic groups. For whites, blacks, and Hispanics there are clusters of neighborhoods across Miami-Dade County that are characterized by high group-specific police stop rates that tend to be in close proximity to other neighborhoods that also have high stop rates. The figures show that white composition is also clustered in space, where predominantly white neighborhoods tend to be contiguous with other predominantly white neighborhoods, and neighborhoods with a small proportion of whites tend to be near similarly nonwhite neighborhoods. This spatial clustering provides evidence for the importance of directly incorporating spatial dependence when analyzing

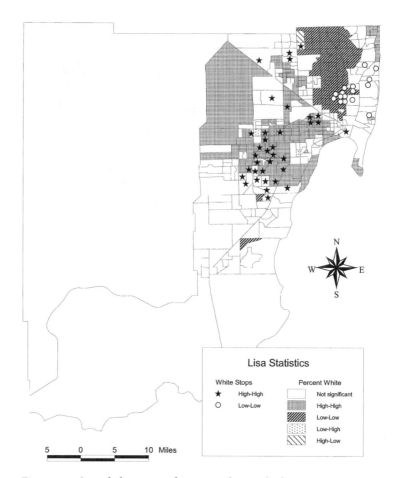

Figure 17.2. Spatial clustering of percent white and white stop rate

police stops, since without doing so, any conclusions based on statistical analyses are likely subject to the problems associated with spatial autocorrelation and must be viewed with caution.

Beyond emphasizing the statistical importance of spatial analytic methods, the clustering shown in each of the figures also allows us to draw some substantive conclusions concerning the degree of overlap between the spatial distribution of police stop rates and the presence of whites in Miami neighborhoods. First, as shown in figure 17.1, while we find that areas with high rates of police stops involving black drivers are in close proximity to other neighborhoods where the police stops of black drivers are also high (represented by stars), we further find that the clustering of high black stop rates tends to be in areas where there is also spatial clustering of whites in the population (represented by a light gray background). Conversely, clusters of low police stop rates involving black drivers (represented by circles) tend to occur where there are clusters of low white population percentage (represented by a dark gray background). That is, there is a clustering of high rates of black stops in areas

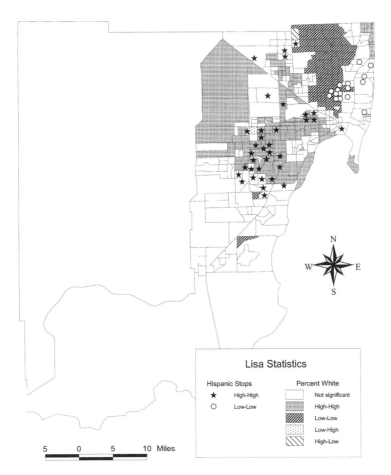

Figure 17.3. Spatial clustering of percent white and Hispanic stop rate

where the presence of whites is also high, and low rates of black stops in areas where the clustering of the white population is also low.

Second, high stop rates of whites and Hispanics tend to cluster in areas where the clustering of whites is either significantly high or low. For example, figure 17.2 shows that there is spatial clustering of high rates of police stops involving white drivers in areas where high percentages of whites also cluster. But there is also spatial clustering of high rates of police stops involving white drivers in areas where the percentage of whites in the population is low. The same pattern is found for Hispanic stop rates, as shown in figure 17.3. In this way, the spatial distribution or cluster patterns of white and Hispanic stop rates are virtually identical. Overall, this spatial analysis reveals distinct patterns between clustering of black stop rates when compared to stop rates of whites and Hispanics in terms of the racial composition of the neighborhoods. That is, the spatial clustering of stop rates among both white and Hispanic drivers is high in areas where the concentration of whites is either high or low. On the other hand, clustering of high rates of black stops only occurs in areas where the percentage of whites in the population is high. We continue to explore this relationship, and other theoretically specified ones, in our spatial multivariate analysis.

Results

We used the GeoDa statistical software program to estimate maximum likelihood spatial regression models of police stop rates for white, black, and Hispanic drivers.[55] When estimating these sorts of spatial regression models, a determination must be made as to which type of spatial dependence is most likely. We have informally described both types in the preceding discussion, but at this point it is helpful to draw a more formal distinction between the two. The form of dependence where unmeasured variables are expected to be highly correlated across proximal neighborhoods is often referred to as "spatial error," which most closely resembles the notion of spatial autocorrelation.[56] An alternative form occurs when the characteristics of one neighborhood are directly and substantively influenced by the characteristics of surrounding neighborhoods. Often referred to as "spatial lag," this form of dependence is more general in the sense that it also subsumes the spatial error form of dependence. As discussed above, spatial lag models conform to our theoretical approach that specifies spatial dependence as a substantive, as well as methodological, concern, and diagnostic tests indicate that the spatial lag model provides the best fit of the data. The results from our spatial lag regression models are displayed in table 17.1.[57] We organize our discussion around our major theoretical arguments and the results of our theorized effects.

Racial Composition and Concentrated Disadvantage

Given the association between the concentration of whites and the rate of group-specific stops shown in the figures, we first focus our attention on the relationship between the racial composition of neighborhoods and rates of stops for each racial and ethnic group. Not surprisingly, we find a positive relationship between the percentage of whites and the black stop rate, while an inverse relationship is found between percentage of whites and the rate at which police officers stop white and Hispanic drivers. This indicates that black stops are more prevalent in areas where there are large concentrations of whites, with the opposite effect for white and Hispanic stops. This is largely congruent with our earlier interpretation of the LISA maps. While the finding for black and whites stops supports our first hypothesis, the negative relationship between the concentration of whites in Miami neighborhoods and Hispanic stops was unexpected. This may be due to the unique racial makeup of Miami-Dade communities, as illustrated in the appendix. That is, while whites make up an estimated 67.5% of the Miami residential population, approximately 54% of the population indicates that they are of Hispanic origin. Given that a large proportion of whites in the Miami-Dade area have Hispanic origins, the likelihood that this group experiences race-biased behavior by police officers decreases. This finding is supported by the cluster patterns found in the maps above, where Hispanic and white stop rates were

TABLE 17.1

Maximum Likelihood Coefficients (and Standard Errors) from the Spatial Regression Equations for Race- and Ethnic-Specific Police Stops Rates in Miami-Dade Communities

	Police Stops by Race or Ethnicity of Driver					
	Black		White		Hispanic	
Concentrated Disadvantage Indicators						
% White Population	0.020**	(.004)	−0.017**	(.003)	−0.008*	(.004)
Concentrated Disadvantage Index[a]	0.001	(.002)	0.002	(.002)	−0.002	(.004)
Social Disorganization Indicators						
Hispanic Index	0.006	(.003)	−0.003	(.002)	−0.008**	(.003)
Residential Mobility	−0.012*	(.006)	−0.003	(.004)	0.00004	(.005)
% Vacant Housing Units	0.021	(.010)	−0.008	(.007)	−0.009	(.008)
Control Variables						
Officer Use of Force Rate (log)	0.797**	(.044)	0.784**	(.030)	0.529**	(.065)
Violent Rate	0.003	(.001)	0.003**	(.001)	0.002	(.001)
% Males in Driving Population[a]	−0.019	(.010)	0.009	(.009)	−0.007	(.013)
Spatial Autocorrelation	0.275**	(.084)	0.563**	(.062)	0.529**	(.065)
Constant	1.95**		2.95**		2.87**	
Pseudo R-Square	.675		.892		.862	
Log Likelihood	−380.7		−370.7		−418.9	
AIC	779.4		759.4		855.8	
N	273		334		336	

*p<.05, **p<.01.
[a] Denotes indicators are race- or ethnic-specific; white indicators exclude persons of Hispanic origins.

clustered in a nearly identical fashion. On the other hand, black drivers experience higher rates of stops by police officers. This finding suggests that racial antagonisms in the Miami area are largely white-black ones, where social control in the form of police stops are concentrated among blacks more so than other groups.

Our findings of a negligible impact of urban disadvantage on racially disaggregated stop rates was also unexpected given the wealth of research documenting the significant impact of disadvantage on neighborhood level crime rates.[58] Neighborhood levels of concentrated disadvantage do not significantly contribute to the stop rates of race and ethnic groups; rather the racial composition of the area appears to be more pertinent to explaining geographical distributions of group-specific police stop rates.[59]

Social Disorganization Theory

A fundamental component of social disorganization theory is that structural barriers influence community-level crime rates, regardless of the race and ethnic characteristics of the residents. Following that principle, we hypothesized that effects of social disorganization indicators would not differ significantly across the group-specific models. Contrary to these expectations, social disorganization constructs differ in significance and magnitude when influencing white, black, and Hispanic stop rates. The Hispanic index has a strong, negative impact on rates of Hispanic stops. That is, an influx of Spanish speakers and a rise in the Hispanic population leads to lower rates at which Hispanics are stopped by local police. Instability in the residential population decreases black stops, while the presence of vacant units, as an indicator of community disorder, has a negligible effect on stop rates, regardless of the race and ethnicity of drivers.

While this analysis offers multiple measures of social disorganization, few indicators derived from the perspective were found to influence rates of traffic stops involving Hispanics or blacks, and none of the social disorganization indicators contribute to our understanding of white stop rates. On the whole, when estimating the relevance of racial composition, disadvantage, and social disorganization indicators to the macro-level study of race, ethnicity, and policing, we find support for theoretical constructs indicative of composition and community disorganization, but concentrated disadvantage is less relevant to police stop rates than has been found in neighborhood-level studies of criminal behavior.

Controls

Police literature consistently reports that the use of force increases with the size of the minority population, as well as when poverty concentration levels are elevated.[60] Informed by this police literature, we control for the level of use of force in our analysis. As shown in table 17.1, we find the expected significant positive relationship between police use-of-force rates and stop rates in all three models. Concerning the impact of other controls, we find that higher rates of violent crime increase the rates at which white drivers are stopped. On the other hand, the level of violent crime in the area does not appear to effect stop rates of Hispanic and black drivers. We also find that an increase in the presence of male drivers does not influence the rates of police stops. That is, the percentage of black, white, or Hispanic male drivers in the area is not significantly related to the police stop rates of these specific groups.

Discussion and Conclusions

The goal of this research was to determine the effects of indicators derived from community-based theories on police stops of blacks, whites, and Hispanics. In addition to conducting theoretically driven research on race, ethnicity, and policing, which has been neglected, we also attempted to address other overlooked issues.[61] First, given the dramatic growth of the Hispanic population across the country, due both to immigration and high fertility rates, we think it is essential to examine not only white and black police stops, but also Hispanic stops. With its large Hispanic, black, and white population, the Miami-Dade area provides a useful context for us to estimate the influence of structural predictors on rates of Hispanic stops as well as those involving black and white drivers. Second, we perform spatial analysis to account for spatial clustering of race- and ethnic-specific police stop rates in relation to the structural characteristics of neighborhoods, as well as surrounding areas. That is, our spatial analysis allows us to account for the influence of other areas in close proximity on the potential for police-citizen contacts within Miami-Dade communities. We now turn to the discussion of our key findings.

Racial Composition and Concentrated Disadvantage

The spatial analysis suggests clear evidence that racial composition affects rates of police stops for race and ethnic groups. In our multivariate models, we find that a higher percentage of whites in a given area increases the rate of black stops, while both white and Hispanic stops decrease. These findings may lend support to the racial threat hypothesis, although much of this research examines the size of the minority population instead of the majority group.[62] The racial threat hypothesis posits that minority groups become increasingly "threatening" to whites as their presence in the population grows, which then increases the use of formal social control to reduce this threat. And there is considerable support for the impact of black percentage on police size, expenditures, use of deadly force, and total arrest rate.[63] Our exploratory spatial analysis takes a different path by showing an apparent clustering of black stops in areas where the white population is high. This pattern may well be the result of formal social control being implemented in the form of police stops when blacks travel to white neighborhoods. Furthermore, we find a cluster of low black stop rates in areas where the white population is also low, which also supports this claim. The multivariate results further support this interpretation by revealing differences in the relationship between racial composition and race- and ethnic-specific stop rates. That is, we find a strong, statistically significant, positive relationship between percentage of whites and black stop rates, while this indicator yields an inverse relationship with white and Hispanic stop rates.

The presence of a large percentage of white residents decreases stop rates of white and Hispanic drivers. This finding was unexpected as Hispanics, much like blacks, are often overrepresented in the criminal justice system[64] and in economically disadvantaged areas.[65] However, we find that the influence of the percentage of whites on the rate of police stops of Hispanics is nearly identical to that of white stops. This finding, as briefly discussed above, is most likely attributable to the unique racial composition of Miami-Dade County, where the majority of white residents are of Hispanic origin. Furthermore, this finding is also consistent with the *contact hypothesis* that residential propinquity increases contact between racial groups and fosters positive attitudes among them.[66] In fact, a growing body of recent research supports the contact hypothesis, showing that higher levels of racial and ethnic integration tend to correspond with lower levels of antagonism and intergroup conflict.[67] Thus, the level of white-Hispanic residential integration is an important consideration in future research on police behavior or the use of formal social control. Yet we failed to find support for the predicted relationship between concentrated disadvantage and stops rates of race and ethnic groups.

Social Disorganization Theory

Multiple indicators of social disorganization were employed in testing our hypothesis concerning the impact of community disorder on police stop rates for all groups. Adhering to this ideology, we predicted higher rates of stops of black, Hispanic, and white drivers as characteristics consistent with neighborhood disorganization increased. However, our results suggest differences in the influence of social disorganization indicators on stop rates by race and ethnicity. Black stops were significantly influenced by residential mobility, yet not in the predicted direction. We find that white stops rates are largely unaffected by social disorganization levels in Miami communities, while Hispanic stop rates were influenced only by the Hispanic index. Here, areas where the presence of persons with Hispanic origin is growing, the stop rates of Hispanics decrease. This may be due to the fact that recent immigrant communities are significantly less likely than native-born Americans to participate in criminal activity. Recent immigrants are also less violent,[68] and immigration tends to reduce crime.[69] These findings suggest that immigration is an important consideration for future research in police behavior at the macro level.

Overall our goal in this research was to contribute methodologically and substantively to the study of spatial and contextual features of neighborhoods, and how these characteristics can contribute to the study of race, ethnicity, and police behavior. We accomplished this by examining variations in police stops relative to the racial composition, level of disadvantage, and social disorganization of neighborhoods in Miami-Dade County. We also account for the spatial proximity of these neighborhoods to other neighborhoods that exhibit similar patterns of race and ethnic police stops. But our study is not without limitation. One limitation might just be our locale —the Miami-Dade area. While Miami-Dade County is in some ways ideal because of the area's divergent racial and ethnic makeup, and because the area is not commonly studied in the policing literature, the relatively large presence of Hispanics in this area (approximately 54% of the total population) might make this area rather unique.[70] In that way, our findings would not be generalizable to other urban areas where Hispanics make up only a small proportion of the population. On the other hand, with continuing rapid increases in the Hispanic population, the number of majority-Hispanic cities, counties, and metropolitan areas across the country will continue to grow, further underscoring the importance of directly incorporating Hispanics, and specifically Hispanic immigration, into our theoretical and empirical models. Indeed, we believe this is an essential avenue for future research on the contextual factors that influence police behavior.

Our examination also reveals significant spatial dependence in group-specific police stop rates, which is unique to the existing literature. Our exploratory spatial data analysis showed considerable spatial clustering in police stops for all three groups, as well as clustering in the racial composition of neighborhoods. The association between these spatial characteristics, which was visually observable in the LISA maps, was confirmed by our spatial regression models. Future research should make greater use of geographic information systems and spatial analytic tools to examine the influence of spatial dependence, both as an important statistical control against overestimating the effects of theoretically derived predictors, and as a tool for evaluating the substantive ways in which proximal neighborhoods influence one another.

Appendix: Mean (and Standard Deviation) Statistics for Dependent and Predictor Variables

TABLE 17.A1

	Black		White		Hispanic	
Dependent Variables						
Stop Rate (log)	5.13	(2.69)	4.97	(2.25)	4.60	(2.28)
Concentrated Disadvantage Indicators						
% White Population	67.53	(30.1)	67.53	(30.12)	67.53	(30.12)
Concentrated Disadvantage Index[a]	48.75	(30.7)	28.19	(19.8)	38.92	(19.66)
Poverty[a]	23.91	(19.5)	17.96	(13.5)	19.69	(13.2)
Jobless[a]	19.89	(13.5)	14.95	(9.8)	17.96	(7.8)
Female-Headed Household with Children[a]	14.52	(14.6)	6.47	(6.04)	8.17	(6.1)
Social Disorganization Indicators						
Hispanic Index	70.58	(41.7)	71.23	(41.8)	69.84	(41.3)
Percent Hispanic	54.36	(29.1)	54.36	(29.1)	54.36	(29.1)
Percent Spanish Speaking Pop. 5 or Older "Not Well" or "Not Well at All"	18.89	(15.5)	18.89	(15.5)	18.89	(15.5)
Residential Mobility	49.06	(12.6)	49.06	(12.6)	49.06	(12.6)
% Vacant Housing Units	7.62	(8.0)	7.62	(8.0)	7.62	(8.0)
Control Variables						
Officer Use of Force Rate (log)	4.11	(2.0)	4.11	(2.0)	4.11	(2.0)
Violent Rate	46.87	(199.3)	46.87	(199.3)	46.87	(199.3)
% Males in Driving Population[a]	47.47	(7.4)	48.67	(5.5)	47.94	(5.1)

[a] Denotes indicators are race- or ethnic-specific; white indicators exclude persons of Hispanic origins.

NOTES

1. Bureau of Justice Statistics, *Prison and jail inmates*

2. Black, *The manners and customs of the police*; Hawkins, *Ethnicity, race, and crime;* Mann, *Unequal justice*; Russell-Brown, *The color of crime*, just to name a few

3. Engel et al., "Theory and racial profiling"; Harris, "'Driving while black'"; Lamberth, "Driving while black"; Lundman and Kaufman, "Driving while black"; Weitzer and Tuch, "Perceptions of racial profiling"

4. Chambliss, "Policing the ghetto underclass"; Smith "The neighborhood context of police behavior"; Smith, "Police response to interpersonal violence"

5. U.S. Bureau of the Census, *American community survey*

6. Hagan and Palloni, "Sociological criminology and the mythology of Hispanic immigration and crime"; Lee and Martinez, "Social disorganization revisited"

7. See Fagan and Davies, "Street stops and broken windows"; Langan et al., *Contacts between police and the public*; Spitzer, *The New York City Police Department's "stop and frisk" practices*

8. Lee et al., "Does immigration increase homicide?"; Martinez, *Latino homicide*

9. Cohen and Tita, "Diffusion in homicide"; Messner et al., "The spatial patterning of county homicide rates"; Morenoff et al., "Neighborhood inequality, collective efficacy, and the spatial dynamics of urban violence"

10. Engel et al., "Theory and racial profiling"

11. Harris, "'Driving while black'"; Lamberth, "Driving while black"; Lundman and Kaufman, "Driving while black"; Weitzer and Tuch, "Perceptions of racial profiling"

12. Harris, "'Driving while black'"

13. Chambliss, "Policing the ghetto underclass"; Fagan and Davies, "Street stops and broken windows"; Smith, "The neighborhood context of police behavior"

14. Fagan and Davies, "Street stops and broken windows"

15. Langan et al., "Contacts between police and the public"

16. Engel and Calnon, "Examining the influence of drivers' characteristics"; Lundman, "Driver race, ethnicity, and gender"; Meehan and Ponder, "Race and place"; Smith and Alpert, "Searching for direction"; Werthman and Piliavin, "Gang members and the police"

17. Smith, "The neighborhood context of police behavior"

18. Fagan and Davies, "Street stops and broken windows"

19. Krivo and Peterson, "The structural context of homicide"; Sampson and Wilson, "Toward a theory of race, crime, and urban inequality"

20. Weitzer and Tuch, *Race and policing in America*; Smith, "The neighborhood context of police behavior"

21. Werthman and Piliavin, "Gang members and the police"

22. Morenoff et al., "Neighborhood inequality, collective efficacy, and the spatial dynamics of urban violence"; Sampson et al., "Assessing neighborhood effects"; Smith, "The neighborhood context of police behavior"; Terrill and Mastrofski, "Situational and officer-based determinants of police coercion"

23. Morenoff et al., "Neighborhood inequality, collective efficacy, and the spatial dynamics of urban violence"; Sampson et al., "Beyond social capital"

24. Anselin et al., "Spatial analyses of crime"

25. Bursik, "Social disorganization and theories of crime and delinquency"; Krivo and Peterson, "The structural context of homicide"; Morenoff et al., "Neighborhood inequality, collective efficacy, and the spatial dynamics of urban violence"; Rose and Clear, "Incarceration, social capital, and crime"; Sampson, "Urban black violence"; Sampson and Wilson, "Toward a theory of race, crime, and urban inequality"

26. Wilson, *The truly disadvantaged*

27. Massey and Eggers, "The ecology of inequality"; Massey and Denton, *American apartheid*; Massey et al., "Disentangling the causes of concentrated urban poverty"

28. Akins, "Racial segregation and property crime"

29. Parker and Maggard, "Structural theories and race-specific drug arrests"

30. Krivo and Peterson, "The structural context of homicide"; Ousey, "Homicide, structural factors, and the racial invariance assumption"; Parker and McCall, "Structural conditions and racial homicide patterns"; Parker et al., "Racial threat, concentrated disadvantage, and social control"

31. Krivo and Peterson, "The structural context of homicide"; Sampson and Wilson, "Toward a theory of race, crime, and urban inequality"

32. Blalock, *Toward a theory of minority group relations*; Brown and Warner, "Immigrants, urban politics, and policing in 1900"

33. Warren et al., "Driving while black"

34. Barlow and Barlow, "Racial profiling"; Brown and Frank, "Race and officer decision making"; Kerner Commission, *National advisory commission on civil disorder*

35. Bureau of Justice Statistics, *Police use of force*

36. Smith, "The neighborhood context of police behavior"; Smith et al., "Equity and discretionary justice"

37. It is important to note that police officers are not deployed evenly or randomly across geographic areas. As policing literature has long documented, police patrols are higher in hot

spots (Sherman and Weisburd, "General deterrent effects"; Koper, "Just enough police presence") and when proactive policing models and specialized units are used (Sherman et al., *Preventing crime*). Disproportionate police deployment can also be based on "calls for service" (Grogger and Ridgeway, "Testing for racial profiling"; Ridgeway, "Assessing the effect of race bias in post-traffic stop outcomes"), which tend to be higher in disadvantaged neighborhoods (see also McMahon et al., *How to correctly collect and analyze racial profiling data*).

38. Shaw and McKay, *Juvenile delinquency and urban areas*

39. Sampson, "Urban black violence"

40. Ousey, "Homicide, structural factors, and the racial invariance assumption"; Parker and McCall, "Structural conditions and racial homicide patterns"; Sampson, "Urban black violence"; Williams and Flewelling, "The social production of criminal homicide"

41. For details, see Ousey, "Homicide, structural factors, and the racial invariance assumption"

42. Morenoff et al., "Neighborhood inequality, collective efficacy, and the spatial dynamics of urban violence"

43. To further take into account errors and other issues pertaining to filling out the cards early in the project, the stop data used here are based on all citizen contact cards filled out from April 1 to Oct 31, 2001. That is, the first two months of data collection, when the officers were still learning and getting use to the idea of filling out cards, were not included in the analysis. Second steps were taken in the research design to estimate if the level of stops made by officers during the study period (i.e., a work "slowdown") and the nature of the information recorded on the contact cards (i.e., race and ethnicity information) was accurate. These efforts to validate the data indicated no significant discrepancies.

44. In terms of missing data, an analysis was conducted to determine if missing cards (i.e., addresses that could not be geocoded because of missing information or errors) differed significantly from known (precisely matched or geocoded) ones and no evidence was found.

45. Smith and Alpert, "Searching for direction"; Grogger and Ridgeway, "Testing for racial profiling"; Ridgeway, "Assessing the effect of race bias in post-traffic stop outcomes"; Warren et al., "Driving while black"

46. Land et al., "Structural covariates of homicide rates"; Ousey, "Homicide, structural factors, and the racial invariance assumption"; Parker and McCall, "Structural conditions and racial homicide patterns"; Stretesky et al., "Space matters"

47. According to the 2000 Census data, 54% of all Miami-Dade residents are of Hispanic origin. Within the Hispanic population, the Miami-Dade area is largely composed of Cubans (681,399 total; over 30% of the total population and over 52% of all Hispanics). The next largest groups are Nicaraguans and Hondurans, each having a little under 100,000 persons.

48. Alpert and MacDonald, "Police use of force"; Mastrofski et al., "Police disrespect toward the public"; Terrill and Mastrofski, "Situational and officer-based determinants of police coercion"; Terrill and Reisig, "Neighborhood context and police use of force"

49. We considered including both use of force and officer complaints in our multivariate models, but issues with collinearity contribute to instability in our parameter estimates when both variables were in the models. We chose to use rate of use-of-force reports because it is more conservative and because of the seriousness of these reports. Further, simply including measure of complaints against officers would not provide an accurate picture, as it does not take into account the result of the complaints.

50. Land et al., "Structural covariates of homicide rates"; Parker and McCall, "Structural conditions and racial homicide patterns"; Stretesky et al., "Space matters"

51. Krivo and Peterson, "The structural context of homicide"; Massey and Eggers, "The

ecology of inequality"; Ousey, "Homicide, structural factors, and the racial invariance assumption"; Wilson, *The truly disadvantaged*

52. Messner et al., "The spatial patterning of county homicide rates"; Morenoff et al., "Neighborhood inequality, collective efficacy, and the spatial dynamics of urban violence"

53. Anselin, "Local indicators of spatial association"

54. All spatial analysis presented in this chapter were generated using a weights matrix based on queen contiguity. Alternative specifications were examined, including rook contiguity and the six nearest neighbors, but the results were substantively identical.

55. Anselin, *GeoDa 0.9 user's guide*

56. Anselin, *Spatial econometrics*

57. We re-estimated the models using spatial Poisson regression. The results did not change substantively from those reported here.

58. Kubrin and Weitzer, "Retaliatory homicide"; Krivo and Peterson, "The structural context of homicide"; Parker and McCall, "Structural conditions and racial homicide patterns"

59. Liska and Chamlin, "Social structure and crime control"; Parker et al., "Racial threat, concentrated disadvantage, and social control"

60. Smith, "The neighborhood context of police behavior"; Terrill and Mastrofski, "Situational and officer-based determinants of police coercion"; Terrill and Reisig, "Neighborhood context and police use of force"

61. Engel and Calnon, "Theory and racial profiling"; Engel et al., "Examining the influence of drivers' characteristics"

62. Liska and Chamlin, "Social structure and crime control"; Parker et al., "Racial threat, concentrated disadvantage, and social control"

63. Liska and Chamlin, "Social structure and crime control"; Jackson and Carroll, "Race and the war on crime"; Liska et al., "Perspectives on the legal order"

64. Walker et al., *The color of justice*

65. Martinez, *Latino homicide*

66. Allport, *The nature of prejudice*

67. Sigelman and Welch, "The contact hypothesis revisited"; Ellison and Powers, "The contact hypothesis"; Oliver and Wong, "Intergroup prejudice"

68. Martinez, *Latino homicide*

69. Lee et al., "Does immigration increase homicide?"; Martinez, *Latino homicide*

70. See Alpert et al., "Investigating racial profiling"; Martinez, "Incorporating Latinos and immigrants"

REFERENCES

Akins, Scott. 2003. Racial segregation and property crime: Examining the mediating effect of police strength. *Justice Quarterly* 20:675–695.

Allport, Gordon W. 1954. *The nature of prejudice*. Boston: Beacon Press.

Alpert, Geoffrey P., and John M. MacDonald. 2001. Police use of force: An analysis of organizational characteristics. *Justice Quarterly* 18:393–409.

Alpert, Geoffrey, Roger Dunham, and Michael R. Smith. 2007. Investigating racial profiling by the Miami-Dade Police Department: A multimethod approach. *Criminology and Public Policy* 6 (1): 201–232.

Anselin, Luc. 1988. *Spatial econometrics*. Boston, MA: Kluwer Academic.

———. 1995. Local indicators of spatial association—LISA. *Geographical Analysis* 27:93–116.

———. 2003. *GeoDa 0.9 user's guide.* Spatial Analysis Laboratory, Urbana-Champaign, IL: University of Illinois.

Anselin, Luc, Jacqueline Cohen, David Cook, Wilpen Gorr, and George Tita. 2000. Spatial analyses of crime. In *Criminal Justice, 2000,* ed. David Duffee. Washington, DC: OJP.

Barlow, David E., and Melissa Hickman Barlow. 2002. Racial profiling: A survey of African American police officers. *Police Quarterly* 5:334–358.

Black, Donald. 1980. *The manners and customs of the police.* New York: Academic Press.

Blalock, Hubert M. 1967. *Toward a theory of minority group relations.* New York: Wiley.

Brown, Robert A., and James Frank. 2006. Race and officer decision making: Examining differences in arrest outcomes between black and white officers. *Justice Quarterly* 23:96–126.

Brown, M. Craig, and Barbara D. Warner. 1992. Immigrants, urban politics, and policing in 1900. *American Sociological Review* 57:293–305.

Bureau of Justice Statistics. 1997. *Police use of force: Collection of national data.* Washington, DC: U.S. Government Printing Office.

———. 2002. *Prison and jail inmates at Midyear 2001, NCJ 191702.* Washington, DC: U.S. Government Printing Office.

Bursik, Robert J. 1988. Social disorganization and theories of crime and delinquency: Problems and prospects. *Criminology* 26:519–551.

Chambliss, William. 1994. Policing the ghetto underclass: The politics of law and law enforcement. *Social Problems* 41:177–194.

Cohen, Jacqueline, and George Tita. 1999. Diffusion in homicide: exploring a general method for detecting spatial diffusion processes. *Journal of Quantitative Criminology* 15:451–493.

Ellison, Christopher G., and Daniel A. Powers. 1994. The contact hypothesis and racial attitudes among black Americans. *Social Science Quarterly* 75:385–400.

Engel, Robin S., and Jennifer M. Calnon. 2004. Examining the influence of drivers' characteristics during traffic stops with police: Results from a national survey. *Justice Quarterly* 21:49–90.

Engel, Robin S., Jennifer M. Calnon, and Thomas J. Bernard. 2002. Theory and racial profiling: Shortcomings and future directions in research. *Justice Quarterly* 19:249–274.

Fagan, Jeffrey, and Garth Davies. 2000. Street stops and broken windows: *Terry,* race, and disorder in New York City. *Fordham Urban Law Journal* 28:457–504.

Grogger, Jeffrey, and Greg Ridgeway. 2006. Testing for racial profiling in traffic stops from behind the veil of darkness. *Journal of the American Statistical Association* 101:878–887.

Hagan, John, and Alberto Palloni. 1999. Sociological criminology and the mythology of Hispanic immigration and crime. *Social Problems* 46:617–632.

Harris, David A. 1997. "Driving while black" and all other traffic offenses: The Supreme Court and pretextual traffic stops. *Journal of Criminal Law and Criminology* 87:544–582.

Hawkins, Darnell J. 1995. *Ethnicity, race, and crime: Perspectives across time and place.* Albany: State University of New York Press.

Jackson, Pamela I., and Leo Carroll. 1981. Race and the war on crime: The sociopolitical determinants of municipal police expenditures in 90 non-southern U.S. cities. *American Sociological Review* 46:290–305.

Kerner Commission. 1968. *National advisory commission on civil disorder.* Washington, DC: U.S. Government Printing Office.

Koper, Christopher. 1995. Just enough police presence: reducing crime and disorderly behavior by optimizing patrol time in crime hot spots. *Justice Quarterly* 12:649–671.

Krivo, Lauren J., and Ruth D. Peterson. 2000. The structural context of homicide: Accounting for racial differences in process. *American Sociological Review* 65:547–559.

Kubrin, Charis E., and Ronald Weitzer. 2003. Retaliatory homicide: Concentrated disadvantage and neighborhood culture. *Social Problems* 50:157–180.

Lamberth, John. 1998. Driving while black: A statistician proves that prejudice still rules the road. *Hartford.* http://www.hartford-hwp.com/archives/45a/192.html.

Land, Kenneth C., Patricia L. McCall, and Lawrence E. Cohen. 1990. Structural covariates of homicide rates: Are there any invariances across time and social space? *American Journal of Sociology* 95:922–963.

Langan, Patrick A., Lawrence A, Greenfield, and Steven K. Smith. 2001. *Contacts between police and the public: Findings from the 1999 national survey.* Washington, DC: U.S. Bureau of Justice Statistics.

Lee, Matthew T., and Ramiro Martinez. 2002. Social disorganization revisited: Mapping the recent immigration and black homicide relationship in northern Miami. *Sociological Focus* 35:363–380.

Lee, Matthew T., Ramiro Martinez, Richard Rosenfeld, et al. 2001. Does immigration increase homicide? Negative evidence from three border cities. *Sociological Quarterly* 42:559–580.

Liska, Allen E., and Mitchell B. Chamlin. 1984. Social structure and crime control among macrosocial units. *American Journal of Sociology* 90:383–395.

Liska, Allen E., Joseph J. Lawrence, and Michael Benson. 1981. Perspectives on the legal order: The capacity for social control. *American Journal of Sociology* 87:413–26.

Lundman, Richard. 2004. Driver race, ethnicity, and gender and citizen reports of vehicle searches by police and vehicle search hits: Toward a triangulated scholarly understanding. *Journal of Criminal Law and Criminology* 94:309–349.

Lundman, Richard, and Robert L. Kaufman. 2003. Driving while black: Effects of race, ethnicity, and gender on citizen self-reports pf traffic stops and police actions. *Criminology* 41:195–221.

Mann, Coramae R. 1993. *Unequal justice: A question of color.* Indianapolis: Indiana University Press.

Martinez, Ramiro. 2002. *Latino homicide: Immigration, violence, and community.* New York: Routledge Press.

———. 2007. Incorporating Latinos and immigrants into policing research. *Criminology and Public Policy* 6 (1): 601–609.

Massey, Douglas S., and Nancy A. Denton. 1993. *American apartheid: Segregation and the making of the underclass.* Cambridge, MA: Harvard University Press.

Massey, Douglas S., and Mitchell L. Eggers, 1990. The ecology of inequality: Minorities and the concentration of poverty, 1970–1980. *American Journal of Sociology* 96:1153–1188.

Massey, Douglas S., Mitchell L. Eggers, and Nancy A. Denton. 1994. Disentangling the causes of concentrated urban poverty. *International Journal of Group Tensions* 24:267–316.

Mastrofski, Stephen D., Michael D., Reisig, and John D. McCluskey. 2002. Police disrespect toward the public: An encounter-based analysis. *Criminology* 40:519–552.

McMahon, J., Garner, J., Davis, R., and Kraus, A. 2002. *How to correctly collect and analyze racial profiling data: Your reputation depends on it!* Washington, DC: U.S. Government Printing Office.

Meehan, Albert J., and Michael C. Ponder. 2002. Race and place: The ecology of racial profiling African American motorists. *Justice Quarterly* 19:399–430.

Messner, Steven F., Luc Anselin, Robert D. Baller, et al. 1999. The spatial patterning of county homicide rates: An application of exploratory spatial data analysis. *Journal of Quantitative Criminology* 15:423–450.

Morenoff, Jeffrey D., Robert J. Sampson, and Stephen W. Raudenbush. 2001. Neighborhood inequality, collective efficacy, and the spatial dynamics of urban violence. *Criminology* 39: 517–558.

Oliver, J. Eric, and Janelle Wong. 2003. Intergroup prejudice in multiethnic settings. *American Journal of Political Science* 47:567–582.

Ousey, Graham. 1999. Homicide, structural factors, and the racial invariance assumption. *Criminology* 37:405–426.

Parker, Karen F., and Scott Maggard. 2005. Structural theories and race-specific drug arrests: What structural factors account for the rise in race-specific drug arrests over time? *Crime and Delinquency* 51:521–547.

Parker, Karen F., and Patricia L. McCall. 1999. Structural conditions and racial homicide patterns: A look at the multiple disadvantages in urban areas. *Criminology* 37:447–477.

Parker, Karen F., Brian J. Stults, and Stephen K. Rice. 2005. Racial threat, concentrated disadvantage, and social control: Considering the macro-level sources of variation in arrests. *Criminology* 43:1111–1134.

Ridgeway, Greg. 2006. Assessing the effect of race bias in post-traffic stop outcomes using propensity scores. *Journal of Quantitative Criminology* 22:1–29.

Rose, Dina R., and Todd R. Clear. 1998. Incarceration, social capital, and crime: Implications for social disorganization theory. *Criminology* 36:441–479.

Russell-Brown, Kathryn K. 1998. *The color of crime: Racial hoaxes, white fear, black protectionism, police harassment, and other macroaggressions.* New York: New York University Press.

Sampson, Robert J. 1987. Urban black violence: The effect of male joblessness and family disruption. *American Journal of Sociology* 93:348–382.

Sampson Robert J., Jeffrey Morenoff, and Felton Earls. 1999. Beyond social capital: Spatial dynamics of collective efficacy for children. *American Sociological Review* 64:633–660.

Sampson, Robert J., Jeffrey D. Morenoff, and Thomas Gannon-Rowley. 2002. Assessing neighborhood effects: Social processes and new directions in research. *Annual Review of Sociology* 28:443–478.

Sampson, Robert J., and William J. Wilson. 1995. Toward a theory of race, crime, and urban inequality. In *Crime and Inequality*, eds. John Hagan and Ruth D. Peterson. Stanford, CA: Stanford University Press.

Shaw, Clifford R., and Henry D. McKay. 1942. *Juvenile delinquency and urban areas: A study of rates of delinquents in relation to differential characteristics of local communities in American cities.* Chicago: University of Chicago Press.

Sherman, Lawrence W., and David A. Weisburd 1995. General deterrent effects of police patrol in crime "hot spots": A randomized, controlled trial" *Justice Quarterly* 12:625–648.

Sherman, Lawrence W., Denise Gottfredson, Doris MacKenzie, John Eck, Peter Reuter, and Shawn Bushway. 1997. *Preventing crime: What works, what doesn't, what's promising.* College Park, MD: National Institute of Justice. http://www.ncjrs.gov/works/.

Sigelman, Lee, and Susan Welch. 1993. The contact hypothesis revisited: Interracial contact and positive racial attitudes. *Social Forces* 71:781–795.

Smith, Douglas A. 1986. The neighborhood context of police behavior. In *Communities and crime*, eds. A. J. Reiss and M. Tonry. Chicago: University of Chicago Press.

———. 1987. Police response to interpersonal violence: Defining the parameters of legal control. *Social Forces* 65:767–782.

Smith, Douglas, Christy Visher, and Laura Davidson. 1984. Equity and discretionary justice: The influence of race on police arrest decisions. *Journal of Criminal Law and Criminology* 75:234–249.

Smith, M., and G. Alpert. 2002. Searching for direction: Courts, social science, and the adjudication of racial profiling claims. *Justice Quarterly* 19:673–703.

Spitzer, Elliot. 1999. *The New York City Police Department's "stop and frisk" practices: A report to the people of the state of New York from the office of the attorney general.* Albany: New York Attorney General's Office.

Stretesky, Paul B., Amie M. Schuck, and Michael J. Hogan. 2004. Space matters: An analysis of poverty, poverty clustering, and violent crime. *Justice Quarterly* 21:817–841.

Terrill, William, and Stephen D. Mastrofski. 2002. Situational and officer-based determinants of police coercion. *Justice Quarterly* 19:215–248.

Terrill, William, and Michael D. Reisig. 2003. Neighborhood context and police use of force. *Journal of Research in Crime and Delinquency* 40:291–321.

U.S. Bureau of the Census. *American community survey, 2005.* Washington, DC: U.S. Department of Commerce.

Walker, Samuel, Cassia Spohn, and Miriam De Lone. 2001. *The color of justice: Race, ethnicity, and crime in America.* 2d ed. New York: Wadsworth.

Warren, Patricia, Donald Tomaskovic-Devey, and William R. Smith. 2006. Driving while black: Bias processes and racial disparity in police stops. *Criminology* 44:709–738.

Weitzer, Ronald, and Steven A. Tuch. 2002. Perceptions of racial profiling: Race, class, and personal experience. *Criminology* 40:435–457.

———. 2006. *Race and policing in America: Conflict and reform.* Cambridge: Cambridge University Press.

Werthman, Carl, and Irving Piliavin. 1967. Gang members and the police. In *The police: Six sociological essays*, ed. David Bordura. New York: John Wiley.

Williams, Kirk R., and Robert L. Flewelling. 1988. The social production of criminal homicide: A comparative study of disaggregated rates in American cities. *American Sociological Review* 53:421–431.

Wilson, William J. 1987. *The truly disadvantaged: The inner city, the underclass, and public policy.* Chicago: University of Chicago Press.

Chapter 18

Revisiting the Role of Latinos and Immigrants in Police Research

Ramiro Martínez Jr.

The scarcity of research on Latinos and policing is one of the most enduring short-comings in the development of race/ethnicity and the criminal justice system scholarship.[1] This oversight is curious since scholars in the 1931 Wickersham Commission report focused on police treatment of Mexican immigrants, a topic central to early work on immigrants and crime, and one pivotal to early studies on the effects of Mexican immigration into the United States.[2] Pioneering research on Latinos and police also include overlooked studies on Border Patrol mistreatment of "illegal" aliens,[3] state police abuse of the Mexican origin in Texas,[4] and the "contentious relationship" between ethnic minorities and urban police departments during World War II.[5] The latter was highlighted by the "zoot-suit hysteria" and police misconduct in the 1940s, when the singling out of Latinos by various facets of the criminal justice system laid the foundation for protracted animosity between the Los Angeles Police Department (LAPD) and the city's Mexican-origin community.[6] In fact, scholars contend that even in the absence of solid data on this topic, the LAPD and general community stereotyped Mexican-origin youth as inherently delinquent for the last half of the 20th century.[7]

Even though early research existed on immigrants and the police, contemporary research on Latino perception of local police, encounters with federal police agents (i.e., , or ICE), or city police by residents of heavily immigrant communities across the United States is scarce.[8] This includes the failure to examine the consequences of stepped-up enforcement of federal immigration policies by local police, or police raids on businesses in search of "illegal" immigrants.[9] The current lack of research is obvious. For example, a recent search of articles published between 1990 and 2006 with keywords "Hispanic" or "Latino" and "police" in *Criminal Justice Abstracts* netted 68 items, but a similar search using "Black" or "African American" and "police" provided 485 articles on this topic. Scholars have understandably directed attention to Black and White attitudinal differences toward the police and documented the perception and prevalence of police misconduct in some African American areas, in particular extremely poor communities, where aggressive police strategies are concentrated.[10] Still researchers interested in examining racial and ethnic variations in experiences with the police and other criminal justice agencies should extend attention to Latinos and foreign-born newcomers.

This failure to conduct research is even more apparent after considering that over the last two decades social scientists have argued that not only is the Latino experience quite different from those of non-Latino Whites and Blacks,[11] but that distinctions also exist among Latino subgroups.[12] Beyond immigration and legality status, these include variations in terms of historical, cultural, political, demographic, economic, and religious patterns.[13] While these differences across the social sciences disciplines are beyond the scope of this chapter, it is again important to recall that ethnic and immigrant groups require attention by criminologists. More important, a historical foundation exists for Latinos and crime, and that starting place should be used to inform contemporary studies while ensuring that the incorporation of Latinos is a routine development in criminological research.

In the remainder of this chapter I argue that when examining Latinos, other immigrant group members (e.g., Caribbean Blacks in southern Florida or Asians on the West Coast) who usually reside in economically disadvantaged communities must also be taken into account. This work would probe the impact of neighborhood disadvantage on violent crime, which is also linked to research on satisfaction with policing in extremely poor communities.[14] Scholars have noted that legal cynicism and dissatisfaction with police are both intertwined with levels of neighborhood disadvantage, an effect that trumps racial differences in attitudes toward the police, even after controlling for neighborhood violent crime rates.[15] Moreover, ecological characteristics of policing also include the use of physical and deadly force at the city level, officer misconduct in police precincts, and slower response times in communities, highlighting research that attitudes toward the police may be a function of neighborhood context and even determinants of police killings. These actions hit young Black males harder than others, but the impact on Latino youths is an open issue, as is the impact of recent immigration and the role of immigrant concentration in shaping police encounters. These issues potentially appear to construct a different story with respect to Latinos, violence, and the police.

This chapter provides suggestions for future research and a conclusion reminding the readers that U.S. society is now a multi-ethnic population and the time has come to routinely examine Latinos in police research. But I also remind the readers that some pioneering research, together with early immigration and crime studies, included issues relevant to Latinos and the police. Prior to turning to what we do and don't know about Latinos and police, I emphasize the consequences of ignoring Latinos.

Why Latino Research?

The need to transcend the Black-White paradigm of U.S. policing research is obvious. Latinos comprise both native (60%) and foreign-born (40%) individuals, making them a very diverse group in terms of historical background, their manner of reception, and year of entry into the United States.[16] The latter is important to acknowledge because the Latina/o population has experienced substantial growth since 1960 due to both rapid migration from Latin American and the Caribbean, and high levels of fertility. Latinos are now the largest racial/ethnic minority group in the United States, a trending that will likely continue to grow in the future.[17]

This growth has implications for the nation. Stereotypes regarding the Latina/o population proliferate in U.S. public discourse, fueled by media reports and perpetuated by some politicians, most of which goes unchallenged even while it contributes to the notion that Latino immigrants are a dangerous threat to the nation.[18] These include stereotypes that they are uneducated peasants, drug dealers, on welfare, and crime-prone.[19] Moreover, new policy mandates for tightening the border and singling out "illegals" who are primarily of Mexican origin is encouraged by politicians and commentators for the sake of enhancing "national security," including the deployment of the National Guard, building a fence on the border between Mexico and the United States, and labeling of "undocumented" immigrants as criminal aliens.[20] Immigration policy now reflects national concern about local crime even though there is little systematic research linking these topics.

The failure to conduct research in this area also means our understanding of Latinos, relative to that of Whites and Blacks, will be underdeveloped. This change requires researchers to consider if Latinos are similarly exposed to police tactics as Black or White residents. If so, does immigration shape the manner in which Latinos are treated by the criminal justice system? As noted above, undocumented Latinos are now being targeted by local and federal police agencies, singled out from others in disadvantaged communities, which sets the stage for potential conflict between police and residents. Much like the neighborhoods studied by pioneering researchers in 1931, these activities are concentrated in economically disadvantaged communities, reminding us that economic conditions shape crime, violence, and perhaps police reactions to residents in some poor neighborhoods. But the outcomes of criminal justice tactics are under-examined for Latinos, and many questions remain unanswered about Latinos and reactions to the police.

For example, while much of the Latino growth is in traditional settlement areas in the southwestern United States, there is substantial movement to new Latino destinations or places where few Latinos resided in previous decades.[21] The emergence of anti-immigrant laws or ordinances have proliferated in these new destination points, aimed at preventing "illegals" from securing housing, and punishing business owners and allowing local police to search for "illegals" or ask about legality status, an issue typically in the federal domain. Take, for example, Hazleton, Pennsylvania, a city with about twenty-three thousand residents, about 5% of whom were Hispanic/Latino according to the 2000 census. In 2006, local officials passed the Illegal Immigration Relief Act, a measure that would have resulted in racial profiling, discrimination, and denial of benefits to legal immigrants. This ordinance imposed fines of up to one thousand dollars to landlords who rented to "illegal" immigrants, denying business permits to corporations who employed undocumented immigrants, and made English the official language of the village.[22] Latinos bore the brunt of the latest anti-immigrant hysteria in Hazelton and other places that implemented similar restrictions.[23] According to Rodríguez and colleagues, the consequences of anti-immigrant/

Latino initiatives are that *all* Latinos, legality aside, are singled out and presumed illegal by politicians and the media.[24]

It is important to note that not only is the composition of the Latino population (e.g., Mexican, Cuban, Puerto Rican, Salvadoran, Dominican, etc.) unlike most other racial and ethnic groups, but they also differ from earlier immigrants. They are growing and estimated to represent about a quarter of the U.S. population by 2030. While still concentrated in the southwestern United States, Latinos are also drawn to other regions of the country and are working in diverse sectors of the economy. Last, they are connected to the home country and send money back to their country of birth. Remittances or money sent from immigrants in the United States is an important source of revenue for many countries in Latin America and the Caribbean. The decline of that money is ominous, shapes interactions with others left behind, as well as their absorption to U.S. society, and potentially creates more poverty in the home country.[25]

Historical Background

This chapter, in part, is motivated by the reminder that early research on Latinos/immigrants has not adequately informed contemporary police studies. In *¡Pobre Raza!* F. Arturo Rosales[26] contributed to the nascent body of research on Latino crime and policing. Rosales made an important contribution to our understanding of early 1900s immigration trends, including how Mexican immigrants responded to the U.S. criminal justice system, to crime and violence within that system, and to non-Latino White hostility that emerged during the era of massive Mexican immigration between the 1890s and the 1930s. Moreover, Rosales reminds us that contemporary border problems, such as the smuggling of liquor, drugs, and "illegal" immigrants, also existed then, as did concerns about an emerging "Mexican problem," a foible attributing an innate propensity to crime to newcomers from south of the Rio Grande.[27] This stereotype is still reflected in contemporary society by politicians and the media but now targets "illegal immigrants," a demographic group most likely to include persons of Mexican origin.[28]

Regarding policing, Rosales[29] contends that immigrant Mexicans experienced the "negative presence of the police system" as soon as they landed on the U.S. side of the border. For example, drawing on historical data including the 1931 Wickersham Commission *Report on Crime and the Foreign Born*, he notes that many Mexican immigrants were disproportionately arrested for disorderly conduct,[30] a "color-less charge" used to "keep them in check," and that "indiscriminate dragnets and brutal arrest tactics" were routine in "Latino" communities.[31] These activities were undoubtedly linked to the widespread stereotype that Mexicans were inclined toward criminality.[32] Warnshuis[33] also quotes a Chicago police sergeant stating, "You know, Indian and Negro blood does not mix very well. That is the trouble with the Mexican; he has too much Negro blood," a stereotype that persists to this day.[34]

In fact, not only did the notion that Mexican Americans were "born criminals" endure, it eventually contributed to national concern about this group, culminating in harsh measures singling out Mexican youths and young adults.[35] By 1943 many residents of the Los Angeles barrios believed that the LAPD regularly violated the rights of Mexican Americans and that police misconduct in the Latino community was routine.[36] In one nationally publicized incident, between June 3 and June 10, 1943, white military service members, civilians, and police officers attacked Mexican American youths dressed in distinct "zoot suits." Many were assaulted and left naked in the LA streets. During the riot, LAPD officers allowed service members to beat and strip the zoot suiters, usually arresting the Mexican American youths for disturbing the peace. In fact, police officers only arrested a handful of service members but jailed over six hundred Mexican Americans.[37] With the police watching on, service members entered bars, theaters, dance halls, restaurants, and even private homes in search of victims. By the end of the rioting, service members were targeting *all* Mexican Americans and even some African Americans. Clearly, for some hostility and animosity defined the relationship between the Latino community and the LAPD long after the end of World War II.[38]

Yet the extent of this enmity was largely ignored by criminology researchers as they directed their attention to race and crime for several decades and ignored Latinos. This is unfortunate because a research foundation existed that could have been built on to inform current research, including learning more from the well-documented police mistreatment of Mexican immigrants in the early half of the century. As early as 1919 the Texas Rangers, a state police force, were involved in "murder; intimidation of citizens; threats against the lives of others; torture and brutality; flogging, horse-whipping, pistol whipping, and mistreatment of suspected persons; incompetency; and disregard for the law."[39] The Texas Rangers were also routinely engaged as strike-breakers and took an active role in protecting employers' interests, interfered with the peaceful farmworkers' strike of 1966–67, and arrested persons without cause.[40]

Moreover, Julian Samora[41] reminds us that the Border Patrol regularly restricted or relaxed the movement of "illegal Mexican aliens" according to business cycles in the agriculture industry. The relaxation of immigrant policy, border-crossing enforcement, and the employment of "illegals" were linked to ebbs and flows in the U.S. border economy. When crops needed to be harvested, the Border Patrol participated in getting workers into the field. In contrast, when crop season ended and the workers were no longer needed, the number of apprehensions and deportations spiked.[42] Thus the periodic roundup of "illegals" was linked to agriculture industry policy and law enforcement practices.

Professor Samora[43] recognized that routine Border Patrol operations were shaped by concerted efforts to thwart "invasions of illegals" crossing the U.S.-Mexican border. Periodic moral panics or financial recessions created concern about the "growing number of Mexican aliens" and undocumented workers. There was also anxiety about perceived high levels of crime at the border and the potential of disease-ridden "aliens" entering the United States. During periods of heightened fear, Border Patrol officers saturated entry points; in 1952 alone they deported over half a million undocumented Mexicans when the decision was made to "close" the border.[44] Over time the Border Patrol redirected their attention elsewhere, and the number of deportees dropped throughout the late 1950s and 1960s.[45]

Thus racial or ethnic conflict existed for some time in the southwestern United States, and future researchers should draw from work produced by these early scholars. The hostile relationship between the Chicano/Latino community and the LAPD lingered for most of the last century, and the long-simmering tension from the LAPD/Zoot suit riot in 1942 should have informed scholars concerned with urban minority group crime, in particular those interested in the causes of urban riots and how police exacerbate racial/ethnic tensions (such as during the 1992 LA riots). The role that border police play in tightening up enforcement of immigration policy is also not new, and work of early scholars laid the foundation for contemporary work on immigration/race/ethnicity and police. Next I draw from a body of ecological research on race and crime, and close with suggestions for future studies.

Latino/Immigrant Neighborhood Disadvantage and Police Research

Much of the recent research on race/ethnicity and crime has been conducted at the aggregate level with official data reported to the police.[46] This literature does not ponder individual variations in propensity to engage in criminal offending, but instead considers variations in violent crime victimization or offending across places such as metropolitan areas or cities.[47] Ecological research on crime and violence also draws attention to the relationship between race/ethnicity and place, whether that is the city, metropolitan, or small community, and proposes that racial disparities are linked to the varying social contexts in which population groups exist. A consistent finding in this literature is that violent crime rates, both offending and victimization, are higher in places with greater proportions of Blacks or African Americans, and this finding persists over time.[48] Most of these studies use homicide or violent crime rates, or counts of racial/ethnic-specific violence as the dependent variable since homicides are routinely detected and reported to the police, but even these studies typically focus on Black or White crime differences.[49]

These aggregate level studies have been valuable because they demonstrate the need to consider racial disparities in crime, and in some cases encourage scholars to push conceptions of race and crime to include Latino composition in crime studies.[50] Indeed, researchers have recently evaluated whether the neighborhood conditions relevant for Black and White violence also apply to Latinos.[51] At the forefront of recent ecological analyses of Latino violence is a series of articles[52] based in the city of Miami, Florida, a heavily impoverished multi-ethnic city with large immigrant Latino and foreign-born Black populations, and high-profile inner-city communities (e.g., Little Haiti, Wynwood, Overtown, Liberty City, and East Little Havana, among others). Latino-specific homicides were analyzed either alone or in comparison with models for native-born Blacks and Whites, and sometimes immigrant Haitians, Jamaicans, or Latino groups such as the Mariel Cubans.[53] All these racial/ethnic/immigrant groups reside in high-crime and disadvantaged communities in need of police services, and regularly encounter police officers, but the extent of positive or negative police-citizen interactions is not clear. Moreover, the Miami studies also note that Latinos usually follow the pattern familiar among Blacks and Whites, in terms of the

all-encompassing effect of concentrated disadvantage or heightened economic problems (although some predictors of Latino homicide are to some extent distinct). Thus
the basic linkages among disadvantage and homicide hold for African Americans,
Haitians, and Latinos in the city of Miami, even in areas dominated by immigrants.
This suggests that a need exists to further examine the interactions between police
and residents, and to explore levels of police treatment, since by extension the study
of Latinos and police encounters at the community level could vary from studies of
Blacks or Whites.

This body of work is important because there is a strong relationship between economic disadvantage, affluence, and violent crime, and this connection has received a
great deal of attention given the racial/ethnic differences in the strength of the association between crime and socioeconomic context at the community level. To a large
extent, this notion is rooted in the claim by Sampson and Wilson that the "sources of
violent crime appear to be remarkably invariant across race and rooted instead in the
structural differences across communities, cities, and states in economic and family
organization," which helps explain the racial/ethnic differences in violence.[54] Thus, as
Sampson and Bean note, the premise is that community-level patterns of racial inequality give rise to the social isolation and ecological concentration of the truly disadvantaged, which in turn leads to structural barriers and cultural adaptations that
undermine social organization and in turn shape crime.[55] Therefore "race" is not a
cause of violence, but rather a marker deriving from a set of social contexts reflecting
racial disparity in U.S. society. This thesis has become known as the "racial invariance" in the fundamental causes of violent crime. Still the racial invariance thesis
has rarely been applied to ethnicity, crime, and policing.[56] While other conceptual or
theoretical overviews on Latino crime and delinquency exist,[57] attention is directed
to macro-level approaches since this is where the bulk of Latino violence research is
located.[58]

The study of neighborhood disadvantage and violence generated similar findings
for Blacks and Latinos in the border cities of San Diego and El Paso.[59] Others studies compare and contrast the characteristics of Black, White, and Latino homicides
in Chicago, Houston, and Los Angeles,[60] or control for social and economic determinants of crime thought to shape racial/ethnic disparities across neighborhoods.[61]
None have found evidence that more immigration means more homicides in a given
area.[62] For the most part these studies also lead to the conclusion that the disadvantage link to homicide is similar for African Americans and Latinos.

Therefore the impact of disadvantage holds in the case of Latinos on the border,
and might be extended to ethnic variations in terms of community-level causes of
violence. By extension it also appears that residents of heavily Mexican-origin communities might have enhanced contact with ICE agents concentrated on or around
the Mexican border, who are increasingly engaged in aggressive crime control strategies designed to stop the movement of undocumented workers into the United States.
Much like the case of young African American males, perceptions of unfair and disrespectful treatment, hand in hand with increased targeting by police in search of
immigration violations and undocumented workers to deport, might affect Latino
males' perception of police. As immigration crackdowns increase, young Latino

adults are singled out regardless of nativity status, which shapes views of police and increases distrust and negative interactions with criminal justice officials. The aggressive targeting by police typically occurs in extremely poor Latino communities, and potentially strains relationships between community members and law enforcement officials.

In sum, this section supports the notion that structural disadvantage matters for violence across racial, ethnic, and even immigrant groups, and that it should also matter for police treatment. However, research on neighborhood contexts and police encounters remain in short supply for Latinos. In short, I hope that future research pays closer attention to potential variations across and within groups of various immigration status, ethnic variations, and perceptions of the police at the neighborhood level.

Recommendations for Future Research

There are a number of other important questions that should be addressed in the future. For example, how does economic disadvantage operate to produce violence within and across Latino groups in similar communities, and in turn, do such dynamics shape ethnic differences in dissatisfaction with the police? Moreover, Latinos reside in areas with high levels of disadvantage, but many Latino communities have high levels of labor market attachment, even though typically it might mean employment in menial jobs. What happens when law enforcement targets specific areas populated by working poor Latinos with aggressive policing tactics designed to subdue immigration policy violations but not necessarily crime? Will native-born Latinos be content with these tactics when pulled off the streets in these sweeps along with documented and undocumented immigrants?

It is not surprising that Latinos disapprove of recently stepped-up immigration enforcement. In a recent survey by the Pew Hispanic Center, Latinos wholeheartedly disapprove of a variety of enforcement measures.[63] Over 80% say that immigration enforcement should be left mainly to the federal authorities rather than the local police; about 76% disapprove of workplace raids; 73% disapprove of the criminal prosecution of undocumented immigrants; and 70% disapprove of the criminal prosecution of employers who hire undocumented immigrants. Most Latinos agree that there has been an increase in the past year in immigration enforcement actions targeted at undocumented immigrants, over one-third of surveyed Latinos say there has been an increase in anti-immigrant sentiment, and a majority of Latinos worry about deportation.

The potential rise of profiling among Latinos is an important topic to consider. In the Pew survey, nearly one-in-ten Latinos, both native- and foreign-born, report that in the past year the police or other authorities have stopped them and asked about their immigration status.[64] Thus, will Latino profiling increase hand in hand with police strategies reacting to the increase in immigration across the nation? This tactic has the potential to create fear and distrust of the police in many Latino communities, where some families are "blended" with immigrant parents and children born and raised in the United States. For example, the Border Patrol recently announced plans to check the documents of Texas residents in the Rio Grande Valley in the event of a hurricane evacuation before they are allowed to board evacuation buses.[65] Some residents of course might not have complete identification in the wake of a natural disaster, but others were concerned that this policy would encourage some to not evacuate, further endangering immigrant communities and burdening agencies engaged in evacuation, rescue, and relief efforts.

This of course has a potential parallel in many immigrant communities. As immigrant Blacks move into older African American areas (e.g., Haitians in Miami), should we expect more or less negative encounters with police profiling in Miami, Miami Shores, North Miami, El Portal, Biscayne Park, and adjacent communities? Will border police, in search of immigrant Blacks, profile African Americans, thereby creating even more hostility in a community resistant to police authority? Miami is an ethnically diverse city, with many Latino groups drawing heavily from the Caribbean basin. Perhaps cities like Los Angeles and Houston, where the Mexican-origin population resides alongside Salvadorans and other Latino group members, provide yet another alternative scenario for the study of Latinos and police.

What is the impact of public or police corruption in the home country for Latino immigrants? It is possible that as disadvantaged as conditions may be, that immigrants may use their sending countries, with even worse economic and political conditions, as reference points when assessing their economic position relative to others, but the impact of this process on police encounters requires more research. For example, research on human smuggling suggests that law enforcement officials actively aid in facilitating "illegal" immigrants exiting their country of origin and entering the United States.[66] Public officials openly request money and gifts to facilitate the immigration process to such an extent that workers in the smuggling business consider public corruption a cost of doing business. These activities probably shape immigrants' perceptions, expectations, and tolerance of American policing. It very well might be that prior experience in the sending country has set such a low standard of expectation that it affects what they will tolerate in the United States. The past experiences of immigrants may shape how they perceive police and the criminal justice system. Given the widespread popularity of immigration crackdowns, researchers should reconsider what works and what doesn't when trying to improve police-citizen relations in Latino communities.

The Alpert and colleagues study of racial/ethnic profiling in unincorporated Miami-Dade, and others like it, provides a foundation for scholars eager to conduct research on racial/ethnic variations in police and citizen encounters, especially those curious about the combined effects of police officer and motorist ethnicity.[67] For example, does police officer ethnicity matter when arresting a driver, issuing a citation, or perhaps any other work-related activity? The growth of Latino populations across the United States has probably sparked an interest in increasing ethnic diversity among many police organizations, but relatively few major departments are primarily Latino, and more research is needed on how the changing ethnic composition of these organizations influences the race/ethnicity and crime relationship. Communities of varying racial/ethnic makeup potentially have unstable relations with criminal justice organizations.[68] Alpert and colleagues also provides a foundation to generate an awareness of how Latino police officers interact with others beyond Miami, especially in the southwestern United States where the history of racial/ethnic relations is very different than in the rest of the country.[69] Perceptions of police by family members, friends, coworkers, school mates, and neighbors of Latino residents routinely remains in short supply.

As I noted above, ecological characteristics of policing also include the use of deadly force at the city level, suggesting that attitudes toward the police and police actions may be a function of neighborhood context. This is an important issue to study, as are the differences and similarities between killings by the police and killings by citizens. For illustrative purposes, I provide data on the race and ethnicity of all homicide victims recorded in the Miami Dade Medical Examiners Office (ME) between the years 1956 to 2002, and break out the figures pre- and post-1980, which is the start of dramatic immigration changes in Miami.[70] These data are useful because the ME Office covers the entire county, which consists of about thirty-five municipalities, such the city of Miami, Hialeah, Miami Gardens, Miami Beach, North Miami, Coral Gables, and many others. It also includes unincorporated Miami-Dade County, which covers suburban and rural areas left over once the cities incorporated.

As can be seen in table 18.1, homicides are relatively rare events and homicides by the police are even rarer. For example, there were 414 police killings in Miami-Dade between 1956 and 2002 and almost 13,000 homicides in that period. Yet the racial and ethnic proportions between police and non-police homicide and time periods are strikingly similar. The percentage of police and non-police homicide victims that are White, Black, and Latino are comparable. If police were killing one racial/ethnic group more than another we should expect variations between types of homicide, but few apparently exist. The differences, however, are between time points. As Latinos moved into Miami throughout the 1980s and 1990s, non-Latino Whites moved out. This is reflected in the *lower* percentage of White homicide victims and *higher* percentage of Latino homicide victims in post-1980 years.

Even though only about 20% of the Miami-Dade population was Black during this period, almost half of all police killings involved Black victims, a racial disparity reflected in the non-police or "criminal" homicide data. Latinos are underrepresented and made up about one-third of police and non-police homicides, even though they now compose most of the total county population. Non-Latino Whites are slightly underrepresented relative to their percentage of the population (20%). Although not definitive, these data suggest that characteristics of police and non-police homicides might be more similar than previously thought.

Conclusion

Clearly, scholars should broaden their focus beyond Blacks and Whites to include Latinos and Latino groups whenever possible in future research on police treatment and the criminal justice system. The growth of Latinos across broad sectors of U.S. society requires a renewed focus on multiple racial/ethnic/immigrant groups when

TABLE 18.1
Police and All Homicides by Race and Ethnicity in Miami-Dade County, 1956–2002
(Number of Homicide Victims Followed by Percentage)

| | Years | | | |
| | 1956–1979 | | 1980–2002 | |
Victim Race/Ethnicity	Police Homicide	Non-police Homicide	Police Homicide	Non-police Homicide
White	56 (33.7%)	1347 (31.8%)	37 (14.9%)	962 (11.2%)
Latino	19 (11.4%)	595 (14.1%)	102 (41.1%)	3586 (41.7%)
Black	88 (53%)	2258 (53.2%)	105 (42.3%)	3997 (46.5%)
Other	3 (1.8%)	41 (1.0%)	4 (1.6%)	48 (0.6%)
TOTAL	166 (3.8%)	4241 (96.2%)	248 (2.8%)	8593 (97.2%)

Source: Data collected by author from homicide logs stored in Miami Dade Medical Examiner Office.

comparing experiences with the police across a variety of communities and regions. Related to the growing ethnic diversity across the nation is the renewed concern about the influx of immigrants and the perpetuation of stereotypes on criminal immigrant Latinos by political commentators, policy makers, and residents in areas with growing immigrant Latino populations.[71] The incorporation of Latinos will help scholars of violent crime, serious delinquency, and policing produce a broader understanding of the race/ethnic and violent crime linkages and expand our focus to include the diverse ecological contexts where Blacks, White, and Latinos reside.[72]

In addition, early scholars had an intimate understanding of the role Latinos and immigrants played in crime and police research in their era.[73] Regrettably, that degree of familiarity seems to have disappeared from much of the recent criminology and policing literature, making it difficult to benefit from the insights arising not only from the violent crime and disadvantage literature but also other areas in the social sciences, especially those found in recent immigration studies.[74] Until we bring Latinos and immigrants back into the study of policing, our understanding of race/ethnicity will be underdeveloped at best.

NOTES

This chapter was initiated while I was a Visiting Scholar at the Center for Mexican American Studies (CMAS) at the University of Houston. I thank the CMAS Center director Tatcho Mindiola for support and the CMAS staff for assistance. I also thank the editors for ubiquitous comments and suggestions.

1. See Peterson and Krivo (2005); Rosenbaum et al. (2005).

2. For review see Rosales (1999: 75–98); see also Warnshuis (1931); Manuel Gamio (1931 [1971]: 140–182), the revered Mexican social scientist, produced pioneering research on Mexican immigration to the United States (also Gamio 1930 [1969]). His study of Mexican labor

and migration during 1926–27 was funded through the Social Science Research Council, generated an enormous amount of data, and produced two books. The life histories of the Mexican immigrants include rich information on their encounters with border and local police.

3. See Julian Samora (1971). In 1953 Professor Samora was the first Mexican American to earn a doctorate in sociology. For more on his pioneering research in immigration, civil rights, public health, and rural poverty, see http://www.samoralegacy.com/. The premier Latino research center in the Midwest is named after him, the Samora Institute (http://www.jsri.msu.edu/).

4. Samora, Bernal and Peña (1979).

5. Mazón (1984); Escobar (1999).

6. Mazón (1984); Escobar (1999).

7. Escobar (1999: 289).

8. But see Engel and Calnon (2004); Kane (2002); Hagan, Shedd and Payne (2005); Menjivar and Bejarano (2004); Reitzel, Rice and Piquero (2004); Weitzer and Tuch (2005).

9. See Capps et al. (2007) for recent exception.

10. Weitzer and Tuch (2005).

11. Moore and Pinderhughes (1993); Martínez (2002).

12. Saenz (2004).

13. For example, see Rodríguez, Sáenz and Menjívar (2008).

14. Sampson and Bartusch (1998).

15. Sampson and Bartusch (1998); Weitzer and Tuch (2002).

16. See Pew Hispanic Center (2006).

17. Again see Rodríguez, Sáenz and Menjívar (2008).

18. See Chavez (2008).

19. Rodríguez, Sáenz and Menjívar (2008).

20. See Martínez (2008).

21. Vásquez, Seales and Marquardt (2008).

22. Rodríguez, Sáenz and Menjívar (2008).

23. Chavez (2008).

24. Rodríguez, Sáenz and Menjívar (2008).

25. Rodríguez, Sáenz and Menjívar (2008).

26. Rosales (1999).

27. Rosales (1999: 3–4).

28. See Martínez (2008) for examples of stereotypes.

29. Rosales (1999: 75).

30. See Warnshius (1931: 279–280).

31. Rosales (1999: 75).

32. Escobar (1999: 14).

33. Warnshuis (1931: 267).

34. See Martínez (2006).

35. Escobar (1999).

36. Escobar (1999: chap. 1).

37. Escobar (1999).

38. Escobar (1999).

39. Quoted in Samora, Bernal and Peña (1979: 12).

40. Samora (1971: 13).

41. Samora (1971: 48–57).

42. Samora (1971).

43. Samora (1971: 33–57).
44. Samora (1971: 51).
45. Samora (1971: 46).
46. See Peterson and Krivo (2005); Sampson and Bean (2006).
47. Peterson and Krivo (2005).
48. Sampson and Bean (2006).
49. See Martínez (2002) for exceptions.
50. Peterson and Krivo (2005).
51. Peterson and Krivo (2005).
52. Martínez (2002); Nielsen, Lee, and Martínez (2005): Nielsen and Martínez (2006).
53. See Martínez (2008); Martínez and Lee (2000).
54. Sampson and Wilson (1995: 41).
55. Sampson and Bean (2006: 8).
56. Sampson and Bean (2006).
57. See Peterson and Krivo (2005).
58. Peterson and Krivo (2005).
59. See Lee, Martínez and Rosenfeld (2001).
60. For review see Peterson and Krivo (2005).
61. Lee, Martínez and Rosenfeld (2001).
62. Martínez (2002).
63. Lopez and Minushkin (2008).
64. Lopez and Minushkin (2008).
65. http://www.nclr.org/content/news/detail/52081.
66. Zhang and Chin (2002).
67. Alpert, Dunham and Smith (2007).
68. Peterson and Krivo (2005).
69. Martínez (2002).
70. See Martínez (2002).
71. Martínez (2006).
72. Peterson and Krivo (2005).
73. See Rosales (1999).
74. Sampson (2008); Martínez (2006).

REFERENCES

Alpert, Geoffrey P., Roger G. Dunham and Michael R. Smith. 2007. "Investigating the Racial Profiling by the Miami-Dade Police Department: A Multimethod Approach." *Criminology and Public Policy* 6: 25–56.

Capps, Randy, Rosa Maria Castañeda, Ajay Chaudry and Robert Santos. 2007. *Paying the Price: The Impact of Immigration Raids on America's Children.* A report by the Urban Institute for the National Council of La Raza.

Chavez, Leo R. 2008. *The Latino Threat: Constructing Immigrants, Citizens, and the Nation.* Stanford, CA: Stanford University Press.

Culver, Leigh. 2004. "The Impact of New Immigration Patterns on the Provision of Police Services in Midwestern Communities." *Journal of Criminal Justice* 32: 329–344.

Engel, Robin and Jennifer M. Calnon. 2004. "Examining the Influence of Drivers' Characteristics During Traffic Stops by Police." *Justice Quarterly* 21: 49–90.

Escobar, Edward J. 1999. *Race, Police, and the Making of a Political Identity: Mexican Americans and the Los Angeles Police Department, 1900–1945.* Berkeley and Los Angeles: University of California Press.

Gamio, Manuel. 1969 (1930). *Mexican Immigration to the United States.* New York: Arno Press and the New York Times.

——. 1971 (1931). *The Life Story of the Mexican Immigrant.* New York: Dover Publications.

Hagan, John, Carla Shedd and M. R. Payne. 2005. "Race, Ethnicity, and Youth Perceptions of Criminal Justice." *American Sociological Review* 70: 381–407.

Kane, Robert J. 2002. "The Social Ecology of Police Misconduct." *Criminology* 40: 867–896.

Lee, Matthew T, Ramiro Martínez, Jr., and Richard Rosenfeld. 2001. "Does Immigration Increase Homicide? Negative Evidence from Three Border Cities." *Sociological Quarterly* 42: 559–80.

Lopez, Mark Hugo and Susan Minushkin. *2008 National Survey of Latinos: Hispanics See Their Situation in the U.S. Deteriorating; Oppose Key Immigration Enforcement Measures.* Washington, DC: Pew Hispanic Center, September 2008.

Martínez, Ramiro Jr. 2002. *Latino Homicide: Immigration, Violence, and Community.* New York: Routledge.

——. 2006. "Coming to America: The Impact of the New Immigration on Crime." In *Immigration and Crime,* edited by Ramiro Martínez, Jr., and Abel Valenzuela, 1–19. New York: New York University Press.

——. 2007. "Incorporating Latinos and Immigrants into Policing Research." *Criminology and Public Policy* 6: 57–64.

——. 2008. "Editorial Introduction: The Impact of Immigration Policy on Criminological Research." *Criminology and Public Policy* 7: 53–58.

Martínez, Ramiro, Jr., and Matthew T. Lee. 2000. *On Immigration and Crime.* In *Criminal Justice 2000: The Nature of Crime: Continuity and Change,* edited by Gary LaFree, Robert J. Bursik, Jr., James F. Short, Jr., and Ralph B. Taylor, 485–523. Washington, DC: National Institute of Justice.

Mazón, Mauricio. 1984. *The Zoot-Suit Riots.* Austin: Center for Mexican American Studies and the University of Texas Press.

Menjivar, Cecila and Cynthia L. Bejarano. 2004. "Latino Immigrants' Perceptions of Crime and Police Authorities in the United States: A Case Study." *Ethnic and Racial Studies* 27: 120–148.

Moore, Joan and Raquel Pinderhughes. 1993. *In the Barrios: Latinos and the Underclass Debate.* New York: Russell Sage Foundation.

Nielsen, Amie L., Matthew T. Lee and Ramiro Martínez, Jr. 2005. "Integrating Race, Place, and Motive in Social Disorganization Theory: Lessons from a Comparison of Black and Latino Homicide Types in Two Immigrant Destination Cities." *Criminology* 43: 837–872.

Nielsen, Amie and Ramiro Martínez, Jr. 2006. "Multiple Disadvantages and Crime Among Black Immigrants: Exploring Haitian Violence in Miami's Communities." In *Immigration and Crime: Race, Ethnicity, and Violence,* edited by Ramiro Martínez, Jr., and Abel Valenzuela, 212–234. New York: New York University Press.

Ong, M. and D. A. Jenks. 2004. "Hispanic Perceptions of Community Policing: Is Community Policing Working in the City?" *Journal of Ethnicity in Criminal Justice* 2: 53–66.

Peterson, Ruth D. and Lauren J. Krivo. 2005. "Macrostructural Analyses of Race, Ethnicity, and Violent Crime: Recent Lessons and New Directions for Research." *Annual Review of Sociology* 31: 331–356.

Pew Hispanic Research Center. 2008. *Statistical Portrait of Hispanics in the United States, 2006.* http://pewhispanic.org/factsheets/factsheet.php?FactsheetID=35.

Reitzel, J. D., S. K. Rice and A. Piquero. 2004. "Lines and Shadows: Perceptions of Racial Profiling and the Hispanic Experience." *Journal of Criminal Justice* 32: 607–616.

Rodríguez, Havidán, Rogelio Sáenz and Cecilia Menjívar. 2008. Preface in *Latinas/os in the United States: Changing the Face of América*. New York: Springer.

Rosales, F. Arturo. 1999. *¡Pobre Raza¡ Violence, Justice, and Mobilization Among Mexico Lindo Immigrants, 1900–1936*. Austin: University of Texas Press.

Rosenbaum, Dennis P., Amie M. Schuck, Sandra K. Costello, Darnell F. Hawkins and Marianne K. Ring. 2005. "Attitudes Toward the Police: The Effects of Direct and Vicarious Experience." *Police Quarterly* 8: 343–365.

Saenz, Rogelio. 2004. *Latinos and the Changing Face of America*. The American People Series, Census 2000. New York: Russell Sage and Population Reference Bureau.

Samora, Julian. 1971. *Los Mojados: The Wetback Story*. Notre Dame, IN: University of Notre Dame Press.

Samora, Julian, Joe Bernal and Albert Peña. 1979. *Gunpowder Justice*. Notre Dame, IN: University of Notre Dame Press.

Sampson, Robert J. 2008. "Rethinking Crime and Immigration." *Contexts* 7: 28–33.

Sampson, Robert J. and Dawn Jeglum Bartusch. 1998. "Legal Cynicism and (Subcultural?) Tolerance of Deviance: The Neighborhood Context of Racial Differences." *Law and Society Review* 32: 777–804.

Sampson, Robert J., and Lydia Bean. 2006. "Cultural Mechanisms and Killing Fields: A Revised Theory of Community-Level Racial Inequality." In *The Many Colors of Crime: Inequalities of Race, Ethnicity, and Crime in America*, edited by Ruth D. Peterson, Lauren J. Krivo, and John Hagan, 8–38. New York: New York University Press.

Sampson, Robert J., and William J. Wilson. 1995. "Toward a Theory of Race, Crime, and Urban Inequality." In *Crime and Inequality*, edited by John Hagan and Ruth Peterson, 37–56. Stanford, CA: Stanford University Press.

Skogan, W. G. and L. Steiner. 2004. "Crime, Disorder, and Decay in Chicago's Latino Community." *Journal of Ethnicity in Criminal Justice* 2: 7–26.

Vásquez, Manuel A., Chad E. Seales and Marie Friedmann Marquardt. 2008. "New Latino Destinations." In *Latinas/os in the United States: Changing the Face of América*, edited by Havidán Rodríguez, Rogelio Sáenz and Cecilia Menjívar, 19–35. New York: Springer.

Warnshuis, Paul L. 1931. "Crime and Criminal Justice Among the Mexicans of Illinois" In *Report on Crime and the Foreign Born*, no. 10, National Commission on Law Observance and Enforcement Report, 265–329. Washington, DC: U.S. Government Printing Office.

Weitzer, Ronald and Steven A. Tuch. 2002. "Perceptions of Racial Profiling: Race, Class, and Personal Experience." *Criminology* 40:435–457.

———. 2005. "Racially Biased Policing: Determinants of Citizen Perceptions." *Social Forces* 83: 1009–1030.

Zhang, Sheldon and Ko-lin Chin. 2002. "Enter the Dragon: Inside Chinese Human Smuggling Organizations." *Criminology* 40: 737–768.

Chapter 19

New Avenues for Profiling and Bias Research
The Question of Muslim Americans

Stephen K. Rice and William S. Parkin

Limited attention has been paid to Muslim Americans' interactions with the justice system and domestic security apparatus. Instead, the "Muslim American experience" has typically been framed by the structural (e.g., matters of assimilation; socioeconomics), sociopolitical (e.g., perceptions of U.S. domestic and foreign policy; a "clash of civilizations"), or codal (religious teachings). In an attempt to chart a course forward, this chapter assesses how perceived injustice and negative emotions (e.g., humiliation, moral outrage) must come to hold a more central position in assessments of deference and defiance among this understudied population.

Introduction

On a July day in 2007, two men on a Washington State ferry were photographed after crew members and passengers noted the pair asking questions and taking pictures in areas that rarely hold interest for tourists. The men, both "dark haired and olive skinned," were reported to have taken photos above- and beneath-deck in a ferry system that has been identified by the Department of Homeland Security as the most likely target for maritime terrorism in the United States.[1] More so than for the photographing of "unusual" behavior—a surveillance activity that has become more commonplace post-9/11[2]—the incident was unusual for the manner in which federal law enforcement called on news agencies to release the men's pictures and for the public to aid in their identification. After approximately ten months, during which time the "Middle Eastern–looking" men were featured on the Federal Bureau of Investigation website, national news broadcasts, and national news publications, it was learned that the two individuals had proactively contacted a U.S. embassy abroad. They were software consultants who had traveled to Seattle in the summer of 2007 for a business conference:

> Turns out the men, both citizens of a European Union nation, were captivated by the car-carrying capacity of local ferries. "Where these gentlemen live, they don't have vehicle ferries. They were fascinated that a ferry could hold that many cars and wanted

to show folks back home," FBI Special Agent Robbie Burroughs said. . . . For someone who rides the ferry every day, taking photos of the car deck is pretty unusual—but not so for "a guy who rides it one time in his life," added FBI Special Agent in Charge David Gomez. . . . They came forward because they worried they'd be arrested if they traveled to the U.S. and so provided proof of their identities, employment and the reason for their trip.[3]

As a result of the nearly year-long scrutiny, Muslim American[4] leaders claimed that the ferry incident became emblematic of the profiling that many Muslim Americans perceive to be underway on mass transit and in Muslim-dominant neighborhoods:[5]

(Rita) Zawaideh, chairwoman of the Seattle-based Arab American Community Coalition, questioned why officials didn't first consult community members, who might have been able to identify the men. "Everyone yelled at me for telling the FBI off," she said. "We're lucky it came out the way it did." Had the men been terrorists, the publicity could have forced them to change tactics and targets, creating a risk for another city, she said. Or the men could have been innocent victims had someone spotted them and "decided to take the law into their own hands," she said.

Aziz Junejo, who hosts a weekly public-access television program and writes a column on Islam for *The Seattle Times*, said he's heard stories about and even experienced more scrutiny on local ferries, particularly when he's with Muslim women who wear traditional head scarves. "We kind of get the walk-by a little slower and a little more noticeable than any others on the boat," he said. "It perpetuates fear, especially in Muslim children who are Americans, first and foremost."[6]

Entering the Fray: Muslim Americans as Profiling/Bias Research Bloc

Anecdotes such as these align with claims of profiling by way of differential treatment at airport screening and on subways as a result of 9/11 and bombings in London, Madrid, and elsewhere.[7] Amid a subtext of a law enforcement machinery that has become more focused on terrorism and intelligence, sometimes to the detriment of traditional functions such as criminal investigation,[8] Muslim Americans are likely to become more prominent within a police profiling and bias literature that has focused principally on African American experiences (and to a lesser degree, Hispanic).[9] As such, this chapter sets out to provide guidance as to how perceived injustice and negative emotions (e.g., humiliation, moral outrage) must come to hold a more central position in assessments of deference and defiance among the understudied Muslim American population—a group that has recently been estimated at 2.4 million nationwide.[10]

As with any formal organization, criminal justice agencies tend to respond to the vagaries of mission creep: as counterterrorism and intelligence gathering become more central to organizational priorities, subsegments of the population such as Muslim Americans may be impacted differentially.[11] Thus violations of the person may correlate with concerns for national security or shifts in the political and demographic landscape.[12] Such processes have been assessed empirically using neighborhood-level measurements to include disadvantage, racial composition, racial inequality, racial immigration, and racial competition on police use of force, police misconduct, and arrest.[13] Facilitators of rioting have also been assessed, as in theses that suggest that police brutality and lack of political support conditioned the neighborhood violence by Arab youth in Paris during 2005.[14]

Such results tie to research that suggests that people's judgments about the fairness of their experiences condition views regarding the legitimacy of authority, and these views subsequently shape compliance with the law.[15] The justice, legitimacy, and compliance chain is thought to be especially relevant in an era of community policing and community justice where police are more reliant on collective problem solving and citizens' exercise of voluntary compliance.[16] This more "horizontal" relationship between police and citizens would appear to be particularly salient here insomuch as police departments and the U.S. Department of Justice have held hundreds of community sensitivity dialogues to educate citizens about Muslim, Arab, and Sikh cultures.[17] It is important to note, however, that tacit categorizations of subgroups as "the Other" may backfire because relative deprivation has been found to spark anger and resentment among those whom perceive inequity.[18] In Europe, for example, perceived attacks on civil rights under the banner "assimilation" (e.g., banning of the hijab) have come to be framed concomitant with the war on terror (hence, as structured anti-Muslim racism).[19] Reflective of similar tensions, Americans of Middle Eastern descent have been described as experiencing humiliation due to a "bizarre catch-22" in which they "are branded white by law but simultaneously reified as the Other. They enjoy neither the fruits of remedial action nor the benefits of white privilege."[20] In one example, Iranian American Tony Zohrehvandi, a software developer with American Airlines, was denied the right to board a flight on his own airline in late 2001 because the pilot "didn't like the way [he] looked." As Zohrehvandi explained: "When I became a citizen and said my pledge of allegiance I said liberty and justice for all—not just for white, blond and blue eyes. It shatters your dreams. Is it going to be like this from now on—every time some idiot takes an action against the U.S., are we going to be singled out again? . . . In this country when I became a citizen, they said 'You're an American.' On [that day I realized] I will never be an American in this country as long as I look like this."[21] Harking to claims of "Driving While Black" on the nation's roadways, accounts such as these have come to be grouped by the catchall phrase "Flying While Arab."[22]

Joining Zohrehvandi is a more widely reported incident that took place on New Year's Day, 2009, when nine members of a Muslim American family were removed from an AirTran Airways flight after two members of the family engaged in what they characterized as a "benign conversation" about the safest place to sit on an airplane (i.e., in the back or over the wings). The family was soon cleared by the FBI but still experienced resistance from the airline, treatment that sparked outrage by advocacy groups such as the Muslim Public Affairs Council and the Council for American-Islamic Relations. As one member of the party, Atif Irfan, explained, "We didn't use any of those buzzwords like bomb or anything like that. . . . Obviously, people . . . gleaned something very different from it—that we were about to attack. People a lot of time, I think, hear what they want to hear," adding that the episode was "humiliating" and something that the family tried not to let become "infuriating."[23]

Experiences such as those of Zohrehvandi and Irfan afford opportunities to better understand how justice concerns may be couched within subgroup and superordinate-group identification. As Huo and colleagues elucidate, "People who identify predominantly with a subgroup may focus on instrumental issues when evaluating a superordinate-group authority, and conflicts with that authority may escalate if those people do not receive favorable outcomes."[24] Note above how Zohrehvandi and Irfan cast themselves as distinctly separate from the security/airline personnel and the community they represent (e.g., Zohrehvandi: "[I realized] I will never be an American in this country as long as I look like this"). Huo and colleagues would likely predict that this form of subgroup identification threatens social cohesion. Consequently, social psychologists have attempted to explicate how forces of social categorization may be harnessed and redirected toward the reduction of intergroup bias.[25]

Affect as Key Component

Per other discussions in the volume (e.g., Tyler and Fagan), it therefore becomes critical for research to incorporate negative affect more centrally in assessments of perceived profiling and bias among Muslim Americans.[26] As such, attention should be drawn to how an individual's background characteristics (e.g., race, ethnicity, sex, faith) intersect with street-level, ad-hoc situations to predict deference or defiance (or as Agnew proffers, how the temporal level between background and situation, what he calls "storylines," takes form).[27] For example, as outlined by Sherman, under what conditions are the implementation of sanctions at the level of the individual or the community perceived as unjust, thereby leading to defiant pride?[28] Such models— while strikingly underdeveloped empirically[29]—would likely predict a dearth of motive-based trust between Muslim Americans and authorities due to a "perfect storm": that of a not-insignificant population becoming poorly bonded to authorities post-9/11 as a result of procedurally and distributively unjust, stigmatizing sanctions at airports and mass transit venues, accusations of collective wrongdoing, and a palpable sense of group surveillance.[30] In 2007, for example, the National Association of Criminal Defense Lawyers and the National Association of Muslim Lawyers complained to then Attorney General Alberto Gonzales that the Justice Department had "smear(ed) the entire Muslim community" with an "overreaching list" of over three hundred Muslim organizations that were attached as unindicted co-conspirators in a Texas terrorism trial. The legal brief described the list as a pattern of the "demonization of all things Muslim" since 2001.[31] The Texas case joined claims of secret monitoring of radiation levels at Muslim sites around the United States between 2001 and 2003.[32]

Rather than default to fundamental attribution error, or the tendency to explain behavior in terms of static personality traits, researchers have found that individuals often express themselves situationally. In Engel's assessment of citizens' interactions with police, for example, she found that perceived fairness was an important complement to the outcomes one received.[33] How do subjective, psychosocial responses manifest? To Homans, emotional responses to injustice are straightforward: those treated fairly will experience positive emotions, while those treated poorly are likely to feel anger.[34] Consistent with this and with the exchange approach to justice, the severity of a perceived injustice is likely to affect individuals' emotional, psychological, and behavioral reactions.[35] For example, Hegtvedt and Markovsky find that individuals who experience outcomes that are out of alignment with what is expected (e.g., with the police) are likely to experience negative emotions, especially when coupled with a perception that he or she is not responsible for the nonproportionality.[36] Relatedly, perceptions of relative deprivation in social interactions are thought to produce psychic discomfort, a dynamic particularly relevant in a time of strict surveillance.[37] In a theoretical sense, negative affect (particularly anger) is thought to be a critical mediator of the processes leading from strains toward antisocial behavior/lack of deference because anger increases felt injury and leads individuals to disregard information that can help resolve situations.[38]

As has been discussed, there is a critical relationship between an individual's interactions with agents of social control, the emotions that may manifest as a result of these interactions, and an individual's willingness to defer to, and accept the legitimacy of, authority.[39] As such, and before continuing to outline how an emotions-based research orientation will afford a better understanding of the Muslim American experience, it is important to outline Muslim Americans' shared histories and social locations (e.g., presuppositions, dispositions). Constructs such as the structural characteristics of neighborhoods, perceived quality of life, perceived discrimination, global versus personally experienced assessments, and intra-ethnic perceptions have already been found to condition public attitudes toward authority.[40] It is to this that we next draw attention.

Shared Histories and Social Locations

Evoking scholarship that suggests that the legacy of slavery affects present-day African American identity development and personality,[41] it is believed that Muslims were introduced to the Americas in the 18th century when Africans arrived via the slave trade.[42] These slaves were forced to convert to Christianity, leaving limited colonial records of belief in Allah and Muhammad. The first mass migration of Muslims choosing to live in the United States started near the end of the 19th century. Seeking to mirror the financial success of Lebanese Christians, these immigrants were unskilled laborers who originated from Middle Eastern regions that today encompass Syria, Lebanon, Jordan, and Palestine. After World War II, Muslims began to emigrate to escape political oppression. For the most part, this wave of immigrants consisted of highly educated and influential members of the communities they left behind.[43] During the 1960s, the United States altered its immigration policies, resulting in an unprecedented growth of Muslim immigrants arriving from Africa and Asia.[44]

Muslim American organizations were slow to develop in the first half of the twentieth century. Before the 1967 Arab-Israeli war, Muslim Americans refrained from becoming active in American politics as they felt that identifying with pro-Arab issues would result in social and economic repercussions.[45] The Nation of Islam was one of two Muslim American organizations to gain national status prior to the Arab-Israeli war, the other being the Muslim Students Association.[46] Even though many foreign-born Muslim Americans view the Nation of Islam as a sectarian religion that is in conflict with Islamic teachings, the organization has attracted many African American converts.[47] During the 1970s and 1980s more Muslim organizations developed, providing a platform for political activism specific to causes affecting the respective communities.[48] This increase in civic engagement coincided with a rise in anti-Muslim sentiments in the United States, due largely in part to the Iranian revolution, the hostage crisis, and the rise of violence in the Middle East.[49] In the 1990s, organizations that lobbied for Muslim Americans became more engaged in local and federal politics. After the terrorist attacks of 9/11, these and similar organizations worked to expose perceived media and public prejudices against the Muslim American community, not to mention claims of law enforcement profiling and bias (e.g., the Muslim Public Affairs Council and the Council for American-Islamic Relations, as discussed above).[50]

Similar to what has happened with African Americans and Hispanics, "anti-Muslim" sentiments tend to reduce all Muslim Americans to a single group, eliminating their distinct ethnicities, religions, and races, as prejudice targets anyone who fits a stereotype.[51] Joining scholarship that indicates that racial and ethnic minorities, particularly African Americans, are overrepresented as offenders by the media,[52] Muslim American men are often portrayed as violent and irrational, and Muslim American women, as oppressed.[53] Most media attention of Islam is unfavorable, focusing especially on terrorism in the Middle East.[54] At times the negative portrayal facilitates fear of victimization and oppression—especially when incidents of terrorism occur.[55] Expressed most vividly, Tehranian argues that the media portrayal of Middle Easterners has morphed into one of the "bloodthirsty terrorist, rabid religious fundamentalist, or misogynistic heathen."[56]

Complementing work that explores the relationship between social structure and perceptions of criminal injustice,[57] opinion polls suggest that living in a pluralist society causes anxiety among some Muslim Americans, especially young people. When interviewed, individuals state that when they were younger they did not always understand why being Muslim sometimes prevented them from participating fully in social life. The pressure to assimilate varies to some degree but tends to be characterized as ever present, with many feeling stigmatized because of religion and ethnic heritage.[58] Domestic policies such as the Patriot Act make it difficult for many Muslim Americans to not feel alienated from a public that is thought to harbor negative perceptions of Islam.[59] Anything that can be linked to Islam may be attacked, a stereotyping that is thought to delegitimize the views of the Muslim American community and to hinder active participation in the political process.[60]

The Numbers

Ronald Weitzer (this volume) explains that in assessing perceived profiling and bias, it is critical to complement individual-level predictors with varied ecological contexts (e.g., neighborhoods, cities, and nations). Toward this end, the Pew Research Center recently published one of the most detailed surveys of the Muslim American population to date, incorporating demographic, political, and social data. The study estimates that there are 1.5 million adult Muslims living in the United States, the majority originating from South Asian and Arab countries. Nearly two-thirds of the 1.5 million are foreign-born, while almost 60% of the native-born (or 20% of all Muslim Americans) are of African American descent. In addition, 60% of the native-born are converts to Islam and 21% are second-generation Muslims.[61] Muslim Americans are spread across the United States, with 32% living in the East, 25% in the South, 18% in the West, and 24% in the Central Great Lakes area.[62] The total population of Muslim Americans in the United States is relatively young, as 74% are under the age of forty-nine (compared to 61% of the general American public).[63]

There is a considerable difference between the racial backgrounds of native-born and foreign-born Muslim Americans. While native-born identify as black 56% of the time, white 31% percent of the time, and Asian 2% percent of the time, foreign-born identify mostly as white (44%), followed by Asian (28%), and finally black (10%). These differences paint a picture of a very diverse and complicated community, especially if one is comparing native-born and foreign-born Muslim Americans. Whether there are important differences in Muslim American perceptions of police profiling and bias inter- and intra-ethnically, intra-faith, and across–birth country remains an outstanding question. In a study of perceived profiling within-ethnicity, for example, Rice, Reitzel, and Piquero found that black Hispanics were more likely than nonblack Hispanics to perceive that profiling was widespread, not justified, and personally experienced.[64]

Even within the population of native-born Muslim Americans, one where the percentage of converts is overwhelmingly African American, there are dissimilarities. For example, 47% of native-born African American Muslims reject the idea of assimilation, believing that Muslim immigrants should maintain both religious and cultural customs native to their country of origin, while the majority of the remaining native-born Muslim Americans believe that immigrant Muslims should attempt to assimilate.[65] For the most part, the descendents of African American converts to Islam have lived in the United States for generations.[66] This history with American culture and customs, especially the link to slavery, may offer an explanation for why there is such a disparity between the views of native-born African American Muslims and non–African American Muslims.[67] Almost half of all Muslim Americans state that they identify as Muslim first, while only 28% identify primarily as American. Native-born Muslims are less likely than foreign-born Muslims to have a favorable view of the communities in which they live, and although more than half of Muslim Americans are not satisfied with the country's overall direction, this rate is more favorable than that of the general public. Interestingly, native-born Muslims are much more likely to believe that mosques should express views politically (68%) when compared to foreign-born Muslims (30%).[68]

As a potential area for scholarship on views of crime and punishment across political philosophy,[69] 7% of native-born Muslims identify as members of the Republican

Party and 78% identify as members of the Democratic Party. While 20% of foreign-born Muslim Americans approved of Republican president George W. Bush's job performance, this was true of only 6% of native-born.[70] Part of the reason that Muslim Americans identify more with Democrats may be the party's stance on the separation of church and state. Some believe that the integration of the two would result in added pressure for their children to be involved with Christian activities in the educational environment, such as prayer sessions. Conversely, however, the Republican Party's stance on traditional family values and admonishment of certain sexual behaviors is also attractive to segments of the Muslim American community.[71] Exit polls indicate that approximately 90% of Muslim Americans voted for Democrat Barack Obama in the 2008 presidential election.[72]

Religion plays a pivotal role in the Muslim American community. Providing a unique opportunity for future research to make fine perceptual "cuts" within-faith, 7% of native-born Muslim Americans identify as Shi'a Muslims, while 50% are Sunni, and 30% claim no denominational affiliation. Sixty-three percent of Muslim Americans believe that modernity and religiosity can comfortably co-exist.[73] Tension exists between older generations and younger generations, however, as the latter attempt to balance the demands of their religion with that of larger society, and the former are influenced by, as well as influence, American popular culture.[74] Even so, young Muslim Americans feel that they are forced to choose between joining a society whose values can be antithetical to Islam, or committing themselves almost entirely to faith.[75]

The events of September 11, 2001, had a profound affect on the Muslim American population. Fifty-nine percent of native-born Muslim Americans believe that is has become more difficult to be a Muslim since 9/11, while only 39% believe that nothing has changed. Important to perspectives that have attempted to understand linkages between perceived discrimination, perceived injustice, and compliance with the law,[76] Muslim Americans identified discrimination, racism, and prejudice as the number one problem facing their communities, while the number two problem was being viewed as a terrorist. Seventy-three percent of native-born Muslims believe that antiterrorism policies single out Muslims, compared to 47% of foreign-born Muslims.[77] Only 26% of Muslim Americans believe that the war on terror is a sincere effort to reduce terrorism. The percentage of Muslim Americans who are very concerned about the increase of Islamic extremism (51%) are higher than Muslims in France (35%), Spain (29%), and Germany (29%). Muslim Americans who have favorable views of al-Qaeda, although still a very small percentage, is higher for Muslims who are native-born (7%) compared to foreign-born (3%).[78]

After September 11, Muslim Americans felt pressure to alter their religiosity, especially portions of it that could be identified visibly. At the same time, however, they reported that the events brought their communities together and solidified their faith.[79] Muslim American females found themselves default representatives of their communities as their men were ostracized by society as suspected terrorists. This status elevation demonstrated that Muslim women were viewed as harmless and not beyond redemption, while the men were viewed as threats.[80] The idea of Muslim

American women as mere victims of a patriarchal religion may be disappearing, however, as increasingly they are being investigated for potential links to terrorism.[81] Such findings may come to inform gendered studies of profiling and bias.[82]

Muslim Americans also report that they feel like they must continuously condemn and apologize for the 9/11 terrorist attacks, as well as reiterate their allegiance to the United States, actions required by no other Americans. Some members of the Muslim American community have taken the opportunity to develop a form of Islam that purposefully separates itself from any association with Arab and Middle Eastern cultures.[83] These individuals have also attempted to create a new identify for themselves by educating a public that believes their religion is inherently violent, oppresses women, and demands antidemocratic governments.[84]

Future Steps: Coupling Shared Histories and Social Locations with Assessments of Negative Emotions, Profiling, and Bias

By affording particularly useful insights into the role of faith, community, political philosophy, assimilation, symbols of terror and responses to terror, and what defines an "American," Muslim Americans provide an opportunity for scholars to better understand perceived profiling, bias, and the effective rule of law. Faith itself, for example —that which defines Muslim Americans as a distinct social group—has been found to shape preferences for punitiveness (e.g., among fundamentalist Christians).[85] It is also important to remember that assessments of the relationship between this subgroup and what has sometimes been cast as super-ordinate group (e.g., domestic security; police) comes at a time when U.S. non-Muslims hold negative views of Muslim Americans (e.g., 27% of Americans say that the federal government should require Muslim Americans to register where they live; 26% assert that mosques should be monitored by federal agents; 29% agree that it is acceptable for the federal government to use undercover agents to infiltrate Muslim organizations).[86] Adding to the trend, a 2005 Gallup poll of American households listed "Nothing" or "I don't know" as 57% of the responses to the question of what one most admires about Muslim societies.[87]

As demonstrated in this volume, criminology and criminal justice are well suited to assess public perceptions of police profiling and bias, and specific threads are well suited to the development of heuristics to better understand links between negative emotions (e.g., humiliation, outrage) and deference or defiance to authority (e.g., Tyler and Fagan; Weitzer, this volume). With regard to "primers" for perceived profiling and perceived bias in Muslim Americans' dealings with authorities, a basic theoretical model incorporating general strain elements may hold promise (see figure 19.1). Put another way, it is important for future research to transition discourse related to the "body" of an African American, Hispanic, or Muslim American (e.g., in stop, search, or seizure) to one also focused on intrapsychic and interpersonal emotional processes.

Both internationally and domestically, a focus on the potential for negative affect among Muslims is apt given the West's covert parceling of Ottoman territories

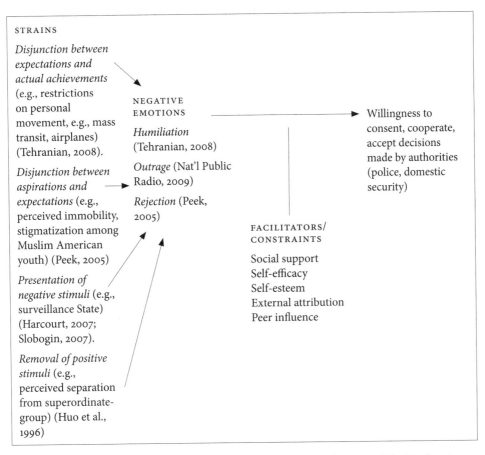

STRAINS

Disjunction between expectations and actual achievements (e.g., restrictions on personal movement, e.g., mass transit, airplanes) (Tehranian, 2008).

Disjunction between aspirations and expectations (e.g., perceived immobility, stigmatization among Muslim American youth) (Peek, 2005)

Presentation of negative stimuli (e.g., surveillance State) (Harcourt, 2007; Slobogin, 2007).

Removal of positive stimuli (e.g., perceived separation from superordinate-group) (Huo et al., 1996)

NEGATIVE EMOTIONS

Humiliation (Tehranian, 2008)

Outrage (Nat'l Public Radio, 2009)

Rejection (Peek, 2005)

FACILITATORS/ CONSTRAINTS

Social support
Self-efficacy
Self-esteem
External attribution
Peer influence

Willingness to consent, cooperate, accept decisions made by authorities (police, domestic security)

Figure 19.1. Basic model for further research: intersections of general strain and the Muslim American experience. General strain theory elements based on Agnew (2006).

after World War I in the Sykes-Picot agreement,[88] accounts of strong disillusionment among disaffected Muslim youth in various countries,[89] strong anger in light of the restriction on Palestinian's movement within the West Bank and Gaza,[90] and accounts from Guantanamo Bay of the pouring of phosphoric liquid, sodomy with chemical lights and broom sticks, and attacks by military working dogs on detainees.[91] Perceived immobility and impotence in the face of state violence, themes which have been developed as threats to social identity in criminology,[92] have also been found to impel extremism among some Muslims.[93] On the domestic front, vitriol may tie to challenges to group self-identification, as in the white supremacist movement's characterization of minorities as threats to "blue-collar Americans."[94]

In sum, as with other minority groups, criminology and criminal justice are well positioned to frame Muslim Americans' "psychological space" in their dealings with police and other agents of social control. More specifically, scholarship will benefit from an agenda that explores the impact of strain, procedural and distributive injustice, humiliation, disgust, and defiance to complement the structural and rational choice theses in extant policing/security scholarship. Further, social markers such as "Muslim" and "Arab" should be disentangled for important perceptual differences within-faith, within- and across-ethnicity, within and across-stated denomination, and across-nation of origin (e.g., U.S., Arab nation, other). Perceptions of police profiling and bias have been shown to be affected by media exposure,[95] so attention should also be paid to whether such mediums intensify the vicarious strain experienced by primed (i.e., susceptible) individuals.[96] Conversely, it will also be important to assess any impact of conciliatory frameworks, such as U.S. President Barack Obama's "new tone in relations" with the Muslim world.[97]

Which research methods are well suited to accomplishing these goals? Broadly speaking, Thoits's call for the geographical mapping of affect provides guidance, as do Maltz's approach to "visualizing" victimization (here, as perceptions tapped at transportation hubs?) and Ajrouch's desire to better understand the network characteristics of immigrant and U.S.-born Muslims vis-à-vis relationship quality, social integration, and discrimination.[98] Further, field-based research concentrating on personal narrative must hold a central position.[99] As Jock Young elicits in his call for cultural criminology, future research in this area requires a *phenomenology* of citizen and police/domestic security interactions, an agenda that captures "its adrenaline, its pleasure and panic, its excitement, and its anger, rage and humiliation, its desperation and its edgework."[100]

NOTES

1. With vessels capable of holding 2,500 people and over 200 vehicles as large as long haul semi-trailer trucks, the Washington State system represents a unique intersection of targeted vulnerabilities in transit infrastructure and trucking security. Yardley, "Debate Swirls"; Department of Homeland Security, *Overview*.

2. Slobogin, *Privacy at Risk*.

3. Green, "Two Ferry Riders."

4. Gil Anidjar argues that there has been "slippage" in the use of terms denoting nationality, ethnicity, and faith (e.g., Muslim versus Arab) (Shaikh, "Religion, Race, and Ethnicity"). For the purpose of this chapter, "Muslim" is utilized in accordance with extant criminal justice scholarship, understanding that it denotes the faith of over one billion individuals in at least fifty-seven countries, the majority of whom who do not reside in Arab countries (Esposito and Mogahed, "Who Speaks for Islam?").

5. Harcourt, "Muslim Profiles."

6. Green, "Two Ferry Riders."

7. See Harcourt's assessment of whether profiling Muslims is an effective counterterrorism measure or whether it violates the principle of nondiscrimination (Harcourt, "Muslim Profiles").

8. Lichtblau, Johnston, and Nixon, "F.B.I. Struggles."

9. The racial and ethnic profiling/bias literature is too extensive to cite here, especially as one incorporates assessments of stop, frisk, and search activity with perceptions of the same. With regard to the former, a helpful resource is this volume's review by Ridgeway and MacDonald; the latter, see Weitzer or Martínez (this volume as well).

10. Pew Research Center, *Muslim Americans*. It is important to note that estimations vary widely, depending on source (p. 10).

11. See Klinger and Grossman ("Who Should Deal with Foreign Terrorists") and Zhao and Hassell ("Policing Styles") regarding the impact of shifting priorities on police practice.

12. Fortman and Myers, "Political Economy."

13. For example, see Kane ("The Social Ecology"), Terrill and Reisig ("Neighborhood Context"), or Parker, Stults, and Rice ("Racial Threat").

14. Schneider, "Police Power."

15. Tyler and Huo, *Trust in the Law*

16. Clear and Karp, *The Community Justice Ideal*; McCluskey, "Compliance, Coercion."

17. "Justice Department's Community Relations Service."

18. Braithwaite, *Taxing Democracy*.

19. Fekete, "Anti-Muslim Racism."

20. Tehranian, *Whitewashed*, p. 36.

21. Ibid., 108.

22. For example, see Baker, "Flying While Arab," which outlines legal questions related to such claims (e.g., unreasonable search, disparate impact, equal protection).

23. National Public Radio, "Muslim Taken Off Plane by AirTran Speaks Out."

24. Huo, Smith, Tyler, and Lind, "Superordinate Identification."

25. See Dovidio et al., "Social Inclusion," p. 247. Also see Huo, Smith, Tyler, and Lind, "Superordinate Identification," p. 40.

26. For a model, see Engel's utilization of the Police-Public Contact Survey (Engel, "Citizen's Perceptions").

27. Agnew, "Storylines." It is important to note that "storylines" are thought to condition crime. It is altogether reasonable to presume that the underlying mechanisms may well relate to deference and defiance vis-à-vis perceptions of profiling and bias on the part of domestic security and police. The years post-9/11 represent conditions "out of the ordinary" (to borrow from Agnew).

28. Sherman, "Defiance, Deterrence."

29. Although see Piquero and Bouffard, "A Preliminary and Partial Test."

30. Motive-based trust is a key concept underpinning process-based regulation. As Tyler and Huo (*Trust in the Law*) explain, motive-based trust relates to "trust in the benevolence of the motives and intensions of the person with whom one is dealing" (within the context here, police and domestic security). "If we believe that someone is honest and acts morally . . . we believe that he or she is motivated by those character traits. Consequently, we interpret that person's decisions and actions in the light of our belief about his or her character, which we see as motivated by moral values. . . . One reason we trust people is that we think we can accurately predict what they will do in the future" (p. 15).

31. MacFarquhar, "Muslim Groups."

32. Clemetson, "F.B.I. Tries to Dispel."

33. Engel, "Citizen's Perceptions."

34. Homans, *Social Behavior*.

35. Hegtvedt and Johnson, "Justice Beyond the Individual."

36. Hegtvedt and Markovsky, "Justice and Injustice."

37. In March 2002, for example, a group of Muslim American leaders accused the Justice Department of racial and religious harassment in light of the DOJ's request that three thousand Muslims living the United States submit to interviews and several raids on homes, businesses, and charities (Kahn, "A Nation Challenged").

38. Agnew, *Pressured into Crime.*

39. Agnew, *Pressured into Crime*; Tyler and Huo, *Trust in the Law*; Sherman, "Defiance, Deterrence."

40. Mastrofski, Snipes, and Supina, "Compliance on Demand"; Reisig and Parks, "Experience"; Rice and Piquero, "Perceptions of Discrimination"; Rice, Reitzel, and Piquero, "Shades of Brown"; Sampson and Bartusch, "Legal Cynicism"; Weitzer, "Racialized Policing."

41. Magnavita, *Theories of Personality*, p. 62.

42. Ghayur, "Muslims in the United States."

43. Haddad, "A Century of Islam in America."

44. Moore, "Muslims in the United States."

45. Shain, "Arab-Americans at a Crossroads."

46. Suleiman "Islam, Muslims, and Arabs in America."

47. Haddad, "A Century of Islam in America."

48. Shain, "Arab-Americans at a Crossroads."

49. Suleiman "Islam, Muslims, and Arabs in America."

50. Moore, "Muslims in the United States."

51. See Brunson, Martínez, and Weitzer (this volume) for assessments of racial/ethnic homogenization. Also see long-standing scholarship on the symbolic assailant (Skolnick, this volume).

52. Gilliam and Iyenger, "Prime Suspects."

53. Naber, "Ambiguous Insiders."

54. Haddad, "A Century of Islam in America."

55. Suleiman "Islam, Muslims, and Arabs in America."

56. Tehranian, *Whitewashed*, p. 7.

57. Hagan and Albonetti, "Race, Class"; Weitzer and Tuch, "Perceptions of Racial Profiling."

58. Peek, "Becoming Muslim."

59. Adbo, "Islam in America."

60. Suleiman "Islam, Muslims, and Arabs in America."

61. Pew Research Center, *Muslim Americans.*

62. Contrary to the thrust of most extant scholarship and media accounts focusing on the United States, one city in the Midwest with a sizable Muslim American population, Dearborn, Michigan (Muslim American population approximately thirty thousand), has been highlighted for the relationship between its police department and Arab and Muslim community. As Aladdin Elaasar (*Silent Victims*) outlines the city's relative lack of backlash violence post-9/11: "the city had a prior working relationship with the . . . community which enabled them to mobilize quickly. . . . Thus long before September 11, officials within the . . . department were familiar with the communities and areas vulnerable to backlash violence. . . . The presence of a specially appointed 'Arab community police officer' before September 11 also allowed police to gain important intelligence. . . . 181 Arab community leaders stated that during the weeks after September 11, most members of the Arab community 'felt safer in Dearborn' than outside it because of the increased and visible police presence in their communities" (pp. 206–208).

63. Hanif, "The Muslim Community in America."

64. Rice, Reitzel, and Piquero, "Shades of Brown."

65. Pew Research Center, *Muslim Americans.* Per the earlier discussion, Huo and colleagues ("Superordinate Identification") suggest that assimilation may hold influence in facilitating group cohesion (e.g., via reinforcing super-ordinate, versus subgroup, ties).

66. Haddad, "A Century of Islam in America."
67. See Weitzer, this volume, for additional guidance regarding native-born versus foreign-born dynamics in assessments of authority.
68. Pew Research Center, *Muslim Americans.*
69. For example, see Lambert, "Worlds Apart."
70. Ibid.
71. Mazuri, "Between the Crescent and the Star-Spangled Banner."
72. Ali, "Islam and Obama."
73. Pew Research Center, *Muslim Americans.*
74. Moore, "Muslims in the United States."
75. Abdo, "Islam in America."
76. For example, see Tyler and Fagan, this volume.
77. Pew Research Center, *Muslim Americans.*
78. Pew Research Center, *Muslim Americans.*
79. Peek, "Becoming Muslim."
80. Elia, "Islamophobia and the 'Privileging' of Arab American Women."
81. Sheth, "Unruly Muslim Women and Threats to Liberal Culture."
82. For example, see Smith, Makarios, and Alpert, "Differential Suspicion."
83. Howell and Shryock, "Cracking Down on Diaspora."
84. Abdo, "Islam in America."
85. Unnever, Cullen, and Applegate, "Turning the Other Cheek."
86. Nisbet and Shanahan, *MSRG Special Report.*
87. Mogahed, "Americans' Views."
88. Sorli, Gleditsch, and Strand, "Why Is There So Much Conflict."
89. Davis, *Martyrs.*
90. "The Hamas Conundrum."
91. Hersch, *Chain of Command.*
92. Anderson, *Code of the Street.*
93. Zuhur, *A Hundred Osamas.*
94. Hamm, "Apocalyptic Violence."
95. Weitzer, this volume.
96. Agnew, "Experienced, Vicarious."
97. Obama: "We can have legitimate disagreements but still be respectful. . . . To the broader Muslim world what we are going to be offering is a hand of friendship" (Cowell, "Obama Signals New Tone").
98. Thoits, "The Sociology of Emotions"; Maltz, "Visualizing Homicide"; Ajrouch, "Arab American Elders." Also see Nobles, this volume.
99. See Brunson, this volume.
100. Young, "Voodoo Criminology."

REFERENCES

Abdo, Geneive. 2005. Islam in America: Separate but unequal. *Washington Quarterly* 28: 7–17.
Agnew, Robert. 2002. Experienced, vicarious, and anticipated strain: An exploratory study on physical victimization and delinquency. *Justice Quarterly* 19: 603–632.
Agnew, Robert. 2006a. *Pressured into crime: An overview of general strain theory.* Los Angeles: Roxbury Publishing.

Agnew, Robert. 2006b. Storylines as a neglected cause of crime. *Journal of Research in Crime and Delinquency* 43: 119–147.

Ajrouch, Kristine J. 2005. Arab American elders: Network structure, perceptions of relationship quality, and discrimination. *Research in Human Development* 2: 213–228.

Ali, Lorraine. November 7 2008. Islam and Obama: American Muslims overwhelmingly voted Democratic. *Newsweek*.

Anderson, Elijah. 1999. *Code of the street*. New York: Norton.

Baker, Ellen. 2002. Flying while Arab: Racial profiling and air travel security. *Journal of Air Law and Commerce* 67: 1375–1405.

Braithwaite, Valerie. 2003. *Taxing democracy: Understanding tax avoidance and evasion*. Hampshire, UK: Ashgate Publishing.

Clear, Todd R., and David R. Karp. 1999. *The community justice ideal: Preventing crime and achieving justice*. Boulder, CO: Westview Press.

Clemetson, Lynette. January 12 2006. F.B.I. tries to dispel surveillance concerns. *New York Times*.

Cowell, Alan. January 27 2009. Obama signals new tone in relations with Islamic world. *New York Times*.

Davis, Joyce. 2003. *Martyrs: Innocence, vengeance, and despair in the Middle East*. New York: Palgrave Macmillan.

Department of Homeland Security. 2007. *Overview: FY 2007 infrastructure protection program final awards*. http://www.dhs.gov/xlibrary/assets/grants_ippawardsfy07.pdf.

Dovidio, John F., Samuel L. Gaertner, Gordon Hodson, Melissa A. Houlette, and Kelly M. Johnson. 2005. Social inclusion and exclusion: Recategorization and the perception of intergroup boundaries. In D. Abrams, M. A. Hogg, and J. M. Marques (eds.), *Social psychology of inclusion and exclusion* (pp. 245–264). Philadelphia: Psychology Press.

Elaasar, Aladdin. 2004. *Silent victims: The plight of Arab and Muslim Americans in post 9/11 America*. Bloomington, IN: AuthorHouse Publishing.

Elia, Nada. 2006. Islamophobia and the "privileging" of Arab American women. *NWSA Journal* 18: 155–61.

Engel, Robin S. 2005. Citizens' perceptions of distributive and procedural injustice during traffic stops with police. *Journal of Research in Crime and Delinquency* 42: 445–481.

Esposito, John L., and Dalia Mogahed. 2007. *Who speaks for Islam? What a billion Muslims really think*. New York: Gallup Press.

Fekete, Liz. 2004. Anti-Muslim racism and the European security state. *Race and Class* 46: 3–29.

Fortman, Bas de Gaay, and Gonwongbay A. Myers. 1992. Political economy of security revisited. *Institute of Social Studies (ISS) Working Chapter Series No. 137*. http://biblio.iss.nl/opac/uploads/wp/wp137.pdf.

Ghayur, M. Arif. 1981. Muslims in the United States: Settlers and visitors. *Annals of the American Academy of Political and Social Science* 454: 150–163.

Gilliam, Franklin D., and Shanto Iyengar. 2000. Prime suspects: The influence of local television news on the viewing public. *American Journal of Political Science* 44: 560–573.

Green, Sara Jean. May 6 2008. Two ferry riders sought by FBI last summer were just tourists. *Seattle Times*.

Haddad, Yvonne. 1986. "A century of Islam in America." Middle East Institute. http://muslim-canada.org/HamdardCentury.html.

Hagan, John, and Celesta Albonetti. 1982. Race, class, and the perception of criminal injustice in America. *American Journal of Sociology* 88: 329–355.

The Hamas conundrum. March 26 2007. *New York Times.*

Hamm, Mark S. 2004. Apocalyptic violence: The seduction of terrorist subcultures. *Theoretical Criminology* 8: 323–339.

Hanif, Ghulam. 2003. The Muslim community in America: A brief profile. *Journal of Muslim Minority Affairs* 23: 303–311.

Harcourt, Bernard. 2007. Muslim profiles post-9/11: Is racial profiling an effective counterterrorist measure and does it violate the right to be free from discrimination? In B. Goold and L. Lazarus (eds.), *Security and human rights* (pp. 73–98). Oxford, UK: Hart Publishing.

Hegtvedt, Karen A., and Cathy Johnson. 2000. Justice beyond the individual: A future with legitimation. *Social Psychology Quarterly* 63: 298–311.

Hegtvedt, Karen A., and Barry Markovsky. 1995. Justice and injustice. In K. S. Cook, G. A. Fine, and J. S. House (eds.), *Sociological perspectives on social psychology* (pp. 257–280). Boston: Allyn and Bacon.

Hersch, Seymour M. 2004. *Chain of command: The road from 9/11 to Abu Ghraib.* New York: HarperCollins.

Homans, George. 1974. *Social behavior: Its elementary forms.* New York: Harcourt Brace Jovanovich.

Howell, Sally, and Andrew Shryock. 2003. Cracking down on diaspora: Arab Detroit and America's "War on Terror." *Anthropological Quarterly* 76: 443–462.

Huo, Yuen J., Heather J. Smith, Tom R. Tyler, and E. Allan Lind. 1996. Superordinate identification, subgroup identification, and justice concerns: Is separatism the problem; is assimilation the answer? *Psychological Science* 7: 40–45.

Justice Department's Community Relations Service to sponsor Arab, Muslim, and Sikh awareness and protocol seminar for law enforcement. 2003. U.S. Department of Justice press release. http://www.usdoj.gov/crs/pramstotpgcounty09252003.htm.

Kahn, Joseph. March 27 2002. A nation challenged: American Muslims; Raids, detentions and lists lead Muslims to cry persecution. *New York Times.*

Kane, Robert J. 2002. The social ecology of police misconduct. *Criminology* 40: 867–896.

Klinger, David A., and Dave Grossman. 2002. Who should deal with foreign terrorists on U.S. soil? Socio-legal consequences of September 11 and the ongoing threat of terrorist attacks in America. *Harvard Journal of Law and Public Policy* 25: 815–834.

Lambert, Eric G. 2005. Worlds apart: The views on crime and punishment among white and minority college students. *Criminal Justice Studies* 18: 99–121.

Lichtblau, Eric, David Johnston, and Ron Nixon. October 18 2008. F.B.I. struggles to handle financial fraud cases. *New York Times.*

MacFarquhar, Neil. August 16 2007. Muslim groups oppose a list of "co-conspirators." *New York Times.*

Magnavita, Jeffrey J. 2001. *Theories of personality: Contemporary approaches to the science of personality.* John Wiley and Sons.

Maltz, Michael D. 1998. Visualizing homicide: A research note. *Journal of Quantitative Criminology* 14: 397–410.

Mastrofski, Stephen D., Jeffrey B. Snipes, and Anne E. Supina. 1996. Compliance on demand: The public's response to specific police requests. *Journal of Research in Crime and Delinquency* 33: 269–305.

Mazuri, Ali. 1996. Between the crescent and the star-spangled banner: American Muslims and U.S. foreign policy. *International Affairs* 72: 493–506.

McCluskey, John. 2001. Compliance, coercion, and procedural justice: An analysis of police-suspect encounters. Paper presented at the 2001 American Society of Criminology (ASC) Conference, Irvine, CA.

Mogahed, Dalia. 2006. Americans' views of the Islamic world. Gallup Poll News Service. http://www.gallup.com/poll/21349/americans-views-islamic-world.aspx.

Moore, Kathleen. 2007. Muslims in the United States: Pluralism under exceptional circumstances. *Annals of the American Academy of Political and Social Science* 612: 116–32.

Naber, Nadine. 2000. Ambiguous insiders: An investigation of Arab American invisibility. *Ethnic and Racial Studies* 23: 37–61.

National Public Radio. January 2 2009. Muslim taken off plan by AirTran speaks out. *All Things Considered.* http://www.npr.org/templates/story/story.php?storyId=98964887.

Nisbet, Erik, and James Shanahan. 2004. *MSRG special report: Restrictions on civil liberties, views of Islam, and Muslim Americans.* Ithaca, NY: Media and Society Research Group. http://www.comm.cornell.edu/msrg/report1a.pdf.

Parker, Karen F., Brian J. Stults, and Stephen K. Rice. 2005. Racial threat, concentrated disadvantage, and social control: Considering the macro-level sources of variation in arrests. *Criminology* 43: 1111–1133.

Peek, Lori. 2005. Becoming Muslim: The development of a religious identity. *Sociology of Religion* 66: 215–242.

Pew Research Center. 2007. *Muslim Americans: Middle class and mostly mainstream.* Washington, DC: Pew Research Center. http://pewresearch.org/assets/pdf/muslim-americans.pdf.

Piquero, Nicole L., and Leana A. Bouffard. 2002. A preliminary and partial test of specific defiance. *Journal of Crime and Justice* 26: 1–21.

Reisig, Michael D., and Roger B. Parks. 2000. Experience, quality of life, and neighborhood context: A hierarchical analysis of satisfaction with police. *Justice Quarterly* 17: 607–630.

Rice, Stephen K., and Alex R. Piquero. 2005. Perceptions of discrimination and justice in New York City. *Policing* 28: 98–117.

Rice, Stephen K., John D. Reitzel, and Alex R. Piquero. 2005. Shades of brown: Perceptions of racial profiling and the intra-ethnic differential. *Journal of Ethnicity in Criminal Justice* 3: 47–70.

Sampson, Robert J., and Dawn J. Bartusch. 1998. Legal cynicism and (subcultural?) tolerance of deviance: The neighborhood context of racial differences. *Law and Society Review* 32: 777–804.

Schneider, Cathy L. 2008. Police power and race riots in Paris. *Politics and Society* 36: 133–159.

Shaikh, Nermeen. 2008. Religion, race, and ethnicity. AsiaSource. http://www.asiasource.org/news/special_reports/anidjar2.cfm.

Shain, Yossi. 1996. Arab-Americans at a crossroads. *Journal of Palestine Studies* 25: 46–59.

Sherman, Lawrence W. 1993. Defiance, deterrence, and irrelevance: A theory of the criminal sanction. *Journal of Research in Crime and Delinquency* 30: 445–473.

Sheth, Falguni. 2006. Unruly Muslim women and threats to liberal culture. *Peace Review* 18: 455–463.

Slobogin, Christopher. 2007. *Privacy at risk: The new government surveillance and the Fourth Amendment.* Chicago: University of Chicago Press.

Smith, Michael, Matthew Makarios, and Geoffrey Alpert. 2006. Differential suspicion: Theory specification and gender effects in the traffic stop context. *Justice Quarterly* 23: 271–295.

Sorli, Mirjam E., Nils P. Gleditsch, and Havard Strand. 2005. Why is there so much conflict in the Middle East? *Journal of Conflict Resolution* 49: 141–165.

Suleiman, Michael. 1999. Islam, Muslims, and Arabs in America: The other of the other of the other. *Journal of Muslim Minority Affairs* 19: 33–47.

Tehranian, John. 2008. *Whitewashed: America's invisible Middle Eastern minority.* New York: New York University Press.

Terrill, William, and Michael D. Reisig. 2003. Neighborhood context and police use of force. *Journal of Research in Crime and Delinquency* 40: 291–321.

Thoits, Peggy A. 1989. The sociology of emotions. *Annual Review of Sociology* 15: 317–342.

Tyler, Tom R., and Yuen J. Huo. 2002. *Trust in the law: Encouraging public cooperation with the police and courts.* New York: Russell Sage Foundation.

Unnever, James D., Francis T. Cullen, and Brandon K. Applegate. 2005. Turning the other cheek: Reassessing the impact of religion on punitive ideology. *Justice Quarterly* 22: 304–339.

Weitzer, Ronald. 2000. Racialized policing: Residents' perceptions in three neighborhoods. *Law and Society Review* 34: 129–155.

Weitzer, Ronald, and Steven A. Tuch. 2002. Perceptions of racial profiling: Race, class, and personal experience. *Criminology* 40: 435–456.

Yardley, William. August 26 2007. Debate swirls around 2 men on a ferry. *New York Times.*

Young, Jock. 2004. Voodoo criminology and the numbers game. In J. Ferrell, K. Hayward, W. Morrison, and M. Presdee (eds.), *Cultural criminology unleashed* (pp. 13–27). London: Glass House Press.

Zhao, Jihong, and Kimberly D. Hassell. 2005. Policing styles and organizational priorities: Retesting Wilson's theory of local political culture. *Police Quarterly* 8: 411–430.

Zuhur, Sherifa. 2005. *A hundred Osamas: Islamist threats and the future of counterinsurgency.* Carlisle, PA: Strategic Studies Institute, U.S. Army War College.

‖‖

Chapter 20

Preventing Racially Biased Policing through Internal and External Controls
The Comprehensive Accountability Package

Michael D. White

Well . . . I'm back over here in the projects, pissing off the natives.[1]

Minority motorists have been treated differently than non-minority motorists during the course of traffic stops on the New Jersey Turnpike. . . . We conclude that the problem of disparate treatment is real —not imagined.[2]

Introduction

The quotes above are related to two infamous cases of police misconduct from the 1990s. The first comes from the Independent Commission on the Los Angeles Police Department (hereafter called the Christopher Commission), which investigated the LAPD in the wake of the Rodney King beating. As part of their investigation, the commission reviewed more than six months of Mobile Digital Terminal (MDT) transmissions and found "an appreciable number of disturbing and recurrent racial remarks," clearly suggesting that "the officers typing the MDT messages apparently had little concern that they would be disciplined for making such remarks."[3] The second quote comes from an interim report authored by a New Jersey State Police Review Team investigating racial profiling. Since the early 1990s, the New Jersey State Police (NJSP) had been accused of engaging in racial profiling, particularly on the New Jersey Turnpike (NJTP). The American Civil Liberties Union (ACLU) filed a number of law suits on behalf of citizens. In *State v. Soto* in 1994–95, evidence presented showed that along a stretch of the NJTP, African Americans made up 13 percent of drivers, 15 percent of vehicles speeding, and 46.2 percent of people stopped by the NJSP. In March 1996, the court ruled that state troopers were engaged in a state-condoned policy of racial profiling, and that the NJSP had failed to monitor, control, or investigate claims of discrimination. In April 1999, then Attorney General Peter Verniero admitted that motorists on the NJTP were stopped and searched based only on the color of their skin.

These LAPD and NJSP cases highlight the pervasive nature of racial bias and its potential impact on police practices. This chapter focuses on the primary mechanisms for preventing and responding to racially biased policing. The foundation of the chapter rests on three important points. First, racially biased policing involves officers taking action against citizens based solely on race or ethnicity. Racially biased policing is discrimination, and as such, it is a form of police misconduct. Racially biased policing includes a wide range of problem behaviors, from racial profiling to use of force. Second, as a form of police misconduct, racially biased policing has severe consequences, including civil litigation and large monetary settlements, poor police-community relations, criminal prosecutions for civil rights violations, and federal intervention. The potentially devastating effects of racially biased policing are far reaching and should not be underestimated. Third, there is a wide range of accountability mechanisms both within and outside police departments that can be employed to combat racially biased policing and other forms of misconduct. This chapter reviews the major internal and external mechanisms, but the author's perspective is that there is no one "magic bullet," or single best accountability mechanism. Each has its advantages and disadvantages, and the best approach for a police department is to employ a number of different mechanisms, each playing an important role in a comprehensive package of accountability.[4]

Internal Control Mechanisms

Traditionally, police departments have been responsible for policing themselves. In recent years, external efforts to control the police have become more common, but primary responsibility for accountability still rests with the police department itself. This section describes the major internal mechanisms for preventing and controlling racially biased police actions, including more traditional tools such as proper recruitment and selection, training, supervision, internal affairs and administrative policy, as well as more recent innovations such as Early Warning systems.

Careful Recruitment and Selection of Personnel

Although it is not always possible to identify racially biased officers at the recruitment stage,[5] effective screening of applicants remains an important part of preventing police misconduct. Recent scandals in Miami, Washington DC, and Los Angeles have been linked to "mass hirings," where departments hired hundreds of officers in a short period of time and did not conduct thorough background and character investigations.[6] Careful recruitment and selection of personnel can serve to weed out many of those who are unfit for police work because of prejudicial attitudes and discriminatory past behavior.

RECRUITMENT: THE FIRST COMPONENT OF ACCOUNTABILITY

The goal of recruitment is to find or attract the best candidates for the position of police officer. Departments employ a variety of strategies to recruit job applicants, such as posting fliers around the community, attending employment workshops at local high schools and colleges, and placing ads in newspapers, radio, and television. More recently, departments rely on the internet by posting job vacancies on their website, allowing candidates to either download application forms or complete them online.

An effective recruitment strategy will reach a wide audience and draw a large number of qualified candidates. The larger the eligible applicant pool, the more selective the department can be in making its hiring decisions. And the more selective a department can be, the greater the likelihood that candidates with racial biases will be weeded out. To reach a wide audience, the recruitment strategy should include a number of things. First, the recruitment effort should use multiple techniques for drawing applicants (outlined above). Although there is a financial commitment up front—in terms of paying for advertisements, sending officers to high school and college career days, and so forth—the department will recoup this money many times over in the long run. Second, an effective recruitment strategy will include special efforts to draw minority and female applicants. Many local police departments have affirmative action plans that require more active recruitment of minorities and women. There is general consensus among scholars and practitioners that fielding a racially and ethnically representative police department can improve police-community relations, diffuse racial tensions, and may even reduce the likelihood of police misconduct. The Commission on Accreditation for Law Enforcement Agencies (CALEA) recommends that the racial makeup of the police department mirror the racial makeup of the community. Also, Fyfe and Kane found that as the NYPD has become more diverse, it "has become better behaved."[7]

Third, the recruitment effort should effectively communicate the basic requirements for employment. Failure to convey these requirements will result in wasted time and effort as the department receives applications from people who are not qualified for the job. Last, the recruitment effort should highlight the benefits and advantages of being a police officer, and present recruits with a realistic picture of what the job is like. Although there is a tendency to focus on the excitement and danger of the job, most police work is neither exciting nor dangerous. Applicants who enter policing with unrealistic expectations (as portrayed on television and in movies) will often become disillusioned, and they may be more likely to quit the profession. If they do not quit, their disillusionment and frustration will often lead to poor job performance, and it may increase the likelihood that they engage in misconduct such as racially biased actions.[8]

SELECTION METHODS

All departments have basic requirements for employment, such as minimum age (usually twenty-one), U.S. citizenship, and at least a high school diploma. If applicants meet these basic requirements, they must also undergo a physical agility test, written exam, oral interview, medical exam, and psychological exam.[9] Police departments will also conduct an extensive background examination that may include a criminal history check, credit check, and interviews of family members, neighbors, and former employers. Among other red flags, departments are looking for any evidence that a candidate possesses prejudicial attitudes that could lead to discriminatory actions on the job.

The overall goal of the recruitment and selection process is to identify those who are most qualified for the job, and who are most likely to carry out their duties with honesty, integrity, and pride. Key qualities in a candidate include an ability to demonstrate good judgment, maintain an even temperament, respect and appreciate diversity, show creativity and problem-solving skills, think on one's feet, handle pressure, and show leadership skills. Candidates who possess these skills will be less likely to engage in racially biased police actions, as well as other forms of misconduct.[10]

Police Training

Careful recruitment and selection must be followed with effective training in the police academy, through field training programs, and through in-service training. At the academy, the goal of training is to provide officers with the basic skills and knowledge necessary to become a police officer. Academy training covers a wide range of topics, including (but not limited to) basic police powers, constitutional law, departmental policies and standards, physical training, use-of-force and firearms training, and proper handling of the mentally ill and domestic violence cases. Officers will also receive blocks of training on ethics and misconduct.

Cadets must receive a clear message at this early stage that racially biased policing is inappropriate, illegal, and that it will not be tolerated. This message can be conveyed through traditional lecture-based instruction, or through scenario-based training where racially biased actions are demonstrated and discussed. Importantly, several scholars have noted that traditional academy training often serves to weed out individuals who do not conform with conservative views or ideology: "A consequence of the police personnel system is that it selects officers who are unable to identify with groups on the margins of traditional society."[11] In some cases, this can foster or compound racialized attitudes.[12] Departments must take care to review their curricula to eliminate this type of training environment.

Following graduation from the academy, officers are typically assigned to a veteran officer for a period of field training (the FTO program). At this stage, the officer applies what he or she has learned in the academy under the guidance and supervision of a more senior officer. The FTO experience is intended to bridge the gap between the classroom environment of the academy and the "real world" of policing on the street. Importantly, this is a formative stage of a police officer's career, and it is critical for field training officers to impart the message that racially biased practices are not consistent with the principles of good policing.

The final form of training is called "in-service," where officers periodically receive additional training on specific issues (e.g., the mentally ill), or as new policies are developed and new tools adopted (e.g., the TASER). Officers also are retrained in several areas to maintain proficiency, such as driving and firearms. In addition, in-service training can be used to "refresh" officers on basic concepts and ethical issues, such as avoiding discriminatory decision making. This retraining sends the message that the department leadership denounces racial bias and expects the same from its officers.

The overall goal of training at all three stages is to provide officers with the skills and knowledge necessary to perform their duties effectively. Fyfe stated that most forms of police misconduct are either intentional or the result of "ineptitude or carelessness," and other scholars have argued that structural features of policing (e.g., poor supervision, isolation, institutional pressures, etc.) are the primary causes of misconduct.[13] Either way, officers who are properly trained are less likely than poorly trained officers to engage in racially biased policing or other forms of misconduct.

Supervision

Policing is an isolated job. Most police officers, particularly in rural areas, will go through an entire shift having little direct contact with a supervisor. Nevertheless, routine supervision of police officers is a critical department task that serves as a foundational element in the agency's effort to insure officer accountability.[14] Weisburd and colleagues reported that nearly 90 percent of police officers surveyed agreed that effective supervision prevents misconduct such as racially biased policing.[15] In particular, sergeants play a vital role in preventing and controlling officer misconduct. Sergeants are primarily responsible for frontline supervision of police officers, and they typically engage in a number of activities to provide proper supervision. Importantly, the sergeant must be held responsible for the behavior of his or her line officers. When sergeants are held to account for the misdeeds of their subordinates, they will be more likely to insure such behavior does not occur. This principle should be maintained up the chain of command, with lieutenants being held responsible for their sergeants' actions, captains being held responsible for their lieutenants' actions, and so on. In short, effective supervision coupled with accountability can greatly reduce the prevalence of racially biased policing.

ACHIEVING EFFECTIVE SUPERVISION

If supervision can reduce racially biased policing, the key then is to provide effective supervision. This can be fostered in a number of different ways. First, the number of officers to be supervised by one sergeant should be limited to eight to twelve.[16] Sergeants who have a "span of control" greater than twelve officers will likely find it difficult to provide sufficient supervision, increasing the potential for misconduct. Second, new sergeants should receive proper instruction in their duties and responsibilities. Quite simply, good supervision can be and should be taught. Third, effective supervision can be made easier if the sergeant not only punishes poor performance, but also rewards good performance.[17] By offering police officers incentives and rewards, the supervisor can create an atmosphere where exceptional performance is valued and sought after. Fourth, if feasible, sergeants should be transferred so they are not responsible for supervising officers who were very recently their peers. Many sergeants find it difficult to supervise officers they have recently worked with, either because officers do not respect their authority, they resent that the sergeant got the promotion and they did not, or because the officers may be aware of the sergeant's own past misdeeds.[18]

Last, effective supervision hinges on the police chief's commitment to accountability. The Mollen Commission stated that "commitment to integrity cannot be an abstract value. . . . It must be reflected not only in the words, but in the deeds, of the Police Commissioner."[19] At its foundation, effective supervision hinges on the "words and deeds" of the chief. Darryl Gates in Los Angeles, Frank Rizzo in Philadelphia, and Harold Breier in Milwaukee demonstrate how attitudes of the chief can send a message to line staff that abusive and racially biased conduct is acceptable.[20] Alternatively, Philadelphia after Rizzo (Morton Solomon), New York after Serpico (Patrick Murphy), and Miami after Liberty City (Bobbie L. Jones and Frederick Taylor) represent cases where meaningful, department-wide reform occurred because of strong leadership that sent a clear message to line officers about what would be tolerated (and more important, what would not).[21]

Murphy put in place systems to hold supervisors and administrators strictly accountable for the integrity and civility of their personnel. He rewarded cops who turned in corrupt or brutal colleagues and punished those who, although personally honest, looked the other way when they learned of misconduct. He used his authority to appoint and demote officers above the rank of captain to weed his department's 450-person executive corps of dead wood and to advance promising young commanders quickly. Murphy used his three and a half years in office to create an environment that loudly and clearly condemned abusive police conduct, those who engaged in it, and—equally important—those who *tolerated* it.[22]

In sum, effective frontline supervision is the cornerstone of internal accountability and is critical to eliminating racially biased policing. If officers believe they will be caught and punished for their racially biased actions or other forms of misconduct, they will be less likely to engage in those activities.[23]

Administrative Guidance

Over the last 30 years, administrative rule making has emerged as the dominant form of discretion control in American policing. Administrative guidance in the form of policies, rules, and procedures communicates to the rank-and-file officers what the department expects, what is considered acceptable, and what will not be condoned.[24] Both CALEA and the American Bar Association (ABA) recommend written rules and policies as an effective manner in which to structure police decision making. Importantly, prior police research has demonstrated that administrative rule making can effectively control police officer behavior in a number of misconduct and racial bias–prone areas, including deadly force, automobile pursuits, use of K-9s, and arrest in domestic violence incidents. Walker reviewed the research examining administrative policies and deadly force, and concluded that: "administrative rules have successfully limited police shooting discretion, with positive results in terms of social policy. Fewer people are being shot and killed, racial disparities in shootings have been reduced, and police officers are in no greater danger because of these restrictions. Officers appear to comply with the rules. This is an accomplishment of major significance and one that provides a model for other discretion control efforts."[25] In this vein, a number of cities and states have passed legislation articulating "no tolerance" for racial profiling and other forms of racial bias. For example, the state of Kentucky recently passed a model policy prohibiting racial profiling: "No state law enforcement agency or official shall stop, detain, or search any person when such action is solely motivated by consideration of race, color, or ethnicity, and the action would constitute a violation of the civil rights of the person."[26]

Yet department policies and rules, by themselves, are not enough to control racially biased policing and other types of misconduct. It is impossible to create rules and policies for every possible situation, and as a result, officers will still employ discretion. However, proper recruitment and selection standards, training, guidance, and supervision can help insure that officers use their discretion wisely. Just as important, the policies must be supported and enforced by the organizational leadership. If the informal norms of the department support racially biased policing, and those who engage in those illicit activities go unpunished, administrative policies become meaningless.

Internal Affairs

The primary task of Internal Affairs is to investigate allegations of misconduct, including racial bias. Investigations by Internal Affairs typically are reactive: the unit receives information about alleged racially biased behavior and investigates to determine whether a violation has occurred. This information can come from a citizen complaint, official report, or from other police officers (supervisors or line officers). Although much of the work conducted by Internal Affairs is reactive, departments are increasingly using proactive investigations to identify problem officers, such as "integrity tests" where incidents fraught with the potential for misconduct are staged and officer responses in those incidents are monitored (i.e., did the officer act in a racially biased manner?).[27]

An effective Internal Affairs unit represents a critical component of a successful departmental response to racially biased policing. There are a number of key issues that will determine the effectiveness of efforts by an Internal Affairs unit to control racially biased actions. First, the unit must have the complete support of the chief.[28] The Internal Affairs commander should report directly to the chief, rather than other managers, as this creates a direct line of communication with the department leadership and demonstrates the importance of the unit and its activities to the rest of the department.[29] Second, the Internal Affairs unit must be given sufficient resources and personnel to complete its tasks.[30] Unfortunately, there is little consensus on optimal size for Internal Affairs units. For example, Sherman found ratios from one investigator to 110 officers to one investigator to 216 officers; when Patrick Murphy took over as commissioner of the NYPD, he reduced the investigator-to-officer ratio from one to 533 to one to 64.[31]

Third, officers assigned to Internal Affairs should receive proper training and instruction. Roles, responsibilities, and the nature of investigations in Internal Affairs are different from other assignments, and for officers to be successful in the unit, they must be adequately prepared for the challenges the new position presents. Fourth, staff selection to the Internal Affairs unit is important. It is important for the officer to want the assignment; otherwise it may perceived as a punishment.[32] Klockars and colleagues stated that a department must create "an environment . . . where assignment to IA is not regarded as a badge of betrayal but as a position of honor and responsibility."[33] Also, the selection criteria for Internal Affairs should itself be rigorous. Officers who have had problems in the past—an excessive number of citizen complaints, disciplinary action, poor performance evaluations, and so forth—are not likely to make good Internal Affairs investigators. Moreover, their reputation as a problem officer among the rest of the department will likely cripple the integrity of the entire unit.

Last, a successful Internal Affairs unit will exist in a department where the informal environment promotes officers bringing information to the unit. Police officers represent a vital source of information about the behavior of their colleagues. Officers know who among them is engaged in racially biased actions. Overcoming the code of silence is difficult but not impossible, and it begins with the chief sending a message that racial bias will not be tolerated, and that officers who report transgressions will be rewarded.

Early Warning Systems

Early Warning (EW) systems are information systems that collect and analyze data on problem behavior, such as incidents of racial bias. The goal of such a system is early identification of problem police officers before their behavior escalates to more serious forms of misconduct. EW systems were first endorsed in 1981 by the United States Commission on Civil Rights and later in 1996 by the U.S. Justice Department conference on police integrity.[34] The first EW systems were developed in the late 1970s by the Miami and the Miami-Dade police departments.[35] More recently, EW systems have been included in consent decrees placed on police agencies by the Civil Rights Division of the Department of Justice (discussed below). Walker and colleagues reported that, by 1999, 27 percent of police departments serving populations of more than fifty thousand people had instituted an EW system, with another 12% of departments in planning stages.[36]

The rationale for an EW system rests on the well-supported theory that a small number of police officers generate most of a department's complaints about problem behavior. Support for the problem police officer theory has been documented in departments across the United States: Houston;[37] Oakland;[38] Los Angeles;[39] Kansas City, MO;[40] Boston;[41] and Washington DC.[42] In most of the cases cited above, the problem officers were readily identifiable, and "police managers ignored patterns of repeated involvement in critical incidents and failed to take any kind of supervisory attention to the officers with the worst records."[43] Accordingly, if a police department can identify and intervene with its problem officers before their behavior escalates, the department can drastically reduce misconduct and significantly improve its relationship with the community. As an illustration, an EW system could identify an officer who has several complaints alleging that he made racial slurs, and intervention through retraining could change his behavior before it escalates into more serious forms of racial bias (e.g., profiling).

An EW system has three basic components: the selection criteria, the intervention, and the post-intervention monitoring.[44] Selection criteria are the behaviors or "red flags" that identify a particular officer as being "at risk." Examples include citizen complaints, use-of-force incidents, involvement in civil litigation, departmental violations and sanctions, and excessive sick days. Although some systems rely on only one indicator, experts recommend a system that uses multiple criteria.[45]

The second component of an EW system is the intervention. Most EW systems are not punitive; rather, they seek to provide problem officers with the necessary counseling and training to change their behavior.[46] The intervention stage is usually a two-step process: first, there is an informal meeting between the officer and his or her supervisor; and second—if deemed necessary after the first meeting—there may be a formal intervention.[47] This may include counseling and additional police training. The final component of an EW system is post-intervention monitoring, as the supervisor "keeps an eye" on the officer to make sure that the problem behavior does not continue. This monitoring can be informal and limited to the immediate supervisor, or formal with significant effort devoted to data collection and analysis, and internal review up the chain of command.

A national evaluation of EW systems concluded that they are expensive, complex and difficult to maintain, requiring a substantial investment in "planning, personnel, data collection, and administrative oversight."[48] The evaluation also found that some systems are "symbolic gestures with little substantive content," while others have proven to be effective in reducing citizen complaints, use of force, and other problem behavior. For example, supervisors in the Pittsburgh Police Department review data from the EW system on a quarterly basis, searching for "any one of eight indicators of racial bias,"[49] including complaints from supervisors, peers or citizens, lawsuits, and normal review of activity reports. An evaluation by the Vera Institute concluded that "the early warning system is the centerpiece of the [Pittsburgh] Police Bureau's reforms in response to the consent decree."[50]

External Mechanisms

Given the long history of police misconduct and the resulting perception that police cannot effectively police themselves, the comprehensive accountability package employed by a department must include external mechanisms—efforts at controlling misconduct that are outside the purview of the police department itself. Many of these accountability measures are well established and have been around since the start of professional policing, such as the criminal law, civil litigation, special investigations, and judicial intervention. Others are more recent innovations, such as U.S. Department of Justice consent decrees and citizen oversight.

The Criminal Law: Prosecuting the Police

Police officers—like any other citizen—can be prosecuted for actions that violate the state penal code. Most states have statutes that address directly the behavior of police officers and others acting in an official capacity when the violation occurs (i.e., official misconduct, abuse of authority). At the federal level, Title 18 of the criminal code includes several sections that have been applied to police officers, including Section 242 (Criminal Liability for Deprivation of Civil Rights) and Section 245 (Violation of Federally Protected Activities).[51]

The criminal law, however, is generally viewed as an ineffective tool in combating police misconduct. Fyfe stated that the criminal law is too vague regarding acceptable behavior by police, and that lay juries lack the expertise necessary to judge matters of professional conduct.[52] Also, the criminal law is a reactive mechanism for controlling officer behavior that plays no practical role in preventing officer misconduct. Arguably, the criminal law could take on a deterrent aspect if it were applied successfully on enough occasions (i.e., certainty, severity, and celerity), but this is simply not the case. Police officers are rarely prosecuted for their transgressions, and when they are, convictions are by no means guaranteed.

At the federal level, the story of applying criminal law to police misconduct is not much different. The Civil Rights Division of the U.S. Department of Justice receives thousands of complaints each year alleging police violation of citizens' civil rights.[53] Of the complaints alleging police misconduct: "about one-third of these complaints are of sufficient substance to warrant investigations. . . . The Department of Justice is very select about the cases it pursues. Of the approximately 3,000 investigations conducted each year, it authorizes only about 50 cases for grand jury presentation and possible indictment."[54] Clearly, federal prosecutions remain rare, leading Skolnick and Fyfe to conclude that "[the Department of] Justice plays virtually no active role in holding local police accountable."[55]

Nevertheless, the nature of criminal trials at both the state and federal level offer some advantages for providing accountability and responding to incidents of racial bias. Criminal trials of police officers are public and typically receive significant media coverage. The media surrounding the trial itself can send a strong message to both the public and department rank and file that racial bias is not tolerated. A criminal trial can also relieve the pressure on the victim of the misconduct, as the prosecutor shoulders the burden of proof. Alternatively, the police officer accused of racial bias receives all the traditional protections of a criminal trial, including innocence until guilt is proven beyond a reasonable doubt. Last, incidents of racial bias often involve violations of state and federal law, and as a matter of law in those cases, criminal prosecution of the officer is necessary and justified.

Civil Litigation: Suing the Police

Police officers can be sued in state and federal court for their actions or failure to act. The number of civil suits against police has increased significantly, from approximately six thousand per year in the late 1960s to as many as thirty thousand per year in the late 1990s.[56] The vast majority of these lawsuits occur in federal court. Although there are a number of federal statutes that can be used by citizens to sue police, the most commonly used statute is the Civil Rights Act of 1871.[57] Section 1983 of the Civil Rights Act of 1871 provides civil and criminal remedies for those whose constitutional rights are violated by persons acting under state authority. Section 1983 states: "Every person, who under color of any statute, ordinance, regulation, custom, or usage, of any State or territory, subjects, or causes to be subjected, any citizen of the United States or other persons within the jurisdiction thereof to the deprivation of any right, privileges, or immunities secured by the Constitution and laws, shall be liable to the party injured in an action at law, suit in equity, or other proper proceeding for redress."

Historically, Section 1983 was used very rarely as an avenue for responding to police misconduct because of inconsistencies in prior court rulings, and the small civil awards one could win against police officers. Beginning in the 1960s, however, rulings in two cases broke down the resistance to filing Section 1983 suits against the police. First, in *Monroe v. Pape* (365 U.S. 167 [1961]), the Supreme Court held that the requirements of Section 1983 (under color of state law) are met whenever a police officer violates a citizen's constitutional rights, regardless of whether their actions also violated state law.[58] This ruling resolved the inconsistency or catch-22 from prior court rulings. In *Monell v. Department of Social Services of the City of New York* (436 U.S. 658 [1978]), the Court ruled that when an agency employee violates an individual's constitutional rights because of the agency's *custom and practice*, the agency as well as the employee may be held liable.[59] Importantly, the Court defined custom and practice broadly enough to include whatever the agency does routinely, whether stated in official policy or not. The *Monell* case led to a dramatic increase in civil litigation against police because it "opened the deep pockets of government treasuries to civil rights plaintiffs."[60] For example, in 2001 the state of New Jersey paid $12.95 million to plaintiffs in a racial profiling lawsuit against the New Jersey State Police. From 1986 to 1990, the city of Los Angeles paid more than $20 million in civil litigation against police officers.[61]

There are a few limitations associated with civil litigation. First, the costs of civil litigation for a police department (and city) go far beyond the awards that are made in specific cases. Police departments must obtain costly liability insurance, must fund a legal staff (or pay for outside legal counsel), and must pay other court-related expenses, in some cases including the fees of plaintiffs' attorneys.[62] Ultimately, these costs are passed along to taxpayers. Second, there is anecdotal evidence suggesting that police have begun to avoid situations—or act differently—because they fear being sued ("litigaphobia"). Although there is no empirical evidence to support this claim, the potential implications are troubling. Many of the other components of the comprehensive accountability package, however, training and supervision in particular, can reduce this potential negative side effect.

The advantages of civil litigation far outweigh its limitations. Many police scholars argue that civil litigation is not only an important way for victims of police misconduct to gain redress; it also is an effective tool for fostering change in police departments. McCoy stated that the increasing costs of civil awards in police mis-conduct suits—and the associated dramatic increases in insurance—forced police departments to take steps to reduce problem behavior.[63] Moreover, many depart-ments have responded to civil liability by adopting written guidelines and instituting training for officers, both of which can decrease the prevalence of all forms of officer misconduct.[64] Given the substantial awards that can now be made (based on the *Monell* case), civil litigation is a critically important component of the comprehensive accountability package.

Judicial Intervention

Courts at all levels play a role in holding police accountable. At the local and state level, judges monitor police decision making at various stages of the criminal proc-ess, including at bail hearings, preliminary hearings, and criminal trials. Appellate courts at the state and federal levels review decisions made by lower courts with re-gard to police behavior, and can issue injunctions that target specific police behavior. An injunction is "a court order that prohibits persons or organizations from engaging in some specific conduct."[65] The injunction can also require that the targeted party engage in some specified manner. There are several cases where plaintiffs have sought injunctive relief from the courts to change police practice (i.e., *Rizzo v. Goode*, 423 U.S. 362 [1976]).

The United States Supreme Court also plays an important role in shaping police behavior through its interpretation of the Constitution and case law. As part of the "Due Process Revolution," the Supreme Court during the late 1950s and 1960s issued a number of watershed rulings that affected police behavior and reshaped police ac-countability. In *Mapp v. Ohio* (367 U.S. 643 [1961]), for example, the Supreme Court established the exclusionary rule, which states that evidence seized illegally cannot be used in court. The Supreme Court has also defined police conduct in numerous other areas, including searches of automobiles, searches with and without warrants, aerial searches, detention and interrogation, pretext/dual motive stops, surveillance, wire-tapping, and entrapment; each of these areas has implications for controlling racially biased policing. Thus judicial intervention has also served as a control on police of-ficer misconduct.

Special Investigations/Commissions

Special or "blue ribbon" commissions have often been formed in response to po-lice misconduct scandals. Commissions are composed of individuals appointed by a city, state, or federal official to investigate police misconduct.[66] These commissions typically hold hearings where witnesses, victims, experts, and police officers offer testimony, and a final report is produced and presented to the police department and city government. Recent examples include the Knapp, Christopher, and Mollen commissions.

But special commissions have limitations. These types of investigations are entirely reactive, formed *after* the misconduct has occurred. In some cases, commissions have subpoena power, but often it is difficult to persuade police officers to testify during the hearing. And of course, those called before the commission may assert their Fifth Amendment protection against self-incrimination. Also, in many cases the special commissions can only make recommendations about reforms and have no power to require the changes be instituted. Police departments can ignore the recommendations of the commission, though doing so may put them at risk of civil liability and result in substantial harm to police-community relations.

Special commissions do serve several important functions as an external accountability mechanism. First, a commission brings together the top scholars, experts, and practitioners in the field to think about police issues and make recommendations for reforms.[67] Second, they are typically well publicized, and because of that publicity, serve to place tremendous pressure on police to begin making those reforms. Third, these types of commissions have had some success in breaking the "code of silence" and convincing officers to testify about the nature and extent of the misconduct (e.g., Michael Dowd's testimony before the Mollen Commission).

U.S. Department of Justice Consent Decrees

A consent decree is "an enforceable agreement reached between two parties involved in a lawsuit."[68] The negotiation of the consent decree is approved by an officer of the court, is binding, and serves to settle the claim. If the party initially being sued complies with the consent decree for a predetermined period of time, that party can then appeal to the court to have the decree dissolved; if the party fails to comply with the decree, the other party can appeal to the court for reinstatement of the original lawsuit.[69] Consent decrees have been used to settle disputes in a wide range of areas, especially conflicts arising between private companies and local governments (i.e., health care issues, pollution, etc.). They have also been used to resolve disputes in criminal justice for some time, most notably claims related to treatment of prisoners. During the 1970s, consent decrees were also used to settle a number of civil suits involving discriminatory hiring practices by police departments.[70]

PATTERN AND PRACTICE LAWSUITS

The 1994 Violent Crime Control Act includes a section that allows the Civil Rights Division of the U.S. Department of Justice to bring a lawsuit against a police department if officers in that department have been engaged in a "pattern or practice" of abuse of citizens' rights.[71] This section greatly expanded the use of consent decrees and facilitates their use as a mechanism for initiating police reform and accountability. Importantly, in a pattern and practice suit, the Civil Rights Division is not seeking financial compensation from the police department. Instead, the government uses the suit to require court-ordered changes in abusive or illegal police practices such as racially biased actions. Since the passage of the Violent Crime Control Act in 1994, the Civil Rights Division has begun fourteen "pattern and practice" investigations. By 2003 six investigations had been completed, resulting in five consent decrees and one memorandum of understanding.

Consent decrees have been put in place in Steubenville, Ohio; Pittsburgh, Pennsylvania; New Jersey (State Police); Los Angeles; and Detroit. Consent decrees have targeted several different types of police misconduct, including racial bias. For example, the consent decree placed on the New Jersey State Police addressed racial profiling. A consent decree typically includes required changes in a number of basic areas such as training, use of force, and citizen complaints. They also often require the development of an Early Warning system and monitoring by an independent authority.

Preliminary research suggests that departments have made significant strides toward complying with the requirements of the decrees. Ortiz stated while under consent decree "the Pittsburgh Police Bureau emerged as a national leader in personnel evaluation and monitoring, traffic stop data collection, and incident reporting policies."[72] Similarly, the monitors of the consent decree against the New Jersey State Police noted that the NJSP "have made significant strides to bring the organization into compliance with the requirements of [the] decree."[73]

Citizen Oversight

There is a long history of police problems in the area of receiving and investigating citizen complaints against individual police officers—particularly with regard to complaints involving racial bias—and citizen oversight has developed as a response to those long-standing problems. Although there are a variety of forms of citizen oversight (see below), the mechanism generally involves review of citizen complaints against the police by individuals who are outside the police department. Citizen oversight boards have four goals: to deter future misconduct; to remove deviant officers; to satisfy individual complainants; and to improve and maintain public confidence in the police.[74] Despite its recent growth, the idea of citizen oversight of the police is still quite controversial, and the arguments for and against it are well defined.[75] The major arguments center on the seriousness of the problem, the fairness and thoroughness of investigations, indicators of effectiveness, and qualifications required for oversight board members to properly assess police actions.

Citizen oversight boards are organized in different ways, with varying degrees of independence from the police department. Boards have varied on at least four important characteristics: (1) who is responsible for the initial investigation and fact-finding, citizens or police; (2) who reviews the completed report, a hearing officer, the board, or a police official; (3) the right of the complainant to appeal; and (4) who imposes the discipline on the officer.[76] The most pure version of citizen oversight (and the rarest) involves an independent organization that receives complaints, employs a cadre of well-trained investigators, holds public hearings and has subpoena power, and makes binding recommendations to the police department.

Research on the impact of citizen oversight of the police is mixed.[77] Experts note that there are some key elements that must be present to at least insure the possibility of effectiveness:

1. A fully functioning civilian review agency needs to investigate complaints, conduct hearings, subpoena witnesses, and report its findings to the police chief and public.

2. Inadequate financing will devastate any system.

3. Civilian review agencies need to be staffed by competent, well-trained investigators who have the authority and the financial backing to carry out investigations.

4. It is simply not possible to have fair and effective civilian review when the hearing officers or panels are biased or less than competent. Police won't ever like civilian review, but they—and the public—are likely to find it more acceptable when investigations and hearings are conducted not by "representative" persons but by hard-nosed, experienced investigators and fair and qualified hearing officers.

5. If a civilian review agency is to work effectively, without unreasonable delay, the oversight system must be afforded access to police witnesses and documents through legal mandate or subpoena power.

6. Both the accuser and the accused are entitled to know the outcome of the hearing and the reasons for the result.[78]

Walker stated that the auditor model of oversight holds the most promise as a reform and accountability mechanism.[79] Under this model, one individual with some degree of legal or policing expertise serves as a full-time independent auditor. The auditor does not receive or investigate individual complaints as they are filed, but rather monitors the entire complaint process, conducts investigations of that process, and make recommendations based on those investigations. There are currently twelve police auditors in the United States, and evidence suggests that several have had a significant impact on police policy and practice—including in areas related to racial bias.[80]

Other Sources of External Accountability

PUBLIC INTEREST GROUPS

There are a number of public interest groups that monitor police behavior and take action when misconduct is alleged. The American Civil Liberties Union (ACLU), Amnesty International, and the National Association for the Advancement of Colored People (NAACP) have long histories of responding to police misconduct, especially racially biased policing. Their activities include preparing written reports and documents, press releases, and assisting in civil and criminal litigation against the police. For example, Amnesty International issued a report in 2004 on racial profiling stating that the practice undermines national security, and that it is so pervasive that it has affected thirty-two million people in the United States.[81] Also, the New York Civil Liberties Union (NYCLU) has vociferously attacked the NYPD for its stop, question, and frisk practices. The NYPD commissioned the RAND Corporation to conduct a study of their field practices. RAND examined more than five hundred thousand stop, question, and frisk (SQF) incidents from 2006, and found that 53 percent of suspects in those SQF incidents were black and 27 percent were Hispanic.[82] The NYCLU notes that nearly 90 percent of those stops resulted in no formal police action (no summons or arrest), and that minorities are disproportionately affected by this practice: "The black community continues to bear the brunt of police stops, blacks continue to be singled out for stops that don't ever result in an arrest, and the police department continues its efforts to justify these practices. Now more than ever, an independent review of the NYPD's stop-and-frisk procedures is necessary."[83] The NYCLU has recently filed suit against the NYPD because of their refusal to make publicly available the SQF data.

THE MEDIA

The media play an important role in police accountability.[84] The television and print media report on police activity on a daily basis, keeping the public informed of police behavior. David Burnham's story in the *New York Times* led to one of the biggest scandals in NYPD history, leading to the creation of the Knapp Commission and the appointment of Patrick Murphy as commissioner, who then instituted dramatic reforms in the department. Perhaps the best example of the media's role as a police accountability mechanism is the Rodney King case. The video footage of the beating was played worldwide, putting tremendous pressure on the Los Angeles Police Department and district attorney's office to take action.[85] Within days of the incident, Chief Daryl Gates publicly denounced the four officers involved in the beating, and the DA's office began a criminal prosecution.[86] Research also shows that the media plays an influential role in shaping individuals' perceptions of the police. After the Rodney King beating, for example, African American and Latino residents' approval of the LAPD dropped a stunning 50 percentage points while approval among whites dropped 43 percentage points.[87] Weitzer also notes that middle-class blacks tend to hold more critical views of the police than their disadvantaged counterparts, and this may be explained by better-educated persons having great exposure to the media (i.e., coverage of police misconduct scandals).[88]

THE PUBLIC

Ultimately, the police are accountable to the public they serve, and the public plays an important role in police accountability. Citizens and citizen groups can place pressure on police departments to initiate reforms. Citizens can file lawsuits against the police to seek redress for inappropriate or illegal police behavior. Just as important, the public can apply pressure on public officials in the city administration, such as the mayor and district attorney. As elected officials, mayors and DAs are hard-pressed to ignore citizen calls for reform without jeopardizing their political careers. Elected officials can initiate police reforms by replacing the police chief, setting up citizen review boards, creating blue-ribbon commissions, and aggressively investigating and prosecuting police misconduct.

Conclusion

Racially biased policing is defined as police officers taking action against citizens based solely on their race or ethnicity. Racially biased policing can involve a wide range of behaviors in varying degrees of seriousness, from racial profiling to use of force to failure to take appropriate action. Regardless of the seriousness, racially biased policing is discriminatory, and as such, it is both illegal and a form of police misconduct. This chapter highlights the accountability mechanisms that can be put in place to prevent and reduce the prevalence of racially biased police actions. Two general categories of mechanisms were reviewed: those that are within the police department (internal) and those that are outside the purview of the department (external).

On the internal side, intensive recruitment, selection, and training can help insure that only the best, most qualified officers are deployed on the street. Candidates who are prone to misconduct such as racial bias will be successfully weeded out. Once on the job, proper supervision and guidance through administrative policy will promote appropriate street behavior, and an effective Early Warning system and proactive Internal Affairs unit will identify problem officers before their behavior escalates to more serious forms of misconduct. Finally, the chief sets the tone for the entire department, and he or she can create an environment where racially biased actions are not condoned, and where officers are held to account for their transgressions.

Still, the long history of failed efforts by police to control their own officers clearly demonstrates the need for additional support through external accountability measures. These measures involve a wide range of stakeholders, including the courts, the prosecutor, the government (state and federal), special interest groups, the media, and the residents of the community. The reception by police to external accountability measures has varied considerably, with a fair amount of outright resistance. The police, however, are accountable to all of these stakeholders, and each plays an important role in preventing and responding to racially biased policing.

Last, there is no single-best accountability mechanism, and the optimal approach for a police department and the community it serves is to rely on a complete accountability package with multiple measures, both internal and external. The measures that make up an accountability package may vary across departments and communities, and that is to be expected given the unique culture, environment, and history of towns and cities—and their police departments—throughout the United States. What becomes critical is that the police department, community, and other stakeholders view their collective roles as equally important, and together, they work to identify the mechanisms of accountability that best meet their specific needs and effectively prevent police misconduct.

NOTES

1. From Los Angeles Police Department Mobile Digital Terminal (MDT) transmissions. Independent Commission on the Los Angeles Police Department, p. 4.

2. New Jersey State Police, *Interim Report of the State Police Review Team Regarding Allegations of Racial Profiling*, p. 4.

3. Independent Commission on the Los Angeles Police Department, pp. 4–8. Other examples that illustrate racial bias include: "sounds like monkey-slapping time"; "hi . . . just got mexercise for the night"; "wees be reedy n about five"; and "don't be flirting with all ur cholo girlfriends."

4. Each of these accountability measures will be given superficial treatment because of page constraints. See Walker, *Taming the System*; and White, *Current Issues and Controversies in Policing*, for more complete coverage of these measures.

5. See Mollen Commission.

6. Skolnick and Fyfe, *Above the Law*; Fyfe and Kane, *Bad Cops*.

7. Fyfe and Kane, *Bad Cops*, p. ii. For divergent perspectives regarding the impact of racial representation in police departments on misconduct (i.e., within-race versus across-race police misconduct), see Alpert and Dunham, *Understanding Police Use of Force*.

8. Skolnick and Fyfe, *Above the Law*.

9. Departments vary in the selection tests they use, and the order in which they use them.

10. Walker and Katz, *The Police in America*; White, *Current Issues and Controversies in Policing*.

11. Kappeler et al., *Forces of Deviance*, p. 91.

12. Tomaskovic-Dewey et al., "Looking for the Driving While Black Phenomena."

13. Fyfe, "Training to Reduce Police-Civilian Violence," p.163; Kappeler et al., *Forces of Deviance*; Armacost, "Organizational Culture and Police Misconduct."

14. Walker and Katz, *The Police in America*.

15. Weisburd et al., *Police Attitudes Toward Abuse*.

16. Walker and Katz, *The Police in America*.

17. Kappeler et al., *Forces of Deviance*.

18. Skolnick and Fyfe, *Above the Law*.

19. Mollen Commission, p. 112.

20. Skolnick and Fyfe, *Above the Law*.

21. Skolnick and Fyfe, *Above the Law*.

22. Skolnick and Fyfe, *Above the Law*, pp. 179–180.

23. Klockars et al., *The Measurement of Police Integrity*.

24. Kappeler et al., *Forces of Deviance*.

25. Walker, *Taming the System*, p. 32.

26. Kentucky State Code 15A.195 (Prohibition against racial profiling).

27. Walker and Katz, *The Police in America*.

28. Walker and Katz, *The Police in America*.

29. Kappeler et al., *Forces of Deviance*.

30. Walker and Katz, *The Police in America*.

31. Sherman, *Police Corruption*; Walker and Katz, *The Police in America*.

32. Walker and Katz, *The Police in America*.

33. Klockars et al., *The Measurement of Police Integrity*.

34. Walker and Alpert, "Early Warning Systems as Risk Management for Police."

35. Walker et al., "Early Warning Systems for Police."

36. Walker et al., "Early Warning Systems for Police."

37. U.S. Commission on Civil Rights, *Who Is Guarding the Guardians?*

38. Toch et al., *Agents of Change*.

39. Independent Commission on the Los Angeles Police Department.

40. "Kansas City Police Go After Their "Bad Boys.""

41. "Wave of Abuse Claims Laid to a Few Officers."

42. "DC Police Lead Nation in Shootings."

43. Walker et al., "Early Warning Systems for Police," p. 201.

44. Walker and Alpert, "Early Warning Systems as Risk Management for Police."

45. Walker and Alpert, "Early Warning Systems as Risk Management for Police."

46. Walker, *The New World of Police Accountability*.

47. Walker and Alpert, "Early Warning Systems as Risk Management for Police."

48. Walker et al., "Early Warning Systems for Police," p. 213.

49. Walker, *The New World of Police Accountability*, p. 114.

50. Vera Institute, *Turning Necessity into Virtue*, p. 37.

51. Kappeler et al., *Forces of Deviance*.

52. Fyfe, "Police Use of Deadly Force."

53. U.S. Commission on Civil Rights, *Who Is Guarding the Guardians?*

54. Epke and Davis, "Civil Rights Cases and Police Misconduct," p. 15.

55. Skolnick and Fyfe, *Above the Law*, p. 211.

56. Silver, *Police Civil Liability*.

57. Kappeler, *Critical Issues in Police Civil Liability*. Following the abolition of slavery, Congress passed the Civil Rights Act of 1871 in an effort to control activities of the Ku Klux Klan and its members.

58. Skolnick and Fyfe, *Above the Law*.

59. Monell, a pregnant employee for the Department of Social Services, requested maternity leave but was informed by her supervisor that department policy was to deny such requests and require pregnant mothers to resign. Monell filed suit, arguing that she and other women were denied equal protection under the law because the Department of Social Services policy only affected female employees.

60. Skolnick and Fyfe, *Above the Law*.

61. Independent Commission on the Los Angeles Police Department.

62. Skolnick and Fyfe, *Above the Law*.

63. McCoy, "Lawsuits Against Police."

64. Skolnick and Fyfe, *Above the Law*.

65. Skolnick and Fyfe, *Above the Law*, p. 207.

66. Grant and Terry, *Law Enforcement in the 21st Century*.

67. Walker and Katz, *The Police in America*.

68. Ortiz, "Consent Decrees," p. 93.

69. Ortiz, "Consent Decrees."

70. Ortiz, "Consent Decrees."

71. Walker and Katz, *The Police in America*.

72. Ortiz, "Consent Decrees," p. 97.

73. Lite et al., *New Jersey Monitor's Fourth Quarterly Report*.

74. Walker, *Police Accountability*.

75. See Walker, *Police Accountability*.

76. Skolnick and Fyfe, *Above the Law*.

77. Walker, *The New World of Police Accountability*.

78. Skolnick and Fyfe, *Above the Law*, pp. 227–228.

79. Walker, *The New World of Police Accountability*.

80. Walker, *The New World of Police Accountability*.

81. Amnesty International (USA), *Threat and Humiliation*.

82. RAND, *Do NYPD's Pedestrian Stop Data Indicate Racial Bias?*

83. "Rand Report Glosses Over Racial Disparities."

84. Walker and Katz, *The Police in America*.

85. Skolnick and Fyfe, *Above the Law*; Kappeler et al., *Forces of Deviance*.

86. The fours officers were all acquitted at the state trial, but two of them (Officers Koon and Powell) were convicted at a subsequent federal civil rights trial, and both served thirty months in prison.

87. Weitzer, "Incidents of Police Misconduct."

88. Weitzer and Tuch, "Race, Class, and Perceptions of Discrimination"; Weitzer and Tuch, "Perceptions of Racial Profiling."

REFERENCES

Alpert, Geoffrey & Roger Dunham. 2004. Understanding police use of force: Officers, suspects, and reciprocity. New York: Cambridge University Press.

Amnesty International. 2004. United States of America: Excessive and lethal force? Amnesty International's concerns about deaths and ill treatment involving police use of tasers. Amnesty International: London (AI Index: AMR 51/139/2004).

Amnesty International (USA). 2004. Threat and humiliation: Racial profiling, national security, and human rights in the United States. New York: Amnesty International (USA).

Armacost, Barbara. 2004. Organizational culture and police misconduct. George Washington Law Review 72: 457–59

DC police lead nation in shootings. 1998, November 15. Washington Post.

Epke, John & Linda Davis. 1991. Civil rights cases and police misconduct. FBI Law Enforcement Bulletin 60: 15.

Fyfe, James J. 1988. Police use of deadly force: Research and reform. Justice Quarterly 5: 165–205.

Fyfe, James J. 1995. Training to reduce police-civilian violence. In And justice for all: Understanding and controlling police abuse of force. Geller, W.A. & Toch, H. (eds.). Washington, DC: Police Executive Research Forum.

Fyfe, James J. & Robert Kane. 2006. Bad cops: A study of career-ending misconduct among New York City police officers: Final report. Washington, DC: National Institute of Justice.

Grant, Heath & Karen J. Terry. 2005. Law enforcement in the 21st century. Boston: Allyn and Bacon.

Independent Commission on the Los Angeles Police Department. 1991. Report of the independent commission on the Los Angeles Police Department. Los Angeles: Independent Commission on the Los Angeles Police Department.

Kansas City police go after their "bad boys." 1991, September 10. New York Times.

Kappeler, Victor E. 2001. Critical issues in police civil liability. 3d edition. Prospect Heights, IL: Waveland Press.

Kappeler, Victor E., Richard D. Sluder, & Geoffrey P. Alpert. 1998. Forces of deviance: Understanding the dark side of policing. Prospect Heights, IL: Waveland Press.

Klockars, Carl, Sanja Kutnjak Ivkovich, William Harver, & Maria Haberfeld. 2000. The measurement of police integrity. Washington, DC: National Institute of Justice.

Lite, Greenberg, DePalma, Rivas, and Public Management Resources. 2001. New Jersey monitors' fourth quarterly report. Available: http://www.state.nj.us/lps/monitors_report_7.pdf.

Mapp v. Ohio, 367 U.S. 643 (1961).

Mayor's Citizen Commission. 1991. A report to Mayor John O. Norquist and the board of fire and police commissioners. Milwaukee: City of Milwaukee.

McCoy, Candace. 1984. Lawsuits against police: What impact do they really have? Criminal Law Bulletin, January–February: 53.

Mollen Commission. 1994. The City of New York commission to investigate allegations of police corruption and the anti-corruption procedures of the police department: Commission report. New York: City of New York.

Monell v. Department of Social Services of the City of New York, 436 U.S. 658 (1978).

Monroe v. Pape, 365 U.S. 167 (1961).

New Jersey State Police. 1999. Interim report of the State Police review team regarding allegations of racial profiling. Trenton: New Jersey State Police.

Ortiz, Christopher. 2005. Consent decrees. In Encyclopedia of law enforcement, Volume 1. Sullivan, L. E. & Rosen, M. S. (eds.). Thousand Oaks, CA: Sage Publications.

RAND. 2008. Do NYPD's pedestrian stop data indicate racial bias? Santa Monica, CA: RAND.

Rand Report Glosses Over Racial Disparities in NYPD's Stop-and-Frisk Practices. 2007, November 20. New York Civil Liberties Union. http://www.nyclu.org/node/1507.

Rizzo v. Goode, 423 U.S. 362, 368–69 (1976).

Sherman, Lawrence W. 1974. Police corruption: A sociological perspective. Garden City, NY: Doubleday Anchor Books.

Silver, Isidore. 2000. Police civil liability. New York: Matthew Bender.

Skolnick, Jerome H. & James J. Fyfe. 1993. Above the law: Police and the excessive use of force. New York: The Free Press.

Toch, Hans, Douglas J. Grant, & Raymond T. Galvin. 1975. Agents of change: A study in police reform. Cambridge, MA: Schenkman.

Tomaskovic-Dewey, David Mason, & Matthew Zingraff. 2004. Looking for the driving while black phenomena: Conceptualizing racial bias processes and their associated distributions. Police Quarterly 7 (1): 3–29.

U.S. Commission on Civil Rights. 1981. Who is guarding the guardians? Washington, DC: Government Printing Office.

Vera Institute. 2002. Turning necessity into virtue. New York: Vera Institute.

Walker, Samuel. 1993. Taming the system: The control of discretion in criminal justice, 1950–1990. New York: Oxford University Press.

Walker, Samuel. 2001. Police accountability: The role of citizen oversight. Belmont, CA: Wadsworth.

Walker, Samuel. 2005. The New world of police accountability. Thousand Oaks, CA: Sage Publications.

Walker, Samuel & Geoffrey P. Alpert. 2002. Early warning systems as risk management for police. In Policing and misconduct. Lersch, K. M. (ed.). Upper Saddle River, NJ: Prentice Hall.

Walker, Samuel, Geoffrey P. Alpert, & Dennis Jay Kenney. 2001. Early Warning systems for police: Concept, history, and issues. In Critical issues in policing. 4th edition. Dunham, R. G. & Alpert, G. P. (eds.). Prospect Heights, IL: Waveland Press.

Walker, Samuel & Charles M. Katz. 2002. The police in America: An introduction. New York: McGraw-Hill.

Wave of abuse claims laid to a few officers. 1992, October 4. Boston Globe.

Weisburd, David, Rosann Greenspan, with Edwin E. Hamilton, Hubert Williams, & Kelly A. Bryant. 2000. Police attitudes toward abuse of authority: Findings from a national study. Washington, DC: Government Printing Office.

Weitzer, Ronald. 2002. Incidents of police misconduct and public opinion. Journal of Criminal Justice 30: 397–408.

Weitzer, Ronald & Steven Tuch. 1999. Race, class, and perceptions of discrimination by the police. Crime and Delinquency 45: 494–507.

Weitzer, Ronald & Steven Tuch. 2002. Perceptions of racial profiling: Race, class, and personal experience. Criminology 40: 435–456.

White, Michael D. 2007. Current issues and controversies in policing. Allyn and Bacon: Boston.

Chapter 21

|||||||||||||||||||||||||||||||||||||||||||||||||||||||||||||||||||||||||||

Democratic Policing
How Would We Know It If We Saw It?

Matthew J. Hickman

At the heart of any discussion about race, ethnicity, and policing is the issue of *fairness*. Fairness in law enforcement is a cornerstone of democratic policing, marked by the fundamental expectation of equal treatment under the law regardless of one's race or ethnicity, gender, religion, sexual orientation, or other extralegal factors. The purpose of this chapter is to reflect on democratic policing in the United States, and to ask some very tough questions regarding how much we really know about fairness in law enforcement. In brief, the problem is that the United States strongly advocates democratic policing abroad, but is not itself fully committed to democratic policing domestically. I discuss these ideas in three parts.

In part I, I explore the nature of democratic policing. I identify themes in discussions of democratic policing, and offer that a common thread is the need for information. I suggest that police behavior is the principal concern of democratic policing and, importantly, the public perception of police behavior. In part II, I discuss the need for national indicators of fairness in policing. It is my belief that fairness in law enforcement can only come to light through systematic and widespread data collection, analysis, and dissemination. The federal government will not be the leader in this regard, for as I will discuss, the process of government data collection with regard to race, ethnicity, and policing can (and has) at times become mired in contradictory political concerns. In part III, I discuss how we can invest in democratic policing through a restructuring of the federal investment in justice statistics, and more importantly, how local police departments can lead the way by exploring the utility of place-based policing, and embracing data collection and public reporting.

I. What Is Democratic Policing?

Discussions of democratic policing generally walk down one of two paths: one path involves discussions of political theory, the nature of democracy, and the role of police in a democracy. This path tends to be more retrospective and concerned with the evolving nature of democratic policing (i.e., democratic policing as a process). Another path generally involves discussions of the core principles or foundations of democratic policing. This path tends to have a more present focus and often seeks to identify "observable" characteristics or indicators thought to be associated with democratic policing (i.e., democratic policing as an end). In either case, discussions of democratic policing are generally focused not on policing in the United States but on the development of democratic policing abroad, primarily in transitional governments. Clearly, the discourse surrounding democratic policing takes on a different tone if one is discussing policing in Seattle, WA, as compared to policing in Iraq or Macedonia.

There appears to be some consensus that democratic policing is best viewed as a process rather than an end. To view democratic policing as a process suggests that the police (and governing bodies) adopt an outlook that requires constant monitoring and evaluation to ensure that democratic ideals are represented. In contrast, to view democratic policing as an end suggests that clear targets can be articulated, and somewhat unrealistically implies that democratic policing has not been attained until those targets are met.

Accountability, Transparency, and Fairness

Three themes consistently emerge from discussions of democratic policing: notions of *accountability*, *transparency*, and *fairness*. With regard to accountability, the focus is not on accountability for the crime control functions of law enforcement, but on adherence to the rule of law (i.e., a focus on the means of policing). Likewise, the focus is not on accountability to the chief executive or elected public officials, but accountability to the public. Minimally, a truly accountable police must first acknowledge police behavior that the public views as a violation of trust, and second, correct the problem. Departments (and governing bodies) that fail on either score cannot be described as accountable to the public.

The idea of transparency in policing suggests that police activities should be open to public scrutiny. Of course, some aspects of law enforcement must necessarily be secret. Police secrecy may be institutionally justified and reinforced as a necessary feature of effective policing. Secrecy may be necessary to protect trade secrets to maintain an edge over the criminal population, or it may be necessary to protect information from the media to maintain the integrity of a criminal investigation. On the other hand, secrecy may be unrelated to the goals and objectives of the police. An extreme case would be the covering up of illegal or immoral activities of officers. Less dramatic is the more common rebuffing of concerned citizens who just want to know about crime in their neighborhood. A related idea is "openness," which suggests that police departments integrate themselves with the citizens served on a number of levels.[1] As a public entity, the police should be accessible to the people, rather than closed off and insular. The concept of openness also echoes the notion that "the police are the people and the people are the police,"[2] and suggests that the police should seek to reflect the population served, if for no other benefit than increased diversity and cultural understanding.

Fairness, as the term is generally used with regard to policing, encompasses ideas related to equality. In its broadest sense, fairness refers to the protection of basic human rights, but as one starts to focus the concept, the discussion turns to ideas about nondiscrimination, nonpartisanship, and equal treatment. Fairness is succinctly summarized in terms of questions posed by Tyler in his discussions of police legitimacy: Are the police objective, unbiased, and consistent in their application of the law? Are the police treating people with dignity, politeness, and respect?[3] Of particular concern is fairness in the treatment of minorities. Researchers generally refer to race/ethnicity as an extralegal variable, a factor that should not influence criminal justice decision making. Thus research often explores the impact of several legally relevant variables on criminal justice decisions (the decision to arrest, for example) while controlling for other characteristics that may or may not influence these decisions. When a significant effect of race on criminal justice decisions rears its ugly head, we then debate about whether that constitutes evidence of racism, actual behavioral differences, or something else.

The common thread linking accountability, transparency, and fairness is that they all require *information* to evaluate whether these democratic ideals are being satisfied as part of the process of democratic policing. Our country is not presently in a position to be able to speak to any of these ideals; we simply don't have the necessary information. Yet we are strong advocates of democratic policing abroad. As part of our country's broader role in advocating global democracy, the U.S. government supports democratic policing through a variety of mechanisms. The total direct expenditures for the support and development of police abroad have been estimated at around $635 million in FY 2004, and indirect expenditures totaled another $293 million.[4] David Bayley does a wonderful job of cataloging expenditures and activities in support of democratic policing abroad.[5]

An indirect example is the U.S. Agency for International Development (USAID), which supports the development of democratic policing as part of its strategy to promote democratic governance. USAID has identified criteria based on four dimensions of democracy: rule of law, good governance, competition, and citizen inclusion.[6] Thus four criteria defining democratic policing are that: (1) the actions of police must be governed by law; (2) police actions must not violate international principles of human rights; (3) the police must be subject to external supervision with respect to both corporate law-enforcement effectiveness and the behavior of individual officers in the performance of their duty; and (4) as a matter of priority, the police must be responsive to the needs of individual citizens.[7] Arguably, it is point number three where our own police are lacking.

A direct example is the International Criminal Investigative Training Assistance Program (ICITAP) administered by the U.S. Department of Justice, and presently funded by the Departments of State and Defense, USAID, and the Millennium Challenge Corporation. ICITAP presently has 16 field offices and 44 country programs, and they reported providing training to over 76,000 foreign participants and holding nearly 1,500 training events during 2007.[8] The ICITAP's more dated Transition to Democratic Policing Development program sought to assist countries in developing democratic policing by conducting assessment and evaluation of existing policies and procedures, as well as community perceptions of the police; development of revised or new policies and procedures, and training; assisting with the implementation of selection, hiring, and training processes; and developing an evaluation program to provide a monitoring mechanism and feedback useful for review of the overall program. It would be interesting to turn this kind of a model on ourselves—I think we might be surprised by what we find in our own country.

Perception and Legitimacy

Although the themes of accountability, transparency, and fairness are useful for organizing thinking about democratic policing, at the risk of great oversimplification I want to suggest that a more operational way to think about democratic policing is that the principal concern of democratic policing is not the behavior of citizens, but rather the behavior of the police. And more to the point, it is not just the behavior of the police, but also the public perception of police behavior. This will be a very uncomfortable idea for many, particularly policing scholars who will recognize threads of Manning's dramaturgical perspective in the linkage of police behavior and public perceptions.[9] This perspective suggests that the inability of the police to succeed at their publicly constructed "impossible" mandate leads to the employment of strategies to manipulate the appearance of crime control (such as the use of arrest statistics), rather than actually addressing public safety. Democratic policing cannot be said to exist where citizens are subject to the deleterious effects of arrest, for example, under this perspective. I want to steer these ideas in a different but related direction.

Police administrators, reformers, and others have long recognized a perceptual component of policing; that is, police behavior has direct consequences for public perceptions of the police. The public presumes that officers have been subjected to a rigorous screening, selection, and training process, and that police agencies are vigilant in monitoring and responding to officer behavior. Because policing is such a visible occupation, involving direct personal contacts with citizens, the presumption of integrity can be eroded by incidents involving poor officer behavior. The public experiences officer behavior through direct police-citizen contact, and indirectly through exposure to the experiences of family, friends, and acquaintances, as well as media reports of police misbehavior and portrayals in the entertainment industry.

It wasn't really until the United States reached a national crisis of race relations and police legitimacy during the 1960s that public opinion data motivated large-scale change efforts to improve the relationship between the police and the communities served. National surveys cited by the 1967 President's Commission on Law Enforcement and the Administration of Justice provided evidence that while the public as a whole exhibited favorable attitudes toward the police, African Americans consistently gave lower ratings on police effectiveness and conduct. One survey found that while only 9% of the public believed police brutality existed in their community, this overall figure included 35% of African American males. The same survey found that two-thirds of whites believed the police were "almost all honest" but that only one-third of African Americans felt so. Ten percent of nonwhites believed the police were "almost all corrupt," compared to less than 2% of whites. Another survey found that 15% of African Americans believed that the police in their communities took bribes, compared to less than 4% of whites.

The 1973 National Advisory Commission on Criminal Justice Standards and Goals considered these findings in writing Standard 1.2: "Every police chief executive immediately should establish and disseminate to the public and to every agency employee written policy acknowledging that police effectiveness depends upon public approval and acceptance of police authority." Further, police departments should periodically survey the public "to elicit evaluations of police service and to determine the law enforcement needs and expectations of the community."

The linkage between officer behavior and public perceptions is demonstrated by research showing that incidents of police misconduct substantially influence public opinion about the police. For example, Weitzer examined public opinion trends in Los Angeles and New York prior to and following several negative incidents.[10] In Los Angeles, these included the 1979 killing of an African American woman, the 1991 Rodney King incident, a 1996 videotaped beating, and the unfolding scandals involving the LAPD's Rampart Division in the late 1990s. A substantial drop in favorable ratings of the police followed each incident. For example, prior to the King incident, the percentage approving of the LAPD's job performance was 80% among Hispanics, 74% among whites, and 64% among blacks. These figures fell to 31%, 41%, and 14%, respectively, following the King incident, and eventually returned to pre-incident levels, although recovery took longer among Hispanics and blacks as compared to whites.[11]

Tyler has characterized this balance between actual and perceived behavior in terms of a contrast between objective measures of police legitimacy (police adherence to norms of conduct) and subjective measures of police legitimacy (public views about police conduct).[12] In discussing the need for a national survey of (subjective) police legitimacy, Tyler argues that public compliance with the law and deference to police authority are dependent on public perceptions of police legitimacy. Low or weak perceptions of legitimacy have direct consequences for the effectiveness of the police. Research has demonstrated moderate correlations between subjective legitimacy and public support for budget increases, greater discretionary authority, and cooperation with the police.[13] Tyler also suggests integrating community survey data into COMPSTAT-like processes.[14] While his focus on subjective measures of legitimacy is important, it should not be taken to suggest that we have adequate objective measures of legitimacy. Tyler offers allegations of police abuse of authority and police shootings as examples; these are far from perfect and are not presently collected in any comprehensive or systematic fashion. We also need to develop these basic objective indicators on a national scale, in concert with Tyler's proposed national study of subjective police legitimacy.

Largely building on Tyler's normative concept of legitimacy, Meares discusses the importance of "lawabiders" as a focus of police marketing efforts. Disparate treatment of minorities has the side effect of reducing minority lawabiders' commitment to governmental authority, and thus erosion of the (subjective) legitimacy of the police. "According to the normative view of compliance, our goal is not to manipulate the cost of crime for lawbreakers but to manipulate the perceptions of government legitimacy that lawabiders hold. In this way, we can hope to embed norms of voluntary compliance intergenerationally to achieve crime reduction."[15] Among many suggestions, Meares notes that alienation of minorities can be alleviated by improving the tracking of racial demographics of arrest, and legitimacy can be enhanced by recognizing that "advertisement is as important as traditional crime policy."[16] Meares notes that "what is critically important is perception rather than outcome. What matters is whether people believe that they count as manifested in the way that authorities behave. Note, however, that what authorities actually think is largely irrelevant. Management of perceptions, then, has great potential for impacting compliance in the new millennium. At the same time, the lack of a necessary connection between perceptions and actual belief suggests a potential dark side to this approach."[17]

The need to monitor and respond to public opinion is clear, and it's an essential part of the process of democratic policing. Somewhat sadly, it doesn't matter if the police are doing great if the public believes that they are not. As previously mentioned, the 1973 National Advisory Commission on Criminal Justice Standards and Goals clearly acknowledged this fact and recognized the need to periodically survey the public. Today, many agencies conduct surveys of the public. In 2000, about one-quarter of the roughly thirteen thousand local police departments in the United States, including more than 60% of those serving populations of one hundred thousand or more residents, surveyed citizens during the prior year.[18] Eighteen percent of all departments, and more than half of the larger departments, inquired about citizen satisfaction with police services.[19] About two-thirds of agencies provided this information to their officers.[20] As encouraging as these statistics may be, they mask great variation in the quality and frequency with which this information is solicited. A great deal of work remains to be done in developing standardized questions that departments can use to accurately gauge public opinion regarding police legitimacy.

II. The Need for National Indicators of Fairness in Policing

The process of democratic policing requires routine examination of law enforcement activity to ensure that it reflects democratic ideals. In short, a democratic government such as ours needs national indicators. This is not a new concept; developed nations of the world employ a variety of indicators to gauge the "health" of their country. In the case of the United States, these include a dizzying array of social and economic indicators regarding employment, education, income, and health. Yet we have hardly anything at all when it comes to information about police behavior. Granted the task is not a small one in a country that boasts nearly eighteen thousand state and local law enforcement agencies.

So we find ourselves in a rather awkward situation. We are a society that is clearly more concerned with the process by which decisions are made than the outcomes of those decisions. It follows that the most important national indicators by which we can gauge the performance of our justice system are those related to fairness in the administration of justice. With regard to the police, then, we should look for evidence not only that our police are enforcing the law while obeying the law, but for a broader array of basic indicators about the quality of police-citizen interactions, use of force, citizen complaints, and, more important, about the role (if any) of race and ethnicity in these aspects of policing.

It is somewhat disturbing, and even somewhat hypocritical given our role as a global advocate of democracy, that the largest democracy in the world actually collects and reports very little of this type of information. As the late professor James J. Fyfe once remarked, "we still live in a society in which the best data on police use of force come to us not from the government or from scholars, but from the *Washington Post*."[21] Likewise, Kane has noted that "it is both ironic and unacceptable that in American democratic society, the police, which function as the most visible representatives of the crime control bureaucracy, collect data on members of the public in the form of arrest and complaint reports without systematically distributing comprehensive data on their own activities that produced those crime statistics."[22]

Current National Indicators, and Politics Thereof

So what kinds of national indicators already exist? At present, the only systematic, national-level data collection on police-citizen interactions is the Police Public Contact Survey (PPCS) administered by the Bureau of Justice Statistics (BJS). The PPCS was the principal federal response to Section 210402 of the Violent Crime Control and Law Enforcement Act of 1994, which requires the attorney general to "acquire data about the use of excessive force by law enforcement officers." The PPCS is a supplement to the National Crime Victimization Survey (NCVS), and the goal is to provide national estimates of the incidence and prevalence of citizen contacts with the police. The PPCS also seeks to describe the nature of those contacts, including whether the police used or threatened the use of force, the specific actions they took, as well as any potentially provoking citizen behaviors. The PPCS has been administered in 1999, 2002, and 2005. The NCVS-based sample for the 2005 PPCS included 80,237 persons age sixteen or older, with completed interviews for 63,943 persons. The sample is weighted to represent a national estimate of 228 million persons age sixteen or older.

With regard to traffic stops, the PPCS has been consistent in documenting that white, black, and Hispanic drivers are stopped by police at similar rates, but that blacks and Hispanics are more likely to be searched by police after being stopped. In 2005, 3.6% of white drivers stopped by police were searched, compared to 8.8% of Hispanic drivers and 9.5% of black drivers. The PPCS has also consistently documented that police use of force is relatively rare (occurring in 0.8% of all traffic stops, and 1.6% of all police contacts), but that males, blacks, and youth are more likely to experience force. This is important information having direct bearing on fairness in policing, and enabling macro-level monitoring and evaluation. In the absence of this type of data, we would be in a position of "not knowing," which means we could not further the process of democratic policing.

The BJS Survey of Inmates in Local Jails (SILJ) also provides some information about police use of force, although BJS has never analyzed or reported on these data. The SILJ is a computer-assisted personal interview conducted with a nationally representative sample of jail inmates, and covering a broad range of topics.[23] Importantly, the SILJ contains items that parallel those included in the PPCS; thus jail inmates are asked about the use or threat of force experienced at the time of their arrest.

Analysis of the inmate data demonstrates that the PPCS underestimates force due to the exclusion of the recently incarcerated (the PPCS accounts for about 87% of the total force incidents derived from both sources), and that the inmate sample is more likely to experience force, a much higher level of force, and is more likely to report injury from force.[24] However, demographic characteristics are substantively similar across the two data sources: males, blacks, and youth are more likely to experience force.[25]

The BJS Law Enforcement Management and Administrative Statistics (LEMAS) survey is presently the most systematic and comprehensive source of national data on law enforcement personnel, expenditures and pay, operations, equipment, and policies and procedures. The LEMAS surveys have been conducted roughly every three years since 1987, and provide national estimates for all state and local law enforcement agencies based on a representative sample of about three thousand agencies. In the 2003 iteration of LEMAS, data were collected on formal citizen complaints about police use of force.[26] The LEMAS data provide information on the volume and rate of complaints as well as complaint dispositions. Importantly, the LEMAS platform can also be used in conjunction with other data (such as Census Bureau data) to explore issues such as minority representation and citizen complaints.[27] The LEMAS complaints data have also found diverse application in the field, including being used to establish "baselines" for larger police departments in their annual reports, as well as in *Monell* litigation involving police departments.[28]

Most recently, the BJS Deaths in Custody Reporting Program (DCRP) has provided national data on arrest-related deaths. DCRP data on law enforcement homicides (both justifiable and unjustifiable) are substantively similar to those obtained by the FBI's Supplemental Homicide Reports (SHR); specifically, 97% of law enforcement homicides involved a male subject, the average age was thirty-three years, more than 80% were killed by a handgun, and about 30% involved a black subject.[29] The DCRP data indicate that about 56% of all arrest-related deaths involved a minority subject (suicide is the only category of arrest-related deaths in which whites are the majority).[30]

With the possible exception of the PPCS, none of these four indicators address fairness in policing in broad terms. All four studies focus on particular decision stages, outcomes, or administrative processes associated with police action; none of them really address the nature and quality of police-citizen interactions. But it's easy to be critical without considering some of the political realities of government data collection—particularly acute when the data bear on race, ethnicity, and policing. A perfect example is the PPCS, which has consistently documented no difference in the rates with which drivers of different races are stopped by police. Once stopped, however, blacks and Hispanics are more likely to have their person or vehicles searched, and are more likely to experience the use or threat of force. As per established BJS procedures, a press release was prepared for purposes of publicly releasing this important report, and it was submitted by the Director to the office of the Principal Deputy Assistant Attorney General (PDAAG) for review. The PDAAG, acting in the political interests of the administration, did not want the secondary finding (regarding racial inequality in searches and the distribution of force) to be mentioned.

New York Times reporter Eric Lichtblau publicly broke the ensuing story in August 2005, about four months after it occurred.[31] The BJS director was subsequently forced out of BJS due to his insistence that these important findings not be tampered with or otherwise "spun" by Justice Department politicals. As Lichtblau reported, the director was formally asked to resign but invoked personnel rules requiring that he be placed elsewhere. In a letter to Attorney General Alberto Gonzales, Rep. John Conyers Jr. (D-Mich.) and other House colleagues formally requested that the attorney general "immediately reinstate" the director.[32] Conyers also separately requested an investigation into these matters by the Government Accountability Office.[33] The *Washington Post* jumped into the fray with coverage of the episode as well as an editorial piece decrying the political interference in justice statistics.[34] And in an op-ed piece, a former BJS director noted that this entire episode simply drew more attention to the racial profiling study.[35] As a postscript, nearly identical findings were again reported from the 2005 PPCS in April 2007. Although the corresponding AP story noted the handling of the 2002 report and subsequent departure of the BJS director, the underlying issue of political interference had ceased to draw much media attention.

Numerous popular authors, news commentators, and journalists have alleged that the Bush administration in general, and the Bush Justice Department in particular, are unique in the degree of information control and secrecy they have exercised.[36] Despite the unquestionable impact of September 11, 2001, on the Justice Department and government broadly, I'm not so certain that this is an uncharacteristic political climate; it is at least not uncharacteristic of other periods in history dominated by conservative politics.[37] For example, political pressure and the creative management of crime statistics during the Nixon administration have been well documented.[38] At the very least, the present administration reinforces the idea that politics and government data are simply inseparable.

So what does this mean for future national data collections focused on fairness in policing? The goal of national data on fairness in policing will not be achieved in the absence of either (a) substantial external pressure, or (b) substantial internal motivation. Unfortunately, public pressure on the federal government to lead the way in providing national data on such issues is apparently not significant, if existent at all. And internal motivation is entirely limited by the individuals who manage and work in these agencies. Scholarly work, and, frankly, the media, does capture the attention of some federal employees in positions to help with internal motivation. Absent individuals having an interest in pursuing these topics, it is difficult to envision any national data collection efforts along these lines in the near future. Federal employees in the agencies charged with conducting, or funding, national data collections will need to lead the way by bringing these issues to the forefront of discussions about the direction of their agencies' research portfolios. Other scholars have argued for national data collections bearing on fairness in policing, and have noted the increased costs associated with these studies in contrast to the stagnant federal budgeting environment,[39] but I don't think many scholars have fully acknowledged the weight of the political dimension.

Quite simply, as long as government bureaucrats in positions to control justice statistics are politically motivated, the "bearing of light" on issues of racial equality in justice will be a slow and controversial process. In my opinion, the likelihood of significant movement in this area is directly related to the presence of federal employees able and willing to take on these issues and, perhaps most important, a management style that permits them to do so.

The goal of national indicators of fairness in policing will also require a rethinking of the federal investment in law enforcement statistics. The current federal investment in national justice statistics is in some ways backward. We spend a lot of money studying crime victims (the NCVS), compiling offenses known to police (the UCR), and, apparently, counting and measuring prisoners in every possible way (BJS corrections programs). If you think of the classic "flowchart" of the criminal justice system, common renderings impose a funnel-like shape in recognition of attrition at each decision stage in the criminal justice process. As such, expenditures on victimization are justifiable since victimization touches the greatest number of people and, as the most important decision makers in the criminal justice process, victims play a strong role in determining what justice "looks like" at subsequent decision stages. But the human resources devoted to the analysis of victimization data simply don't match. The overall investment in law enforcement statistics is nothing short of pathetic considering that the police decision to arrest constitutes the second-most important decision stage in the criminal justice process.[40]

In sum, if you were to superimpose an image of federal resource allocations to justice statistics on top of the classic flowchart of the criminal justice system, it might be somewhat funnel-shaped, but (with the exception of victimization statistics) it would most likely point in the opposite direction. Until the federal investment in justice statistics is restructured, the goal of national indicators of fairness in policing will be unattainable.

III. Investing in Democratic Policing

In short, I believe it is time for this country to put its money where its mouth is, and invest in the idea of democratic policing. The process of democratic policing—a reflection of constant monitoring and evaluation to ensure that democratic ideals are represented—demands it. Current federal justice statistics and research mechanisms (NIJ and BJS) will need significant internal change. In a broad sense, they will need to develop a management style that actually encourages government-led research and development, and they will need to recruit personnel with active research agendas to carry it out. Perhaps more important is a restructuring of current investments in justice statistics; a fivefold increase in financial and human resources devoted to law enforcement statistics would not be inappropriate. Minimally, human and financial resources for justice statistics should be proportional to both the impact on citizens lives (for example, victimization affects the greatest number of people), and the relative importance in the criminal justice decision making process, which is largely a reflection of the impact on subsequent decision stages. In the absence of movement toward these goals, the federal government will not be effective in the development of national indicators of fairness in policing, and thus will not lead the way toward democratic policing.

Instead, I believe that local police departments can lead the way on three fronts. First, there seems to be some promise and momentum behind the idea of "place-based policing" not only as an organizing principle for the business of policing, but as part of the process of democratic policing. Second, it is clear that, independent of place-based policing, democratic policing will require wholesale change in performance monitoring and assessment. Third, in the spirit of transparency and accountability, consistent public reporting on fairness in policing is not only required but can conceivably have more positive benefits to the agency than negative. I'll discuss each of these in turn.

Place-based policing, in a nutshell, focuses police efforts on places rather than people; on the context in which criminal behavior occurs, rather than the individuals involved in crimes.[41] Building on the growing acceptance of hot spots, place-based policing holds that the units of analysis associated with "place" are contingent on the nature of underlying crime problems. This means moving beyond addresses with a high volume of calls for service, and toward recognition that the appropriate units of analysis may be a collection of street blocks, street segments, storefronts, or other micro-level place units. Police departments will need to move away from traditional organizational schema that emphasize precinct or district definitions of place, and toward a more fluid definition of place. This extends to the organization of policing and deployment practices as well as the methods by which data are compiled and analyzed.

The expected benefits of place-based policing include greater efficiency in the allocation of resources, relatively time-stable targets for police interventions, and greater effectiveness.[42] The greater efficiency in resource allocation derives from the idea that the concentration of crime is greater at places than in people, and thus the police have to target a greater number of people than places to address an equivalent proportion of crime. The time-stable nature of places is demonstrated by crime trajectories of places (which seem to evidence stability over multiple years), as contrasted to variability in individual offending over time. The notion that places are more stable than people is somewhat intuitive, and this characteristic will increase the efficiency of police interventions directed at places. Finally, the effectiveness of place-based policing is supported by growing evidence in the literature on hot-spots policing strategies.

Weisburd discusses some interesting ethical and legal concerns surrounding place-based policing. He notes that "place-based policing offers a target for police interventions that is less protected by traditional legal guarantees. The common law and our legal traditions have placed less concern over the rights of places than the rights of individuals. It is not that police can do what they like at places. Rather, the extent of constitutional and procedural guarantees has at times been relaxed where places are targeted. When it is established that places are crime targets or deserve special protection, it becomes easier to legally justify enforcement in regard to individual offenders."[43] I'd like to extend these ideas by adding the possibility that the adoption of place-based policing may also help to insulate the police from allegations of racially biased policing. To the extent that the police have truly adopted place-based strategies (i.e., the notion that places are the targets of their efforts, not people), the racial characteristics of offenders seem to become less relevant. Of course, the key assumption is that targets are objectively selected for intervention. Place-based policing suggests that selection would be based on quantitative hot-spot type analyses, which should reinforce objectivity.

A second and related area is the need for wholesale change in the way local police departments measure and assess their performance. No longer should we concern ourselves primarily with monthly and annual fluctuations in UCR offenses known to the police. To be sure, crimes and offenders are the bread and butter of policing, and law enforcement strategy and resource allocations should be designed around these key facets of law enforcement. But first and foremost the police need to know *how* their officers are enforcing the law. Public opinion needs to become part of performance evaluation. This means more than an annual or sporadic survey; a much more significant marketing approach will be necessary if the police are to be effective at the management of public perceptions of the police.

Finally, the process of democratic policing requires consistent public reporting on fairness in law enforcement. I would like to challenge every local police department, in their next annual report (and if they don't have an annual report, they ought to start doing one), to try leaving the crime statistics for the appendix. Instead try leading the publication with statistics on the number of citizen complaints and complaint dispositions, official use-of-force incidents, and to the extent possible, provide data by race and ethnicity. Provide the racial demographics of arrests and traffic stops. This doesn't mean that we are emphasizing the "bad" in policing; rather we are trying to establish a baseline regarding officer behavior, and initial public reaction (which can then be managed), then steer it toward an emphasis on the "good."

Take the wind out of the sails of those who would claim racial bias; collect, analyze, and disseminate the data, and make it publicly available. Lay all the cards on the table and let the debates run. No one can justly punish a police department for being forthcoming on these issues. As the controversy surrounding the PPCS statistics aptly demonstrates, you only draw more attention (and negative attention, at that) by trying to hide or ignore it. Perhaps most important, you can't fix a problem you don't know to exist. And denying the existence of a problem doesn't make the problem go away; it only suggests ignorance, which may become the basis for legal action. In discussing some practical reasons for police departments to collect information on police behavior, Kane notes that it enables them to identify problem officers and practices, identify policies that work and those that do not, and insulate themselves to some degree from pattern or practice lawsuits (where poor record-keeping practices may result in negative outcomes).[44] Kane notes that in his experience defending police departments, when he could acquire data, the analyses more often than not demonstrated equitable practices with regard to disciplinary and other matters. In this regard, he suggests that "by collecting and allowing public access to data on coercive processes and outcomes, police departments might dispel several myths and stereotypes that some members of the public erroneously maintain of the police."[45] This alone is worth the investment.

NOTES

1. Skolnick, 1999.
2. National Advisory Commission, 1973, p. 330.
3. Tyler, 2002, p. 80.
4. Bayley, 2006.
5. Ibid.
6. U.S. Agency for International Development, 2005.
7. Hume & Miklaucic, 2005.
8. ICITAP, 2008.
9. Manning, 1977.
10. Weitzer, 2002.
11. The foregoing discussion of the perceptual component of policing is drawn from Hickman, 2006a.
12. Tyler, 2002.
13. Ibid.
14. Ibid.
15. Meares, 2007, p. 3.
16. Ibid., p. 5.
17. Ibid., p. 6.
18. Hickman and Reaves, 2003.
19. Ibid.
20. Ibid.
21. Fyfe, 2002, p. 99.
22. Kane, 2007, p. 776.
23. For detail, see James, 2004.
24. Hickman, Piquero & Garner, 2009.
25. Ibid.
26. See Hickman, 2006b. In my previous career as a statistician at BJS, I became interested in different possible methods for collecting national data on police use of force. I was motivated by the dearth of national data, but more so by Fyfe's work on the lack of data on the use of deadly force, which led me to informally consult with him on a number of occasions. In the course of our conversations it became clear that one less-than-perfect, but viable, option was to harness the BJS Law Enforcement Management and Administrative Statistics (LEMAS) survey. After extensive discussions with Fyfe and other policing scholars, I made the decision to incorporate items in the LEMAS survey instrument to collect departmental data on citizen complaints about police use of force. These data were collected from large agencies as a type of pilot study that, in my mind, if successful, would lead to broader collection efforts, perhaps including the collection of available demographic information about complainants. I also viewed this pilot study as a necessary step toward the eventual long-term goal of collecting administrative records of force incidents on a national scale. This initial effort was indeed successful, providing evidence that police departments were in fact willing and able to provide this type of "sensitive" information to the federal government, with the usual caveats regarding data quality and large-scale establishment surveys.
27. Hickman and Piquero, 2009.
28. Futterman, Mather & Miles, in press.
29. Mumola, 2007, p. 2.
30. Ibid., p. 13.
31. See Lichtblau, 2005a: "The planned announcement noted that the rate at which whites,

blacks and Hispanics were stopped was 'about the same,' and that finding was left intact by Ms. Henke's office, according to a copy of the draft obtained by the *New York Times*. But the references in the draft to higher rates of searches and use of force for blacks and Hispanics were crossed out by hand, with a notation in the margin that read, 'Do we need this?' A note affixed to the edited draft, which the officials said was written by Ms. Henke, read 'Make the changes,' and it was signed 'Tracy.' That led to a fierce dispute after Mr. Greenfeld refused to delete the references, officials said. Ms. Henke, who was nominated by Mr. Bush last month to a senior position at the Department of Homeland Security, said in a brief telephone interview that she did not recall the episode."

32. A copy is on file with the author and available upon request.

33. And the GAO did subsequently conduct an investigation that cleared BJS of any wrongdoing. See GAO, 2007.

34. See Eggen, 2005; Lichtblau, 2005b; Washington Post, 2005.

35. See Bessette, 2005: "Ironically, virtually identical data were contained in the previous BJS study on police contacts and were properly identified in the corresponding press release. In March 2001, BJS released a comparable study of police contacts in 1999. On the second page of the two-page press release (still available on the BJS website), it was duly noted that 'Black and Hispanic motorists (11 percent each) were more likely than whites (5 percent) to be physically searched or have their vehicles searched.' This information entered the public domain with nary a ripple of controversy."

36. For example, Lichtblau, 2008.

37. My tenure in the federal government, just over seven years, was not long by federal standards. I recognize that it also represents a somewhat biased cross-sectional view of politics in the Justice Department, given the years of my employment (2000–2007). I entered on the tail end of President Clinton's second term, and left during President Bush's second term, having served under Attorneys General Janet Reno, John Ashcroft, and Alberto Gonzales.

38. Seidman and Couzens, 1974.

39. For example, Tyler, 2002.

40. When I was at BJS, the law enforcement unit consisted of two people, including myself. We typically sought external funding (from other federal agencies with shared research interests) to support law enforcement data collections. In contrast, other programs at BJS were clearly overstaffed, and as most of their data collections were sole-sourced to the U.S. Bureau of the Census, extremely cost-inefficient.

41. Weisburd, 2008.

42. Ibid.

43. Ibid., p. 8.

44. Kane, 2007, p. 775.

45. Ibid., p. 775.

REFERENCES

Bayley, David. 2006. Changing the guard: Developing democratic police abroad. Oxford University Press.

Bessette, Joseph. 2005. The injustice department: Why was Lawrence Greenfeld fired? Weekly Standard, October 17.

Eggen, Dan. 2005. Official in racial profiling study demoted. Washington Post, August 25.

Futterman, Craig, Mather, H. Melissa, and Miles, Melanie. (In press). The use of statistical evidence to address police supervisory and disciplinary practices: The Chicago Police Department's broken system. Civil Rights Litigation and Attorney Fees Annual Handbook (v. 23). Eagan, MN: Thomson/West.

Fyfe, James J. 2002. Too many missing cases: Holes in our knowledge about police use of force. Justice Research and Policy 4: 87–102.

Government Accountability Office. 2007. Bureau of justice statistics: Quality guidelines generally followed for Police-Public Contact Surveys, but opportunities exist to help assure agency independence. GAO-07-340. Washington, DC: GAO.

Hickman, Matthew J. 2006a. Integrity in policing. In Encyclopedia of police science (3d edition), ed. Jack R. Greene. New York: Routledge.

Hickman, Matthew J. 2006b. Citizen complaints about police use of force. Washington, DC: Bureau of Justice Statistics.

Hickman, Matthew, and Piquero, Alex. (2009). Organizational, administrative, and environmental correlates of complaints about police use of force: Does minority representation matter? Crime and Delinquency 55: 3–27.

Hickman, Matthew J., Piquero, Alex R., and Garner, Joel H. (2009). Toward a national estimate of police use of non-lethal force. Criminology and Public Policy 7: 563–604.

Hickman, Matthew J., and Reaves, Brian. 2003. Local police departments, 2000. Washington, DC: Bureau of Justice Statistics.

Hume, Elizabeth, and Miklaucic, Michael. 2005. Exorcising demons of the past: Seizing new opportunities to promote democratic policing. Presentation at the 2005 USAID Summer Seminar Series, July 7, 2005.

International Criminal Investigative Training Assistance Program. 2008. About ICITAP. Washington, DC: ICITAP.

James, Doris J. 2004. Profile of jail inmates, 2002. Washington, DC: Bureau of Justice Statistics.

Kane, Robert J. 2007. Collect and release data on coercive police actions. Criminology and Public Policy 6(4): 773–780.

Lichtblau, Eric. 2008. Bush's law: The remaking of American justice. New York: Pantheon.

———. 2005a. Profiling report leads to a demotion. New York Times, August 24.

———. 2005b. Democrats want official to be reinstated over report on profiling. New York Times, August 26.

Manning, Peter. 1977. Police work. Cambridge, MA: MIT Press.

Meares, Tracey L. 2007. Law enforcement for lawabiders. Washington, DC: Police Foundation.

Mumola, Christopher J. 2007. Arrest-related deaths in the United States, 2003–2005. Washington, DC: Bureau of Justice Statistics.

National Advisory Commission on Criminal Justice Standards and Goals. 1973. Police. Washington, DC: Government Printing Office.

President's Commission on Law Enforcement and Administration of Justice. 1967. Task force report: The police. Washington, DC: Government Printing Office.

Reaves, Brian A., and Hickman, Matthew J. 2002. Census of state and local law enforcement agencies, 2000. Washington, DC: Bureau of Justice Statistics.

Seidman, David, and Couzens, Michael. 1974. Getting the crime rate down: Political pressure and crime reporting. Law and Society (Spring): 457–493.

Skolnick, Jerome H. 1999. On democratic policing. Washington, DC: Police Foundation.

Tyler, Tom R. 2002. A national survey for monitoring police legitimacy. Justice Research and Policy 4: 71–86.

U.S. Agency for International Development. 2005. At freedom's frontiers: A democracy and governance strategic framework. Washington, DC: USAID.

Washington Post. 2005. Lowering profiling's profile. August 26.

Weisburd, David. 2008. Place-based policing. Washington, DC: Police Foundation.

Weitzer, Ronald. 2002. Incidents of police misconduct and public opinion. Journal of Criminal Justice 30: 397–408.

Chapter 22

Moving Beyond Profiling
The Virtues of Randomization

Bernard E. Harcourt

Racial profiling is best understood as a type of law enforcement technique that relies, at least in theory, on actuarial methods to target individuals and resources. The
only legitimate justification for racial profiling—for the deliberate and affirmative
use of race in policing—would be that the method serves as a type of statistical discrimination that more effectively and efficiently allocates law enforcement resources.
Although racial profiling is never really based on scientific evidence of differential
offending rates—given that it operates in a hidden manner and is generally denied
—profiling can only ever be justified if there are true offending differentials between racial groups; otherwise, there is no reason whatsoever to engage in statistical
discrimination.

In this sense, racial profiling simply represents one instance of a larger category
of actuarial methods in policing and punishment—a larger category that now per-
meates the field of criminal law and its enforcement. From the use of the IRS Dis-
criminant Index Function to predict potential tax evasion and identify which tax
returns to audit, to the use of drug-courier profiles to identify suspects to search at
airports, to the use of risk-assessment instruments to determine pretrial detention,
length of criminal sentences, prison classification, and parole eligibility, prediction
instruments increasingly determine individual outcomes in our policing, law enforcement, and punishment practices. More and more, we use risk-assessment tools
to identify whom to search, when to punish more, and how to administer the penal
sanction.

Most of us view this larger trend with hope rather than alarm. Many scholars,
criminal justice practitioners, and public citizens embrace the turn to actuarial methods as a more efficient, rational, and wealth-maximizing tool to allocate scarce law
enforcement resources.[1] When it comes time to identify violent sexual predators,
drug traffickers, tax cheats, or dangerous recidivists, we increasingly put our faith in
actuarial instruments.[2] The simple fact is, we believe that the police can detect *more*
crime with the *same* resources if they investigate suspects who are at *greater* risk of
criminal offending; and courts can reduce *more* crime if they incapacitate for *longer*
periods convicted criminals who were *more* likely to recidivate. Most of us believe
that the use of *reliable* actuarial methods in criminal law represents progress. No one,

naturally, is in favor of spurious stereotypes and erroneous predictions. But to most of us, it simply makes common sense to decide whom to search based on reliable predictions of criminal behavior, or whom to incarcerate based on dependable estimates of future reoffending. Many even believe that it is alright to use ethnicity at the border, national origin or Islamic religion at the airports, and possibly race in the inner city *if* these are reliable proxies of danger.[3] It has today become second nature to think about just punishment through the lens of actuarial prediction.

In a recent book, *Against Prediction: Profiling, Policing, and Punishing in an Actuarial Age* (University of Chicago Press, 2007), I challenge this common sense understanding and set forth three compelling reasons why we should be skeptical of—rather than embrace—the new actuarial paradigm. First, the reliance on predictions of future criminality may undermine the primary goal of law enforcement, namely reducing crime. Though this may sound counterintuitive, it is surprisingly correct: the use of probabilistic methods may increase the overall amount of targeted crime depending on the relative responsiveness of the profiled individuals (in comparison to the responsiveness of those who are not profiled) to the shift in the level of law enforcement. The ultimate effect on crime will depend on how members of the two different groups react to changes in policing or punishment: if the higher-offending, profiled persons are *less* responsive to the policy change, then the overall amount of profiled crime in society will likely *increase*. In other words, profiling on higher past, present, or future offending may be entirely counterproductive to the central aim of law enforcement—crime minimization.

Second, the reliance on probabilistic methods produces a distortion in the carceral population. It creates an imbalance between, on the one hand, the distribution of demographic or other group traits among the actual offender population and, on the other hand, the distribution of those same traits among the population of persons with criminal justice contacts, such as arrest, conviction, probation, incarceration, parole, or other forms of supervision and punishment. Simply put, the profiled population becomes an even larger proportion of the carceral population—larger in relation to its representation among actual offenders—than the nonprofiled population. This in turn aggravates and compounds the difficulties that many of the profiled individuals have obtaining employment, pursuing educational opportunities, or simply leading normal family lives. These are significant social costs that are most often overlooked in the crime and punishment calculus—overlooked primarily because these individuals are *guilty* of a criminal offense. They are likely to fuel increased crime rates.

There are, naturally, other costs to consider as well. Psychologist Tom Tyler has demonstrated how perceptions of the legitimacy of criminal justice procedures affect the willingness of citizens to abide by the law.[4] Lawrence Sherman has also discussed the need to better minimize offender defiance through fair and just procedures that do not stigmatize the offender—calling for what Sherman coins "emotionally intelligent justice."[5] Other commentators have properly emphasized the link between targeted enforcement—particularly in the case of racial profiling—and increased police misconduct. So, for instance, the implementation of a targeted policing strategy focused on increased stop-and-frisk searches on the streets of New York City in the 1990s was accompanied with disproportionate searches of African American and Latino citizens, as well as a sharp rise in the number of civilian complaints of police misconduct, including brutality.[6] Still others have focused on the direct costs on families and the incarcerated.[7] In *Against Prediction*, I emphasize the negative consequences associated with the potential ratchet effect, but I only do so because others have properly emphasized these other costs.

Third, the proliferation of actuarial methods has begun to bias our conception of just punishment. The perceived success of predictive instruments has rendered more natural theories of punishment that function more smoothly with prediction. It favors theories of selective incapacitation and sentencing enhancements for offenders who are at greater risk of future dangerousness. Yet these actuarial instruments represent nothing more than fortuitous advances in technical knowledge from disciplines, primarily sociology in the early twentieth century, that at the time had no normative stake in the criminal law. The originators, scholars like the preeminent sociologist Ernest Burgess at the University of Chicago, were interested only in trying to accurately predict future behavior; they had no investment in theories of just punishment. They were intervening as pure behavioral scientists. As a result, these technological advances were, in effect, exogenous shocks to the legal system, and this raises very troubling questions about what theory of just punishment we would have independently embraced and how it is, exactly, that we have allowed technical knowledge, somewhat arbitrarily, to dictate the path of justice.

These three arguments should severely temper our embrace of the new actuarial turn in the field of crime and punishment. To be sure, the force of these arguments will resonate differently in different punishment and policing contexts. But they are at their strongest in the case of racial profiling of African American and Hispanic individuals, for example when they are targeted as drivers on the nation's highways and our city streets. This, for several reasons: first, given the likely differentials in responsiveness to policing among the different racial groups, racial profiling on the highways probably *increases* the overall amount of criminal activity in society. If we assume rational action theory, any likely increase in drug and other offending among whites, as a result of their accurate perception that the police are focusing on African Americans and Hispanics, would probably exceed the potential reduction in drug offending among minorities. The logic here is that any explanation for possible offending differentials (whether it be socioeconomic background, limited employment alternatives, or acculturation) would also predict lower elasticity to policing among the higher offending group. Second, and dispensing with rational choice assumptions, racial profiling likely produces a ratchet effect resulting in a disproportionate representation of minorities with correctional contacts in relation to their representation in the offending population—a ratchet that operates along one of the most troubling lines, namely race and ethnicity. It is precisely the type of ratchet that can only aggravate our tragic legacy of racial discrimination in this country. And it has significant negative effects on the educational, employment, and social outcomes of members of minority groups. Third, profiling on the highways for drug contraband involves a law enforcement objective—the war on drugs—whose net benefits are, at the very least, debatable and, certainly, highly contested. Finally, racial profiling tends to distort our conception of just punishment, especially our shared ideal that similarly situated offenders should be treated similarly, regardless of skin color.[8]

The starting point of this chapter, then, is that the use of predictive methods such as racial profiling are likely to be counterproductive to the law enforcement objective of reducing crime, and therefore that there is no justification for racial profiling. There are, of course, a number of other, perhaps more important problems with racial profiling that have nothing to do with its efficiency at combating crime. There are problems of equal treatment, of racial discrimination, of the ethical treatment of others, as well as many other concerns. But the truth is, we do not even need to address those larger ethical and political issues if the use of racial profiling does not accomplish the law enforcement objective of reducing crime, because then there is absolutely no reason to profile in the first place. There is no longer any justification whatsoever.

This initial premise is fully set forth and defended at length in *Against Prediction*. There, I dissect with mathematical equations, economic models, and graphs the claims of a number of economists who contend that the use of racial profiling can improve the efficiency of policing by increasing the number of successful searches.[9] Their argument runs as follows: Assuming that people respond rationally to the increased cost of offending—assuming rational action theory—targeting more police resources at a higher-offending population will reduce their rate of offending (given the greater likelihood of being detected and punished). If we assume, in addition, that minorities have a higher offending rate than whites, then the optimal level of profiling occurs when the offending rate of minorities declines to the same level as the offending rate of whites. At that point, the police will maximize the number of successful police interventions and have no legitimate interest in profiling minorities to any greater extent. The economists verify these conclusions with accurate mathematical equations and economic models.

But even under these assumptions, racial profiling may actually *increase* the overall societal rate of offending.[10] It all depends on the relative responsiveness of the two groups—the profiled minorities and the nonprofiled whites—to policing. If minorities are *less* responsive to policing than whites, then their decrease in offending will be outweighed, in absolute numbers, by the more elastic responsiveness of whites—that is, by the increased offending of whites in response to the fact that they are being policed less. This is true despite the fact that the overall number of successful police interventions *increases*—despite the fact that the police are detecting and punishing *more* crime. I demonstrate this in *Against Prediction*[11] and will not rehearse the argument further here, but start instead from the point where I ended there—namely that the use of prediction in the context of racial profiling is likely to be counterproductive to the law enforcement objective of reducing crime. In a nutshell, there is no justification for racial profiling.

Where then does this leave us? The answer is *randomization*. Instead of racial profiling, we need to police race-blind, which, it turns out, is no different from selecting randomly by race. And not only race-blind, but entirely randomly: we should not substitute other types of profiling for racial profiling *because the same arguments concerning comparative elasticities apply to all other group traits.* Profiling along any dimension will increase overall crime in society if the profiled group is less elastic to policing along that dimension. In other words, we are left in the position of having to rely on randomness in policing and punishment. Instead of targeting our policing on higher-offending populations, we should instead police in a race-neutral and offending-neutral manner, and select our policing targets and allocate our police resources in a more random way. I realize this goes against the grain of policing.[12] It is not, however, something we should be afraid of. To the contrary, it is something we should embrace.

Instead of endorsing the actuarial turn in criminal law and the use of racial profiling, I argue that we should celebrate the virtues of randomization. Random sampling is the only way to achieve a carceral population that reflects the actual offending population. As such, random sampling is the only way to fulfill a central moral intuition regarding just punishment, namely that similarly situated individuals should have the same likelihood of being apprehended when they offend, *regardless of race, ethnicity, gender, or class.* Randomization also avoids the risk that actuarial methods will increase the overall amount of crime in society where the targeted population is less elastic to policing.

Naturally, random sampling does not mean searching any citizen without probable cause, granting parole by lottery, or pulling prison sentences out of a hat. Randomization has a limited and narrow definition: it means making criminal justice determinations blind to predictions of future dangerousness. In the policing context, randomization is simple: law enforcement should randomly sample IRS tax filings for audits or use numerical sequencing for consensual car searches on the highway. In terms of policing, randomization means sampling from among suspects where there is probable cause. In the sentencing area, randomization means something quite different, but no less straightforward: it means imposing a sentence based on a proper and independent metric and then avoiding the effects of the actuarial, by eliminating prediction-based devices such as parole. Randomization does not mean drawing names arbitrarily in deciding whom to parole; it means, instead, eliminating the effects of predictions of future offending.

The baseline presumption in the criminal law should favor *randomized* policing and punishment. Criminal law enforcement and correctional institutions should be blind to predictions of criminality based on group characteristics. In sum, we should adopt a presumption *against* prediction.

The close analysis of the economic models of racial profiling liberates us to explore the virtues of randomization. Once it is shown that the use of predictions of future offending may actually increase the overall crime rate in society, it becomes clear that we can and should reexamine our presuppositions about the role of randomness in policing. In this chapter, I explore the virtues of randomization, looking not only at the narrow question of policing, but more broadly at the larger issues of punishment and the administration of the criminal sanction.

The Virtues of Randomization

Justifications of racial profiling, it turns out, are a symptom of a much larger problem in the fields of policing, criminal law, and punishment theory—namely the fact that so often our empirical claims and theorizing take a leap of faith. The economic model of racial profiling is a perfect example: the economists had essentially assumed in their model of racial profiling that minorities are as responsive to policing as whites, if not more. If they had not made that crucial assumption, then their own models would have demonstrated to their own satisfaction that racial profiling will actually increase the amount of crime in society—which is most definitely not an "efficient" outcome. Their claims were mathematically verified, but only if we assumed something about the relative elasticity of the two groups that we have no ground to believing. (In fact, if minorities have a higher offending rate than whites, it is far more likely that the cause of that difference, perhaps lower employment opportunities, would lower their responsiveness to policing in comparison to whites.)

This, I take it, is a gap within their own model: even assuming deterrence—which itself is, to many, a leap of faith[13]—there is a gap over which these economists took possibly another leap of faith. But this is merely a symptom of a larger problem, one that points in many ways to the virtues of randomization. In much modern theorizing about policing and punishment, there always comes this moment when the empirical facts run out or the deductions of principle reach their limit—or both—*and yet the reasoning continues.* There is always this moment, ironically, when we take a leap of faith. It is no accident that it is always there, at that precise moment, that we learn the most about the researcher—that we can read from the text and decipher a vision of just punishment that is never entirely rational, never purely empirical, and never fully determined by the theoretical premises of the author. In each and every case, our modern texts on policing and punishment let slip a leap of faith—a choice about how to resolve a gap, an ambiguity, an indeterminacy in an argument of principle or fact. Racial profiling may be the perfect illustration of this, but it is by no means the only one.[14]

It is precisely when we reach that gap that we should turn instead to *randomization.* Where our social scientific theories run out, where our principles run dry, we should leave the decision making to chance. We should no longer take a leap of faith, but turn instead to the coin toss, the roll of the dice, the lottery draw—in sum, to randomization and chance. And we should do so, I almost hesitate to say, *throughout* the field of crime and punishment.

In the realm of searches, surveillance, and detection, law enforcement agencies should turn either to completeness or to random sampling. The Internal Revenue Service could audit tax returns at random using a social security number lottery system. The Transportation Security Administration could search every passenger at the airport, or randomly select a certain percent based on a computer generated algorithm using last names. The Occupational Safety and Health Administration could investigate employer compliance by randomly selecting on employer tax identification number. In these and other prophylactic law enforcement investigations, the agency could very easily replace profiling—which rests on uncertain assumptions about responsiveness and rational action—with randomization.

In choosing law enforcement priorities, governmental agencies should begin allocating resources by chance. The local district attorney's office, as well as the federal prosecutor's office, could select annual enforcement targets (as between, for instance, public corruption, insider trading, drug enforcement, or violent crimes) by lottery. State highway policing authorities could distribute patrol cars through a randomized mapping system using heavily trafficked roads and interstate highways. The Bureau of Alcohol, Tobacco, and Firearms could choose between equal-impact initiatives on the basis of an annual lottery draw.

And yes, even in the area of sentencing and corrections, courts and prison administrators should start thinking about relying more heavily on chance. Judges could impose sentences, following conviction, based on a draw from within a legislatively prescribed sentencing range; the range could easily be determined, for instance, by felony classifications. The department of corrections could assign prisoners to facilities on a random basis within designated escape-risk or security-level categories. Prisoners in need of drug, alcohol, or mental health treatment could be assigned to comparable programs based on a lottery draw.

The common gesture running through all these suggestions is to question and, ultimately, to reject social engineering through policing and the criminal sanction. The desire to stop and refuse to take leaps of faith represents nothing more, in practice, than *stopping to engineer* persons and social relations through punishment. The central impulse is precisely to resist shaping people by means of the penal sanction—and thereby to wipe the policing and punishment field clean of speculative social science and indeterminate principle.

Possible Objections and Responses

Why Turn to Randomization?

Some may ask, of course, "Why turn to randomization?" There are other alternatives. We could simply stick with what we have done in the past: do what we did before, use the same punishments as earlier generations. We could heed the status quo. The problem is, their judgments were precisely the product of years and years of uncritical leaps of faith. We will have learned nothing from the exercise of critical reason. Alternatively, we could turn to the democratic process and allow the legislature to decide. But in the end, their vote will reflect nothing more than prejudice, ideology, bias, and, again, leaps of faith. We could decide simply to impose our tastes and aesthetic preferences, but that seems obnoxious and irrational.

We must turn instead to randomization *because we have no other choice*. We must turn to the lottery because it is the only way to act *within the bounds of reason*. We must turn to randomization *by default*. Sure, randomization may have some positive values. It may remind us that our knowledge claims are limited. It may remind us of the frightening role of ideology in our punishment practices. It may help gather information. By using a form of random sampling, we may in fact learn a lot about the world of deviance that surrounds us. Randomization may offer more transparency in our policy making. And in fact, it may be more efficient than the alternative. But none of these are the reason we turn to randomization. We turn instead because there is no alternative that satisfies critical reason.

But Where Exactly Do We Stop?

How far exactly shall we go with this? Once we have begun to roll the dice, how will we know when to stop? If we use a lottery *within* sentencing ranges, why not then draw *all* sentences from the same urn? Why not determine guilt by the toss of a coin? Why not even decide whom to accuse by drawing lots? This is, after all, the whole point of Jorge Luis Borges's brilliant short story "The Lottery of Babylon" (1941). Once you go down the path of chance, the road may well lead to hell. How far are we willing to go and how will we know when to stop?

"The Lottery in Babylon" gives life to this fear. In Babylon, Borges tells us, the lottery started simply as a game of chance played by commoners. A drawing of lots intended only to promote commerce and entertain. Soon enough, though, to draw more interest in the lottery, the lottery would include not just winning draws, but also some unlucky ones. At first, those unlucky draws would impose a monetary fine, but soon enough those unlucky draws would lead to some days in jail. And why limit the winning draws to monetary gain? "Certain moralists," the narrator in Borges's tale tells us, "argued that the possession of coins did not always bring about happiness, and that other forms of happiness were perhaps more direct."[15] And so, a winning draw might include appointment to the state council or the imprisonment of one's enemy, and over time, the rewards and losing hands became more and more extreme, and along with that the power of the state (which Borges refers to as "the Company") grew and grew.

Eventually, the Company began to add layers on layers of chance, to the point where, today, the narrator tells us, "our customs are now steeped in chance." But it's not a pretty fate. "Like all the men of Babylon," the narrator tells us, "I have been proconsul; like all, I have been a slave. I have known omnipotence, ignominy, imprisonment. Look here—my right hand has no index finger. . . . Once, for an entire lunar year, I was declared invisible—I would cry out and no one would heed my call, I would steal bread and not be beheaded."[16] Borges writes, "I owe that almost monstrous variety to an institution—the Lottery—which is unknown in other nations, *or at work in them imperfectly or secretly.*"[17]

Borges's tale raises a troubling question: if we do indeed turn to chance, how will we know where to stop? If we accept the coin toss for searches, then why not for the arrest or the conviction as well? Why stop at the first police contact? Why not extend randomness to the guilt determination? This is the slippery slope of randomization that leads, ultimately, to the "Lottery in Babylon." Where is the natural limit of randomization once you have gone down the path of chance?

The response: the central claim here is *not* that we can know *nothing*. We have some basic intuitive knowledge that no one can dispute. As an empirical matter, we know that searching someone is less intrusive than arresting and detaining them. We know that punishing an entirely innocent person is wrong. We know that if we execute someone, we are not going to be able to rehabilitate them. As a matter of principle, we know that murdering an innocent person is worse than stealing their wallet. We can use these minimal ingredients of certainty to set limits to the use of chance. So, for instance, we do not draw punishments for murder and pocket picking from the same urn. We do not decide whom to accuse by drawing lots. These elementary forms of knowledge allow us to rest our policing and punishment practices minimally on very basic notions of proportionality. There *are* some natural limits to the use of randomization.

We only turn to chance when *our social science and principles run out.* The easy cases are where our social science findings rest on bad evidence, weak data, or faulty models, where there is no scientific evidence at all, or where there are competing and equally plausible hypotheses that are all similarly nonfalsified—in other words, when we do not have reliable social science findings to rely on. This, I take it, can hardly be contested. No one wants to affirmatively and intentionally police or punish another human being on the basis of bad science or no science at all.

Ultimately, the degree of uncertainty in the policing and punishment field is not complete, but radical. The model of nonfalsification alone is not adequate to sort social science theories apart. We need, in addition, a mechanism that distinguishes between social science hypotheses that intermediate though consciousness and those that do not. By way of illustration, consider four theories dear to the field of policing: (a) rational choice theory, (b) the broken-windows theory, (c) legitimation theory, and (d) incapacitation theory. The first three operate through the intermediary of human consciousness. In each case, the theories depend on actors believing certain things and conforming their behavior accordingly. The first assumes that individuals pursue their self-interest or maximize their utility, and that, accordingly, when the cost of offending goes up, they will offend less. It is a theory that requires us to accept the idea that individuals—whether knowingly or unconsciously—conform their behavior to calculated expectations of success or failure. The second and third theories—broken-windows and legitimation theories—also depend on people taking cues from their social or physical environment (a disorderly neighborhood in one case, a discourteous or insolent police officer in another) and adapting their behavior accordingly. All three of these theories require a defined process of the human intellect and a decision about behavior. They require the intermediation of human consciousness. They are neither true nor false, just not-yet-falsified-properly, nor clearly falsifiable in the near future. In contrast, the fourth theory involves what we might call "social physics." If we physically detain an individual and isolate her from the free world, she will not commit statutory offenses on the outside. This is a matter of social physics, not modern social science. Similarly, transportation made it physically impossible for a convict to offend in the original jurisdiction.

The first type of theories are far too susceptible to ideology. I say "ideology" in the sense that social scientific theories that intermediate through consciousness are shaped by historical, social, and familial contexts that change over time and are affected by the very punitive practices that we implement. In this area, there is a feed-back mechanism—what Ian Hacking refers to as a "looping effect."[18] The practices and categories we deploy shape us as subjects and change the way we respond to those very practices. As a result, these theories will necessarily be filled with ideologi-cal commitments, biases, and prejudices. They need to be eliminated from the field of policing and punishment. Only the second type are respectable hypotheses for the twenty-first century. To be sure, it narrows the range of acceptable empirical and principled claims. But that's all for the better; it will entail less social engineering.

Randomization Today

As Jon Elster suggests, "We have a strong reluctance to admit uncertainty and inde-terminacy in human affairs. Rather than accept the limits of reason we prefer the rit-uals of reason."[19] Yet randomization is by no means foreign to the law—and not just in François Rabelais's vivid imagination.[20] A number of states statutorily prescribe a flip of the coin to resolve election ties. Wisconsin law, for instance, provides that "if 2 or more candidates for the same office receive the greatest, but an equal number of votes, the winner shall be chosen by lot in the presence of the board of canvassers charged with the responsibility to determine the election."[21] Similarly, Louisiana law expressly states that "in case of a tie, the secretary of state shall invite the candidates to his office and shall determine the winner by the flip of a coin."[22] In New Mexico, it's a poker hand that resolves a tie.[23] Courts as well have turned to chance to re-solve election disputes.[24] A number of courts also partition disputed land by lot or chance.[25]

Randomness also surfaces across a number of policing strategies, including sobri-ety checkpoints and the random selection of airline passengers for further screening at airports. Even efficiency-oriented police administrators at times oppose targeted profiling of higher-risk suspects. New York City's police commissioner, Raymond Kelly, for instance, opposes ethnic profiling in defensive counterterrorism measures such as stop-and-search programs at New York City subway entrances.[26] We have become increasingly accustomed to randomized searches in a number of different areas, including "the compelled provision of urine samples for drug testing of law enforcement officers, jockeys, railroad workers, and other classes of employees."[27] We have also become accustomed to metal detectors and X-ray machines that screen practically all people entering government buildings or embarking on planes.

Chance also plays a large role in the detection of crime: who gets apprehended and who does not most often turns on luck. As R. A. Duff writes, "One burglar is caught because the police are mounting a blitz on burglaries in that area at that time; another escapes detection because he happens to commit his burglary at some other place or time. . . . In these and other ways the actual fate within the criminal system of two equally guilty offenders may be partly a matter of chance: one loses our in the criminal lottery, while the other wins."[28] Yet few of us object to these "detection lot-teries." Few of us find that they seriously infringe on our sense of justice.[29] Even fixed sentencing schemes have a significant element of chance. A lot turns on the luck of the draw regarding which judge—lenient or stern—presides over the sentencing.[30]

Efficiency and Deterrence

Nevertheless, a call for more randomization will undoubtedly meet with great resistance. Many will instinctively protest that the use of chance is far less efficient than profiling or targeting higher offenders—that it is wasteful to expend law enforcement resources on low-risk offenders. There's no point conducting extra airport security checks on elderly grandmothers in wheelchairs and families with infants—or "Girl Scouts and grannies," as one recent commentator writes.[31] As I demonstrate in *Against Prediction* with equations and graphs, however, profiling on the basis of group offending rates may in fact be counterproductive and may actually cause more crime even under very conservative assumptions regarding the comparative elasticities of the different populations.[32] We have no good theoretical reason to believe that targeted enforcement would be efficient in decreasing crime or would increase, rather than decrease, overall social welfare.

More sophisticated economists may respond that targeting enforcement on groups that are more responsive, at the margin, would maximize the return of any law enforcement investment.[33] But here we face an empirical void. What we would need is reliable empirical evidence concerning both the comparative offending rates and the comparative elasticities of the targeted and nontargeted populations. I derive the exact equation for this in *Against Prediction*.[34] The problem is not the reliability of the evidence, it's that it simply does not exist.[35] If there ever was a place to avoid taking leaps of faith, surely it would be here, where there is no empirical data whatsoever.

The conventional wisdom among law-and-economists is that increasing the probability of detection serves as a greater deterrent to crime than increasing the amount of the sanction because of the high discount rate imputed to criminals—namely because convicts purportedly do not give much weight to extra years of incarceration in the distant future.[36] Assuming this is true, the decision to embrace randomization in sentencing should have no effect on deterrence. Using a sentencing lottery to determine the length of incarceration from within a sentencing guideline range, rather than using a grid that profiles based on prior criminal history, gun use, or other factors, would not change the *certainty* of the expected sentence and need not change the *amount* of the expected sentence.

Some behavioral law-and-economists had argued that the certainty of a criminal sentence—the fact that the size of a criminal sanction is fixed and known ahead of time—may deter criminals more effectively than uncertain sentences and, on those grounds, had argued against sentencing lotteries.[37] More recent research involving actual experimental research, however, suggests that uncertainty regarding a sanction may be *more* effective at deterring deviant behavior. Experiments by Alon Harel, Tom Baker, and Tamar Kugler reveal that a sentencing lottery may in fact be more effective at deterring deviant behavior than fixed sentences.[38] Other psychological experiments have similarly shown individuals to be averse to ambiguity.[39]

Just Punishment and Moral Luck

Randomization in sentencing will likely meet much greater resistance, not just because of efficiency concerns but also because of considerations of just punishment and desert. Flipping a coin to decide how to sentence an accused may qualify perhaps as the grossest and most repulsive instance of injustice—as the quintessential illustration of a miscarriage of justice. In striking down the death penalty in *Furman v. Georgia* in 1972, Justice Potter Stewart famously compared the death penalty to being struck by lightening. It was precisely this character of randomness, of the chance event, that the Court found most troubling about the practice. The random imposition of punishment is barbaric. Justice Stewart famously wrote:

> These death sentences are cruel and unusual in the same way that being struck by lightning is cruel and unusual. For, of all the people convicted of rapes and murders in 1967 and 1968, many just as reprehensible as these, the petitioners are among a capriciously selected random handful upon whom the sentence of death has in fact been imposed. My concurring Brothers have demonstrated that, if any basis can be discerned for the selection of these few to be sentenced to die, it is the constitutionally impermissible basis of race. But racial discrimination has not been proved, and I put it to one side. I simply conclude that the Eighth and Fourteenth Amendments cannot tolerate the infliction of a sentence of death under legal systems that permit this unique penalty to be so wantonly and so freakishly imposed.[40]

Justice, we believe, is about having right reasons, about justifying an outcome. Justice and justification are tightly related. We want to be able to explain why we believe someone guilty or sentenced to death, and not just why, but for what valid reason. "Because it was heads" is not a valid answer. In a 1987 Tanner Lecture, Jon Elster reviewed the arguments for randomization and discussed a number of legal areas where lotteries might make sense. Yet he refused to see any room for a lottery in the criminal law. "I do not think there are any arguments for incorporating lotteries in present-day criminal law," Elster concluded.[41]

The professions seem to agree. In one notorious incident in 1982, a state court judge in Brooklyn, New York, used a coin toss to determine a jail sentence.[42] The judge, Alan Friess, was presiding over the criminal sentencing of a defendant convicted of pocket picking. The parties were plea-bargaining over a sentence of thirty days in jail (which Friess was inclined to impose) or twenty days (which the defendant obviously preferred), when Friess offered the defendant a gamble. "I'm prepared to allow you to decide your own fate," Friess reportedly told the defendant, "and if you're a gambling man, I'll permit you to flip a coin for that purpose." Heads, the defendant would get thirty days, tails, twenty. The defendant agreed, called tails, and won. Friess sentenced him to twenty days.[43]

The legal establishment responded swiftly. Friess was charged with judicial misconduct for the coin toss,[44] and resigned while the charges were pending. Despite his resignation, the state commission on judicial conduct held hearings to determine whether to bar Friess from ever serving again as a judge in New York. A couple of judges defended Friess. One reportedly testified that a coin toss "is no more bizarre than the way in which I have seen [sentencing] done on thousands of occasions."[45] Another judge, Louis Rosenthal, also from the Brooklyn bench, confessed using a similar approach to speed up the arraignments of individuals charged with dealing three-card monte. Rosenthal testified that he'd give dealers the choice between pleading guilty or playing a hand themselves. He'd then write down three outcomes on separate pieces of chapter: a five-hundred-dollar fine, thirty days in jail, or discharge. "I'm going to mix up these chapters, and he's going to pick one," Rosenthal testified. "They would always plead guilty—they were afraid of the thirty days. . . . They knew the odds were against them."[46] (Rosenthal also resigned from the bench.)

The commission was not impressed and came down hard on Friess, finding that he had "exhibited extraordinarily poor judgment, utter contempt for the process of law, and the grossest misunderstanding of the role and responsibility of a judge in our legal system. . . . He has severely prejudiced the administration of justice and demonstrated his unfitness to hold judicial office." Friess was barred from ever serving again as a judge in New York.[47] "A court of law is not a game of chance," the commission declared. "The public has every right to expect that a jurist will carefully weigh the matters at issue and, in good faith, render reasoned rulings and decisions. Abdicating such solemn responsibilities, particularly in so whimsical a manner as respondent exhibited, is inexcusable and indefensible."[48]

Most academics agree—or at least suggest that we, as a community, should tend to agree. "We insist upon deliberate, self-conscious decisionmaking," Judith Resnik suggests. "The coin flip offend[s] this society's commitment to rationality. Whether or not a judge's mental processes, when pronouncing a sentence of twenty or thirty days, actually amount to anything more than a mental coin flip, the community wishes judicial rulings to appear to be the product of contemplative, deliberate, cognitive processes."[49]

A large body of philosophical and legal literature has grown around the issue of luck in criminal sentencing, much of it tied to the larger debate over what Bernard Williams and Thomas Nagel coined "moral luck."[50] Most of the commentators oppose the use of chance.[51] Yet surprisingly, as a legal matter, the role of luck has been universally embraced in this country and in the West. Most jurisdictions in the United States impose a lesser sentence or half the punishment for attempts; beyond our borders, reduced punishment for attempts has achieved "near universal acceptance in Western law."[52]

What accounts for this almost universal academic rejection of chance in criminal sentencing? The reason, I would suggest, is that we desperately want to believe that there is a rational alternative. We cling to the idea that there is a better way, a more rational way, a more morally acceptable way. As Elster explains, "Since human beings are meaning-seeking animals, they are uncomfortable with the idea that events are merely sound and fury, signifying nothing. Human beings are also reason-seeking animals. They want to have reasons for what they do, and they create reasons when none exist. Moreover, they want the reasons to be clear and decisive, so as to make the decision easy rather than close."[53]

In discussing penal lotteries, R. A. Duff observes that lotteries in general are justified only when "there is no other practicable or morally acceptable way of distributing the benefit or burden in question."[54] Lotteries are justified as a default mechanism when there is no other morally justifiable way: "What justifies such lotteries. . . is the fact that it is either impossible to eliminate them, or possible to reduce or eliminate them only at an unacceptably high cost."[55]

Duff has it right. What justifies lotteries, morally, is the lack of an alternative. Where he has it wrong, though—and where everyone seems to have it wrong—is in believing that *there is a rational alternative*. The fact is, we have hunches. We take leaps of faith. But we do not have good evidence or determined principles that resolve the policing or sentencing ambiguities. Policing and sentencing lotteries make sense, in the end, precisely because *we have no better choice*.

Conclusion

In the end, randomization is not only right because racial profiling is wrong; it may also be right because we need to stop taking leaps of faith in policing and punishment. There is an alternative. Whenever we are at the precipice of reason, faced with competing empirical hypotheses that have not been falsified, or an indeterminate principle, or questionable assumptions, we need to stop using reason: stop rationalizing which hypothesis makes more sense, stop marshalling better reasons for one derivation of principle over another, stop legitimizing the questioned assumption. Instead, we should turn to chance. Resolve the indeterminacy by drawing straws, flipping a coin, pulling numbers from a hat, running a randomized computer algorithm. We need to let chance take over when empirics and reason end. This would represent, in some sense, the end of policing and punishment as a transformative practice—as a practice intended to change mortals, to correct delinquents, to treat the deviant, to deter the super predator. We would have sanitized policing and punishment: no longer the field of social engineering, but also no longer about moral education, nor about social intervention. That, it seems, would be step forward for us all.

NOTES

1. *See, e.g.,* Schauer, 2003; Knowles, Persico, and Todd, 2001; Hernández-Murillo and Knowles, 2003; Sperry, 2005; Ellmann, 2002; Weitzer and Tuch, 1999 and 2002 (finding that general perceptions regarding racial profiling are shaped by respondents' race, experiences with police discrimination, and exposure to media).

2. *See, generally,* Harcourt, 2007a:7–16 (describing the use of parole prediction tools, tax-evasion algorithms, sex-offender prediction instruments, and drug-courier profiles, among other actuarial tools in use today).

3. *See, e.g.,* Ellmann 2002; Sperry, 2005. The use of the "drug-courier" profile at airports is constitutionally permitted, is a well-recognized practice in law enforcement, has been studied,

and, according to its proponents, has shown to be effective, *see* Harcourt, 2007:a15–16 and 103–106; in addition, the United States Supreme Court has condoned the use of ethnic features in border policing, *see* Harcourt, 2006.

4. Tyler, 1990 and 1998.

5. Sherman, 2003.

6. *See, generally*, Harcourt, 2001:166–175.

7. The NAACP Legal Defense Fund, for instance, has done a study in Mississippi looking at the cost of pretrial detention to the community in terms of lost income of the prisoners and loss of ability to support their families.

8. I demonstrate this at length in Harcourt, 2007a:195–214 ("A Case Study on Racial Profiling").

9. *See, e.g.*, Knowles, Persico, and Todd, 2001; Hernández-Murillo and Knowles, 2003.

10. Harcourt, 2007a:111–144.

11. Harcourt 2007a:132–136.

12. Though it does go against the grain of policing, there have been initiatives that have attempted to "randomize away" police action based on ascribed characteristics. The Canberra reintegrative shaming experiment and the Minneapolis domestic violence experiment are two cases on point (Sherman, Strang, and Woods, 2000; Sherman and Berk, 1984).

13. The trouble with most research on deterrence is that it is extremely difficult to divorce the effects of deterrence from those of incapacitation—from the fact that increased law enforcement will also result in more imprisonment and thus greater incapacitation of criminal offenders. The National Academy of Sciences appointed a blue-ribbon panel of experts to examine the problem of measuring deterrence in 1978—led by Alfred Blumstein, Jacqueline Cohen, and Daniel Nagin—but the results were disappointing: "Because the potential sources of error in the estimates of the deterrent effect of these sanctions are so basic and the results sufficiently divergent, no sound, empirically based conclusions can be drawn about the existence of the effect, and certainly not about its magnitude" (Blumstein, Cohen, and Nagin, 1978:42; *see also* Nagin, 1978:95 and 135; Spelman, 2000:97). Little progress has been made since then. As Steven Levitt suggested in 1998, "few of the empirical studies [regarding deterrence of adults] have any power to distinguish deterrence from incapacitation and therefore provide only an indirect test of the economic model of crime" (1158 n.2).

14. Another illustration is the modern policing practice of order maintenance, or "broken windows." In the early 1990s, several major U.S. cities began implementing order-maintenance strategies, most notably New York City, where in 1994 then mayor Rudolph Giuliani and his first police commissioner, William Bratton, put in force the "quality-of-life initiative." The order-maintenance strategies rested on the "broken windows" theory—the idea that minor neighborhood disorder like graffiti and loitering, if left unattended, will cause serious criminal activity (Wilson and Kelling, 1982:31; Harcourt, 2001:23–27; Harcourt and Ludwig, 2006:278–287). During the 1990s, several proponents of order-maintenance declared that the broken windows theory had been empirically verified (Kelling and Coles, 1996:24). They rested this assertion on the findings of a 1990 study by Skogan titled *Disorder and Decline*. Subsequent research discovered several gapping flaws in the study that undermine confidence in the findings (Harcourt, 2001:59–78). Today, the social scientific support for the broken windows theory rests principally on a 2001 study coauthored by George Kelling and William Sousa. The trouble with the Kelling and Sousa study is that they do not control for what statisticians call "mean reversion." An examination of their data reveals that those precincts that experienced the *largest drop* in crime in the 1990s were the ones that experienced the *largest increases* in crime during the city's crack epidemic of the mid to late 1980s. In a recent study with Jens

Ludwig, we demonstrate that the declines in crime observed in New York City in the 1990s are exactly what would have been predicted from the rise and fall of the crack epidemic, even if New York had not embarked on its broken windows policing strategy (Harcourt and Ludwig, 2006:315). Jens Ludwig and I call this "Newton's Law of Crime": what goes up, must come down, and what goes up the most, tends to come down the most. What it represents, in effect, is a competing hypothesis that more fully explains the relationship between crime and policing. There's another empirical gap and leap of faith.

15. Borges, 1998:102.

16. Borges, 1998:101.

17. Borges, 1998:101.

18. Hacking, 2006:2.

19. Elster, 1987:108.

20. Rabelais, 1999, III:39. You may recall the giant, Gargantua, and his son, Pantagruel, from the wonderful writings of François Rabelais. In the third book, Pantagruel goes to visit a number of professionals, including a doctor, a priest, and a judge. We meet Judge Bridlegoose in chapter 39 of the Third Book—appropriately entitled "How Pantagruel was present at the trial of Judge Bridlegoose, who decided causes and controversies in law by the chance and fortune of the dice." Judge Bridlegoose was himself on trial, accused of returning an inequitable sentence. He represented himself and argued, in his defense, that his eyes have gotten bad with age and that he must have misread the dice that he and every other judge used to sentence people. In Rabelais's satirical writings, all judges in truth turned to chance to determine legal outcomes.

21. Wis. Stat. Ann. § 5.01(4) (2005). *See, generally,* Choper, 2001:340 n.22 (collecting the following other sources: Mo. Rev. Stat. 162.492 [2000] [1978 Amendment deleted former subsec. 6, which provided that a tie vote would be determined by the flip of a coin]; N.D. Cent. Code 16.1–11–38, 16.1–14–0, 16.1–15–29, 40–21–17, 58–04–15 [2000] ["In case of a tie vote the nominee or nominees must be determined by a coin flip"]).

22. La. Rev. Stat. 46:1410(C)(3) (2005).

23. Reuters, 2000 (describing practice of using "one hand of five-card poker"); N.M. Stat. Ann. 1-13-11 (2000) ("candidate chosen by lot . . . in the event of a tie vote").

24. *See, e.g.,* Huber v. Reznick, 437 N.E.2d 828, 839 (Ill. App. 1982) (holding that trial court did not err in choosing a coin flip as the method of determining the winner of the tie vote by lot).

25. *See, generally,* Zitter, 1999.

26. *See* Harcourt, 2007b.

27. *Edmond,* 1999.

28. Duff, 1990:26–27.

29. There are also historical instances of randomness in sentencing. One is the decimation of a military regiment as a form of punishment for mutiny: "Each soldier is punished for his part in the mutiny by a one-in-ten risk of being put to death. It is a fairly pure penal lottery, but not entirely pure: the terror of waiting to see who must dies is part of the punishment, and this part falls with certainty on all the mutineers alike" (Lewis 1989:58).

30. Harel and Segal, 1999:292.

31. Sperry, 2005.

32. Harcourt, 2007a, 129–132; Harcourt, 2007b.

33. Margoliath, 2007.

34. Harcourt 2007a:133.

35. There may be one single exception. Avner Bar-Ilan and Bruce Sacerdote have a working chapter from 2001 that explores the comparative responsiveness to an increase in the

fine for running a red light along several dimensions (finding that the elasticity of red light running with respect to the fine "is larger for younger drivers and drivers with older cars," equivalent for drivers "convicted of violent offenses or property offenses," and smallest, within Israel, for "members of ethnic minority groups"). A handful of other chapters come close, but do not address the key issue of comparative elasticities. Paul Heaton's 2006 work on the effect of eliminating racial profiling policies in New Jersey on the offending of minorities, "Understanding the Effects of Anti-profiling Policies," explores the elasticity of the profiled group; however, the study involves de-policing of the profiled group and not a substitution onto white motorists. As a result, there is no change in the elasticity or offending of whites, and therefore Heaton's study does not address how the elasticity of black offenders compares to that of whites.

36. Polinsky and Shavell, 1999:12.

37. Harel and Segal, 1999:280.

38. Baker, Harel, and Kugler, 2004.

39. Harel and Segal, 1999:291.

40. *Furman*, 1972:309–310 (STEWART, J., concurring).

41. Elster, 1987:157.

42. Shipp 1983a; Resnick, 1984:610.

43. Van Natta, 1996.

44. The complaint alleged one other incident: apparently, on another occasion, Friess asked courtroom spectators for a show of hands on whom to believe in a harassment case (Shipp 1983a, 1983b).

45. Shipp, 1983b.

46. Herman and Johnston, 1983.

47. Shipp, 1983a.

48. Shipp, 1983a.

49. Resnik, 1984:610–611.

50. Williams, 1981:20–39; Nagel, 1979:24–38.

51. Kadish, 1994:680; Lewis, 1989:58; Kessler, 1994:2237; Duff, 1990; Von Hirsch, 1976: 72–73.

52. Kadish, 1994:679.

53. Elster, 1987:174–75.

54. Duff, 1990:26.

55. Duff, 1990:27.

REFERENCES

Baker, Tom, Alon Harel, and Tamar Kugler. 2004. "The Virtues of Uncertainty in Law: An Experimental Approach." *Iowa Law Review* 89:443–494.

Bar-Ilan, Avner and Bruce Sacerdote. 2001. "The Response to Fines and Probability of Detection in a Series of Experiments." National Bureau of Economic Research (Cambridge, MA) Working Chapter No 8638 (December).

Blumstein, Alfred, Jacqueline Cohen, and Daniel Nagin. 1978. "Report of the Panel on Research on Deterrent and Incapacitative Effects," in Alfred Blumstein et al., *Deterrence and Incapacitation: Estimating the Effects of Criminal Sanctions on Crime Rates*, Washington, DC: National Academy of Sciences.

Borges, Jorge Luis. 1998 (1941). "The Lottery in Babylon," in *Collected Fictions*, 101–106. Trans., Andrew Hurley. New York: Penguin Putnam.

Choper, Jesse H. 2001. "Why the Supreme Court Should Not Have Decided the Presidential Election of 2000." *Constitutional Commentary* 18:335–357.

Duff, R. A. 1990. "Auctions, Lotteries, and the Punishment of Attempts." *Law and Philosophy* 9:1 (February):1–37.

Ellmann, Stephen. 2002. "Racial Profiling and Terrorism." *New York Law School Law Review* 46:675–730.

Elster, Jon. 1987. "Taming Chance: Randomization in Individual and Social Decisions." *The Tanner Lectures on Human Values* (delivered at Brasenose College, Oxford University). May 6 and 7.

Hacking, Ian. 2006. "Kinds of People: Moving Targets." *The Tenth British Academy Lecture.* Read April 11, at the British Academy. Available at http://www.britac.ac.uk/pubs/src/brit acad06/index.html.

Harcourt, Bernard E. 2001. *Illusion of Order: The False Promise of Broken Windows Policing.* Cambridge MA: Harvard University Press.

———. 2006. "The Road to Racial Profiling," in *Criminal Procedure Stories* (ed. Carol Steiker). New York: Foundation Press.

———. 2007a. *Against Prediction: Profiling, Policing, and Punishing in an Actuarial Age.* Chicago: University of Chicago Press.

———. 2007b. "Muslim Profiles Post 9/11: Is Racial Profiling an Effective Counterterrorist Measure and Does It Violate the Right to be Free from Discrimination?" in *Security and Human Rights* (eds. Benjamin Goold and Liora Lazarus). Oxford: Hart Publishing.

Harcourt, Bernard E. and Jens Ludwig. 2006. "Broken Windows: New Evidence from New York City and a Five-City Social Experiment." *University of Chicago Law Review* 73:1 (Winter):271–316.

Harel, Alon and Uzi Segal. 1999. "Criminal Law and Behavioral Law and Economics: Observations on the Neglected Role of Uncertainty in Deterring Crime." *American Law and Economics Review* 1:1/2:276–312.

Heaton, Paul. 2006. "Understanding the Effects of Anti-Profiling Policies." Working chapter available at http://home.uchicago.edu/~psheaton/workingpapers/racialprofiling.pdf (March).

Hernández-Murillo, Rubén and John Knowles. 2003. "Racial Profiling or Racist Policing? Testing in Aggregated Data." Working chapter available at http://www.econ.upenn.edu/~jknowles/research/HK.htm (April 18).

Kadish, Sanford. 1994. "The Criminal Law and the Luck of the Draw." *Journal of Criminal Law and Criminology* 84:679–702.

Kelling, George and Catherine M. Coles. 1996. *Fixing Broken Windows: Restoring Order and Reducing Crime in Our Communities.* New York: The Free Press.

Kelling, George L. and William H. Sousa, Jr. 2001. "Do Police Matter? An Analysis of the Impact of New York City's Police Reforms." Civic Report No 22, Manhattan Institute Center for Civic Innovation (December).

Kessler, Kimberly D. 1994. "The Role of Luck in Criminal Law." *University of Pennsylvania Law Review*, 142:6 (June):2183–2237.

Knowles, John, Nicola Persico, and Petra Todd. 2001. "Racial Bias in Motor Vehicle Searches: Theory and Evidence." *Journal of Political Economy* 109:203–232.

Levitt, Steven. 1998. "Juvenile Crime and Punishment." *Journal of Political Economy* 106:6 (December):1156–1185.

Lewis, David. 1989. "The Punishment that Leaves Something to Chance." *Philosophy and Public Affairs* 18:1 (Winter):53–67.

Margoliath, Yoram. 2007. "In Defense of Prediction." *Law and Social Inquiry*, forthcoming.

Nagel, Thomas. 1979. "Moral Luck," in *Mortal Questions*. Cambridge: Cambridge University Press.

Nagin, Daniel. 1978. *General Deterrence: A Review of the Empirical Evidence*, in Alfred Blumstein et al., *Deterrence and Incapacitation: Estimating the Effects of Criminal Sanctions on Crime Rates*, Washington, DC: National Academy of Sciences.

Polinsky, Mitchell and Steven Shavell. 1999. "On the Disutility and Discounting of Imprisonment and the Theory of Deterrence." *Journal of Legal Studies* 28:1–16.

Pratt, John and Mark Brown (eds). 2000. *Dangerous Offenders: Punishment and Social Order.* London: Routledge.

Rabelais, François. 1999 (1546). *Le Tiers livre des faits et dits heroïques du bon Pantagruel*, in *Les Œuvres romanesques*. Trans. Françoise Joukovsky. Paris : Honoré Champion Éditeur.

Resnik, Judith. 1984. "Precluding Appeals." *Cornell Law Review* 70:603–624.

Schauer, Frederick. 2003. *Profiles, Probabilities, and Stereotypes*. Cambridge, MA: Harvard University Press.

Sherman, Lawrence W. 2003. "Reason for Emotion: Reinventing Justice with Theories, Innovations, and Research: 2002 ASC Presidential Address." *Criminology* 41(1):1–38.

Sherman, Lawrence W. and Richard A. Berk 1984. *The Minneapolis Domestic Violence Experiment*. Washington, DC: Police Foundation Reports. Available at http://www.police foundation.org/pdf/minneapolisdve.pdf.

Sherman, Lawrence W., Heather Strang, and Daniel J. Woods. 2000. *Recidivism Patterns in Canberra Reintegrative Shaming Experiments (RISE)*. Canberra, Australia: Australian National University, Research School of Social Sciences, Centre for Restorative Justice.

Spelman, William. 2000. "The Limited Importance of Prison Expansion," in *The Crime Drop in America* (ed. Alfred Blumstein and Joel Wallman). New York: Cambridge University Press.

Tyler, Tom R. 1990. *Why People Obey the Law*. New Haven, CT: Yale University Press.

———. 1998. "Trust and Democratic Governance," in *Trust and Governance* (ed. Valerie Braithwaite and Margaret Levi). New York: Russell Sage Foundation.

Von Hirsch, Andrew. 1976. *Doing Justice*. New York : Hill and Wang.

Weitzer, Ronald and Steven Tuch. 1999. "Race, Class, and Perceptions of Discrimination by the Police." *Crime and Delinquency* 45:494–507.

———. 2002. "Perceptions of Racial Profiling: Race, Class, and Personal Experience." *Criminology* 40:435–456.

Williams, Bernard. 1981. *Moral Luck*. Cambridge: Cambridge University Press.

Wilson, James Q. and George L. Kelling. 1982. "Broken Windows." *Atlantic Monthly*, March, 29–38.

Zitter, Jay M. 1999. "Judicial Partition of Land by Lot or Chance." *American Law Reports* 4(32): 909.

Newspaper Articles and Court Cases

Edmond v. Goldsmith, 183 F3d 659 (7th Cir 1999), affd, *City of Indianapolis v. Edmond*, 531 US 32 (2000).

Furman v. Georgia, 408 U.S. 238 (1972).

Herman, Robin and Laurie Johnston. 1983. "New York Day by Day," *New York Times*, February 10, Section B, page 3 (Metro Desk).

Reuters. 2000. "Election 2000; The Presidency; High Stakes; If Vote Is Tied in New Mexico, Poker Hand Could Settle It," *Newsday*, November 15, page A05.

Shipp, E .R. 1983a. "Friess Is Barred From Ever Being New York Judge," *New York Times*, April 7, Section B, page 3 (Metro Desk).

———. 1983b. "2 Justices Defend Friess at Hearing on Misconduct," *New York Times*, February 6, Section 1, page 33 (Metro Desk).

Sperry, Paul. 2005. "When the Profile Fits the Crime," *New York Times*, July, 28, available at http://www.nytimes.com/2005/07/28/opinion/28sperry.html.

Van Natta, Don, Jr. 1996. "Doubting Harolds: Looking Inside a Judge's Mind," *New York Times*, April 7, Section 4, page 3 (Week in Review).

About the Contributors

Geoffrey P. Alpert is Professor in the Department of Criminology and Criminal Justice at the University of South Carolina. His books include *Managing Accountability Systems for Police Conduct: Internal Affairs and External Oversight* (with J. Noble) and *Understanding Police Use of Force: Officers, Suspects, and Reciprocity* (with R. Dunham), which was recently published by Cambridge University Press.

Rod K. Brunson is Associate Professor in the Department of Criminology and Criminal Justice at Southern Illinois University, Carbondale.

Garth Davies is Assistant Professor in the School of Criminology at Simon Fraser University. He is the author of *Crime, Neighborhood, and Public Housing* (LFB Scholarly Publishing, 2006).

Robin S. Engel is Associate Professor in the Division of Criminal Justice at the University of Cincinnati and Director of the University of Cincinnati Policing Institute.

Jeffrey A. Fagan is Professor of Law and Public Health and Director of the Center for Crime, Community, and Law at Columbia University. He is author (with Frank Zimring) of *Changing Borders of Juvenile Justice* (University of Chicago Press, 2000) and editor (with several others) of *Legitimacy and Criminal Justice in Comparative Perspective* (2008, Russell Sage Foundation Press).

The late *James J. Fyfe* was Distinguished Professor of Law, Police Science, and Criminal Justice Administration at the John Jay College of Criminal Justice and Deputy Commissioner of Training with the New York City Police Department at the time of his death in 2005. Fyfe coauthored *Above the Law* (with Jerome H. Skolnick, 1993) and the most recent edition of O. W. Wilson's classic *Police Administration* (with Jack Greene and William Walsh, 1996).

Amanda Geller is Associate Research Scientist at Columbia University.

Bernard E. Harcourt is the Julius Kreeger Professor of Law and Criminology and Professor of Political Science at the University of Chicago. He is the author of *Against Prediction: Profiling, Policing, and Punishing in an Actuarial Age* (University of Chicago Press, 2007), *Language of the Gun: Youth, Crime, and Public Policy* (University of Chicago Press 2005), and *Illusion of Order: The False Promise of Broken Windows Policing* (Harvard University Press, 2001).

David A. Harris is Professor of Law at the University of Pittsburgh School of Law. He is the author of *Good Cops: The Case for Preventive Policing* (The New Press,

2005) and *Profiles in Injustice: Why Racial Profiling Cannot Work* (The New Press, 2002).

Matthew J. Hickman is Assistant Professor in the Department of Criminal Justice at Seattle University.

Delores Jones-Brown is Professor in the Department of Law, Police Science, and Criminal Justice Administration at John Jay College, City University of New York. She is also the Director of the John Jay College Center on Race, Crime, and Justice. She is the author of *Race, Crime, and Punishment* and coeditor of *Policing and Minority Communities: Bridging the Gap* and *The System in Black and White: Exploring the Connections Between Race, Crime, and Justice.*

Robert J. Kane is Associate Professor in the School of Criminology and Criminal Justice at Arizona State University.

Charles F. Klahm IV is Assistant Professor of Criminal Justice at St. Joseph's College, New York. He received his PhD from the University of Cincinnati in 2009.

John Lamberth is the CEO of Lamberth Consulting.

Erin C. Lane is Student Services Advisor at the Youth Automotive Training Center, a nonprofit school for delinquent, disadvantaged, and at-risk youth in southern Florida.

John MacDonald is the Jerry Lee Assistant Professor of Criminology at the University of Pennsylvania.

Ramiro Martínez Jr. is Professor of Criminal Justice at Florida International University. He authored *Latino Homicide: Immigration, Violence, and Community* (Routledge, 2002), and edited *Immigration and Crime: Race, Ethnicity, and Violence* (New York University Press, 2006).

Marcinda Mason is a Research Analyst at the Research Triangle Institute.

Brian A. Maule is Adjunct Lecturer of Sociology at John Jay College of Criminal Justice and is enrolled in the Criminal Justice Doctoral program at the Graduate Center of the City University of New York.

Matt R. Nobles is an Assistant Professor of Criminal Justice at Washington State University.

Karen F. Parker is Professor in the Department of Sociology and Criminal Justice at the University of Delaware. She recently published a book by NYU Press titled *Unequal Crime Decline: Theorizing Race, Urban Inequality, and Criminal Violence.*

William S. Parkin is a doctoral student in the PhD Program in Criminal Justice at the City University of New York (CUNY).

Meaghan Paulhamus is a doctoral student in the School of Criminology and Criminal Justice at Arizona State University.

Alex R. Piquero is Professor in the College of Criminology and Criminal Justice at Florida State University. He is the author of *Key Issues in Criminal Careers Research: New Research from the Cambridge Study in Delinquent Development* (with Alfred Blumstein and David P. Farrington) (Cambridge University Press, 2007).

Stephen K. Rice is Assistant Professor in the Department of Criminal Justice at Seattle University.

Greg Ridgeway is Director of RAND's Safety and Justice Program and the Center for Quality Policing, a Senior Statistician, and a Professor of Policy Analysis in the Pardee RAND Graduate School.

Jessica Saunders is Associate Social Scientist for the RAND Corporation.

Jerome H. Skolnick is Codirector of the Center for Research in Crime and Justice, New York University School of Law, and Claire Clements Dean's Chair Emeritus, University of California at Berkeley, Boalt School of Law. Professor Skolnick has published many books, including *Crisis in American Institutions* (HarperCollins, 10th ed., 1997) (with Elliot Currie), *Above the Law: Police and the Excessive Use of Force* (with James Fyfe) (The Free Press, 1993), *Justice Without Trial: Law Enforcement in Democratic Society* (Macmillan, 3rd ed., 1993), *Criminal Justice: A Casebook* (with Malcolm Feeley and John Kaplan) (Foundation Press, 5th ed., 1991), and *The New Blue Line: Police Innovation in Six American Cities* (with David Bayley) (The Free Press, 1986).

William R. Smith is Associate Professor in the Department of Sociology and Anthropology at North Carolina State University. He has authored *Paroling Authorities: Recent History and Current Practice* (with Edward Rhine and Ronald W. Jackson) (American Correctional Association, 1991) and *Social Structure, Family Structure, Child Rearing, and Delinquency: Another Look* (University of Stockholm, 1991).

Brian J. Stults is Assistant Professor in the College of Criminology and Criminal Justice at Florida State University.

Rob Tillyer is Assistant Professor in the Department of Criminal Justice at the University of Texas at San Antonio.

Donald Tomaskovic-Devey is Professor of Sociology at the University Massachusetts–Amherst. He authored *Recapitalizing America* (Routledge, 1983) and *Gender and Racial Inequality at Work* (Cornell University Press, 1993).

Tom R. Tyler is University Professor at New York University. He teaches in the Psychology Department and the Law School. He is the author of many books, including *Why People Obey the Law* (Yale University Press, 1990) and *Trust in the Law: Encouraging Public Cooperation with the Police and Courts* (with Y. J. Huo) (Russell-Sage Foundation, 2002).

Patricia Warren is Assistant Professor in the College of Criminology and Criminal Justice at Florida State University.

Ronald Weitzer is Professor in the Department of Sociology at George Washington University. His books include *Policing Under Fire: Ethnic Conflict and Police-Community Relations in Northern Ireland* (SUNY Press, 1995) and *Race and Policing in America: Conflict and Reform* (with Steven Tuch) (Cambridge University Press, 2006).

Valerie West is Assistant Professor of Criminal Justice at John Jay College of the City University of New York.

Michael D. White is Associate Professor in the School of Criminology and Criminal Justice at Arizona State University. He is author of *Current Issues and Controversies in Policing* (Pearson/Allyn Bacon, 2007).

Matthew Zingraff is Associate Dean for Research in the College of Humanities and Social Sciences at George Mason University.

Index